FINANCE
Introduction To Markets, Institutions & Management

Ronald W. Melicher, University of Colorado
Merle T. Welshans, Washington University

8th Edition

COLLEGE DIVISION South-Western Publishing Co.

Cincinnati Ohio

FB65HA

Copyright © 1992

by SOUTH-WESTERN PUBLISHING CO.

Cincinnati, Ohio

Sponsoring Editor: James Keefe
Developmental Editor: Alice Denny
Production Editors: Rhonda Eversole
                          Mark Sears
Production House: Julia Chitwood

Designer: Craig LaGesse Ramsdell
Cover and Interior Photography:
  Diana Fleming
Marketing Manager: Scott Person

2 3 4 5 6 7 8 9 MT 9 8 7 6 5 4 3 2

Printed in the United States of America

Library of Congress Cataloging-in-Publication Data

Melicher, Ronald W.
    Finance : introduction to markets, institutions & management /
Ronald W. Melicher, Merle T. Welshans. — 8th ed.
      p.   cm.
    Includes bibliographical references and index.
    ISBN 0-538-81214-1
    1. Finance.   2. Finance—United States.   I. Welshans, Merle T.
II. Title.
HG173.M398   1992
332'.0973—dc20   91-25587
                                        CIP

PREFACE

The Eighth Edition of *FINANCE: Introduction to Markets, Institutions and Management* is designed for the first course in finance. We believe that a basic understanding of the complex world of finance should begin with a survey course that covers an introduction to financial markets, institutions, and management. The subject matter of this book includes the entire scope of the financial system and its functions: (1) the markets in which funds are traded, (2) the institutions that participate in and aid the flow of funds, and (3) the principles of financial management that guide the participants in making sound decisions.

For the student taking only one course in finance, this text provides a meaningful survey of the basics of finance in a single term. The student who continues in finance will be able to progress more effectively because it provides the necessary background for further courses in financial management, monetary policy, bank management, government finance, and securities markets. Because the text thoroughly examines the financial structure of our economy, it is also appropriate for business majors who will eventually be managers seeking funds for business and other operations.

ORGANIZATION AND CHANGES

FINANCE is organized around four major topics. The first is the financial system of the United States. The second part focuses on business financing and management. Financing other sectors of the economy is covered in the third part. The fourth part discusses monetary, fiscal, and debt management policies.

Several changes and revisions have taken place in the Eighth Edition of *FINANCE*. Some of the major developments are summarized below.

Part 1, which consists of six chapters, has been revised and updated to reflect current developments in the U.S. and international financial systems. We begin with a discussion of the role of finance in the economy and then cover characteristics of the U.S. monetary system. Banking structure and banking operations continue to undergo rapid change. Competition among depository institutions and with other financial institutions has been encouraged and fostered by recent legislation. International banking has grown in both scope and importance. As a result of these developments, Chapter 3 was completely rewritten. The remaining chapters in Part 1 focus on the Federal Reserve System, the expansion and contraction of the money supply, and the savings and investment process.

Part 2 covers both financial management topics and business financing sources in a seven-chapter sequence. After an introduction to business finance, the discussion turns to the functions of financial planning and working capital management that involve managing the firm's current assets and current liabilities. Sources of short-term business financing are then covered.

The time value of money concept and related problems are discussed early in Chapter 10. Then our attention focuses on the management of fixed assets and methods for selecting among available capital investment projects. The formulas and techniques are presented without subjecting students to excessive rigor. The remaining chapters in Part 2 cover the management of long-term debt and equity funds, sources of long-term business financing, and markets for long-term business funds.

Part 3 also consists of seven chapters, divided into three sections. Chapters 14 and 15 deal with government financing at the federal level and at the state and local level. Chapter 14 discusses the federal debt and the role of foreign capital in financing the deficit. Chapters 16 and 17 include a discussion of consumer financing, and Chapter 18 covers residential real estate. Chapter 19 was extensively revised to reflect the changes in the structure of the Farm Credit Administration. Chapter 20 has been expanded to include discussion of foreign exchange markets and management of the financial aspects of international transactions.

Part 4 includes five chapters. Chapter 21 provides, in a presentation that can be readily understood by students, an introduction to monetary policy, fiscal policy, and debt management. This is followed by chapters covering recent developments in the areas of interest rate levels, changes in the price level, business fluctuations and international payment problems, and monetary and fiscal policy actions.

TEACHING AND LEARNING AIDS

The Eighth Edition of *FINANCE* has been heavily edited to improve readability and student understanding. Each chapter begins with a list of learning objectives that identify important topics that should be understood as a result of studying the chapter. The key terms with brief definitions are given in the margins where they first occur and are also included in the glossary (with expanded definitions) at the end of the book.

Each chapter ends with discussion questions and, where relevant, problems. All problems can be solved manually, but those that may be solved using the South-Western *Decision Assistant* software are clearly marked with an icon in the margin. *Decision Assistant* is a computerized toolkit (available to adopters) that allows students to use and master the concepts presented in the chapter. Suggested readings for each chapter are also presented.

A feature new to this edition of *FINANCE* is self-test questions at the end of each chapter. Most chapters also contain one or two self-test problems. Since answers are provided, these items permit students to have immediate feedback on their understanding of material presented in the chapter.

Boxed items throughout the book provide examples of actual events and current topics. They are designed to demonstrate and illustrate concepts and practices in the dynamic field of finance.

A much expanded *Instructor's Manual* is available to instructors who adopt this book. It contains a section of general comments about the purpose and use of *FINANCE* as well as detailed teaching outlines, answers to end-of-chapter discussion questions and problems, and suggestions for quizzes for each chapter. Information about and suggestions for use of the *Decision Assistant* tools is presented. Transparency masters of many of the figures from the text are also provided in the manual. In addition, the manual includes an extensive test bank of over 1,500 true-false and multiple-choice examination questions with answers.

The test bank is also available for use with MicroSWAT III test generation software, which is available to instructors who adopt

FINANCE. This easy-to-use, menu-driven software allows an instructor to quickly and efficiently produce quality tests. It includes a word processor for entering, editing, and scrambling questions and a grade book. The software requires an IBM or IBM-compatible personal computer with a minimum of 320K memory and two floppy disk drives or a hard disk drive.

ACKNOWLEDGMENTS

We have benefited greatly from discussions with and helpful suggestions from colleagues at Washington University and the University of Colorado. Several reviewers also provided constructive comments and suggestions as this Eighth Edition was being developed. We especially want to thank

Hector P. Agostini
Middlesex Community College

Stewart Bonem
Cincinnati Technical College

Gerard A. Cahill
Florida Institute of Technology

James A. Fetters
Mattatuck Community College

Marshall Giller
Ferris State College

Edward Krohn
Miami-Dade Community
  College

Bruce R. Kuhlman
University of Toledo

Lucille S. Mayne
Case Western Reserve University

Jim Nead
Vincennes University

Elmer Reiter
Delaware Valley College

John Sullivan
North Shore Community College

Doug Wakeman
Meredith College

M. Raquibuz Zaman
Ithaca College

for their help. Likewise, comments from students and teachers who have used prior editions of this book are also greatly appreciated.

We thank Julia Chitwood for her meticulous copy editing. We also thank Alice Denny, our developmental editor, and the other staff members at South-Western who worked diligently to bring this book to its completion. Finally, we wish to thank our families for their understanding and support during the writing of the Eighth Edition.

Ronald W. Melicher
Merle T. Welshans

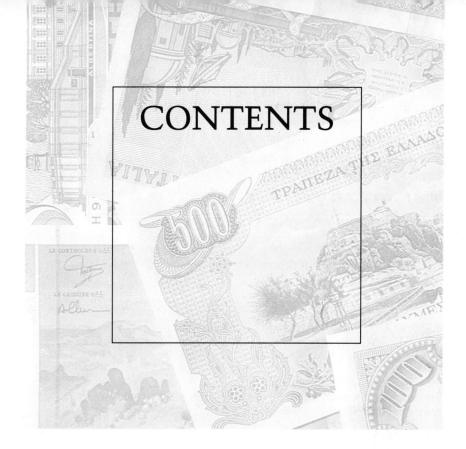

CONTENTS

PART 3
FINANCING OTHER SECTORS OF THE ECONOMY

A. GOVERNMENT FINANCING

PART 4
MONETARY, FISCAL, AND DEBT MANAGEMENT POLICIES

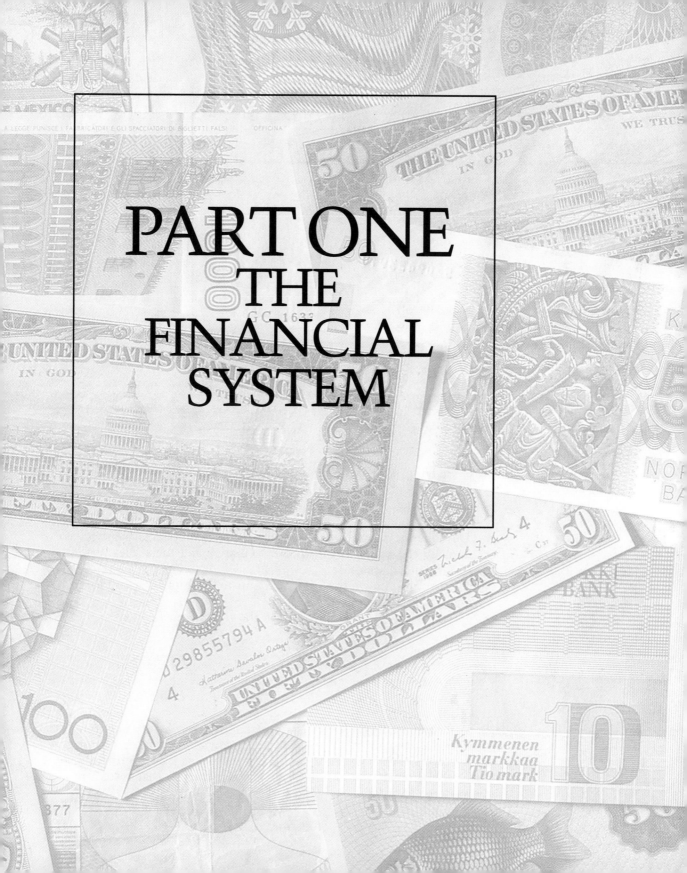

PART ONE
THE
FINANCIAL
SYSTEM

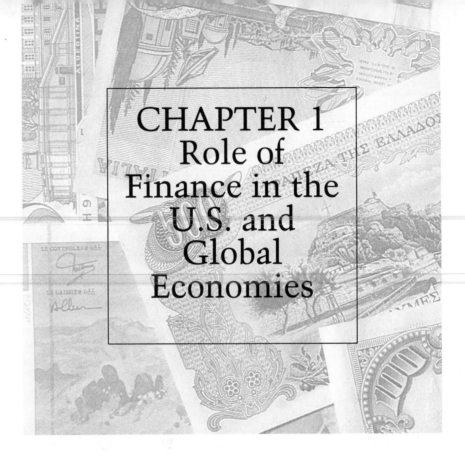

CHAPTER 1
Role of Finance in the U.S. and Global Economies

After studying this chapter, you should be able to:
- Define finance at both the macro and micro levels.
- Explain what finance is about.
- Identify and discuss some finance career opportunities.
- Describe the basic requirements of an effective financial system.
- Identify the major financial intermediaries and their roles in the U.S. financial system.
- Identify and explain the types of claims to wealth that are traded in the U.S. financial markets.
- Describe the financial functions in the U.S. financial system.

We begin this textbook by asking two questions. First, what is finance? Second, what career opportunities are available in the field of finance? While these questions could be discussed at much greater length, even brief answers will help develop an understanding of the materials in this book.

After addressing these two basic questions, we will turn our attention to the discussion of an effective financial system. A modern market economy such as ours could not function as it does without an effective financial system. Intelligent participation in that system requires some knowledge of finance.

WHAT IS FINANCE?

Finance can be defined at both the overall or macro level and the organization or micro level. **Finance** at the *macro level* is the study of financial institutions and financial markets and how they operate within the financial system in both the U.S. and global economies. Finance at the *micro level* is the study of financial planning, asset management, and fund raising for businesses and financial institutions.

Finance has its origins in economics and accounting. Economists use a supply-and-demand framework to explain how the prices and quantities of goods and services are determined in a free-market economic system. Accountants provide the record-keeping mechanism for showing ownership of the financial instruments used in the flow of financial funds between savers and borrowers. Accountants also record revenues, expenses, and profitability of organizations that produce and exchange goods and services.

Large-scale production and specialization of labor can exist only if there is an effective means of paying for raw materials and final products. Business can obtain the money it needs to buy capital goods such as machinery and equipment only if a mechanism has been established for making savings available for investment. Similarly, federal and other governmental units, such as state and local governments and tax districts, can carry out their wide range of activities only if efficient means exist for raising money, for making payments, and for borrowing.

Financial markets, financial intermediaries, and financial management are crucial elements of well-developed financial systems. Financial markets provide the mechanism for allocating financial resources or funds from savers to borrowers. **Financial intermediaries** are firms, such as banks and credit unions, that engage in financial activities to aid the flow of funds from savers to borrowers. Financial management in business involves the efficient use of financial resources in the production and exchange of goods and services. The goal of the financial manager in a profit-seeking organization is to maximize the owners' wealth. This is accomplished through effective financial planning and analysis, asset management, and the acquisition of financial capital. These same functions must be performed by financial managers in not-for-profit organizations to provide a desired level of services at acceptable costs.

finance
study of how institutions, markets, and individual firms operate within the financial system

financial intermediaries
bring about the flow of funds from savers to borrowers

CAREER OPPORTUNITIES IN FINANCE

Career opportunities in finance are generally found in four areas. The first area is business financial management. Larger firms typically divide their finance activities into treasury and control functions,

**FINDING A JOB
IN BUSINESS OR
FINANCE**

One of the reasons for studying a finance book is to improve your job opportunities. This book provides you with a basic knowledge about the field of finance. Of course, entry-level jobs in business and management are available in a number of areas in addition to finance. These include accounting, marketing and sales, production and operations, information systems and processing, human resources and public administration, research and development, and technical and professional services.

Finding a job requires a basic knowledge of the job search process. Time, effort, and research are required to identify potential employers. Résumés must be properly developed, and application letters and forms prepared. You should be prepared for topics that are likely to be covered during the initial interview. An excellent guide to careers in business and a detailed description of the job search process is provided in annual issues of *Peterson's Business and Management Jobs,* (Peterson's Guides, P.O. Box 2123, Princeton, NJ 08543).

Readers interested in finance careers will find *Careers in Finance* to be quite useful (published by the Financial Management Association, University of South Florida, Tampa, FL 33620). It describes finance job opportunities in corporate finance, portfolio management, working capital management, corporate real estate and taxes, general accounting, and banking in terms of basic functions, primary job responsibilities, and types of decisions required. This booklet is provided to members of student chapters of the Financial Management Association, which are located on many college campuses.

while smaller firms often combine both. The *treasurer* is responsible for managing the firm's cash, acquiring and managing the firm's assets, and selling stocks and bonds to raise the financial capital necessary to conduct business. The *controller* is responsible for cost accounting, financial accounting, and tax record-keeping activities. Entry-level career opportunities might begin in cash management or asset acquisition activities in the treasurer's department or cost accounting activities in the controller's department.

A second opportunity area is with financial intermediaries. For example, banks offer the opportunity to start a finance career in consumer or commercial lending. The entry-level job is usually financial analyst, who evaluates loan applicants for their credit worthiness and ability to repay. Successful analysts advance to assistant loan officer and then loan officer levels. Similar positions are available with savings and loans (S&Ls), credit unions, and other financial institutions.

A third area for a finance career is the securities markets field. At the entry level, one might begin as an account executive who sells stocks and bonds to individual and institutional customers. An account executive may also handle the management of client funds consistent with the client's risk-taking objectives. Careers in the securities area also include being a securities analyst or a securities trader for brokerage firms. Other opportunities include managing securities portfolios for bank trust departments and life insurance companies.

A fourth area for a career in finance involves government or not-for-profit organizations. Finance opportunities at the federal or state government level include managing cash funds, making asset acquisition decisions, and obtaining borrowed funds. Not-for-profit organizations such as hospitals also need expert financial managers to manage assets, control costs, and obtain funds.

Many businesses engaged in producing and marketing products and services in foreign markets offer their employees opportunities for international job assignments. Large U.S. banks also offer international job experience for some of their employees through foreign operations.

We have only touched on a few of the many career opportunities in the finance field. Because finance is dynamic and ever changing, new opportunities will certainly occur in the future. However, after studying the materials in this book, the reader will be better prepared for a business career, possibly even one in the field of finance.

BASIC REQUIREMENTS FOR AN EFFECTIVE FINANCIAL SYSTEM

An effective financial system needs an efficient monetary system. It also must be able to allow capital formation by channeling savings into investment. Lastly, to complete the investment process, there must be markets in which to buy and sell claims to wealth, such as real estate or financial assets.

The monetary system must provide an efficient medium for exchanging goods and services. A way to measure prices, such as the dollar in the U.S. economy or the pound sterling in the British economy, is a basic requirement. This is called a *unit of account*. The unit of account must be universally accepted if exchange is to function smoothly. Its value must remain reasonably stable if it is to be used widely. And there must be convenient means to pay for goods and services purchased, whether the purchase is a pack of chewing gum or a business worth millions of dollars. This means that the monetary system must operate with monetary institutions, instruments such as stocks and bonds, and procedures geared to the needs of the economy.

capital formation
the creation of produc-
tive facilities such as
buildings, tools, and
equipment

A financial system must make possible the creation of capital on a scale large enough to meet the demands of the economy. ***Capital formation*** takes place whenever resources are used to produce buildings, machinery, or other equipment to be used in the production of goods for consumer or producer use. In a simple economy, such as a self-sufficient, one-person farm, this process takes place directly. The farmer creates capital by building a new barn.

In a highly developed economy, capital formation takes place indirectly. If individuals, businesses, or governmental units do not need to spend all of their current income, they save some of it. If these savings are placed with some type of financial intermediary, they will be made available in the form of loans to others who use them to buy buildings, machinery, or equipment. The indirect process of capital formation can work only if the proper legal instruments and financial intermediaries exist. Then savers will feel secure transferring the use of their savings to businesses and other institutions who need them.

A third essential feature of the financial system is that it provides markets for the transfer of financial assets, such as stocks and bonds, and for the conversion of such assets into cash. Markets are necessary for capital formation. They encourage investment by providing the means for savers to quickly and easily convert their claims into cash when needed. For example, millions of people are willing to invest billions of dollars in AT&T, IBM, and other companies because the New York Stock Exchange makes it possible to sell their shares to other investors easily and quickly.

FINANCIAL INTERMEDIARIES IN THE UNITED STATES

The current system of financial intermediaries that exists in the United States, like the monetary system, developed to meet the changing needs of our economy. Because the U.S. economy is closely tied to the economies of other nations, our financial intermediaries must continually respond to changes in the global economy as well. For example, today banks are willing to exchange foreign currencies for U.S. dollars and vice versa, as well as lend to foreign businesses.

Five Types of Financial Intermediaries

depository institutions
commercial banks, sav-
ings and loans, savings
banks, and credit unions

The basic kinds of financial intermediaries that play active roles in the U.S. financial system are shown in Figure 1.1. First are the ***depository institutions***, which are commercial banks, savings and loan associations, savings banks, and credit unions. These institutions play an important role in the channeling of individuals' savings into loans to governments (by purchasing their debt issues), loans to businesses, and home mortgages.

The second category, *contractual savings institutions*, are so classified because they involve relatively steady inflows of money. Life insurance companies receive steady inflows in the form of insurance premium payments. Likewise, pension funds for both private and government programs receive contributions on a regular basis. These institutions play an active role in supplying long-term funding by purchasing corporate stocks and bonds, mortgages, and government securities.

Investment institutions make up the third major category in our financial system. These institutions combine the relatively small amounts of savings from many individuals and invest the total in financial assets. Mutual funds purchase corporate stocks and bonds as well as government securities. REITs, or real estate investment trusts, invest in property and mortgages. Money market funds invest in short-term debt securities. While individual investors can invest directly in such securities, investment institutions offer small investors diversification and experienced management of their funds.

The fourth category consists of *finance companies.* These companies provide loans directly to consumers and businesses. Sales and consumer finance companies lend to individuals. Sales finance companies finance installment loan purchases of automobiles and other durable goods. Consumer finance companies provide small loans to individuals and households. Businesses that are unable to obtain financing from commercial banks often turn to commercial finance companies for necessary loans. Thus, finance companies play an important role in our financial system. They provide loanable funds to consumers and businesses that are not obtainable from depository institutions.

The fifth category consists of *securities market institutions* that are involved in the savings-investment process and/or the marketing and transferring of claims to wealth. (There are many kinds of securities market institutions so it is important to know that only selected ones are shown in Figure 1.1.) Creating or issuing new securities or other claims to wealth takes place in the **primary securities market**. The **secondary securities market** involves the transfer of existing securities from old investors to new investors.

Credit-reporting and credit-rating organizations aid lenders in deciding whether to extend credit to consumers and businesses. Finally, in recent years government credit-related agencies (such as the Government National Mortgage Association) have taken an increasingly active role in the marketing and transferring of real estate mortgages.

Among the listed institutions, mortgage banking firms play an important role in the origination of real estate mortgages by bringing together borrowers and lenders. Investment banking and brokerage

primary securities market
market involved in creating and issuing new securities, mortgages, and other claims to wealth

secondary securities market
market for transferring existing securities between investors

firms are often involved in marketing new stock and bond securities issued by businesses. And brokerage houses, along with organized securities markets, handle the transfer of stocks and bonds among investors.

Few of today's financial intermediaries existed during the American colonial period. Only commercial banks and insurance companies (life and property) can be traced back prior to 1800. Savings banks and S&Ls began developing during the early 1800s. Investment banking firms and organized securities exchanges also can be traced back to the first half of the 1800s. No new major financial intermediaries evolved during the last half of the nineteenth century. Credit unions, pension funds, mutual funds, and finance companies began during the early part of the twentieth century. This was true for government involvement in credit-related agencies as well.

Financial intermediaries in other market economies are generally different in name and organizational structure from their U.S. counterparts. However, they carry out financial functions similar to those described in Figure 1.1. In addition, two international financial institutions exist to promote stability and growth in international finance and trade. Both the International Monetary Fund and the World Bank, which are affiliates of the United Nations, were founded at the end of World War II and have important roles in today's global economy. The

✳FIGURE 1.1   Major Intermediaries in the U.S. Financial System

DEPOSITORY INSTITUTIONS	FINANCE COMPANIES
Commercial banks Savings and loan associations (S&Ls) Savings banks Credit unions	Sales finance companies Consumer finance companies Commercial finance companies
CONTRACTUAL SAVINGS INSTITUTIONS	**SELECTED SECURITIES MARKET INSTITUTIONS**

Life insurance companies
Private pension funds
State and local government
  retirement funds
	Mortgage banking companies
	Investment bankers and brokerage companies
	Organized securities markets
	Credit-reporting organizations
	Government credit-related
	  agencies

INVESTMENT INSTITUTIONS	

Investment companies and
  mutual funds
Real estate investment trusts
  (REITs)
Money market mutual funds	

International Monetary Fund (IMF) focuses on maintaining orderly conditions in foreign exchange markets by providing facilities where member countries can borrow foreign currencies to correct temporary payment imbalances with other countries. The IMF is an outgrowth of the Bretton Woods agreements and will be discussed in Chapter 2. The **World Bank** encourages international trade by providing long-term loans to developing countries for basic capital projects designed to support their domestic development. Funds for loans made by the World Bank are obtained by selling bonds in developed countries.

International Monetary Fund (IMF) provides means for United Nations' countries to borrow money

World Bank provides loans to developing countries

Financial Intermediation

Intermediation is the process by which savings are accumulated in depository institutions and, in turn, lent or invested. During the 1970s and 1980s, the great bulk of all funds flowing into the credit markets was supplied by depository institutions. The role of depository institutions has increased significantly since the 1920s. At that time over half the net increase in the financial assets of households was in the form of securities purchased directly in the credit markets. By the 1980s these purchases accounted for only a small amount of the financial savings of households. The remainder, except for net additions to currency holdings, flowed through depository institutions.

intermediation the accumulation and lending of savings by depository institutions

The role of depository institutions has grown because they offer a variety of investment opportunities in which savers are interested. Notes, bonds, and shares of stock offered by institutions seeking long-term funds are not the assets which most savers are willing to purchase and hold. Depository institutions offer savers safety of principal, easy access to funds, convenience, and availability in small amounts.

Small savers also prefer depository institutions because of the relatively high cost of making small transactions for securities. It is also more difficult to make transactions in securities markets than it is to put funds into a depository institution. Government guarantees of deposit safety through FDIC insurance and supervision has also made depository institutions attractive to small savers. Lastly, there is a multitude of choices among depository institutions, each of which is competing for the saver's funds. This has led to a variety of services and conveniences for the saver as well as attractive rates of return.

In years of strong demand for credit and strong restraint on the money supply, such as the early 1980s, the percentage of funds moving through depository institutions to the credit markets has decreased significantly. These are referred to as periods of **disintermediation**. During these times, rapid shifts of sources of funds create difficulties in the economy by impeding the flow of funds to such sectors as housing, which rely heavily on loans from depository institutions.

disintermediation periods when there is a significant decrease in funds moving through depository institutions to the credit markets

CLAIMS TO WEALTH   *explain*

real assets
land, buildings,
machinery, inventory,
and precious metals

financial assets
claims against the
income or assets of others

Claims to wealth may be in the form of real assets or financial assets. **Real assets** would include the direct ownership of land, buildings, machinery, inventory, and even precious metals. **Financial assets,** also called *intangible assets* or *intangibles*, represent claims against the income and assets of those who issued them. Financial assets are claims against individuals, businesses, financial intermediaries, and governments in the form of obligations or liabilities. For example, a firm's debt obligations are financial assets to those who hold them, but represent liabilities of that firm. Real assets in the form of inventory, machinery, and buildings often back the financial claims or liabilities issued by businesses.

However, relatively few of the many types of financial assets actually require the use of financial markets. Checkable deposits, such as checking accounts and share drafts, and time deposits, such as savings accounts held in depository institutions, are also examples of financial assets. In fact, all kinds of promissory notes or "IOUs" represent financial assets to their holders. Also included is currency issued by the U.S. government. When held by the public, currency is a financial asset. At the same time, it is a financial liability to the government.

Only certain financial assets in the form of securities and debt instruments are marketed and traded in the financial markets. Financial markets are frequently divided into money and capital markets in addition to the previously mentioned primary and secondary markets. **Money markets** are the markets where debt instruments of one year or less are traded. **Capital markets** include longer-term debt securities such as notes and bonds, debt instruments such as mortgages, and corporate stocks.

money markets
markets where debt
instruments of one year
or less are traded

capital markets
markets for longer-term
debt securities

Figure 1.2 indicates the major types of financial assets that are traded in the financial markets. Since the U.S. government actively borrows through debt financing, its short- and longer-term financial claims, such as treasury bills (T-bills) and notes and bonds, are very important in both the money and capital markets. Federal agencies, for example the Farm Credit Banks and Federal Home Loan Mortgage Corporation, and state and local governments generally issue longer-term financial claims that trade in the capital markets.

commercial paper
short-term unsecured
promissory notes

negotiable certificates of
deposit
debt instruments of
$100,000 or more issued
by banks that can be
traded in the money
markets

Businesses are active in both financial markets. Some businesses finance a portion of their needs by issuing debt instruments in the form of short-term unsecured promissory notes called **commercial paper**. Corporations also issue large amounts of stocks and bonds to meet their financing needs. Real estate mortgages, created to finance residential and other properties, are also traded in the capital markets.

Negotiable certificates of deposit (CDs) are debt instruments issued by depository institutions to depositors. CDs pay annual inter-

FIGURE 1.2   Claims to Wealth Traded in U.S. Financial Markets

MONEY MARKET INSTRUMENTS	CAPITAL MARKET SECURITIES AND INSTRUMENTS
U.S. Treasury bills	U.S. Treasury notes and bonds
Negotiable certificates of deposit	U.S. Government agency bonds
Bankers' acceptances	State and local government
Federal funds	bonds
Commercial paper	Corporate bonds
Repurchase agreements	Corporate stocks
	Real estate mortgages

est and at maturity pay back the original deposit. Those in denominations of $100,000 or more are negotiable, that is, readily exchangeable in the money markets. **Bankers' acceptances** are created as a result of international trade. They are a promise of payment at some future date, similar to a check, issued by a firm and guaranteed by a bank. Acceptances represent an obligation of the accepting or guaranteeing bank and are fully marketable. **Federal funds** are overnight loans between depository institutions of the deposits that these institutions maintain at their Federal Reserve Banks. **Repurchase agreements** are short-term loans in which treasury bills serve as collateral. Each of these money market instruments and capital market securities and instruments will be described in detail in this book.

Markets for financial assets are also important for the continued development of international trade and finance in a global economy. An important element is a uniform world-wide currency. While U.S. currency has been readily available in many foreign countries for many years, most international trade involves the transfer of deposits between banks. Until the development of Eurodollars, deposits denominated in U.S. dollars were held only in U.S. banks. This situation hindered growth in international trade.

Eurodollars are U.S. dollars deposited in banks outside the United States, usually in European banks. American banks can borrow these deposits from other banks or from their own foreign branches when they need funds. Eurodollars have become an internationally accepted currency denominated in U.S. dollars for conducting trade in a global economy. **Eurocurrencies,** a more broadly-based term, refers to all foreign currency deposits held in banks outside the countries of origin.

Bonds represent the primary method for raising funds in many countries. These debt instruments are traditionally denominated in the currency of the countries where they are sold. A more recent development in international bond markets is the issuance of **Eurobonds**, which are bonds denominated in currencies other than those of the countries in which they are marketed. The Eurobond market has

bankers' acceptances
a promise of future payment issued by a firm and guaranteed by a bank

federal funds
temporary excess reserves that are loaned to banks by the Fed

repurchase agreements
short-term loans using Treasury bills as collateral

Eurodollars
U.S. dollars placed in foreign banks

Eurocurrencies
all non-U.S. currencies held by banks outside their country of origin

Eurobonds
bonds denominated in currencies other than that of the country where they are sold

expanded rapidly in recent years because the market is largely unregulated and interest on the bonds is generally tax-free because these
bonds are unregistered and there is no record of ownership. Eurobond
issuers can move more quickly and with greater flexibility than can, for
example, those in the U.S. bond market.

FINANCIAL FUNCTIONS IN THE U.S. SYSTEM

In our economy, the government and private financial intermediaries of
many kinds have developed instruments and procedures to perform the
financial functions listed in Figure 1.3. These financial functions may,
in turn, be viewed as characteristics of the financial system which
evolved to support our modern market economy.

Creating Money

money
anything that is gener-
ally accepted as payment

Money may be defined as anything that is generally accepted as payment for goods and services and for discharging debts. The value of
money lies in its purchasing power. It is the most generalized claim to
wealth, since it can be exchanged for almost anything else. Most
transactions in a modern economy involve money, and most would not
take place if money were not available.

One of the most significant functions of the financial system is
creating money, which serves as a medium of exchange. In the United
States, the Federal Reserve System has primary responsibility for the
amount of money that is created, although most of the money is
actually created by depository institutions. A sufficient amount of

FIGURE 1.3   Characteristics of an Effective Financial System

BASIC REQUIREMENTS	FINANCIAL FUNCTIONS
I. Monetary System	1. Creating money
	2. Transferring money
II. Savings-Investment Process	3. Accumulating savings
	4. Lending and investing money
III. Claims-to-Wealth Structure	5. Marketing financial assets
	6. Transferring financial assets

money is essential for economic activity to take place at an efficient rate. However, if too much money is made available, its value tends to fall and prices go up. When this happens, *inflation* occurs.

Transferring Money

Individuals and businesses hold money for purchases or payments they expect to make in the near future. One way to hold money is in checkable deposits at depository institutions. When money is held in this form, payments can easily be made by check. The check is an order to the depository institution to transfer money to the party who received the check. This is a great convenience, since checks can be written for the exact amount of payments, can be safely sent in the mail, and provide a record of payment. Today, institutions can also transfer funds between accounts electronically, making payments without paper checks. Funds transfers can be made by telephone or at remote terminals connected to a bank's computer.

Accumulating Savings

A function performed by financial intermediaries is the accumulation or gathering together of individual savings. Most individuals, businesses, and organizations do not want to take the risks involved in having cash on hand. Even if cash amounts are relatively small, they are put into a depository institution for safekeeping. When all the deposits are accumulated in one place, they can be used for loans and investments in amounts much larger than any individual depositor could supply. Depository institutions regularly conduct advertising campaigns and other promotional activities to attract deposits.

Lending and Investing Money

Another basic function of financial intermediaries is lending and investing. The money that has been put into these intermediaries may be loaned to businesses, farmers, consumers, institutions, and governmental units. It may be loaned for varying time periods and for different purposes, such as to buy equipment or to pay current bills. Some financial intermediaries make loans of almost all types. Others specialize in only one or two types of lending. Still other financial intermediaries invest all or part of their accumulated savings in the stock of a business or in debt obligations of businesses or other institutions.

Marketing Financial Assets

A business may want to sell shares of ownership, called stock, to the general public. It can do so directly, but the process of finding individuals interested in investing funds in that business is likely to be difficult, costly, and time-consuming. A particular financial intermediary, an investment banking firm, can handle the sale of shares of ownership. The function of the investment banking firm is essentially one of merchandising.

Transferring Financial Assets

Several types of financial intermediaries facilitate or assist the processes of lending and of selling securities. If shares of stock are to be sold to the general public, it is desirable to have a ready market in which such stocks can be resold when the investor desires. The several stock exchanges serve this purpose. If lending is to be done effectively, it is necessary to have readily available up-to-date information on the applicants for loans. Various types of credit-checking agencies exist to meet this need.

THE PLAN OF STUDY

The subject matter of this book includes the entire scope of the financial system and its functions. You will learn about the markets in which funds are traded and the institutions that participate in and assist these flows of funds. And you will study the principles and concepts which guide these institutions in making sound decisions.

Part 1 deals with the financial system in the U.S. economy and its role in the global economy. Financial functions, intermediaries, and instruments are considered briefly in this chapter. Other chapters in Part 1 deal with the U. S. monetary system and the role of depository institutions and the Federal Reserve System in providing money and credit to meet the needs of the economy. We conclude Part 1 with Chapter 6, which focuses on the savings-investment process and its major role in our modern market economy.

Part 2 looks at the financial system as it relates to the business sector of the economy. We begin with an introduction to business finance. This includes coverage of financial management objectives and the need to conduct financial analysis to attain these objectives. The next chapter focuses on financial planning and working capital management. This is followed by a discussion of the sources of short-term business financing. Then the discussion turns to the management of fixed assets and the mix of debt and equity funds found in organizations. The next chapter deals with the sources of long-term business financing, followed by one on the time value of money and fixed-assets management. Chapter 13, the last in Part 2, covers the markets for long-term business funds.

We devote a great deal of attention to business financing for several reasons. Firms typically use the financial markets for a large portion of the funds they need for current operations and capital investment. Because business profits are so sensitive to financial decisions, theories and concepts of financial management are carefully discussed. Business finance principles are also applicable to other areas of finance, including the management of financial institutions. In addition, a significant part of the financial system is involved in meeting the demands for funds in the business sector of the economy.

Part 3, Chapters 14 through 20, is concerned with meeting the demand for funds in other sectors of the economy. Three basic sectors are identified. Section A of Part 3 deals with financing for governmental needs. The first chapter considers the financing of the federal government. The next looks at financing of state and local governments.

Section B deals with short and long-term financing for the consumer. The initial chapters discuss the role of consumer financing in the economy and the institutions and procedures available for providing credit to consumers. A third chapter focuses on mortgages used to finance the purchase of residential real estate.

Section C of Part 3 covers the institutions and procedures developed to supply funds in specialized areas. It discusses financing of agriculture and international trade and foreign investment.

Part 4 focuses on monetary, fiscal, and debt management policies. The first chapter, Chapter 21, examines the role of the Federal Reserve System in establishing monetary policy. It also considers the relationship of the Treasury to the supply of money and credit in the financial markets. Then we focus attention on the structure and level of interest rates in relation to monetary and fiscal policies. This is followed by two chapters exploring the relationships between monetary policies and price levels, business fluctuations, and international financial equilibrium. The last chapter traces the impact of recent monetary and fiscal-policy actions on our market economy.

KEY TERMS

bankers' acceptances	disintermediation
capital formation	Eurobonds
capital markets	Eurocurrencies
commercial paper	Eurodollars
depository institutions	federal funds

finance   negotiable certificates of deposit
financial assets   primary securities market
financial intermediaries   real assets
intermediation   repurchase agreements
International Monetary Fund   secondary securities market
money   World Bank
money markets

DISCUSSION QUESTIONS

1. What is finance? Provide a brief overview of the field.
2. Indicate some of the finance career opportunities that are available to business students today.
3. What are the basic requirements of an effective financial system?
4. Identify and briefly describe the structure of financial intermediaries in the United States.
5. What is meant by the term financial intermediation?
6. How do real assets and financial assets differ?
7. Briefly describe the differences between the money and capital markets.
8. Identify and briefly describe the types of claims to wealth that are traded in U.S. financial markets.
9. Briefly explain the terms Eurodollars, Eurocurrencies, and Eurobonds.
10. Identify and describe the financial functions or characteristics of the financial system that evolved to support the U.S. economy.

SELF-TEST QUESTIONS

1. The basic requirements for an effective financial system in a developed economy include:

    a. a monetary system
    b. a savings-investment process
    c. markets for the transfer of financial assets
    d. all of the above

2. Which one of these financial intermediaries focuses on maintaining orderly conditions in foreign exchange markets?

    a. commercial banks
    b. the World Bank
    c. International Monetary Fund
    d. commercial finance companies

3. Which of the following claims to wealth traded in U.S. financial markets is a money market instrument?
    a. commercial paper
    b. U.S. Treasury notes and bonds
    c. corporate bonds
    d. real estate mortgages

4. U.S.-dollar-denominated deposits held in banks outside the United States are referred to as:
    a. negotiable certificates of deposit
    b. bankers' acceptances
    c. federal funds
    d. Eurodollars

5. The savings-investment process involves which of the following financial functions:
    a. creating and transferring money
    b. accumulating savings and lending and investing money
    c. marketing and transferring financial assets
    d. all of the above

SUGGESTED READINGS

Cook, Timothy Q., and Bruce J. Summers (eds.). *Instruments of the Money Market*, 5e. Federal Reserve Bank of Richmond, 1981.

Edmister, Robert O. *Financial Institutions*, 2e. New York: McGraw-Hill. 1986. Chap. 1.

Henning, Charles N., William Pigott, and Robert H. Scott. *Financial Markets and the Economy*, 5e. Englewood Cliffs, NJ: Prentice-Hall, 1988. Chap. 1.

Mishkin, Frederic S. *The Economics of Money, Banking, and Financial Markets*, 2e. Glenview, IL: Scott, Foresman and Co., 1989. Chap. 3.

Rose, Peter S. *Money and Capital Markets*, 3e. Homewood, IL: BPI/Irwin, 1989. Chaps. 1 and 2.

Shapiro, Alan C. *Multinational Financial Management*, 3e. Boston: Allyn & Bacon, 1989. Chap. 3.

ANSWERS TO SELF-TEST QUESTIONS   1. d   2. c   3. a   4. d   5. b

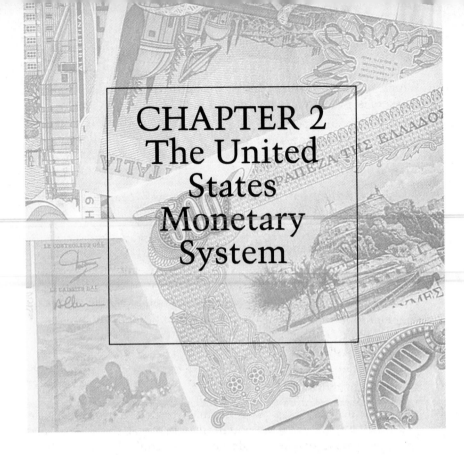

CHAPTER 2
The United States Monetary System

After studying this chapter, you should be able to:
- Describe the functions of money.
- Give a brief overview of the historical development of our monetary system.
- Define the bimetallic standard as used in the United States.
- Describe the history of paper money in the United States.
- Explain why it is important to have a monetary standard that serves as a standard of value.
- Explain what is important in defining the money supply and define the M1 money supply.
- Briefly explain the M2, M3, and L definitions of the money supply.

The essential role of a monetary system in the operation and development of a financial system was explained in Chapter 1. In this chapter the nature and functions of money are developed more fully. Also, the nature of the monetary system of the United States is described and analyzed. Consideration is also given to the monetary standard upon which the system is based and to the types of money currently used to meet the needs of the economy.

Although our focus is on the U.S. monetary system, today we operate in a global economy. Thus we must interact with other monetary systems. For example, a change in either the Japanese or German monetary systems will directly impact the U.S. monetary system. For example, when the Bundesbank (the German central bank) acts to increase interest rates in Germany, the value of the U.S. dollar weakens relative to the German mark. This increases the cost of products imported into the United States unless the Federal Reserve takes countering actions.

THE NATURE AND FUNCTIONS OF MONEY

In the preceding chapter, money was defined as anything generally accepted as a means of paying for goods and services and of discharging debts. This function of money is generally referred to as that of serving as a **medium of exchange.** This is the basic function of money in any economy. However, money also serves as a store of purchasing power and as a standard of value.

medium of exchange
the basic function of money

Money may be held as a **store of purchasing power** that can be drawn on at will. This may be done shortly after it is received or after it has been held for a period of time. While money is held, it is a liquid asset and provides its owner with flexibility. But the owner pays for this flexibility by foregoing the potential return that could be earned through investment or the satisfaction that could be gained from spending it for goods and services. Furthermore, money can perform its function as a store of purchasing power only if its value is relatively stable.

store of purchasing power
when money is held as a liquid asset

The function of serving as a store of purchasing power can also be performed by an asset other than money if that asset can be converted into money quickly and without significant loss of value. We refer to this quality—the ease with which an asset can be exchanged for money or other assets—as **liquidity.** Money is perfectly liquid since it is a generally accepted medium of exchange. Other assets, such as savings deposits held at depository institutions, approach the liquidity of money. The existence of such liquid assets reduces the need for holding money itself as a store of purchasing power.

liquidity
how easily an asset can be exchanged for money

The third function of money—as a **standard of value**—means that prices and contracts for deferred payments are expressed in terms of the monetary unit. Prices and debts are usually expressed in terms of dollars without stating whether the purchase will be cash or credit. The function of money as a standard by which to judge value is circular. The value of money may be stated in terms of the goods it will buy; a change in prices generally reflects a change in the value of money. If money is to perform its function as a standard of value, it is essential that the value of the monetary unit be relatively stable.

standard of value
a function of money that occurs when prices and debts are stated in terms of the monetary unit

DEVELOPMENT OF MONETARY SYSTEMS

We have answered the question of what money is, but we have not yet said what items serve as money. The answer to this may not be as simple as it seems at first. A look at the history of money reveals that the answer has changed over time, just as a monetary system changes to meet the changing needs of an economy. We can infer much about these developments from the available evidence and from practices still in use in more primitive economies.

Barter

Primitive economies consisted largely of self-sufficient units or groups that lived by means of hunting, fishing, and simple agriculture. There was little need or occasion to exchange goods or services. Even in such economies, however, some trade took place.

barter
exchange of goods or services without using money

As economies became more developed, the process of exchange became important. Some individuals specialized, to a degree at least, in herding sheep, raising grain, or as gold- and silversmiths. To aid exchanges of goods for goods, called **barter**, tables of relative values were developed from past experience. For example, a table might show the number of furs, measures of grain, or amount of cloth agreed to equal one cow. This arrangement eased exchanges, but the process still had many serious drawbacks. For example, if a person had a cow and wanted to trade it for some nuts and furs, he or she would need to find someone who had an excess of both these items to trade. The need for a simpler means of exchange led to the development of money.

Early Development of Money

The record of the early development of money is very sketchy. In all probability traders found that some items, such as furs and grain, were traded more frequently than others. Since these items could be easily traded, traders could afford to accept them in exchange when they did not need them. They probably also found it convenient to figure the value of less frequently traded goods in terms of more frequently traded items. This is because the system gave traders a familiar yardstick with which to value goods.

This system developed in much the same way in some prisoner of war camps in Germany during World War II. Cigarettes were used as a general medium of exchange since they could always be traded for other goods or services. Values of all types of goods were quoted in cigarettes even when there was no intention of exchanging them.

Records from early economies show that many items useful for food or clothing were used as a general medium of exchange and, to some degree at least, as a unit for measuring value. Included were grain, salt, skins, spices, tea, seeds, and cattle. Some early economies made use of such commodities as beads, ivory, bird feathers, gold, and silver because there was a general demand for personal ornaments. Objects that were used as tools or in making tools, such as animal claws, fishhooks, shark teeth, and stone discs, were also used. All of these items were generally accepted in exchange because they could be used for further exchange or as food, clothing, tools, or ornaments.

Traders accepted these items as long as they felt certain they could use them again in future trading. This meant that the supply of the item had to be limited in relation to the desires of individuals in the economy to have the item. In early economies this was generally true of items such as grains, cattle, and tools. Items of ornamentation could likewise be used as a general medium of exchange only if there was an unfilled demand for them. For example, Native Americans valued wampum beads as a decoration and were not able to get enough of them to meet the desires of everyone. Therefore, such beads served as a general medium of exchange.

Use of Precious Metals as Money

When commodities were used as a medium of exchange, goods could be valued in terms of the item used as money and could be exchanged for it. This process, however, was still clumsy and time-consuming. For example, if furs were used, they were bulky and difficult to carry. Furthermore, arguments could arise over the quality of the furs. It was also necessary to make a trade of goods equal to one, two, three, or more skins since furs lost value when cut into pieces.

The transition from the use of commodities like furs as money to the use of precious metals was probably a gradual one. The advantages of precious metals eventually led to their general usage. Gold and silver were in great demand for ornamentation because they were durable, beautiful, and could be shaped. The supply of these metals was limited enough so that very small amounts had great value. This made them easy to carry around as money. Furthermore, they could be refined into the pure metal rather easily, making their quality uniform. Various quantities could also be weighed out so that exchanges of varying values could be made. In time, coins with a certain weight of metal in them were developed. Since an unscrupulous trader could cover less valuable metals with gold or produce coins with short weight, the process of coinage needed regulation to make coins generally uniform. For that reason, coining money and determining its value has been a governmental function in some cultures for about twenty-five hundred years.

Metal coins and other commodities that served as early forms of money are sometimes referred to as ***full-bodied money.*** They had a value equal to their value as commodities. Since they were money, they served as a standard of value—that is, the worth of other commodities was expressed in units of this monetary commodity. When governments undertook the function of coining money, they formalized the standard. They established by law the basic money unit in terms of the weight and fineness, or parity, of precious metals such as gold. This standardization also provided a convenient medium of exchange for trade between nations.

Representative Money

The earliest forerunners of private banks were goldsmiths, specialists in weighing, assaying, and storing precious metals. Individuals would pay these early "banks" to store their gold for safekeeping. The stored gold would be carefully evaluated, and a receipt issued verifying its weight and fineness. It was often more convenient to conduct a transaction by signing over the receipts rather than handing over the gold itself. Gold was cumbersome and dangerous to transport. Also, the recipients would often have more confidence in the expert evaluation of the gold's weight and fineness stated on the receipt than in their own evaluation. As the receipts or notes circulated more freely, they became the first representative full-bodied paper money.

Since early modern times, governments have also issued money in the form of paper. Gold and silver coins are difficult to protect and carry around for large transactions. To ease exchange, governments issued paper money to represent certain quantities of gold or silver that were kept on deposit by the government to back such paper. The paper was generally accepted as a medium of exchange because the persons accepting it knew they could get the precious metal when and if they wanted it.

After they were developed, banks also issued paper money backed by precious metals. At first this was done without specific authorization by governmental authorities. However, as time went on, governments regulated the issuance of paper money by the banks. Paper money backed by gold or silver circulated freely. As long as individuals felt certain they could exchange it for the precious metal behind it, they felt no need to do so.

These types of paper money were ***representative full-bodied money*** because such a government note or bank note represented a specific amount of gold or silver in storage in a government or bank vault. For localized transactions, the paper was exchanged freely. Holders of the paper rarely had a need to present the paper for redemption in metal. Gradually the paper circulated more widely, and eventually even merchants of different nations would accept the paper money issued by reputable banks and governments. Since only a small number of notes would be redeemed during a given period of time, there was relatively little turnover of the precious metal in the vaults. This situation led to the evolution of modern monetary systems.

✳ Credit Money

As the paper circulated, the gold sat in vaults, with only a fraction of it being redeemed during any period of time. Like the goldsmiths before them, bankers went into the loan business, lending either gold itself or issuing additional receipts or notes. In so doing the bankers issued notes for more gold than they actually had in their vaults. As long as the bankers did not experience an unusually high number of customers presenting notes for redemption at the same time, they found this to be a safe and profitable way of doing business. And as long as the depositors were confident that the gold could be redeemed, they were usually content to leave it safely on deposit. This practice not only represents one of the earliest examples of credit money, but also describes the origins of our modern fractional reserve system of banking and money creation, which will be discussed in Chapter 5.

The general acceptance of paper money as a medium of exchange, with no intention of redeeming it for the precious metal behind it, made possible the issuance of paper money with no such backing. From time to time, money was issued based only on the general credit of a government and on the provision that such money was **legal tender**, acceptable to pay taxes and to fulfill contracts calling for payment in lawful money. This is the case today in the United States and in other countries. Since this money is proclaimed to be money by law or a decree known as a fiat, it is sometimes called **fiat money.**

legal tender
money backed only by government credit

Banks also issued paper money without metallic backing. As such issues were brought under regulation, the banks were required to have some metallic backing for their paper money. They also had to have some form of collateral, such as government bonds, for the remainder of the face value of the money they issued. The privilege of private banks to issue paper money of any type became more and more restricted and has been abolished in all countries in recent years. The only banks that issue any significant amounts of paper money today are central banks, which are owned or controlled by the national government of the country.

fiat money
legal tender proclaimed to be money by law

Any circulating medium which has little real value relative to its monetary value is called **credit money.** Almost all money circulating in the world today is some form of credit money—money which does not consist of or represent a specific valuable commodity. Rather, its value depends on its general acceptance based on the credit of its issuer.

credit money
money worth more than what it is made of

THE U.S. MONETARY SYSTEM

While barter was undoubtedly important in early U.S. history, the government moved swiftly towards a monetary system based on precious metals. Today the U.S. monetary system uses credit money, and money transfers are often conducted electronically.

Early Legislation

*bimetallic standard
monetary standard
based on two metals,
usually silver and gold*

The first monetary act in the United States was passed in 1792, and provided for a bimetallic standard. A ***bimetallic standard*** is one based upon two metals—in this case, silver and gold. The dollar, which was set up as the unit of value, was defined as 371.25 grains of pure silver or 24.75 grains of pure gold. Thus, the metal in the silver dollar was 15 times the weight of the metal in the gold dollar, making a ratio of 15 to 1 between the metals when minted. Provision was made for gold coins in denominations of $2.50, $5, and $10, and for silver coins in denominations of $1, 50¢, 25¢, 10¢, and 5¢. All of these coins contained silver equal to their full face value, the 10¢ piece one tenth as much as the silver dollar, and so on. In addition, provision was made for copper token coins in one-cent and half-cent denominations. Unlike full-bodied coins, ***token coins*** are worth more as money than the value of the metal they contain.

*token coins
coins containing metal
of less value than their
stated value*

The bimetallic standard was difficult to maintain because the market ratio between silver and gold, which was about 15 to 1 in 1792, soon changed to about 15.5 to 1. Consequently, little gold was brought to the mint for coinage because it was found to be worth more in the open market. The few gold coins that were minted soon disappeared from circulation. In 1834 Congress changed the official mint ratio to 16 to 1. This reversed the situation rather than remedying it. Gold was now overvalued at the mint. Gold coins became abundant, but silver coins disappeared from circulation. Officially the bimetallic standard lasted until 1900, but the United States had in fact been on a gold standard since the 1830s. Full-bodied coins actually circulated until 1934, and the dollar was defined in terms of gold until the 1970s.

Credit Money in the United States

Except for brief experiments beginning with the War of 1812, the federal government did not become a major issuer of credit money until the Civil War. However, twice during the early years of the country it chartered a national bank authorized to do so. During the years that the First and Second Banks of the United States existed, a reliable paper currency circulated nationally in significant quantities. However, each of these banks was chartered for only twenty years, and for political reasons, neither of the charters was renewed by Congress.

Prior to 1792, many foreign coins circulated in the United States. In addition to establishing a bimetallic standard, the Monetary Act of 1792 provided for the continued use of foreign coins until U.S. coins were produced in sufficient quantities. Spanish silver dollars were to be accepted as full legal tender. They weighed 415 grains nine-tenths pure, which gave them a silver content of 373.5 grains. They could be legally used to discharge debts, and creditors could not insist on payment in any other type of money if the debt was stated in Spanish dollars. All lighter Spanish dollars and all other foreign coins were to be accepted only for their actual value in metal. These provisions were unrealistic, since to carry them out meant weighing coins at every transaction. Most foreign coins were of short weight due to long periods of use, while the U.S. coins were of full weight. The result was that U.S. coins were hoarded and foreign coins were circulated. Therefore, the 1792 monetary act resulted in an early monetary system that relied almost exclusively on the use of foreign coins.

FOREIGN COINS IN THE EARLY AMERICAN ECONOMY

Various state-chartered banks also issued bank notes. Except for the years that the national banks existed, the lack of uniform regulation made these state bank issues inconsistent and unreliable. They were frequently accepted only at a discount any distance from the issuing bank, and were sometimes not redeemable even there. Bank-issued money will be discussed in more detail in the next chapter.

To help finance the Civil War, Congress authorized the issue of paper money. It was officially known as United States Notes and popularly called **greenbacks.** This was fiat money; the notes were legal tender, but were not redeemable for gold or silver. In addition, in 1863 Congress established the National Banking System, which authorized nationally chartered banks to issue notes. The National Bank notes were carefully controlled and were backed by government securities. In effect, Congress allowed newly chartered banks to issue credit money and lend it to the Treasury. This helped finance the war, and it also provided another reliable source of credit money. At the same time, notes of state banks, which had been a source of confusion in the economy because of their unreliability, were taxed out of existence. Thus, for the first time, this country had a uniform national currency.

In 1878, the Treasury began issuing silver certificates backed by silver stored in its vault. These certificates continued to serve as the principal small-denomination currency in circulation until 1967. In 1914, the Federal Reserve System, known as the Fed, began operations,

greenbacks
money issued by the U.S. government to help finance the Civil War

Collectors of old coins and paper currency are referred to as *numismatists*. Although authorized in 1792, the first U.S. silver dollar carried a 1794 mint date. As might be expected, the 1794 dollar is quite rare today and is very valuable even in worn condition. Minting silver dollars was stopped in 1804 before being resumed again in 1836. So-called liberty head or Morgan dollars were first minted in 1878 and continued into 1921. The peace-type silver dollar became available in 1921. It continued to be minted through 1935 when the production of silver dollars ceased. Eisenhower dollars were minted during 1971–1978 and were followed by the ill-fated Susan B. Anthony dollars, which were minted from 1979 to 1981.

The history of U.S. currency is as interesting as the history of U.S. coins. For example, the first paper money was issued by the U.S. government in the form of U.S. Treasury notes in conjunction with the War of 1812. U.S. large-size currency was much larger than that in use today. It came into circulation with the U.S. note series of 1862. Later, large-size currency also included silver certificates, gold certificates, and Treasury notes. Federal Reserve bank notes began with the series of 1918. National bank notes were issued between 1863 and 1928. Large-size U.S. government currency and national bank notes are avidly sought by collectors today. The smaller, current size U.S. currency began in 1929 (series of 1928) with the issuance of U.S. notes and silver certificates. It continues today in the form of Federal Reserve notes.

Good information on U.S. silver dollars and other coins is provided in a variety of publications including: *A Guide Book of United States Coins*, 43e. by R. S. Yeoman (Racine, WI: Western Publishing Co., 1990). Further information on U.S. paper currency is available in the *Standard Catalog of United States Paper Money*, 9e. by Chester L. Krause and Robert E. Lemke (Lola, WI: Krause Publications, 1990) as well as many other sources.

and Federal Reserve notes replaced national bank notes. In 1967, Federal Reserve notes also replaced silver certificates and are the only paper currency of significance in the economy today.

Demand Deposits

The process of making exchange more and more convenient did not stop with the widespread use of paper money. *Demand deposits* have a long history, but their growth was especially rapid after the national banking system was established and state banks could no longer issue bank notes. Rather than issuing a note in a specific denomination, a bank allows the holder of a deposit to transfer ownership of that deposit by means of a check—an order to the bank to make payment to another party. Today most transactions for any but small amounts are made by checks drawn on banks or other depository institutions. Demand and checkable deposits take the advantages of paper money one step further. Demand deposits are issued only by commercial banks and do not earn interest. Today, there are many forms of checkable deposits issued by all types of depository institutions that earn interest. They currently make up the bulk of our money supply. With these deposits, the holder does not physically hold, or risk losing, anything. Checks can be safely sent in the mail and can be used to make payments in any specific amounts.

Electronic Funds Transfer Systems

Though not actually a form of money, *electronic funds transfer systems* (EFTS) greatly enhance the efficiency of the payments mechanisms used in our economy. They can be considered another evolutionary step in our monetary system. With EFTS, individuals, businesses, and governments can receive and disburse funds electronically instead of through the use of checks. Transfers can be made between deposit accounts even nationwide, potentially reducing or eliminating the physical handling of checks.

electronic funds transfer systems
electronic method of receiving and disbursing funds

Several EFTS applications are currently in use. Employers can have their employees' wages deposited directly in their checking accounts, rather than issuing payroll checks. Individuals can have regular payments such as mortgage payments or insurance premiums automatically deducted from their accounts. Electronic funds transfers by telephone, for payment of utility bills, credit card balances, and so forth, are increasingly in use. The automated teller machine, which accepts deposits, arranges transfers between accounts, and dispenses cash, has also become commonplace.

THE MONETARY STANDARD AND THE VALUE OF MONEY

One of the functions of money is that it serves as a standard of value. Prices are stated in units of money, and an individual's wealth is frequently expressed in monetary terms. But the value of money is its purchasing power. When money was full-bodied, this was clear, at least in terms of a commodity with widely recognized value. This is quite different from the case today, when the monetary unit is not fixed in terms of any commodity.

When gold coins made up the money supply, the value of money was constant in terms of gold. This, of course, did not guarantee a constant purchasing power of gold. For instance, after the discovery of America, tons of gold flowed into Europe; and prices there rose sharply in terms of gold. Nevertheless, this sudden increase in the availability of gold was an exceptional case. Throughout most of history, the value of gold has been stable enough to provide a useful standard of value. Silver has also served as a monetary standard in the past.

When representative full-bodied paper money was issued, the standard remained the precious metal which the paper represented. Paper money that is easily redeemable for metal retains the value of that metal as its standard. Until 1900 the United States was officially on a bimetallic standard. However, differences between the official values and the market values of the two metals made it difficult to keep them both in circulation at the same time. For this reason, first silver and later gold served as the accepted monetary standard. As long as people were confident that the paper money issued by the banks was redeemable for gold or silver, it retained the value of a certain weight of metal, and people were willing to hold and circulate the paper.

However, during the Civil War the government printed paper currency and temporarily suspended redemption in metal. We were in effect on an inconvertible paper standard. Although there was an implied promise to redeem these notes at some time in the future, no time was specified, and the U.S. notes became the standard money. National bank notes could be exchanged for U.S. notes, so these had equal purchasing power. However, metal coins virtually disappeared from circulation, and prices in terms of paper money rose dramatically. Since the money in circulation could not be exchanged for gold or silver, its value became dependent on its acceptability in trade: the amount of goods and services it could be exchanged for. This in turn depended on people's confidence in the monetary authority—confidence in both its restraint in maintaining the relative scarcity of the money and its ability to maintain the money's status as legal tender. The dollars of both the Confederacy and the Union lost value as paper money was printed and prices rose during the Civil War. Over time, however, the U.S. notes regained their prewar purchasing power while the value of Confederate money fell to zero.

The de facto, or actual, gold standard was restored after the Civil War. However, after a century of monetary experiments, both gold and silver have now been completely removed from any monetary role in our economy. The Treasury does own some gold and silver, but there is no minimum reserve of these metals backing any of our money. They are traded freely in markets just as are other commodities. Our monetary standard is the paper dollar, issued by the Fed. No one doubts the ability of our government to enforce the legal status of the paper dollar;

however, its purchasing power, and thus its value, depends on its relative scarcity. It is one of the responsibilities of the Fed to regulate the supply of money to maintain its purchasing power. Some level of growth in the money supply is necessary to support and sustain real, adjusted for inflation, economic growth in our free-enterprise system. At the same time, a too-rapid growth in the money supply is believed to be inflationary. **Inflation** is a rise or increase in the prices of goods and services that is not offset by increases in their quality. An increase in the general price level of all goods and services in our economy leads to a decline in the purchasing power of money.

inflation
a rise in prices not offset by increases in quality

THE INTERNATIONAL MONETARY SYSTEM

The international monetary system was historically tied to the gold standard. During the early seventeenth century, Great Britain returned to the gold standard. Many other countries then followed Great Britain's lead. This caused an international gold standard to dominate international trade during the 1880–1914 period. A breakdown in the gold standard occurred during World War I, and less formal exchange systems continued during the world-wide depression of the 1930s and during World War II.

In 1944, many of the world's economic powers met at Bretton Woods, New Hampshire. They agreed to an international monetary system which was tied to the U.S. dollar or gold via fixed or pegged exchange rates. One ounce of gold was set equal to $35. Each participating country then had its currency pegged to either gold or the U.S. dollar. This system of fixed exchange rates became known as the Bretton Woods System and was maintained through 1971.

By early 1973, major currencies were allowed to "float" against each other, resulting in a flexible or floating exchange rate system. While free market forces are allowed to operate today, central monetary authorities attempt to intervene in exchange markets when they believe that exchange rates between two currencies are harming world trade and the global economy. This actually makes the current international monetary system a "managed" floating exchange rate system.

Virtually all international transactions now involve the exchange of currencies or checkable deposits denominated in various currencies. Exchanges occur either for goods and services, for financial claims, or for other currencies. The value of one currency relative to another, or their **exchange rate,** depends on the supply of and demand for each currency relative to the other. The supply of a currency in international markets depends largely on the imports of the issuing country, that is, how much of their currency they spend in world

exchange rate
value of one currency in terms of another

markets. Demand for a currency depends on the amount of exports that currency will buy from the issuing country. Demand also depends on the confidence of market participants in the restraint and stability of the monetary authority issuing the currency. If demand for a particular currency falls relative to its supply, the exchange rate falls and the international purchasing power of that nation's money supply drops. This can be caused by domestic inflation, political instability, or an excess of imports over exports. On the other hand, if a currency is widely accepted, the demand for it may be increased by the desire of people worldwide to hold it as an international medium of exchange. Such is the case of the U.S. dollar. It is widely held by foreigners because of its general acceptance and ability to hold its value. International finance is discussed in detail in Chapter 20.

THE U.S. MONEY SUPPLY & next 5 pages

No full-bodied or representative full-bodied money is in use in the United States today. All of our money is credit money. The Treasury issues token coins, and the Fed issues paper currency. The rest of the money supply is issued by depository institutions, and is held in checking accounts and similar deposits. As we have seen, the composition of the stock of money has changed over the years. In fact, some of the most dramatic changes have occurred quite recently. Because of the large number of deposit accounts and other financial instruments, the question of how much money there is no longer has a simple answer. Before we can count the money supply, we must know what to count.

Defining the Money Supply

There are two things we want to keep in mind when defining the money supply. First, we want to include in our definition only those things that perform the functions of money. Second, we want the definition to be useful. We have already discussed the effect the money supply has on economic activity and the importance of controlling it. Our definition should correspond to some measurable quantity that is clearly related to economic activity. This implies that it should consist of a set of categories we can actually measure; it would do us no good to include components which cannot be counted or separated from accounts we want to exclude.

Money serves three functions: it is a standard of value, a medium of exchange, and a store of purchasing power. The standard of value in our system is the dollar. Many assets, including many financial assets, are evaluated in dollar units, but not all are money. However, anything not measured in dollar units is disqualified—for example, gold is not money in our system. Many things also serve as a store of value, including financial assets and many real assets. Many of these are preferable to money as long-term stores of wealth, either because they earn interest or otherwise increase in value, or because they provide a flow of services to the owner. However, if we hold an asset as a store of purchasing power, we need to consider its liquidity, or the ease with which it can be converted into other assets. No other asset is as liquid as money, because money is itself a medium of exchange. Money does not need to be converted into anything else before it can be spent or used to make a payment. It is this liquidity of money that is the most helpful in narrowing our definition of the money supply.

However, even liquidity is not completely clear in today's sophisticated financial system, where so many financial assets, such as various accounts at depository institutions, are so readily interchangeable. And when we consider that our definition of money includes a measurable set of assets which can be used in the economy, our choice becomes less certain. Very generally, our reasoning goes like this. The money supply is a measure of purchasing power in the economy. We expect the amount of purchasing power to have some correspondence with the volume of transactions actually made, and this should correspond with other measures of economic activity. Historically we have observed this to be generally true: too much money in circulation has led to an excessive amount of spending and has been inflationary; too little has restrained the economy and led to recession. Thus we need to define the money supply to include those stores of purchasing power which have a close relationship with spending and other measures of economic activity.

We look to the Fed as the ultimate authority in defining the money supply. It has responsibility for controlling the money supply and is also the source of most monetary data. Using the considerations discussed here, the Fed has come up with several alternative definitions of the money supply. The basic definition, M1, corresponds to the strict functional criteria above. It comprises those assets which are themselves acceptable in exchange and are normally held with the intention of spending them in the immediate future.

The second definition, M2, includes all of M1 plus a number of assets which may be held primarily as savings for some future expenditure. At the same time, these savings are readily convertible into M1 and thus may be held by some individuals or firms for immediate expenditure. In other words, M2 is a broader definition than M1 and is designed to be a more accurate measure of purchasing power. Although M1 more closely defines what has been traditionally considered money, some observers find M2 to be more consistently related to measures of economic activity.

**HOW THE
DEFINITION OF
THE MONEY
SUPPLY HAS
CHANGED**

In a simple economy in which metallic coins were used, it was easy to define money, since only one form of generally accepted medium of exchange was in use. As forms of payment increased to meet the needs of the economy, defining money became more complex. Differences of opinion developed about the items that should be included in the money supply. One of the most common traditional definitions of the money supply included currency and coin in the hands of the public and demand deposits held by the public in commercial banks. Deposits of one bank in another bank were excluded since such funds were not currently available for spending. Checks and other items in the process of collection were also excluded to avoid double counting. Likewise, U.S. government deposits were excluded. An alternative definition of the money supply included time and savings deposits held by the public in commercial banks and savings banks.

By 1975, the traditional money supply measure was defined as M1 by the Fed. The M2 measure added time deposits and savings deposits held by the public in commercial banks to M1 but did not include certificates of deposit with denominations of $100,000 or more. At that time, M3 included all of the items in M1 and M2 plus deposits at savings banks and S&Ls. By 1980, credit union shares had been added to the M3 definition and the Fed even had M4 and M5 definitions of the money supply. By 1984, the Fed had carefully defined the money supply definitions in use today for M1, M2, M3, and L.

M3 is a still broader measure than M2. A fourth measure is so broad and so far removed from our functional definition of money that the Fed designates it L, setting it off as a measure of liquid assets. L is a very broad measure of purchasing power, including everything in the other definitions plus a number of assets which can easily be sold to provide money for expenditures.

Measuring the Money Supply

Even if the Fed did not define and publish measures of the money supply, it would collect most of the data necessary to do so in performing its central banking functions. Figures collected from depository institutions are totaled according to the definitions established, and money stock measures are published and released weekly. Since not all depository institutions report to the Fed every week, some estimation is necessary. These figures are then revised and adjusted as more complete information becomes available. A summary of the definitions of the money stock measures and their relationships is shown in Figure 2.1.

M1 MONEY SUPPLY
The basic definition of the money supply, and the one referred to here unless stated otherwise, is M1. It measures transactions balances.

FIGURE 2.1
Definitions of Money Supply Measures and Totals for June, 1990

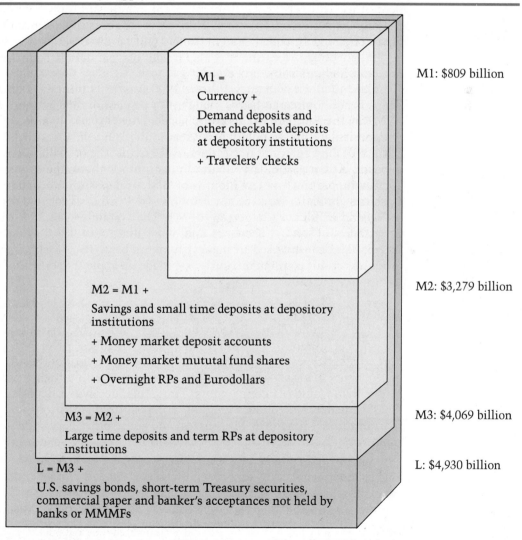

M1 =

Currency +

Demand deposits and other checkable deposits at depository institutions

+ Travelers' checks

M1: $809 billion

M2 = M1 +

Savings and small time deposits at depository institutions

+ Money market deposit accounts

+ Money market mututal fund shares

+ Overnight RPs and Eurodollars

M2: $3,279 billion

M3 = M2 +

Large time deposits and term RPs at depository institutions

M3: $4,069 billion

L = M3 +

U.S. savings bonds, short-term Treasury securities, commercial paper and banker's acceptances not held by banks or MMMFs

L: $4,930 billion

Source: *Federal Reserve Bulletin*, October 1990: A13.

These are sums of money that can be spent without first converting them to some other asset, and which are held for anticipated or unanticipated purchases or payments in the immediate future. These include currency, such as coin and Federal Reserve notes; checkable deposits at banks, S&Ls, savings banks and credit unions; and travelers' checks. Essentially, only those amounts that represent the purchasing power of units in our economy other than the federal government are counted. Specifically excluded are vault cash and deposits of other depository institutions, the Fed, the federal government, and foreign banks and governments. The vault cash and deposits belonging to depository institutions do not represent purchasing power and are therefore not money. However, they serve as reserves, an important element of our financial system which will be discussed in the next several chapters. Adjustment is also made to avoid double counting of checks which are being processed.

The M1 stock of money in June 1990 was $809 billion.[1] Demand deposits at commercial banks made up 34 percent of this amount. The share made up of demand deposits has declined, especially since other checkable deposits were authorized nationwide by the Depository Institutions Deregulation and Monetary Control Act of 1980. Demand deposits took a particularly sharp dip, and other checkable deposits a sharp jump, in the first few months of 1981, as depositors shifted funds to the newly authorized accounts. In June 1990, other checkable deposits accounted for over 36 percent of M1. They include negotiable order of withdrawal (NOW) accounts and share draft accounts, which pay interest and can be used to make payments by writing a check. The other important component, currency, made up about 29 percent of the M1 money measure.

M2 MONEY SUPPLY

The Fed's second definition of the money stock, M2, is a broader measure of purchasing power than M1. It includes all of M1 plus several other types of highly liquid financial assets. Most of these other components are assets that provide their owners with a higher rate of return than would M1 components. These include savings deposits and small time deposits (under $100,000) at depository institutions, money market mutual fund (MMMF) shares, and some other very short-term money market instruments, such as overnight repurchase agreements and Eurodollars.[2] Some of the owners of these assets hold them as

---

1. *Federal Reserve Bulletin* (October 1990): A13.
2. A repurchase agreement is essentially a way of making a loan. The lender buys an asset, usually securities, from the borrower, thus providing funds to the borrower. The borrower repays by buying back the asset at a prearranged time and price. Overnight repurchase agreements (RPs) and Eurodollars are repaid the next day; term RPs are held for longer periods of time.

long-term savings instruments. Since they are very liquid, however, some individuals and firms hold them even though they plan to spend the funds within a few days. M1 thus understates purchasing power by the amount of these M2 balances held for transaction purposes.

The components of M2 illustrate the difficulties the Fed has faced in drawing the boundaries of these definitions. For example, money market mutual funds provide limited check-writing privileges, and can therefore be used for transaction purposes. Some analysts argue on this basis that MMMF balances should be a part of M1. The Fed has included MMMF balances in M2 but not in M1. This is because they are so different from our traditional money components, and because they are believed to be used more as savings instruments than as transactions balances. On the other hand, it can be argued that small time-deposits should be excluded from M2 because they are not, in practice, very liquid. Holders of these deposits who wish to cash them in before maturity are penalized by forfeiting some of the interest they have earned. However, small time deposits are included because they are considered to be close substitutes for some of the other savings instruments included in M2. As Figure 2.1 shows, M2 is over four times as large as M1, and small time-deposits make up the bulk of the difference between the two money stock measures.

M3 AND L MONEY SUPPLIES

M3 includes all of M2 plus some large money market instruments, large time deposits (over $100,000), and term repurchase agreements. These instruments are frequently held by corporations and wealthy individuals, allowing them to earn market rates of interest on large cash balances while still maintaining their liquidity.

L is the Fed's broadest measure of money that is available to the public. It adds to M3 a variety of liquid assets, including the public's holdings of U.S. savings bonds, short-term Treasury securities, commercial paper, and bankers' acceptances.[3] All of these represent stored purchasing power of their owners and are thus potentially related to economic activity. The relationship is an uncertain one, because some of the asset owners will hold these liquid assets for years, while others will convert them to cash and spend the funds within a few days. One reason the Fed defines so many measures of money and liquid wealth is that economists have different opinions as to which measure is most consistently related to spending and other economic activity.

We will see during the remaining chapters in Part 1 that a major objective of the Fed is to regulate and control the supply of money and the availability of credit. The Fed sets target growth rates for M1, M2,

---

3.   Commercial paper and bankers' acceptances are instruments of short-term business credit. They will be discussed in more detail in Chapters 9 and 20.

and M3, but not for L, and attempts to keep actual growth of these money stock measures close to the targets. This task, however, is not an easy one since the banking system has the capacity to expand or contract the money supply. Furthermore, we will see that there are other factors affecting the money supply which are not under the control of our central bank.

Figure 2.2 illustrates the growth of M1, M2, and M3 during the period 1982–1990. As mentioned earlier, some growth of the money stock or supply is necessary to support and sustain real growth in our economy. However, a too rapid rate of money supply growth may be inflationary. In fact, most economists agree that rapid rates of growth of the money supply contributed to the high rate of inflation during the 1970s and early 1980s.

The M1 measure grew at an unsteady pace since the start of the 1980s, while the other two measures grew more smoothly. Part of the reason for this is decreasing regulation and increasing competition among financial institutions, which has led to the growth of new types of accounts. This evolution of the financial system makes it increasingly difficult to define consistent measures of the money supply. For example, during 1980 and 1981 money market mutual funds grew rapidly because they paid a high rate of interest and were highly liquid. As funds were shifted from demand deposits to MMMFs, M1 declined,

FIGURE 2.2   Money Stock Measures, 1982–1990

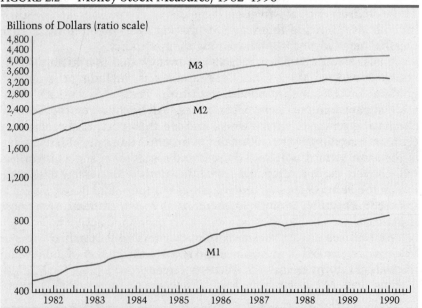

Source: *Economic Indicators*, Council of Economic Advisers (August 1990).

although no real change in purchasing power had taken place. M2 was not affected by the shift, since both demand deposits and MMMFs are counted in M2. Beginning in 1983, some funds were shifted from MMMFs into Super-NOW accounts, a type of account offered by depository institutions that pays competitive interest rates and is counted in M1. Thus, different growth rates of the money supply measures may result from the way they are defined. This is another reason why the Fed keeps track of several measures of the money supply.

KEY TERMS

barter
bimetallic standard
credit money
electronic funds transfer
    systems
exchange rate
fiat money
full-bodied money
greenbacks

inflation
legal tender
liquidity
medium of exchange
representative full-bodied
    money
standard of value
store of purchasing power
token coins

DISCUSSION QUESTIONS

1. What are the basic functions of money?
2. Briefly describe the development of money, from barter to the use of precious metals.
3. What is meant by a bimetallic standard?
4. Describe the development and use of paper money in the United States.
5. What is credit money? What is fiat money?
6. What are some examples of current electronic funds transfer systems?
7. Describe the historical relationship between monetary standards and the value of money in the United States.
8. Briefly describe the development of the international monetary system.
9. What factors are important in defining the money supply?
10. Describe the M1 definition of the money supply and indicate the relative significance of the M1 components.
11. How does M2 differ from M1? Which measure is probably more closely related to economic activity?
12. Describe the M3 and L measures of the money supply.

PROBLEM

Obtain a current issue of the *Federal Reserve Bulletin*. Compare the present size of M1, M2, M3, and L money stock measures with the June 1990 figures presented in this chapter. Also find the current sizes of these M1 components: currency, travelers' checks, demand deposits, and other checkable deposits. Express each component as a percentage of M1 and compare your percentages with those presented at the end of the chapter.

SELF-TEST QUESTIONS

1. The three functions of money are:
   a. medium of exchange, store of purchasing power, and a measure of liquidity
   b. conduit for international trade, store of purchasing power, and standard of value
   c. medium of exchange, store of purchasing power, and standard of value
   d. inflation hedge, measure of liquidity, and medium of exchange

2. Metal coins that have intrinsic value equal to their value as commodities are referred to as:
   a. full-bodied money
   b. token coins or money
   c. credit money
   d. fiat money

3. An increase in the general overall prices of goods and services that is not offset by increases in the quality of those goods and services is termed:
   a. liquidity
   b. inflation
   c. full-bodied goods and services
   d. store of purchasing power

4. The current international monetary system is a:
   a. gold standard system
   b. fixed exchange rate system
   c. free-market floating exchange rate system
   d. "managed" floating exchange rate system

5. Which one of the following items is *not* part of the M1 definition of the U.S. money supply?
    a. currency
    b. demand deposits at depository institutions
    c. savings and small time deposits at depository institutions
    d. checkable deposits at depository institutions

SUGGESTED READINGS

Abdullah, Fuad A. *Financial Management for the Multinational Firm.* Englewood Cliffs, NJ: Prentice-Hall, 1987. Chap. 2.

Bordo, Michael David. "The Classical Gold Standard: Some Lessons for Today." *Review,* Federal Reserve Bank of St. Louis (May 1981): 2–17.

Friedman, Milton, and Anna J. Schwartz. *A Monetary History of the United States, 1867–1960.* Princeton, NJ: Princeton University Press, 1963.

Kaufman, George G. *The U.S. Financial System,* 4e. Englewood Cliffs, NJ: Prentice-Hall, 1989. Chap. 2.

Kidwell, David S., and Richard L. Peterson. *Financial Institutions, Markets, and Money,* 4e. Hinsdale, IL: The Dryden Press, 1990. Chap. 1.

Rose, Peter S. *Money and Capital Markets,* 3e. Homewood, IL: BPI/Irwin, 1989. Chap. 2.

Shapiro, Alan C. *Multinational Financial Management,* 3e. Boston: Allyn & Bacon, 1989. Chap. 3.

Tatom, John A. "Recent Financial Innovations: Have They Distorted the Meaning of M1?" *Review,* Federal Reserve Bank of St. Louis (April 1982): 23–32.

Wood, John H. "The Demise of the Gold Standard." *Economic Perspectives,* Federal Reserve Bank of Chicago (November/December 1981):13–23.

ANSWERS TO SELF-TEST QUESTIONS   1. c   2. a   3. b   4. d   5. c

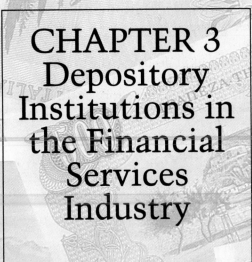

CHAPTER 3
Depository Institutions in the Financial Services Industry

After studying this chapter, you should be able to:

- Describe the early history of the nation's depository institutions.
- Discuss the significance of recent legislation as it relates to the operation of the nation's depository institutions and the implications for businesses and individuals.
- Explain how our banking system obtains funds for operations and how these funds are committed to use.
- Evaluate the significance of trends in concentration within the banking system.
- Describe how banking is becoming an increasingly international business.

The financial services industry encompasses virtually every aspect of the financial mechanisms that serve our competitive enterprise economy. This book describes the major financial services of the nation's depository institutions, as well as investment banking and consumer financing. We will also touch on various less well-known services such as leasing, trade credit, and factoring, all of which depend upon our depository institutions. The four types of depository institutions are commercial banks, savings and loan associations (S&Ls), savings banks, and credit unions. The nature and functions of these institutions are described in the following pages.

Depository institutions play an integral part in the management of the monetary system. They accumulate and lend idle funds, handle the transfer of money, and provide for its safekeeping. These institutions provide the bulk of short-term loans to businesses for day-to-day working capital purposes. In addition, they provide part of the long-term financing required by industry, commerce, and agriculture. They play an important part in financing the construction of millions of homes, and are an important source of personal loans. Depository institutions also provide loans to the federal government as well as to state and local governments.

HISTORY OF THE U.S. BANKING SYSTEM

The structure of the modern **banking system** includes commercial banks, savings and loans, mutual savings banks, and credit unions. It is the result of historical forces as well as of current banking requirements. Banking, like most forms of economic activity, is subject more to the forces of tradition than to those of innovation. Yet, despite the great influence of early banking practices and legislation on today's banking, the evolution of banks to meet the requirements of the modern industrial economy has been effective and successful. We must not assume, however, that the present structure of banking is here to stay. To meet the requirements of a dynamic economy, changes are constantly taking place in banking practices, regulation, and legislation. An understanding of banking in the United States today, therefore, requires an understanding of the development of the banking system in the economic history of the country.

*banking system
commercial banks, savings and loans, mutual savings banks, and credit unions*

Before the Civil War

Until the Civil War banking in the United States developed under circumstances that explain much of the apparent confusion and difficulty that accompanied its development. The population lived for the most part on farms. Families were self-sufficient, and transportation and communications were poor. The friction between those who supported a strong central government and those who did not existed in the early years of our history as it does today. The country had little experience in money and financial management, and much controversy raged over the power to charter and regulate banks.

EARLY CHARTERED BANKS
During the colonial period there were small unincorporated banks that were established to ease the shortage of capital for businesses. Their operations consisted largely of issuing their own paper money. Outside

of the larger towns, deposit banking was of minor significance. It was not until 1782 that the first incorporated bank, the Bank of North America, was created. It was established in Philadelphia by Robert Morris to assist in financing the Revolutionary War. This bank set a good example for successful banking—its notes served as a circulating monetary medium, it loaned liberally to the U.S. government, and it redeemed its own notes in metallic coins upon demand. Two years later the Bank of Massachusetts and the Bank of New York were established. These three incorporated banks were the only such banks until 1790.

THE FIRST BANK OF THE UNITED STATES
Alexander Hamilton was the first Secretary of the Treasury of the United States. For several years he had harbored the idea of a federally chartered bank that would adequately support the rapidly growing economy and would give financial assistance to the government during its crises. His recommendations were submitted to the House of Representatives of the United States in 1790, and in 1791 a twenty-year charter was issued to the First Bank of the United States. This bank served the nation effectively by issuing notes, transferring funds from region to region, providing useful service to the government, and curbing the excessive note issues of state banks by presenting such notes periodically for redemption. However, strong opposition existed to the renewal of its charter, and it ceased operations in 1811. The antagonism of state banking interests was an important cause of the demise of the First Bank.

Following the expiration of the charter of the First Bank of the United States, the number of state banks increased rapidly, as did the volume of their note issues. Abuses of banking privileges were extensive. The capital of many banks was largely fictitious, and there was a flood of irredeemable notes issued to the public.

THE SECOND BANK OF THE UNITED STATES
The Second Bank of the United States was chartered primarily to restore order to the chaotic banking situation that had developed after the First Bank of the United States ceased operations. Like the First Bank of the United States, it received a twenty-year federal charter. It began operations in 1816 and, after a short period of mismanagement, set upon a course of reconstructing sound banking practices. It ably served individuals, businesses, and the government. It accepted deposits, made loans, and issued notes. Furthermore, it restrained the note-issuing practices of state banks by periodically presenting their notes for redemption. The Second Bank of the United States also played a most important and efficient role as fiscal agent for the government. As fiscal agent it received all deposits of government funds and reported regularly on all government receipts and expenditures.

In 1833 President Andrew Jackson and many of his associates began such a vigorous campaign against the Second Bank of the United States that it became apparent its charter would not be renewed when it expired in 1836. President Jackson claimed that the Bank was being run to benefit private interests and was operated in such a way as to weaken government policies. Like the First Bank of the United States, it became a victim of political pressure. Not until 1863 was another bank in the United States to receive a federal charter.

STATE BANKS FROM 1836 TO THE CIVIL WAR

When the Second Bank's charter expired, the excesses that had plagued the period 1811–1816 began again. This period is characterized as one of "wildcat" banking. Although many state banks operated on a conservative and very sound basis, the majority engaged in risky banking practices through excessive note issues, lack of adequate bank capital, and insufficient reserves against their notes and deposits.

Because the notes of even the well-established banks were often of inferior quality, it was easy for skillful counterfeiters to increase the denomination of notes. Also, because of the poor communications that existed between various sections of the country, it was often quite difficult for a banker to be certain whether notes presented for payment were real. Skillfully prepared counterfeit notes frequently circulated with greater freedom than did the legitimate notes of weak and little known banks.

In spite of the many abuses of state banks during this period, New York, Massachusetts, and Louisiana originated highly commendable banking legislation, much of which provided the basis for the establishment of the National Banking System in 1863.

Entry of Thrift Institutions

The chaotic banking conditions of the early 1800s left individuals with few safe institutions in which they could place their savings. The lack of safe depository institutions, in turn, inhibited the effective development of home financing. The rapidly growing population depended to a large extent on individual financial arrangements to meet its need for housing. The accumulated savings of most individual home buyers, then, as now, was simply not enough to buy a house. In response to this problem, two new forms of depository institutions, known as **thrift institutions**, came into being: savings banks and S&Ls.

thrift institutions
savings and loans, mutual savings banks, and credit unions

SAVINGS BANKS

Savings banks made their appearance in 1812, emphasizing individual thrift savings and safety of principal. The accumulation of funds by these savings banks was invested primarily in home mortgages. Very often the trustees of these banks were prominent local citizens, serving without pay, who regarded their service as an important civic duty. Although the approximately 500 savings banks now in operation are confined almost entirely to the New England area, New York State, and New Jersey, their contribution to both savings accumulation and home financing has been enormous. Today they have assets of nearly $500 billion, most of which is invested in mortgage loans.

SAVINGS AND LOAN ASSOCIATIONS

S&Ls first came on the scene in 1831. First known as building societies, then as building and loan associations, their basic mission was to provide home mortgage financing. While home financing was important to the savings banks, it was the fundamental basis of savings and loan operations. In distinguishing between these two important forms of depository institutions, it might be said that originally the savings banks' emphasis was on thrift and the safety of savings while the emphasis of the S&Ls was on home financing. In contrast with the limited geographic expansion of savings banking, savings and loan activity spread throughout the United States. There are now more than 3,000 associations and many times that number of association branches in the nation. At the present time, the S&Ls of the nation have assets of approximately $1.25 trillion dollars invested largely in mortgage loans.

CREDIT UNIONS

Credit unions, which now have assets of approximately $185 billion, came on the American scene much later than the other thrift institutions. As cooperative nonprofit organizations, they exist primarily to provide member depositors with consumer credit. They are made up of individuals who possess common bonds of association such as occupation, residence, or church affiliation. These institutions derive their funds almost entirely from the savings of their members. It was not until the 1920s that credit unions became important as a special form of depository institution.

Credit unions are discussed further in Chapter 17. Savings banks and S&Ls are discussed in detail in Chapter 18.

Legislation To Govern the Banking System

2 banking systems

THE NATIONAL BANKING ACT

In 1864 the National Banking Act made it possible for banks to receive federal charters. This legislation provided the basis for our present national banking laws. As in the cases of the First and the Second Bank of the United States, the reasons for federal interest in the banking system were to provide for a sound banking system and to curb the excesses of the state banks. An important additional purpose of the National Banking Act was to provide financing for the Civil War. Secretary of the Treasury Salmon P. Chase and others believed that government bonds could be sold to the nationally chartered banks, which could in turn issue their own notes based in part on the government bonds they had purchased.

Through the National Banking Act, various steps were taken to promote safe banking practices. Among other things, minimum capital requirements were established for banks with federal charters, loans were regulated with respect to safety and liquidity, a system of supervision and examination was instituted, and minimum reserve requirements against notes and deposits were established. In general, these reform measures were constructive. However, in some instances they have been regarded as altogether too restrictive. For example, loans were forbidden against real estate. Much of the criticism of the national banking system, in fact, was caused by the inflexibility of its rules. Many of its limitations were either modified or eliminated in 1913 with the establishment of the Federal Reserve System (Fed).

The National Banking Act did not establish a system of central banks. It only made possible the chartering of banks by the federal government. The Federal Reserve Act of 1913 brought to the American economy a system of central banks. The Federal Reserve System was designed to eliminate many of the weaknesses that had persisted under the National Banking Act and to increase the effectiveness of commercial banking in general. It included not only strong central domination of banking practices but also many services for commercial banks. The influence of the Fed is described in Chapter 4.

THE DEPOSITORY INSTITUTIONS DEREGULATION AND MONETARY CONTROL ACT

In 1980, President Jimmy Carter signed into law the Depository Institutions Deregulation and Monetary Control Act. This act represents a major step toward deregulating banking in the United States and improving the effectiveness of monetary policy. We will generally refer to this legislation as the Monetary Control Act throughout the text and will here describe the two main provisions of the Act: deregulation and monetary control.

Depository Institutions Deregulation

This major part of The Monetary Control Act was designed to reduce or eliminate interest rate limitations imposed on the banking system, increase the various sources of funds, and expand the uses of the funds of S&Ls. One significant change affected the Fed's Regulation Q, which established interest rate ceilings on time and savings deposits. Except for the zero ceiling on demand deposits, which remains in effect, all other provisions of Regulation Q were phased out by March 31, 1986. Furthermore, state-imposed interest rate ceilings were substantially modified, and existing state restrictions on deposit interest rates for insured institutions were eliminated.

To enable depository institutions to compete effectively for funds that were flowing in large amounts to money market mutual funds, NOW accounts (negotiable orders of withdrawal) were authorized. Money market mutual funds became available in large numbers as sponsored and promoted primarily by investment banks and mutual funds groups. The NOW accounts had interest rates more competitive with those of the money market mutual funds but continued to be subject to Regulation Q during the phase-out period. Credit unions were permitted to issue draft accounts which to all intents and purposes were the same as the NOW accounts. Federal deposit insurance was increased from $40,000 to $100,000 for each account. This large increase in deposit protection, although politically popular at the time, is now described as an undue expansion of protection. The U.S. Treasury has stated that it undermined market discipline and enabled depository institutions to make high-risk loans for which the taxpayers in the long run have become liable.

In order to enhance competition among depository institutions, Title IV of The Monetary Control Act amended the Home Owners' Loan Act of 1933. Federally chartered S&Ls were permitted to invest up to one fifth of their assets in corporate debt securities, commercial paper, and consumer loans. Prior residential mortgage loan restrictions relating to geographical areas and first mortgage lending requirements were removed. Greater authority was also permitted for granting real estate development and construction loans by federally chartered S&Ls. In addition, federal savings banks were allowed to make a small number of commercial loans and accept some checkable deposits.

Monetary Control

The Monetary Control Act was designed to extend the Fed's control to thrift institutions and to commercial banks that are not members of the System. This was accomplished by extending both reserve requirements and general controls to these institutions. Because the Fed had more stringent regulations than many state regulatory agencies, many commercial banks had given up their membership in the System to become state-chartered nonmember banks. The Monetary Control Act, therefore, has had the effect of halting the declining System membership by transferring much regulatory control from the state to the federal level.

In the past, reserve requirements imposed by the Fed applied only to member banks. The requirements were based on a complicated formula involving size, location, and type of charter. These differential reserve requirements have now been eliminated. Even foreign banks and offices operating in this country have been included in these simplified reserve requirements. Along with the broadening of control by the Fed, there has also been a broadening of privileges to those institutions brought under its control. All depository institutions may now borrow from the Fed on the same basis, and the fee schedule for services rendered by the Fed applies to all regulated depository institutions.

To summarize, The Monetary Control Act permits both greater competition for deposits and more flexibility in the holding of assets by depository institutions. Thus, as institutions become more alike, similarities in their financial management are likely to increase.

THE GARN-ST GERMAIN DEPOSITORY INSTITUTIONS ACT

There had been high hopes that The Monetary Control Act would have a quick and beneficial effect on the banking system as well as on the effectiveness of monetary control by the Fed. However, this was not the case. Of special significance was the dramatic increase in interest rates in late 1980 and 1981. S&Ls and savings banks were faced with heavy increases in their cost of funds as depositors shifted from low-interest passbook savings to the higher yielding NOW accounts and savings certificates. Furthermore, since the NOW accounts continued to be subject to ceiling rates under Regulation Q, money market mutual funds had a clear competitive advantage in attracting funds. Rapidly increasing federal deficits and troubles in the automobile and housing industries added to the demand for legislation to address these problems. The Garn-St Germain Act of 1982 resulted.

Although The Garn-St Germain Act had many provisions, its principal focus was to assist the savings and loan industry, which had deteriorated to dangerous levels. Depository institutions in general were authorized, to among other things, issue a new money market deposit account with no regulated interest rate ceiling; S&Ls were authorized to make nonresidential real estate loans, commercial loans, and to issue variable-rate mortgages.

PROTECTION OF DEPOSITORS' FUNDS

The various legislative measures described above were all designed to enable depository institutions to adjust to the changing circumstances confronting them. Some of the measures, however, became the sources of critical problems.

The Savings and Loan Crisis of the 1980s

Authorization to invest funds in a wide range of higher yielding investments permitted many savings and loan associations to run wild by
supporting speculative office buildings and other such ventures. This
resulted not only in overbuilding at inflated costs but, as the promoters
were unable to honor the terms of their loan contracts, many S&Ls
became insolvent. Because the deposits of these associations were
largely protected by the Federal Savings and Loan Insurance Corporation (FSLIC), the federal government was obliged to provide a safety net
for the depositors at a cost of $500 billion or more to taxpayers. The
Federal Savings and Loan Insurance Corporation, discussed here and in
Chapter 18, had insured the deposits of most S&L depositors since the
early 1930s. Federal financial assistance to the FSLIC was made possible through legislation approved by Congress in 1988. Legislators
created the Resolution Trust Corporation to take over and liquidate the
assets of failed associations. As depositors withdrew funds for investment in other institutions, high interest rates continued to be a burden
to S&Ls in their attempt to remain solvent.

Additional legislation came in 1989 under the title Financial Institutions Reform, Recovery, and Enforcement Act (FIRREA). This legislation included numerous provisions and financial resources designed
to strengthen the nation's depository institutions and their federal deposit insurance programs. Special features of this legislation included
stronger capital standards for thrift institutions and enhanced enforcement powers for the federal government.

Commercial banks have suffered some of the same difficulties as
the S&Ls. However, losses from international loans, agricultural loans,
and loans to the petroleum industry, have been more significant for
commercial banks—many banks had to be merged with other banks.
Savings banks and credit unions experienced some difficulties as well
but to a lesser extent. Because of the seriousness of the problems of the
nation's depository institutions, many sections of this text will stress
the specific nature of these problems and the attempts to resolve them.

Insurance for Deposit and Share Accounts

Insurance protection for deposits at depository institutions was started
during the Great Depression to restore the confidence of depositors.
The Federal Deposit Insurance Corporation (FDIC), the Federal Savings
and Loan Insurance Corporation (FSLIC), and the National Credit
Union Share Insurance Fund (NCUSIF) were established under federal
legislation to protect deposits in banks, S&Ls, and credit unions—in
that order. Over the years the limitation on deposit account insurance
was increased until by 1980 it had been set at $100,000 per account.

The financial difficulties discussed above resulted not only in the failure of many S&Ls but also the bankruptcy of the FSLIC. The reserves held by the FSLIC were not enough to meet the claims of depositors of bankrupt S&Ls, and its functions were transferred to the FDIC in 1989. The Treasury has transferred huge amounts of capital to the FDIC to cover the losses of S&L depositors. Furthermore, capital has been needed to cover losses from a significant increase in commercial bank failures. Additional large transfers of capital will likely occur as the magnitude of increased losses is recognized. As of January 1991 approximately 420 federally insured thrifts were listed as insolvent. It is estimated that from 700 to 800 institutions may ultimately need to be sold, reorganized, or liquidated.

There is little doubt that deposit insurance will continue to exist. It is also obvious that radical changes will have to be made if, after the resolution of the present crisis, we are to avoid future burdens on taxpayers resulting from deposit insurance programs. Suggestions for solving these problems include eliminating all deposit insurance, reducing insurable deposits limits to protect only the small deposits, levying higher premiums on depository institutions for the insurance, and having more strict regulatory and supervisory control. In September 1990, the premium for the insurance was raised.

FUNCTIONS OF THE BANKING SYSTEM

Modern depository institutions perform six functions. The most basic functions are (1) accepting deposits and (2) granting loans. In accepting deposits, banks provide a safe place for the public to keep money for future use. Individuals and businesses seldom wish to spend their money as it becomes available; without depository facilities such funds may lie idle. The banking system puts the accumulated deposits to use through loans to persons and businesses having immediate use for them. The result of this pooling of funds is their more effective use.

Along with accepting deposits and granting loans, depository institutions provide (3) safekeeping for depositors, (4) efficient and economical transfer of payments through check-writing procedures, and (5) record keeping for depositors through regular reporting procedures.

When granting personal or business loans, the banking system carries out its function of (6) risk selection. A banker's refusal to finance an ill-conceived venture protects assets. It may also be in the best interest of the prospective operators of the new venture, by preventing them from engaging in an activity that will result in loss. The objective in business risk selection is the careful distribution of loan funds to those businesses with the best chances of success, which makes possible the most efficient development of the nation's resources.

ASSETS AND SOURCES OF FUNDS FOR DEPOSITORY INSTITUTIONS

Types of depository institution assets and the sources of the funds with which these assets are acquired are shown in Figure 3.1.

Assets

The principal assets of all depository institutions are cash, securities, and loans.

CASH

Cash includes funds in the depository institution's vault and deposits at its Reserve Bank or other banks. A certain minimum of vault cash is needed to meet the day-to-day currency requirements of customers. The amount of cash required may be small compared to total resources. This is because the typical day's operation will result in approximately the same amount of cash deposits as cash withdrawals. A margin of safety, however, is required to take care of those periods when for one reason or another withdrawals greatly exceed deposits.

FIGURE 3.1   Depository Assets and Sources of Funds

ASSETS	SOURCES OF FUNDS
CASH Vault cash and cash due from banks Reserves at Federal Reserve Bank Deposits at other banks	DEPOSITS Checkable deposits Savings and time deposits

SECURITIES
U.S. government securities
State and local government securi-
  ties
Other securities
Capital stock of the Federal
  Reserve Bank or Federal Home
  Loan Bank
	OTHER LIABILITIES AND
	DEFERRED CREDITS
	Discounts and fee collected but
	  not yet earned
	Funds borrowed from Federal
	  Reserve Bank or Federal Home
	  Loan Bank

LOANS Secured loans Unsecured loans and discounts Real estate mortgages	OWNER'S EQUITY Common and preferred stock Surplus Retained earnings Share accounts (for credit unions)
OTHER ASSETS Interest receivable Buildings and furniture Prepaid expenses	

The appropriate amount of cash that a depository institution should carry depends largely upon the character of its operations. For example, a bank that has some very large accounts might be expected to have a larger volume of unanticipated withdrawals (and deposits) than a bank that has only small individual accounts. An unpredictable volume of day-to-day withdrawals requires, of course, a larger cash reserve.

The second cash item, designated "reserves at Federal Reserve Bank," is considerably greater than vault cash. Depository institutions are required to keep a percentage of their deposits as reserves either with the Reserve Bank in their districts or in the form of vault cash. The Monetary Control Act requires uniform reserve amounts for all depository institutions in order to enhance monetary control and competitive fairness. As withdrawals are made and total deposit balances decrease, the amount of the required reserves also decreases. The vault cash reserves that have been freed may then be used to help meet withdrawal demands.

Cash in other banks refers to the common practice used by smaller banks of keeping substantial deposits with banks in large cities. These correspondent relationships with other banks speed the clearing of drafts and other credit instruments by routing such instruments through their large city correspondents. They also provide immediate access to information regarding the money markets of the large cities.

SECURITIES

Securities are the second major group of assets. Securities include those of the U.S. government, state governments, and municipalities. Also included are other securities and capital stock of the Federal Reserve Bank and Federal Home Loan Bank, held as investments. Holding the capital stock of its Reserve Bank is a requirement for all member banks of the Fed. The same is true for S&Ls that are members of the Federal Home Loan Bank System.

LOANS

The third group of asset items includes several classifications of loans: first, secured loans that are payable on demand; second, those secured loans that have definite maturities; third, unsecured loans and discounts with definite maturities; and, finally, real estate mortgages.

In a **secured loan,** specific property is pledged as collateral for the loan. In the event the borrower fails to repay the loan, the lending institution will take the assets pledged as collateral for the loan. In all cases, the borrower is required to sign a note specifying the details of the indebtedness; but unless specific assets are pledged for the loan, it is classified as unsecured. An **unsecured loan** represents a general claim against the assets of the borrower. It is the usual arrangement

secured loan
loan backed by collateral

unsecured loan
loan that is a general claim against the borrower's assets

between the small businesses and the lender, whereby amounts are borrowed periodically for meeting a payroll, accumulating an inventory, or for other short-term working capital purposes.

The distinction between a loan and a discount is an important one. A loan customarily includes a specified rate of interest. The interest must be paid with the principal amount of the loan when the loan contract matures. With a discount arrangement, the interest is deducted from the stated amount of the note at the time the money is loaned. The borrower receives less than the face value of the note, but repays the full amount of the note when it matures.

A given discount rate results in a higher cost of borrowing than an interest loan made for the same rate. This is true because under the discount arrangement less actual money is received by the borrower, although the amount paid for its use is the same. For example, if $500 is borrowed on a loan basis at an interest rate of 10 percent for one year, at maturity $500 plus $50 interest must be repaid. On the other hand, if the $500 is borrowed on a discount basis and the rate is 10 percent, a deduction of $50 from the face value of the note is made and the borrower receives only $450. At the end of the year, the borrower repays the face amount of the note, $500. In the first case, the borrower has paid $50 for the use of $500; in the second case, $50 has been paid for the use of only $450. The effective rate of interest, therefore, on the discount basis is approximately 11.1 percent compared with the even 10 percent paid when the $500 was borrowed on a loan basis.

OTHER BANK ASSETS
The remaining assets are less important than those previously discussed. They include interest that has been earned on bonds and notes but not yet received, bank buildings and furniture, office supplies, and prepaid expenses such as insurance premiums paid in advance.

Almost 80 percent of the assets of commercial banks are in the form of loans. However, in contrast with S&Ls and savings banks, less than one-third of all loans are for real estate mortgages. S&Ls and savings banks, on the other hand, have nearly three quarters of their assets in the form of real estate mortgages and mortgage-backed securities. The assets of credit unions are largely consumer loans with a small percentage in government securities. Some credit unions also make home mortgage loans, although such mortgage financing typically constitutes a small percentage of their total assets.

Sources of Funds

There are two major sources from which depository institutions acquire their capital funds and liabilities. Owners' equity represents the initial investment and retained earnings of the owners of the institutions. Liabilities represent the funds owed to depositors and others from whom the bank has borrowed. The most important liability of a depository institution consists of its deposits of various kinds, but the other liabilities should be understood also.

DEPOSITS

Several types of deposits—traditionally grouped as checkable, savings, and time deposits—make up the principal liabilities of all depository institutions. Checkable deposits are the checking accounts of individuals, businesses, and other institutions. These deposits may be withdrawn on demand, that is, the institution agrees to pay the depositor immediately when requested to do so. The depositor normally utilizes a check to request the bank to make payment.

In practice, depository institutions also make savings deposits immediately available to depositors on demand. However, they are legally permitted to require written notification up to thirty days in advance of withdrawal. All savings deposits and time deposits earn interest. Most time deposits are **certificates of deposit** (CDs), which have a stated maturity and either pay a fixed rate of interest or are sold at a discount. A smaller category of time deposits is special club accounts such as Christmas and vacation savings clubs.

certificates of deposit (CDs)
time deposits with a stated maturity

Although records reveal that commercial banks issued certificates of deposit as early as 1900, a major innovation in the early 1960s resulted in a tremendous growth in their importance. CDs were issued in negotiable form, which meant they could be bought and sold. The vastly increased use of negotiable CDs in the 1960s caused a secondary market for them to develop. Today, CDs issued by depository institutions are purchased and sold in the money markets as readily as most forms of debt obligations. The depository institutions of the nation have used negotiable CDs as a means of attracting much larger deposits from businesses and other institutions.

OTHER LIABILITIES AND DEFERRED CREDITS

The second category of liabilities is represented by items having a far smaller dollar significance than that of deposits. In brief, these include liabilities not yet payable—such as accrued taxes, interest, and wages—and the receipt of fees and other charges for which service has not yet been rendered. Funds borrowed from a Reserve Bank or Federal Home Loan Bank or other banks are also reflected here.

OWNERS' EQUITY

The owners' equity category includes stock, surplus, and retained earnings. At the time a bank is formed, stock is purchased by the owners of the bank or by the public. In the case of credit unions, the members buy shares. From time to time additional stock may be sold to accommodate bank expansion. The surplus account is an accounting convenience to which the excess from the sale of stock at a price above its par or stated value per share is credited. When dividends are paid, the retained earnings account is reduced. These accounts constitute the primary equity of a depository institution.

On the balance sheets of many depository institutions today, there may be an item designated as "capital notes" in the equity section. These notes, always placed below the claims of bank depositors, reflect long-term borrowing on the part of the bank for purposes of bolstering the equity section. Although, like deposits, they are liabilities of the depository institutions that issue them, reserve requirements do not apply to them.

The owners' equity section of the balance sheet for all depository institutions is of special interest to various groups. Losses from operations are reflected immediately in this section. It would be expected that this would create a strong incentive for prudent management. Yet it is also true that the smaller the owners' investment relative to a given level of revenues and profits, the larger the percentage return per dollar of owners' investment. If the owners' investment is quite small compared to the total assets of the firm, the owners may consider their risks to be negligible relative to large potential profits. For this reason, all regulatory authorities have emphasized the importance of an adequate ratio of the owners' equity to deposits or assets.

The agencies that insure deposits have a critical interest in the safety of the institution. The losses now being recorded by many of the nation's S&Ls have not only exhausted their equity accounts but have also destroyed the agency that insured their depositors. Depositors, too, have an interest in the adequacy of the owners' equity or capital account. Although it is expected that the federal government will make good on the insured liabilities of the failed S&Ls there is no absolute guarantee that it will be done now or in the future. The financial well-being of the entire nation depends upon a stable and thriving system of depository institutions. For this reason much attention is directed not only to the quality of a firm's loans and investments but also to its capital-to-deposits ratio. The size of adequate ratio percentage differs for each class of assets. For example, federal government obligations among a firm's assets would require a small percentage. A commercial real estate investment, on the other hand, may require a much higher ratio. A composite of these various risk categories is developed to obtain a single percentage figure described as the firm's *risk-based capital ratio.*

In late 1988 the three bank regulatory bodies—the Federal Deposit Insurance Corporation, the Fed, and the Office of the Comptroller of Currency—adopted new capital adequacy standards for commercial banks. A minimum 8 percent risk-based capital ratio will be required by the end of 1992. These revised standards were arrived at in cooperation with the monetary authorities of eleven industrialized countries. Their goal was to bring foreign banking offices in this country into conformity with the requirements of domestic banks. For many years foreign banking offices had a competitive advantage over domestic banks since they were not subject to domestic requirements. With lower capital ratios they could offer better loan terms and still provide an adequate return on their capital accounts. The added risk for the low capital ratios of these foreign banking offices was borne by their home offices.

CONCENTRATION IN COMMERCIAL BANKING CONTROL

Concentration in banking control has taken a number of forms because banks, like other businesses, have increased their scope and volume of operations to accommodate the growing economy. The change in structure of the U.S. banking system has been especially significant since 1970. Since then there has been a strong trend toward branch banking and bank holding company arrangements.

Branch Banking

Branch banks are those banking offices that are controlled by a single parent bank. One board of directors and one group of stockholders control the home office and the branches. Some of our branch banking systems are very small, involving perhaps only two, three, or four branches. Others are quite large, extending over an entire state or several states and having many branches. The laws of some states prevent the operation of branch banking. Other states permit the operation of branch offices only within limited areas, and still others permit branch operation on a state-wide scale.

*branch banks
bank offices under a
single bank charter*

One of the particular merits of branch banking is that these systems are less likely to fail than independent unit banks. In a branch banking system, a wide diversification of investments can be made. Therefore, the temporary reverses of a single community are not as likely to cause the complete failure of an entire banking chain. This is true primarily of those branch systems that operate over wide geographical areas rather than in a single metropolitan area.

The independent bank cannot rely on other banks to offset local economic problems. It is on this point that branch banking operations appear to have their strongest support. The record of bank failures in the United States is one of which the banking system as a whole cannot be proud. However, opponents of branch banking have pointed out that failure of a system of banks, although less frequent, is far more serious.

There are also conflicting points of view when the pros and cons of branch banking are voiced by bank customers. The placement of branches in or near shopping centers, airports, and other centers of activity is convenient for consumers. The ability to make deposits or to withdraw funds at a branch is a special advantage for the elderly. Businesses may satisfy very large borrowing requirements by dealing with a bank that has been able to grow to a substantial size through its branch operations. In certain unit-banking states, though, it is common for the largest businesses to maintain their basic banking operations with banks located in money centers such as New York, Chicago, or San Francisco. This is because local banks cannot provide the variety of services and the amount of credit available from the very large banks. On the other hand, businesses may find an advantage in the highly competitive actions of many unit banks. Branches, of course, will not compete with each other, which means that a rejected loan application by one branch is a rejection by all of the branches of the bank. Small businesses especially may find it helpful to be able to "shop" among unit banks.

The resistance to branch banking has come primarily from small unit banks located in rural areas. The political power of these banks was used effectively for many years to prevent competition from the branches of urban financial center banks. S&Ls, on the other hand, have enjoyed far more flexibility in establishing branches. This advantage of the S&Ls has eroded some commercial bank opposition to branch banking. Since 1970, the number of states permitting branch banking has increased significantly. Currently, 35 states allow unlimited statewide branching or statewide expansion through acquisition of existing banks. Eleven states allow only limited branching, but two of these have passed legislation that will permit statewide branching in the future. Only four states remain unit banking states, allowing no branching. These are Colorado, Illinois, Montana, and Wyoming. At year-end 1951, branches accounted for only 26 percent of all bank offices. At year-end 1989, branches accounted for 75 percent of all banking offices. The increase in the proportion of branches is shown in Figure 3.2.

Bank Holding Companies

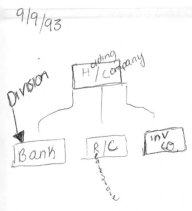

bank holding company company that holds voting power in two or more banks through stock ownership

The **bank holding company** is a device whereby two or more individual banks are controlled through one company that has voting control. The policies of banks thus controlled by such a holding company are determined by the parent company and coordinated for the purposes of that organization. The holding company itself may or may not engage in direct banking activities, and the banks that are controlled by the holding company may operate branches.

FIGURE 3.2   Banks and Branches Since 1915

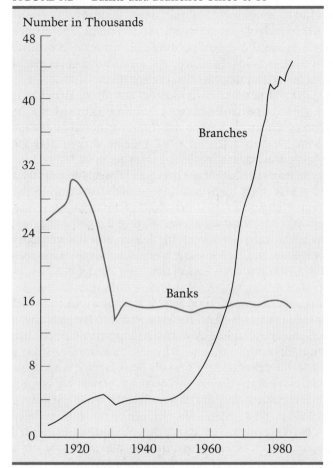

Source: *1989 Historical Chart Book*, Board of Governors of the
Federal Reserve System, 82.

Little control was exercised over bank holding companies until the
depression years of the early 1930s. Bank holding companies did not
come under the jurisdiction of either state or federal control unless
they also engaged directly in banking operations themselves. The Banking Act of 1933 and the Securities Acts of 1933 and 1934 imposed
limited control on bank holding companies, but it remained for the
Bank Holding Company Act of 1956 to establish clear authority over
these operations.

The Bank Holding Company Act defined a bank holding company
as one which directly or indirectly owns, controls, or holds the power
to vote 25 percent or more of the voting shares of each of two or more
banks. The Bank Holding Company Act Amendments of 1966 estab-

lished uniform standards to evaluate the legality of bank holding company acquisitions. But it remained for the Bank Holding Company Amendments of 1970 to provide the basis for modern bank operations. These amendments provide that bank holding companies can acquire companies having activities "closely related to banking," such as credit card operations, insurance, and data processing services.

By the end of 1987, 70 percent of domestic commercial banking assets were held by subsidiary banks of bank holding companies. The total number of banks controlled by bank holding companies had increased from 723 in 1969 to 4,465 in 1987. During this period the number of bank holding companies increased from 86 to 975.

A major development of the last few years has been the merging of financially troubled S&Ls with bank holding companies. Among the largest of these mergers is that of Western S&L of Phoenix, Arizona, which was acquired by BankAmerica Corp. The collapse of the real estate market in Arizona has resulted in the bankruptcy of virtually every S&L in that state, including Western. S&Ls in the southwestern part of the United States have been especially hard hit by the boom-and-bust in the real estate market. Bank holding companies have acquired financially distressed commercial banks as well as S&Ls. As of 1990, each monthly issue of the *Federal Reserve Bulletin* lists approved mergers of S&Ls and commercial banks with bank holding companies.

The liberalization of regulations relating to interstate banking is as significant as the liberalization of branch banking within states. At this time 45 states permit the acquisition of banks by out-of-state bank holding companies. In contrast, only one state permitted interstate banking before 1982. Although the majority of state laws still limit entry to banking organizations from nearby states, called regional reciprocal, some states are beginning to permit entry on a nationwide basis, known as national reciprocal or open-entry, as indicated in Figure 3.3.

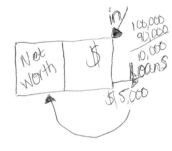

INTERNATIONAL BANKING

The growth of international banking in recent years has been just as dramatic as the growth of interstate banking. The United States has long maintained banking facilities on either a branch or agency basis in foreign countries, and other countries have had banking representation in the United States. However, the burst of expansion in these facilities in recent years now gives banking a strongly international character. Foreign interests have been attracted to commercial banking in the United States just as they have been attracted to business firms in general. The growing financial strength of certain foreign nations and the attraction of competitive lending opportunities in the United States

FIGURE 3.3   Interstate Banking Regulation in 1989

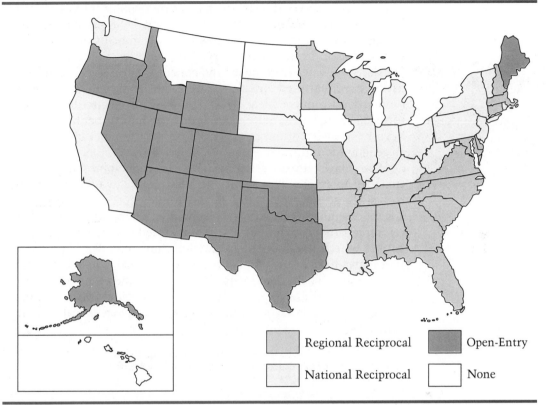

Source: *Economic Review*, Federal Reserve Bank of Dallas (November 1989): 16.

are among the factors generating this interest. Foreigners found special opportunity for commercial banking in the United States because they were not subject to the same restrictions as domestic banks. For example, foreign banks were able to engage in interstate banking long before domestic banks. A "level playing field" for all banks, both domestic and foreign, was largely achieved through the passage of the International Banking Act of 1978.

The "level playing field" for commercial banks in the United States has not meant "level" banking interests throughout the world. Japan, as well as other countries, continues to offer regulatory resistance in those countries to U.S. banking interests. Further, Japan's favorable balance of trade has made it necessary to invest abroad to accommodate its large accumulation of foreign wealth. That nation's high savings rate adds to this need for foreign investment. Japanese banks have invested heavily in commercial banking throughout the world as they have in nonbanking enterprises. From 1984 to 1988, the share of international banking assets held by Japanese banks grew from 23 percent to almost 40 percent. There are now 100 branches and agencies of Japanese banks in the United States as well as a number of relatively large subsidiaries of Japanese banks. Japanese banks now have about 14 percent of the banking market in the United States; they are especially important in California. To a lesser extent European banking interests, especially those of Great Britain and West Germany, have also moved into U.S. banking. Hong Kong and British banks have established important positions in the U.S. commercial lending market. Commercial banking in the U.S. is now truly international.

nonbank financial conglomerates large corporations that offer various financial services

NONBANK FINANCIAL CONGLOMERATES

In competition with the large bank holding companies are the **nonbank financial conglomerates.** These financial supermarkets have now become dominant in many areas of financial service. Without the regulatory constraints of the banking system, there is virtually no limit to the scope of their activities.

The first conglomerate that comes to mind is Sears Roebuck & Company. It owns virtually every form of significant financial service, including mortgage insurance, real estate management, consumer finance, leasing, commercial banking, auto and fire insurance, and investment banking. Of special interest is the acquisition of the investment banking firm of Dean Witter Reynolds, Inc. by Sears. Other investment banking firms have been acquired by financial conglomerates. For example, Prudential Insurance Company purchased the Bache Group Securities, Inc., and Travelers Insurance purchased Dillon Reed and Company. Other major conglomerates include General Electric Company, Primerica, and American Express Company.

Firms such as General Motors, Ford, International Harvester, and others have for many years owned financial subsidiaries to support sales. However, the "supermarket" conglomerates of today come close to creating their own financial universes. Early in this chapter we saw that one of the purposes of The Monetary Control Act and The Garn-St Germain Act was to enable banks, S&Ls, savings banks, and credit unions to compete on equal terms with the money market mutual funds of the conglomerates. These acts have provided help in the competitive race with the nonbank conglomerates, but depository institutions continue to operate at a distinct disadvantage.

KEY TERMS

bank holding company
banking system
branch banks
certificates of deposit
nonbanking financial
    conglomerates

secured loan
thrift institutions
unsecured loan

DISCUSSION QUESTIONS

1. Describe the composition of depository institutions that make up the banking system.

2. Compare the operations of commercial banks during the nation's colonial period with those of today's modern commercial banks.
3. How vital a role has the banking system played in the development of the United States economy? Has its importance decreased or increased with industrialization?
4. Distinguish between commercial banks and thrift institutions.
5. Why was it considered necessary to create the Federal Reserve System when we already had the benefits of the National Banking Act?
6. Comment on the objectives of The Depository Institutions Deregulation and Monetary Control Act of 1980.
7. Why was the Garn-St Germain Depository Institutions Act thought to be necessary?
8. Describe the principal functions of the four depository institutions that make up the banking system.
9. Why do regulatory authorities insist on certain minimum capital requirements for depository institutions before they may begin operations?
10. What are the sources of capital for depository institutions? Why would an institution wish to increase its capital after operations had begun and its initial capital requirements were met?
11. Bank regulatory authorities recently increased the standard for the ratio of primary capital to total assets. Why was this action taken?
12. To what extent is concentration in banking control in the United States increasing? For the remainder of the century do you anticipate a degree of concentration comparable to that of Canada and Great Britain?
13. Describe the functions assigned to the Resolution Trust Corporation created in 1988.
14. In 1989, the Financial Institutions Reform, Recovery, and Enforcement Act was passed. What are the special features of this legislation?
15. Describe the development and significance of international banking.
16. Comment on the problems faced by the Federal Deposit Insurance Corporation.

PROBLEM

From a recent issue of the *Federal Reserve Bulletin*, identify, on a consolidated basis for all commercial banks, a) the dollar amount of the principal sources of funds and b) the dollar amount of the principal uses to which the funds were applied. For each source and use of funds, compute the percentage represented by each relative to the total sources and uses.

SELF-TEST QUESTIONS

1. From the period 1836 until the Civil War, the banking system was dominated by:
   a. the Second Bank of the United States
   b. the First Bank of the United States
   c. savings banks
   d. state chartered banks

2. The National Banking Act of 1964:
   a. provided for the creation of a central bank
   b. provided for the creation of a group of central banks
   c. made possible the chartering of banks by the federal government
   d. was repealed because of a host of unrelated amendments

3. Thrift depositories came into existence in the early 1800s primarily to:
   a. provide a financial basis for home financing
   b. provide safe depositories for individual savers
   c. assist consumer finance institutions
   d. provide high rates of interest income for savers

4. Commercial banks obtain the bulk of their loanable funds from:
   a. depositors
   b. the issue of certificates of deposit
   c. the sale of bank stock
   d. the sale of subordinated debenture bonds

5. Interstate banks are now:
   a. permitted on a reciprocal basis by all states
   b. considered desirable but not yet permitted
   c. permitted in a majority of states on a regional basis
   d. not permitted in any state

SELF-TEST PROBLEM

You are in the market for a $700 loan that you plan to repay in one year. One institution quotes a "discount loan" basis of 8 percent. Another institution quotes a rate of 8.5 percent on a "loan" basis. Compare the attractiveness of the two quotes on an interest-cost basis.

SUGGESTED READINGS

Amel, Dean F., and Michael J. Jacowski. "Trends In Banking Structure since the Mid-1970s." *Federal Reserve Bulletin* (March 1989): 120–131.

Clair, Robert T., and Paul K. Tucker. "Interstate Banking and the Federal Reserve: A Historical Perspective." *Economic Review*, Federal Reserve Bank of Dallas (November 1989): 1–20.

Corrigan, E. Gerald. "Trends in International Banking in the United States and Japan." *Quarterly Review*, Federal Reserve Bank of New York (Autumn 1989): 1–6.

Dewey, D.R. *Financial History of the United States*, 12e. New York: Longmans, Green & Co., 1934.

Edmister, Robert O. *Financial Institutions*. New York: McGraw-Hill, 1986. Part 3.

Hammond, Bray. *Banks and Politics in America from the Revolution to the Civil War*. Princeton, NJ: Princeton University Press, 1957.

Hempel, George H., Alan B. Coleman, and Donald G. Simonson. *Bank Management*, 2e. New York: John Wiley & Sons, 1986. Parts II and III.

Kuprianov, Anatoli, and David L. Mengle. "The Future of Deposit Insurance: An Analysis of the Alternatives." *Economic Review*, Federal Reserve Bank of Richmond (May/June 1989): 3–15.

ANSWERS TO SELF-TEST QUESTIONS   1. d   2. c   3. b   4. a   5. c

SOLUTION TO SELF-TEST PROBLEM

The interest cost of the "loan"-basis 8.5 percent quote is 8.5 percent. The "discount"-basis 8 percent quote provides an effective interest rate of 8.7 percent (rounded). Calculation: $56 is deducted from the $700 loan principal, providing you with $644. (The $56 is 8 percent of $700.) The $56 cost divided by the funds available for your use of $644 is 8.7 percent.

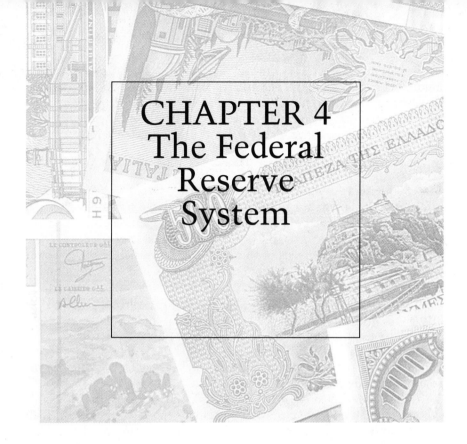

CHAPTER 4
The Federal Reserve System

After studying this chapter, you should be able to do the following:
*   Identify the major financial and banking problems that gave rise to the Federal Reserve System in the United States.
*   Describe the general structure of the Federal Reserve System.
*   List and discuss the functions of the Federal Reserve System.
*   Explain the methods by which the Federal Reserve System carries out the important function of controlling the size of the money supply.
*   Describe the ways in which the Reserve Banks accommodate the clearance and collection of checks.

U.S. BANKING PRIOR TO WORLD WAR I

In order to understand the importance of the Federal Reserve Act of 1913 it is important to review the weaknesses of the banking system that gave rise to that Act. Although the National Banking Act had resulted in substantial improvements in banking practices, certain weaknesses persisted and as the economy expanded, new problems developed. The National Banking Act provided a sound basis for the holding of reserves and the issuance of notes by banks. As we shall see, however, the constraints on note issuance, in the interest of prudent bank management, made it difficult for banks to meet the credit needs of an expanding economy. These matters are discussed below.

Weaknesses of the Banking System

One of the main weaknesses of the banking system in the late 1800s was the arrangement for holding reserves. A large part of the reserve balances of banks was held as deposits with large city banks, in particular with large New York City banks. Banks outside of the large cities were permitted to keep part of their reserves with their large city bank correspondents. Certain percentages of deposits had to be retained in their own vaults. These were the only alternatives for holding reserve balances. During periods of economic stress, the position of these large city banks was precarious because they had to meet the deposit withdrawals by their own customers as well as by the smaller banks. The frequent inability of the large banks to meet such deposit withdrawal demands resulted in extreme hardship for the smaller banks whose reserves they held.

Another weakness of the banking system under the National Banking Act was the method used to issue bank notes. In an effort to provide the nation with a sound national currency, no provision had been made for the expansion or contraction of national bank notes to reflect variations in business activity. The volume of national bank notes was governed not by the needs of business but rather by the availability and price of government bonds.

The National Banking Act provided that national banks could issue their own notes only against U.S. government bonds the banks held on deposit with the Treasury. Note issues were limited to 90 percent of the par value, as stated on the face of the bond, or the market value of the bonds, whichever was lower. When bonds sold at prices considerably above their par value, the advantage of purchasing bonds as a basis to issue notes was eliminated.

For example, if a $1,000 par value bond were available for purchase at a price of $1,150, the banks would not be inclined to make such a purchase since a maximum of $900 in notes could be issued against the bond, in this case 90 percent of par value. The interest that the bank could earn from the use of the $900 in notes would not be great enough to offset the high price of the bond. When government bonds sold at par or at a discount, on the other hand, the potential earning power of the note issues would be quite attractive and banks would be encouraged to purchase bonds for note issue purposes. The volume of national bank notes, therefore, depended on the government bond market rather than the seasonal or cyclical needs of the nation for currency.

Central Banking

The U.S. financial system of the late 1800s appeared to suffer not so much from the shortcomings of the National Banking Act as from the lack of an effective banking structure. Yet a single theme ran through the proposals and counterproposals that preceded the enactment of the Federal Reserve Act: opposition to a strong central banking system. The vast western frontiers and the local independence of the southern areas created distrust of centralized financial control. This distrust was made all the more pointed by the experience, during the years immediately preceding enactment of the Federal Reserve Act, of trust-busting under President Theodore Roosevelt. Many of the predatory practices of the large corporate combinations were at that time being made public through legislative commissions and investigations.

The controversy between industrial and financial centers on the one hand and the less well developed western and southern states persists to a certain extent to the present time. The senatorial arrangement of two senators from each state is a reflection of this perceived need for adequate representation on the political front. A strong central bank could be counted on, it was assumed at the time, to support restrictive monetary practices at the expense of the credit needs of outlying areas. The financial panic of 1907 illustrates the well justified suspicion of the financial centers of the nation. Trust companies during the early years of this century were comparatively unrestricted by law. Many of these companies branched out into commercial banking and kept inadequate reserves. Inadequacy of reserves made them vulnerable to the first signs of economic downturns. The failure of many of these trust companies resulted in a major financial panic and accompanying strengthening of distrust of centralized financial power.

The United States was one of the last major industrial nations to adopt a permanent system of central banking. However, many financial and political leaders had long recognized the advantages of such a system. These supporters of central banking were given a big boost by the financial panic of 1907. The central banking system adopted by the United States was, in fact, a compromise between the system of independently owned banks in existence in this country and the central banking systems of such countries as Canada, Great Britain, Spain, and Germany. This compromise took the form of a series of central banks, each representing a specific region of the United States. The assumption was that each central bank would be more responsive to the particular financial problems of its region.

In many respects, a central bank resembles a commercial bank with regard to services performed. A central bank lends money to its members; it is required to hold reserves; it is given the responsibility of creating money, generally through bank notes and deposits; and it has stockholders and a board of directors as well as other characteristics of a commercial bank. In contrast with a commercial bank, a central bank does not necessarily operate for profit, but it has a primary responsibility for influencing the cost, availability, and supply of money. It facilitates the operations of the commercial banks with both the business community and the government.

Guaranteed to be on Test

STRUCTURE OF THE FEDERAL RESERVE SYSTEM

Under the authority of the Federal Reserve Act of 1913, twelve Federal Reserve districts were established. Each Federal Reserve district is served by a Federal Reserve Bank, and the activities of the twelve banks are in turn coordinated by a board of governors located in Washington, DC. The members of the Board of Governors are also members of the Federal Open Market Committee. The Federal Advisory Council provides advice and general information to the Board of Governors. The organizational structure of the Federal Reserve System is shown in Figure 4.1.

The Federal Reserve System (Fed) did not replace the system that existed under the National Banking Act but rather was superimposed upon it. Certain provisions of the National Banking Act, however, were modified to permit greater flexibility of operations.

Federal Reserve Membership

The Federal Reserve Act provided that all national banks were to become members of the Fed. In addition, state-chartered banks, as well as trust companies, were permitted to join the system if they could show evidence of a satisfactory financial condition. The Federal Reserve Act also required that all member banks purchase capital stock of the Reserve Bank of their district up to a maximum of 6 percent of their paid-in capital and surplus. In practice, however, member banks have had to pay in only 3 percent; the remainder is subject to call at the discretion of the Fed. Member banks are limited to a maximum of 6 percent dividends on the stock of the Reserve Bank that they hold. The Reserve Banks, therefore, are private institutions owned by the many member banks of the Fed.

State-chartered banks and trust companies are permitted to withdraw from membership with the Fed six months after written notice has been submitted to the Reserve Bank of their district. In such cases, the stock originally purchased by the withdrawing member is canceled, and a refund is made for all money paid in.

As of year-end 1989, 6,018 of the nation's 14,990 commercial banks were members of the Fed. This appears to be a rather small coverage of

FIGURE 4.1 Organization of the Federal Reserve System

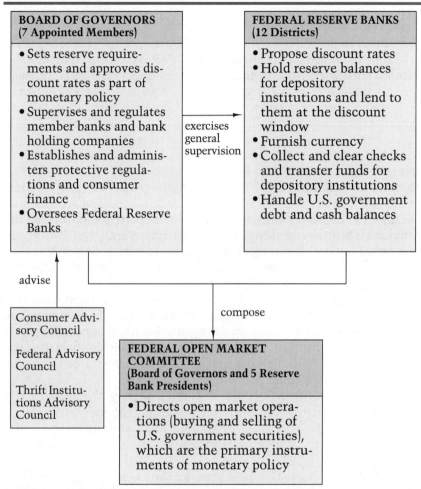

banks by the Federal Reserve compared with the 96 percent of all commercial banks that carry insurance under the provisions of the Federal Deposit Insurance Corporation. These member banks, however, hold approximately 70 percent of the deposits of all commercial banks. Even this figure understates the importance of the Federal Reserve in the nation's financial system. As indicated in Chapter 3, the Monetary Control Act has generally eliminated distinctions between banks that are members of the Fed and other depository institutions by applying comparable reserve and reporting requirements to all these institutions.

Federal Reserve Banks

DIRECTORS AND OFFICERS

Each Reserve Bank has corporate officers and a board of directors. The selection of officers and directors, however, is unlike that of other corporations. Each Reserve Bank has on its board nine directors, who must be residents of the district in which they serve. The directors serve terms of three years, with appointments staggered in such a way that three directors are appointed each year. In order to assure that the various economic elements of the federal reserve districts are represented, the nine members of the board of directors are divided into three groups: Class A, Class B, and Class C.

Both Class A and Class B directors are elected by the member banks of the federal reserve district. The Class A directors represent member banks of the district, while the Class B directors represent nonbanking interests. These nonbanking interests are commerce, agriculture, and industry. The Class C directors are appointed by the Board of Governors of the Federal Reserve System. These persons may not be stockholders, directors, or employees of existing banks.

The majority of the directors of the Reserve Banks are elected by the member banks of each district. However, the three nonbanking members of each board appointed by the Board of Governors of the Federal Reserve System are in a more strategic position than the other board members. One member appointed by the Board of Governors is designated chairperson of the board of directors and federal reserve agent, and a second member is appointed deputy chairperson. The federal reserve agent is the Board of Governors' representative at each Reserve Bank. He or she is responsible for maintaining the collateral that backs the Federal Reserve Notes issued by each Reserve Bank.

Each Reserve Bank also has a president and first vice-president who are appointed by its board of directors and approved by the Board of Governors. A Reserve Bank may have several additional vice-presidents. The president is responsible for executing policies established by the board of directors and for the general administration of Reserve Bank affairs. All other officers and personnel of the Reserve Bank are subject to the authority of the president.

FEDERAL RESERVE BRANCH BANKS

In addition to the twelve Reserve Banks, 25 branch banks have been established. These branch banks are located for the most part in geographical areas not conveniently served by the Reserve Banks themselves. For this reason, the geographically large western Federal Reserve districts have a majority of the Reserve Branch Banks. The San Francisco district has four, the Dallas district has three, and the Atlanta district has five branch banks. The New York federal reserve district, on the other hand, has only one branch bank, while the Boston district has no branches. The cities in which Reserve Banks and their branches are located are shown in Figure 4.2.

Board of Governors

The Board of Governors of the Federal Reserve System is composed of seven members. Each member is appointed for a term of fourteen years. The purpose of the fourteen-year term undoubtedly was to reduce political pressure on the board. Board members can be of any political party, and there is no specific provision concerning the qualifications a member must have. All members are appointed by the President of the United States with the advice and consent of the Senate. One member is designated as the chairperson and another as the vice-chairperson.

The appointive power of the President and the ability of Congress to alter its structure makes the Board of Governors a dependent political structure. However, it enjoys much independence in its operations by virtue of popular support by the public. The Board of Governors of the Federal Reserve System is, in fact, one of the most powerful monetary organizations in the world. The chairman of the board plays an especially influential role in policy formulation. Since the board attempts to achieve its goals without political considerations, disagreement between the administration in power and the board is common. From time to time pressures from Congress or the President have undoubtedly influenced the board's decisions, but its semi-independence generally prevails.

In addition to setting the nation's monetary policy, the board gives direction and coordination to the activities of the twelve Reserve Banks under its jurisdiction. The board reviews and approves the discount-rate actions of the twelve Reserve Banks. The board is responsible for approving the applications of state-chartered banks applying for membership in the system. It is also responsible for recommending the removal of officers and directors of member banks when they break rules established by the Fed and other regulatory authorities. In addition, the board implements many of the credit control devices that have come into existence in recent decades such as the Truth-in-Lending Act, the Equal Credit Opportunity Act, and the Home Mortgage Disclosure Act.

There is general agreement that in carrying out its various functions the Fed has achieved much respect and confidence on the part of the citizens of the nation. The semi-independence of the system reassures most people that raw politics does not shape policy. From the viewpoint of competition among depository institutions, small firms especially benefit from the backing afforded by their Reserve Banks.

FIGURE 4.2   The Federal Reserve System

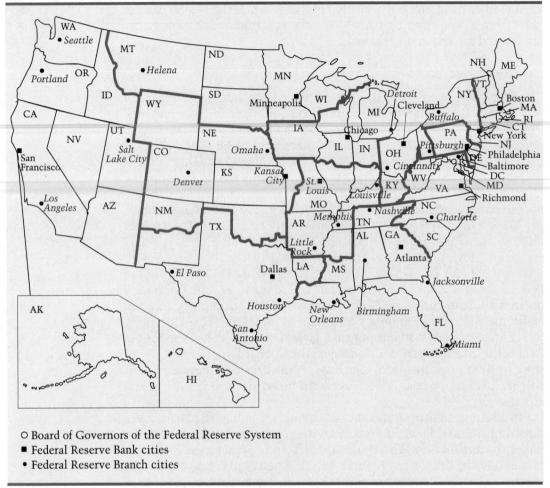

○ Board of Governors of the Federal Reserve System
■ Federal Reserve Bank cities
• Federal Reserve Branch cities

Source: Board of Governors of the Federal Reserve System.

The net result has been an improvement of both the stability and growth of the economy.

Federal Open Market Committee

As early as 1922, efforts were made to coordinate the timing of purchases and sales of securities by the Federal Reserve Banks in order to achieve desirable national monetary policy objectives. The Federal Open Market Committee, with the additional powers granted to it by the Banking Act of 1935, has full control over all open market operations of the Reserve Banks. This committee (FOMC) consists of the seven members of the Board of Governors of the Fed plus five presidents of Reserve Banks.

FUNCTIONS OF THE FEDERAL RESERVE SYSTEM

The primary responsibility of a central bank is to regulate the supply of money, and therefore regulate its cost and availability. By exercising its influence on the monetary system of the United States, the Fed performs a unique and important function: the promotion of economic stability. It is notable that the system's broad powers to affect economic stabilization and monetary control were not present when the Fed came into existence in 1913. At that time, the system was meant to provide for the contraction and expansion of the money supply as dictated by economic conditions, serve as bankers' banks in times of economic crisis, provide a more effective check clearance system, and establish a more effective regulatory system. Much of these responsibilities initially fell to the twelve Reserve Banks, but as the scope of responsibility for the monetary system was broadened, power was concentrated with the Board of Governors. Today the responsibilities of the Fed may be described as those relating to monetary policy, to supervision and regulation, and to services provided for depository institutions and the government.

Monetary Policy Functions

In Part 4 of this text the monetary policies of the Fed are described in somewhat greater detail, especially as they relate to the fiscal policy of the federal government. The pursuit of desirable policies requires close cooperation between the Fed and the U.S. Treasury. For its part, the Fed influences the economy by affecting the availability of depository institutions' reserves, thereby influencing monetary and credit conditions. The Fed affects the reserves through open market operations, changing reserve requirements, and by changing the discount rate at which loans are made to depository institutions.

The control of depository reserves enables the Fed to affect a substantial measure of control on the entire economy. For example, if the board feels there is a growing threat of inflation resulting from booming economic activity, it may take action to reduce reserves through one or more of the three devices cited above. As reserves are reduced, depository institutions become more selective in their lending activity. In addition, they usually increase the interest rates on their loans. The result is downward pressure on the housing market, since most homes are purchased with mortgage financing. Businesses too find it more expensive to carry or add inventories, and attempts to increase prices to offset the burden of higher interest rates may be met with consumer resistance. These factors, along with many others, serve to slow down the economy.

Increasing the reserves of depository institutions has the opposite effect, and loans become more readily available at lower interest rates. Home buying picks up as mortgage payments are lowered; businesses enter into new ventures as lenders take a more optimistic view; factories replace old equipment; and communities may be encouraged to build roads, schools, parks, and other public facilities. The three principal monetary control devices that affect the depository reserves of the nation are described in the following pages.

OPEN MARKET OPERATIONS

*Open market operations
buying and selling of
securities by the Federal
Reserve to alter the
supply of money*

Open market operations, carried out under the general direction of the Federal Open Market Committee, are the most powerful and flexible monetary policy tool of the Federal Reserve. **Open market operations** are the purchases or sales of large blocks of obligations, ordinarily those of U.S. government Treasury Bills. Although not restricted to the purchase and sale of government obligations, the large size of these transactions requires a broad and highly active market that can accommodate the transactions without being distorted or disrupted itself.

For example, assume the Open Market Committee decides to buy $100 million of obligations to stimulate the economy. The purchase is ordinarily made from large money-center banks or from specialized bond dealers. Payment is made by issuing a check drawn on the Federal Reserve. When presented to the Fed for payment, reserves of the presenting bank are increased. If the seller of the obligations is not a bank, its reserves at its bank are increased as the check is presented for credit to its account. The check is then forwarded to the Fed for credit to the seller's bank. These increased reserves increase the deposit-creation potential of the banking system.

If the Federal Reserve wishes to lower the money-creation potential of the nation's depository institutions, it will sell securities rather than purchase them. By so doing, it absorbs reserves as purchasers of the securities make payment.

The location of the Reserve Bank of New York allows it to play a special role in the conduct of monetary policy. The trading desk of the Open Market Committee is located in that bank and all purchases and sales on behalf of the system are carried out at that location. Located in the financial capital of the world, the Federal Reserve Bank of New York is in a particularly good position to observe interest rate and money market trends and to convey information to the Federal Reserve Board in Washington, DC.

HOLDING RESERVES OF DEPOSITORY INSTITUTIONS

One of the basic measures provided by the Federal Reserve Act of 1913 was the institution of a better system of maintaining reserves for the banks of the nation. The shortcomings of the system of holding reserves under the National Banking Act were understood, and an improved system was needed before progress could be made toward stabilizing the banking system. To accomplish this, member banks were to keep a specified percentage of their deposits on reserve with the Reserve Bank of their district.

The Monetary Control Act, as noted in Chapter 3, has radically changed the nature of reserve requirements. Thrift institutions and agencies and branches of foreign banks are now required to maintain reserves with Reserve Banks. Although member banks of the Fed must maintain reserves either in their own vaults or with Reserve Banks, nonmembers may maintain reserves with certain large city banks.

LENDING TO DEPOSITORY INSTITUTIONS

It was believed that if the Reserve Banks were to serve effectively as bankers' banks, they would have to be able to lend to their member banks at times when those banks needed additional funds. Such a lending arrangement answers one of the principal problems of the National Banking Act, its inflexible currency system. Loans to depository institutions by the Reserve Banks may take two forms. In one the borrowing institution may receive an *advance,* or loan, secured by its own promissory note together with eligible paper it owns. In the second, the borrower may *discount,* or sell to the Reserve Bank, its **eligible paper**. Eligible paper includes securities of the U.S. Government and federal agencies, promissory notes, mortgages of acceptable quality, and bankers' acceptances.

eligible paper
short-term promissory notes eligible for discounting with Federal Reserve banks

The Monetary Control Act provides access to advances and discounts for other depository institutions as well as for member banks. As of March, 1991, the rate charged for loans was 6 percent. The rate may be lowered or raised to encourage or discourage, as desired, depository institutions' participation in the loan program. And the rate will vary at times from one Reserve Bank to another. Differences in rates among Reserve Banks generally result from a desire to equalize the general flow of credit throughout the nation.

Supervisory and Regulatory Functions

As the central bank for the nation, the Federal Reserve has a basic responsibility for the financial stability of the economy. This responsibility, shared with other agencies of the government, is directed primarily toward the depository institutions of the nation. A strong and stable depository system is vital to the growth and the stability of the entire economy. Depository *supervision* is primarily concerned with the safety and soundness of individual firms. It involves oversight to ensure that depository institutions are operated carefully. Depository *regulation* relates to the issuance of specific rules or regulations that govern the structure and conduct of operations.

SPECIFIC SUPERVISORY RESPONSIBILITIES

On-site examination of depository institutions is one of the System's most important responsibilities. This function is shared with the federal Office of the Comptroller of the Currency (OCC), the Federal Deposit Insurance Corporation, and state regulatory agencies. Although the Federal Reserve is authorized to examine all member banks, in practice it limits itself to state-chartered member banks and all bank holding companies. It cooperates with state examining agencies to avoid overlapping examining authority. The Office of the Comptroller directs its attention to nationally chartered banks and the FDIC supervises insured nonmember commercial banks.

In addition to these three federal banking supervisory agencies, two federal agencies have primary responsibility for supervising and regulating nonbank depository institutions. The National Credit Union Administration (NCUA) has the responsibility for supervising and regulating credit unions and the Office of Thrift Supervision (OTS) has responsibility for all other nonbank depository institutions. The examination of a nonbank depository institution generally entails (1) an appraisal of the soundness of the institution's assets; (2) an evaluation of internal operations, policies, and management; (3) an analysis of key financial factors, such as capital and earnings; (4) a review for compliance with all banking laws and regulations; and (5) an overall determination of the institution's financial condition.

The Federal Reserve conducts on-site inspections of parent bank holding companies and their nonbank subsidiaries. These inspections include a review of nonbank assets and funding activities to ensure compliance with the Bank Holding Company Act. Bank holding companies and their nonbank subsidiaries were discussed in Chapter 3.

The Federal Reserve has broad powers to regulate the overseas activities of member banks and bank holding companies. Its aim is to allow U.S. banks to be fully competitive with institutions of host countries in financing U.S. trade and investment overseas. Along with the OCC and the FDIC, the Federal Reserve also has broad oversight authority for the supervision of all federal and state-licensed branches and agencies of foreign banks operating in the United States.

SPECIFIC REGULATORY RESPONSIBILITIES

The Federal Reserve has legal responsibility for the administration of the Bank Holding Company Act of 1956, the Bank Merger Act of 1960, and the Change in Bank Control Act of 1978. Under these acts, the Fed approves or denies the acquisitions of banks and other closely related nonbanking activities by bank holding companies. Furthermore, it permits or rejects changes of control and mergers of banks and bank holding companies.

The Federal Reserve has responsibilities for writing rules or enforcing a number of major laws that offer consumers protection in their financial dealings. In addition to consumer protection laws, the Federal Reserve, through the *Community Reinvestment Act*, encourages depository institutions to help meet the credit needs of their communities for housing and other purposes while maintaining safe and sound operations. This is particularly true in neighborhoods of families with low or moderate income.

Service Functions

As the operating arm of the nation's central bank, the Reserve Banks provide a wide range of important services to depository institutions and to the U.S. Government. The most important of these services is the payments mechanism, a system whereby billions of dollars are transferred each day. Other services include electronic fund transfers, net settlement facilities, safekeeping and transfer of securities, and serving as fiscal agent for the United States.

THE PAYMENTS MECHANISM

The *payments mechanism* has many aspects, including providing currency and coin, processing and clearing checks, providing for the settlement of checks, and wire transfers.

Currency and Coin

Notwithstanding comments heard about the nation's trend toward a "cashless society," we remain highly dependent on currency and coin. It is the Federal Reserve's responsibility to ensure that the economy has an adequate supply to meet the public's demand. Currency and coin are put into or retired from circulation by the Reserve Banks, which use depository institutions for this purpose. Virtually all currency in circulation is in the form of Federal Reserve Notes. These notes are printed by the Bureau of Engraving and Printing of the U.S. Treasury.

Check Clearance and Collection

One of the Fed's important contributions to the smooth flow of financial interchange is facilitating the clearance and collection of checks of the depository institutions of the nation. Each Reserve Bank serves as a clearinghouse for all depository institutions in its district, provided that they agree pay the face value on checks forwarded to them for payment.

- *The Truth in Lending Act* requires disclosure of the "finance charge" and the "annual percentage rate" of credit along with certain other costs and terms to permit consumers to compare the prices of credit from different sources. This act also limits liability on lost or stolen credit cards.
- *The Fair Credit Billing Act* sets up a procedure for the prompt correction of errors on a revolving charge account and prevents damage to credit ratings while a dispute is being settled.
- *The Equal Credit Opportunity Act* prohibits discrimination in the granting of credit on the basis of sex, marital status, race, color, religion, national origin, age, or receipt of public assistance.
- *The Fair Credit Reporting Act* sets up a procedure for correcting mistakes on credit records and requires that records be used only for legitimate business purposes.
- *The Consumer Leasing Act* requires disclosure of information to help consumers compare the cost and terms of one lease of consumer goods with another and to compare the cost of leasing versus buying on credit or for cash.
- *The Real Estate Settlement Procedures Act* requires disclosure of information about the services and costs involved at the time of settlement when property is transferred from seller to buyer.
- *The Electronic Fund Transfer Act* provides a basic framework regarding the rights, liabilities, and responsibilities of consumers who use electronic transfer services and of the financial institutions that offer them.
- *The Federal Trade Commission Improvement Act* authorizes the Federal Reserve Board to identify unfair or deceptive acts or practices on the part of banks and to issue regulations to prohibit them.

Source: *The Federal Reserve System—Purposes & Functions*, Board of Governors of the Federal Reserve System, Washington, DC, 1984.

An example of the check-clearance process through the Reserve Banks will demonstrate the facility with which these clearances are made at the present time. Assume that the owner of a business in Sacramento, California, places an order for merchandise with a distributor in San Francisco. The order is accompanied by a check drawn on the owner's depository in Sacramento. This check is deposited by the distributor with its depository in San Francisco, at which time the distributor receives a corresponding credit to its account with the depository. The distributor's depository will then send the check to the Reserve Bank of its district, also located in San Francisco. The Reserve Bank will in turn forward the check to the depository in Sacramento on which the check was originally drawn. The adjustment of accounts is accomplished at the Reserve Bank through an alternate debit and credit to the account of each depository institution concerned in the transaction. The San Francisco depository, which has honored the check of its customer, will receive an increase in its reserve with the Reserve Bank, while the depository in Sacramento will have its reserve decreased by a corresponding amount. The depository in Sacramento will then reduce the account of the business on which the check was written. Hence, the exchange is made with no transfer of currency.

Check clearance between Federal Reserve Districts.   If an order was also placed by the Sacramento firm with a distributor of goods in Chicago, the check would be subject to an additional step in being cleared through the Fed. The Chicago distributor, like the San Francisco distributor, deposits the check with the depository of its choice and in turn receives an increase in its account. The Chicago depository deposits the check for collection with the Reserve Bank of Chicago, which then forwards the check to the Reserve Bank of San Francisco. The Reserve Bank of San Francisco, of course, then presents the check for payment to the depository on which it was drawn. Thus there are two routes of check clearance: the *intradistrict settlement*, where the transaction takes place entirely within a single federal reserve district, and the *interdistrict settlement*, in which there are relationships between banks of two federal reserve districts.

As previously described, Reserve Banks are able to minimize the actual flow of funds by increasing or decreasing reserves of the participating depository institutions. In the same way, the Interdistrict Settlement Fund eliminates the flow of funds between the Reserve Banks needed to make interdistrict settlements. The Interdistrict Settlement Fund in Washington, DC, has a substantial deposit from each of the Reserve Banks. These deposit credits are alternately increased or decreased, depending upon the clearance balance of the day's activities on the part of each Reserve Bank. At a certain hour each day, each Reserve Bank informs the Interdistrict Settlement Fund by direct wire of the amount of checks it received the previous day that were drawn upon depository institutions in other Federal Reserve Districts. The deposit of each Reserve Bank with the Interdistrict Settlement Fund is increased or decreased according to the balance of the day's check-clearance activities.

Check clearance through Federal Reserve branch banks.   Branch banks of the Reserve Banks enter into the clearance process in a very important way. If a check is deposited with a depository located closer to a Reserve branch bank than to a Reserve Bank, the branch bank, in effect, takes the place of the Reserve Bank. The Federal Reserve facilitates the check-clearing services of the Reserve Banks and their branches by maintaining a small group of regional check-processing centers.

Check routing.   Over one quarter of the total personnel of the twelve Reserve Banks are engaged in the task of assisting in the check-clearance process by the Fed. Great effort has been exercised to make this task easier, and much timesaving machinery has been introduced into the operation. Fundamental to the clearance process is a machine that has the ability to "read" a system of symbols and numerals, shown in Figure 4.3. Although these symbols are slightly different from conventional numbers, they are easily read by human eyes as well. Information about the clearance process is printed on the lower part of the check form in magnetic ink that contains iron oxide. Processing machines can read this information directly from checks. The system has been named Magnetic Ink Character Recognition (MICR). In addition to the clearance symbol, depository institutions with compatible electronic accounting equipment include a symbol for each customer's account. This makes it possible to electronically process checks for internal bookkeeping purposes. Banks continue to include the older check routing symbol in the upper right-hand corner of their checks. It is useful for physically sorting checks that are torn or otherwise unsuitable for electronic sorting.

Transfer of credit.   The Fed provides for the transfer of hundreds of millions of dollars in depository balances around the country daily. The communication system called Fedwire may be used by depository institutions to transfer funds for their own accounts, to move balances at correspondent banks, and to send funds to another institution on behalf of customers.

Electronic funds transfers.   The tremendous growth in volume of check clearance and the relatively high cost of wire transfers through the Federal Reserve leased system, have resulted in efforts to bring computers into the process. While the use of credit cards has taken some pressure off check-clearance facilities, the problem remains. Credit cards, of course, permit payment for many transactions to be completed with a single check at the end a the billing cycle. Established in the early 1970s, automated clearinghouses (ACHs) have grown into a nationwide clearing and settlement mechanism for electronically originated debits and credits. Examples of such transfers are the direct deposit of payments for wages, pensions, social security, and so on to

FIGURE 4.3   Check Routing Symbols

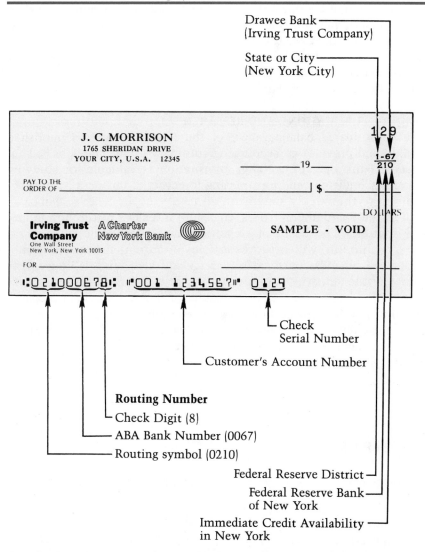

the payee's account at his or her depository institution. In spite of the speed and convenience of electronic transfers, the growth of this process has not been as great as had been hoped.

THE FED AS GOVERNMENT FISCAL AGENT

A substantial portion of the employees of the Fed hold jobs that are directly related to its role as **fiscal agent** for the U.S. government. The

fiscal agent
role of the Fed in collecting taxes, issuing checks, and other activities for the Treasury

services include holding the Treasury's checking accounts, assisting in the collection of taxes, transferring money from one region to another, and selling, redeeming, and paying interest on federal securities. The federal government makes most of its payments to the public from funds on deposit at the Reserve Banks. The Fed also acts as fiscal agent for foreign central banks and international organizations such as the International Monetary Fund.

REPORTS, PUBLICATIONS, AND RESEARCH

The consolidated balance sheet of the Reserve Banks is published weekly and provides an accounting summary of all phases of Federal Reserve Bank operations. This information is valuable for studying business conditions and formulating forecasts of business activity. In addition to the weekly statement, all twelve of the Reserve Banks, as well as the Board of Governors, engage in intensive research in monetary matters. The Board of Governors makes available the *Federal Reserve Bulletin*, which carries articles of current interest to economists and business persons in general and also offers a convenient source of the statistics compiled by the Fed. The *Bulletin* is a convenient secondary source for certain statistical series and data prepared by other government agencies and private organizations such as the F.W. Dodge reports on construction contracts, and the New York Stock Exchange reports on stock prices and sales.

KEY TERMS

eligible paper   open market operations
fiscal agent

DISCUSSION QUESTIONS

1. To what extent did the Federal Reserve Act of 1913 supplant bank regulation and operation under the National Banking Act?
2. The Federal Reserve Act of 1913 provided for the establishment of a group of central banks. How do the operations of a central bank differ from those of a commercial bank?
3. Describe the organizational structure of the Federal Reserve System.
4. Banking and large, medium, and small businesses are represented

on the board of directors of each Reserve Bank. Explain how this representation is accomplished.

5. What is meant by Reserve Branch Bank? How many such branches exist, and where are most of them located geographically?

6. The Federal Reserve System is under the general direction and control of the Board of Governors of the Federal Reserve System in Washington, DC. How are members of the Board of Governors appointed? To what extent are they subject to political pressures?

7. Discuss the structure, the functions, and the importance of the Federal Open Market Committee.

8. Reserve Banks have at times been described as bankers' banks due to their lending powers. What is meant by this statement?

9. Explain the usual procedures for examining national banks. How does this process differ from the examination of member banks of the Federal Reserve System holding state charters?

10. Explain the process by which the Reserve Banks provide the economy with currency and coin.

11. Describe how a check drawn on a commercial bank but deposited for collection in another bank in a distant city might be cleared through the facilities of the Federal Reserve System.

12. What is the special role of the Federal Reserve Interdistrict Settlement Fund in the check-clearance process?

13. In what way do the Reserve Banks serve as fiscal agents for the U.S. government?

PROBLEMS

1. You are a resident of Seattle, Washington and maintain a checking account with a bank in that city. You have just written a check on that bank to pay your tuition. Describe the process by which the banking system enables your college or university to collect the funds from your bank?

2. As the executive of a bank or thrift institution you are faced with an intense seasonal demand for loans. Assuming that your loanable funds are inadequate to take care of the demand, how might your Reserve Bank help you with this problem?

SELF-TEST QUESTIONS

1. The creation of the Federal Reserve System and its central banking arrangement was long in coming compared to other industrialized nations because:

a. of the nation's poor communication system in early years
b. of the physical size and diversity of the nation
c. the existing system worked quite well
d. of general opposition to a strong central banking system

2. A central bank serves the nation:

a. as a source of consumer credit when it's not otherwise available
b. by influencing the cost, availability, and supply of money
c. as a secondary source of funds for home financing
d. as the "strong right arm" of the U.S. Treasury

3. Sales and purchases of securities by the Federal Reserve System are carried out by:

a. the Federal Open Market Committee
b. the Federal Advisory Council
c. the U.S. Treasury
d. each Reserve Bank for its own account

4. Reserve Banks are responsible for:

a. more than 90 percent of all currency in circulation
b. insuring bank deposits up to $100,000 for each depositor
c. the appointment of members of the Board of Governors of the System
d. all bank examinations and supervision

5. The Federal Reserve Board has responsibility for:

a. establishing margin requirements on stock market credit
b. setting interest rates on consumer credit
c. establishing the terms and conditions of real estate credit
d. setting interest rates for bank-issued certificates of deposit

SPECIAL SELF-TEST QUESTION

Identify the Federal Reserve Bank or branch that serves your home town.

SUGGESTED READINGS

Edmister, Robert 0. *Financial Institutions.* New York: McGraw-Hill, 1986. Part 5.

Greenspan, Alan. "Innovation and Regulation of Banks in the 1990s," *Federal Reserve Bulletin* (December 1988): 783–787.

Kaufman, George G. *The U.S. Financial System,* 4e. Englewood Cliffs, NJ: Prentice-Hall, 1989. Chaps. 27 and 28.

Kidwell, David S., and Richard L. Peterson. *Financial Institutions, Markets, and Money*, 4e. Hinsdale, IL: The Dryden Press, 1990. Chaps. 6 and 10.

Meulendyke, Ann-Marie. *U.S. Monetary Policy and Financial Markets*. Federal Reserve Bank of New York, 1990.

Rose, Peter S. *Money and Capital Markets*, 3e. Homewood IL.: BPI/Irwin, 1989, Chap. 22.

Summers, Bruce J. "Electronic Payments in Retrospect," *Economic Review*, Federal Reserve Bank of Richmond (March/April 1988): 16–19.

ANSWERS TO SELF-TEST QUESTIONS   1. d   2. b   3. a   4. a   5. a

SOLUTION TO SPECIAL SELF-TEST QUESTION

For most towns or cities it will not be too difficult to determine the nearest Federal Reserve Bank or branch—simply refer to Figure 4.2. Additional help may be provided by referring to the map of districts in the back of each issue of the *Federal Reserve Bulletin*.

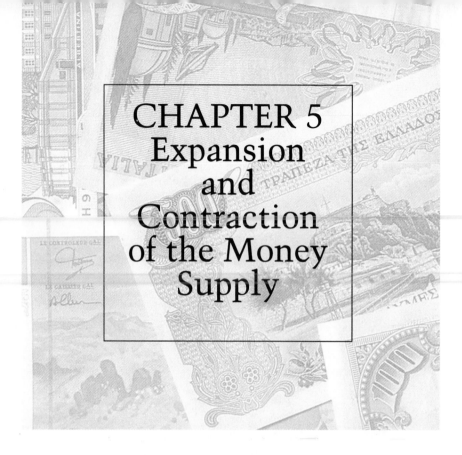

CHAPTER 5
Expansion and Contraction of the Money Supply

After studying this chapter, you should be able to:
- Describe the current backing for U.S. Federal Reserve Notes and indicate how the backing has changed over time.
- Discuss how the expansion of the money supply takes place in the U.S. banking system.
- Discuss the process by which contraction of the money supply takes place.
- Briefly summarize the factors that affect bank reserves.
- Explain the meaning of the monetary base and money multiplier.
- Explain what is meant by the velocity of money and give reasons why it is important to control the money supply.

The Federal Reserve System (Fed) attempts to regulate and control the supply of money and the availability of credit. This is because the size of the total money supply compared to the demands put upon it influences the supply of funds available for investment. The relationship between the money supply and demand in turn affects the level of prices and economic activity in our market economy. Therefore, the process by which the money supply is increased and decreased is a very important factor in the success of the economy.

You will recall that the M1 money supply is made up of cash (currency and coins) and checkable deposits in depository institutions. Since only a small part of the money supply is made up of coins, changes in the money supply are under the control of the banking system—the Fed and depository institutions. This chapter begins with a discussion of the changes in the volume of Federal Reserve notes and of coins. Next, it examines how the checkable deposit part of the money supply is expanded and contracted by the banking system. Then we discuss the factors that affect reserves in our banking system. The final sections of the chapter briefly explore the concept of a money "multiplier" and the importance of regulating and controlling the money supply.

It is important to note here that the level of savings is the primary factor which determines the supply of funds available for investment in any given time period. The savings and investment process will be explored in detail in the next chapter.

CHANGES IN THE VOLUME OF FEDERAL RESERVE NOTES AND COINS

Federal Reserve notes may be issued by the Fed with a backing of gold certificates, SDRs,[1] eligible paper, or U.S. government and agency securities. Eligible paper in the form of business notes and drafts provides little collateral today. Instead, Federal Reserve notes have been increasingly backed by government securities. At the end of January 1990, the backing for $234.5 billion in Federal Reserve notes was $11.1 billion of gold certificates, $8.5 billion of SDRs, and $214.9 billion of U.S. government and agency securities.[2]

Although Federal Reserve notes are not tied to changes in business volume as directly as when they were backed primarily by commercial paper, they still maintain their elastic character. The supply of notes expands and contracts to meet changes in the demand for currency. For example, when the Christmas shopping season ends, the public has less need for currency. Businesses deposit in their banks the money they have earned. The commercial banks turn this excess currency over to their Reserve Bank, thus reducing the supply of Federal Reserve notes.

The money supply is also increased when coins are issued by the Treasury. When the Treasury issues additional coins in response to the

---

1. As was noted in Chapter 2, Special Drawing Rights (SDRs) are a form of reserve asset or "paper gold" created by the International Monetary Fund. Their purpose is to provide worldwide monetary liquidity and to support international trade.
2. *Federal Reserve Bulletin*, (April 1990): A10.

demands of one of the Reserve Banks, it receives a credit to its account at that Reserve Bank. When the Treasury draws checks on its account (e.g., for a social security payment), the funds are transferred to the general public. As these funds are deposited in a commercial bank, they become available to the banking system as additional funds. As banks in turn deposit the funds in a Reserve Bank, the banks increase their reserve balances.

THE CHECKABLE DEPOSIT PORTION OF THE MONEY SUPPLY

Discussion of checkable deposit expansion and contraction tradition- ally has focused on the commercial banking system. This is because until recently only commercial banks were able to offer demand or checkable deposits. Now all other depository institutions can offer checkable deposits and thus affect the nation's money supply. While we will continue to refer to the expansion and contraction of checkable deposits in terms of the "banking system," we are now including the other depository institutions in addition to commercial banks. Also, to shorten our discussion, we will refer to checkable deposits simply as "deposits."

The banking system of the United States can change the volume of deposits as the needs for funds by individuals, businesses, and govern- ments change. This ability to alter the size of the money supply is based on the use of a *fractional reserve system*. In our fractional reserve system, banks must hold with the Fed reserves equal to a certain percentage of their deposits. To understand the deposit expansion and contraction process, one must study the operations of banks as units in a banking system and the relationship of bank loans to deposits and to bank reserves.

primary deposit
deposit that adds new reserves to a bank

derivative deposit
deposit of funds that were borrowed from the reserves of primary deposits

In analyzing deposit expansion, it is helpful to make a distinction between primary deposits and derivative deposits. For example, the deposit of a check drawn on the Fed is a **primary deposit** because it adds new reserves to the bank where deposited and to the banking system. **Derivative deposits** occur when reserves created from primary deposits are made available to borrowers through bank loans. Borrowers then deposit the loans so they can write checks against the funds. When a check is written and deposited in another bank, there is no change in total reserves of the banking system. The increase in reserves at the bank where the check is deposited is offset by a decrease in reserves at the bank on which the check is drawn. Banks must keep reserves against both primary and derivative deposits.

Checkable Deposit Expansion

When reserves were first required by law, the purpose was to assure depositors that banks had the ability to handle withdrawals of cash. This was before the establishment of the Federal Reserve System, which made it possible for a healthy bank to obtain additional funds in time of need. Depositor confidence is now based on deposit insurance and more complete and competent bank examinations by governmental agencies. Today, the basic function of reserve requirements is to provide a means for regulating deposit expansion and contraction.

Deposit creation takes place as a result of the operations of the whole system of banks, but it arises out of the independent transactions of individual banks. To explain the process, therefore, we will consider the loan activities of a single bank. First we will focus on the bank itself; then we will examine its relationship to a system of banks. This approach is somewhat artificial since a bank practically never acts independently of the actions of other banks, but it has been adopted to clarify the process. Furthermore, it helps to explain the belief of some bankers that they cannot create deposits since they only loan funds placed on deposit in their banks by their depositors. This analysis shows how a system of banks in which each bank is carrying on its local activities can do what an individual banker cannot do.

For illustration, let us assume that a bank receives a primary deposit of $10,000, and that it must keep reserves of 20 percent against deposits. The $10,000 becomes a cash asset to the bank as well as a $10,000 liability since it must stand ready to honor a withdrawal of the money. The bank statement, ignoring all other items, would then show the following:

ASSETS		LIABILITIES	
Reserves	$10,000	Deposits	$10,000

Against this new deposit of $10,000 the bank must keep required reserves of 20 percent, or $2,000. Therefore, it has $8,000 of excess reserves available. Excess reserves are reserves above the level of required reserves.

It may appear at first glance that the banker could proceed to make loans for $40,000, since all that is needed is a 20 percent reserve against the resulting checkable deposits. If this were attempted, however, the banker would soon be in difficulty. Since bank loans are usually obtained just before a demand for funds, checks would very likely be written against the deposit accounts almost at once. Many of these checks would be deposited in other banks, and the bank would be faced with a demand for cash as checks were presented for collection. This demand could reach the full $40,000. Since the bank has only $8,000 to meet it, it could not follow such a course and remain in business.

The amount that the banker can safely lend is the $8,000 of excess reserves. If more is lent, the banker runs the risk of not being able to make payments on checks. After an $8,000 loan, the books show:

ASSETS		LIABILITIES	
Reserves	$10,000	Deposits	$18,000
Loans	8,000		

If a check were written for the full amount of the derivative deposit ($8,000) and sent to a bank in another city for deposit, the lending bank would lose all of its excess reserves. This may be seen from its books, which would appear as follows:

ASSETS		LIABILITIES	
Reserves	$ 2,000	Deposits	$10,000
Loans	8,000		

In practice, a bank may be able to loan somewhat more than the $8,000 in this example. This is because banks frequently require their customers to keep an average deposit balance of about 15 to 20 percent of the loan. The whole of the additional $1,500 to $2,000 cannot safely be loaned since an *average* balance of $1,500 to $2,000 does not prevent the full amount of the loan being used for a period of time. With an average balance in each derivative deposit account, however, all accounts will not be drawn to zero at the same time. Therefore, some additional funds will be available for loans.

It may be argued that a banker will feel sure that some checks written against the bank will be redeposited in the same bank and that therefore larger sums can be lent. However, since any bank is only one of thousands, the banker cannot usually count on such redeposits of funds. Banks cannot run the risk of being caught short of reserves. Thus, when an individual bank receives a new primary deposit, it cannot lend the full amount of that deposit but only the amount available as excess reserves. From the point of view of an individual bank, therefore, deposit creation appears impossible. Since a part of every new deposit cannot be loaned out due to reserve requirements, the volume of additional loans is less than new primary deposits.

What cannot be done by an individual bank can be done by the banking system. This occurs when many banks are expanding loans and derivative deposits at the same time. To illustrate this point, assume that we have an economy with just two banks, A and B. This example can be realistic if we assume further that Bank A represents one bank in the system and Bank B represents all other banks combined. Bank A, as in our previous example, receives a new primary deposit of $10,000 and is required to keep reserves of 20 percent against deposits. Therefore, its books would appear as follows:

BANK A

ASSETS		LIABILITIES	
Reserves	$10,000	Deposits	$10,000

A loan for $8,000 is made and credited as follows:

BANK A

ASSETS		LIABILITIES	
Reserves	$10,000	Deposits	$18,000
Loans	8,000		

Assume that a check is drawn against it almost immediately and deposited in Bank B. The books of the two banks would then show the following:

BANK A				**BANK B**			
ASSETS		LIABILITIES		ASSETS		LIABILITIES	
Reserves	$ 2,000	Deposits	$10,000	Reserves	$ 8,000	Deposits	$ 8,000
Loans	8,000						

The derivative deposit arising out of a loan from Bank A has now been transferred by check to Bank B where it is received as a primary deposit. Bank B must now set aside 20 percent as required reserves and may lend or reinvest the remainder. Its books after such a loan would appear as follows:

BANK B*

ASSETS		LIABILITIES	
Reserves	$ 8,000	Deposits	$14,400
Loans	6,400		

*after making a loan equal to its excess reserves

Assume that a check is drawn against the derivative deposit of $6,400 arising out of the loan by Bank B. This reduces its reserves and deposits as follows:

BANK B

ASSETS		LIABILITIES	
Reserves	$ 1,600	Deposits	$ 8,000
Loans	6,400		

The check for $6,400 will most likely be deposited in a bank, in our example in Bank A or Bank B itself, since we have assumed that only two banks exist. In the U.S. banking system, it may be deposited in one of the approximately 14,000 banks, or in one of thousands of other depository institutions.

Deposit expansion as when a bank makes a loan can take place in the same way when it buys securities. Assume, as we did in the case of a bank loan, the following situation:

BANK A

ASSETS		LIABILITIES	
Reserves	$10,000	Deposits	$10,000

Securities costing $8,000 are purchased and the proceeds credited to the account of the seller, giving the following situation:

BANK A

ASSETS		LIABILITIES	
Reserves	$10,000	Deposits	$18,000
Investments	8,000		

Assume that a check is drawn against the seller's deposit and is deposited in Bank B. The books of the two banks would then show:

BANK A

ASSETS		LIABILITIES	
Reserves	$2,000	Deposits	$10,000
Investments	8,000		

BANK B

ASSETS		LIABILITIES	
Reserves	$ 8,000	Deposits	$ 8,000

Just as in the case of a loan, the derivative deposit has been transferred to Bank B where it is received as a primary deposit.

At each stage in the process, 20 percent of the new primary deposit becomes required reserves, and 80 percent becomes excess reserves that can be loaned out. In time, the whole of the original $10,000 primary deposit will have become required reserves, and $50,000 of deposits will have been credited to deposit accounts, of which $40,000 will have been loaned out.

Table 5.1 further illustrates the deposit expansion process for a 20 percent reserve ratio. A primary deposit of $1,000 is injected into the banking system, making excess reserves of $800 available for loans and investments. Eventually, $5,000 in checkable deposits will be created.

The multiple expansion in the money supply created by the banking system through its expansion of deposits also can be expressed in formula form as follows:

$$\frac{\text{Increase in excess reserves}}{\text{Reserve ratio}} = \text{Change in checkable deposits}$$

TABLE 5.1   Multiple Expansion of Deposits—20 Percent Reserve Ratio

	ASSETS				LIABILITIES
	RESERVES			LOANS AND	CHECKABLE
	TOTAL	(REQUIRED)	(EXCESS)	INVESTMENTS	DEPOSITS
INITIAL RESERVES PROVIDED:	$1,000	$ 200	$800	$ -0-	$1,000
EXPANSION: Stage 1	1,000	360	640	800	1,800
Stage 2	1,000	488	512	1,440	2,440
Stage 3	1,000	590	410	1,952	2,952
Stage 4	1,000	672	328	2,362	3,362
Stage 5	1,000	738	262	2,389	3,689
Stage 6	1,000	790	210	2,951	3,951
Stage 7	1,000	832	168	3,161	4,161
Stage 8	1,000	866	134	3,329	4,329
Stage 9	1,000	893	107	3,463	4,463
Stage 10	1,000	914	86	3,571	4,571
⋮	⋮	⋮	⋮	⋮	⋮
Final stage	$1,000	$1,000	$ -0-	$4,000	$5,000

In the example presented in Table 5.1, the maximum expansion in the money supply (checkable deposits component) would be:

$$\frac{\$1,000}{0.20} = \$5,000$$

which is the same as the final stage figure shown for checkable deposit liabilities. The maximum increase in deposits (and money supply) that can result from a given increase in excess reserves is called the **money multiplier**. The money multiplier is equal to 1 divided by the reserve ratio. For our example, $m = 1 \div 0.20 = 5$. In our complex economy, however, there are several factors or "leakages" that reduce the ability to reach the maximum expansion in the money supply depicted in this simplified example.

Ripple effect

money multiplier
the ratio formed by 1 divided by the reserve ratio, which indicates maximum expansion possible in the money supply increase

Offsetting or Limiting Factors

Deposit creation can go on only to the extent that the activities described actually take place. If for any reason the proceeds of a loan are withdrawn from the banking system, no new deposit arises to continue the process. A new deposit of $10,000 permits loans of $8,000 under a 20 percent required reserve; but if this $8,000 were used in currency transactions without being deposited in a bank, no deposit could be created. It is the custom of doing business by means of checks that makes deposit creation possible.

In the examples above, no allowance was made for currency withdrawal or cash "leakage" from the system. In actual practice, as the volume of business in the economy increases, some additional cash is withdrawn for hand-to-hand circulation and to meet the needs of business for petty cash.

Money may also be withdrawn from the banking system to meet the demand for payments to foreign countries, or foreign banks may withdraw some of the money they are holding on deposit in U.S. banks. The U.S. Treasury may withdraw funds it has on deposit in banks. All of these factors reduce the multiplying capacity of primary deposits.[3]

Furthermore, this process can go on only if excess reserves are actually being loaned by the banks. This means that banks must be willing to lend the full amount of their excess reserves and that acceptable borrowers must be available who have a demand for loans.

Contraction of Deposits

When the need for funds by business decreases, deposit expansion can work in reverse. Expansion takes place as long as excess reserves exist and the demand for new bank loans exceeds the repayment of old loans. Deposit contraction takes place when old loans are being repaid faster than new loans are being granted and banks are not immediately investing these excess funds.

Assuming that Bank A has no excess reserves, let us see the effect of a loan being repaid. Before the borrower began to build up deposits to repay the loan, the banks's books showed:

BANK A

ASSETS		LIABILITIES	
Reserves	$ 2,000	Deposits	$10,000
Loans	8,000		

The borrower of the $8,000 must build up his or her deposit account by $8,000 in order to be able to repay the loan. This is reflected on the books as follows:

BANK A

ASSETS		LIABILITIES	
Reserves	$10,000	Deposits	$18,000
Loans	8,000		

After the $8,000 is repaid, the books show the following:

---

3. The nonbank public's decisions to switch funds between checkable deposits and time or savings deposits also will influence the ability to expand the money supply and credit. This will be explored later in this chapter.

BANK A

ASSETS		LIABILITIES	
Reserves	$10,000	Deposits	$10,000

If no new loan is made from the $10,000 of reserves, deposit contraction will result. This is true because $8,000 of funds have been taken out of the banking system to build up deposits to repay the loan and are now being held idle by Bank A as excess reserves. As we shall see, taking out $8,000 of reserves may be cumulative on the contraction side just as it was during expansion.

Assume that the $8,000 of deposits built up to repay the loan came from Bank B, which before these funds were withdrawn had no excess reserves and showed the following situation on its books:

BANK B

ASSETS		LIABILITIES	
Reserves	$ 2,000	Deposits	$10,000
Loans	8,000		

The withdrawal of $8,000 of deposits would require a sale of the bank's securities or a loan from its Reserve Bank or from another bank that might have excess funds to lend. If we assume a loan was made, Bank B's books would then show:

BANK B

ASSETS		LIABILITIES	
Reserves	$ 400	Deposits	$ 2,000
Loans	8,000	Loan from Reserve Bank	6,400

Reserves must remain at $400 since this amount is the required 20 percent reserve on the $2,000 of deposits. In order to pay off its debt to the Reserve Bank, this bank will probably refuse to renew the $8,000 loan when it comes due. In order to pay that loan, the borrower must build up her or his deposit by $8,000. The books now show:

BANK B

ASSETS		LIABILITIES	
Reserves	$ 8,400	Deposits	$10,000
Loans	8,000	Loan from Reserve Bank	6,400

This enables the bank to pay its loan to the Reserve Bank as follows:

BANK B

ASSETS		LIABILITIES	
Reserves	$ 2,000	Deposits	$10,000
Loans	8,000		

After the $8,000 loan from the bank is repaid, the situation is as follows:

BANK B

ASSETS		LIABILITIES	
Reserves	$ 2,000	Deposits	$ 2,000

In building up the $8,000 deposit to repay the loan, the lender took $8,000 out of another bank in the system, which in turn led this bank to refuse to renew other loans for this $8,000 amount. In building up deposit balances to repay the loans, funds were withdrawn from other banks, which makes deposit contraction cumulative just like deposit expansion. It cannot be stopped by a bank selling securities to meet a demand for funds when it does not have excess reserves. This is because when someone buys the securities, funds are normally withdrawn from another bank in the system to pay for them. This leads to contraction just as when the adjustment to deficient reserves is a loan from the Reserve Bank that is repaid by the bank by reducing the amount of its loans outstanding.

FACTORS AFFECTING BANK RESERVES

The extent to which deposit expansion or contraction can and does take place is governed by the level of a bank's excess reserves. This is true for an individual bank and for the banking system as a whole. Therefore, the factors which affect the level of bank reserves are significant in determining the size of the money supply. **Total reserves** in the banking system consist of reserve balances and vault cash used to meet reserve requirements. Reserve balances are deposits held at the Reserve Banks by commercial banks and other depository institutions. Vault cash is currency, including coin, held on the premises of these institutions.

Total reserves can be divided into two parts: The first, **required reserves**, is the minimum amount of total reserves that a depository institution must hold. The percentage of deposits that must be held as reserves is called the **reserve ratio**. The second part of total reserves is **excess reserves**, the amount by which total reserves exceed required reserves. If required reserves are larger than the total reserves of an institution, the difference is called **deficit reserves**.

Two kinds of factors affect total reserves: those that affect the currency holdings of the banking system and those that affect deposits at the Fed. Currency flows in response to changes in the demand for it by households and businesses. Reserve balances are affected by a variety of transactions involving the Fed and banks, which may be initiated

total reserves
deposits held in Federal Reserve Banks and cash in depository institutions

required reserves
the minimum amount of total reserves that a depository institution must hold

reserve ratio
the percentage of deposits that must be held as reserves

excess reserves
the amount that total reserves are greater than required reserves

deficit reserves
the amount that required reserves are greater than total reserves

by the banking system or the Fed, by the Treasury or by other factors. Although the Fed does not control all of the factors which affect the level of bank reserves, it does have the ability to offset increases and decreases. Thus it has broad control over the total reserves available to the banking system.

Changes in the Demand for Currency

Currency-flows into and out of the banking system affect the level of reserves of the banks receiving the currency for deposit. Let us assume that an individual or a business finds they have excess currency of $100 and deposit it in Bank A. Deposit liabilities and the reserves of Bank A are increased by $100. The bank now has excess reserves of $80, assuming a 20 percent level of required reserves. These reserves can be used by the banking system to create $400 in additional deposits. If the bank does not need the currency but sends it to its Reserve Bank, it will receive a $100 credit to its account. The volume of Federal Reserve Notes in circulation is decreased by $100. These transactions may be summarized as follows:

1. Deposits in Bank A are increased by $100 ($20 in required reserves and $80 in excess reserves).
2. Bank A's deposit at its Reserve Bank is increased $100.
3. The amount of Federal Reserve Notes is decreased by $100.

The opposite takes place when the public demands additional currency. Let us assume that a customer of Bank A needs additional currency and cashes a check for $100. The deposits of the bank are reduced by $100, and this reduces required reserves by $20. If the bank has no excess reserves, it must take steps to get an additional $80 of reserves either by borrowing from its Reserve Bank, demanding payment for a loan or not renewing one which comes due, or by selling securities. When the check is cashed, the reserves of the bank are also reduced by $100. If the bank has to replenish its supply of currency from its Reserve Bank, its reserve deposits are reduced by $100. These transactions may be summarized thus:

1. Deposits in Bank A are reduced by $100 ($20 in required reserves and $80 in excess reserves).
2. Bank A's deposit at its Reserve Bank is reduced $100.
3. The amount of Federal Reserve notes in circulation is increased by $100.

Federal Reserve System Transactions

Transactions of banks with the Fed and changes in reserve requirements by the Fed also affect either the level of total reserves or the

HOLIDAY-
RELATED
CHANGES IN
THE MONEY
SUPPLY

Changes in the components of the money supply typically occur during holiday periods, with the most pronounced change taking place during the Christmas season. These changes are beyond the immediate control of the Fed, which must anticipate and respond to them in order to carry out its money-supply growth targets. Following are the money supply (M1) component figures in billions of dollars for the end of 1989 and the beginning of 1990 as reported in the *Federal Reserve Bulletin*:

	NOV. '89	DEC. '89	JAN. '90
Currency	$221.0	$225.3	$222.9
Travelers' checks	7.0	6.9	7.0
Demand deposits	281.6	291.6	283.0
Other checkable deposits	282.1	288.4	289.5
M1	$791.7	$812.1	$802.4

Notice the surge in currency outstanding between November and December 1989 and the subsequent decline during January 1990. This substantial increase in circulating currency prior to the Christmas holidays requires adjustment by the Fed in its effort to control the money supply. As large amounts of cash are withdrawn from depository institutions, deposit contraction might occur unless the Fed moves to offset it by purchasing government securities in the open market.

Also notice the substantial increase in demand deposits between November and December 1989 and the subsequent decline in early 1990. This also seems to reflect the public's surge in spending during the Christmas holiday season and the payment for many of the purchases in early 1990. The Fed, in its effort to control bank reserves and the money supply, also must take corrective actions to temper the impact of these wide swings in demand deposit amounts over time.

degree to which deposits can be expanded with a given volume of reserves. Such transactions are initiated by the Fed when it buys or sells securities, by a depository institution when it borrows from its Reserve Bank, or by a change in Federal Reserve float. These are examined here in turn, and then the effect of a change in reserve requirements is described. Finally, we will look at Treasury transactions, which can also affect reserves in the banking system.

OPEN MARKET OPERATIONS

When the Fed, through its open market operations, purchases securities such as government bonds, it adds to bank reserves. The Fed pays for the bonds with a check. The seller deposits the check in an account and receives a deposit account credit. The bank presents the check to the Reserve Bank for payment and receives a credit to its account. When the Fed buys a $1,000 government bond, the check for which is deposited in Bank A, the transactions may be summarized as follows:

1. Bank A's deposit at its Reserve Bank is increased by $1,000. The Reserve Bank has a new asset—a bond worth $1,000.
2. Deposits in Bank A are increased by $1,000 ($200 in required reserves and $800 in excess reserves).

The opposite takes place when the Fed sells securities in the market.

In contrast to the other actions that affect reserves in the banking system, open market operations are entirely conducted by the Fed. For this reason they are the most important policy tool the Fed has to control reserves and the money supply. Open market operations are conducted virtually every business day, both to smooth out ups and downs caused by other transactions, and to implement changes in the money supply called for by the Federal Open Market Committee.

DEPOSITORY INSTITUTION TRANSACTIONS

When a bank borrows from its Reserve Bank, it is borrowing reserves; so reserves are increased by the amount of the loan. Similarly, when a loan to the Reserve Bank is repaid, reserves are reduced by that amount. The transactions when Bank A borrows $1,000 from its Reserve Bank may be summarized as follows:

1. Bank A's deposit at its Reserve Bank is increased by $1,000. The assets of the Reserve Bank are increased by $1,000 by the note from Bank A.
2. Bank A's excess reserves have been increased by $1,000. It also has a new $1,000 liability—its note to the Reserve Bank.

This process is reversed when a debt to the Reserve Bank is repaid.

FEDERAL RESERVE FLOAT

Changes in Federal Reserve float also affect bank reserves. Float arises out of the process of collecting checks handled by Reserve Banks. **Federal Reserve float** is the temporary increase in bank reserves that results when checks are credited to the reserve account of the depositing bank before they are debited from the account of the banks on which they are drawn. Checks drawn on nearby banks are credited almost immediately to the account of the bank in which they were deposited and debited to the account of the bank on which the check was drawn. Under Fed regulations, all checks are credited one or two

Federal Reserve float
temporary increase in bank reserves from checks credited to one bank's reserves and not yet debited to another's

days later to the account of the bank in which the check was deposited. It may take longer for the check to go through the collection process and be debited to the account of the bank upon which it is drawn. When this happens, bank reserves are increased, and this increase is called float. The process by which a $1,000 check drawn on Bank B is deposited in Bank A and credited to its account before it is debited to the account of Bank B may be summarized:

1. Bank A transfers $1,000 from its Cash Items in the Process of Collection to its account at the Reserve Bank. Its reserves are increased by $1,000.
2. The Reserve Bank takes $1,000 from its Deferred Availability Account and transfers it to Bank A's account.

Thus, total reserves of banks are increased temporarily by $1,000. They are reduced when Bank B's account at its Reserve Bank is reduced by $1,000 a day or two later.

Changes in reserve requirements change the amount of deposit expansion that is possible with a given level of reserves. With a reserve ratio of 20 percent, excess reserves of $800 can be expanded to $4,000 of additional loans and deposits. If the reserve ratio is reduced to 10 percent, it is possible to expand $800 of excess reserves to $8,000 of additional loans and deposits. When the reserve ratio is lowered, additional expansion also takes place because part of the required reserves becomes excess reserves. This process is reversed when the reserve ratio is raised.

Bank reserves are also affected by changes in the level of deposits of foreign central banks and governments at the Reserve Banks. These deposits are maintained with the Reserve Banks at times as part of the monetary reserves of a foreign country and may also be used to settle international balances. A decrease in such foreign deposits with the Reserve Banks increases bank reserves; an increase in them decreases bank reserves.

TREASURY TRANSACTIONS

Bank reserves are also affected by the transactions of the Treasury. They are increased by spending and making payments and decreased when the Treasury increases the size of its accounts at the Reserve Banks. The Treasury makes almost all of its payments out of its accounts at the Reserve Banks, and such spending adds to bank reserves. For example, the recipient of a check from the Treasury deposits it in a bank. The bank sends it to the Reserve Bank for collection and receives a credit to its account. The Reserve Bank debits the account of the Treasury. When a Treasury check for $1,000 is deposited in Bank A and required reserves are 20 percent, the transactions may be summarized as follows:

1. The deposits of Bank A are increased by $1,000, its required reserves by $200, and excess reserves by $800.
2. Bank A's reserves at the Reserve Bank are increased by $1,000.
3. The deposit account of the Treasury at the Reserve Bank is reduced by $1,000.

Treasury funds from tax collections or the sale of bonds are generally deposited in its accounts in banks. When the Treasury has a need for payment funds from its accounts at the Reserve Banks, it transfers funds from commercial banks to its accounts at the Reserve Banks. This process reduces bank reserves. When $1,000 is transferred from the account in Bank A and required reserves are 20 percent, transactions may be summarized as follows:

1. The Treasury deposit in Bank A is reduced by $1,000, required reserves by $200, and excess reserves by $800.
2. The Treasury account at the Reserve Bank is increased by $1,000, and the account of Bank A is reduced by $1,000.

The Treasury is the largest single depositor at the Fed. The volume of transfers between the account of the Treasury and the reserve accounts of banks is large enough to cause significant changes in reserves in the banking system. For this reason, the Fed closely monitors the Treasury's account and often uses open market operations to minimize its effect on bank reserves. This is accomplished by purchasing securities to provide reserves to the banking system when the Treasury's account increases, and selling securities when the account of the Treasury falls to a low level.

The effect on bank reserves is the same for changes in Treasury cash holdings as it is for changes in Treasury accounts at the Reserve Banks. Reserves are increased when the Treasury decreases its cash holdings, and reserves are decreased when it increases such holdings.

Summary of Transactions Affecting Bank Reserves

The previously discussed transactions which change the volume of bank reserves or the ability of banks to expand deposits are summarized in Figure 5.1. Important roles are played by the nonbank public, the Fed, and the U.S. Treasury in deciding currency holdings. The Fed, of course, provides the major impact. First the Fed establishes the reserve ratio that banks must hold against their deposits. The impact of a 20 percent reserve ratio on checkable deposits was illustrated in simplified examples earlier in this chapter. In addition to changing the reserve ratio, the Fed can alter bank reserves through its open-market operations and its loan policies to banks. Loans are encouraged or discouraged on the basis of the discount rate and the willingness of the Fed to make loans.

FIGURE 5.1   Transactions Affecting Bank Reserves

NONBANK PUBLIC	FEDERAL RESERVE SYSTEM	UNITED STATES TREASURY
Change in the non-bank public's demand for currency to be held outside the banking system	Change in reserve ratio Open-market operations (buying and selling government securities) Change in bank borrowings Change in float Change in foreign deposits held in Reserve Banks Change in other Federal Reserve accounts	Change in Treasury spending out of accounts held at Reserve Banks Change in Treasury cash holdings

Bank reserves are also affected by other transactions involving the Fed. Included are changes in the amount of float, foreign deposits held in Reserve Banks, and various other Fed accounts.

Finally, Treasury transactions can influence the level of reserves in the banking system. Treasury spending from its accounts held in Reserve Banks, transfers of funds to those accounts from the banking system, and changes in its holdings of cash all alter bank reserves.

THE MONETARY BASE AND THE MONEY MULTIPLIER

Earlier in this chapter we examined the deposit multiplying capacity of the banking system. Recall that, in the situation shown in Table 5.1, excess reserves of $1,000 were introduced into the banking system with a 20 percent reserve ratio, resulting in a deposit expansion of $5,000. This can also be viewed as a money multiplier of 5.

In our complex financial system, the money multiplier is not quite so straightforward. It will be useful to focus on the relationship between the monetary base and the money supply in order to better understand the complexity of the money multiplier. The **monetary base** is defined as banking system reserves plus currency held by the public. More specifically, the monetary base consists of reserve deposits held in Reserve Banks, vault cash or currency held by depository institutions, and currency held by the nonbank public. Thus the monetary base can either be used as cash holdings for the public or as reserves to support bank deposits. The monetary base (MB) times the money multiplier (m) produces the M1 definition of the money supply. It can be expressed in formula form as:

monetary base
banking system reserves plus currency held by the public

$MB \times m = M1$

The size and stability of the money multiplier is important because the Fed can control the monetary base, but it cannot directly control the size of the money supply. Changes in the money supply are caused by changes in the monetary base, in the money multiplier, or in both. The Fed can change the size of the monetary base through open market operations or changes in the reserve ratio. The money multiplier is not constant. It can and does fluctuate over time depending on actions taken by the Fed as well as by the nonbank public and the U.S. Treasury.

As of January 1990, the money multiplier was approximately 2.8 as determined by dividing the $802.4 billion M1 money stock by the $288.7 billion monetary base.[4]

Taking into account the actions of the nonbank public and the Treasury, the formula for the money multiplier in today's financial system[5] can be expressed as:

$$m = \frac{1 + k}{r(1 + t + g) + k}$$

where

r is the ratio of reserves to total deposits (checkable, noncheckable time and savings, and government)

k is the ratio of currency held by the nonbank public to checkable deposits

t is the ratio of noncheckable deposits to checkable deposits

g is the ratio of government deposits to checkable deposits.

Let's illustrate how the size of the money multiplier is determined by returning to our previous example of a 20 percent reserve ratio. Recall that in a more simple financial system, the money multiplier would be determined as $1/r$ or $1/.20$, which equals 5. However, in our complex system we also need to consider leakages into currency held by the nonbank public, noncheckable time and savings deposits, and government deposits. Let's further assume that the reserve ratio applies to total deposits, a k of 20 percent, a t of 10 percent, and a g of 5 percent. The money multiplier then would be estimated as:

$$m = \frac{1 + .20}{.20(1 + .10 + .05) + .20} = \frac{1.20}{.43} = 2.8$$

4. *Federal Reserve Bulletin* (April 1990): A12 and A13.
5. The reader interested in understanding how the money multiplier is derived will find a discussion in most money and banking textbooks.

Of course, if a change occurred in any of the components, the money multiplier would adjust accordingly as would the size of the money supply.

IMPORTANCE OF CONTROLLING THE MONEY SUPPLY

velocity of money
the rate of circulation of
the money supply

At this point, we should ask why it is important to regulate and control the supply of money. The money supply (M1) is linked to the gross national product (GNP) via the velocity or turnover of money. More specifically, the **velocity of money** measures the rate of circulation of the money supply. It is expressed as the average number of times each dollar is spent on purchases of goods and services and is calculated as nominal GNP (GNP in current dollars) divided by M1. Changes in the growth rates for money supply ($M1_g$) and money velocity ($M1V_g$) affect the growth rate in real economic activity ($RGNP_g$) and the rate of inflation (I_g) and can be expressed in equation form as follows:

$$M1_g + M1V_g = RGNP_g + I_g$$

For example, if the velocity of money remains relatively constant, then a link between money supply and nominal GNP should be observable. Likewise, after nominal GNP is adjusted for inflation, the resulting real GNP growth can be examined relative to M1 growth rates. Changes in money supply have been found to lead to changes in economic activity.

The ability to predict M1 velocity, in addition to money supply changes, is important in making successful monetary policy. Fed M1 growth targets need to take into consideration expected velocity movements in order to achieve the desired effects on real GNP and inflation. It would be naive, however, to believe that regulating and controlling the supply of money and credit is all that is needed to manage our complex economy. As we shall see in later chapters, economic activity is also affected by government actions concerning government spending, taxation, and the management of our public debt.

KEY TERMS

deficit reserves
derivative deposits
excess reserves

Federal Reserve float
monetary base
money multiplier

primary deposits   total reserves
required reserves   velocity of money
reserve ratio

DISCUSSION QUESTIONS

1. Explain how Federal Reserve Notes are supported or "backed" in our financial system.
2. Why is the expansion and contraction of deposits by the banking system possible in our financial system?
3. Trace the effect on its accounts of a loan made by a bank that has excess reserves available from new deposits.
4. Explain how deposit expansion takes place in a banking system consisting of two banks.
5. Explain the potential for deposit expansion when required reserves average 10 percent and $2,000 in excess reserves are deposited in the banking system.
6. What is the process of deposit contraction?
7. Trace the effect on bank reserves of a change in the amount of cash held by the public.
8. Describe the effect on bank reserves when the Federal Reserve sells U.S. government securities to a bank.
9. Summarize the factors that can lead to a change in bank reserves.
10. What is the difference between the monetary base and total bank reserves?
11. Briefly describe what is meant by the money multiplier and indicate the factors that affect its magnitude or size.
12. Define the velocity of money and explain why it is important to anticipate changes in money velocity.
13. Why does it seem to be important to regulate and control the supply of money?

PROBLEMS

1. Determine the maximum deposit expansion in a financial system where the reserve ratio is 11 percent, initial excess reserves are $1 million, and there are no currency or other leakages. What would the money multiplier be? What would your answers be if the reserve requirement had been 9 percent?
2. Assume a financial system has a monetary base of $25 million. The reserve ratio is 10 percent and there are no leakages in the system. What is the size of the money multiplier? What will be the system's

money supply? How would the money supply change if the reserve ratio is increased to 14 percent?

3. A complex financial system has these relationships: the ratio of reserves to total deposits is 12 percent and the ratio of noncheckable deposits to checkable deposits is 40 percent. In addition, currency held by the nonbank public amounts to 15 percent of checkable deposits. The ratio of government deposits to checkable deposits is 8 percent, and the monetary base is $300 million.
   a. Determine the size of the M1 money multiplier and the size of the money supply.
   b. If the ratio of currency in circulation to checkable deposits were to drop to 13 percent, what would be the impact on the money supply?
   c. What would happen to the money supply if the reserve requirement increased to 14 percent while noncheckable deposits to checkable deposits fell to 35 percent? Assume the other ratios remain as originally stated.

4. Obtain a current issue of the *Federal Reserve Bulletin* and use it to:
   a. Find M1 and the monetary base and then estimate the money multiplier.
   b. Determine the nominal gross national product (GNP in current dollars). Estimate the velocity of money using M1 from the first part and nominal GNP.
   c. Indicate how the money multiplier and the velocity of money have changed between two recent years.

5. Determine the change in checkable deposits and the money multiplier for a simple financial system where the reserve ratio is .15, initial excess reserves are $1,000, and there are no other leakages or adjustments in the system. (Use the Money Multiplier and Deposit Expansion tool.)

6. A complex financial system has the following relationships. The ratio of reserves to total deposits is 12 percent, and the ratio of noncheckable deposits to checkable deposits is 40 percent. In addition, currency held by the nonbank public amounts to 15 percent of checkable deposits. The ratio of government deposits to checkable deposits is 8 percent and the initial reserves are $300 million. (Use the Money Multiplier and Deposit Expansion tool.)
   a. Determine the size of the M1 money supply and the M1 multiplier.
   b. What will happen to the financial system's M1 money supply and money multiplier if the reserve requirement increases to 14 percent while the ratio of noncheckable deposits to checkable deposits falls to 35 percent? Assume the other ratios remain as originally stated.

SELF-TEST QUESTIONS

1. U.S. Federal Reserve notes are primarily backed by which one of the following items?
   a. gold certificates
   b. Special Drawing Rights
   c. U.S. government and agency securities
   d. silver coins and bullion

2. Deposits that add new reserves to the bank where they are deposited are called:
   a. primary deposits
   b. derivative deposits
   c. secondary deposits
   d. Special Drawing Rights

3. Total reserves in the banking system consist of:
   a. currency and coin
   b. reserve deposits and secondary deposits
   c. vault cash and derivative deposits
   d. reserve deposits and vault cash

4. Transactions that affect bank reserves can be initiated by the:
   a. nonbank public
   b. Federal Reserve System
   c. United States Treasury
   d. all of the above

5. Banking system reserves plus currency held by the nonbank public is referred to as the:
   a. money supply
   b. monetary base
   c. monetary multiplier
   d. monetary requirement

SELF-TEST PROBLEM

Determine the maximum deposit expansion in a financial system where the reserve requirement is 12 percent, initial excess reserves are $100,000, and there are no currency or other "leakages." What would be the money multiplier? What would your answers be if the reserve requirement is only 8 percent?

SUGGESTED READINGS

Cacy, J. A. "Recent M1 Growth and Its Implications." *Economic Review*, Federal Reserve Bank of Kansas City (December 1985): 18–23.

Cooper, S. Kerry, and Donald R. Fraser, *The Financial Marketplace*, 2e. Reading, MA: Addison-Wesley, 1990. Chap. 6.

Gramley, Lyle E. "Financial Innovation and Monetary Policy." *Federal Reserve Bulletin* (July 1982): 393–400.

Harrison, William B. *Money, Financial Institutions, and the Economy*. Plano, TX: Business Publications, 1985. Chap. 9.

Henning, Charles N., William Pigott, and Robert H. Scott. *Financial Markets and the Economy*, 5e. Englewood Cliffs, NJ: Prentice-Hall, 1988. Chap. 5.

Kidwell, David S., and Richard L. Peterson. *Financial Institutions, Markets, and Money*, 4e. Hinsdale, IL: The Dryden Press, 1990. Chap. 7.

Roley, V. Vance. "The Demand for M1 by Households: An Evaluation of its Stability." *Economic Review*, Federal Reserve Bank of Kansas City (April 1985): 17–27.

ANSWERS TO SELF-TEST QUESTIONS   1. c   2. a   3. d   4. d   5. b

SOLUTION TO SELF-TEST PROBLEM

Maximum deposit expansion: $100,000/.12 = $833,333
Money multiplier: 1/.12 = 8.333
Maximum expansion for an 8% reserve requirement: $100,000/.08 = $1,250,000
Money multiplier for an 8% reserve requirement: 1/.08 = 12.5

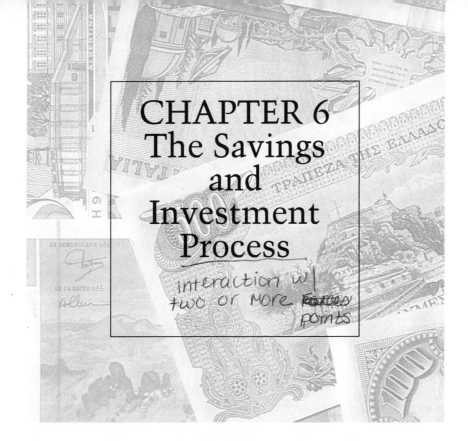

CHAPTER 6
The Savings and Investment Process

interaction w/ two or more ~~field~~ points

After studying this chapter, you should be able to:
- Briefly describe the historical role of savings in the United States.
- Describe how financial assets and liabilities are created.
- Identify the major sources of savings in the United States.
- Explain how funds flow from savings into investments.
- Identify and describe the factors that affect savings.

Capital formation is the creation of productive physical facilities such as buildings, tools, equipment, and roads. The process of adding to the amount or stock of these real assets produces growth in our economy. Recall from Chapter 1 that an effective financial system provides the funds needed for capital formation by channeling savings into investment. The savings-investment process in the U.S. financial system begins by first accumulating savings in financial intermediaries; these institutions, in turn, lend and invest the savings.

Financial investment occurs when claims to wealth in the form of financial assets are purchased or when debt obligations are repaid. **Real investment** takes place when savings are used to create or acquire wealth in the form of real assets. Savers may directly engage in making real investments or they may make financial investments that are transferred into real investments.

financial investment
occurs when financial assets are purchased or debt obligations are repaid

real investment
takes place when savings are used to create or acquire real assets

109

savings
the accumulation of cash and other financial assets

Savings are the accumulation of cash and other financial assets, such as savings accounts and corporate securities. Changes in the level of savings for individuals and corporations are measured by current income minus tax payments and total spending. Governments, too, may save when their revenues exceed their spending. This definition embraces two types of savings: voluntary savings and contractual savings. **Voluntary savings** are simply financial assets set aside for use in the future. **Contractual savings** include such savings as the accumulation of reserves in insurance and pension funds. Contractual savings are not determined by current decision. They are disciplined by previous commitments which the saver has some incentive to honor.

voluntary savings
financial assets set aside for future use

contractual savings
savings accumulated on a regular schedule by prior agreement

HISTORICAL ROLE OF SAVINGS IN THE U.S.

As the size of U.S. businesses expanded, it became increasingly important that large amounts of financial capital be accumulated and converted to business use. The corporate form of organization provided a convenient and flexible legal arrangement for bringing together available financial capital. These advantages of the corporation over sole proprietorship, or private ownership, and partnership are described in Chapter 7.

> Bonds - promise to pay in the future.

Developments in public transportation were often too costly and speculative for private promoters to undertake. The magnitude of early canal, turnpike, and railroad construction was such that the government undertook much of the financing of these projects. In fact, until the end of the 19th century, governmental units contributed more funding to these efforts than did private interests. Since this government financing was accomplished largely through bond issues rather than current revenues, the ultimate source of funds was the savings of individuals who bought the bonds.

Foreign Sources of Savings

Large amounts of the securities sold by both government and private promoters were purchased by foreign investors. Foreign capital played a decisive role in the development of the nation's early transportation system.

The huge role that foreign capital played in the economic development of the United States is paralleled by the developing nations of today. These nations now face many of the financial problems that the United States experienced during its early years. Private savings in many of these countries is negligible because almost all current income must be used for immediate consumption. Individual nations and such international organizations as the World Bank supply large amounts of capital to the developing nations of the world to increase their productive capacity.

The flow of development capital not only stimulates economic expansion in these countries but it also makes their capital much more efficient. For example, speedier transportation reduces the amount of goods in transit, thus releasing working capital for other purposes. In due time, as internal capital formation increases, it is hoped that the need for foreign capital will be eliminated and that these countries can then enjoy an independent capital formation process.

Domestic Supply of Savings

As capital formation began increasing at a faster and faster rate after the Civil War, the demand for funds also increased. Wealthy Americans and foreign investors could no longer provide funds at a rapid enough rate. Britain was investing heavily in India because of political commitments, and the other European countries were not large or wealthy enough to continue supplying funds in quantities adequate to sustain our growth. The American family soon took over the function of providing savings for the capital formation process. Per capita income rose to a level where American families could afford luxuries well beyond the subsistence level and could save part of what they had earned. Thus, the United States gradually developed to the stage where it could generate sufficient capital to finance its own expansion. Ultimately the result was a change in our status from a debtor nation to a creditor nation.

THE CREATION OF FINANCIAL ASSETS AND LIABILITIES

It is common practice today to view the U.S. financial system as comprising four basic economic units: individuals, business firms, financial intermediaries, and governments (federal, state, and local). At any point in time, these units are likely to be holders of real and financial assets. They are also likely to have certain financial liabilities or obligations. And, to the extent that their holdings of real and financial assets exceed their financial liabilities, these economic units will have net worth or owners' equity positions. These concepts will become clearer as we proceed.

In addition to measuring an economic unit's assets, liabilities, and net worth position as of a specific point in time, we are also interested in how these components change over a time period such as one year. This is because, for any measured time period, some of the basic economic units may be savings surplus units while others may be savings deficit units.

Savings surplus occurs when an economic unit, such as individuals taken as a group, has current savings that exceed its direct investment in real assets. These surplus savings are made available to savings deficit units. For example, business firms as a group are often unable to meet all of their plant and equipment investment needs out of earnings retained in the business, which are profits remaining after taxes and, in the case of corporations, after the cash dividends are paid to stockholders.[1] When this occurs there is a **savings deficit** situation and it becomes necessary to acquire funds from a savings surplus unit.

Figure 6.1 illustrates how financial assets and liabilities are created when balancing savings surplus and savings deficit units. The process might begin with a group of individuals placing their savings in time deposit accounts at a commercial bank. The bank might, in turn, loan some of these deposits to a savings deficit business firm that wishes to purchase more equipment. This process of channeling savings into investment through the use of a financial institution or intermediary results in the creation of two types of financial assets and two types of financial liabilities. The time deposits represent financial assets to the individuals who save funds. At the same time, these time deposits are financial liabilities to the commercial bank. Likewise, the business loan represents a financial asset to the commercial bank but a financial liability to the borrowing firm. It should be recognized that the total system remains in balance because the increase in time deposits held by the group of individuals results in a corresponding increase in their net worth, and the business loan is used to increase that firm's real assets.[2]

At this point we should distinguish between direct securities and debt instruments and those that are indirect. **Direct securities,** such as corporate stocks and bonds, are contracts between the savers and the borrowers themselves. The same instrument represents the financial asset of the saver and the claim or liability on the borrower. Direct financial transactions may be handled by brokers or other intermediaries, but the instruments do not represent a claim or obligation of the intermediary. In **indirect financing,** the intermediary creates and is a party to separate instruments with the ultimate lenders and the borrowers. In the example above, the business loan and the time deposits are indirect instruments. The business firm owes money to the bank, and the bank owes money to the individuals, but the firm and the

savings surplus
occurs when current savings exceed direct investment

savings deficit
occurs when investment exceeds income

direct securities
direct contracts between savers and borrowers

indirect financing
financing created by an intermediary

---

1. Earnings retained is referred to as the operating savings of business firms and corporations. Gross savings is calculated by adding depreciation charges (designed to reflect the using up of productive assets) to retained earnings. In theory, if depreciation funds were actually set aside, they would be available to replace real assets as they wear out.
2. The individuals receive safety of principal, liquidity, and a return on their savings over time. At the other end, the business firm anticipates earning a return on its investment in real assets that is higher than the interest cost on the bank loan. The bank, of course, earns compensation for facilitating the savings and investment process.

FIGURE 6.1   Creation of Financial Assets and Liabilities

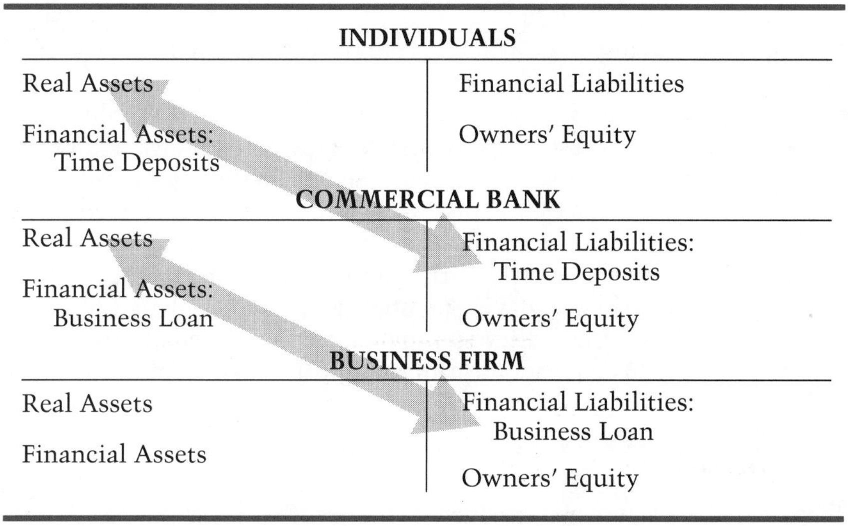

INDIVIDUALS	
Real Assets	Financial Liabilities
Financial Assets: Time Deposits	Owners' Equity

COMMERCIAL BANK	
Real Assets	Financial Liabilities: Time Deposits
Financial Assets: Business Loan	Owners' Equity

BUSINESS FIRM	
Real Assets	Financial Liabilities: Business Loan
Financial Assets	Owners' Equity

individuals have no direct relationship. Indirect instruments could have been avoided in the above example if the individual had supplied funds directly to the business firm by purchasing bonds issued by that firm.[3] This would have resulted in the creation of one type of financial asset—bond securities held by the individuals—and one type of financial liability—bond securities issued by the business firm.

Transactions involving both direct and indirect securities initially occur in primary markets. Many of these securities can be sold by their owners, the original lenders, in secondary markets. Secondary market transactions allow the owners of securities to convert them to cash prior to the time the original borrower has agreed to repay the indebtedness, in order to reclaim their savings for other purposes. Such transactions do not affect the original borrowers except that their debt is now owed to someone else. However, secondary markets provide liquidity to the original lenders, and this feature is important in attracting savings to certain primary markets. For example, the New York Stock Exchange is a secondary market. Its existence makes it easier for corporations to sell new issues of stock to individuals and other organizations in the primary market.

3.   There are reasons, of course, why the individuals might not choose to invest directly in the firm's bonds. If they are small savers, they may be unable to individually purchase a bond. There is also less liquidity and safety of principal in such investments. Thus financial institutions and intermediaries can play an important role in channeling savings into investments.

MAJOR SOURCES OF SAVINGS

An important savings sector in the economy is personal savings. It is from individuals that most financial intermediaries accumulate capital. Individuals as a group consistently represent a savings surplus unit. Corporations also represent an important source of savings. However, their large demand for investment funds, as is also the case for unincorporated business firms, generally results in a net need for external funds. While financial intermediaries can also save, their primary role in our financial system is to aid the savings-investment process. Our governments on balance have operated as a savings deficit unit in recent years. Thus, the ability to provide adequate funds to meet our investment needs is dependent primarily on the savings of individuals and corporations.

Personal Savings

Table 6.1 shows personal savings during recent years in the United States. The savings rate, which is personal saving as a percent of disposable personal income, has been averaging a comparatively low 3 to 6 percent in recent years. However, the dollar amount of personal savings exceeded $206 billion in 1989.

Private individuals maintain savings for a number of reasons. They set aside a part of their current income for the acquisition of costly durable consumer goods, such as cars and appliances. Savings are set aside by individuals to meet unforeseeable financial needs. These savings are not set aside for specific future consumption; instead, they represent emergency or "rainy-day" funds. Individuals may also save for such long-term foreseeable spending as children's college education or for retirement. For short periods of time people may save a portion of current income simply because desirable goods and services are not available for purchase.

There are a number of media in which to maintain savings, ranging in liquidity from cash balances to pension funds. Three factors usually

TABLE 6.1   Personal Savings in the United States (in Billions of Dollars)

	1987	1988	1989
Personal income	$3,777.6	$4,064.5	$4,428.7
Less: taxes & other payments	571.7	586.6	648.7
Disposable personal income	$3,205.9	$3,477.8	$3,780.0
Less: personal outlays	3,104.1	3,333.1	3,573.7
Personal savings	$ 101.8	$ 144.7	$ 206.3
Savings rate (personal savings/ disposable personal income)	3.2%	4.2%	5.5%

Source: *Federal Reserve Bulletin* (April 1990): A54.

influence a person's choice of medium: liquidity, degree of safety, and return.

CASH BALANCES

The most liquid form of savings that an individual can maintain is cash. Cash savings are generally in the form of checkable deposits and pocket cash. People maintain this liquidity in order to meet current commitments or to make purchases in the very near future. Cash savings may also be hoarded. These hoards are not held for specific consumption purposes but rather out of distrust of depository institutions or because an individual wants monetary wealth to be close at hand. Hoarded funds are withdrawn from circulation and add nothing to the capital formation process. Figure 6.2 shows that checkable deposits and currency declined as a percent of disposable income between the 1950s and 1980s and is currently below the 15 percent level.

TIME AND SAVINGS DEPOSITS

A wide choice of facilities providing both safety of principal and a reasonable return is available to the individual saver. The combination of easy access to funds and regular earning power resulted in a substantial rate of growth for time and savings deposits during the 1950s and 1960s. More recently, financial assets have been directed towards money market deposit accounts (MMDAs) and money market fund shares. These offer limited check-writing privileges and returns based on the investment of money market funds in bank certificates of deposit and corporate commercial paper. Household investments in large time deposits (amounts of $100,000 or more) also grew rapidly during the 1970s and early part of the 1980s, as shown in Figure 6.2.

INSURANCE RESERVES AND PENSION FUNDS

The contractual savings embodied in insurance reserves and pension funds grew rapidly as a percent of disposable personal income during the 1950s. Growth in this area of financial assets accelerated again during the 1980s. Figure 6.2 shows that life insurance and pension fund reserves continue to account for an increasing portion of total household assets. Individuals may acquire life insurance through private organizations and may belong to private pension plans or funds. Retirement funds are the principal form of individual savings provided by state and local governments. The federal government accumulates reserves for the accounts of individuals through the Old-Age and Survivors Insurance Trust Fund, the Disability Insurance Trust Fund, the National Service Life Insurance Fund, and others. These savings of individuals as represented by government-held reserves are invested primarily in the obligations of federal, local, and state governments. As such, they satisfy a part of the demand for funds by governments.

FIGURE 6.2   Financial Assets Held by Households (as Percent of Disposable Personal Income)

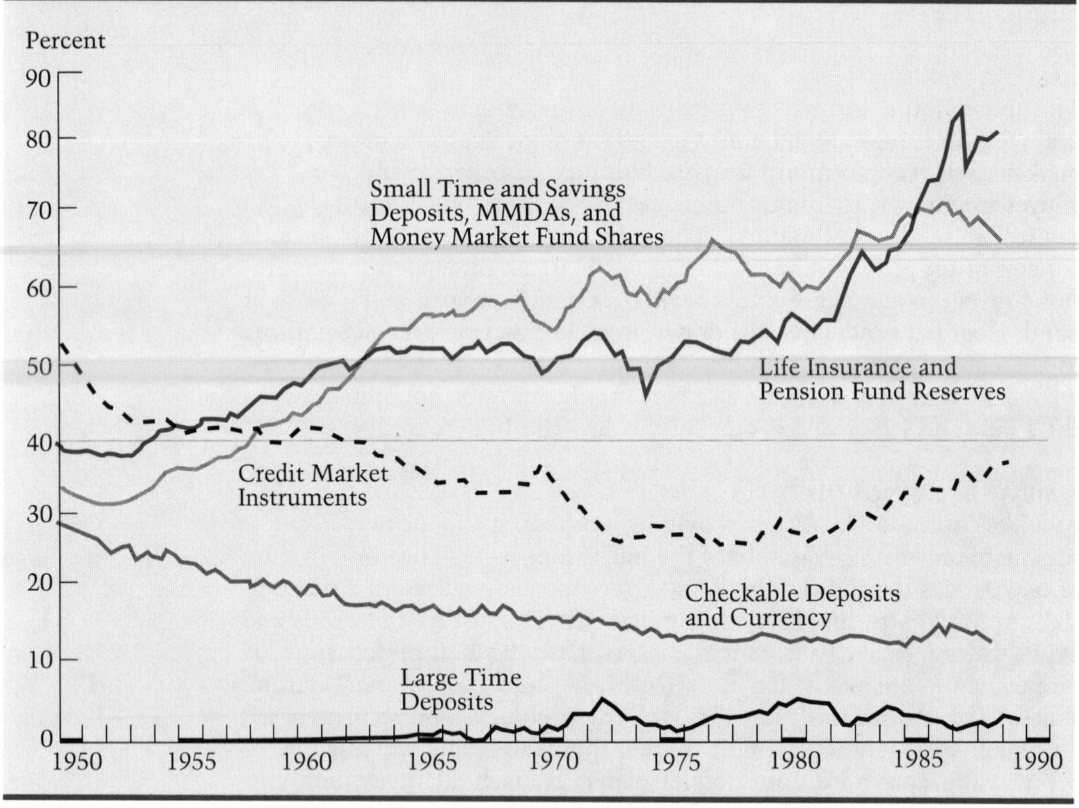

Source: *1989 Historical Chart Book*, Board of Governors of the Federal Reserve System, p. 68.

SECURITIES

Because of the wide diversity of securities—corporate stock, corporate bonds, and government securities—individuals can usually find a security that is well suited to their special savings objectives. For persons desiring growth of principal, corporate stocks with the likelihood of growth are available. These stocks usually provide a lower current income to the saver than is available from most other securities. Other savers may place primary emphasis on stability of principal for liquidity purposes. The stocks of public utilities and other recession-resistant companies serve this purpose, as do high-grade corporate and government bonds. There is a wide spectrum of risk, growth potential, and yield in which virtually every saver who chooses securities as a savings medium can find a place for funds consistent with his or her own individual objectives and preferences. Figure 6.2 illustrates the relative importance of corporate and government credit market debt instruments.

SAVINGS HABITS
OF AMERICANS

Savings by individuals provides a crucial source of funds for investment purposes. Everyone must decide what portions of their disposable personal income to spend or to save. U.S. income tax laws stemming from the Great Depression of the 1930s were designed to encourage spending rather than saving. In order to stimulate economic activity, savings were heavily taxed. As a consequence, the savings rate has been relatively lower in the United States compared with Japan and the industrialized countries of Western Europe.

Following are U.S. personal savings rates, or personal savings as a percent of disposable income, by five-year intervals beginning with 1960.

U.S. SAVINGS RATES

1960	5.8%
1965	7.0
1970	8.1
1975	9.2
1980	7.1
1985	5.1

Notice that the savings rate increased from a level less than 6 percent in 1960 to over 9 percent by 1975. Tax reform in the form of lower personal income tax rates in the mid-1960s and in the 1970s may have contributed to this higher personal savings rate. However, the savings rate declined to just over 5 percent by 1985. Since then, as discussed in this chapter, the rate has fallen as low as the 3 to 4 percent level before showing some recovery.

Source: *Savings Institutions Sourcebook,* Chicago: United States League of Savings Institutions, and the *Federal Reserve Bulletin.*

Shares of investment companies add to the importance of common stock as a form of individual savings. These shares have played a large role for the saver with limited funds because of they are readily available in small quantities. Investment companies have also instituted convenient procedures for accumulating shares on a regular basis out of current income.

Corporate Savings

Table 6.2 shows corporate savings during recent years in the United States. Corporations save by producing profits after taxes and then not paying all of these profits out to investors in the form of dividends. The proportion of after-tax profits retained in the organization is referred to

TABLE 6.2
Corporate Savings in the United States (in Billions of Dollars)

	1987	1988	1989
Profits before taxes	$266.7	$306.8	$287.3
Less: tax liabilities	124.7	137.9	129.0
Profits after taxes	$142.0	$168.9	$158.2
Less: dividends	98.7	110.4	122.1
Undistributed profits	$ 43.3	$ 58.5	$ 36.2
Retention rate (undistributed profits/profits after taxes)	30.5%	34.6%	22.9%

Source: *Federal Reserve Bulletin* (April 1990): A35.

as *undistributed profits.* Notice that corporations retained between about 23 and 35 percent of their after-tax profits in recent years, with a dollar amount of corporate savings of approximately $36 billion in 1989. In addition to undistributed profits, funds generated through business operations include the conversion of operating assets to financial assets through depreciation allowances. This reflects an accounting convention designed to show the using up of real assets.

Corporate saving for short-term working capital purposes is by far the most important reason for accumulating financial assets. Seasonal business changes create an uneven demand for corporate operating assets, such as inventories and accounts receivable. And because of these seasonal changes, cash inflow is seldom in just the right amount and at the right time to accommodate the increased levels of operating assets. Quarterly corporate income tax liabilities also impose the necessity of accumulating financial assets. The short-term accumulation of financial assets on the part of business corporations does not add to the level of long-term savings of the economy as a whole. However, these funds do enter the monetary stream and become available to users of short-term borrowed funds. As such, these short-term savings serve to meet a part of the demand for funds of consumers, government, and other businesses. These savings are typically held by a corporation in the form of checkable deposits with commercial banks, short-term obligations of the federal government, commercial paper, and certificates of deposit issued by commercial banks. These financial assets meet the requirements of safety and liquidity.

Corporations also engage in the savings process for purposes of meeting planned spending in the future. Reserves are often set up to provide all or part of the cost of construction, purchase of equipment, or major maintenance and repairs to existing facilities. Savings committed to these purposes are often invested in securities that have longer maturities and higher yields than those held for short-term business purposes. These securities include the debt obligations of both corporations and government and, to a limited extent, corporate stock.

FLOW OF FUNDS FROM SAVINGS INTO INVESTMENTS *Know the relationship*

Individuals represent the most important source of savings in our financial system. As we have discussed, they may invest their savings directly in bonds, stocks, and real estate mortgages or indirectly by placing their savings with financial intermediaries.

Table 6.3 shows the importance of private financial intermediation as a source of funds supplied to credit markets. Total funds supplied, excluding corporate equities, increased from about $693 billion in 1987 to $767 billion in 1988 before dropping to about the 1987 level in 1989. Approximately 81 percent of these total funds were provided in 1987 through financial intermediation. Although the ratio of financial intermediation funds to total funds supplied declined to approximately 71 percent in 1989, the role of financial intermediation continues to be extremely important to the savings and investment process. The dollar amount of funds supplied by commercial banks, insurance and pension funds, and other finance intermediaries increased between 1987 and 1989. In contrast, thrift institutions supplied fewer funds in 1989 compared with 1987 and 1988.

Table 6.4 shows how funds were used or raised in the credit markets by borrowing sector and by instrument. Borrowing by households is the single largest borrowing sector. During 1989, households borrowed

TABLE 6.3   Sources of Funds to Credit Markets in the United States (in Billions of Dollars)

	1987	1988	1989
Total funds supplied to domestic nonfinancial sectors	$693.2	$767.0	$695.2
Funds advanced by private financial intermediaries:			
Commercial banks	136.8	155.3	171.6
Thrift institutions	136.8	120.5	− 75.3
Insurance and pension funds	210.9	194.9	177.1
Other financial intermediaries	76.3	87.4	219.0
Total	$560.8	$558.2	$492.4
Financial intermediation funds as a percent of total funds supplied	80.9%	72.8%	70.8%

Note: Corporate equities were not included above.

Source: *Federal Reserve Bulletin* (June 1990): A43.

TABLE 6.4   Funds Raised in the Credit Markets (in Billions of Dollars)

	1987	1988	1989
Net borrowing by domestic nonfinancial sectors	$693.2	$767.0	$695.2
By borrowing sector:			
U.S. government	144.9	157.5	149.8
State & local governments	33.6	29.8	24.7
Households	271.9	287.9	258.5
Farms	–10.6	–7.5	.3
Nonfarm noncorporate	107.9	91.9	65.9
Corporate	145.5	207.5	196.0
Total	$693.2	$767.0	$695.2
By instrument:			
U.S. government securities	$144.9	$157.5	$149.8
Tax-exempt obligations	34.1	34.0	24.2
Corporate bonds	99.9	120.8	114.2
Mortgages	324.5	307.7	255.5
Consumer debt	32.9	51.1	46.1
Bank loans	10.8	38.4	33.0
Other debt	46.0	57.5	72.4
Total	$693.2	$767.0	$695.2
Total net new share issues	14.3	–117.9	–60.9

Note: External corporate equity funds were not included above.

Source: *Federal Reserve Bulletin* (June 1990): A42.

$259 billion or about 37 percent of the total borrowings by domestic nonfinancial sectors. Borrowing by the U.S. government has been relatively stable in recent years and in 1989 accounted for 22 percent of the total borrowings.

Corporate borrowing now ranks second in importance, with a 1989 level of about 28 percent of total net borrowings (versus about 21 percent for 1987). Also noteworthy is the level of borrowing by state and local governments and the generally negative net borrowing by the farm sector, reflecting the farming difficulties in the 1980s.

Table 6.4 also shows recent borrowing activities by instrument. Mortgage borrowing amounted to about $256 billion in 1989 and comprised about 37 percent of total borrowings. The mortgage category consists largely of home mortgages and to a lesser extent, in order of importance, commercial property mortgages, multifamily residential mortgages, and farm mortgages. Household borrowing is primarily in the form of home mortgages and consumer debt. The second largest instrument for raising borrowed funds is U.S. government securities, which approached $150 billion in 1989 and comprised about 22 percent of total borrowings. Corporate bonds were in third place in borrowing importance in 1989.

The significance of borrowing by the corporate sector is somewhat obscured because corporations use a variety of debt instruments to meet their borrowing needs. For example, corporations issue their own bonds, take out commercial property mortgages, obtain bank loans, and acquire other debt, such as by issuing their own short-term promissory notes. Corporations also raise funds by issuing shares of stock. However, total net new share issues tend to be quite volatile from year to year, as shown at the bottom of Table 6.4. In fact, because of acquisitions and other corporate buyouts, there were negative amounts of net new equity funds in 1988 and 1989.

FACTORS AFFECTING SAVINGS

Among the several factors influencing the total amount of savings that exist in any given time period are: levels of income, economic expectations, cyclical influences, and the life stage of the individual saver or corporation. The precise relationship between savings and consumption is the subject of much debate and continuing study, however, and we limit our observations here to broad generalizations.

Levels of Income

For our purposes, savings have been defined as current income minus tax payments and consumption spending. Keeping this definition in mind, let us explore the effect of changes in income on the levels of savings of individuals. As income falls, the individual attempts to maintain his or her present standard of living as long as possible. In so doing, the proportion of his or her consumption spending increases and total savings diminish. As income is further reduced, the individual may be forced to curtail consumption spending, and this results in a lower standard of living. Such reduction is reasonably limited, however, since the basic needs of the individual, or family unit, must be met. Not only will personal savings be eliminated under circumstances of drastic reductions in income, but the individual may also **dissave,** that is, spend accumulated savings rather than reduce further consumption spending.

dissave
to liquidate savings for consumption uses

As income increases, the individual will again be in a position to save. However, the saving will not necessarily begin immediately, since it may be desirable to buy many things that had to be foregone during the low-income period. The amount of this need, notably for durable consumer goods, largely determines the rate of increase in savings during periods of income recovery.

On the whole, income levels are closely associated with levels of employment. Changes in business activity, in turn, influence employment levels. Downturns in the economy during 1970 and 1974–1975 resulted in declines in employment levels and correspondingly lowered levels of income. Employment also suffered during the first part of the 1980s when unemployment levels rose to post-World War II highs, in excess of 10 percent.

Economic Expectations

The anticipation of future events has a significant effect on savings. If individuals believe that their incomes will decrease in the near future, they may tend to curtail their current spending in order to establish a reserve for the expected period of low income. A worker anticipating a long and protracted labor dispute may increase current savings as partial protection against the financial impact of a strike.

Expectations of a general increase in price levels may also have a strong influence upon the liquidity that savers want to maintain. The prospect of price increases in consumer durable goods may cause an increase in their sales as individuals try to buy before prices increase. Savings are thus quickly converted to consumer spending. Corporate savings too may be reduced as a result of price increase expectations. In addition to committing funds to plant and office equipment before price increases take place, corporations typically increase their inventory positions. As for the individual, the prospect of an interruption in the supply of inventory because of a labor strike or other cause often results in a rapid stockpiling of raw materials and merchandise. The prospect of price decreases and of large production capacity has the opposite effect—the liquidity and financial assets of a business increase relative to its operating assets.

Unprecedented price increases during the inflationary 1970s led many individuals to develop the philosophy of "buy it now because it will cost more later." This resulted in a classic example of the impact of price increase expectations on the spend-save decisions of individuals. When the economy began recovering during 1975, employment and income levels also began rising. The personal savings rate increased in 1975 before it began declining under the pressure of renewed price inflation during the latter part of the 1970s. As previously noted, the personal savings rate remained low throughout the 1980s.

Economic Cycles

While changes in levels of income may be caused mainly by cyclical movements in the economy, they do not represent the complete effect that the cycle has on savings. Cyclical movements affect not only the amounts but also the types of savings.

To illustrate this point, let us observe the effect that changes in economic activity have on the shifting of savings from one type to another, notably between time and savings deposits at commercial banks or thrift institutions and other media. Short-term interest rates usually decrease during a period of economic downturn or recession for such money market instruments as U.S. Treasury bills, commercial paper, and obligations of U.S. government agencies. This was the case during the latter part of 1974 and into 1975. Short-term money market rates also tend to remain relatively low during the early stages of economic recovery or expansion, such as occurred during 1976. However, as the economy continues to expand, short-term interest rates begin to move up rapidly, as occurred during 1977 and 1978. These money market rates usually peak at about the same time that a peak in economic activity occurs. For example, short-term interest rates peaked in early 1980 and in mid-1981 just prior to economic downturns.

Until recently, interest rates paid on time and savings deposits (excluding large negotiable CDs) held at commercial banks and thrift institutions were regulated and thus varied little with economic activity. Financial intermediation took place so long as the interest rates on time and savings deposits exceeded money market rates. However, disintermediation became particularly pronounced during periods when money market interest rates grew higher than interest rate ceilings set on time and saving deposits. Passage of the Depository Institutions Deregulation and Monetary Control Act of 1980 called for the elimination of rate ceilings on time and savings deposits. This act seems to have caused the lessening of cyclical swings between intermediation and disintermediation during the 1980s.

Life Stages of the Individual Saver

The pattern of savings over an individual's life span follows a somewhat predictable pattern when viewed for the total population. An individual saves very little during the youthful years simply because little income is produced. One's income has increased considerably by the time he or she has matured and begun to raise a family. Expenses, however, have also increased during these early family-forming years; one's savings are typically limited to those accruing to life insurance reserves. By the time the individual reaches middle age, two factors come into play that result in increased savings. First, income is typically much higher than at any previous time; second, the expense of raising children has been reduced or eliminated. Thus it is this middle-aged group that saves the most.

At retirement the individual's income is sharply reduced. He or she may now begin the process of dissaving. Pension fund payments along with accumulated savings are drawn upon for current living expenses.

The level of savings of individuals is therefore a function of the age composition of the population as a whole. A population shift to a large proportion of individuals in the productive middle-age years would result in a greater savings potential.

Life Stages of the Corporation

Just as the financial savings of an individual are governed in part by age, so the financial savings generated by a business firm are a function of its life stage. It is true, of course, that all business firms do not proceed through a fixed life-stage cycle. To the extent, however, that a firm experiences the typical pattern of vigorous early growth and ultimate maturity and decline, its flow of financial savings may experience a predictable pattern.

During the pioneering and early expansion years of a successful business, the volume of physical assets typically increases rapidly. So rapid is this growth, the firm is unable to establish a strong position with respect to its financial assets. Indeed, it is during these years of the corporate life cycle that there is a large need for borrowed capital. At this time the corporation is typically a heavy user of financial assets rather than a provider.

More intensive market penetration and expanding geographic areas of distribution make it possible for the firm to continue its growth. Continuing profitable expansion becomes more difficult, however, as the managerial talent of the firm reaches the limit of its ability to direct and control operations and as competing firms in the industry also grow. The combination of a slow-down in expansion and a continuing large flow of cash generation results in financial savings. As the enterprise matures and ceases to expand, it reaches its peak of savings. Earnings are high, and commitment of funds to increased operating assets is reduced or eliminated.

As the firm begins to decline in the final phase of the life cycle, its ability to create financial savings is reduced. During the early years of the decline of a business, however, it may continue to provide a reasonably high level of financial savings. This is true, notwithstanding lower profits, because of the conversion of physical assets to financial assets through depreciation allowances.

As the final stages of decline are reached, the firm is unable to generate further financial savings and is probably perpetuating itself largely on the basis of the sustaining power of its previously accumulated financial assets.

KEY TERMS

contractual savings
direct securities
dissave
indirect financing
investment

savings
savings deficit
savings surplus
voluntary savings

DISCUSSION QUESTIONS

1. What are savings? Differentiate between voluntary and contractual savings.
2. Briefly describe the historical role of savings in the United States.
3. Compare savings surplus and savings deficit units and indicate which economic units are generally one type or the other.
4. Describe and illustrate how financial assets and liabilities are created through the savings-investment process involving financial intermediaries.
5. What types of savings media are available to individuals?
6. How and why do corporations save?
7. Which types of institutions are the major sources of funds through financial intermediation? Indicate the relative importance of these institutions as suppliers of funds.
8. Explain in terms of borrowing sector the relative importance of funds raised in the credit markets.
9. Identify and explain the relative importance of debt instruments used to raise funds in the credit markets.
10. Describe the principal factors that influence the level of savings by individuals.
11. How do economic cycle movements affect the media or types of savings by businesses?
12. Why are the financial savings generated by a business a function of its life cycle?

PROBLEM

Obtain a current issue of the *Federal Reserve Bulletin* and determine:
a. the current personal savings rate in the United States.
b. the amount of current corporate savings as reflected in the amount of undistributed profits.

c. the amount of total funds supplied to domestic nonfinancial sectors through financial intermediaries for the most recent available year. Also indicate the relative importance of several financial intermediaries in the financial intermediation process.

d. For the most current year, indicate by both borrowing sector and by instrument the relative significance of funds raised in the credit markets.

SELF-TEST QUESTIONS

1. Savings are the accumulation of cash and other financial assets and are generally classified into which of the following two categories?
    a. voluntary and contractual savings
    b. primary and secondary savings
    c. personal and governmental savings
    d. voluntary and corporate savings

2. Which one of the following is an example of indirect financing?
    a. corporate bonds
    b. corporate stocks
    c. business bank loan
    d. U.S. government bonds

3. The personal savings rate is calculated as:
    a. personal savings divided by personal outlays
    b. personal savings divided by disposable personal income
    c. disposable personal income divided by personal outlays
    d. personal income divided by personal outlays

4. As a percent of disposable personal income, which one of the following financial assets held by households is the largest?
    a. large time deposits
    b. checkable deposits and currency
    c. credit market instruments
    d. life insurance and pension fund reserves

5. Which one of the following instruments generates the largest amount of funds annually in the credit markets?
    a. U.S. government securities
    b. corporate bonds
    c. mortgages
    d. bank loans

SUGGESTED READINGS

Dougall, Herbert E., and Jack E. Gaumnitz. *Capital Markets and Institutions*, 5e. Englewood Cliffs, NJ: Prentice-Hall, 1986.

Edmister, Robert O. *Financial Institutions*, 2e. New York: McGraw-Hill, 1986. Chap. 2.

Rose, Peter S. *Money and Capital Markets*, 3e. Homewood, IL: BPI/Irwin, 1989. Chap. 2.

Savings Institutions Sourcebook. Chicago: United States League of Savings Institutions, 1989.

Van Horne, James C. *Financial Market Rates and Flows*, 3e. Englewood Cliffs, NJ: Prentice-Hall, 1990.

Wilson, John F., Elizabeth M. Fogler, James L. Freund, and Guido E. van der Ven. "Major Borrowing and Lending Trends in the U.S. Economy, 1981–85." *Federal Reserve Bulletin* (August 1986): 511–524.

ANSWERS TO SELF-TEST QUESTIONS   1. a   2. c   3. b   4. d   5. c

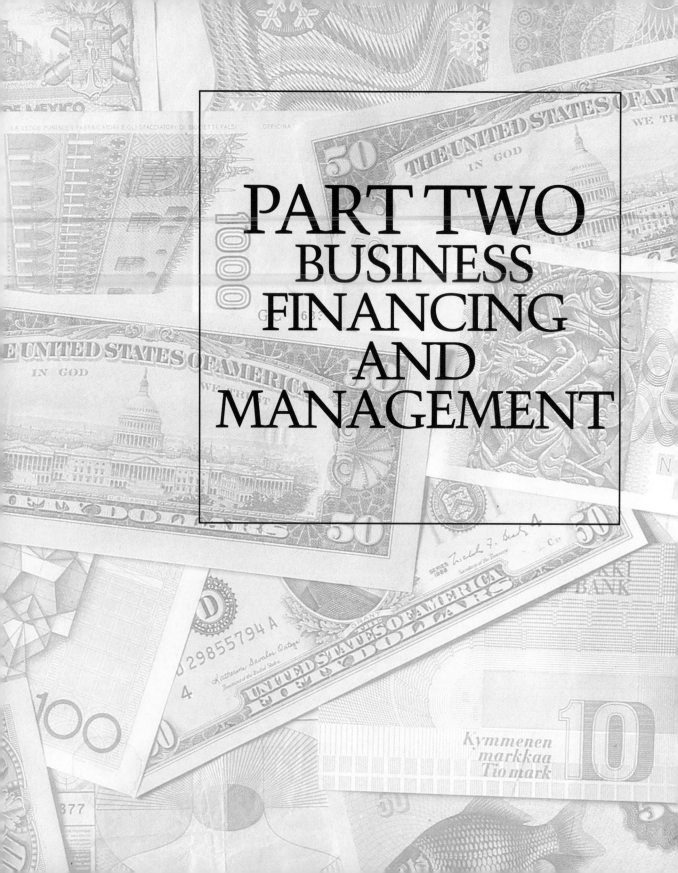

PART TWO
BUSINESS FINANCING AND MANAGEMENT

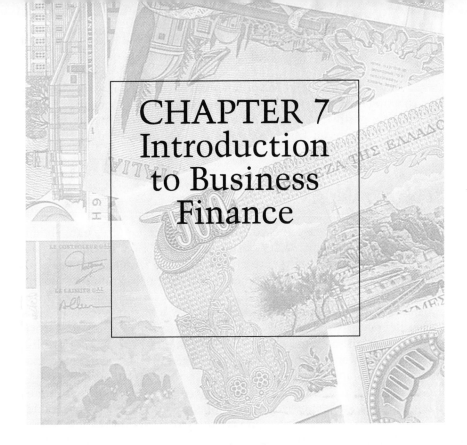

CHAPTER 7
Introduction
to Business
Finance

After studying this chapter, you should be able to:
- Describe different forms of business organization.
- Indicate the objective of financial management and identify its basic functions.
- Provide a brief description of the balance sheet.
- Provide a brief description of the income statement.
- Briefly explain the meaning of financial analysis and show how it is applied.
- Explain the Du Pont system of financial analysis.

All businesses require money to run their operations. Money is needed to provide plant and equipment and to support current operations. Some firms require very little capital, and the industries in which these firms operate have a vast number of competitors. Any field of activity that requires little financial capital is open to a host of people who want to establish their own business. At the other extreme, there are businesses that require huge amounts of financial capital to operate even on a minimum scale. The cement and steel industries, for example, because of their capital requirements have only a few large firms dominating the market.

129

After discussing the forms of business organization, we will examine the financial management functions needed by successful businesses. To perform these functions, the financial manager must understand the basic financial statements and the role of financial analysis.

STARTING A BUSINESS

In our market economy, individuals have the freedom to establish any legal business of their own choosing. However, they must have adequate financial capital of their own or be able to arrange the necessary financing. The success of a businessperson in raising funds for operations is governed by the extent that profits can be produced from operations. This means that a person starting a business must possess either the necessary financial capital to support initial operations until there is a profit, or must show unusual potential for making profits. Typically, the would-be owner must have the funds, since the potential for profit is seldom great enough to attract financial supporters.

The world's resources are limited. There is only a certain amount of labor, suitable land, appropriate buildings, and other factors of production that the businessperson can control. Command over these scarce resources is a measure of success in business operation and financing. Business financing, therefore, is the process of acquiring the factors of production necessary to conduct business operations.

In contrast to a controlled economy where factors of production are allocated by central planning authorities, allocation of these factors is largely automatic under the market system. Resources flow smoothly to those businesses that, through their past operations and the promise of profitable future operations, are able to pay for them. It is true, of course, that mistakes are made. Investors often invest in a firm only to find that its performance does not measure up to expectations. The result is a loss or decrease in the value of the investment. This risk is part of the market system. By the same token, the investor or the financial intermediary who assumes an unusually large risk does so with the full expectation that, if things go well with the firm, the rewards for the investment will be very great. Where the possible risk is very small, the potential reward is small.

Therefore, investment funds flow both to risky firms and very safe firms. There is simply a difference in the investor's risk and return expectation. Some investors prefer to maintain a minimum risk; they must, of course, be satisfied with a modest return on their investment. Other individuals and institutions assume large risks in the hopes of achieving substantial returns.

Good
Bad
UGly

Diff between
S & C

FORMS OF BUSINESS ORGANIZATION IN THE UNITED STATES

Three major forms of business ownership are used in the United States: proprietorship, partnership, and corporation. Proprietorships are the most widely used form although they are generally the smallest organizations in terms of assets. About 70 percent of U.S. firms are proprietorships, about 10 percent are partnerships, and the remaining 20 percent are corporations. The choice of a legal form of organization for a business is a strategic matter from many points of view. Managerial lines of authority and control, legal responsibility, and the allocation of income and risk are all directly related to the form the organization takes. In this chapter we look at the relationship between the legal form of organization and its sources and methods of financing and its allocation of risk.

Proprietorship

The **proprietorship** is a business venture that is owned by a single individual who personally receives all profits and assumes all responsibility for the debts and losses of the business. Proprietorships far outnumber all other forms of business organization in the United States. However, the economic power of these firms, as measured by number of employees and size of payrolls, is far less than that of the nation's corporations.

proprietorship
a business owned by one person who is responsible for all assets and liabilities

The savings of the owner and funds that may be borrowed from friends, relatives, and banks may be sufficient for the operation of a typical small business. The investment made by the owner is called *equity capital* or owner's equity. As the business grows and larger investments in capital are required, the owner may reach the point where additional funds cannot be borrowed without an increase in owner's equity. Lenders will generally insist on an increase in the owner's equity because that equity provides a margin of safety for the lender.

This point is where the proprietorship form of organization displays its basic weakness. In many cases, the owner's original investment exhausts his or her personal resources and often those of friends and relatives. Unless profits from the venture are great enough to meet the increased equity needs, the firm is prevented from achieving its maximum growth. At this stage it may be necessary to adopt a form of organization more appropriate for capital-raising purposes.

Another weakness of proprietorship is that the owner's liability for debts of the firm is unlimited. Creditors may take not only the assets of the business to settle claims but also the personal assets of the proprietor. Thus the proprietor may find his or her home and personal property under claim if the assets of the business are not sufficient to meet the demands of creditors. The unlimited liability of the owner is, therefore, a serious disadvantage of the proprietorship.

Partnership

partnership
a business owned by two or more people who share ownership responsibilities

A **partnership** form of business organization exists when two or more persons own a business operated for profit. Although the partnership resembles the proprietorship to some degree, technically there are important differences.

Undoubtedly, one of the major reasons for the popularity of the partnership arrangement is that it allows individuals to pool their resources of money, property, equipment, knowledge, and business skills without the complications that often accompany incorporation. A partnership form may exist from the beginning of a business operation. In other cases, a firm that began as a proprietorship may reach the point where additional growth is impossible without increased equity capital. Converting to a partnership arrangement is one method of increasing the equity capital of a firm.

The number of partners that may be taken into a business venture is theoretically unlimited. However, the managerial difficulties and conflicts arising with many partners limit their number to a practical size. Thus the partnership, like the proprietorship, eventually suffers from a lack of large amounts of equity capital. While it is unusual to find more than a few partners in an industrial or commercial firm, some public accounting firms have dozens and even hundreds of partners. Such businesses usually use a modification of the general partnership arrangement.

Like the proprietor, the members of a partnership team risk their personal assets as well as their investments in the business venture. In addition, if one of the partners negotiates a contract that results in substantial loss, each partner suffers a portion of the loss, based on a previously determined agreement on distribution of profits and losses. The other partners may, however, sue the offending partner if there is any violation of the articles of copartnership.

More serious, perhaps, is a partner's liability for the actions of the business. Under partnership law, each partner has unlimited liability for all the debts of the firm. This permits creditors to claim assets from one or more of the partners if the remaining partners are unable to cover their share of the loss.

limited partnership
a partnership in which some partners have liability only to the extent of their investment

The **limited partnership** is a modification of the partnership in which one or more general partners combine with one or more limited partners. The limited partners, much like the shareholders in a corporation, are liable for debts of the business only to the extent of their investment. The general partners are governed by the federal laws concerning partnerships, while the limited partners are governed by individual state laws. The limited partnership comes into existence only after the state accepts and approves a proper application by the general partners.

Corporation

In the case of Dartmouth College versus Woodward in 1819, Chief Justice of the Supreme Court John Marshall described the status of the **corporation** so exactly and clearly that his description has since become the generally accepted definition. It reads in part:

A corporation is an artificial being, invisible, intangible, and existing only in contemplation of law. Being the mere creature of law, it possesses only those properties which the charter of its creation confers upon it, either expressly, or as incidental to its very existence ... Among the most important are immortality and individuality—properties by which a perpetual succession of persons are considered as the same and may act as a single individual.

corporation
a form of business organization that exists as a legal entity with limited liability for stockholders and managers

Sub-chapter

"C"   "S"

income tax   NO income tax
                state tax
no limit   limited Stockholder

profit or loss
goes to stock-
holders

unlimited   Limited = 25
Stockholders

This definition emphasizes the corporation as a legal entity, which means that the law has created an artificial being that has the rights, duties, and powers of a person. The definition includes the concept of many people united into one body that does not change its identity with changes in ownership. Finally, the definition suggests that a corporation may have unending life.

A corporation that has existed only a short time, like most new ventures, usually finds it difficult to attract investment funds from outsiders. The corporate form of organization does not by itself assure a flow of investment funds into the business. Rather, it removes several of the barriers to the flow of capital that exist in other forms of business organization. But it is only after a corporation has become well established and offers attractive returns for investors that these special features of the corporate form become significant. One of the important reasons corporations can accumulate large sums of capital is that they are allowed to sell capital stock. The stock may be offered to existing stockholders or to new investors in amounts suited to their purposes.

1993
1st year

$10 \times 10,000 = 1M$ — 10%

Time on Jan 1993

One of the advantages for corporate stockholders is the limitation on liability. Ordinarily, creditors and other claimants may look only to the assets of the corporation for satisfaction of their claims. They cannot take the personal assets of the owners (stockholders). This advantage is particularly appealing to the owner of a business who has built up considerable personal wealth and has other business interests.

The limitation on liability may also make it possible for promoters of new ventures to attract wealthy investors who would otherwise be unwilling to risk claims against their personal property. Limited liability may be possible in certain circumstances in noncorporate forms of business, but the safety is not as great as that provided by the corporate form.

The limitation on stockholder liability for debts of a corporation is seldom sufficient reason to incorporate a small business whose owner's personal assets are already largely invested in it. In this situation there is little risk on the part of the owner beyond his or her personal investment. Furthermore, the corporate form of organization may not always protect stockholders from personal risk beyond their investment when a business is relatively new or in a weak financial condition. Creditors may simply require that one or more of the stockholders add their signatures to the obligation of the corporation, making them personally liable for the obligation. After a corporation has established a good credit reputation, however, creditors and suppliers seldom insist on personal guarantees on the part of the stockholders.

Another important advantage of the corporation is the ease with which ownership may be transferred. Corporate stock may be transferred freely from one person to another. The purchaser of this stock then has all the rights and privileges formerly held by the seller. The corporation is not a party to the transfer of ownership and has no power to interfere with the sale or purchase of its stock. In contrast, there must be unanimous approval of the members of a partnership before a new partner can be brought into the business.

MULTINATIONAL AND STATELESS CORPORATIONS

The growth of international trade over the past few decades has led to a global marketplace and a world economy. Many businesses have responded to these economic developments by becoming multinational corporations (MNCs). A *multinational corporation* is a firm that generates a substantial portion of its revenues from sales made in countries other than its home country. During the 1970s, the term multinational corporation was largely associated with U.S. firms that moved to expand their domestic operations by selling in foreign markets. These firms often made large asset investments in foreign countries as well. Large corporations in other countries engaged in similar activities during the 1980s.

Today, some multinational corporations actually earn a majority of their revenues from countries outside their home countries. The term "stateless" corporation was introduced in a recent article in *Business Week* (14 May 1990: 98–106) to describe this new breed of firm. Following are examples of so-called stateless corporations:

COMPANY	HOME COUNTRY	PERCENT OF 1989 SALES OUTSIDE HOME COUNTRY
Nestlé	Switzerland	98%
Volvo	Sweden	80
Michelin	France	78
Sony	Japan	66
Bayer	W. Germany	65
Colgate	United States	64
Honda	Japan	63
IBM	United States	59
Coca-Cola	United States	54

Income Tax Considerations

In addition to financing and risk factors, income tax liabilities also may differ for each form of business organization selected. Income from partnerships and proprietorships is combined with other personal income for tax purposes. Corporations, in contrast, are taxed as separate entities. The Tax Reform Act of 1986 provided that, beginning in 1988, corporations were to be taxed at the following rates on their taxable income:

15% on the first $50,000
25% on the next $25,000
34% on amounts over $75,000

A corporation with taxable income of $60,000 has a marginal tax rate of 25 percent, while another corporation with taxable income of $100,000 is in the 34 percent marginal tax bracket. Taxes on the corporation with $60,000 in income are calculated as follows:

$$.15 \times \$50,000 = \$\ 7,500$$
$$.25 \times 10,000 = \underline{2,500}$$
$$\$10,000$$

The dollar amount of income taxes paid is based on the firm's average tax rate. Dividing the tax of $10,000 by the $60,000 income produces an average tax rate of 16.7 percent. Of course, as a firm's taxable income gets larger, the average tax rate will approach the maximum marginal tax rate of 34 percent. Whether or not an owner or owners would have a lower tax liability if the business were taxed as a proprietorship or partnership depends upon the owners' personal income tax bracket.

Small businesses can sometimes qualify as *S corporations* under the Internal Revenue Code. These organizations receive the limited liability of a corporation but are taxed as proprietorships or partnerships. A corporation pays taxes on its taxable income. Then, if cash

CORPORATE TAX LAW CHANGES DURING THE 1980'S

The amount of income taxes paid by corporations was substantially affected by the passage of two major tax laws during the 1980s. The Economic Recovery Act of 1981 stimulated the economy by allowing businesses to write off their depreciable assets more quickly through the accelerated cost-recovery system (ACRS). Also, an investment tax credit which acts as an offset against existing tax liability was made available on the purchase of new equipment as a further stimulus to economic activity. The top marginal rate or tax bracket was kept at 46 percent for taxable incomes above $100,000.

The Tax Reform Act of 1986 provided for a substantial reduction in corporate income tax rates with a new maximum rate of 34 percent. Following is a brief comparison of the corporate tax under the 1981 and 1986 laws:

NET INCOME	1981 LAW	1986 LAW
Up to $25,000	15%	15%
$25,000 to $50,000	18	15
$50,000 to $75,000	30	25
$75,000 to $100,000	40	34
Over $100,000	46	34

However, in order to partially counter the impact of these lower corporate income tax rates, the 1986 law revised the ACRS to provide for less attractive depreciation schedules. In addition, the investment tax credit was repealed, the favored rate on long-term capital gains (over short-term gains) was eliminated, and an alternative minimum corporate tax rate was instituted.

from profits is distributed as dividends to stockholders, the stockholders must pay personal income taxes. This double taxation is avoided by the S corporation because the business is taxed as a proprietorship or partnership. Whether or not this taxation option is selected depends upon the level of the owner's personal tax bracket.

Businesses also have the opportunity of carrying operating losses backward for three years and forward for fifteen years to offset taxable income. A new business corporation that loses, for example, $50,000 the first year can only offset taxable income earned in future years. However, initial losses by a new proprietorship or partnership can be first carried back against personal income taxes paid by owners, permitting them tax refunds. This can be helpful for a new business that has limited funds.

FINANCIAL MANAGEMENT FUNCTIONS   *Why?*

Not cash related
1. Depreciation
2. reserve for bad debt

The overall objective of financial management is to maximize the value of the owners' investment or equity in the firm. To be successful in this endeavor, the financial manager must effectively carry out the functions of financial planning and analysis, asset management, and the raising of funds.

Financial Planning and Analysis

In order to plan, it is necessary to look forward. We all have perfect hindsight, but foresight is what determines the success of a business. Long-range plans covering several years must be prepared to project growth in sales, assets, and employees. First, a sales forecast needs to be made that includes expected developments in the economy and that reflects possible competitive pressures from other businesses. The sales forecast then must be supported by plans for an adequate investment in assets. For example, a manufacturing firm must invest in plant and equipment to produce an inventory of products that will fill sales orders. Asset investment plans call for, in turn, plans indicating the size of financing needs. Adequate investment in human resources must be planned for as well.

In addition to long-range plans or budgets, the financial manager is concerned with near-term cash inflows and outflows associated with business operation. Cash flows are often monitored on a daily basis for large firms while small firms may make only monthly cash budgets. An unexpected shortage of cash causes financial problems for the financial manager. Having failed to plan for such a need in advance, he or she may have to seek a loan from a bank or other lender when the firm is out of money.

Budget - Future events next year

Financial analysis goes hand in hand with successful financial planning. The established firm must conduct a financial analysis of past performance to aid in developing realistic future plans. The new firm should analyze the performance characteristics of other firms in the same industry before making plans. Financial analysis is conducted primarily through the examination of financial ratios, such as the ratio of profits to sales. These are viewed either historically over time or by comparing ratios with other firms in the industry. Some basics of financial analysis will be discussed later in this chapter. Financial planning will be covered in Chapter 8.

Asset Management   *Asset Control*

Successful financial planning means that the financial manager must decide on the amount and mix of assets necessary to generate the forecasted level of sales and profits. Investments in fixed assets are necessary to support sales. For manufacturing firms, plant facilities and machinery are necessary to produce the firm's products. In addition to fixed assets, the firm must carry adequate amounts of current assets. Inventory must be accumulated for the purpose of making sales. Cash balances must be maintained to carry on day-to-day transactions, and receivables may be incurred if sales are made on credit. The management of current assets will be addressed further in Chapter 8, while the acquisition and management of fixed assets will be covered in Chapter 10.

Raising Funds

Once financial plans have been made and asset needs planned for, the financial manager must acquire or raise the short-term and long-term funds necessary to support the firm's assets. Trade credit may be requested from suppliers, short-term bank loans may be obtained, or other current liabilities may be used. Long-term sources of financing may come from profits, the owner's own equity contributions, or long-term borrowing.

In smaller firms, the operator of the business may take total responsibility for the finance functions. In fact, in small firms, the owner usually administers all facets of the business' operations. It is because of this that the small business finds itself at a special disadvantage. Few people have the overall ability to effectively perform the many challenging functions required by even the small business. On the other hand, the medium and large business may, by virtue of size, assign an individual or group of individuals to these special functions and in so doing achieve the efficiency that comes from specialization of talent.

Sources of short-term financing will be discussed in Chapter 9, while long-term debt and equity funds are covered in Chapters 11 and 12. Chapter 13 covers the merchandising and facilitating agencies involved in long-term business financing.

ACCOUNTING AND FINANCIAL STATEMENTS

The financial manager needs a basic understanding of the accounting and financial statements used by businesses in order to carry out his or her financial management functions. It is important to know both the firm's financial position at a point in time and changes in its financial position over time. This financial information indicates the performance of the firm and reflects the success of the financial manager and other officers.

The financial manager's overall objective is to maximize the value of the owners' investment. This objective is consistent with a long-run view of the operation of the firm. However, there is a potential internal conflict in U.S. corporations due to the separation between stockholder ownership and management control. U.S. managers are often faced with the reality that their own compensation and advancement is dependent on short-run accounting profits and company stock prices. Because of this, U.S. managers are frequently accused of managing for the short-run, while Japanese managers and other foreign competitors supposedly make decisions which are consistent with their firms' long-run objectives.

CORPORATE ECONOMIC GOALS AND OBJECTIVES

Too much emphasis on short-run results may produce short-sighted managers. For example, there is a lot of pressure in major U.S. corporations today to "streamline." This may risk the ability of U.S. firms to compete internationally if over time research activities, plant and equipment investments, and potential new products are cut to improve short-run performance. U.S. managers must consider the long-run implications of their short-run decisions. More specifically, financial managers must evaluate the long-run impact as they carry out the functions of financial planning and analysis, asset management, and the raising of funds.

The Balance Sheet

For purposes of understanding the uses and sources of funds and the allocation of risk for businesses, it is necessary to look at the balance sheet. The **balance sheet** is a summary or report that shows the assets and the sources of financing of a business on a particular date. It reveals two broad categories of information: (1) the **assets** owned by a business and (2) the creditors' claims and the owners' equity in the business assets. The creditors' claims, which are the financial obligations of the business, are referred to as **liabilities**.

balance sheet
a report showing the assets and liabilities of a business

assets
items of ownership convertible into cash

liabilities
financial obligations of a business

The balance sheet is like a snapshot, revealing the condition of a business on a given date. Like a cutaway section of an automobile motor, however, the balance sheet also reveals much of the inner workings of the structure. The various types of assets indicate at once the results of recent business operations and the capacity for future operations. The creditors' claims and the owners' equity in the assets reveal the sources from which these assets have been derived. The term *balance sheet* itself indicates a relationship of equality between the assets of the business and the sources of funds used to obtain them that may be expressed as follows:

Assets = Liabilities + Owners' equity

The simplified balance sheet of a manufacturing firm shown in Figure 7.1 reveals this equality of assets and the financial interests in the assets. The financial interests in the assets, as noted above, are the creditors' claims and owners' interests. We shall, in the following pages, discuss the composition of this balance sheet. Our specific objective will be to relate the assets to the sources of funds for obtaining them.

CURRENT ASSETS

The balance sheet of the Kenwood Manufacturing Company reveals, among other things, that the business had assets as of December 31 of $500,000. The assets of the company have been classified into two groups: current assets and fixed assets.

current assets
assets that will be used in the near future

The **current assets** of a business include cash and other assets that may reasonably be expected to be converted into cash, sold, or used in the near future through the normal operations of the business. The

FIGURE 7.1   Balance Sheet for Kenwood Manufacturing Company

BALANCE SHEET
DECEMBER 31, 1991

ASSETS	
Cash and marketable securities	$ 25,000
Accounts receivable	100,000
Inventories	125,000
Total current assets	$250,000
Gross plant and equipment	$275,000
Less accumulated depreciation	–75,000
Net plant and equipment	$200,000
Land	50,000
Total fixed assets	$250,000
Total assets	$500,000
LIABILITIES AND OWNERS' EQUITY	
Accounts payable	$ 75,000
Notes payable (bank, 10%)	20,000
Accrued liabilities	30,000
Total current liabilities	$125,000
Mortgage debt (12%)	100,000
Total liabilities	$225,000
Owner's equity	275,000
Total liabilities and owner's equity	$500,000

principal current assets of a business are typically its cash and marketable securities, accounts receivable, and inventories.

Cash and Marketable Securities

This includes cash on hand and cash on deposit with banks, marketable securities, such as commercial paper issued by other firms, and U.S. government securities in the form of Treasury bills, notes, and bonds.

Accounts and Notes Receivable

Accounts receivable generally arise from the sale of products, merchandise, or services on credit. The buyer's debts to the business are generally paid according to the credit terms of the sale. Some firms also have notes receivable. A ***note receivable*** is a written promise by a debtor of the business to pay a specified sum of money on or before a stated date. Such notes are ordinarily made payable to the order of a particular firm or person or to "bearer." Notes receivable may come into existence in several ways. For example, overdue accounts receivable may be converted to notes receivable at the insistence of the seller or upon special request by the buyer. Notes receivable may also occur as a result of short-term loans made by the business to its employees or to other persons or businesses. These notes may be held until maturity or converted into cash immediately by selling them to a bank or other purchaser.

accounts receivable
obligations due from credit sales

note receivable
an asset in the form of money due to a firm by a certain date

Most credit sales of goods and services by businesses in the United States are made on the basis of accounts-receivable financing. However, for the bank, loan company, or other such financial institution, notes receivable represent one of their principal assets because their customers are required to sign notes as evidence of loans.

Inventories

The materials and products that a manufacturing firm has on hand are shown as *inventories* on the balance sheet. Generally, a manufacturing firm categorizes its inventories in terms of raw materials, goods in the process of manufacture, and finished goods. Sometimes the balance sheet will reveal the amount of inventory in each of these categories.

FIXED ASSETS

Fixed assets are the physical facilities used in the production, storage, display, and distribution of the products of a firm. These assets normally provide many years of service. The principal fixed assets are plant and equipment and land.

fixed assets
a firm's plant, equipment, and land

In a manufacturing firm, a large investment in plant and equipment is usually required. As products are manufactured, some of the economic value of this plant and equipment lessens. This is called *depreciation* and accountants reflect this using up of real assets by charging off depreciation against the original cost of plant and equipment. Thus the net plant and equipment at any point in time is supposed to reflect their remaining useful lives. The net is calculated by subtracting the amount of depreciation that has accumulated over time from the gross plant and equipment.

Some firms own only the land or real property on which their buildings or manufacturing plants are constructed. Other firms may own other land for expansion or investment purposes. The original cost of land owned is reflected on the firm's balance sheet.

OTHER ASSETS

Businesses occasionally include other assets on their balance sheets. For example, a firm might show some *prepaid expenses* as assets to reflect the prepayment of rent and insurance expenses. These are listed as assets because the time period that has been covered by the rental and insurance payments has not yet expired. Businesses may also list *intangible assets*. Intangible assets are nonphysical and include such items as patent rights and a firm's goodwill.

LIABILITIES

Liabilities are the debts of a business. They come into existence through direct borrowing, purchases of goods and services on credit, and the accrual of obligations such as wages and income taxes. Liabilities are classified as current and long-term.

Current Liabilities

current liabilities
business debts that must be paid in one year

The **current liabilities** of a business may be defined as those obligations that must be satisfied within a period of one year. They are the accounts payable, notes payable, and accrued liabilities that are to be met out of current funds and operations. Although the cash on hand plus marketable securities of the Kenwood Manufacturing Company is only $25,000 compared with current liabilities of $125,000, it is expected that normal business operations will convert receivables and inventory into cash in time to meet current liabilities as they become due.

accounts payable
debts from credit purchases

Accounts payable. *Accounts payable* are debts that arise primarily from the purchase of goods on credit terms. An account payable is not evidenced by a note. Although it lacks some of the legal force of a note, its convenience and simplicity have made it very popular. Accounts payable, as well as notes payable, arising from the purchase of inventory on credit terms represent *trade credit* financing as opposed to direct short-term borrowing from banks and other lenders. An account payable shown in a balance sheet is reflected as an account receivable on the balance sheet of the firm from which goods were purchased.

Notes payable.   A *note payable* is a written promise to pay a specified amount of money to the order of a creditor on or before a certain date. These notes may arise from the purchase of goods or services on a credit basis, from direct short-term borrowing, or in settlement of accounts payable that have not been satisfied according to the terms of the original purchase agreement. The most common occurrence of a note payable takes place when a business borrows money from a bank on a short-term basis for the purchase of materials or for other current operating requirements. The transaction that creates the note payable on a firm's balance sheet is reflected as a note receivable on the balance sheet of the firm to which the money is owed.

*note payable
a liability in the form of a debt to be paid by a certain date*

Accrued liabilities.   Amounts owed but not yet due for such items as wages and salaries, taxes, and interest on notes are called *accrued liabilities*. They are included in the current liabilities section of the balance sheet. Of special importance is the tax accrual, which often is the largest single current liability of the business.

*accrued liabilities
amounts owed but not yet due*

Long-Term Liabilities

Business debts with maturities greater than one year are *long-term liabilities*. The length of maturity depends upon the confidence of lenders in the business and the nature of the security that the business may offer for the loans. When a long-term debt approaches its maturity date, that is, when it is due within a year from the date of the balance sheet, the debt is transferred to the current liabilities section.

*long-term liabilities
debts with maturities greater than one year*

One of the most common methods used by businesses for obtaining a long-term loan is to offer a mortgage to a lender. A *mortgage* is a transfer of title to property that is given by a debtor to a creditor as security for the payment of the debt. Mortgages contain a provision that such transfer of title becomes void when the debt is paid according to the terms agreed upon. In the event that the borrowing business fails to meet the obligations of the loan contract, the mortgage may be foreclosed. That is, the property may be seized through appropriate legal channels and sold in order to satisfy the indebtedness.

*mortgage
an interest in real property used as security for a debt*

OWNERS' EQUITY

All businesses have owners' equity in one form or another. *Owners' equity* is the investment of the owners or owner in the business. It initially results from a cash outlay for the purchase of assets to operate the business. In some cases, the owners of a business may place their own assets, such as machinery, real estate, or equipment with the firm for its operation. In addition to contributing cash or property, owners' equity may also be increased by allowing profits to remain with the business. On the balance sheet, the amount of owners' equity is always

*owners' equity
investment of an owner or owners in a business*

represented by the difference between total assets and total liabilities of the business. It reflects the owners' claims on the assets of the business as opposed to the creditors' claims.

In the case of a corporation, the owners' equity is usually broken down into several different accounts. First is the *common stock account*, which reflects the number of outstanding shares of common stock carried at a stated or par value. For example, a corporation may have issued 10,000 shares of common stock with a par value of $1, shown as a $10,000 value on its balance sheet. If the stock had actually been sold for $5 per share, then the $4 above the par value per share would have been placed in a ***paid-in capital account*** (or surplus account) in an amount of $40,000 ($4 × 10,000 shares). A third account, ***retained earnings***, reflects the retention or growth of earnings or profits within the corporation. Together these three accounts comprise the corporation's common or owners' equity.

paid-in capital account
owners' equity from a
corporation's stock sold
above par value

retained earnings
owners' equity accumu-
lated as profits within
the corporation

The Income Statement

income statement
statement itemizing the
net profit or loss of a
firm during a specified
time period

The ***income statement*** reflects the change in a firm's financial position over time. This statement indicates the extent to which the assets shown on the balance sheet have been used to support revenues or sales for the firm. The expenses incurred in generating those revenues or sales are also shown on the income statement. Finally, the interest costs associated with financing some of the firm's assets with liabilities, along with the payment of income taxes, are subtracted in the income statement. The result is the net profit or income, or in some cases the loss, available to the owners of the business. A simplified income statement for the Kenwood Manufacturing Company is shown in Figure 7.2.

FIGURE 7.2   Income Statement for Kenwood Manufacturing Company

INCOME STATEMENT YEAR-END 1991	
Net revenues or sales	$700,000
Cost of goods sold	450,000
Gross profit	$250,000
General and administrative expenses	$115,000
Selling and marketing expenses	36,000
Depreciation	25,000
Interest	14,000
Total additional expenses	$190,000
Net income before income taxes	$ 60,000
Income taxes	10,000
Net income	$ 50,000

NET REVENUES OR SALES

The starting point of the income statement reflects the revenues or sales generated from the operations of the business. Quite often gross revenues are larger than net revenues. This is due to sales returns and allowances that may occur over the time period reflected in the income statement. Sometimes when customers make early payment on their bills, cash discounts are given by the firm. Also, if customers buy in very large quantities, trade discounts may be given. Thus discounts will reduce gross revenues.

COSTS OR EXPENSES

The typical firm is faced with two types of expenses: variable and fixed. **Variable costs** are those types of expenses that vary directly with sales. For example, a substantial part, if not all, of the expense contained in cost of goods sold would be variable. **Fixed costs** include those expenses such as general and administrative expenses that must be paid regardless of the volume of sales generated by the firm.

*variable costs
expenses that vary
directly with sales
fixed costs
costs not related to sales*

Cost of Goods Sold

The costs of producing or manufacturing the products sold to earn revenues are grouped under cost of goods sold. These expenses are largely variable and reflect costs directly involved in production, such as raw materials, labor, and overhead.

General and Administrative Expenses

These expenses are largely fixed in nature and cover requirements such as record keeping and preparing financial and accounting statements. Utility costs not directly associated with product manufacturing and the salaries of administrative personnel are also included.

Selling and Marketing Expenses

These expenses reflect the costs associated with selling the firm's products. This includes salaries and/or commissions generated by the sales force as well as promotional and advertising expenditures.

Depreciation Expense

This expense item reflects the reduction in the economic value of the firm's plant and equipment caused by manufacturing the firm's products. It is for the time period covered by the income statement. This one-time-period depreciation is accumulated over time and appears in the balance sheet as previously noted.

Interest Expense

When a portion of a firm's assets are financed with liabilities, interest costs or charges usually result. This is true for notes payable, bank loans, and mortgage loans. Interest is recorded as an expense on the income statement.

INCOME TAXES

Businesses are required to pay income taxes on any profits. Profits are defined as income remaining after all other expenses have been deducted from revenues. Effective income tax rates can vary substantially depending on whether the firm is organized as a proprietorship, partnership, or corporation.

NET INCOME

The net income or profits remaining after income taxes are paid reflects the earnings available to the owners of the business. This income may be retained in the business to reduce existing liabilities, increase current assets, and/or acquire additional fixed assets. On the other hand, some or all of the income may be distributed to the owners of the business.

Other Financial Statements

statement of cash flows
statement showing how funds are obtained and used

In addition to the balance sheet and income statement, businesses provide a **statement of cash flows**. This is sometimes referred to as a *sources and uses of funds statement*. Information is taken from both the income statement and the balance sheet to show how the firm obtained funds during the accounting period and how those funds were used. For example, funds may be obtained through profits, borrowing, and selling equity securities. Uses of funds include purchasing fixed assets, building up inventories, and repaying loans.

cash transactions statement
statement that records cash received and disbursed

   Another useful financial statement is the **cash transactions statement**. It differs from the other financial statements in that it records only the actual receipt or disbursement of cash. For example, a cash sale will show up immediately in this statement, whereas a sale made on credit will not be recorded until the receivables are actually collected. The cash transactions statement is used by firms to manage their day-to-day cash activities and to forecast short-term borrowing needs.

FINANCIAL ANALYSIS   *Def.*

trend (or time series) analysis
comparison of a firm's financial ratios over several years

Financial analysis evaluates the past performance of a firm by examining *financial ratios*. Two kinds of financial analysis can be conducted. Financial ratios may be compared over several years for the same firm to identify positive and negative trends. This method of comparison is referred to as **trend** or **time series analysis**. The second method compares the firm's ratios against industry ratios and is known as ***industry comparative analysis***.

Analysis of financial statements can also be conducted by expressing individual accounts on a percentage basis. For example, each asset, liability, and equity item on the balance sheet is expressed as a percentage of total assets. Likewise, each expense and income item on the income statement is expressed as a percentage of net sales. This process is referred to as the preparation of "common size" financial statements. Possible changes in percentage relationships can then be examined over time for a single firm. Or a firm can be compared with another firm or the industry within which it operates.

industry comparative analysis
comparison of a firm's financial ratios to industry ratios

Financial Ratios   *Know 3*

Ratio - need two #'s to compare

Financial analysis is designed to cover four areas of a business. ***Liquidity ratios*** show the ability of the business to meet its short-term obligations as they come due. These ratios focus on the relationship between the firm's current assets and current liabilities. ***Asset utilization ratios*** show how well the firm uses its assets to support or generate sales. ***Financial leverage ratios*** indicate the extent to which assets are financed by borrowed funds and other liabilities. Total liabilities are often expressed as a percentage of total assets or as a percentage of stockholders' equity. The final area of financial analysis is firm profitability. ***Profitability ratios*** generally are of two types. Net income is expressed as a percentage of net sales to show the degree of income profitability. Profitability is also measured by relating net income to total assets or to stockholders' equity.

liquidity ratios
information showing a firm's ability to meet short-term obligations
asset utilization ratios
information showing how effectively assets are being used
financial leverage ratios
ratios that show the extent that assets are financed by liabilities
profitability ratios
ratios comparing profits with sales, assets, or stockholders' equity

We will be exploring these various ratio measures in greater detail in the remaining chapters of Part 2. However, at this time we can increase our understanding of financial analysis by examining a financial model or system that uses the profitability and asset utilization dimensions.

The Du Pont System

A system of financial analysis developed by the Du Pont Corporation provides a very valuable aid to the financial manager. It focuses on firm profitability as measured by the rate of return on assets. The return on assets is derived by dividing net income by total assets. This system can be briefly expressed as follows:

$$\frac{\text{Net income}}{\text{Total assets}} = \frac{\text{Net sales}}{\text{Total assets}} \times \frac{\text{Net income}}{\text{Net sales}}$$

Return on assets = Asset turnover × Profit margin

Two ratio components when multiplied together give the return on assets. The asset turnover component, expressed as net sales divided by total assets, indicates the extent to which assets have been effectively used to produce sales. The higher the asset turnover ratio the more effective their use. Income statement profitability is reflected in the size of the profit margin—the higher the percentage, the more profitable the firm.

Firms in some industries are able to achieve high asset turnovers but low profit margins, and vice versa. For example, retail food chains have high utilization of assets. In other words, they make small asset investments compared to sales generated but have very low profit margins and only average returns on assets. The chemical and steel industries, in contrast, are very capital intensive and thus require large investments in assets to support their sales. Firms in these industries must earn higher than average profit margins to produce average asset returns.

The Du Pont system when applied to the 1991 data for the Kenwood Manufacturing Company in Figures 7.1 and 7.2, indicates a return on total assets of 10 percent. This is based on a turnover of assets of 1.4 times and a profit margin of 7.143 percent as the following calculations show:

$$\frac{\$50,000}{\$500,000} = \frac{\$700,000}{\$500,000} \times \frac{\$50,000}{\$700,000}$$

$$10\% \quad = \quad 1.4 \quad \times \quad 7.143\%$$

This information by itself, however, is of limited value to the financial manager without prior information. For example, the return on assets for 1990 for Kenwood might have been 11 percent based on net income of $44,000 and total assets of $400,000. We might ask why the return on assets declined. If sales were $600,000 in 1990, then the asset turnover would have been 1.5 ($600,000/$400,000) with a profit margin of 7.33 percent ($44,000/$600,000). Thus the decline in 1991 in the return on assets occurred because of poorer utilization of assets and lower profits on sales.

Kenwood's financial manager would want to investigate further why performance was poorer in 1991 compared with 1990. He or she might expand the basic model to include the major components of both the balance sheet and income statement. A graphic expansion of the Du Pont system of financial analysis is shown in Figure 7.3. As we will see later, a more detailed examination of individual asset items can be conducted. This examination would show which items caused Kenwood's total assets to increase more rapidly than sales between the two years. Likewise, the various expense items could be examined more closely to identify which contributed to the decline in the profit margin.

The financial manager should also consider comparing Kenwood's financial performance against industry averages during the same two

FIGURE 7.3   Expansion of the Du Pont System of Financial Analysis

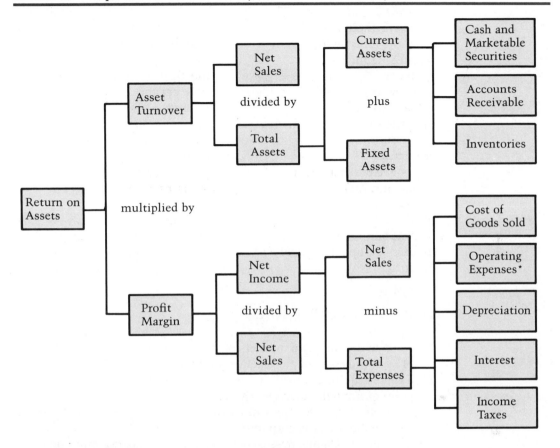

*Includes general, administrative, selling, and marketing expenses.

years. This comparison will show whether other firms in the industry have been similarly affected. For example, if industry averages had shown a return on assets of 12 percent in each of the two years and asset turnovers of 1.5 and profit margins of 8 percent, then there would be reason for concern. The financial manager should determine the specific reasons for Kenwood's below-industry-average performance and then take the necessary steps to improve financial performance in the future.

Financial analysis is an important financial management tool. By calculating and comparing financial ratios, the financial manager can evaluate past financial performance and use this information in planning for the firm's future. Financial analysis is also useful in monitoring the success of financial plans over time.

KEY TERMS

accounts payable	limited partnership
accounts receivable	liquidity ratios
accrued liabilities	long-term liabilities
assets	mortgage
asset utilization ratios	note payable
balance sheet	note receivable
cash transactions statement	owner's equity
corporation	paid-in capital account
current assets	partnership
current liabilities	profitability ratios
financial leverage ratios	proprietorship
fixed assets	retained earnings
fixed costs	statement of cash flows
income statement	trend (or time series) analysis
industry comparative analysis	variable costs
liabilities	

DISCUSSION QUESTIONS

1. How do the financial markets of the nation accommodate the needs of both the risky business effort and the well-established firm?
2. Explain the relationship between risk and return from the standpoint of financial managers and investors.
3. What are the differences in owner liability in proprietorships and partnerships versus corporations?
4. The ability of a business to obtain capital is in part a function of its legal form of organization. Explain.
5. What are some of the income tax considerations in selecting a particular form of business organization?
6. Briefly identify and describe the functions of financial management.
7. Explain and contrast: (1) current assets versus fixed assets, (2) accounts receivable versus notes receivable, and (3) accounts payable versus notes payable.
8. Briefly identify and describe the major types of expenses that must be met or covered by a manufacturing firm.
9. What accounting and financial statements in addition to balance sheets and income statements are used by the financial manager?
10. What kinds of financial analysis comparisons can be made in evaluating a firm's financial ratios?
11. Identify and briefly describe the four areas of a firm that are analyzed through financial ratios.

?'s on Quiz

12. What is the focus of the Du Pont system of financial analysis? What are the two major components of the system? Also, describe how the system is related to both the balance sheet and income statement.

PROBLEMS

1. Determine the marginal and average tax rates under the 1986 tax law for corporations with the following amounts of taxable income: (a) $60,000, (b) $150,000, and (c) $500,000.
2. The Dayco Manufacturing Company had the following financial statement results for last year. Net sales were $1.2 million with net income of $90,000. Total assets at year-end amounted to $900,000.
   a. Calculate Dayco's asset turnover ratio and its profit margin.
   b. Show how the two ratios in part a. can be used to determine Dayco's rate of return on assets.
   c. Dayco operates in the same industry as Kenwood Manufacturing, whose industry ratios are:
      Return on assets: 10.5%
      Asset turnover: 1.5 times
      Profit margin: 7%
      Compare Dayco's performance against the industry averages.
3. Next year Kenwood Manufacturing (discussed in the chapter) expects its sales to reach $900,000 with an investment in total assets of $600,000. Net income of $70,000 is anticipated.
   a. Use the Du Pont system to compare Kenwood's anticipated performance against its 1991 results and hypothetical results for 1990. Comment on your findings.
   b. How would Kenwood compare with the industry if the industry ratios (see Problem 2) remain the same the next year?
4. Following are selected financial data in thousands of dollars for the Hunter Corporation.

	1990	1991
Current assets	$ 400	$ 500
Fixed assets, net	600	700
Total assets	$1,000	$1,200
Current liabilities	$ 200	$ 250
Long-term debt	200	200
Common equity	600	750
Total liabilities and equity	$1,000	$1,200
Net sales	$1,200	$1,500
Total expenses	−1,100	−1,390
Net income	$ 100	$ 110

a. Calculate Hunter's rate of return on total assets in 1990 and in 1991. Did the ratio improve or worsen?

b. Use Figure 7.3 in the chapter to diagram the expanded Du Pont system for Hunter for both 1990 and 1991. Insert the appropriate dollar amounts for each stage except the last (figures not given).

c. Use the Du Pont system to calculate the return on assets for the two years, and determine why they changed.

5. Following are financial statements for the Genatron Manufacturing Corporation for 1990 and 1991.

a. Apply the return on assets financial model (the Du Pont system) to both the 1990 and 1991 financial statements' data.

b. Explain how financial performance differed between 1990 and 1991.

GENATRON MANUFACTURING CORPORATION

BALANCE SHEET	1990	1991
Cash	$ 50,000	$ 40,000
Accts. Receivable	200,000	260,000
Inventory	450,000	500,000
Total Current Assets	$ 700,000	$ 800,000
Fixed Assets, Net	300,000	400,000
Total Assets	$1,000,000	$1,200,000
Accts. Payable	$ 130,000	$ 170,000
Bank Loan, 10%	90,000	90,000
Accruals	50,000	70,000
Total Current Liabilities	$ 270,000	$ 330,000
Long-term Debt, 12%	300,000	400,000
Common Stock, $10 par	300,000	300,000
Capital Surplus	50,000	50,000
Retained Earnings	80,000	120,000
Total Liabilities & Equity	$1,000,000	$1,200,000

INCOME STATEMENT	1990	1991
Net Sales	$1,300,000	$1,500,000
Cost of Goods Sold	780,000	900,000
Gross Profit	$ 520,000	$ 600,000
Expenses:		
General & Administrative	$ 150,000	$ 150,000
Marketing	130,000	150,000
Depreciation	40,000	53,000
Interest	45,000	57,000
Earnings Before Taxes	$ 155,000	$ 190,000
Income Taxes	62,000	76,000
Net Income	$ 93,000	$ 114,000

6. This problem uses the two years' of financial statement information contained in Problem 5. Assume that the data shown for 1990
   are for the ACE Company and the data shown for 1991 are for the
   KING Company. (Use the Financial Statement Analysis tool.)
   a. Prepare "common size" financial statements for both firms.
   b. Determine each firm's asset turnover ratio, profit margin, and
      rate of return on assets.

SELF-TEST QUESTIONS

1. "All owners have unlimited liability for all debts of the firm" is
   associated with which one of the following types of business organization?
   a. proprietorship
   b. partnership
   c. limited partnership
   d. corporation

2. The maximum corporate income tax rate established under the Tax
   Reform Act of 1986 is:
   a. 15 percent
   b. 30 percent
   c. 34 percent
   d. 46 percent

3. Which one of the following is *not* considered to be a major financial
   management function?
   a. financial planning and analysis
   b. asset management
   c. raising funds
   d. managing the firm's accounting system

4. Which one of the following financial statements conveys a relationship of equality between assets and liabilities plus owners' equity?
   a. balance sheet
   b. income statement
   c. statement of changes in financial position
   d. cash flow statement

5. Financial analysis is designed to cover four areas or dimensions of
   the firm. Which one of the following does not belong?
   a. liquidity ratios
   b. asset utilization ratios
   c. financial leverage ratios
   d. source and use of funds ratios

SELF-TEST PROBLEM

The Eagle Manufacturing Company had the following financial statement results for last year. Net sales were $1 million with net income of
$70,000. Total assets at year end amounted to $800,000.
a. Calculate Eagle's asset turnover ratio and its profit margin.
b. Show how the two ratios in part a. can be used to determine Eagle's
    rate of return on assets.
c. Eagle operates in the same industry as Kenwood Manufacturing, for
    which the industry ratios are:
    Return on assets: 10.5%
    Asset turnover: 1.5 times
    Profit margin: 7%
    Compare Eagle's performance against the industry averages.

SUGGESTED READINGS

Block, Stanley B., and Geoffrey A. Hirt. *Foundations of Financial Management*, 5e.
    Homewood, IL: Richard D. Irwin, Inc., 1989. Chaps. 2 and 3.
Harrington, Diana R., and Brent D. Wilson. *Corporate Financial Analysis*, 3e. Home-
    wood, IL: BPI/Irwin, 1989. Chap. 1.
Helfert, Erich A. *Techniques of Financial Analysis*, 6e. Homewood, IL: Richard D. Irwin,
    1987.
Higgins, Robert C. *Analysis for Financial Management*, 2nd ed. Homewood, IL: Richard
    D. Irwin, 1989. Chaps. 1 and 2.
Seitz, Neil. *Financial Analysis: A Programmed Approach*, 3e. Reston, VA: Reston
    Publishing Co., 1984. Chap. 1.
Fraser, Lyn M. *Understanding Financial Statements*, 2e. Reston, VA: Reston Publishing
    Co., 1988.

ANSWERS TO SELF-TEST QUESTIONS   1. b   2. c   3. d   4. a   5. d

SOLUTION TO SELF-TEST PROBLEM

a. Asset turnover ratio = $1,000,000/$800,000 = 1.25
    Profit margin = $70,000/$1,000,000 = .07 or 7%
b. Return on assets (ROA) = 1.25 × 7% = 8.75%

	RETURN ON ASSETS	ASSET TURNOVER	PROFIT MARGIN
Industry	10.50%	1.50	7.0%
Eagle	8.75	1.25	7.0

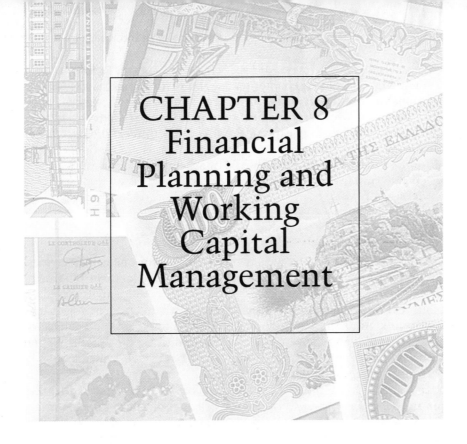

CHAPTER 8
Financial Planning and Working Capital Management

After studying this chapter, you should be able to:
- Describe the concept of financial planning and explain the steps involved in estimating external financing needs.
- Explain cost-volume-profit analysis and operating leverage concepts.
- Explain what is meant by the short-term operating cycle and describe its impact on working capital needs.
- Identify and briefly explain the factors that affect short-term financing requirements.
- Describe the motives underlying the management of cash and marketable securities.
- Briefly explain what is involved in accounts receivable management and indicate how it is carried out.
- Describe inventory management from the standpoint of the financial manager.

Financial planning is crucial to successful financial management. Sales must be forecasted and assets acquired to support the anticipated sales. The financial manager must decide how to finance the assets using a combination of internally generated profits and external funds. External financing must be planned in terms of the desired mix between debt and equity funds.

155

The first part of this chapter focuses on planning the assets to sales relationship and the financing mix. We then explore the firm's short-term operating cycle and the link between financial planning and the management of working capital. Broadly defined, **working capital** includes the firm's current assets and current liabilities. Our final emphasis is on management of cash and marketable securities, accounts receivable, and inventories.

working capital
the current assets and
liabilities of a firm

FINANCIAL PLANNING

Financial planning begins with a sales forecast for one or more years. These sales forecasts are the basis for written financial plans referred to as *budgets*. For established firms, sales forecasts are usually based on historical sales data that are used in statistical analyses to project into the future. Adjustments may be made to reflect possible changes in sales growth due to expected economic conditions, new products, and so forth. For example, a firm's sales may have been growing at a 10 percent average annual rate in the past. However, if a recession is anticipated, management might forecast only a 5 percent growth rate for the next year or two. In contrast, a booming economic climate might be associated with a 15 percent annual growth rate. New firms without sales histories have to rely on information from the experiences of other firms in their industry. Accurate sales forecasting is an essential element of successful financial management.

Asset Investment Requirements

Once the sales forecast has been made, plans must be made to acquire the assets necessary to support the new sales level. The relationship of assets and sales is shown in the asset turnover ratio, which was defined in Chapter 7 as net sales divided by total assets. While all firms strive to increase this ratio to improve asset utilization and profitability, the size of the ratio is significantly influenced by characteristics of the industry within which the firm operates. Capital intensive electric utilities might have asset turnover ratios as low as .33, indicating that they require $3 of investment in assets in order to produce $1 in revenues. In contrast, retail food chains with asset turnovers as high as 10 would require a $.10 investment in assets to produce $1 in sales. A typical manufacturing firm has an asset turnover of about 1.5, or about $.67 invested in assets per $1 in sales.

Recall from the last chapter that Kenwood Manufacturing had an asset turnover ratio of 1.4 based on 1991 sales of $700,000 and total assets of $500,000. By taking the inverse of this ratio, total assets divided by net sales, we can express assets as a percent of sales, which would be 71.4 percent ($500,000/$700,000). This is the percent-of-sales method for forecasting asset investment requirements. For example, a 10 percent forecasted increase of $70,000 in net sales ($700,000 × 10%) would result in an anticipated new asset investment of about $50,000 ($70,000 × 71.4%).

Figure 8.1 shows each major balance sheet item expressed as a percent of sales for 1991 for Kenwood. Notice that the sum total for all the assets is 71.4 percent as we calculated above. Actual asset investment required to support a specific sales increase may be altered if either of two developments occur: if the asset turnover ratio increases or certain fixed assets do not have to be increased.

First, if Kenwood could improve its asset turnover ratio to the industry average of 1.5 times, then assets would be only 66.7 percent of sales. This would mean that a $70,000 increase in sales would require an asset investment of about $46,700, or roughly $2,300 less than the earlier calculation. Second, fixed assets such as land or buildings might not have to be increased each year along with an increase in sales. The deciding factor usually is whether the firm currently has excess production capacity. For example, according to Figure 8.1, if only current assets are expected to increase with sales next year, then the asset investment requirements would be about $25,000 ($70,000 × 35.7%).

FIGURE 8.1
Percent-of-Sales Balance Sheet for Kenwood Manufacturing Company (1991)

ASSETS	DOLLAR AMOUNT	PERCENT OF SALES ($700,000)
Cash and marketable securities	$ 25,000	3.6%
Accounts receivable	100,000	14.3
Inventories	125,000	17.8
Total current assets	$250,000	35.7%
Net plant and equipment	$200,000	28.6%
Land	50,000	7.1
Total fixed assets	$250,000	35.7%
Total assets	$500,000	71.4%
LIABILITIES AND OWNERS' EQUITY		
Accounts payable	$ 75,000	10.7%
Notes payable (bank)	20,000	2.8
Accrued liabilities	30,000	4.3
Total current liabilities	$125,000	17.8%
Mortgage debt	100,000	14.3
Total liabilities	$225,000	32.1%
Owners' equity	275,000	39.3
Total liabilities and owners' equity	$500,000	71.4%

A greater than 10 percent sales growth for Kenwood would require an even larger investment in new assets. A much lower asset investment would be needed for an expected growth of, say, only 5 percent. And existing assets might even be reduced if sales decline.

Internally Generated Financing

Internally generated funds for financing new asset investments come from profits. Let us return to the Kenwood Company to illustrate planning for internally generated funds. Let's assume that the $50,000 asset investment scenario will be what is needed next year. We are now ready to plan how these assets will be financed from anticipated profits or external sources. Recall from Chapter 7 that during 1991 Kenwood earned $50,000 in net income on net sales of $700,000 for a profit margin of 7.14 percent. If net sales are expected to rise by 10 percent next year to $770,000 and the profit margin is expected to hold, then profits would be projected at about $55,000 ($770,000 × 7.14%). The amount of profit retained in the firm would show up as an increase in owners' equity, or retained earnings in the case of corporations. This would be more than adequate to finance the $50,000 investment in new assets.

However, let's further assume that management plans to pay out about one half of the profits, or $27,500, to the owners of the company. This would leave only $27,500 ($55,000 – $27,500) in internally generated funds to finance the $50,000 in assets. The remaining $22,500 in assets would have to be financed with external funds. These can be either short-term debt, long-term debt, or equity funds. Let's consider how the financial manager might plan the mix of short-term and long-term funds from external sources.

External Financing Requirements

Kenwood can expect that a portion of its asset financing requirements will be met by almost "automatic" increases in certain current liability accounts such as accounts payable and accrued liabilities. To meet planned sales increases, more credit purchases of materials will be necessary to produce the products to make sales. Increases would also be expected in accrued wages and taxes. These "automatic" liability accounts reduce the need for other external financing since they allow the firm to acquire additional inputs without an immediate cash outlay.

Figure 8.1 shows that accounts payable plus accrued liabilities were about 15 percent of sales in 1991 for Kenwood. Based on a 10 percent expected increase in sales, accounts payable and accrued liabilities would be expected to provide about $10,500 ($70,000 × 15%) in spontaneous short-term funds. This would leave an external financing need for Kenwood of about $12,000 ($22,500 minus $10,500) in order to cover the asset investment requirements. Management might choose to borrow the amount from a commercial bank, issue long-term debt, or request more equity funds from the owners.

To summarize briefly, the amount of new external funds needed to finance asset additions can be calculated as follows:

1. Forecast the dollar amount of expected sales increase.
2. Determine the dollar amount of new asset investments necessary to support the sales increase.
3. Subtract the expected amount of internally generated profits from the planned asset investments.
4. Subtract the amount of spontaneous increases expected in accounts payable and accrued liabilities from the planned asset investments.
5. The remaining dollar amount of asset investments determines the external financing needs (EFN).

For the Kenwood example we have:

$$EFN = \$50,000 - \$27,500 - \$10,500 = \$12,000$$

Determining the Financing Mix

Figure 8.2 depicts increases in the investment in assets. Increases in the investment in fixed assets and current assets will be consistent with rising sales over time. Seasonal sales variations in a business also affect the demand for current assets. Inventories must be increased to meet seasonal needs, and receivables will go up as sales increase. The added need for funds will disappear as inventories are reduced by sales and accounts receivable are collected. Thus seasonal variation in sales requires only temporary additional investments in current assets.

Figure 8.2 also depicts a recommended pattern for financing the assets. Prudent financial managers should practice the principle of **hedging**. Hedging calls for the matching of average maturities of a firm's assets with its liabilities and owners' equity. Cash funds are necessary to meet liabilities as they come due. Consequently, it is desirable to have assets maturing when liabilities are maturing. Following this principle implies that fixed assets should be financed with long-term debt and owners' equity funds. On the other hand, fluctuating current assets associated with seasonal operations should be financed with short-term liabilities.

The normal level of current assets actually reflects a "permanent" investment in cash, accounts receivable, and inventories needed to support sales. While individual accounts are collected and products sold, they are replaced by others. This causes the level of investment in these assets to remain constant. A portion of this investment will be offset by the "permanent" levels of accounts payable and accrued liabilities that behave similarly to the permanent current assets. How-

hedging
matching the average maturities of a firm's assets with its liabilities and equity

FIGURE 8.2   Asset Investment and Financing Relationships

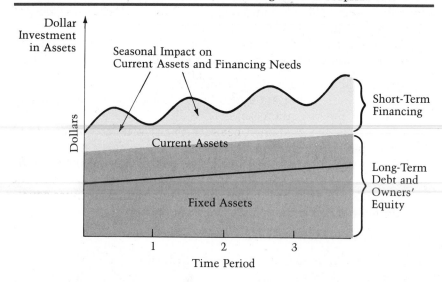

ever, the remaining portion of normal current assets requires long-term financing. To finance these assets with a short-term bank loan would be inconsistent with the hedging principle because permanent current assets have in effect long-term maturities.

Cost-Volume-Profit Analysis

Cost-volume-profit (CVP) analysis represents another tool used by managers for financial planning purposes. For example, let's assume that a firm is considering developing, manufacturing, and selling a basic accounting-system software product at $100 per copy. The variable costs—raw materials and direct labor—are estimated at $50 per unit. Fixed costs—various administrative and departmental overheads —allocated to this product are expected to be $40,000. Management is interested in knowing what level of operating profit will occur if unit sales are 1,000 per year.

The operating profit or earnings before interest and taxes (EBIT) relationship can be set up as follows:

$$EBIT = P(Q) - [VC(Q) + FC]$$

where

P = selling price per unit
Q = quantity sold

VC = variable cost per unit, and
FC = fixed costs

In our example, we have:

EBIT = $100(1,000) – [$50(1,000) + $40,000]
     = $100,000 – [$50,000 + $40,000]
     = $100,000 – $90,000
     = $10,000

Thus, if sales reach 1,000 units per year, the firm expects an operating profit of $10,000.

Management may also want to know how many units of the software product will have to be sold in order to break even. That is, what volume needs to be reached so that the amount of total revenues equals total costs (variable costs plus fixed costs). The breakeven point in units (BE) can be calculated as follows:

$$BE = \frac{FC}{(P - VC)}$$

Again, using the above example, we have:

$$BE = \frac{\$40,000}{(\$100 - \$50)}$$

$$= \frac{\$40,000}{\$50}$$

= 800 units

This can be confirmed by substituting the relevant information in the above operating profit equation as follows:

EBIT = $100(800) – [$50(800) – $40,000]
     = $80,000 – [$40,000 – $40,000]
     = $80,000 – $80,000
     = 0

The breakeven point in units, depicted graphically in Figure 8-3, occurs when total revenues equal total costs. The breakeven point in sales dollars is equal to the selling price per unit times the breakeven point in units. In our example, we have $100 times 800 units or $80,000.

Degree of Operating Leverage

The variability of sales or revenues over time indicates a basic operating business risk which must be considered when developing financial plans. Furthermore, financial managers may multiply or magnify the sales variability risk through asset management decisions that affect kinds of cost. For example, changes in the amount of net income shown

FIGURE 8.3   Cost-Volume-Profit Relationships

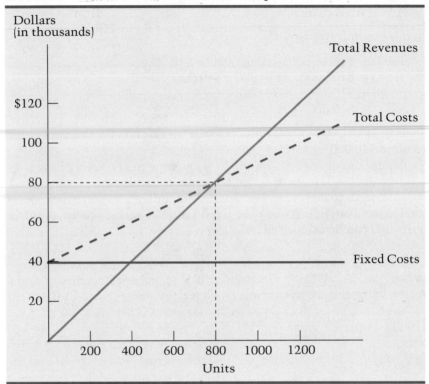

on the income statement are affected by changes in sales and the use of fixed versus variable costs. The following portion of an income statement illustrates this point.

Net sales	$700,000
Less: variable costs (60% of sales)	420,000
fixed costs	200,000
Earnings before interest and taxes	$ 80,000

The cost of goods sold for many firms will be largely variable in nature. That is, the cost of raw materials and labor will vary directly with the amount of goods produced and sold. Fixed operating costs are typically general and administrative overhead expenses and depreciation expenses. Marketing expenses may be fixed if the sales force is paid a flat salary, or variable if the sales personnel are paid on a commission basis. Some estimate of the proportion of variable and fixed costs is important when conducting financial planning.

For example, let's examine the impact of both a 10 percent decrease and a 10 percent increase in next year's sales on the firm's operating income or earnings before interest and taxes (EBIT). The revised partial income statement would appear as follows:

	PERCENT CHANGE IN SALES	
	−10%	+10%
Net sales	$630,000	$770,000
Less: variable costs (60% of sales)	378,000	462,000
fixed costs	200,000	200,000
Earnings before interest and taxes	$ 52,000	$108,000
Percent change in operating income (EBIT)	−35%	+35%

This example illustrates the potential importance of the *degree of operating leverage* (DOL) to financial planning. The degree of operating leverage quantifies the responsiveness of operating income to changes in the level of output. If net sales increase by 10 percent next year, from $700,000 to $770,000, the increase will be magnified 3.5 times in terms of operating income. An increase in operating income from $80,000 to $108,000 is a $28,000 or 35 percent increase ($28,000/$80,000 = 35%). Thus, a 35 percent change in operating income divided by a 10 percent change in net sales produces a 3.5 times magnification or leverage. DOL also works in reverse and provides negative leverage when net sales decline. Sophisticated financial planning models take into consideration the impact of operating leverage when projecting the next year's net income.

THE SHORT-TERM OPERATING CYCLE AND WORKING CAPITAL NEEDS

The link between financial planning and the management of working capital, including both current assets and current liabilities, can be described in terms of the firm's *short-term operating cycle*. Estimating the time it takes to complete the cycle relative to the level of operations will indicate two things: It gives 1) the size of the investment in accounts receivable and inventories, and 2) the extent to which financing will take place through accounts payable.

How the Short-term Cycle Works

Figure 8.4 depicts the short-term operating cycle, also called cash-to-cash cycle, for a manufacturing firm that has an existing fixed asset investment in plant and equipment. Raw materials must be purchased.

FIGURE 8.4   The Short-Term Cash-to-Cash Operating Cycle

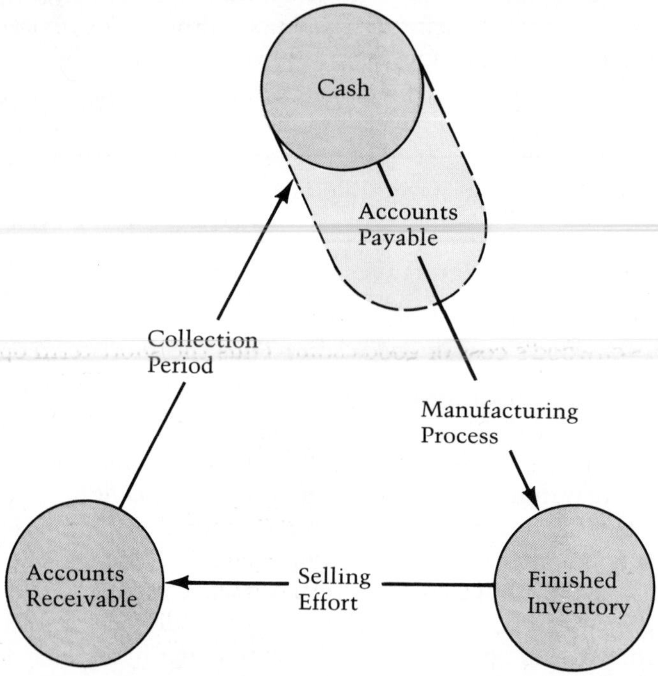

If these are credit purchases, then accounts payable are created, providing initial financing for a period. Then, movement through the manufacturing process will result in finished goods. Inventories, made up of raw materials, work-in-process, and finished goods, must be financed.

The manufacturing firm must also make a selling effort which may produce a certain amount of credit sales. The resulting accounts receivable must be financed as well. Finally, the firm must conduct a collection effort to turn credit sales into cash.

As the firm moves through its short-term operating cycle, accrued liabilities (not depicted in Figure 8.4) may also arise. For example, the manufacturing process is likely to lead to a level of wages payable, and to the extent that the firm is profitable there may be taxes payable. Increases in these accounts provide temporary financing in the same manner as accounts payable.

Working Capital Requirements

The average time it takes a firm to complete its short-term operating cycle will indicate the size of investment needed in accounts receivable and inventories, as well as the amount of financing provided by accounts payable. For example, Kenwood's production process might require on average 70 days to go from raw materials to finished products and another 30 days before the finished goods are sold. This amounts to an average inventory cycle of 100 days. Let's also assume that Kenwood extends credit to customers and has an accounts receivable cycle of 51.4 days based on its net sales. The combined cycle for inventories and accounts receivable is 151.4 days. This is the average time needed to complete the firm's short-term operating cycle if Kenwood does not purchase raw materials on credit.

However, let's assume that materials are purchased on credit terms from suppliers so that the accounts payable cycle averages 60 days based on Kenwood's cost of goods sold. Thus the short-term operating cycle would be reduced to 91.4 days (151.4 days minus 60 days). We can also express the short-term operating cycle in days as follows:

Inventory cycle	100 days
Accounts receivable cycle	51.4 days
	151.4 days
Accounts payable cycle	–60 days
Short-term operating cycle	91.4 days

Based on a 360-day year, this implies that Kenwood's short-term operating cycle would turn over on average about 3.9 times a year (360/91.4). It should be noted that the receivables cycle for many firms is longer than the payables cycle. If this had been the case for Kenwood, the operating cycle would have been longer and the turnover lower.

Now we can develop an idea about the size of the investments needed in inventories and accounts receivable. First of all, the inventory turns over about 3.6 times a year (360/100). If Kenwood has an annual cost of goods sold of $450,000 from producing its products, the average inventory on its balance sheet would be estimated at $125,000 ($450,000/3.6). In essence, we divide the cost of goods sold by the average number of times the inventory turns over during the year. Accounts receivable turn over on average 7 times (360/51.4) a year. However, because net sales include a markup or profit in addition to cost of goods sold, we use net sales for estimating the investment in accounts receivable. Kenwood had net sales of $700,000. Dividing this figure by the turnover for accounts receivable would provide an average investment of $100,000 ($700,000/7). Thus the combined investment found by adding inventories and accounts receivable would be $225,000.

Accounts payable turn over 6.1 times (360/60) a year. To estimate the financing provided by accounts payable we divide the cost of goods sold of $450,000 by the turnover of 6 and get $75,000. This would leave a net accounts receivable and inventories financing need of $150,000 ($225,000 – $75,000). Part of this need likely would be met by the firm's accrued liabilities. Some cash is also needed to carry on Kenwood's day-to-day operations. The remaining financing of current assets thus would have to come from short-term bank loans and/or long-term funds.

Net Working Capital

Short-term financing is used primarily to finance the current assets of a business. If a business relied entirely upon short-term financing for its current asset requirements, the total current assets of the firm would be equal to the total current liabilities. The balance sheet of most successful businesses, however, will reveal an excess of current assets over current liabilities. This excess reflects the extent to which long-term financing has contributed to the support of the current asset requirements of the firm. The portion of current assets financed through long-term financing is *net working capital*. This amount is determined by subtracting total current liabilities from total current assets.

net working capital
funds remaining after subtracting current liabilities from current assets

The balance sheet for the Kenwood Manufacturing Company, shown in Figure 8.1, allows us to examine Kenwood's net working capital position. Kenwood has current assets of $250,000 and current liabilities of $125,000. Therefore, it has $125,000 in net working capital. This net working capital is supported by the mortgage debt and/or owners' equity.

The net working capital is a measure of the financial soundness of a firm. In general, the greater the net working capital of a firm, the less difficulty it will have meeting short-term obligations. The existence of adequate net working capital is so important to a firm that it has become one of the prime tests of strength. Creditors place great emphasis on it in determining whether or not to extend credit.

The importance of providing for part of the current asset requirements of a business through long-term financing may be illustrated by a theoretical and highly improbable situation in which long-term financing has not been provided. For example, if in Kenwood's balance sheet the current liabilities had been $250,000, resulting from each current liability account being doubled and owners' equity reduced by $125,000, there would be no net working capital.

The current liabilities of such a firm would fall due periodically and would have to be paid out of cash. The cash and marketable securities are $25,000. Therefore, only that much indebtedness could be retired on the date of the balance sheet. It is true though that the accounts receivable and the inventory would in time be converted into cash as the firm moves through its operating cycle. However, the business would be in an extremely precarious position. In the event that receivables and inventory were not converted into cash on schedule, the firm would be unable to meet its current obligations. The answer to this problem is to provide part of the current asset requirements through long-term financing. With current assets amounting to substantially more than current liabilities, the chance that the business will have too little cash to meet its obligations is greatly reduced.

An adequate net working capital makes it possible for the firm to meet its debts promptly. Furthermore, it will be able to take discounts that may be available for early payment for purchases of raw materials and other goods. The firm that can make cash payments may also pay a lower price for its purchases. Or it may have access to higher quality merchandise at the same price because of its better bargaining position. Suppliers of materials as well as banks regard very highly the firm with a strong net working capital position. This ensures a continuing flow of funds and supplies during peak periods of seasonal activity and makes it possible for the firm to expand as long-term growth opportunities become available.

Liquidity Ratios

The net working capital or short-term financial position of a firm is expressed not only in terms of dollars but also in relative terms through liquidity ratios. One relationship is the **current ratio**; it is found by dividing total current assets by total current liabilities. Although the net working capital and the current ratio are simply alternative ways of expressing the short-term financial position of a firm, each has its particular usefulness.

current ratio
total current assets divided by total current liabilities

The current ratio is particularly useful in comparing the financial positions of firms of varying sizes. For example, Kenwood has total current assets of $250,000 and total current liabilities of $125,000. Thus, the current ratio is two to one and the net working capital is $125,000. Another firm, engaged in similar business activities, may have total current assets of $500,000 and total current liabilities of $250,000. Its current ratio is two to one, but the net working capital is $250,000. In this example, the net working capital of the latter firm is twice that of Kenwood. Yet it is clear that it is a matter of proportion; the latter firm may simply be a larger enterprise doing a larger volume of business. The current ratio of each firm, however, is two to one, revealing the similarity of their short-term financial positions.

A second liquidity ratio, the acid-test ratio, is often used along with the current ratio in order to better assess a firm's ability to meet its short-term obligations as they come due. The **acid-test ratio** excludes inventories from current assets before dividing by current liabilities because it is uncertain whether all assets can be easily converted into cash. For comparison purposes, both the current and acid-test ratios are shown as follows for Kenwood:

acid-test ratio
current assets minus inventories divided by current liabilities

CURRENT RATIO	ACID-TEST RATIO
$\dfrac{\text{Current assets}}{\text{Current liabilities}}$	$\dfrac{\text{Current assets minus inventories}}{\text{Current liabilities}}$
$\dfrac{\$250{,}000}{\$125{,}000} = 2{:}1$	$\dfrac{\$250{,}000 - \$125{,}000}{\$125{,}000} = 1{:}1$

An acid-test ratio of one to one is considered good. Current liabilities can be covered through the collection of accounts receivable and the use of cash and marketable securities.

FACTORS AFFECTING SHORT-TERM FINANCING

Determining the proper proportion between short-term and long-term financing depends upon an evaluation of many factors affecting the business. The nature of the demand for funds is basic and will be considered first in this section. Then we will consider a series of other factors involved, such as risks, cost, flexibility, the ease of future financing, and other qualitative factors.

Nature of the Demand for Funds

The nature of the demand for funds depends in part on the industry in which a business operates and on the characteristics of the business itself. It also depends on such factors as the seasonal variation in sales and output and on the trend of growth of the company. The need for funds also depends upon fluctuations in sales over the business cycle.

INDUSTRY AND COMPANY FACTORS

The nature of a company and the industry of which it is a part have a significant effect on financing decisions. An industry which has a need for large amounts of fixed capital can do more long-term financing than one which has a relatively small investment in fixed assets. Electric power companies, for example, have heavy investments in fixed assets and relatively little investment in current assets. The same is true of telephone companies, railroads, and gas companies. While manufacturing companies often require substantial investments in fixed assets for manufacturing purposes, they also have significant investments in inventories and receivables. Thus, as was the case for Kenwood, manufacturers generally have a more equal balance between current and fixed assets than electric utility and telephone companies.

Large retail stores often lease their quarters, but they hold substantial assets in the form of inventories and receivables. Thus, they are characterized by relatively high current asset to fixed asset mixes. At the same time, retail stores are characterized by relatively high total asset turnovers. That is, even though a large portion of their assets are in the form of current assets, it takes a relatively small investment in total assets in order to make $1 in revenues. This high asset turnover, however, is generally offset by low profit margins for many retail operations.

We need to make two points at this time. First, the level of total assets needed to support a given level of sales is significantly influenced by the industry characteristics within which the firm operates. Second, the composition of the asset structure, or current assets versus fixed assets, of an industry and of a firm within that industry is a significant factor in determining the relative proportions of their long-term and short-term financing.

The competitive structure of an industry is also significant. In an industry in which prices and profits fluctuate widely, as is the case in some basic metals industries, it is poor policy to incur a large proportion of debt. The same is true of oligopolistic industries (ones with very few producers) in which price wars can disrupt normal cost and price relationships. In industries in which demand is relatively stable and prices are regulated, such as utilities, a greater proportion of debt financing is generally safe.

The size and age of a company and stage in its financial life cycle may also influence financing decisions. A small, new company's only source of funds may be the owner and possibly his or her friends. Some long-term funds may be raised by mortgaging real estate and buying equipment on installment, and some current borrowing may be possible to meet seasonal needs. As a business grows it has more access to short-term capital from finance companies and banks. Further along, its growth and good record of profitability may enable a business to arrange longer-term financing with banks or other financial agencies such as insurance companies. At this stage in its financial development, it may also expand its group of owners as well by issuing stock to people other than the owner and a few friends.

The next stage in financial development is one in which stock is widely enough held and the financial record of a company is such that brokerage firms will make a secondary market in the company's stock. In addition to buying and selling shares of existing stock, brokerage firms at this stage may also be willing to sell stock of the company, bonds or notes in a small-scale public offering in the primary securities market.

The last stage in the financial life cycle is one in which stock is widely enough held that it is listed on a regional and finally on a national stock exchange. New issues of stock and bonds can then be sold to the general public through a large group of investment banking houses. At these two stages in its financial life cycle, a company will be able to obtain short-term credit on reasonable terms.

The growth prospects of a company also have an effect on financing decisions. If a company is growing faster than the rate at which it can finance its funds from internal sources, it must give careful consideration to a plan for long-term financing. Even if it can finance its needs in the current situation from short-term sources, it may not be wise to do so. Sound financial planning calls for raising long-term funds under the most favorable conditions. This may call for such financing at intervals of several years.

SEASONAL VARIATION

Our earlier discussion of Figure 8.2 pointed out that seasonal variations in sales affect the demand for current assets. Inventories are built up to meet seasonal needs, and receivables go up as sales increase. The peak of receivables will come after the peak in sales, the intervening time depending on the credit terms and payment practices of customers. Accounts payable will also go up as inventories are purchased, again with a lag depending on terms and payment policies. The difference between the increase in current assets and accounts payable should be financed by short-term borrowing. That is because the need for added funds will again disappear as inventories are reduced by sales and accounts receivable are collected. When a need for additional funds is financed by a short-term loan, such a loan is said to be self-liquidating since funds are made available to repay it as inventories and receivables are reduced.

SALES TREND

The trend of sales of a business also affects the current position. As sales grow, fixed assets and current assets must also grow to support the sales growth, as depicted in Figure 8.2. In fact, the growth rates for sales and assets will be the same as long as the asset-turnover ratio remains constant. This need for funds is ongoing unless the upward trend of sales is reversed, because higher asset levels are necessary to support higher sales levels. If the need for funds is met by current borrowing, the loan could not be repaid without added investment by the owners. It would have to be renewed indefinitely. The sum of money involved would go up year by year as the trend continued upward. Even if there were no seasonal need for extra funds, short-term borrowing could not be used indefinitely to supply the added funds. In time, the current ratio would drop to such a level that no financing institution would provide additional funds. The only alternative then is long-term financing.

CYCLICAL VARIATIONS

The need for current funds is also increased when there is an upswing in the business cycle or the cycle in an industry. Since the cycle is not regular in timing or degree, it is hard to predict exactly how much, or for how long, added funds will be needed. The need should be estimated for a year ahead in the budget and checked quarterly. When the volume of business decreases, the need for funds will again decrease. If the business is also growing, the need will not necessarily return to its former level because of an economic downturn. It is even possible that for a time during the downturn the need will increase temporarily. This is because the circular flow of cash slows down as receivables are collected more slowly and inventories move more slowly and drop in value.

If cyclical needs for funds are met by current borrowing, the loan will not be self-liquidating in a year. It may be self-liquidating over a complete cycle except for the increased needs due to the sales growth trend. There are hazards in financing these needs on a short-term basis. The lending institution may demand payment of all or part of the loan as business turns down. Funds may be needed more than ever at this stage of the cycle, and the need may last until receivables can be collected and inventory can be reduced. A more conservative approach would make use of longer-term financing.

Risks and Financing Decisions

The risks which affect all business operations also affect the financing of the business. These risks can be divided into three categories: (1) business risks, (2) purchasing power risk, and (3) interest rate risk.

BUSINESS RISKS

Business risks arise out of the operation of the business itself as well as from outside economic forces. The extent to which changes in the economy impact on the business operations of the firm and its industry indicates the degree of **macroeconomic business risk**. This business cycle impact, which was just discussed, is reflected in the degree of variability in a firm's sales and profits. In general, the higher the level of macroeconomic business risk, the more risky it is to use debt financing.

macroeconomic business risk
the impact on a firm from changes in the economy

Internal business risk arises from several factors. There is a risk of loss of property due to fire, flood, and the like. Such risks can and must be covered by insurance before any financing can be done. There is a risk in small and medium-sized firms of loss due to the death of a key figure in the business. Such a risk can be covered by insurance on the lives of key officials. In some cases, however, no amount of money will offset the loss sustained if a business does not progress as it did before

internal business risk
risk of the loss of property or key personnel

a key official died. Profits may be too low to attract new capital, or losses may result because of inept management in any area.

The uncertainty about profits is one of the reasons why a small or medium-sized business generally cannot do any significant amount of long-term borrowing except through mortgages on general-use real estate. The business must rely on short-term borrowing and owners' equity to meet its needs. Suppliers of short-term loans will generally be protected if a reasonable amount of insurance exists. This allows the business to continue operations in the event of misfortune and will give the lending institution time to assess the situation. If the lender feels the risk is too great, it can reduce the loan or call for payment before the business gets into financial difficulties.

PURCHASING POWER RISK

purchasing power risk
business risk of signifi-cant price increases

Some risks which are primarily of a financial nature have an effect on short-term financing policies, even though they primarily affect long-term financing. One of these financial risks is the **purchasing power risk** that results from changes in prices. As the price level increases, a business has problems since it takes more dollars to do the same volume of business. This affects short-term financing almost immediately because part of the purchasing power in cash balances and receivables is lost when prices go up. This loss is offset to the extent that current assets are financed by current or long-term borrowing. This is because loan agreements call for repayment in dollars that now have less purchasing power. However, the total dollar amount of current assets to be financed will be greater than before the price rise, which also means a larger dollar amount of net working capital will be needed.

INTEREST RATE RISK

interest rate risk
business risk of a fast rise in interest rates

Another financial risk which has some effect on short-term financing is **interest rate risk**. If interest rates rise significantly in a short period of time, the added cost may affect profit margins unless prices can be raised to offset the added cost. Such increases were especially significant in 1973 and 1974 and at the beginning of the 1980s. Increased interest costs were avoided by firms that had set up long-term financing in periods of more moderate interest rates.

Cost of Financing

Another factor to consider when making finance decisions is the cost of short-term financing compared with alternative sources of financing. Short-term interest rates on business loans have generally been lower than long-term interest rates since the depression of the 1930s. But there have been exceptions, especially in periods of tight money such as 1973–1974 and 1980–1981. When interest rates on short-term borrowing are lower than on long-term borrowing, there is an incentive to use short-term financing as much as possible.

It is usually less costly to engage in short-term financing than to sell additional equity interests in a business. Persons who purchase additional equity interests in the business will share the profits with the existing owners. During periods of normal business activity, these profits usually represent a far greater return on investment than the costs of short-term financing. Hence, the existing owners of the business can increase their own earnings through short-term financing to the extent that the earnings on assets acquired through short-term financing exceed their costs. Both forms of long-term financing, debt and equity, may therefore be more costly than the usual forms of short-term financing.

1.) Interest cost

2.) Opportunity cost

Cost can also be a limiting factor in current borrowing. As the percentage of current assets financed by current borrowing goes up, interest charges become higher. If the lending institution feels it isn't safe to increase an unsecured loan, they may lend larger sums only on a secured basis, such as an accounts-receivable loan or an inventory loan. The financing arrangements for secured loans include added clerical costs, warehouse fees, and the like, which increase the effective cost of borrowing.

Other Factors in Short-Term Financing

Short-term borrowing has several additional advantages over other forms of financing. Short-term borrowing has more flexibility than long-term financing since a business can borrow only those sums needed currently. Because of the cost and time needed to obtain long-term funds, such financing is usually used to take care of future needs. If, during a period of general business expansion, an enterprise obtains its additional current asset requirements entirely through long-term financing, it may be burdened with excess funds during a subsequent period of general business contraction. Using short-term financing along with long-term financing, therefore, creates a flexibility of operations that is not possible with long-term financing alone. As the need for assets decreases, the firm may simply repay its short-term obligations. The long-term obligations of a business may in some cases be retired (repaid) when the funds from such financing are no longer required. However, this action often involves a penalty for prepayment of the obligation.

Short-term financing also has advantages that result from continuing relationships with a bank or other financial institution. The firm that depends almost entirely upon long-term financing for its needs will not enjoy the close relationship with its bank that it might otherwise. A record of frequent borrowing from and prompt repayment to a bank is an extremely important factor in sound financial management. A bank will make every effort to accommodate business customers who do this with loans at all times. The enterprise that has not established this type of working relationship with its bank will scarcely be in a position to seek special loans when it has emergency needs. The credit experience of a business with short-term financing may be the only basis on which its potential long-term lenders will be able to judge it. Hence, the business that intends to seek long-term loans may wish to establish a good credit reputation based on its short-term financing.

Offsetting these advantages of short-term financing is the factor of frequent renewals. Even though short-term credit is usually easy to obtain, time and effort must be spent on it at frequent intervals due to the short duration of these loans. And when business decreases, a great deal of negotiation may be required to receive needed credit.

Frequent maturities also create an added element of risk. The bank or finance company can call the loan whenever it is due. Even if a revolving credit agreement is used, it runs for a limited period of time only. Borrowing costs may also rise if short-term interest rates increase. A company in a temporary slump due to the business cycle or some internal problem could possibly work out its problems in time with adequate financing. If the company had acquired funds on a long-term basis, it might have covered its difficulties, or at least have a better chance to solve them. On the other hand, if it relies heavily on short-term financing, its loans may be reduced or not renewed, which may make it nearly impossible to recover and even lead to liquidation.

MANAGEMENT OF CURRENT ASSETS

Management of current assets involves the administration of cash and marketable securities, accounts receivable, and inventories. On the one hand, the financial manager should strive to minimize the investment in current assets because of the cost of financing them. On the other hand, adequate cash and marketable securities are necessary for liquidity purposes, acceptable credit terms are necessary to maintain sales, and appropriate inventory levels must be kept to avoid running out of stock and losing sales. Successful management thus requires a continual balancing of the costs associated with investment in current assets.

Cash and Marketable Securities Management

transactions motive
demand for cash needed to carry out daily operations

Business firms should strive to minimize their cash holdings. Some cash is necessary to carry on day-to-day operations. This is the ***transactions motive*** or demand. If cash inflows and outflows could be projected with virtual certainty, the transactions demand for cash could theoretically be reduced to zero. Most businesses prepare cash flow forecasts or budgets, trying to predict the amount of cash holdings they will need. However, most firms are forced to hold some cash because of cash flow uncertainties and because compensating balances are often required on loans from commercial banks.

Marketable securities are held primarily to meet **precautionary motives**. These are demands for funds that may be caused by unpredictable events, such as delays in production or shipments or in the collection of receivables. Marketable securities can be sold to pay for such liquidity problems. In the event of strong seasonal sales patterns, marketable securities can also be used to reduce wide fluctuations in short-term financing requirements.

precautionary motive
demand for funds to handle unpredictable events

Marketable securities may also be held for **speculative motives**. In certain instances a firm might be able to take advantage of unusual cash discounts or price bargains on materials if it can pay quickly with cash. Marketable securities are easily converted into cash for such purposes.

speculative motive
demand for funds to take advantage of unexpected price bargains or discounts

For an investment to qualify as a marketable security it must be highly liquid, that is it must be readily convertible to cash without a large loss of value. Generally this requires that it have a short maturity and that an active secondary market exists so that it can be sold prior to maturity if necessary. The security must also be of high quality, with little chance that the borrower will default. U.S. Treasury bills offer the highest quality, liquidity, and marketability. Other investments that serve well as marketable securities include negotiable certificates of deposit (CDs) and commercial paper, both of which offer higher rates but are more risky and less liquid than Treasury bills. Business firms can also hold excess funds in money market accounts, or they can purchase bankers' acceptances or short-term notes of U.S. government agencies.

Accounts Receivable Management

The management of receivables involves conducting credit analysis, setting credit terms, and carrying out collection efforts. Taken together, these decision areas determine the level of investment in accounts receivable.

CREDIT ANALYSIS

Credit analysis involves appraising the credit worthiness or quality of a potential customer. That is, should credit be extended? The decision is made on the basis of the applicant's character, capacity, capital, collateral, and conditions—the five C's of credit analysis. **Character** is the ethical quality of the applicant upon which one can base a judgment about his or her willingness to pay bills. **Capacity** is the ability to pay

character
the willingness of a borrower to pay bills
capacity
the ability of a borrower to pay bills

**WORKING
CAPITAL
MANAGEMENT**

Proper management of working capital is essential to the success of a firm. Working capital represents a substantial portion of total assets, and its management requires a substantial amount of the financial manager's time. For manufacturing firms, current assets have historically accounted for more than 40 percent of total assets, while current liabilities have averaged over 25 percent of total liabilities and equity. Inventories account for a little less than 20 percent of total assets and are followed in importance by accounts receivable, which amount to slightly more than 15 percent of assets. Cash and marketable securities usually constitute about 5 percent of total assets for manufacturing firms. Working capital as a percentage of total assets is even more important for retail firms and service businesses. Current working capital percentages are available in the Federal Trade Commission's *Quarterly Financial Report for Manufacturing, Mining, and Trade.*

The importance of working capital management is further supported by a survey of chief financial officers by Lawrence J. Gitman and Charles E. Maxwell, the results of which they discuss in "Financial Activities of Major U.S. Firms: Survey and Analysis of Fortune's 1000" (*Financial Management*, Winter 1985: pp. 57–65). Twenty-seven percent of survey respondents selected working capital management as the financial activity they considered to be of greatest importance. Financial planning and budgeting ranked first with 59 percent. Furthermore, the respondents reported spending slightly more than 30 percent of their time on the management of working capital.

capital
owners' equity compared to liabilities—credit worthiness

collateral
assets to provide security for credit

conditions
the economic climate and state of the business cycle

bills and often involves an examination of liquidity ratios. **Capital** indicates the adequacy of owners' equity relative to existing liabilities as the underlying support for credit worthiness. **Collateral** reflects whether assets are available to provide security for the potential credit. **Conditions** refer to the current economic climate and state of the business cycle. They are an important consideration in assessing whether the applicant can meet credit obligations.

Once a firm has established its credit quality standards, credit analysis is used to determine whether an applicant should be granted credit, rejected, or falls into a "marginal" category. Whether or not credit should be extended to marginal applicants depends on such factors as the prevailing economic conditions and the extent to which the selling firm has excess production capacity. During periods of economic downturn and excess capacity, a selling firm may need to sell to lower quality applicants who may be slow paying but are not likely to default.

Credit-Reporting Agencies

Several sources of credit information are available to aid a firm in deciding whether to extend credit. ***Credit bureaus*** exist to obtain credit information about business firms and individuals. They are nonprofit institutions, established and supported by the businesses they serve.

credit bureau
an organization that provides credit information about businesses or individuals

The local mercantile, or business, credit bureau provides a central record for credit information on firms in the community. Bureau members submit lists of their customers to the bureau. The bureau determines the credit standing of these customers by contacting other bureau members who have extended credit to them. Thus, a member firm need only contact its credit bureau for information on prospective customers rather than deal with many individual firms.

The exchange of mercantile credit information from bureau to bureau is accomplished through the National Credit Interchange System. Credit bureau reports are factual rather than analytical, and it is up to each credit analyst to interpret the facts.

Local retail credit bureaus have been established to consolidate and distribute credit information on individuals in the community. These organizations are generally owned and operated by participating members on a nonprofit basis. A central organization known as the Associated Credit Bureaus of America enables local retail credit bureaus in the United States to transmit credit information from bureau to bureau.

U.S. businesses selling to foreign customers encounter all the problems involved in a domestic sale, such as credit checking, plus several others. Among these are increased distance, language differences, complicated shipping and government regulations, differences in legal systems, and political instability. To help exporters with these problems, the National Association of Credit Management established the Foreign Credit Interchange Bureau. Just as local credit bureaus increase their information on business credit risks by pooling credit and collection experience, so the members of the Foreign Credit Interchange Bureau have established a central file of information covering several decades of credit experience. The Bureau is located in New York to serve the numerous export and financial organizations there that do business overseas.

Some private firms also operate as credit-reporting agencies. The best known is Dun & Bradstreet, which has been in operation for well over a century and provides credit information on businesses of all kinds. The information that is assembled and evaluated is brought into the company through many channels. The company employs full- and part-time employees for direct investigation, communicates directly with business establishments by mail to supplement information files, and obtains the financial statements of companies being evaluated. All information filed with public authorities and financial and trade papers is carefully gathered and analyzed to produce a credit analysis. The basic service supplied to the manufacturers, wholesalers, banks, and insurance companies who subscribe to Dun & Bradstreet is rendered in two ways: through written reports on individual businesses and through a reference book.

A Dun & Bradstreet report is typically divided into five sections: (1) rating and summary, (2) trade payments, (3) financial information, (4) operation and location, and (5) history. In addition, they publish a composite reference book of ratings on thousands of manufacturers, wholesalers, retailers, and other businesses six times per year.

CREDIT TERMS AND COLLECTION EFFORTS

trade credit
credit extended to customers for purchases

Credit extended on purchases to a firm's customers is called **trade credit** and will be discussed more fully in Chapter 9. This credit appears as accounts payable on the balance sheet of the customer, and as receivables to the seller. The seller sets the terms of the credit. For example, the firm might require full payment in 60 days, expressed as net/60. If all customers pay promptly in 60 days, this would result in a receivables turnover of 360/60 or six times a year.[1] Thus, annual net sales of $720,000 would require an average receivables investment of $120,000. A change in credit terms or in the enforcement of the terms through the collection effort will alter the average investment in receivables. The imposition of net/50 day terms would lead to an increase in the receivables turnover to 7.2 (360/50) times and the average investment in receivables would decline to $100,000 ($720,000/7.2). If it costs, say, 15 percent to finance assets, then the $20,000 reduction in receivables would result in a savings of $3,000 ($20,000 × 15%).

We are assuming that a reduction in the credit period and in the receivables portion of the short-term operating cycle will not cause lost sales. The financial manager must be very careful not to impose credit terms that will lower sales and cause lost profits, which would more than offset any financing cost savings.

The collection effort involves administering past due accounts. Techniques include sending letters, making telephone calls, and even making personal visits for very large customers with past due bills. If the customer continues to fail to pay a bill, then the account may be turned over to a commercial collection firm. If this fails, the last resort is to take legal action.

average collection period
the average amount of time that accounts receivable are outstanding

A lax collection policy may result in the average collection period for receivables being substantially longer than the credit period stated in the terms. The **average collection period** is the accounts receivables divided by the net sales divided by 360. For example, a firm might sell on credit terms of net/60 days and have net sales of $720,000 and an

---

1.   The turnover of current asset accounts such as receivables and inventories, like total assets turnover, is an asset utilization ratio. A higher ratio implies better usage of assets.

accounts receivable balance of $150,000. For this firm, the average collection period is:

$$\frac{\text{Accounts receivable}}{\text{Net sales} \div 360} = \frac{\$150,000}{\$720,000 \div 360} = \frac{\$150,000}{\$2,000} = 75 \text{ days}$$

This shows that the accounts receivable are outstanding an average of 75 days instead of the 60-day credit period. Tightening the collection effort might reduce the average collection period to 60 days and the accounts receivable balance to $120,000.

Lowering a firm's credit standards or customer credit quality will also cause the average collection period to lengthen—poorer quality customers are slower payers. Thus the financial manager must balance the advantages of increased sales from more customers against higher receivable investments and increased collection costs.

Inventory Management

Inventory administration is primarily a production management function. The length of the production process and the production manager's willingness to accept delays will influence the amount invested in raw materials and work-in-process. The amount of finished goods on hand may vary depending on the firm's willingness to accept stockouts and lost sales.

Costs of owning raw materials, such as financing, storage, and insurance, need to be balanced against the costs of ordering the materials. Production managers attempt to balance these costs by determining the optimal number of units to order that will minimize inventory costs of total raw materials.

Financial managers are concerned with minimizing the overall inventory investment in order to hold down financing costs. In other words, they try to increase the use of these assets by achieving a high inventory turnover. Let's assume that a firm's cost of goods sold is $600,000 and it has inventories on hand of $100,000. We measure the **inventory turnover** as follows:

inventory turnover
the cost of goods sold divided by inventories

$$\frac{\text{Cost of goods sold}}{\text{Inventories}} = \frac{\$600,000}{\$100,000} = 6 \text{ times}$$

If the firm is able to increase its inventory turnover to, say, eight times, then the investment in inventories could be reduced to $75,000 ($600,000/8) and some financing costs would be saved. However, if a tight inventory policy is imposed, lost sales due to stockouts could result in lost profits that more than offset financing cost savings. Thus the financial manager must balance possible savings against potential added costs when managing investments in inventories.

The "just in time" inventory control system is gaining increased acceptance by firms that are trying to reduce the amount of inventories they must carry. Under this system, substantial coordination is required between the manufacturer and its suppliers so that materials needed in the manufacturing process are delivered just in time to avoid halts in production. For example, automobile manufacturers who used to keep a two-week supply of certain parts now place orders on a daily basis and expect daily shipment and delivery.

KEY TERMS

acid-test ratio
average collection period
capacity
capital
character
collateral
conditions
credit bureau
current ratio
hedging
interest rate risk

internal business risk
inventory turnover
macroeconomic business risk
net working capital
precautionary motive
purchasing power risk
speculative motive
trade credit
transactions motive
working capital

DISCUSSION QUESTIONS

1. How is the process of financial planning used to estimate asset investment requirements?
2. Explain how financial planning is used to determine a firm's external financing requirements.
3. Explain how businesses should strive to finance their asset structures with short-term and long-term funds.
4. Briefly describe a manufacturing firm's short-term operating cycle. How is its length determined?
5. Explain the relationship among current assets, current liabilities, and net working capital. Why is it necessary to have adequate net working capital?
6. What factors affect the nature of the demand for short-term versus long-term funds?
7. Describe the various risks that should be analyzed in making financing decisions.

8. Prepare a list of advantages and disadvantages of short-term borrowing relative to other financing decisions.
9. Describe several motives or reasons for holding cash and marketable securities. What characteristics should an investment have to qualify as an acceptable marketable security?
10. What are the five C's of credit analysis?
11. Describe the various credit-reporting agencies that provide information on business credit applicants.
12. How do credit terms and collection efforts affect the investment in accounts receivable?
13. How is the financial manager involved in the management of inventories?

PROBLEMS

1. The Jackman Company had sales of $1,000,000 and net income of $50,000 last year. Sales are expected to increase by 20 percent next year. Selected year-end balance sheet items were:

Current assets	$400,000
Fixed assets	500,000
Total assets	$900,000
Current liabilities	$200,000
Long-term debt	200,000
Owners' equity	500,000
Total liabilities and equity	$900,000

   a. Express each balance sheet item as a percent of last year's sales.
   b. Estimate the new asset investment requirement for next year, assuming no excess production capacity.
   c. Estimate the amount of internally generated funds for next year, assuming all profits will be retained in the firm.
   d. If all current liabilities are expected to change spontaneously with sales, what will be their dollar increase next year?
   e. Estimate Jackman's external financing requirements for next year.
2. The Kenergy Company is planning to manufacture and sell electronic alarm clocks. Raw materials for each clock will be $3 and direct labor per clock will amount to $6. Fixed administrative overhead costs will amount to $24,000. The clocks are expected to sell for $15 each.
   a. Find the breakeven point in units. What is the sales breakeven point?
   b. How much profit or loss will occur if 5,000 clocks are sold? What if only 3,000 clocks are sold?

3. Pretty Lady Cosmetic Products has an average production process time of 40 days. Finished goods are kept on hand for an average of 15 days before they are sold. Accounts receivable are outstanding an average of 35 days, and the firm receives 40 days of credit on its purchases from suppliers.
   a. Estimate the average length of the firm's short-term operating cycle. How often would the cycle turn over in a year?
   b. Assume net sales of $1,200,000 and cost of goods sold of $900,000. Determine the average investment in accounts receivable, inventories, and accounts payable. What would be the net financing need considering only these three accounts?

4. The Robinson Company has the following current assets and current liabilities for these two years:

	1990	1991
Cash and marketable securities	$ 50,000	$ 50,000
Accounts receivable	300,000	350,000
Inventories	350,000	500,000
Total current assets	$700,000	$900,000
Accounts payable	$200,000	$250,000
Bank loan	-0-	150,000
Accruals	150,000	200,000
Total current liabilities	$350,000	$600,000

   a. Calculate the net working capital for Robinson in 1990 and 1991. What happened?
   b. Compare the current ratios between the two years. Also compare the acid-test ratios between 1990 and 1991. Comment on your findings.

5. The Robinson Company from Problem 4 had net sales of $1,200,000 in 1990 and $1,300,000 in 1991.
   a. Determine the receivables turnover in each year.
   b. Calculate the average collection period for each year.
   c. Based on the receivables turnover for 1990, estimate the investment in receivables if net sales were $1,300,000 in 1991. How much of a reduction in the 1991 receivables occurred?

6. The Robinson Company had a cost of goods sold of $1,000,000 in 1990 and $1,200,000 in 1991.
   a. Calculate the inventory turnover for each year. Comment on your findings.
   b. What would have been the amount of inventories in 1991 if the 1990 turnover ratio had been maintained?

7. Following are financial statements for the Genatron Manufacturing Corporation for the years 1990 and 1991:

BALANCE SHEET	1990	1991
Cash	$ 50,000	$ 40,000
Accounts receivable	200,000	260,000
Inventory	450,000	500,000
Total current assets	$ 700,000	$ 800,000
Fixed assets, net	300,000	400,000
Total assets	$1,000,000	$1,200,000
Bank loan, 10%	$ 90,000	$ 90,000
Accounts payable	130,000	170,000
Accruals	50,000	70,000
Total current liabilities	$ 270,000	$ 330,000
Long-term debt, 12%	300,000	400,000
Common stock, $10 par	300,000	300,000
Capital surplus	50,000	50,000
Retained earnings	80,000	120,000
Total liabilities and equity	$1,000,000	$1,200,000

INCOME STATEMENT	1990	1991
Net sales	$1,300,000	$1,500,000
Cost of goods sold	780,000	900,000
Gross profit	$ 520,000	$ 600,000
General and administrative	150,000	150,000
Marketing	130,000	150,000
Depreciation	40,000	53,000
Interest	45,000	57,000
Earnings before taxes	$ 155,000	$ 190,000
Income taxes	62,000	76,000
Net income	$ 93,000	$ 114,000

a. Calculate Genatron's dollar amount of net working capital in each year.
b. Calculate the current ratio and the acid-test ratio in each year.
c. Calculate the average collection period and the inventory turnover ratio in each year.
d. What changes in the management of Genatron's current assets seem to have occurred between the two years?

8. Genatron Manufacturing Corporation is interested in estimating its short-term cash operating cycle for 1991. Begin by calculating the inventory turnover, the accounts receivable turnover, and the accounts payable turnover. Then determine the short-term operating cycle using a 360-day year.

9. Genatron Manufacturing expects its sales to increase by 10 percent in 1992. Estimate the firm's external financing needs by using the

percent-of-sales method for the 1991 data. Assume that no excess capacity exists and that one-half of the 1992 net income will be retained in the business.

10. Genatron wants to estimate what will happen to its income before interest and taxes if its net sales change from the 1991 level of $1,500,000. Refer to Genatron's 1991 income statement, shown in Problem 7, where the income before interest and taxes is $247,000. Assume that the cost of goods sold are variable expenses and that the other operating expenses are fixed.

   a. Calculate the expected amount of income before interest and taxes for both a 10 percent decrease and a 10 percent increase in net sales for next year.

   b. Determine the percentage change in income before interest and taxes given your calculations in part a., and determine the degree of operating leverage.

11. Associated Containers Company is planning to manufacture and sell plastic pencil holders. Direct labor and raw materials will be $2.28 per unit. Fixed costs are $15,300 and the expected selling price is $3.49 per unit. Note: Use the Cost-Volume-Profit Analysis tool to solve this problem.

   a. Determine the breakeven point (where operating profit is zero) in units and dollars.

   b. How much profit or loss before interest and taxes will there be if 10,825 units are sold?

   c. What will the selling price per unit have to be if 13,650 units are sold in order to break even?

   d. How much will variable costs per unit have to be in order to break even if only 9,500 units are expected to be sold and the selling price is $3.49?

12. This problem uses the two years of financial statements data provided in Problem 7 for the Genatron Manufacturing Corporation. Note: Use the Financial Statement Analysis tool.

   a. Calculate and compare each current assets account as a percentage of total assets for that year.

   b. Calculate and compare each current liabilities account as a percentage of total liabilities and equities for that year.

   c. Calculate the current ratio and the acid-test ratio for each year. Describe the changes in liquidity, if any, that occurred between the two years.

   d. Calculate the average collection period and the inventory turnover for each year. Describe the changes that occurred, if any, in the management of accounts receivable and inventory between the two years.

SELF-TEST QUESTIONS

1. The principle of hedging calls for:
    a. matching of average maturities of a firm's assets with its liabilities and equity
    b. matching of dollar amounts of current assets with fixed assets
    c. matching of short-term financing with fixed assets
    d. matching of fixed assets with sales volume

2. Which one of the following activities is *not* a major component of the short-term cash operating cycle?
    a. manufacturing process
    b. selling effort
    c. collection period
    d. asset investment decisions

3. Which one of the following categories of risk is *not* considered to affect the financing of business firms?
    a. macroeconomics business risk
    b. transactions risk
    c. purchasing power risk
    d. interest rate risk

4. Business firms hold cash and marketable securities for which of the following reasons or motives?
    a. transactions, precautionary, and goodwill motives
    b. precautionary, speculative, and goodwill motives
    c. transactions, precautionary, and speculative motives
    d. precautionary, goodwill, and transactions motives

5. Management of current assets does *not* involve which one of the following areas?
    a. cash and marketable securities
    b. accounts receivable
    c. inventory
    d. plant and equipment

SELF-TEST PROBLEM

The Deuter Steel Products company has an average production process time of 30 days. Finished goods are kept on hand for an average of 15 days before they are sold. Accounts receivable are outstanding on average for 30 days and Deuter receives 40 days of credit on its purchases from suppliers.

a. Estimate the average length of Deuter's short-term operating cycle. How often would the cycle turn over in a year?

b. Assume that Deuter has net sales of $1,200,000 and a cost of goods sold of $1,000,000. Determine the average investment in accounts receivable, inventories, and accounts payable. What would be the net financing need considering only these three accounts?

SUGGESTED READINGS

Brigham, Eugene F. *Fundamentals of Financial Management*, 5e. Hinsdale, IL: The Dryden Press, 1989. Chaps. 8 and 19.

Gitman, Lawrence J. and Charles E. Maxwell. "Financial Activities of Major U.S. Firms: Survey and Analysis of Fortune's 1000." Financial Management (Winter 1985): 57–65.

Harrington, Diana R., and Brent D. Wilson. *Corporate Financial Analysis*, 3e. Homewood, IL: BPI/Irwin, 1990. Chaps. 2 and 3.

Pinches, George E. *Essentials of Financial Management*, 3e. New York: Harper & Row, 1990. Part Six.

Richards, Verlyn D., and Eugene J. Laughlin. "A Cash Conversion Cycle Approach to Liquidity Analysis." *Financial Management* (Spring 1980): 32–38.

Welshans, Merle T. "Financial Management." *Encyclopedia of Professional Management*. New York: McGraw-Hill, 1985. Pp. 304–313.

ANSWERS TO SELF-TEST QUESTIONS   1. a   2. d   3. b   4. c   5. d

SOLUTION TO SELF-TEST PROBLEM

a. Inventory cycle   45 days (30 + 15)
    Accounts receivable cycle   30 days
                                              75 days
    Accounts payable cycle   –40 days
    Short-term operating cycle   35 days

    Operating cycle turnover = 360/35 = 10.3 times

b. Inventory turnover = 360/45 = 8 times
    Cost of goods sold = $1,000,000
    Average inventory investment = $1,000,000/8 = $125,000
    Accounts receivable turnover = 360/30 = 12 times
    Net sales = $1,200,000
    Average accounts receivable investment = $1,200,000/12 = $100,000
    Accounts payable turnover = 360/40 = 9 times
    Cost of goods sold = $1,000,000
    Average accounts payable financing = $100,000/9 = $111,111

    Net financing needs:
    Inventory investment $125,000
    Accounts receivable investment   100,000
                                             $225,000
    Less accounts payable financing   111,111
                                             $113,889

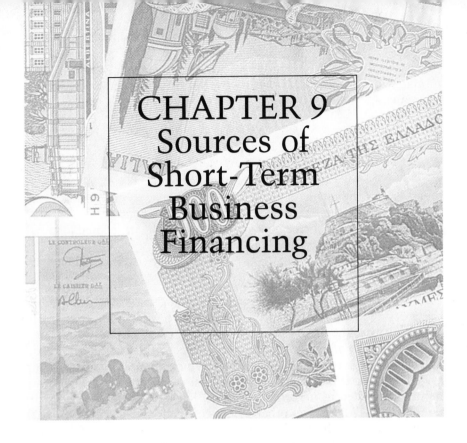

CHAPTER 9
Sources of Short-Term Business Financing

After studying this chapter, you should be able to:

- Identify the types of unsecured loans made by commercial banks to business borrowers.
- Describe the use of accounts receivable, inventory, and other sources of security for bank loans.
- Explain the characteristics, terms, and costs of trade credit.
- Explain the role of commercial finance companies in providing short-term business financing.
- Briefly describe how factors function as a source of short-term business financing.
- Describe how the Small Business Administration aids businesses in meeting short-term borrowing needs.
- Describe how and why commercial paper is used as a source of short-term financing by large corporations.

The tremendous resources of the nation's banking system make commercial banks the largest provider of short-term loan funds for businesses. Short-term funds also come in the form of trade credit extended between businesses. Other important sources of short-term funds are commercial finance companies, factors, and the Small Business Administration. Commercial paper is yet another source of short-term financing.

COMMERCIAL BANK LENDING OPERATIONS

The typical loan from a bank to a business is unsecured. When future prospects for the business are good, the pledge of specific assets of the business is not needed to secure the loan. Although in recent years many banks require a pledge of specific assets, the unsecured loan still remains the primary type of loan arrangement.

Bank Lines of Credit

line of credit
amount of credit a bank will extend to a business

list 3 or 4 things

There is often an agreement between a business and a bank regarding the amount of credit that the business will have at its disposal. The loan limit that the bank establishes for each of its business customers is called a **line of credit**. Lines of credit cost the business only the normal interest for the period during which money is actually borrowed. Under this arrangement, the business does not wait until money is needed to negotiate the loan. Rather, it files the necessary financial statements and other evidences of financial condition with the bank prior to the need for credit. The banker is interested in how well the business has fared in the past and in its probable future. This is because the line of credit is generally extended for a year at a time. The banker may require that other debts of the business be subordinated to, or come after, the claim of the bank.

Under a line of credit program, major changes in the operation of a business may be subject to the approval of the bank. A major shift or change in management personnel or in the manufacture or sale of particular products can greatly influence the future success of a company. Hence, the bank, having contributed substantially to the resources of the business, is necessarily interested in these activities. The bank may also seek information on the business through organized credit bureaus, through contact with other businesses having dealings with the firm, and through other banks.

In the event that the business needs more money than was anticipated at the time the line of credit was set up, it may request the bank to increase the limit on its line of credit. It must be prepared, however, to offer very sound evidence of the need for additional funds and the ability of the business to repay the increased loan from business operations. A request for an increased line of credit frequently occurs when a business is growing and needs more and more capital to make its growth possible. Although banks generally insist that expansion be financed with long-term funds, following the principle of hedging discussed in Chapter 8, they may assist growth by temporarily providing a part of the increased needs. The business that is unable to obtain additional unsecured credit from its bank may seek a secured loan from the bank or other lenders. These other forms of borrowing are discussed later in this chapter.

Nearly all banks require a **compensating balance** of from 10 to 20 percent of unsecured loans outstanding to be kept on deposit by the business. The most frequently cited justification for this requirement is that since banks cannot lend without deposits, bank borrowers should be required to be depositors also. Banks usually also require their business customers to "clean up" their lines of credit for a specified period of time each year—generally a minimum of two weeks. That is, they pay off their debts to the bank for this period of time.

*compensating balance
the average amount a
borrower must keep on
deposit with the lender*

Revolving Credit Agreements

The officers of a business may feel rather certain that an agreed upon line of credit will provide the necessary capital requirements for the coming year. However, there is always the possibility that conditions will change and the bank may have to reduce or withdraw its extension of credit. This possibility is normally included in the original agreement. The bank is obligated to make good on its line of credit only so long as conditions make it possible to do so.

The well-established business with an excellent credit rating may be able to obtain a revolving credit agreement. A **revolving credit agreement** is a commitment in the form of a standby agreement for a guaranteed line of credit. In addition to paying interest for the use of money for the period of the loan, the business must pay a commission or fee to the bank based on the amount of money it has on call during the agreement period. This additional commission is charged because the bank must meet loan demands regardless of changes in business conditions.

*revolving credit
agreement
a commitment by a
bank to a guaranteed
line of credit*

Accounts Receivable Financing

The business that does not qualify for an unsecured bank loan or that has emergency needs for funds in excess of its line of credit may offer a pledge of accounts receivable as security. This banking practice stems in part from the competition banks have experienced from commercial finance companies, which will be discussed later. When banks use accounts receivable as security, they make the same sort of credit investigation as they do for unsecured loans. Particular attention is given to the collection practices of the business and to certain characteristics of its accounts receivable.

The bank may spot-check the receivables of the firm and may in some cases analyze each account to determine how quickly the firm's

HOW CHANGES
IN COMMERCIAL
BANK LENDING
RATES AFFECT
THE ECONOMY

The cost of short-term bank borrowing to finance working capital needs often determines whether businesses make a profit. During periods of very high bank rates, the cost of carrying inventories and accounts receivable may be far greater than a firm's profit margins. The problem is often compounded by the fact that short-term interest rates are usually high when an economic downturn begins. Inventories tend to build up and credit customers begin to pay more slowly during the early stages of an economic downturn. Paying high short-term interest rates can frequently cause operating losses and even bankruptcy for many firms.

Financial managers found the early 1980s to be a very difficult time for financing and managing their working capital. The *prime rate*, which is the lowest rate offered by commercial banks to their highest quality business borrowers—others pay higher rates—reached a historical high of 21.5 percent in December 1980. This, coupled with unstable business conditions, caused major operating problems for U.S. businesses. Year-end prime rates for the 1980s, as reported in the *Federal Reserve Bulletin*, were:

YEAR	PRIME RATE
1980	21.50%
1981	15.75
1982	11.50
1983	11.00
1984	10.75
1985	9.50
1986	7.50
1987	8.75
1988	10.50
1989	10.50

Economic growth and business profits typically result from relatively low short-term bank borrowing rates. Because of the substantial decrease in prime rate levels and more stable economic conditions, many business financial managers found it easier to manage their firms' working capital during the last half of the 1980s.

customers make payments. It is also important for the bank to know something about these customers. Their ability to pay their debts will strongly influence how well the business applying for the loan will be able to collect payment.

In addition, the bank studies the type and quality of goods that are sold. For if the merchandise is inferior, there may be objections from the customers and hence slower payment of bills. Accounts receivable are of little value as security for a loan if large quantities of merchandise are returned and the amount of accounts receivable is reduced accordingly.

ACCOUNTS RECEIVABLE LOAN LIMITS

The Bank Management Commission of the American Bankers Association recommends that a loan based on the security of accounts receivable should generally be no more than 80 percent of the gross receivables. Furthermore, it recommends that this amount should be reduced by any trade discounts allowed to customers and by the normal percentage of merchandise returns. If there is reason to believe that many of the loan applicant's customers are not suitable risks, or if adequate credit ratings are not available, the bank will lend a lower percentage of the face value of the receivables.

TECHNICAL FEATURES OF ACCOUNTS RECEIVABLE FINANCING

Under the accounts receivable loan arrangement, there is, in addition to the basic interest charge, a fee to cover the extra work that is needed for such a loan. The bank must periodically check the books of the business in order to see that it is, in fact, living up to the terms of the agreement. At the time the loan is made, individual accounts on the ledger of the business are clearly designated as having been pledged for the bank loan. Only those accounts suitable for collateral purposes for the bank are designated. When these accounts are paid in full or become unsatisfactory, they are replaced by other accounts.

In addition to designating pledged accounts in the ledger of the borrowing firm, the bank also requires a schedule of the accounts and a copy of all shipping invoices involved. The business must also execute an assignment, or legal transfer, of these accounts to the bank. A sample copy of a promissory note for this type of loan is shown in Figure 9.1.

As the business receives remittances on the accounts that have been assigned for the loan, they must be turned over to the bank separately from other funds. The bank also reserves the right to make a direct audit of the business' books from time to time and to have an outside accounting firm examine the books periodically. The accounting firm frequently verifies a certain percentage of the accounts receivable by mail, much as it does in a regular audit. Checking the accounts in this routine manner leaves customers of the business unaware that their accounts have been pledged as collateral for a loan.

Businesses that use their receivables as collateral for bank loans often prefer to keep this knowledge from their customers. It could be

FIGURE 9.1   Promissory Note

$ 24,744.00   New York   October 15,   19--

Ninety days _____ after date we promise to pay

to the order of Irving Trust Company

Twenty-four thousand seven hundred forty-four no/100-------------- Dollars,

at IRVING TRUST COMPANY, NEW YORK. Value received

If any maker, endorser or guarantor hereof shall suspend business, become insolvent, offer settlement to any creditors, commit an act of bankruptcy, make any bulk sale, assignment for the benefit of creditors, mortgage, pledge or transfer, of accounts receivable or other property, in trust or otherwise, or any false representation or fail to furnish information or permit inspection of books or records on demand of the Trust Company, or fail to pay any obligation when due, or there be filed by or against it any petition in bankruptcy or proceeding under any law relating to the relief of debtors, or for the appointment of a receiver of its property, or if an execution or warrant of attachment be issued against any of its property, or any judgment be entered against it, or if an individual, he shall die, or if a corporation, it be dissolved or its capital be impaired, or if for any other cause the protection of the Trust Company in its sole discretion so requires, all liabilities of the undersigned to the Trust Company, including this note, shall, at the option of the Trust Company, mature and become due and payable without demand or notice, which are hereby waived. The undersigned further promise(s) to pay to the Trust Company the expenses, including reasonable attorneys' fees, incurred in the collection or attempted collection of this note. If this note is signed by more than one maker they shall be jointly and severally bound.

THE NOBEL CORPORATION

Authorized Signer

seen as an indication of weakness on the part of the business. Although businesses using this form of loan arrangement are frequently in a financially weak condition, this is not always the case. Some firms that are financially sound use accounts receivable financing because they feel it has advantages for them over other loan arrangements. Manufacturing companies appear to be the largest users of accounts receivable financing. In particular, this is true of manufacturers of food products, textiles, leather products, furniture, paper, iron, steel, and machinery.

Inventory Loans

A business may use its inventory as collateral for a loan in much the same manner that it may borrow on its receivables. The bank evaluates the physical condition of the firm's inventory and the inventory's general composition. Staple items that are in constant demand serve well as collateral for a loan. Style and fashion items such as designer clothes are not as acceptable as collateral except for brief periods of time. Firms that use inventory as collateral usually do so because they are not in a position to obtain further funds on an unsecured basis.

The bank may protect itself when lending to a business that is using inventory as collateral either by having title to the goods assigned to the bank or by taking a chattel mortgage (a mortgage on personal property) on the inventory. In other cases, a trust receipt instrument may be used. When title to the inventory is assigned to the bank, clear title to this inventory cannot pass from the business to its customers until the loan is paid off or other collateral is substituted for the merchandise. Under a trust receipt arrangement, the bank retains ownership of the goods until they are actually sold in the regular course of business.

WAREHOUSING INVENTORY

In some cases when inventory is used as collateral, the bank may insist that the inventory be placed in a bonded and licensed warehouse. The receipt issued by the warehouse is then turned over to the bank, which holds it until the loan is repaid. A sample copy of a warehouse receipt for stored merchandise is shown in Figure 9.2.

Need for Field Warehousing

It is frequently inconvenient for a business to deliver large bulky items of inventory to a warehouse for storage. This problem is solved by using field warehouses. A field warehousing enterprise has the power to establish a *field warehouse* on the grounds of the borrowing business establishment. Field warehouses differ from the typical public warehouse in that (1) they serve a single customer—that customer on whose property the field warehouse is established, and (2) they exist only until the loan is repaid. The field warehouse could be a cattle ranch, a grain elevator, or a lake on which logs are temporarily stored.

field warehouse
a warehouse set up on the property of a borrowing business to store collateral inventory

FIGURE 9.2   Warehouse Receipt

LAWRENCE SYSTEMS, INC.

ORIGINAL WAREHOUSE RECEIPT

NOT INSURED

NON-NEGOTIABLE

RECEIVED FROM: Wood Lumber and Moulding Company
FOR STORAGE IN   Any Town, Any State
LOCATED AT (STREET)   111 A Street

SUBJECT TO ALL THE TERMS AND CONDITIONS CONTAINED HEREIN AND ON THE REVERSE SIDE HEREOF FOR THE ACCOUNT OF AND TO BE DELIVERED WITHOUT SURRENDER OF THIS WAREHOUSE RECEIPT UPON WRITTEN INSTRUCTION OF

FILL IN → ___ First National Bank of Any Town ___
WAREHOUSE RECEIPT HOLDER

S1-5	02	1218A	S154	11-12-83	51734	Depositor's Declared Values for which the Warehouseman Assumes No Responsibility
RCPT. TYPE	REG. CODE	WAREHOUSE NO.	HOLDER NO.	DATE	RECEIPT NO.	

ITEM	CODE NO.	NO. OF UNITS	SAID TO BE OR CONTAIN	UNIT VALUES	EXTENSION (DJM)
	0001	1,151	M. bd. ft. logs pine	105.00	120,855.00
	0002	958	M. bd. ft. logs white fir	80.00	76,640.00
	0003	1,523	M. bd. ft. logs douglas fir	105.00	159,915.00
	0004	621	M. bd. ft. logs cedar	65.00	40,365.00
		4,253			397,775.00

CAUTION: LAWRENCE SYSTEMS, INC. WILL NOT BE RESPONSIBLE FOR THE QUANTITIES SHOWN HEREON UNLESS TOTAL NUMBER OF UNITS IS TYPED BELOW.

TOTAL ► Four million, two hundred fifty-three thousand board feet

Stored under field warehousing arrangement. Subject to lien for storage, handling and other charges as per contract and lease with the industry served. A general lien is claimed for charges and expenses in regard to other goods deposited by the same depositor. Transfers of merchandise not complete unless made on the books of the warehouse company.

"By agreement goods of same kind or grade may be commingled and where authorized by law unlike units shall be deemed fungible and treated as equivalents."

LAWRENCE SYSTEMS, INC.

BY ► _____
BONDED WAREHOUSE MANAGER
(Do not accept this warehouse receipt if any corrections or changes appear hereon.)

In setting up a field warehouse, it is usually necessary for the warehouse operator to first obtain a lease on that portion of the property which is to be used for warehousing purposes. Then he or she must establish fences, barriers, walks, and other postings to indicate clear possession of the property. This is done to avoid accidental or deliberate removal of stored items during the general course of business operations. A guard may be posted in order to check on the safety of the warehoused goods, or a room may be sealed and the seal inspected periodically to make sure the company is honoring its agreement.

There must also be a complete statement of the commodities or items that are to be warehoused, and agreements must be made about the maintenance of the property, proper fire precautions, insurance, and other necessary physical requirements. Under certain circumstances, the warehouse operator is authorized to release a certain quantity of goods by the day, week, or month to make possible a rotation of merchandise. Under this arrangement, physical inventories must be taken from time to time.

Extent of Field Warehousing

Field warehouses are in operation throughout the United States but are concentrated in the central and Pacific coast regions. It is estimated that from 10,000 to 12,000 field warehouses are in existence at any given time. Nearly all forms of merchandise that may be safely warehoused have at one time or another been stored in them. Canned goods, miscellaneous groceries, lumber, timber, and building supplies fill about two-fifths of all field warehouses in this country. Those banks that make loans involving commodities will generally accept field warehouse receipts as collateral.

COST OF INVENTORY LOANS

Inventory loans are somewhat more expensive than unsecured loans to business borrowers. The higher cost is due in part to the cost of warehousing operations, and also because the borrower's credit rating may be low. Bank interest rates for warehouse loans are ordinarily somewhat higher than for unsecured loans.[1] In addition, a warehouse fee of from ¾ of 1 percent to 2½ percent of the loan, depending upon size and other factors, must be paid.

Inventory loans have become popular in part because of factors influencing the size of inventory holdings. Businesses want to take advantage of cash discounts on volume purchases when they can get the cash at reasonable rates. Constant production throughout the year rather than just prior to anticipated sales results in a firm's holding a

---

1.   Inventory loans, like receivable loans, are also made by commercial finance companies. Their interest rates are usually higher than those charged by banks.

larger average inventory. This, in turn, requires a larger commitment of inventory funds by the company. These funds may be obtained by using the inventories themselves, stored in a warehouse, as the basis for a bank loan.

Loans Secured by Stocks and Bonds

Stocks and bonds are often used as collateral for short-term loans. These securities are welcomed as collateral primarily because of their marketability and their value. If the securities are highly marketable, and if their value is high enough to cover the amount of the loan requested even if the stock's price goes down somewhat, a banker will not hesitate to extend a loan. Securities listed on one of the national exchanges are preferred since frequent price quotations are available. Banks will usually loan from 60 to 70 percent of the market value of listed stocks, and from 70 to 80 percent of the market value of high-grade bonds. In 1934 the Board of Governors of the Federal Reserve System established maximum percent-of-market-value limits on loans secured by stocks or bonds when the purpose of the loan is to purchase or deal in listed stocks.[2]

Only assignable stocks and bonds are eligible for this type of collateral financing, with the exception of nonassignable U.S. Savings Bonds. When assignable securities are placed with a bank, a **stock or bond power** is executed that authorizes the bank to sell or otherwise dispose of the securities should it become necessary to do so to protect the loan. (See Figure 9.3.)

stock or bond power *authorizes a lender to dispose of securities assigned as loan collateral*

Other Forms of Security for Bank Loans

Security for short-term bank loans may also include such things as the cash surrender value of life insurance policies, guarantee of a loan by a party other than the borrower, notes, and acceptances.

LIFE INSURANCE LOANS

Small businesses frequently find it possible to obtain needed short-term bank loans by pledging the cash surrender value, or the amount they will receive upon cancellation, of life insurance policies. The policies must be assignable, and many insurance companies insist that their own assignment forms be used for such purposes. Because of the safety afforded the bank by the cash surrender values, these loans usually carry a lower interest rate than loans on other types of business collateral. Another reason for the favorable rates is that the borrower could borrow directly from the insurance company. Even so, bank

2.   The operations of the securities exchanges and the limitations on borrowing for purposes of dealing in securities are discussed in Chapter 13.

FIGURE 9.3   Irrevocable Stock or Bond Power

```
                    IRREVOCABLE STOCK OR BOND POWER

         FOR VALUE RECEIVED, the undersigned does (do) hereby sell, assign and transfer to


    The Third National Bank of St. Louis, Missouri

                                                        53-0822721
                                                  (SOCIAL SECURITY OR TAXPAYER IDENTIFYING NO.)
                         100     shares of the Common stock of  Black River Timber Company
    IF STOCK,
    COMPLETE          represented by Certificate(s) No(s).  143001                    inclusive,
    THIS
    PORTION           standing in the name of the undersigned on the books of said Company.


    IF BONDS,                                          bonds of
    COMPLETE          in the principal amount of $              , No(s).               inclusive,
    THIS
    PORTION           standing in the name of the undersigned on the books of said Company.


              The undersigned does (do) hereby irrevocably constitute and appoint
                         my             attorney to transfer the said stock or bond(s), as the case may be,
              on the books of said Company, with full power of substitution in the premises.
    Dated  June 17, 19--

        IMPORTANT – READ CAREFULLY
    The signature(s) to this Power must corre-          Penelope H. Plack
    spond with the name(s) as written upon the
    face of the certificate(s) or bond(s) in every
    particular without alteration or enlargement
    or any change whatever. Signature guarantee
    should be made by a member or member organ-       (PERSON(S) EXECUTING THIS POWER SIGN(S) HERE)
    ization of the New York Stock Exchange, mem-
    bers of other Exchanges having signatures on
    file with transfer agent or by a commercial            SIGNATURE GUARANTEED
    bank or trust company having its principal
    office or correspondent in the City of New York.
```

interest rates have been higher in recent years than those of insurance companies to their policyholders. As a result, there has been an increase in the number of these loans made by insurance companies. The functions and financial operations of insurance companies are covered in Chapter 12.

COMAKER LOANS

Many small businesses find it necessary to provide the bank with a guarantor in the form of a cosigner to their notes. It is expected that the cosigner has a credit rating at least as satisfactory as, and usually far better than, the firm requesting the loan.

DISCOUNTING NOTES AND ACCEPTANCES

The act of discounting a credit instrument (notes or acceptances) with a bank may technically be considered as a sale rather than a pledge of collateral. However, because the discounted instruments are endorsed by the seller, the seller is contingently liable. That is, the seller remains liable in the event of default. The discount of credit instruments by a firm with its bank is a form of bank credit.

Short-term financing available to businesses, including multinational corporations (MNCs), is similar worldwide. Loans from banks are the most important source of short-term interest-bearing financing around the world. As in the United States, these bank loans are frequently in the form of lines of credit.

SOURCES OF INTERNATIONAL SHORT-TERM BUSINESS FINANCING

Trade credit, both interest bearing and noninterest-bearing, is the most important overall source of short-term business financing in the U.S. and elsewhere. This type of credit becomes increasingly more complex, however, at the international level. The process of obtaining information about the quality of potential customers is made more difficult because of both geographical distances and language barriers. Characteristics of trade credit involving importers and exporters are discussed in Chapter 20.

MNCs can also issue their own short-term debt instruments that are known as Euronotes or Eurocommercial paper. These notes are usually denominated in U.S. dollars and issued by businesses outside the United States. In general, Euronotes are denominated in a currency that is not the national currency of the country where the notes are issued.

Promissory Notes

A promissory note signed by a customer may be required by a firm when it is not certain of the credit standing of its customer. (The use of a promissory note to bind a credit sale, as noted earlier, is not common in most fields of business activity.) Notes are advantageous to a business because they do not require further proof of the claim against a customer. The additional advantage of negotiability makes it possible for the business to sell these notes to its bank or other financing agency. Except for the few areas of business activity where notes are commonly used, however, banks are cautious in their purchase of such instruments. They often indicate weak credit situations.

Acceptances

Another type of receivable instrument that arises out of the sale of merchandise and which may be sold to a bank is the acceptance. An **acceptance** is a receivable from the sale of merchandise on the basis of a draft or bill of exchange drawn against the buyer or the buyer's bank. The accepted draft or bill of exchange is returned to the seller of the merchandise where it may be held until the date payment is due. During this period, the business may discount such acceptances with its bank. Again the seller is contingently liable for these discounted

acceptance
a receivable instrument arising from the sale of merchandise

acceptances. The use of the banker's acceptance is discussed in detail in Chapter 20 in connection with an international shipment of goods.

TRADE CREDIT

The most important single form of short-term business financing is the credit extended by one business organization to another. The open accounts receivable together with longer-term notes receivable—taken by manufacturers, wholesalers, jobbers, and other businesses that sell products or services to businesses—are known as trade credit. The following discussion excludes credit resulting from the sale of goods to the ultimate consumer, which is considered in Chapters 16, 17, and 18.

Characteristics of Trade Credit

The establishment of trade credit is the least formal of all forms of financing. It involves only an order for goods or services by one business and the delivery of goods or performance of service by the selling business. The purchasing business receives an invoice stating the terms of the transaction and the time period within which payment is to be made. The purchaser adds the liability to accounts payable; the seller adds the claim to accounts receivable. In some situations, the seller may insist upon written evidence of liability on the part of the purchaser. Such written evidence is usually in the form of a note that is payable by the purchaser and as a note receivable by the seller. In both situations, the open account and the use of a note, trade credit as a form of short-term financing has been used. Before a business organization delivers goods or performs a service for another business, it must determine the ability and willingness of the purchaser to pay for the order. The responsibility of such credit analysis in most businesses belongs to the credit manager.

Terms for Trade Credit

Sales may be made on terms such as cash, E.O.M. (end of month), M.O.M. (middle of month), or R.O.G. (receipt of goods). Or such terms as 2/10, net/30 may be offered, which means the purchaser may deduct 2 percent from the purchase price if payment is made within 10 days of shipment; but if not paid within 10 days, the net amount is due within 30 days. Such discounts to purchasers for early payment are common and are designed to provide incentive for prompt payment of bills. Occasionally, sellers offer only net terms such as net/30 or net/60.

A cash sale, contrary to its implication, usually involves credit. This is because the purchaser is often permitted a certain number of days within which to make payment. For example, a sale of merchandise in which the purchaser is permitted up to ten days to pay may be considered a cash transaction, but credit is outstanding to the purchaser for that period of time. Even for the firm that purchases products entirely on a cash basis, the volume of accounts payable outstanding on its books at any one time may be large.

Cost of Trade Credit

When trade credit terms do not provide a discount for early payment of obligations, there is no cost to the buyer for such financing. Even when discounts are available, it may seem that there is no cost for trade credit since failing to take the early payment discount simply requires the purchaser to pay the net price. There is a cost involved, however, when a discount is not taken. For example, with terms of 2/10, net/30, the cost is the loss of the 2% discount that could have been taken if payment were made within the 10-day period. In this situation, the buyer has trade credit without cost only for the first ten days.

In order to calculate the comparative cost of trade credit and bank credit, the cost of the trade credit must be reduced to an annual interest rate basis. For example, if the terms of sale are 2/10, net/30, the cost of trade credit is the loss of the 2 percent discount that the purchaser fails to take if she or he extends the payment period from ten days up to 30 days. The lost 2 percent is the cost of trade credit for those 20 days. Two percent for 20 days is the same as 36 percent for 360 days. If we also consider that it is the discounted price (invoice price minus % discount) that is being financed and use a conventional 360-day year, the approximate effective cost (EC) is:

$$EC = \frac{\% \text{ Discount}}{100\% - \% \text{ Discount}} \times \frac{360 \text{ Days}}{\text{Credit period} - \text{Discount days}}$$

For our 2/10, net/30 example,

$$EC = \frac{2\%}{100\% - 2\%} \times \frac{360}{30 - 10} = 2.04\% \times 18 = 36.7\%$$

This shows that the cost of trade credit typically is far in excess of bank rates. Thus it is usually worthwhile to borrow funds to take advantage of cash discounts on trade credit. Failure to take advantage of the trade discount is the same as borrowing from the vendor at the calculated, or effective cost, rate of interest.

Volume of Trade Credit

While it is difficult to measure the actual amount of outstanding trade credit in the United States, estimates can be made. Federal Trade Commission records for all manufacturing corporations show trade accounts well in excess of $100 billion. Notes and accounts receivable of all nonfinancial U.S. corporations exceed $700 billion. Trade credit is particularly heavy in the construction industry and in wholesaling operations, and it is a more important financing source for smaller firms than larger firms.

Sources of Funds for Trade Credit

Trade credit, unlike other forms of short-term financing, does not involve providing money to the user. The net effect, however, is very much the same since it enables the user to acquire goods or services without immediate payment. The firm that provides trade credit must be able to do so from its general resources. If a firm has such a strained financial position that it is unable to extend credit terms similar to other firms in its industry, it operates at a severe if not impossible competitive disadvantage. Trade credit provided by a firm is reflected in its balance sheet as a current asset, specifically as notes receivable and accounts receivable. Sources of funds for carrying trade credit are very much the same as for other current assets. Sources include purchasing products on the basis of trade credit, short-term borrowing, long-term financing, and retaining profits from operations.

Reasons for Using Trade Credit

The cost of trade credit in most lines of business activity is high when discounts are missed. However, it should not be assumed that high cost necessarily makes trade credit an undesirable source of short-term financing. It can be, in fact, the most important form of financing for small and growing businesses that are unable to qualify for short-term credit through customary financial channels.

For the firm that has access to low-cost credit from banks or other financial institutions, it is reasonable to expect wise managers to take advantage of discounts. For the firm that does not have recourse to a line of credit, the question is not the cost of trade credit. Rather the business must compare the profit that can be made from the sale of output acquired through trade credit with the cost of the trade credit itself.

The firm in a weak financial condition will find trade credit more readily available than bank credit. The bank stands to gain only the interest on the loan if repayment is made, but it will lose the entire sum loaned if the borrower's obligation is not met. The manufacturer or merchant, on the other hand, has a profit margin on the goods sold. If the purchaser fails to meet the obligation, the seller loses at most the cost of the goods delivered to the purchaser.

COMMERCIAL FINANCE COMPANIES

Shortly after the turn of the century, the first commercial finance company in the United States was chartered. Since that time, the number of these institutions has increased to more than five hundred. Some of these organizations are small, offering limited financial services to their customers, while others have vast resources and engage in broadly diversified programs of business lending.

Operating Characteristics of Commercial Finance Companies

The **commercial finance company** is an organization without a bank charter that advances funds to businesses by (1) discounting accounts receivable, (2) making loans secured by chattel mortgages on machinery or liens on inventory, or (3) financing deferred-payment sales of commercial and industrial equipment. These companies are also known as commercial credit companies, commercial receivables companies, and discount companies.

commercial finance company
an organization with no bank charter that makes loans to businesses

Commercial finance companies—such as C.I.T. Financial Corporation, Commercial Credit Company, and Walter E. Heller International —offer much the same services as do commercial banks for accounts-receivable financing and inventory financing. Accounts-receivable financing was, in fact, originated by commercial finance companies and only later was it adopted by commercial banks.

Commercial finance companies grew to their present number because they were completely free to experiment with new and highly specialized types of credit arrangements. Also, state laws concerning lending on the basis of accounts receivable were generally more favorable to these nonbanking organizations. A third factor is that they were able to charge high enough rates to make a profitable return on high-risk loans. Frequently these rates were far above rates bankers were permitted to charge.

As noted in the definition of commercial finance companies, these organizations also lend money using inventory as collateral and finance the sale of commercial and industrial equipment on a deferred-payment basis. This type of financing is used primarily in fields where there is a high percentage of small retail businesses, such as household appliances, hardware, plastics, drugs, paper, food products, paint, wallpaper, and leather.

Accounts Receivable Loans

When a commercial finance company sets up a loan secured by receivables, it enters into a contract with the borrower. The contract provides for the acceptance of the borrower's open accounts receivable as collateral for a loan. The company specifies those accounts that are acceptable as collateral and, as a rule, will only lend an amount less than the total value of the receivables pledged for the loan. The excess of receivables pledged over the actual amount of the loan provides a margin of safety for adjustments in outstanding accounts resulting from goods returned.

TERMS AND LOAN CHARGES

The cost of loans offered by commercial finance companies on the basis of receivables as collateral varies widely with the size of the lending company. In recent years the effective yearly rates on loans by the larger companies, which do most of the accounts-receivable financing by finance companies, have ranged from 15 to 20 percent. Higher interest rates are not uncommon among small finance companies. This is because these companies generally deal with local firms whose receivables are smaller in amount and more expensive to handle than the receivables of the firms financed by the larger companies. Also, the small finance company cannot achieve the economies of large-scale operation.

Volume and Sources of Commercial Finance Company Loans

Commercial finance company loans outstanding on accounts receivable total several billions of dollars. These companies also provide a vast amount of credit for businesses by financing commercial vehicles, industrial and farm equipment, and other types of business credit. The Board of Governors of the Federal Reserve System estimates the total volume of business credit outstanding by the commercial finance companies to be more than $200 billion.

The equity position of commercial finance companies is considerably greater than that of banks; however, these organizations do not operate on equity capital alone. Additional long-term capital is acquired by selling debenture, or unsecured, bonds. In addition, commercial banks lend a large volume of money at wholesale rates to commercial finance companies, which in turn lend it to business borrowers at retail rates. Nonbank financial intermediaries, as well as commercial and industrial firms, often find it advantageous to invest their temporary surplus funds in the notes of commercial finance companies. These sources of short-term funds permit the commercial finance companies to meet their peak loan demands without having too much long-term debt, only part of which would be used during slack lending periods.

Reasons for Using Commercial Finance Companies

When viewing the average cost of 15 to 20 percent for commercial finance company loans, the question may arise as to why a borrower would under any circumstances use these companies. As a matter of fact, the business that has ample current assets and is in a highly liquid position may be well advised to rely on other sources of short-term financing. However, the business that is without a short-term financial problem at one time or another is the exception rather than the rule. During periods when business is most brisk and growth possibilities most favorable, the need for additional short-term funds becomes unusually pressing.

The business first requests an increase in its bank line of credit. Failing this, an additional loan from the bank may be secured by pledging either inventory or receivables as collateral. However, not all banks actively engage in this type of financial arrangement. Thus it may be necessary to deal with a commercial finance company. Commercial finance companies are able to operate through a system of branches on a regional or national basis, unhampered by restrictions on branch operations. Therefore, they can acquire the volume of business necessary to cover overhead and provide the needed diversification of risks for high-risk financing. Several bank holding companies have purchased or established commercial finance companies to take advantage of their special operating characteristics.

FACTORS   *Defin.*

The *factor*, like the commercial finance company, engages in accounts-receivable financing for businesses. In contrast with the commercial finance companies, however, the factor purchases the accounts outright and assumes all credit risks. Under this arrangement, customers whose accounts are sold are notified that their bills are payable to the factor. The task of collecting on the accounts is thus shifted from the seller of the accounts to the factor.

factor
an organization that engages in accounts receivable financing by purchasing accounts and assuming all risks

Despite the long history of these companies, their growth has taken place largely within the last thirty years. The origin of factoring was in the textile industry. Since most of the selling and credit-reporting agencies in the textile field are located in New York City, most of the nation's factors can be found there. In addition to serving the textile industry, factors have also proved useful in such fields as furniture, shoes, bottle making, paper, toys, and furs.

Operating Characteristics of Factors

Assume that a business is experiencing financial difficulties for the first time in several years because of increasing levels of inventory and receivables. The firm is well managed and has been able to secure adequate financing through an unsecured line of credit with its bank for several years. In order to take advantage of expanded business opportunities, however, it needs to supplement its usual sources of current funds. At this time, the business may use the services of a factor.

The factor draws up a contract establishing the duties and obligations of each party. This contract includes the conditions under which accounts may be sold to the factor, the responsibility for the payment of these accounts, the collection procedures to be followed, and the method of reporting balances due. The contract also provides that the accounts so established be assigned to the factor and that invoices for sales to these customers, together with the original shipping documents, be delivered daily to the factor. All sales must be approved by the factor before goods are delivered; sales are subject to rejection if the credit rating of the customer does not meet the factor's standards. Daily reports must be given to the factor on all credits, allowances, and returns of merchandise. The contract also stipulates the charges for the factoring service.

The credit analysis department is the heart of the factoring organization since it must conserve the factor's assets and also be in constant contact with its clients. Members of the factor's credit department must be not only extremely prompt and accurate in their credit analyses but also, because they work closely with the firm's clients, must retain the goodwill of the companies that use its services.

Charges and Terms for Factoring

The charge for factoring is in two parts. First, interest is charged on the money advanced. Second, a factoring commission or service charge is figured as a percentage of the face amount of the receivables. This charge typically ranges from 3/4 of 1 percent to 1 1/2 percent of the face amount of the accounts financed. The commission charge is determined after considering such things as the volume of the client's sales, the general credit status of the accounts being factored, and the average size of individual accounts.

As further financial protection, the factor reserves from 5 to 15 percent of the total amount of receivables factored to make adjustments, such as for merchandise that is returned to the seller. This portion of the receivables is returned to the seller if it is not needed for adjustment purposes.

Volume and Sources of Funds

The number of firms engaged exclusively in factoring operations has decreased in recent years through merger with or acquisition by firms engaged in other commercial financing activities. However, the dollar volume of factoring operations is increasing and spreading into many lines of business where it was formerly unknown. Each year several billions of dollars of financing is supplied to American businesses through the factoring of open accounts receivable.

Like the commercial finance companies, factors obtain their operating funds through a combination of equity capital, long-term borrowing, short-term borrowing, and profits from operations. Although most factors obtain equity capital directly from the small group of persons actively engaged in the factoring company, at least one factor has sold common stock to the general public.

Benefits and Drawbacks of Using Factoring Services

Although a factor's services may be used by a firm that is unable to secure financing through customary channels, financially strong companies may at times use these services to good advantage. In fact, factors are of greatest benefit to those companies that are enjoying very great success with respect to sales and growth. We have noted that during such periods companies experience extreme shortages of working capital. The sale of receivables without recourse (no contingent liability for their collection) has the effect of substituting cash for accounts receivable. This may make even greater growth and profitability possible in the long run.

Some firms factor their receivables not because it is the only form of financing available to them, but because of other considerations. First, the cost of doing business through credit sales is definite and can be figured in advance because the factor assumes all risks of collection. This is, in effect, a form of credit insurance. Second, factoring eliminates overhead, including bookkeeping costs, the maintenance of a credit department, and the expenses of collecting delinquent accounts. Unless a firm factors all of its receivables, however, completely eliminating credit department expenses would not be possible. A further advantage, but of a less tangible nature, is that factoring frees the management of a business from concern with financial matters and permits it to concentrate on production and distribution.

In recent years, factoring has become increasingly important in supporting export sales. The firm that is unfamiliar with the problems of financing international shipments of goods is relieved of all such details by factoring foreign receivables.

Although factoring services are regarded highly by some businesses, others offer objections to their use. The two reasons cited most frequently are the cost and the implication of financial weakness. The cost of factoring is unquestionably higher than the cost of borrowing from a bank on the basis of an unsecured loan. However, it is difficult to conclude without reservation that the net cost is higher. The elimination of overhead costs that would otherwise be necessary plus the reality that management need not concern itself with financial matters may completely offset the additional cost involved in factoring.

With respect to the implication of financial weakness, many borrowers prefer to avoid the factoring plan in favor of the nonnotification plan available through commercial finance companies. In this way they avoid having their customers make direct payments to the factor. Outside the textile field, where factoring has long played an important role, businesses often make every effort to avoid letting their customers know that their accounts are being used to secure financing because of the implication of financial weakness.

THE SMALL BUSINESS ADMINISTRATION

The Small Business Administration (SBA) was established by the federal government to provide financial assistance to small firms that are unable to obtain loans through private channels on reasonable terms. Created in 1953, the SBA provides, in addition to loans, a wide variety of services through its more than 100 field offices.

The Use of SBA Loans

The reason businesses use SBA loans is explained by the stated objectives of the SBA: to enable deserving small businesses to obtain financial assistance otherwise not available through private channels on reasonable terms. When the SBA was established, it was recognized that the economic development of the nation depended in large part upon the freedom of new business ventures to enter into active operation. Yet the increased concentration of investable funds with large institutional investors, such as life insurance companies, investment companies, and others, had made it increasingly difficult for new and small business ventures to attract investment capital.

If a firm is able to obtain financing elsewhere, its loan application to the SBA is rejected. An applicant for a loan must prove that funds needed are not available from any bank, that no other private lending sources are available, that issuing securities is not practicable, that financing cannot be arranged through the disposal of business assets, and that the personal credit of the owners cannot be used. These loans may not be used for paying existing creditors or for speculative purposes.

Financing Policies of the SBA

The SBA assists in financing small enterprises in three ways: it may make direct loans to businesses; it may participate jointly with private banks in extending loans to businesses; or it may agree to guarantee a bank loan. The SBA can make direct loans of up to $150,000. When participating with banks in making loans, the SBA's share may not exceed $150,000. In guaranteeing loans, the SBA may extend its guarantee to 90 percent of a bank loan or $500,000, whichever is less.

In addition to the business lending activities described above, the SBA has been vested with the responsibility for several related financial activities. These include loans to development companies, disaster loans, lease guarantees, surety bond support, minority enterprise programs, procurement assistance, and support for investment companies that service small businesses.

FINANCING TERMS AND CHARGES
SBA working capital loans are limited to seven years, while regular business loans have a maximum maturity of 25 years. The SBA sets the interest rates on its direct loans and on its share-of-participation loans. It also sets a maximum allowable rate which banks can charge on guaranteed loans. These rates are adjusted periodically by the SBA to reflect changes in market conditions.

Volume and Sources of Funds

During the very early days of its operation, the SBA encouraged lending to small businesses by local credit pools throughout the country. A change in policy, though, resulted in more active lending by the SBA. The amount of loans the SBA can guarantee is considerably larger than the funds it has available for direct loans. Several billions of dollars in loans are always outstanding, most of which were made on a guaranty basis through commercial banks rather than directly by the SBA.

The SBA operates on a revolving fund periodically renewed by Congress. The total of business loans which have been approved far exceeds the revolving fund because of repayments and because a portion of the amount approved is the participation share of commercial banks.

COMMERCIAL PAPER ISSUERS AND DEALERS

Large U.S. corporations of high credit quality can issue or sell commercial paper, which is short-term promissory notes. These notes are backed solely by the credit quality of the issuer. Commercial paper may be sold directly by the issuer to financial institutions or other investors. Alternatively, it can be sold to **commercial paper houses** or dealers who purchase the promissory notes to resell them to individuals or businesses. A fee based on the amount of notes purchased, charged to the issuer of the notes, provides the basic income of commercial paper dealers.

commercial paper house
organization that buys and sells short-term promissory notes

Operations of Commercial Paper Houses

A firm that wishes to obtain funds from a commercial paper house must have an unquestioned reputation for sound operation. First the commercial paper house makes a thorough investigation of the firm's financial position. If it appears that the notes of the firm can be sold with little difficulty, an agreement is made for the outright sale of a block of the firm's promissory notes to the commercial paper house. They, in turn, will resell these notes as quickly as possible to banks, managers of pension funds, business corporations that have surplus funds, or other investors. The notes are usually prepared in denominations of $100,000 or more with maturities ranging from a few days to 270 days. The size of the notes and the maturities, however, can be adjusted to suit individual investor requirements.

Commercial Paper House Terms and Charges

A commercial paper house will pay the borrower the face amount of the notes minus the interest charge and a fee that may be as low as ⅛ of 1 percent calculated on an annual basis. The interest charge is determined by the general level of prevailing rates in the money market and the strength of the borrowing company. When these notes are resold to banks and other lenders, only the prevailing interest charge is deducted from the face value of the notes. Hence, the commercial paper house receives the fee as compensation for the negotiation.

Volume of Commercial Paper Financing

The volume of commercial paper has expanded dramatically in recent years. At the end of December 1989, nonfinancial companies had over $129 billion in commercial paper outstanding, most of which was dealer placed. At the same time, financial companies had over $186 billion outstanding in dealer-placed paper, and their directly placed paper amounted to more than $209 billion.[3] Fewer than ten commercial paper houses, located for the most part in New York City, dominate the dealer-placed market. These dealers serve borrowers such as finance companies, manufacturers, wholesalers, retailers, and public utilities.

Advantages of Using Commercial Paper Financing

The most important reason for directly issuing commercial paper or using commercial paper dealers is that the cost of borrowing is generally less than regular bank rates. Also, the need for compensating bank balances that increase interest costs on short-term bank loans is

3. *Federal Reserve Bulletin* (May 1990): A23.

avoided. Loan restrictions on the amount that can be borrowed from a single bank may also favor the issuance of commercial paper by large corporations.

Industrial firms and other nonbank lenders often purchase commercial paper as a more profitable alternative than Treasury bills. In recent years, commercial paper has provided a yield above that of short-term government securities. Although commercial banks were historically the main purchasers of commercial paper, now paper is actively held by industrial corporations, money market mutual funds, and other lenders. Corporations have increased their purchases of commercial paper as a convenient and profitable means of investing excess cash.

KEY TERMS

acceptance	field warehouse
commercial finance company	line of credit
commercial paper house	revolving credit agreement
compensating balance	stock or bond power
factor	

DISCUSSION QUESTIONS

1. What is meant by an unsecured loan? Are these loans an important form of bank lending?
2. Explain what is meant by a bank line of credit. Describe the revolving credit agreement and compare it with the bank line of credit.
3. When might a business seek accounts receivable financing?
4. What safeguards may a bank establish to protect itself when it lends on the basis of a customer's receivables pledged as collateral for a loan?
5. When a business firm uses its inventory as collateral for a bank loan, how is the problem of storing and guarding the inventory accomplished for the bank?
6. Discuss other forms of collateral that a business may use in securing loans from a commercial bank.
7. What is meant by trade credit? Briefly describe some of the possible terms for trade credit.
8. What are the primary reasons for using trade credit for short-term financing?
9. Under what circumstances would a business secure its financing through a commercial finance company?

10. Describe how a factor differs from a commercial finance company in terms of accounts-receivable financing.
11. Why would a business use the services of a factor?
12. What is the purpose of the Small Business Administration? How does the SBA provide financing to businesses?
13. What is meant by commercial paper and how important is it as a source of financing?
14. Briefly describe the role and operations of commercial paper dealers or houses.

PROBLEMS

1. A supplier is offering your firm a cash discount of 2 percent if purchases are paid for within 10 days; otherwise the bill is due at the end of 60 days. Would you recommend borrowing from a bank at an 18 percent annual interest rate in order to take advantage of the cash discount offer? Explain your answer.
2. Assume that you have been offered cash discounts on merchandise that can be purchased from either of two suppliers. Supplier A offers trade credit terms of 3/20, net/70, while supplier B offers 4/15, net/80. What is the approximate effective cost of missing the cash discounts from each supplier? If you could not take advantage of either cash discount offer, which supplier would you select?
3. Obtain a current issue of the *Federal Reserve Bulletin* and determine the changes in the prime rate that have occurred since the end of 1988. Comment on any trends in the data.

SELF-TEST QUESTIONS

1. A short-term bank loan that is unsecured is referred to as:
   a. a line of credit
   b. an accounts-receivable loan
   c. an inventory loan
   d. a life insurance policy loan

2. The most important form of short-term business financing is:
   a. a revolving credit agreement
   b. accounts-receivable financing
   c. inventory loans
   d. trade credit

3. An organization that engages in accounts-receivable financing by purchasing the accounts outright is referred to as a:

   a. field warehouse firm
   b. commercial finance company
   c. factor
   d. commercial paper house

4. The Small Business Administration assists in the financing of small businesses in which of the following ways?

   a. by making direct loans to businesses
   b. by participating jointly with banks in extending loans to businesses
   c. by guaranteeing bank loans to businesses
   d. all of the above

5. Large U.S. corporations of high credit quality can issue or sell short-term promissory notes called:

   a. revolving credit agreements
   b. commercial paper
   c. trade credit
   d. inventory loans

SELF-TEST PROBLEM

Assume that you have been offered cash discounts on merchandise that can be purchased from either of two suppliers. Supplier A offers trade credit terms of 3/15, net/60, while supplier B offers 4/10, net/70. What is the approximate effective cost of not taking the cash discounts from each supplier?

SUGGESTED READINGS

Block, Stanley B., and Geoffrey A. Hirt. *Foundations of Financial Management*, 5e. Homewood, IL: Richard D. Irwin, Inc., 1989. Chap. 8.

Brady, Thomas R. "Changes in Loan Pricing and Business Lending at Commercial Banks." *Federal Reserve Bulletin* (January 1985): 1–13.

Gitman, Lawrence J. *Principles of Managerial Finance*, 5e. New York: Harper & Row, 1988. Chap. 18.

Moskowitz, L. A. *Modern Factoring and Commercial Finance*. New York: Crowell Publishing. 1977.

Van Horne, James C. *Fundamentals of Financial Management*, 7e. Englewood Cliffs, NJ: Prentice-Hall, 1989. Chaps. 11 and 12.

Walker, Ernest W., and J. William Petty II. *Financial Management of the Small Firm*, 2e. Englewood Cliffs, NJ: Prentice-Hall, 1986. Chap. 14.

Weston, J. Fred, and Eugene F. Brigham. *Essentials of Managerial Finance*, 9e. Hinsdale, IL: The Dryden Press, 1990. Chap. 14.

ANSWERS TO SELF-TEST QUESTIONS   1. a   2. d   3. c   4. d   5. b

SOLUTION TO SELF-TEST PROBLEM

Supplier A:

$$EC = \frac{3\%}{100\% - 3\%} \times \frac{360}{60 - 15} = 3.09\% \times 8.0 = 24.72\%$$

Supplier B:

$$EC = \frac{4\%}{100\% - 4\%} \times \frac{360}{70 - 10} = 4.17\% \times 6.0 = 25.02\%$$

CHAPTER 10
Time Value of Money and Fixed-Assets Management

After studying this chapter, you should be able to:

- Explain what is meant by the time value of money and describe compounding.
- Describe discounting to determine present values.
- Explain and apply the process for valuing long-term debt and equity securities.
- Briefly explain how relevant cash flows are determined for capital budgeting decision purposes.
- Identify and describe the methods or techniques used to make proper capital budgeting decisions.
- Briefly discuss the possible need for risk adjustments when making fixed-asset investment decisions.

The profitability of a firm is affected to the greatest extent by the success of its financial manager in making fixed-asset investment decisions. These decisions require major financing commitments and impact on the firm for many years. A fixed-asset decision will be sound only if it produces a stream of future cash inflows that cover the investment cost and earn the firm an acceptable rate of return.

In order to evaluate fixed-asset investments, we must first understand the mathematics of finance known as compounding and discounting. These concepts are also used to show how prices or values in debt and equity financial instruments change over time. The first part of this chapter focuses on the time value of money. Then we turn to the management of fixed assets.

TIME VALUE OF MONEY

Most individuals have experienced compounding by watching a savings account "grow" or increase over time when interest is reinvested. Discounting is the opposite of compounding, as we will see following the discussion of basic compounding concepts.

Financial calculators or computer software, such as the *Decision Assistant* that accompanies this textbook, will perform the calculations and procedures discussed in this chapter. However, we first describe the calculation procedures in detail to enhance the understanding of the logic involved in the time-value-of-money concepts. By first working the problems the "long way," the follow-the-steps format of financial calculators and computer software should make more sense. We encourage students to use all three computational approaches.

Compounding to Determine Future Values

Let's begin by discussing how a savings account works. Assume you have $1,000 to invest now and a bank offers you an 8 percent interest rate. Another bank will pay 10 percent interest and both banks will compound your money annually. If you invest for only one year, at the end of the year you would receive, in addition to your original $1,000, $80 interest ($1,000 × 0.08) from the first bank, and $100 ($1,000 × 0.10) from the second bank. While the $20 difference is not great, it has some significance to most of us.

compounding
when an investment earns interest that is reinvested along with the principal

To understand compounding, let's assume that you leave the investment with a bank for ten years. **Compounding** means that interest earned each year plus the principal will be reinvested at the stated rate. For example, the first bank accepts your $1,000 investment now, adds $80 at the end of one year, reinvests the $1,080 for the second year at 8 percent, and so forth. Table 10.1, a partial future-value table, shows how a $1 investment will grow or increase in value over a ten-year period. Notice under the 8 percent column that an initial value of $1 will be worth 1.080 at the end of one year (1.000 × 1.080) and 1.166 by the end of the second year (1.080 × 1.080). At the end of ten years, the initial 1.000 would have increased to a future-value interest factor (FVIF) of 2.159. Multiplying this factor by the $1,000 investment gives a future value of $2,159 on your initial investment.

Table 10.1 also shows how a $1 investment will grow in value at a 10 percent interest rate. Notice that the FVIF at the end of ten years

TABLE 10.1   Future Value Interest Factor of $1 (FVIF)

YEAR	5%	6%	7%	8%	9%	10%
1	1.050	1.060	1.070	1.080	1.090	1.100
2	1.102	1.124	1.145	1.166	1.188	1.210
3	1.158	1.191	1.225	1.260	1.295	1.331
4	1.216	1.262	1.311	1.360	1.412	1.464
5	1.276	1.338	1.403	1.469	1.539	1.611
6	1.340	1.419	1.501	1.587	1.677	1.772
7	1.407	1.504	1.606	1.714	1.828	1.949
8	1.477	1.594	1.718	1.851	1.993	2.144
9	1.551	1.689	1.838	1.999	2.172	2.358
10	1.629	1.791	1.967	2.159	2.367	2.594

would be 2.594, making your investment worth $2,594 ($1,000 × 2.594). Now the difference between the 8 percent and 10 percent rates is much more significant, $435 ($2,594 – $2,159). Thus we see the advantage of being able to compound at even slightly higher interest rates over a period of years.

The compounding concept can be expressed in equation form as

$$FV = PV(1 + i)^n$$

where FV is the future value, PV is the present value, i is the interest rate, and n is the number of periods in years. For our 8 percent, ten-year example, we have

$$FV = \$1,000(1 + 0.08)^{10}$$

$$= \$1,000(2.159)$$

$$= \$2,159$$

Notice that the $(1 + i)^n$ part of the equation is the FVIF factor shown in Table 10.1. Table 1 in the Appendix is a more complete FVIF table.

Many finance computations involve cash flows that occur over several years. When the cash flow stream is constant or level in each time period it is called an **annuity**. For example, suppose you are going to save $1,000 per year for three years at an 8 percent interest rate. This is an *annuity due* problem because cash flows occur at the beginning of each time period. You calculate the future value of this annuity as follows:

annuity
a constant cash flow in each time period

$$FV \text{ annuity due} = \$1,000(1.08)^3 + \$1,000(1.08)^2 + \$1,000 (1.08)^1$$

$$= \$1,000(1.260) + \$1,000(1.166) + \$1,000(1.080)$$

$$= \$1,000(1.260 + 1.166 + 1.080)$$

$$= \$1,000(3.506)$$

$$= \$3,506$$

Notice that the first $1,000 would earn interest compounded at 8 percent for three years while the second $1,000 would earn interest for two years and the third $1,000 would earn interest for only one year. The future value interest factor for an annuity due (FVIFAD) may be calculated with a financial calculator or by using the formula given below Table 2 in the Appendix.

Annuity problems may also involve level cash flow amounts that occur at the end of each period starting with the first cash flow at the end of the first year. This type of annuity is referred to as an *ordinary annuity* and can be illustrated by our $1,000, 8 percent rate, three-year annuity. Only now the first $1,000 will be invested at the end of the first year. The appropriate calculations would be:

$$\text{FV ordinary annuity} = \$1,000(1.08)^2 + \$1,000(1.08)^1 + \$1,000(1.08)^0$$

$$= \$1,000(1.166) + \$1,000(1.080) + \$1,000(1)$$

$$= \$1,000(3.246)$$

$$= \$3,246$$

Table 10.2 is a partial table that can be used for finding future values of ordinary annuities. Notice that the table gives the future-value interest factor for an ordinary annuity (FVIFA) for three years at 8 percent as 3.246, which is the same as we just calculated. We can express the future value of an ordinary annuity in general terms as

$$\text{FV ordinary annuity} = \text{Annual payment} \times \text{FVIFA}$$

Table 2 in the Appendix is a more comprehensive table for finding FVIFA factors for ordinary annuities.

Discounting to Determine Present Values

Most financial management decisions involve present values rather than future values. For example, a financial manager who is consider-

TABLE 10.2   Future Value Interest Factor for a $1 Ordinary Annuity (FVIFA)

YEAR	5%	6%	7%	8%	9%	10%
1	1.000	1.000	1.000	1.000	1.000	1.000
2	2.050	2.060	2.070	2.080	2.090	2.100
3	3.152	3.184	3.215	3.246	3.278	3.310
4	4.310	4.375	4.440	4.506	4.573	4.641
5	5.526	5.637	5.751	5.867	5.985	6.105
6	6.802	6.975	7.153	7.336	7.523	7.716
7	8.142	8.394	8.654	8.923	9.200	9.487
8	9.549	9.897	10.260	10.637	11.028	11.436
9	11.027	11.491	11.978	12.488	13.021	13.579
10	12.578	13.181	13.816	14.487	15.193	15.937

ing purchasing an asset wants to know what the asset is worth now rather than at the end of some future time period. The reason that an asset has value is because it will produce a stream of future cash benefits. To determine its value now in time period zero, we have to translate the future cash benefits to the present. This procedure is called **discounting**.

Let's illustrate discounting with a simple example involving a loan. Assume that a borrower offers to pay you $1,000 at the end of one year in return for a $1,000 loan now. If you are willing to accept a zero rate of return you might make the loan. Most of us would not jump at an offer like this! Rather, we would require some return on our loan. To receive a return of, say, 8 percent, you would lend less than $1,000 now. The amount to be lent would be determined by dividing the $1,000 that is due at the end of one year by one plus the interest rate of 8 percent ($1,000/1.08). This results in a loan amount of $926. If you required a 10 percent rate of return, you would lend only $909 ($1,000/1.10).

Table 10.3, a partial present-value table, illustrates the present value of having to wait to receive $1 sometime in the future. Notice under the 8 percent column that a value of $1 to be received one year from now would have a present value of 0.926. To receive $1,000 at the end of one year, the present value would be $926 ($1,000 × 0.926). Table 10.3 further shows that if one had to wait ten years to receive $1 and the discount rate were 8 percent, the present value interest factor (PVIF) would be only 0.463. Thus a $1,000 future receipt would have a present value of $463 ($1,000 × 0.463).

The discounting concept can be expressed in equation form as

$$PV = \frac{FV}{(1+i)^n}$$

$$= FV\left(\frac{1}{(1+i)^n}\right)$$

where the individual terms are the same as those defined for the

discounting a method of determining the present value of cash flows to be received in the future

TABLE 10.3 Present Value Interest Factor of $1 (PVIF)

YEAR	5%	6%	7%	8%	9%	10%
1	0.952	0.943	0.935	0.926	0.917	0.909
2	0.907	0.890	0.873	0.857	0.842	0.826
3	0.864	0.840	0.816	0.794	0.772	0.751
4	0.823	0.792	0.763	0.735	0.708	0.683
5	0.784	0.747	0.713	0.681	0.650	0.621
6	0.746	0.705	0.666	0.630	0.596	0.564
7	0.711	0.665	0.623	0.583	0.547	0.513
8	0.677	0.627	0.582	0.540	0.502	0.467
9	0.645	0.592	0.544	0.500	0.460	0.424
10	0.614	0.558	0.508	0.463	0.422	0.386

There are a number of ways of acquiring a million dollars. Probably the easiest legal way is to inherit it. As for those of us who won't do that, we must save a portion of our disposable personal income and then live long enough to take advantage of compounding interest. For example, if you could invest $10,000 now, the following combinations of annual compound interest rates and time periods would make you a millionaire.

INTEREST RATE	AMOUNT OF TIME
5%	94.4 years
10%	48.3 years
15%	33.0 years
20%	25.3 years

Notice that at a 5 percent compound rate it would take over ninety-four years to accumulate $1 million. This is probably not acceptable (or possible) for most of us. Even if we could compound our interest at a 20 percent annual rate, it would take a little more than twenty-five years to become a millionaire.

An alternative approach would be to create an investment annuity of $10,000 per year. The following chart shows the time required to become a millionaire under the assumptions of both an ordinary annuity, where the first investment will be made one year from now, and an annuity due, where the first investment is made now.

INTEREST RATE	AMOUNT OF TIME	
	ORDINARY ANNUITY	ANNUITY DUE
5%	36.7 years	35.9 years
10%	25.2 years	24.3 years
15%	19.8 years	18.9 years
20%	16.7 years	15.8 years

With this approach the time required, particularly at higher interest rates, is more feasible. Compounding at 5 percent would still require making annual investments for about thirty-six years to accumulate $1 million. At 10 percent, it would take you only twenty-four to twenty-five years to attain that goal. Of course the most critical factor, which might be easier said than done, is whether you will be able to come up with $10,000 per year out of your disposable personal income. Good luck!

future-value equation. Notice that the future-value equation has simply been rewritten to solve for the present value. For the $1,000,

8 percent, ten-year example, we have

$$PV = \$1,000\left(\frac{1}{(1+0.08)^{10}}\right)$$

$$= \$1,000\left(\frac{1}{2.159}\right)$$

$$= \$1,000\,(.463)$$

$$= \$463$$

Notice that the $1/(1+i)^n$ part of the equation represents the PVIF shown in Table 10.3. An expanded listing of present value interest factors is given in Table 3 in the Appendix.

Many present-value problems also involve cash flow annuities. Usually these are ordinary annuities—cash inflows are assumed to begin at the end of the first year and the end of each year thereafter for the duration of the cash flow stream. Let's assume that we will receive $1,000 per year beginning one year from now for a period of three years at an 8 percent discount rate. The appropriate calculations would be:

$$\text{PV ordinary annuity} = \$1,000\left(\frac{1}{(1.08)^1}\right) + \$1,000\left(\frac{1}{(1.08)^2}\right) + \$1,000\left(\frac{1}{(1.08)^3}\right)$$

$$= \$1,000(.926) + \$1,000(.857) + \$1,000(.794)$$

$$= \$1,000(2.577)$$

$$= \$2,577$$

Notice that the first $1,000 would be discounted for only one year, the second $1,000 for two years, and the third $1,000 for three years, reflecting when each of the cash inflows is to be received. We can express the present value of an ordinary annuity in general terms as

PV ordinary annuity = annual receipt × PVIFA

Table 10.4 is a partial table that can be used for determining the present values of ordinary annuities. Notice that the present-value interest factor for three years at 8 percent is 2.577, which is the same as we just calculated. A more comprehensive PVIFA table is Table 4 in the Appendix.

Occasionally there are present value annuity-due problems. For example, leasing arrangements often require the person leasing equipment to make the first payment at the time the equipment is delivered. A financial calculator or computer software program can be used to calculate the appropriate interest factor for an annuity-due problem. Or it may be found by using the formula given in the Appendix for converting PVIFA values to annuity-due values (PVIFAD).

TABLE 10.4
Present Value Interest Factor for a $1 Ordinary Annuity (PVIFA)

YEAR	5%	6%	7%	8%	9%	10%
1	0.952	0.943	0.935	0.926	0.917	0.909
2	1.859	1.833	1.808	1.783	1.759	1.736
3	2.723	2.673	2.624	2.577	2.531	2.487
4	3.546	3.465	3.387	3.312	3.240	3.170
5	4.329	4.212	4.100	3.993	3.890	3.791
6	5.076	4.917	4.767	4.623	4.486	4.355
7	5.786	5.582	5.389	5.206	5.033	4.868
8	6.463	6.210	5.971	5.747	5.535	5.335
9	7.108	6.802	6.515	6.247	5.995	5.759
10	7.722	7.360	7.024	6.710	6.418	6.145

Determining Annual Annuity Payments

In addition to finding present and future values of annuities, there are many instances in which we might want to determine a constant periodic payment—for example, the periodic payment amount necessary to pay off, or amortize, a loan or real estate mortgage. Let's assume that a lender offers you a $20,000, 10 percent, three-year loan that is to be fully amortized with three annual payments. The first payment will be due one year from the loan date. How much will you have to pay each year?

This is a present-value problem because the $20,000 is the worth of the loan now. The annual payment[1] can be found by rearranging the present value of an ordinary annuity equation to read

$$\text{Annual payment} = \frac{\text{PV ordinary annuity}}{\text{PVIFA}}$$

We can find the present-value interest factor of the annuity (PVIFA) by returning to Table 10.4 and finding the factor at 10 percent for three years, which is 2.487. With this information we can now determine the required annual payment:

$$\text{Annual payment} = \frac{\$20,000}{2.487} = \$8,041.82$$

This shows that you will have to pay, in round numbers, $8,042 each year for three years to pay off the loan.

Table 10.5 illustrates the repayment process with a loan amortization schedule. Since the interest rate is 10%, the first year you will pay

1. Annual receipts or annual payments can be used interchangeably in present-value annuity problems depending on whether the problem is viewed from the standpoint of receiving or paying cash flows.

TABLE 10.5   Sample Loan Amortization Schedule

YEAR	ANNUAL PAYMENT	INTEREST PAYMENT	PRINCIPAL REPAYMENT	LOAN BALANCE
0	–	–	–	$20,000
1	$8,042	$2,000	$6,042	13,958
2	8,042	1,396	6,646	7,312
3	8,042	731	7,311*	-0-

*Because of rounding, the final principal repayment is off by $1.

interest of $2,000 ($20,000 × 0.10). Subsequent interest payments are based on the remaining loan balances, which are smaller each year (also referred to as the declining balance). Since $6,042 ($8,042 – $2,000) of the first year's $8,042 payment is used to repay part of the principal, the second year's interest payment will only be $1,396 ($13,958 × 0.10). The third and last payment covers the final year's interest of $731 plus the remaining principal balance.

This loan amortization process is the same as that used to determine monthly payments on home mortgages. However, because the discounting interval is very short, it would be unwieldy to calculate the monthly payment "the long way" for a typical 30-year loan. Therefore a financial calculator or computer program is used.

More Frequent Compounding or Discounting Intervals

There are many situations in which compounding or discounting may occur more often than annually. For example, recall from the beginning of this chapter the $1,000 that could be invested at one bank at an 8 percent annual interest rate for ten years. Remember that the future value at the end of ten years was:

$$FV = \$1,000\,(1.08)^{10}$$

$$= \$1,000\,(2.159)$$

$$= \$2,159$$

Now let's assume that another bank offers the same 8 percent interest rate but with semiannual (twice a year) compounding. We can find the future value for this investment by first dividing the annual interest rate of 8 percent by the number of times compounding is to take place during the year (0.08/2 = 0.04). We also need to increase the total number of periods to reflect semiannual compounding. To do this, multiply the number of years for the loan times the frequency of compounding within a year (10 years × 2 = 20 periods). The solution for the semiannual compounding example would be:

$$FV = \$1,000 \ (1.04)^{20}$$
$$= \$1,000 \ (2.191)$$
$$= \$2,191$$

The 2.191 future-value interest factor (FVIF) can also be found in Table 1 in the Appendix.

Notice that semiannual compounding will result in $32 more than the $2,159 earned with annual compounding. It follows that more frequent compounding, such as quarterly or monthly, produces even higher earnings.

The process described above also applies to discounting problems when discounting occurs more frequently than annually. The use of financial calculators and computer software is more expedient as the frequency of compounding or discounting within a year increases.

The Valuation of Long-term Debt and Equity Securities

The values of bonds and stocks are also affected by time-value-of-money concepts. Thus, future receipts of interest, dividends, and possible price appreciation help to determine the value of a stock or bond today.

VALUATION OF BONDS

Long-term debt usually provides for periodic payments of interest plus the return of the principal at maturity. Most corporate bonds are issued in $1,000 denominations. To illustrate how a corporate bond's value is calculated, let's assume that a bond with $1,000 face value has a stated interest rate of 9 percent and a ten-year life before maturity. Thus an investor will receive $90 ($1,000 × 0.09) at the end of each year in interest and will receive $1,000 at the end of ten years.[2] We determine the bond's present value based on the interest rate required by investors on similar quality bonds. For example, let's assume investors require a 9 percent rate of return. We then would discount the $90 annuity portion of the bond at the PVIFA at 9 percent for ten years, which is 6.418 (see Table 10.4). Since the $1,000 principal will be received only at the end of ten years, we use the 0.422 PVIF at 9 percent for ten years from Table 10.3. Taking these together we have

$$\$90 \times 6.418 = \$ \ \ 578$$
$$\$1,000 \times 0.422 = \underline{\ \ \ 422}$$
$$\text{Bond value} = \$1,000$$

---

2.   In actual practice, most bonds pay interest semiannually. For example, this bond might pay $45 every six months over the ten years, making a total of twenty payment periods.

Thus the bond is worth $1,000 and will remain so as long as investors receive a 9 percent rate of return.

However, what if investors required a 10 percent return, or yield, on bonds of similar quality? The bond must then fall in price to compensate for the fact that only $90 in interest is still being paid annually. The appropriate discount factors at 10 percent for ten years from Tables 10.3 and 10.4 would be:

$$\begin{aligned}
\$90 \times 6.415 &= \$553 \\
\$1,000 \times 0.386 &= \underline{386} \\
\text{Bond value} &= \$939
\end{aligned}$$

Thus an investor would be willing to pay only $939 for the bond. Although interest remains $90 per year, a new investor would earn a 10 percent return because she or he would pay only $939 now and get back $1,000 at the end of ten years. It should now be clear why bond prices change with changes in interest rates. Of course, if investors required less than a 9 percent return for bonds of this quality, then the above-described bond would have a value greater than $1,000.[3]

VALUATION OF STOCKS

Investors in common stocks expect to receive adequate compensation in the form of cash dividend yield and price appreciation, or growth, for undertaking investment risk. This concept is often expressed in equation form as

$$\text{Expected return} = \frac{\text{Dividends}}{\text{Stock price}} + \text{Growth}$$

For example, if investors expect to receive cash dividends next year of $2 per share and the common stock is currently selling for $40 per share, the expected dividend yield would be 5 percent ($2/$40). This would not likely be considered an adequate total return. Consequently, investors in this common stock would expect some price appreciation over time. If the current $40 stock price is expected to rise to $43 over the next year, then the appreciation would be 7.5 percent ([$43 – $40]/$40). If this one-year increase is expected to be the long-run average growth, then the total expected return is

$$\text{Expected return} = 5\% + 7.5\% = 12.5\%$$

We can also rewrite the above relationship by solving for the stock price:

$$\text{Stock price} = \frac{\text{Dividends}}{\text{Expected return} - \text{Growth rate}}$$

3. Alternatively, if we knew the current price for a bond, we could solve for the implied "internal rate of return" to the investor. This is a technique we will discuss later in the chapter.

Now, if we know that investors expect a 12.5 percent rate of return, that the expected growth rate is 7.5 percent, and that the stock is expected to pay $2 per share in cash dividends next year, we can solve for the present value of the stock by substituting the term *stock value* for *stock price*.

$$\text{Stock value} = \frac{\$2}{0.125 - 0.075} = \frac{\$2}{0.05} = \$40$$

Notice that the estimated stock value is the same as the current stock price in our example. However, if investors were to reduce their expected return to 11.5 percent because of lower inflation expectations for the economy, the stock-value estimate would increase as follows:

$$\text{Stock value} = \frac{\$2}{0.115 - 0.075} = \frac{\$2}{0.04} = \$50$$

We would expect the actual stock price to adjust upward to the estimated stock value as the lower inflation expectations are incorporated into security values by investors. Stock prices change over time in response to changes in investor-expected returns (influenced by changes in interest rates), growth rates, and cash dividend levels.

In general, investments in stocks are considered riskier than those in bonds. This is because stock prices fluctuate more widely than bond prices; also there is greater uncertainty about the returns from stocks. Bond investors depend largely on interest income and the knowledge that a bond will be worth $1,000 at maturity as long as the issuer does not default. On the other hand, stock dividends and stock price appreciation are much more uncertain. Thus stockholders must expect and receive, over the long run, higher returns than bondholders to compensate for the risk. As interest rates rise, stockholders must anticipate even higher returns, and vice versa.

The typical risk-return relationship between long-term debt and equity securities is depicted in Figure 10.1. Long-term U.S. government securities are considered to have virtually no risk of default. Because of their safety, investors require only a moderate rate of return on these bond investments. Corporate bonds are riskier, so investors expect higher returns as compensation for assuming greater default risk. As we just discussed, common stocks are even riskier on average, and investors must be compensated accordingly with higher average returns. Stated differently, we can view the risk-return relationships shown in Figure 10.1 as an investor "indifference curve" for securities of varying degrees of risk.

For a particular firm at a specific point in time, its stockholders or owners will expect a higher rate of return than its long-term debt holders. As we now look at the management of fixed assets, it is

FIGURE 10.1
Risk-Return Relationship for Long-term Securities

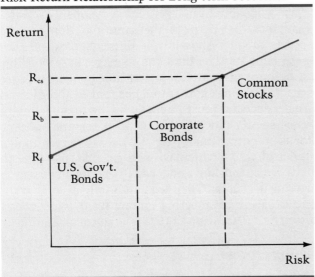

important to keep this in mind. The financial manager must set a rate of return that the firm needs to earn on its asset investments in order to cover the cost of debt and still leave an adequate rate of return for the owners. The combined rate necessary to cover the cost of debt and equity funds is the firm's **cost of capital**.

cost of capital
the rate needed to cover
the cost of debt and
equity funds

MANAGEMENT OF FIXED ASSETS

Fixed-assets management involves making proper capital budgeting decisions. The financial manager must compare capital expenditures for plant and equipment, against the cash-flow benefits that will be received from these investments over several years. When properly adjusted benefits exceed expenditures, these projects will help increase the firm's value.

It is investment in fixed assets that provides the basis for the manufacturing firm's earning power or profitability. Plant and equipment are employed to manufacture inventories that will be sold for profit, produce cash inflows, and make the firm more valuable. Proper capital-budgeting decisions must be made by the financial manager for this to occur. The types of decisions include: whether to replace existing equipment with new equipment; whether to expand existing product lines by adding more plant and equipment similar to that in use; or whether to expand into new product areas requiring new types of fixed assets.

There are other types of capital-management decisions. For example, two or more machines that perform the same function may be available from competing suppliers, possibly at different costs and with different expected cash benefits. The financial manager is responsible for choosing the best of these alternatives. In addition, projects that are not in direct competition with one another must be ranked according to their expected returns; a decision must be made by the financial manager about which projects will be included in the firm's capital budget.

We are able to focus on only a small part of what is a very complex topic. In the remainder of this chapter, we will first discuss how to determine relevant cash expenditures and cash benefits involved in making capital budgeting decisions. Then we will briefly discuss available techniques for evaluating or selecting among fixed-asset investments. This is followed by a discussion of risk-related considerations.

The Capital Budgeting Process

The capital budgeting process involves the preparation and analysis of a "business case" request for funding, and usually consists of the following five stages:

1. Identification
2. Development
3. Selection
4. Implementation
5. Follow-up

The identification stage involves finding potential capital investment opportunities and identifying whether a project involves a replacement decision and/or revenue expansion. Development requires estimating relevant cash inflows and outflows. It also involves discussing the pros and cons of each project; sometimes asking: "What if we don't do it?"

The third stage, selection, involves applying the appropriate capital budgeting techniques to help make a final accept or reject decision. Projects that are accepted then must be implemented (the fourth stage) in a timely fashion. Finally, past decisions need to be periodically reviewed with a follow-up analysis to determine whether they are meeting expectations. When this is done, sometimes it is necessary to terminate or abandon previous decisions.

MULTINATIONAL CORPORATION INVESTMENT CONSIDERATIONS

The multinational corporation (MNC) must go through the same capital budgeting process just described. In addition, however, MNCs need to consider possible added political and economic risks when making their decisions. Risk adjustments may be necessary due to the possibility of seizure of assets, unstable currencies, and weak foreign economies. MNCs must also consider the impact of foreign exchange controls and foreign tax regulations on a project's cash flows in relation to the final amounts that may be paid to the parent MNC.

Determining Relevant Cash Flows

The decision of whether to invest in a fixed asset begins with the development of a schedule of relevant cash flows. For many fixed-asset investments, all cash outlays occur at the time of purchase. For example, let's assume that a producer will sell you a machine press for $18,000. It will cost you an additional $2,000 for transporting and installing the press. The sum of these expenditures is $20,000 and represents the initial outlay now, which is referred to as time-period zero.

Potential after-tax cash inflows to be derived from operating the machine press are more difficult to assess. The producer's specifications about the machine press's output will be helpful. If the firm has previously purchased similar machine presses, it can also use past experiences to assess the cost of producing annual inventories and the resulting before-tax cash benefits from their sale. Adjustments then must be made for tax payments, so that after-tax cash inflows can be directly compared with the initial investment outlays that are payable out of after-tax dollars.

Let's assume that the machine press will have a five-year life and then it will be discarded. Cash revenues from the sale of inventories produced by the machine press are expected to be $12,000 per year. Cash operating expenses associated with the use of the press are estimated at $5,600 per year. The firm also is entitled to "write off," or depreciate, the machine press for income tax purposes. Let's assume that $4,000 ($20,000/5 years) can be depreciated each year[4] and that the firm has a 25 percent income tax rate.

The relevant annual after-tax cash earnings can be estimated as follows:

Cash revenues	$12,000
Cash operating expenses	– 5,600
Cash earnings before depreciation	$ 6,400
Depreciation	– 4,000
Cash earnings before taxes	$ 2,400
Income taxes (25%)	– 600
Cash earnings after taxes	$ 1,800

4. Current income tax laws specify methods for depreciating business assets. These specifications are referred to as the modified accelerated cost recovery system (MACRS).

It is important to understand that the $1,800 represents cash earnings after taxes and not the after-tax cash inflow. This is because depreciation does not involve actual cash disbursements; it is only an accounting bookkeeping entry for income tax purposes. To figure the cash inflow after taxes, we would start with the $6,400 in cash earnings before depreciation and subtract the $600 in income taxes that were paid in cash. The annual cash inflow after taxes is $5,800 ($6,400 – $600). Most computer software models arrive at cash inflows after taxes by beginning with the cash earnings after taxes, in this case $1,800. The amount of the depreciation ($4,000), which did not involve any actual outflow of cash, is added back to arrive at the inflow ($5,800).

The after-tax cash outflows and inflows can now be combined into the following schedule for the five-year life of the machine press:

YEAR	CASH FLOW
0	–$20,000
1	5,800
2	5,800
3	5,800
4	5,800
5	5,800

In the example of the machine press, a $20,000 initial investment is expected to produce a stream of benefits amounting to $29,000 over a five-year period ($5,800 × 5). This is a net benefit of $9,000 ($29,000 – $20,000). Would you recommend investing in the machine press? If money had no time value, the answer would definitely be yes. Instead of making a quick decision, however, we must first consider some capital budgeting evaluation techniques.

Capital Budgeting Techniques

Methods or techniques for selecting among fixed-asset investments provide the basis for making proper capital budgeting decisions. Any approach needs to reflect the fact that cash outlays for plant and equipment occur now, while the benefits occur in the future. Three methods—payback period, net present value, and internal rate of return—are widely utilized.

payback period method
evaluation technique
that determines the time
it will take to recover an
initial investment in
fixed assets

PAYBACK PERIOD
The **payback period method** determines the time in years it will take to recover the initial investment in fixed assets. Let's return to our earlier machine press example that requires a $20,000 cash outlay and

Business firms are allowed to depreciate their fixed assets based on a stated schedule. The amount of depreciation allowed is important because it reduces the amount of income tax liability, therefore increasing the amount of cash inflows after taxes that are expected from investments in fixed assets. Financial managers make their capital budgeting decisions by comparing the after-tax cash flow benefits with the dollar amount of the investment. In some cases, the size of the depreciation expenses will have a major impact on whether or not to go ahead with a capital budgeting project.

HOW DEPRECIATION CAN INFLUENCE CAPITAL BUDGETING DECISIONS

The Economic Recovery Tax Act of 1981 provided a major overhaul of allowed depreciation expenses by instituting the accelerated cost recovery system (ACRS). This system is intended to stimulate business investment in plant and equipment. Under the Tax Reform Act of 1986, business assets such as computers, copiers, and autos fall into a five-year property class and are written off over six years. This is because of the half-year convention that treats any asset as if it were in service for six months of the year it was bought. Manufacturing equipment, fixtures, and office furniture are considered to be seven-year property class assets and must be depreciated over an eight year period. Following are the annual depreciation percentages allowed for the five-year and seven-year property classifications.

YEAR	5-YEAR	7-YEAR
1	20%	14%
2	32	25
3	19	17
4	12	13
5	11	9
6	6	9
7		9
8		4
	100%	100%

will produce after-tax cash inflows of $5,800 per year for five years. We will refer to this alternative as Project A. Another machine press investment, Project B, will cost $25,000 but is expected to provide a stream of after-tax cash inflows beginning with $4,000 the first year and ending with $10,000 in the fifth year. The cash flow streams are summarized as follows for the two projects:

YEAR	PROJECT A	PROJECT B
0	−$20,000	−$25,000
1	5,800	4,000
2	5,800	4,000
3	5,800	8,000
4	5,800	10,000
5	5,800	10,000

The payback period method may be used to compare the two investments to determine which one recovers its initial outlay more quickly. In cases where the cash benefits form an annuity, the payback period is easily calculated:

$$\text{Payback period} = \frac{\text{Initial outlay}}{\text{Annual cash inflow}}$$

For Project A we have: payback period = $20,000/$5,800 = 3.4 years.

Cash inflows for Project B will total $16,000 ($4,000 + $4,000 + $8,000) for the first three years. This leaves $9,000 ($25,000 − $16,000) still unrecovered. It will take an additional 0.9 of the fourth year ($9,000/ $10,000) before the investment is fully recovered. Thus the payback period for Project B is 3.9 years. Based solely on the payback-period technique, Project A would be chosen over Project B because it recoups its investment more quickly.

However, the payback-period evaluation method suffers from two basic drawbacks. First, the technique does not consider the time value of money. The second limitation is that all cash flows beyond the payback period are ignored. Notice that Project B will return $10,000 in cash inflow in year five, which is substantially more than Project A's fifth year cash inflow. The possible significance of this difference is overlooked by the payback period method.

NET PRESENT VALUE

net present value method *evaluation technique that calculates the present value of all cash inflows from a project's operations minus the initial investment*

The **net present value method** overcomes the shortcomings of the payback period by considering the time value of money as well as all expected after-tax cash inflows. A project's net present value is calculated as the present value of all cash inflows for the life of the property less the initial investment or outlay. When the net present value is positive that means that the project's returns are greater than its investment plus financing costs. A project is acceptable because the firm's value will increase.

In order to apply the net present value method, we need to know the firm's required rate of return for discounting purposes. This required rate, which the financial manager has determined, should reflect the cost of long-term debt and equity capital funds. For this problem, let's assume that the required rate of return or cost of capital is 10 percent.

We can now apply the net present value technique to the cash flows for Projects A and B, which are shown in Table 10.6. The cash flows are multiplied by the 10 percent PVIF from Table 10.3 to get the present values. Notice that there is no discount for the initial outlays because they occur before any time has passed (i.e., in year zero). Positive net present values are shown for both projects. This means that an investment in either project will provide a rate of return that is greater than 10 percent. However, Project A, with the higher net present value of $1,982, is preferable to Project B, which has a net present value of $988.

A short-cut method can be used to calculate the net present value for Project A. Since the cash inflows form an annuity we could have used the FVIFA at 10 percent for five years from Table 10.4, which is 3.791. The net present value then can be calculated:

$$\$5,800 \times 3.791 \quad = \quad
\begin{array}{rl}
\$21,988 & \text{PV cash inflows} \\
\underline{-20,000} & \text{Initial outlay} \\
\$\ 1,988 & \text{Net present value}
\end{array}$$

The $1,988 net present value figure differs slightly from the $1,982 shown in Table 10.6 due to a rounding of the present-value interest factors in Table 10.3. When cash inflows are not in the form of an annuity, as in the case of Project B, the longer calculation process shown in Table 10.6 must be used to find the net present value.

Projects with negative net present values are not acceptable to a firm. They provide returns lower than the cost of capital and would cause the value of the firm to fall. Clearly, it is important for the financial manager to make capital budgeting decisions on the basis of their expected impact on the firm's value.

INTERNAL RATE OF RETURN

While the net present value method tells us that both Projects A and B provide expected returns that are greater than 10 percent, we do not know the actual rates of return. The ***internal rate of return method*** is

internal rate of return method
finding the rate of return that causes the net present value to be zero

TABLE 10.6   Net Present Value Calculations

	PROJECT A			PROJECT B		
YEAR	CASH FLOW	× 10% PVIF	= PRESENT VALUE	CASH FLOW	× 10% PVIF	= PRESENT VALUE
0	−$20,000	1.000	−$20,000	−$25,000	1.000	−$25,000
1	5,800	0.909	5,272	4,000	0.909	3,636
2	5,800	0.826	4,791	4,000	0.826	3,304
3	5,800	0.751	4,356	8,000	0.751	6,008
4	5,800	0.683	3,961	10,000	0.683	6,830
5	5,800	0.621	3,602	10,000	0.621	6,210
	Net Present Value	=	$1,982	Net Present Value	=	$988

designed to calculate the actual return rate by finding the return that causes the net present value to be zero—that is, when the present value of the cash inflows equals the project's initial investment.[5] A trial-and-error process is used to find the internal rate of return (IRR).

Let's illustrate the IRR process first for Project A. Because the cash inflows form an annuity, the IRR is easy to find. We divide the initial outlay (PV annuity) by the cash inflow annuity amount (annual receipt) to arrive at the present value interest factor for an ordinary annuity.

$$\text{PVIFA} = \frac{\text{PV annuity}}{\text{Annual receipt}}$$

Notice that this is simply a rearrangement of the present value of an annuity equation and is the same as the payback period equation. For Project A the PVIFA is 3.448 ($20,000/5,800).

We know this PVIFA of 3.448 is for five years. By turning to Table 4 in the Appendix, Present Value of a $1 Ordinary Annuity, we can read across the five-year row until we find a PVIFA close to 3.448. It falls between 3.605 (12 percent) and 3.433 (14 percent) but is much closer to the PVIFA at 14 percent. Thus the internal rate of return for Project A is a little less than 14 percent.

The trial-and-error process used to find the IRR for Project B is shown in Table 10.7. Discounting the cash flows at a 10 percent rate results in a positive net present value of $988, as we previously calculated. A positive net present value indicates that we need to try a higher discount rate, such as 12 percent. The 12 percent present-value interest factors are taken from Table 3 in the Appendix, Present Value of $1. Notice that when the cash flows are discounted at a 12 percent rate, the net present value becomes minus $514. This indicates that the IRR

TABLE 10.7   Internal Rate of Return Calculations, Project B

YEAR	CASH FLOW	× 10% PVIF	= PRESENT VALUE	CASH FLOW	× 12% PVIF	= PRESENT VALUE
0	−$25,000	1.000	−$25,000	−$25,000	1.000	−$25,000
1	4,000	0.909	3,636	4,000	0.893	3,572
2	4,000	0.826	3,304	4,000	0.797	3,188
3	8,000	0.751	6,008	8,000	0.712	5,696
4	10,000	0.683	6,830	10,000	0.636	6,360
5	10,000	0.621	6,210	10,000	0.567	5,670
	Net Present Value	=	$988	Net Present Value	=	−$514

5.   This method is also used to find the "yield to maturity" on bonds. We will discuss bond yields more fully in Chapter 22.

actually falls between 10 and 12 percent. Since minus $514 is closer to zero than $988, the IRR is a little above 11 percent.

If discounting at a 12 percent rate had yielded a positive net present value for Project B, then a higher discount rate would have been applied. This process is continued until the net present value approaches zero and the IRR is reached.

The higher IRR for Project A is consistent with the higher net present value we previously found. Both projects are acceptable because they provide returns that are higher than the 10 percent cost of capital. However, since we want only one machine press, we would select Project A over Project B.

Risk-Related Considerations

The degree of risk associated with expected cash inflows may vary substantially among different fixed-asset investments. For example, a decision about whether to replace an existing machine with a new, more efficient machine would not involve substantial cash inflow uncertainty. This is because the firm already has some operating experience for the existing machine. Likewise, expansion in existing product lines allows the firm to base cash inflow expectations on past operating results. These capital budgeting decisions can be made by discounting at the firm's cost of capital because they are comparable in risk to the firm's other assets.

Expansion projects involving new areas and product lines are usually associated with greater cash inflow uncertainty. In order to compensate for this greater risk, financial managers often apply risk-adjusted discount rates to these cash flows. A **risk-adjusted discount rate** contains a risk premium that is added to the firm's cost of capital. For example, let's use the previously presented data for Projects A and B to illustrate the use of risk-adjusted discount rates. Let's assume that Project A involves expansion in an existing product line, whereas Project B is for a new product. The firm's 10 percent cost of capital would be the appropriate discount rate for Project A. Recall that this would result in a net present value of $1,982.

In contrast, a higher discount rate for Project B's cash flows of possibly 12 percent—the 10 percent cost of capital plus a 2 percentage point risk premium—might be judged appropriate by the financial manager. Recall from Table 10.7 that this would result in a net present value of minus $514. Thus, on a risk-adjusted basis, Project A would still be acceptable to the firm, but Project B would be rejected. Making adjustments for risk differences is a difficult but necessary task if the financial manager is to make capital budgeting decisions that will increase the value of the firm.

risk-adjusted discount rate
risk premium added to a firm's cost of capital

KEY TERMS

annuity   internal rate of return method
compounding   net present value method
cost of capital   payback period method
discounting   risk-adjusted discount rate

DISCUSSION QUESTIONS

1. Describe the process of compounding.
2. What is an annuity? How do ordinary annuities and annuities due differ?
3. What is meant by discounting? Give an illustration.
4. Describe the process for determining the size of a constant periodic payment that is necessary to fully amortize a loan.
5. How is the present value of a corporate bond determined?
6. Briefly describe what is meant by the risk-return relationship for long-term securities.
7. Why is proper management of fixed assets crucial to the success of a firm?
8. Briefly describe the capital budgeting process, and identify some additional considerations faced by multinational corporations.
9. What types of cash flows are important in making capital budgeting decisions? What is meant by an after-tax cash inflow?
10. Describe the payback method for making capital budgeting decisions.
11. What is meant by a project's net present value? How is it used for choosing between projects?
12. Identify the internal rate of return method and describe how it is used in making capital budgeting decisions.
13. How are risk-adjusted discount rates used?

PROBLEMS

1. Determine the future values if $5,000 is invested in each of the following situations: (a) 5 percent for ten years, (b) 7 percent for seven years, and (c) 9 percent for four years.
2. Assume you are planning to invest $5,000 each year for six years and will earn 10 percent per year. Determine the future value of this annuity if your first $5,000 is invested now. How would your answer change if you waited one year before making the first investment?

3. Determine the present value if $15,000 is to be received at the end of eight years and the discount rate is 9 percent. How would your answer change if you had to wait six years to receive the $15,000?

4. What is the present value of a loan that calls for the payment of $500 per year for six years if the discount rate is 10 percent and the first payment will be made one year from now? How would your answer change if the $500 per year occurred for ten years?

5. Determine the annual payment on a $15,000 loan that is to be amortized over a four-year period and carries a 10 percent interest rate. Also prepare a loan amortization schedule for this loan.

6. Assume a $1,000 face value bond pays interest of $85 per year and has an eight-year life. If investors are willing to accept a 10 percent rate of return on bonds of similar quality, what is the present value or worth of this bond? How would the value change if investors wanted an 8 percent rate of return?

7. A machine can be purchased for $10,500 including transportation charges, but installation costs will require $1,500 more. The machine is expected to last four years and produce annual cash revenues of $6,000. Annual cash operating expenses are expected to be $2,000, with depreciation of $3,000 per year; the firm has a 30 percent tax rate. Determine the relevant after-tax cash flows and prepare a cash flow schedule.

8. Use the information in Problem 7 to determine the machine's relevant cash flows.
   a. Calculate the payback period for the machine.
   b. If the firm's cost of capital is 10 percent, would you recommend buying the machine?
   c. Estimate the internal rate of return for the machine.

9. The Sanders Electric Company is evaluating two projects for possible inclusion in the firm's capital budget. Project M will require a $37,000 investment while Project O's investment will be $46,000. After-tax cash inflows are estimated as follows for the two projects:

YEAR	PROJECT M	PROJECT O
1	$12,000	$10,000
2	12,000	10,000
3	12,000	15,000
4	12,000	15,000
5		15,000

   a. Determine the payback period for each project.
   b. Calculate the net present value for each project based on a 10 percent cost of capital. Which, if either, of the projects is acceptable?
   c. Determine the approximate internal rate of return for Projects M and O.

10. Project R requires an investment of $45,000 and is expected to produce after-tax cash inflows of $15,000 per year for five years. The basic cost-of-capital rate is 10 percent.
   a. Determine the payback period and the net present value for Project R. Is the project acceptable?
   b. Now, assume that the appropriate risk-adjusted discount rate is 14 percent. Calculate the risk-adjusted net present value. Is the project acceptable after adjusting for its greater risk?
   c. Calculate the approximate internal rate of return.

11. Assume the financial manager of the Sanders Electric Company in Problem 9 believes that Project M is comparable in risk to the firm's other assets. In contrast, there is greater uncertainty concerning Project O's after-tax cash inflows. Sanders Electric uses a 4 percentage point risk premium for riskier projects. The firm's cost of capital is 10 percent.
   a. Determine the risk-adjusted net present values for Project M and Project O, using risk-adjusted discount rates where appropriate.
   b. Are both projects acceptable investments? Which one would you choose?

12. The Franklin Corporation's common stock is currently selling for $50 per share. Management expects to pay out cash dividends amounting to $4 per share next year. Furthermore, the stock is expected to appreciate at a 4 percent annual compound growth rate in the future.
   a. Determine the total annual rate of return stock investors can expect.
   b. Estimate Franklin's stock value if the growth rate is expected to be only 2 percent in the future. Assume other factors remain constant.
   c. Estimate Franklin's stock value if the expected rate of return declines to 11 percent because of lower future inflation expectations. Assume other factors remain constant.
   d. Determine the cost of equity capital (this is the same as the investors' expected return) for Franklin if next year's expected dividend is $3, the stock is expected to sell for $54 per share at the end of next year, and the current stock price is $50 per share.

13. Use the Present and Future Value of a Lump Sum tool to answer the following questions:
   a. What would be the future value of $15,555 invested now if it earns interest at 14.5 percent for seven years?
   b. What would be the future value of $19,378 invested now if the money remains deposited for eight years and the annual interest rate is 18 percent?

c. How would your answer in part b. change if interest on your investment is compounded quarterly?

14. Use the Present and Future Value of a Lump Sum tool to answer the following questions:
    a. What is the present value of $359,000 that is to be received at the end of 23 years if the appropriate discount rate is 11 percent?
    b. How would your answer in part a. change if semiannual discounting were used?
    c. How would your answer in part a. change if monthly discounting were used?

15. Use the Present and Future Value of an Annuity tool to answer the following questions:
    a. What would be the future value of $7,455 invested annually for nine years beginning one year from now if the annual interest rate is 19 percent?
    b. What would be the present value of a $9,532 annuity for which the first payment will be made beginning one year from now, payments will last for 27 years, and the annual interest rate is 13 percent?
    c. How would your answer in part b. change if quarterly discounting occurred and $2,383 is invested at the end of each quarter?

16. A $1,000 face value bond issued by the Dysane Company currently pays total annual interest of $79 per year and has a thirteen-year life. Use the Bond Yield to Maturity and Bond Valuation tool to answer the following questions about it:
    a. What is the present value, or worth, of this bond if investors are currently willing to accept a 10 percent annual rate of return on bonds of similar quality?
    b. How would your answer in part a. change if interest payments are made semiannually (i.e., $39.50 every six months) by the Dysane Company?
    c. How would your answer in part b. change if, one year from now, investors only required a 6.5 percent annual rate of return on bond investments similar in quality to the Dysane bond?

17. The BioTek Corporation has a basic cost of capital of 15 percent and is considering investing in either or both of the following projects. Project HiTek will require an investment of $453,000, while Project LoTek's investment will be $276,000. The following after-tax cash flows (including the investment outflows in year zero) are estimated for each project.

YEAR	PROJECT HITEK	PROJECT LOTEK
0	−$453,000	−$276,000
1	132,000	74,000
2	169,500	83,400

3	193,000	121,000
4	150,700	54,900
5	102,000	101,000
6	-0-	29,500
7	-0-	18,000

Use the Present Value, Future Value, and Internal Rate of Return of a Series of Cash Flows tool to evaluate these two projects.

a. Determine the present value of the cash inflows for each project and then calculate their net present values by subtracting the appropriate dollar amount of capital investment. Which, if either, of the projects is acceptable?

b. Calculate the internal rates of return for Project HiTek and Project LoTek. Which project would be preferred?

c. Now assume that BioTek uses risk-adjusted discount rates in order to adjust for differences in risk among different investment opportunities. BioTek projects are discounted at the firm's cost of capital of 15 percent. A risk premium of 3 percentage points is assigned to LoTek types of projects, while a 6 percentage point risk premium is used for projects similar to HiTek. Determine the risk-adjusted present value of the cash inflows for LoTek and HiTek and calculate their risk-adjusted net present values. Should BioTek invest in either or even both HiTek and LoTek projects?

SELF-TEST QUESTIONS

1. Time value of money problems can be solved by using which of the following methods?
    a. equations and appropriate time-value-of-money tables
    b. a financial calculator
    c. an appropriate computer software program
    d. all of the above

2. When solving for the future value of an amount deposited now, which one of the following factors would *not* be an input?
    a. present value amount
    b. 1 plus the interest rate
    c. 1 divided by the sum of 1 plus the interest rate
    d. number of periods to compound over

3. Assume that you currently hold a ten-year maturity bond with a stated interest rate of 12 percent. What will happen to the bond's

value if next month investors require a 10 percent yield on bonds of similar quality? The bond value will:

a. increase
b. decrease
c. remain unchanged
d. be worth $1,000

4. Which one of the following is *not* one of the stages in the capital budgeting process?

a. identification
b. development
c. argumentation
d. selection

5. Which of the following capital budgeting techniques does *not* explicitly consider the time value of money?

a. payback period
b. net present value
c. internal rate of return
d. all of the above

SELF-TEST PROBLEMS

1. Assume you are planning to invest $100 each year for four years and will earn 10 percent per year. Determine the future value of this annuity if your first $100 is invested now. How would your answer change if you waited one year before making the first investment?

2. The Consolidated Company is evaluating a project, code named MXG, for possible inclusion in the firm's capital budget. Project MXG will require a $40,000 investment. After-tax cash inflows are estimated as follows:

YEAR	PROJECT MXG
1	$12,000
2	12,000
3	12,000
4	12,000

a. Determine the payback period for the project.
b. Calculate the net present value for the project based on a 10 percent cost of capital. Is the project acceptable?
c. Determine the approximate internal rate of return for Project MXG.

SUGGESTED READINGS

Bierman, Harold Jr., and Seymour Smidt. *The Capital Budgeting Decision*, 7e. New York: Macmillan, 1988.

Brigham, Eugene E. *Fundamentals of Financial Management*, 5e. Hinsdale, IL: The Dryden Press, 1989. Chaps. 9, 10, and 11.

Gitman, Lawrence J., and Vincent A. Mercurio. "Cost of Capital Techniques Used by Major U.S. Firms." *Financial Management* (Winter 1982): 21–29.

Pinches, George E. *Essentials of Financial Management*, 3e. New York: Harper & Row, 1990. Chaps. 8, 9, and 10.

Shao, Stephen P. *Mathematics for Management and Finance*, 6e. Cincinnati: South-Western Publishing Co., 1991.

Shapiro, Alan C. *Multinational Financial Management*, 3e. Boston: Allyn and Bacon, 1989. Chap. 17.

ANSWERS TO SELF-TEST QUESTIONS   1. d   2. c   3. a   4. c   5. a

SOLUTIONS TO SELF-TEST PROBLEMS

1. First investment now (annuity due problem):
   $100 (6.105 − 1) = $100 (5.105) = $510.50
   First investment at end of 1 year (ordinary annuity problem): $100 (4.641) = $464.10

2. a. Payback period for project MXG: $40,000/$12,000 = 3.3 years
   b. Project MXG PVIFA at 10% for 4 years = 3.170
      $12,000 × 3.170   = $38,040
                          −40,000
      Net present value: −$1,960
      Do not accept Project MXG.
   c. Internal rate of return for Project MXG:
      PVIFA = $40,000/$12,000 = 3.333
      Turning to Table 10.4 and the 4-year row, we find the 3.333 is slightly higher than 3.312 at 8%, indicating the IRR is slightly less than 8%.

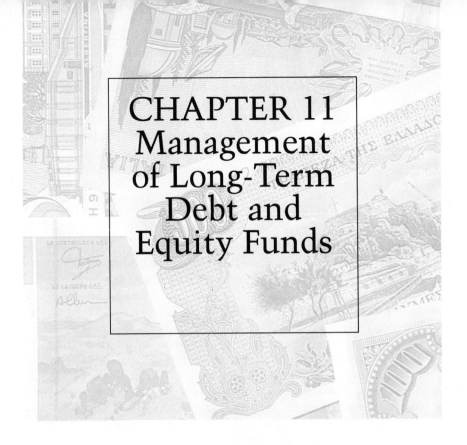

CHAPTER 11
Management of Long-Term Debt and Equity Funds

After studying this chapter, you should be able to:

- Identify the major sources of long-term funds available to corporations.
- Describe internal versus external financing and explain why dividend policy and practices are important.
- Explain the term *corporate equity capital* and describe the types of equity securities.
- Explain the term *debt capital* and describe the types of debt securities.
- Explain the role of the return and risk factors in choosing a long-term financing mix.
- Describe and discuss the impact of flexibility, control, timing, and availability factors on the financing mix decision.

Raising funds to finance assets is an important financial management function. In Chapter 8 we discussed the need to apply the principle of hedging as it related to matching the average maturities of a firm's assets and liabilities. This was followed by a discussion of working capital management, including the principal instruments of short-term financing. We are now ready to return to long-term debt and equity funds.

We begin by describing the relative importance of sources of funds for corporations. This is followed by a discussion of internal versus external financing. Then characteristics of bonds and stocks, securities that are unique to corporate organization, are covered. The final section focuses on long-term external financing policies and examines the mix between debt and equity funds.

INTERNAL VERSUS EXTERNAL FINANCING

Long-term financing for most businesses is usually made up of both internal and external forms. For some types of business, in fact, there may be little need for any type of financial support from the capital markets. These corporations that require little investment in fixed assets (for example, firms operating in service industries) rely almost exclusively upon internally generated funds. Other businesses, such as high technology firms, because of rapid growth and small amounts of internally generated funds relative to capital needs, may be forced to go often to the capital markets to finance their requirements. But the decision to use internal versus external financing is not based simply on whether internal funds are inadequate to meet the needs of the business. Rather, businesses must balance internal and external financing in a way that provides them with the best overall financial position.

The proportion of internal to external financing varies over the business cycle. During periods of economic expansion, it is customary for firms to rely more on external funds because investment opportunities grow faster than internally generated funds. During periods of economic contraction the reverse is true. As profitable investment opportunities become fewer, the rate of investment is reduced and reliance on external capital markets decreases.

Internal Financing

Corporations as a group rely heavily on internal financing sources to help meet their asset needs. Table 11.1 shows these sources for several recent years. Internal sources include capital consumption allowances and after-tax corporate profits not distributed as cash dividends to stockholders. We often refer to these undistributed profits as retained earnings. Notice that in 1989 corporate profits after taxes amounted to $159.3 billion and that $122.1 billion was paid out in dividends. This left $37.2 billion, or 23.4 percent of after-tax profits, retained by the corporations.

Capital consumption, or depreciation, allowances provide the major source of internally generated funds available to corporations. They are usually viewed as providing for the replacement of worn-out

TABLE 11.1
Annual Sources of Funds for Corporations (in Billions of Dollars)

	1985	1987	1989
INTERNALLY GENERATED FUNDS			
Profits after taxes	$131.4	$142.0	$159.3
Less dividends	81.6	98.7	122.1
Undistributed profits	$ 49.8	$ 43.3	$ 37.2
Capital consumption allowances	253.7	281.7	317.1
Total	$303.5	$325.0	$354.3
Dividend payout ratio (dividends/profits after taxes)	62.1%	69.5%	76.6%
NEW SECURITY ISSUES			
Corporate bonds	$165.8	$325.8	$201.0
Corporate preferred stocks	6.5	10.1	6.2
Corporate common stocks	29.0	43.2	26.0
Total	$201.3	$379.1	$233.2
Percent of total security issues:			
Corporate bonds	82.4%	85.9%	86.2%
Corporate preferred stocks	3.2	2.7	2.7
Corporate common stocks	14.4	11.4	11.1

Sources: Capital consumption allowances are from the "Economic Report of the President" (February 1990): 308. The remaining data are from the *Federal Reserve Bulletin*, (May 1990): A34 and A35.

fixed assets. Table 11.1 shows that capital consumption allowances amounted to $317.1 billion in 1989 and accounted for over 85 percent of the total amount of internally generated funds.

External Financing

Corporations also satisfy a substantial portion of their annual need for funds from external sources. Short-term funds come from increases in trade credit, bank loans, and by issuing short-term promissory notes. Long-term funds are obtained by issuing corporate bonds and stocks. Table 11.1 shows that the total of new security issues amounted to $233.2 billion in 1989, which was about two-thirds of the internally generated funds. Most of the security issues funds come from corporate bond sales. In fact, corporate bonds exceeded 85 percent of total new security issues in 1987 and 1989.

Corporate preferred stocks account for only a small portion of funds raised through new security issues. In contrast, corporate common stocks accounted for 14 percent of the funds raised through new security sales in 1985. The relative importance of common stock issues fell in 1987 and 1989 to about 11 percent.

Dividend Policy

Who Cares?

One of the most important aspects of both external and internal financing is a firm's dividend policy. A liberal dividend payout may be seen favorably by the stockholders, but it also reduces internally generated funds available for investment. It is important for corporate management to adopt a dividend policy that provides the company with a reasonable amount of retained earnings and also appeals to investors so that the public issues of securities will sell at favorable prices. Table 11.1 shows that business corporations paid out between 62 and 77 percent of their profits after taxes as dividends for the years 1985, 1987, and 1989.

Keep in mind that the capital markets are made up of many investors, each with individual investment goals and objectives. It is the task of the financial manager to orient the company's practices to appeal to the maximum number of investors in the capital markets. The company that pursues a policy of paying no dividends and retaining as much of its earnings as possible will probably find few investors interested in its stock. This is because many investors need current dividend income.

There are large differences in payout practices among different industries. The aerospace industry was characterized by an average cash dividend payout ratio, or dividends divided by earnings, of less than 40 percent during the 1980s. Over the same period, the average payout ratio for the electric utility industry was approximately 70 percent. Dividend payout policies can also vary substantially among firms in the same or related industries.

MAINTAINING CONSISTENT DIVIDEND PRACTICES

Once a dividend policy is established by a corporation, investors may be disturbed by changes in it. For this reason corporations tend to move slowly in changing their dividend paying practices. Companies in the same industry may have diverse dividend paying practices and yet individually pursue these practices with great success. For example, one company may have a liberal dividend policy and enjoy strong support in the capital markets. Another firm in the same line of activity may have a very conservative dividend policy and also enjoy strong market support. Yet, if each company tried to adopt the policy of the other, it is possible that both would experience criticism from their stockholders. Consistency, then, plays an important role in the dividend paying practices of the corporation.

The necessity of consistency reduces the possibility of coordinating the generation of funds with the need for those funds for investment purposes. If firms could use their earnings at any time they were needed and then pay out what is left as dividends, retained earnings would be a very convenient source of funds for investment. For most firms, however, retained earnings must be first used for dividends, which have first priority in the administration of income.

The ability to generate earnings adequate to pay cash dividends and allow for some earnings retention is influenced to a large extent by the firm's profit margin. Recall that the Du Pont system of financial analysis expresses the return on assets as a function of the asset turnover times the profit margin. Changes in the profit margin, or net income divided by net sales, given a stable dollar dividend policy, can cause substantial variation in earnings retention from year to year.

DIVIDENDS AND TAXES

Corporate income tax matters also influence the use of internal versus external financing. Although the corporation must pay income tax on its earnings, the stockholders have no personal income tax liability if the earnings are not distributed to them. The case is often made, therefore, that business should retain a maximum of earnings on behalf of its stockholders since this would prevent an immediate personal tax liability for them. However, corporate income tax regulations attempt to prevent corporations from using this device as an unfair tax shield. Unless the firm invests retained earnings in due time in business operations, an "undue accumulation of earnings" tax may be levied against the firm. The provision for possible tax penalties is contained in Section 531 of the Revenue Act of 1954.

Not all stockholders may wish to reinvest their portion of the firm's earnings in the corporations whose stocks they hold. Presumably a shareholder knows the dividend policies of the companies in which investments are planned and will, therefore, choose companies whose dividend practices suit his or her income needs and tax situation. If a company changes its dividend practice, the investor can simply sell the stock. In the case where a company has increased its retained earnings at the expense of stockholder dividends, the investor who sells stock can only hope that the reinvestment of earnings will be reflected in a higher market price for the stock.

LONG-TERM CORPORATE SECURITIES

The long-term capital funds for corporations are of two broad forms: equity capital and debt capital. Equity capital is obtained by selling shares of stock in the corporation. These shares may be divided into several classes, each having specified benefits and privileges with respect to ownership status in the corporation. In contrast to the equity capital of a corporation, debt capital represents funds obtained from creditors rather than from owners. Such capital may be obtained through direct negotiations with a lender or the sale of notes or bonds to many lenders.

Corporate Equity Capital

corporate equity capital
financial capital supplied by a corporation's owners through the purchase of shares of stock

stock certificate
represents ownership claim in a corporation

Corporate equity capital is the financial capital supplied by the owners of a corporation. This ownership claim is represented by the **stock certificate**, as shown in Figure 11.1. The stock certificate shows the type of stock held by the owner, the name of the company, the name of the stock's owner, and the signatures of certain company officers. Stock certificates are generally issued for 100 shares or multiples thereof. The stock certificate also has a space on the reverse for its assignment in the event that it is transferred to another person. As a protection against forgery, all signatures on transferred stock certificates must usually be

FIGURE 11.1   Common Stock Certificates

certified by a commercial bank's representative or a stock broker. If a stock certificate is lost, however, an individual may request a duplicate certificate. The corporation, in return, will generally require that a bond or surety be posted by the stockholder to protect the corporation if the lost certificate should later be presented.

When a stockholder sells his or her shares, the assigned stock certificate is forwarded to the company by the broker, and it is destroyed by the secretary of the corporation. A new certificate is issued to the new owner, whose name will then be carried on the stock record. For larger corporations an official transfer agent, generally a trust company or a bank, is appointed to accomplish this task. The larger corporations may also have an independent stock registrar to supervise the transfer of securities.

The common stock of a corporation may be assigned a **par value**, or stated value, in the certificate of incorporation. It usually bears little relationship to the current price or book value of the stock. If the corporation sells stock for less than the par value, the owners of the stock may become liable to creditors for the difference between the selling price and the par value if the company fails. Thus the limited liability of the stockholders may be lost. This technicality seldom creates any difficulty, however, since most stock is first sold at or above its par value. In addition, legal devices exist to protect against this contingent liability in such instances. Aside from the possibility that stock might be sold at less than its par value, par value has little significance. In fact, most states permit corporations to issue no-par stock which has no contingent liability. Equity securities of the corporation may be grouped broadly into two classes: common stock and preferred stock.

par value
stated value of stock

COMMON STOCK

Common stock represents ownership shares in a corporation. The outstanding characteristic of common stock is its complete claim to business profits that remain after the holders of all other classes of debt and equity securities have received their stipulated returns. It is generally the voting privilege of the common stockholders that governs the selection of the corporation's board of directors. The board of directors, in turn, exercises general control over the firm. For these reasons, the holders of common stock may be regarded as the basic owners of the corporation.

common stock
ownership shares in a corporation

The common stockholders' favorable position with respect to dividends and control of the corporation is offset by the fact that, during periods when profits are low, other claims may completely absorb available funds, leaving little or nothing for the common stockholders. The common stockholders, therefore, may expect less stability with respect to the amount of their dividends. They often receive considerably greater yield than other security holders during prosperous periods and generally less during periods of distress.

The common stockholders also have low priority when a business venture is liquidated. All creditors must receive their claims in full; preferred stockholders must, as a rule, be paid in full before common stockholders receive proceeds from liquidation. As with dividends, all liquidation proceeds remaining after prior obligations are all settled accrue to the common stockholders. It is seldom, however, that a corporation that has been forced to liquidate will provide enough proceeds to take care of the claims of creditors and preferred stockholders. Common stockholders generally receive little, if anything from liquidation proceedings. The common stockholders, therefore, are affected hardest by business failure, just as they enjoy the primary benefits of business success.

Common stock may be divided into special groups, generally Class A and Class B, in order to permit the acquisition of additional capital without diluting the control of the business. When a corporation issues two classes of common stock, it will often give voting rights to only one class, generally Class B. Except for voting, owners of Class A stock will usually have most, if not all, of the other rights and privileges of common stockholders. Issuing nonvoting equity securities is opposed by some government agencies, including the Securities and Exchange Commission, because it permits the concentration of ownership control. The New York Stock Exchange refuses to list the common stock of corporations that issue nonvoting classes of common stock.

PREFERRED STOCK

preferred stock
stock with priority claim over common stock for earnings and generally a stated dividend

Preferred stock is an equity security that has several stated preferences over common stock. In contrast with common stock, preferred stock generally carries a stated dividend. The dividend is specified as either a percentage of par value or as a fixed number of dollars per year. For example, a preferred stock may be a 9-percent preferred, meaning that its annual dividend participation is not to exceed 9 percent of its par or stated value. The dividend for no-par preferred stock is stated in terms of a dollar amount, for example, "preferred as to dividends in the amount of $9 annually." The holder of the preferred stock accepts the limitation on the amount of dividends as a fair exchange for the priority held in the earnings of the company.

As has been noted, before common stockholders receive any dividends, preferred stockholders must receive their full dividend. Preferred stock, therefore, offers the investor something of a compromise between basic equity securities like common stock and credit instruments such as bonds and long-term notes. Because preferred stocks are frequently nonvoting, many corporations issue them as a means of obtaining equity capital without diluting the control of the current stockholders.

Preferred stock may have special features. For example, it may be cumulative or noncumulative. **Cumulative preferred stock** requires that before dividends on common stock are paid, preferred dividends must be paid not only for the current period but also for all previous periods in which no preferred dividends were paid. It is important to remember that the preferred stockholders cannot force the payment of their dividends. They may have to wait until earnings are adequate to pay dividends. Cumulative preferred stock offers some protection for those periods during which dividends are not declared.

cumulative preferred stock
shares that require payment for all previous unpaid dividend periods before common stock dividends are paid

Noncumulative preferred stock, on the other hand, makes no provision for the accumulation of unpaid dividends. The result may be that management may be tempted to declare preferred dividends only when it appears that sufficient earnings are available to pay common stock dividends as well. Practically all modern preferred stock is cumulative.

noncumulative preferred stock
shares that do not require accumulated payment of unpaid dividends

Callable preferred stock gives the corporation the right to retire the preferred stock at its option. **Convertible preferred stock** has a special provision that makes it possible to convert it to common stock of the corporation at the stockholder's option. This, like many of the special features that preferred stock may have, exists primarily to attract investors to buy securities at times when distribution would otherwise be difficult.

callable preferred stock
shares that can be retired by the corporation at its option

convertible preferred stock
shares that can be converted to common stock at the stockholder's option

Debt Capital

In addition to the financial capital provided by the owners of the corporation, funds may also be secured from creditors on a long-term basis. *Debt capital*, however, must be preceded by an equity investment in the corporation on the part of the stockholders. Creditors generally require a contribution by the owners before committing their own funds to the corporation. Uses for borrowed funds may be the same as those for equity funds: acquisition of additional land, buildings, and equipment.

Holders of debt capital have certain rights and privileges not possessed by the holders of equity capital in a corporation. A debt instrument holder may force the firm to abide by the terms of the debt contract even if the result is reorganization or dissolution of the firm. The periodic interest payments due the holders of debt securities must be paid, therefore, if the corporation is to survive. In the event of liquidation, the holders of debt securities have priority over stockholders up to the limit of their claim against the corporation. Like preferred stock, corporate bonds may carry such special provisions as conversion rights in order to enhance their original sale.

Offsetting the advantage of this preferred position, the yield to which the creditors of a successful corporation are entitled is usually considerably less over a period of years than that available to the owners of equity securities. Also, as long as the corporation meets its contractual obligations, the creditors have little voice in its management and control, except for those formal agreements and restrictions that are stated in the loan contract.

Long-term corporate debt securities fall into two categories: secured obligations and unsecured obligations. Secured obligations are generally referred to as mortgage bonds, while unsecured obligations are called debenture bonds. Although ownership of many shares of stock may be evidenced by a single stock certificate, the bondholder has a separate security for each bond owned. On the face of the bond itself appear a description of the rights and obligations of the corporation and the bondholder. This includes the denomination of the bond (usually $1,000), maturity, interest rate, periods of interest payments, and the specific nature of the claim of the bond.

trust indenture
document stating a bond's contractual terms

If the bond contract is too complicated and extensive to be included on the face of the bond, this information is set out in a ***trust indenture***. This document is extensive and includes in great detail the various provisions of the loan arrangement. The trust indenture provides the basis for the settlement of disputes about the responsibilities and rights of the parties to the contract. It is essential that it be carefully preserved, normally by a trustee designated by the corporation. It is the trustee's duty to protect the indenture and enforce its provisions.

When there is a direct loan arrangement established between a corporation and a single lending institution, corporate notes may be used rather than bonds. Although long-term corporate notes are less formal in nature than bonds, they usually include many restrictive covenants not required for the typical short-term promissory note. Long-term corporate notes may also be used when a group of institutions negotiates jointly with a borrowing corporation.

MORTGAGE BONDS

mortgage bonds
corporate bonds secured by real property

Mortgage bonds are debt obligations secured by specifically pledged property. As a rule the mortgage applies only to real estate, buildings, and other assets classified as real property. For a corporation that issues bonds to expand its plant facilities, the mortgage usually includes only a lien, or legal claim, on the facilities to be constructed. As an interesting historical note, the opposite has been true of most railway expansions. Originally, railway construction was done in a piecemeal fashion. Extensions of track and facilities took place over a period of many years. Mortgage bonds issued to finance track extensions often included a lien on all the roadbed previously constructed as well as on the additional track.

When a parcel of real estate has more than one mortgage lien against it, the mortgage first filed for recording at the appropriate government office, generally the county recorder's office, has priority. The bonds outstanding against the mortgage are known as *first mortgage bonds*. The bonds outstanding against all mortgages subsequently recorded are known by the order in which they are filed, such as second or third mortgage bonds. Because first mortgage bonds have priority with respect to asset distribution if the business fails, they generally provide a lower yield to investors than the later liens. However, the second or third mortgage bonds of a strong company may be considered by investors to be safer than the first mortgage bonds of a less well-established company.

Mortgage bonds are of different types. A ***closed-end mortgage bond*** is sold under an arrangement that does not permit the sale of additional bonds secured by assets pledged as security for the first bond issue. Alternatively, an ***open-end mortgage bond*** is one in a continuing sale of bonds secured by the same mortgage. As a rule, under an open-end mortgage there is also a stipulation that additional real property that the company acquires automatically becomes a part of the property secured under the mortgage.

closed-end mortgage bond
allows only a single issue of bonds secured by one mortgage

open-end mortgage bond
allows for continuing sale of bonds secured by the same mortgage

DEBENTURE BONDS

Debenture bonds are unsecured obligations and depend on the general credit strength of the corporation for their security. They represent no specific pledge of property; their holders are classed as general creditors of the corporation equal with the holders of promissory notes and trade creditors. Debenture bonds are used by governmental bodies and by many industrial and utility corporations.

debenture bond
corporate bond that is not secured by property

THE LONG-TERM FINANCING MIX

The mix between debt and equity funds used to finance a firm's assets is an important financial management consideration. Because the cost of borrowed funds traditionally is fixed, debt can often be used to increase rates of return to the firm's owners, or stockholders in the case of corporations. Of course this higher potential return must be balanced against higher financial risk and combined leverage effects to determine the impact on the firm's value. Other conditions that impact on the mix between debt and equity capital are: flexibility, corporate control, timing, and availability.

Impact of Borrowing on Rates of Return

In Chapter 7 we introduced the Du Pont financial model or system, which expressed the rate of return on assets as follows:

$$\frac{\text{Net income}}{\text{Total assets}} = \frac{\text{Net sales}}{\text{Total assets}} \times \frac{\text{Net income}}{\text{Net sales}}$$

Return on assets = Asset turnover × Profit margin

Recall that this model was applied using financial statements for the Kenwood Manufacturing Company, shown here as Figures 11.2 and 11.3. The result was a 10 percent return on assets for Kenwood calculated on the basis of the following data:

$$\frac{\$50,000}{\$500,000} = \frac{\$700,000}{\$500,000} \times \frac{\$50,000}{\$700,000}$$

$$10\% = 1.4 \times 7.143\%$$

If a firm finances all of its assets with equity funds, then the return on assets would be the same as the return to the owners. However, almost all firms make use of current liabilities, and many also finance

FIGURE 11.2   Balance Sheet for the Kenwood Manufacturing Company

BALANCE SHEET
DECEMBER 31, 1991

ASSETS	
Cash and marketable securities	$ 25,000
Accounts receivable	100,000
Inventories	125,000
Total current assets	$250,000
Gross plant and equipment	$275,000
Less accumulated depreciation	75,000
Net plant and equipment	$200,000
Land	50,000
Total fixed assets	$250,000
Total assets	$500,000
LIABILITIES AND OWNERS' EQUITY	
Accounts payable	$ 75,000
Notes payable (bank, 10%)	20,000
Accrued liabilities	30,000
Total current liabilities	$125,000
Mortgage debt (12%)	100,000
Total liabilities	$225,000
Owners' equity	275,000
Total liabilities and owners' equity	$500,000

FIGURE 11.3
Income Statement for the Kenwood Manufacturing Company

**INCOME STATEMENT
YEAR ENDED DECEMBER 31, 1991**

Net revenues or sales	$700,000
Cost of goods sold	450,000
Gross profit	$250,000
General and administrative expenses	$115,000
Selling and marketing expenses	36,000
Depreciation	25,000
Interest	14,000
Total additional expenses	$190,000
Net income before income taxes	$ 60,000
Income taxes	10,000
Net income	$ 50,000

some of their assets with long-term debt. This gives the firm an opportunity to provide the owners with a rate of return on owners' equity that is higher than the rate of return on assets. Financial leverage makes this possible.

FINANCIAL LEVERAGE RATIOS
Financial leverage ratios, as noted in Chapter 7, indicate the extent to which assets are financed by borrowed funds and other liabilities. The **debt ratio**, total liabilities divided by total assets, is a common way of measuring financial leverage. We can calculate the debt ratio for Kenwood Manufacturing using the balance sheet data shown in Figure 11.2:

debt ratio
total liabilities divided by total assets

$$\text{Debt ratio} = \frac{\text{Total liabilities}}{\text{Total assets}} = \frac{\$225,000}{\$500,000} = 0.45 \text{ or } 45\%$$

This means that 45 percent of Kenwood's total assets are financed with debt funds.

To interpret the significance of the debt ratio, we must compare it over time for Kenwood or against the debt ratios of other firms in the same industry. For example, if the industry average is 40 percent, then Kenwood would be considered to be more risky than the industry average. A 50 percent industry ratio would make Kenwood relatively less risky. When a firm deviates substantially from industry norms, it may be severely penalized in the marketplace for its long-term securities. This possible consequence will be covered more fully in our discussion of risk implications.

An alternative way of expressing financial leverage is through the **equity multiplier ratio**, which is defined as total assets divided by

equity multiplier ratio
total assets divided by owners' equity

owners' equity. The calculation for Kenwood would be:

$$\text{Equity multiplier ratio} = \frac{\text{Total assets}}{\text{Owners' equity}} = \frac{\$500,000}{\$275,000} = 1.82$$

This means that the owners' investment is multiplied 1.82 times with debt funds to finance Kenwood's total assets. Notice that the equity multiplier can be found by knowing the debt ratio, and vice versa. For example, if debt is used to finance 45 percent of the total assets, then 55 percent is financed with equity funds. Dividing 1 by 0.55 gives the equity multiplier of 1.82.

The Du Pont return-on-assets model can be expanded into a return-on-owners'-equity model by using the equity multiplier ratio as follows:

$$\frac{\text{Net income}}{\text{Owners' equity}} = \frac{\text{Net sales}}{\text{Total assets}} \times \frac{\text{Net income}}{\text{Net sales}} \times \frac{\text{Total assets}}{\text{Owners' equity}}$$

$$\begin{array}{ccccc}\text{Return} \\ \text{on equity}\end{array} = \begin{array}{c}\text{Asset} \\ \text{turnover}\end{array} \times \begin{array}{c}\text{Profit} \\ \text{margin}\end{array} \times \begin{array}{c}\text{Equity} \\ \text{multiplier}\end{array}$$

Inserting the appropriate data for Kenwood from Figures 11.2 and 11.3 gives:

$$\frac{\$50,000}{\$275,000} = \frac{\$700,000}{\$500,000} \times \frac{\$50,000}{\$700,000} \times \frac{\$500,000}{\$275,000}$$

$$18.2\% = 1.4 \times 7.14\% \times 1.82$$

Thus, while Kenwood was able to earn a 10 percent return on assets, the firm provided its owners with an 18.2 percent return on their equity investment because debt funds were used to finance nearly one half of the firm's assets.

In addition to a firm's rate of return on owners', or common, equity, common stock investors are also interested in the firm's earnings per share (EPS). For example, if Kenwood Manufacturing is a corporation with 25,000 shares of common stock outstanding, the EPS would be calculated as follows:

$$EPS = \frac{\text{Net income}}{\text{Shares outstanding}}$$

$$= \frac{\$50,000}{25,000}$$

$$= \$2$$

Higher EPS levels are generally an indication of higher profits.

Investors are also interested in knowing how their firm will be valued in the stock market. The relationship between a firm's stock price and its earnings per share (EPS) is called its **price-earnings ratio** (P/E). For example, if Kenwood's stock is trading at $20 per share, then the P/E ratio is:

price-earnings ratio
*a firm's stock price
divided by its earnings
per share*

$$P/E \text{ ratio} = \frac{\text{Stock price}}{\text{EPS}}$$

$$= \frac{\$20}{\$2}$$

$$= 10$$

In general, the higher the P/E ratio, the greater the confidence by investors that the firm's EPS will continue to grow in the future.

FINANCIAL RISK IMPLICATIONS

The process of using debt funds in an effort to increase the rate of return to owners is termed **trading on the equity**. Recall that we discussed earlier how equity investment must precede debt financing in a business. Hence, a corporation's bonds or notes are sold on the strength of the underlying equity capital.

trading on the equity
using borrowed funds to increase the rate of return

Trading on the equity by a firm can either result in positive or negative financial leverage. **Positive financial leverage** will occur as long as the rate of return earned on borrowed funds is higher than their cost. For example, the cost of long-term debt for the Kenwood Company was 12 percent (see Figure 11.2). If Kenwood can earn more than 12 percent on the investment of these funds in assets, then positive financial leverage will result. Since interest is deductible for tax purposes, the return on assets is figured before interest and taxes. Kenwood had a net income before taxes of $60,000 in 1991 (see Figure 11.3). Adding back interest of $14,000 gives an income before interest and taxes of $74,000. Dividing $74,000 by the firm's total assets of $500,000 gives an average return of almost 15 percent. This figure is higher than the 12 percent cost, indicating that positive financial leverage existed for Kenwood on its long-term debt.

positive financial leverage
when the rate of return on borrowed funds is greater than their cost

Negative financial leverage occurs when the interest cost of borrowing is more than the rate of return being earned on the assets. It is important to understand the leverage effect of long-term corporate debt. As the percentage return to stockholders increases substantially during periods of highly profitable operations, so the return to stockholders is lowered during periods of low profits. If the earnings before interest fall below the amount needed to meet interest obligations on the bonds, the firm will be insolvent and might be forced into bankruptcy.

negative financial leverage
when the interest cost of borrowing is more than the return on assets

A study of the mix of long-term debt and owners' equity for various types of businesses reveals a wide range. In industries that experience only minor operating changes and reverses over the business cycle, we generally find a greater use of borrowed capital than in firms that are subject to wide cyclical swings. For example, the utility companies that have relatively stable revenues can capitalize to a much greater extent through borrowed capital than can most industrial corporations.

The capital structure, or mix between long-term debt and owners' equity, is usually expressed on a percentage basis. For example, the capital structure for Kenwood Manufacturing, taken from Figure 11.2, is expressed as follows:

	DOLLAR AMOUNT	PERCENT
Long-term debt	$100,000	27%
Owners' equity	275,000	73
Total capital	$375,000	100%

Long-term debt has a weight of 27 percent of Kenwood's capital structure, with owners' equity constituting 73 percent.

optimal capital structure
an industry's ideal mix between long-term debt and equity funds

An **optimal capital structure** reflects the ideal mix between long-term debt and equity capital for the industry within which the firm operates. Firms continually strive for the ideal capital structure, which is, other things being equal, likely to be a mix close to the industry average.

An optimal capital structure minimizes the cost of debt and equity funds and maximizes the value of the firm. Substantial deviations from an optimal capital structure will increase the cost of capital. Some long-term debt is valuable to a firm because it is less costly than equity funds, and the interest is tax deductible. However, too much long-term debt will cause substantial increases in the cost of both debt and equity funds because of concern over the firm's ability to meet its interest and principal payments.

Excessive use of debt will also result in lower bond quality ratings by such organizations as Moody's and Standard & Poor's. Lower bond quality ratings result in higher interest costs because of greater perceived risk, and vice versa. Thus internal policy decisions about capital structure and debt ratios must be influenced by how outsiders view the strength of the firm's financial position.

weighted average cost of capital
the after-tax cost of a firm's capital weighted by the optimal capital structure mix

Calculating the cost of capital by using a **weighted average cost of capital** (WACC) can be illustrated using the data for Kenwood Manufacturing. Let's assume that bonds can be sold at a 12 percent interest rate and that Kenwood has a 30 percent tax rate. In addition, management believes that its stockholders expect a 15 percent rate of return from dividends and stock price appreciation. This is 3 percent more than the cost of long-term debt.[1] Since interest is deductible for tax purposes, we multiply the 12 percent before-tax rate by 0.70 (one minus

1.   The general risk premium approach for estimating the cost of equity capital is based on examining the "spread" between bond returns (either government or corporate) and stock returns. Two other approaches used to estimate the cost of equity capital are (1) the dividend-yield plus capital-appreciation method and (2) the capital-asset-pricing method.

A business firm's cost of common equity capital is viewed as being the same as the rate of return expected by investors in the firm's common stock. One approach to estimating expected return is the dividend-yield-plus-growth-model, which was briefly discussed in Chapter 10.

ESTIMATING THE COST OF COMMON EQUITY CAPITAL

A second approach for estimating expected returns involves measuring risk premiums. One form can be expressed as:

Expected return = Risk-free rate + Risk premium

The risk-free rate is the rate on long-term government securities, and the risk premium reflects the added compensation expected by investors for engaging in riskier investments.

The **capital asset pricing model** (CAPM) is a specific form of the general risk premium approach. It measures risk differences in terms of the sensitivity of a firm's stock price to an overall market average such as Standard & Poor's 500 Stock Index. The index of sensitivity is referred to as the stock's beta (β). The CAPM model is expressed as

capital asset pricing model
a model used to determine the expected return of a stock by comparing its risk to an overall market average

Expected return = $RF + (ERM - RF)\beta$

where RF is the prevailing risk-free rate and ERM is the expected overall return on the market. The expected return on a stock is a function of the RF plus a risk premium, measured as the difference between ERM and the RF times the beta.

For example, let's assume that the risk-free rate is 8 percent, the expected return on the market is 12 percent, and the firm's stock has a beta of 1, meaning it is equal in risk to the market average. We then estimate the expected return on the stock as follows:

Expected return = $8\% + (12\% - 8\%)1 = 8\% + 4\% = 12\%$

It should not come as a surprise that the expected return on the firm's stock is the same as the expected return on the overall market because here the risks are comparable. In contrast, if the firm's stock is riskier than the market average and the stock's beta is 1.5, then the expected return would be:

Expected return = $8\% + (12\% - 8\%)1.5 = 8\% + 6\% = 14\%$.

Of course, if the firm's stock is considered to be less risky than the market average, the stock's beta would be less than 1 and the expected return would be less than that expected for the overall market.

the 0.30 tax rate) to arrive at an after-tax cost of 8.4 percent. Now, using the previously determined optimal capital structure weights, we calculate the after-tax cost of capital as follows:

	WEIGHT	×	AFTER-TAX COST	=	COMPONENT COST
Long-term debt	0.27	×	0.084	=	0.023
Owners' equity	0.73	×	0.150	=	0.109
			Cost of capital:		0.132 = 13.2%

This 13.2 percent (13% rounded) cost of capital should be used as Kenwood's discount rate for making future capital budgeting decisions.

Large corporations typically have their owners', or common, equity divided into three separate accounts—common stock, capital surplus, and retained earnings. Thus the sum of these accounts will comprise the common equity portion of the capital structure, and each equity account will usually be assigned the same percentage cost.

Our illustration for the Kenwood Company used the dollar book values for long-term debt and owners' equity to determine the capital structure weights. Although this is the typical method, some financial managers prefer using market values for weighting purposes. To do this, the current value of the firm's bonds has to be determined. Then, the market value of the common equity is calculated as the product of the current common stock price times the number of shares of common stock that are outstanding.

COMBINED OPERATING AND FINANCIAL LEVERAGE EFFECTS

We observed in Chapter 8 that the variability of sales or revenues over time is a basic business operating risk. Furthermore, when managers have fixed operating costs, such as general and administrative overhead expenses, a change in net sales will result in a greater change in operating income or earnings before interest and taxes (EBIT). This is due to the magnification produced by operating leverage. In a similar fashion, when money is borrowed at a fixed interest rate, financial leverage will be created. As a result, a change in the firm's EBIT will produce a magnified change in the firm's net income. The use of both operating and financial leverage produces a compound impact when a change in net sales occurs. Thus, from an overall risk perspective, it is important for the financial manager to combine the degrees of operating and financial leverage so as to form an acceptable combined leverage effect.

Let's illustrate this concept with a full income statement for last year and both a 10 percent decrease and a 10 percent increase in net sales for next year, as follows:

	LAST YEAR	NEXT YEAR	
		−10%	+10%
Net sales	$700,000	$630,000	$770,000
Less: variable costs (60% of sales)	420,000	378,000	462,000
Less: fixed costs	200,000	200,000	200,000
Earnings before interest and taxes	$ 80,000	$ 52,000	$108,000
Less: interest expenses	20,000	20,000	20,000
Income before taxes	$ 60,000	$ 32,000	$ 88,000
Less: income taxes (30%)	18,000	9,600	26,400
Net income	$ 42,000	$ 22,400	$ 61,600
Percent change in operating income (EBIT)		−35.0%	+35.0%
Percent change in net income		−46.7%	+46.7%

To clarify this magnification concept, we can directly estimate the combined effect of operating and financial leverage. First the degree of operating leverage (DOL) is estimated as

$$DOL = \frac{Contribution\ profit}{EBIT}$$

where the contribution profit (net sales minus variable costs) is divided by the earnings before interest and taxes. Thus

$$DOL = \frac{\$700,000 - \$420,000}{\$80,000}$$

$$= \frac{\$280,000}{\$80,000}$$

$$= 3.5$$

The degree of financial leverage (DFL) reflects the impact of interest expenses on profitability and is estimated as

$$DFL = \frac{EBIT}{EBT}$$

where EBT is the earnings or income before taxes. Thus,

$$DFL = \frac{\$80,000}{\$60,000}$$

$$= 1.333$$

Finally, the degree of combined leverage (DCL) can be directly estimated by dividing the contribution profit by earnings before taxes:

$$DCL = \frac{\text{Contribution profit}}{\text{EBT}}$$

$$= \frac{\$700,000 - \$420,000}{\$60,000}$$

$$= \frac{\$280,000}{\$60,000}$$

$$= 4.67$$

We can also find the degree of combined leverage by finding the product of the DOL and the DFL as follows:

$$DCL = DOL \times DFL$$

$$= 3.5 \times 1.333$$

$$= 4.67$$

By knowing the DCL factor, we can now estimate next year's change in net income, assuming no major change occurs in the income tax rate. This is done by multiplying the expected percentage change in net sales by the DCL of 4.67. For example, a 10 percent increase in net sales will result in net income increasing by 46.7 percent (10 percent times the combined leverage factor of 4.67).

Of course, combined leverage works in both directions, and a decline in net sales might place the firm in a difficult financial position. Furthermore, it is important to note that the degrees of operating, financial, and combined leverages depend upon the current level of sales. Next year, when the sales level is different, the degrees of leverage will reflect the impact of a sales change from that new level.

Flexibility

In the sections about short-term financial policies in Chapter 8, we saw that one of the important reasons for the use of short-term borrowing is seasonal business change. If a business needs funds for only six or seven months of the year, it may be far cheaper to use short-term borrowing rather than long-term funds on which interest must be paid throughout the year. By the same token, the business cycle itself causes changes in the firm's financial requirements. There are always periods in the life of a business when there are fewer investment opportunities or when the demand for the firm's products may temporarily decrease. A capital structure that allows for change during these periods is a great advantage. A large company with many different debt securities that have staggered maturities may find, during a period of economic contraction, that it is wise to simply pay off a maturing bond. The company can retire the issue out of the increasing liquidity that results when working assets move from inventories and accounts receivable into cash.

In other situations the business may engage in temporary ventures that will be ended either at some set future date or at the discretion of management. Here, too, a type of financing that can be eliminated if no longer needed becomes appropriate. Debt financing may be accomplished with maturities suited to the expected period of need for funds. Thus debt financing holds an important advantage over preferred stock or common stock financing because equity securities do not have a stated maturity that would make it possible to retire them conveniently. It should be mentioned here that a lease arrangement for fixed assets is advantageous because the lease term may be set to coincide with the duration of the need for the assets. The lease arrangement is described in Chapter 12.

Corporate Control

Although the control of a corporation is usually administered by its board of directors, ultimate control rests with the stockholders, who hold stock with voting rights. Stockholders elect the members of the board of directors, who are in turn responsible to the stockholders. Many stockholders in large corporations do not exercise their voting rights. Thus it is possible and often true that stockholders owning less than a majority of the total stock are able to control the election of the board of directors and, hence, have ultimate control over all activities of the corporation.

The device of classifying common stock as voting and nonvoting lessens the control of corporate affairs by those who own only a small part of all capital investment. The same is true, in some cases, of the issue of nonvoting preferred stock. Some states require that all stock, regardless of its class, be voting stock. This requirement is apparently designed to permit all stockholders to participate in corporate activity.

A growing firm that has prospered under its existing management may lack the capital necessary to take advantage of available opportunities. Yet management may not desire additional stockholders because of the voting privileges the new investors would have. The financial capital needed might require selling so much new stock that the existing stockholders would own proportionately less stock and therefore lose control of the affairs of the company. Many firms have avoided expansion rather than risk losing control through the sale of stock.

Corporate bonds and notes, in contrast, provide no voting rights. Therefore, management frequently prefers this form of financing. Although bond and note holders have no voting privilege, frequently contractual provisions exist that limit the actions of the directors of the business. For example, before the loan is made, the borrower may be required to agree that dividends will not be distributed to stockholders if the net working capital of the firm falls below a stated minimum. When the debt is retired, management is freed from such restrictions.

Timing

The sale of securities by a corporation and the type of securities sold depends in large measure upon existing conditions in the capital markets. A wise policy with respect to long-term financial planning makes it possible to capitalize on changing market conditions. For example, during a period of economic recession when business is at a low ebb, interest rates are typically at low levels as well. At the same time, common stock prices are down. Under these conditions, if additional funds are needed for expansion or to retire maturing debt, it becomes much more attractive to do so through the sale of debt securities rather than through the sale of common stock.

During the early expansion phase of the business cycle, when business opportunities and investment plans are increasing, it is also advantageous to borrow on a long-term basis even though interest rates may be rising somewhat. After a long period of economic expansion, however, pressure on capital resources and on the capital markets is such that interest rates reach very high levels. Then all corporations except those with the very strongest credit risks may find it difficult to borrow additional funds. At these times most common stock prices are typically still high, and thus it is attractive for the corporations to sell new shares of stock.

The ability of a corporation to take advantage of these changing conditions in the capital markets is dependent on the maintenance of a favorable capital structure—one that allows it to easily maneuver between debt issues and common stock issues. The business that has exhausted its long-term borrowing power may find itself forced to sell common stock at a time when stock prices are depressed. This is a high cost situation because more shares have to be issued to raise a specific amount of funds. Long-term financial policy, therefore, must be geared to probable future needs as well as those of the moment.

Availability

Just as financial management must consider flexibility and timing in its plans, so too it must recognize that availability may dictate the type of securities to be sold. Small and medium-sized firms may simply not have access to the capital markets to sell stock. On the other hand, owning plant and equipment may provide suitable collateral for long-term borrowing. At times a business may be able to borrow only if it provides the lender with some form of additional potential return.

Recently it has become customary for even large institutional lenders, such as insurance companies, to insist upon additional opportunities for reward. One reason for this has been the strong price inflation of recent years, which has made lenders try to protect themselves against the lowering of the dollar's value. Lenders may try to accomplish this by insisting that borrowers make available supplementary benefits, such as a percentage of gross or net income or the use of convertible securities or stock options. With the issuance of convertible bonds or preferred stock, the holder of the security has the immediate fixed-income yield and safety that they provide. Furthermore, if the business becomes more prosperous, the holder can convert the securities at a predetermined ratio into common stock of the company. This makes it possible to enjoy the benefits received by the common stockholders as the firm prospers.

In some instances very strong corporations may resort to the use of convertible securities when common stock prices are below levels considered acceptable to the company. Convertible securities are issued with the expectation that when the price of the company's common stock recovers, these securities will be called for redemption, thus forcing the holders to convert their securities to the common stock of the company. The holders of convertible securities have a specified time period within which they must convert their securities once the company has called them for redemption. If holders don't convert their securities, they will be redeemed at the call price, which is lower. The net effect of this device is that stock is ultimately sold at a price considered satisfactory to the company.

KEY TERMS

callable preferred stock
capital asset pricing model
closed-end mortgage bonds
common stock
convertible preferred stock
corporate equity capital
cumulative preferred stock
debenture bonds
debt ratio
equity multiplier ratio
mortgage bonds
negative financial leverage

noncumulative preferred stock
open-end mortgage bonds
optimal capital structure
par value
positive financial leverage
preferred stock
price-earnings ratio
stock certificate
trading on the equity
trust indenture
weighted average cost of capital

DISCUSSION QUESTIONS

1. What are the major sources of long-term funds available to business corporations? Indicate their relative importance.
2. Describe the relationship between internal and external financing in meeting the long-term financial needs of a firm.
3. Why is it important to establish dividend payout policies and then maintain consistency in dividend payment practices?
4. List the principal features of a stock certificate. How are stock certificates transferred from person to person?
5. List and briefly explain the special features usually associated with preferred stock.
6. Distinguish between the types of corporate debt securities.
7. Describe the link between a firm's rate of return on equity and its rate of return on total assets as calculated under the Du Pont system of analysis.
8. Explain what is meant by trading on the equity. Also briefly describe the difference between positive and negative financial leverage.
9. Why is it important for a firm to minimize its weighted average cost of capital?
10. It is sometimes said that long-term debt financing provides a greater degree of flexibility to financial managers than issuing either preferred or common stock. Why?
11. What is meant by the concept of corporate control as it relates to a firm's capital structure?
12. Briefly explain how the factors of timing and availability affect the mix between debt and equity capital.

PROBLEMS

1. The Schumacher Company had the following financial statement results for last year. Net sales were $2 million with net income of $120,000. Total assets at year-end amounted to $1,600,000 and total liabilities were $900,000.
   a. Calculate Schumacher's asset turnover ratio and profit margin.
   b. Calculate Schumacher's debt ratio and its equity multiplier ratio.
   c. Show how the two ratios in part a. can be used to determine Schumacher's rate of return on assets.
   d. Expand the return-on-assets model expressed in part c. to a return-on-owners'-equity model. Comment on the difference between the two rate of return calculations.
2. Next year Kenwood Manufacturing Company expects its sales to reach $900,000 with an investment in total assets of $600,000.

Total liabilities are estimated to be $325,000, and net income of $70,000 is anticipated.

    a. Estimate Kenwood's debt ratio and equity multiplier for next year. How do these ratios compare with the 1991 results given on pages 253 and 254?

    b. The average industry debt ratio is 50 percent and the equity multiplier is 2. Compare these averages with Kenwood's ratios for 1991 and for next year's projections.

    c. Apply the return-on-owners'-equity model based on the projected data and compare it with the results for 1991.

    d. Calculate the rate of return on assets using Kenwood's projected data. Comment on how it compares with the return on equity ratio.

3. Following are selected financial data in thousands of dollars for the Hunter Corporation:

	1990	1991
Current assets	$ 400	$ 500
Net fixed assets	600	700
Total assets	$1,000	$1,200
Current liabilities	$ 200	$ 250
Long-term debt	200	200
Common equity	600	750
Total liabilities and equity	$1,000	$1,200
Net sales	$1,200	$1,500
Total expenses	1,100	1,390
Net income	$ 100	$ 110

    a. Calculate Hunter's return-on-owners'-equity ratio in 1990 and 1991. Did the ratio improve or get worse?

    b. Expand the ratio results in part a. into a return-on-equity model with its three major components and determine what changes occurred between the two years.

4. Use the data for Hunter in Problem 3 to work this problem.

    a. Determine the percentage weights for long-term debt and common equity in Hunter's capital structures in 1990 and 1991.

    b. Assume that Hunter has to pay a 12 percent interest rate on its long-term debt and is in the 30 percent income tax bracket. The firm believes that its common equity carries a 4 percentage-point premium over its interest rate on debt. Based on this information, calculate the firm's after-tax cost of long-term debt and its cost of common equity.

    c. If Hunter's 1991 capital structure is considered optimal, determine the firm's weighted average cost of capital.

5. The Nutrex Corporation wants to calculate its weighted average cost of capital. Its target capital structure weights are 40 percent

long-term debt and 60 percent common equity. The before-tax cost of debt is estimated to be 10 percent and the company is in the 40 percent tax bracket. The current risk-free interest rate is 8 percent on long-term government bonds. The expected return on the market is 13 percent and the firm's stock beta is 1.8.

  a. Estimate Nutrex's expected return on common equity using the capital asset pricing model.
  b. Calculate the after-tax weighted average cost of capital.

6. Following are financial statements for the Genatron Manufacturing Corporation for the years 1990 and 1991:

BALANCE SHEET	1990	1991
Cash	$ 50,000	$ 40,000
Accounts receivable	200,000	260,000
Inventory	450,000	500,000
Total current assets	$ 700,000	$ 800,000
Fixed assets (net)	300,000	400,000
Total assets	$1,000,000	$1,200,000
Bank loan, 10%	$ 90,000	$ 90,000
Accounts payable	130,000	170,000
Accruals	50,000	70,000
Total current liabilities	$ 270,000	$ 330,000
Long-term debt, 12%	300,000	400,000
Common stock, $10 par	300,000	300,000
Capital surplus	50,000	50,000
Retained earnings	80,000	120,000
Total liabilities and equity	$1,000,000	$1,200,000

INCOME STATEMENT	1990	1991
Net sales	$1,300,000	$1,500,000
Cost of goods sold	780,000	900,000
Gross profit	$ 520,000	$ 600,000
General and administrative	150,000	150,000
Marketing expenses	130,000	150,000
Depreciation	40,000	53,000
Interest	45,000	57,000
Earnings before taxes	$ 155,000	$ 190,000
Income taxes	62,000	76,000
Net income	$ 93,000	$ 114,000

  a. Apply the return-on-owners'-equity model to both the 1990 and 1991 financial statements data. Expand the Du Pont return-on-assets model to include the equity multiplier. Explain how the financial performance differed between the two years.

b. Estimate Genatron's capital structure component weights based on the assumption that the 1991 capital structure represents the desired target mix. Now calculate the weighted average cost of capital based on an after-tax cost of new debt of 9 percent and an estimated common equity cost of 15 percent.

7. The Browning Corporation had sales last year of $500,000. Variable operating expenses were 70 percent of sales and fixed costs were $100,000. The firm has fixed interest expenses of $10,000 per year and is in the 30 percent income tax bracket.

a. Determine Browning's earnings before interest and taxes (i.e., its operating income) and its net income.

b. Show how the operating income and net income figures would change under both a 10 percent decrease in sales and a 10 percent sales increase.

c. Calculate the degree of operating leverage (DOL), the degree of financial leverage (DFL), and the degree of combined leverage (DCL).

8. This problem uses the two years of financial statement data provided in problem 6 for the Genatron Manufacturing Corporation. Note: Use the Financial Statement Analysis tool to perform the following analyses.

a. Calculate the asset turnover, the profit margin, and the return on assets for each of the two years.

b. Calculate the debt ratio, the equity multiplier, and the return on equity for each of the two years.

c. Calculate the earnings per share (EPS) for each year based on 30,000 shares of outstanding common stock.

d. Describe how the financial performance changed between the two years.

9. This problem uses the capital structure portion of the 1991 balance sheet for the Genatron Corporation as presented in Problem 6. Note: Use the Weighted Average Cost of Capital tool.

a. Calculate the weighted average cost of capital based on book value weights. Assume an after-tax cost of new debt of 8.63 percent and a cost of common equity of 16.5 percent.

b. The current market value of Genatron's long-term debt is $350,000. The common stock price is $20 per share and there are 30,000 shares outstanding. Calculate the WACC using market value weights and the component capital costs in part a.

c. Recalculate the WACC based on both book value and market value weights assuming that the before-tax cost of debt will be 18 percent, the company is in the 40 percent income tax bracket, and the after-tax cost of common equity capital is 21 percent.

10. The Miller Fan Corporation sold 55,687 ceiling fans last year at an average sales revenue of $115 per fan. Variable costs amounted to an average of $89 per fan and total fixed operating costs were $955,800. Fixed interest expenses were $163,000 last year, the firm was in the 40 percent income tax bracket, and there are 50,000 shares of common stock outstanding. Note: Use the Breakeven and Combined Leverage Analysis tool.
    a. Calculate the operating breakeven point in units and the firm's earnings per share.
    b. Calculate the degree of operating leverage, the degree of financial leverage, and the degree of combined leverage for the Miller Fan Corporation.
    c. Calculate the results if only 42,500 ceiling fans had been sold last year.

SELF-TEST QUESTIONS

1. The largest annual supply of funds for business corporations comes from which one of the following sources?
    a. undistributed profits
    b. issuance of bonds
    c. issuance of preferred stocks
    d. issuance of common stocks

2. The terms of a bond contract are set out in which of the following documents?
    a. debenture
    b. trust indenture
    c. mortgage
    d. lien

3. The return-on-owners'-equity model is expressed as the product of which of the following factors or ratios?
    a. asset turnover and profit margin
    b. asset turnover and equity multiplier
    c. profit margin and equity multiplier
    d. asset turnover, profit margin, and equity multiplier

4. What is the process of using debt funds in an effort to increase the rate of return to owners or stockholders?
    a. trading on the equity
    b. finding the weighted cost of capital
    c. determining an optimal capital structure
    d. the degree of combined leverage

5. Which of the following conditions affect the mix between debt and equity capital in a firm's capital structure?
    a. flexibility
    b. flexibility and control
    c. flexibility, control, and timing
    d. flexibility, control, timing, and availability

SELF-TEST PROBLEMS

1. Handi-Tool Manufacturing Company had the following financial statement results for last year. Net sales were $2 million with net income of $100,000. Total assets at year-end amounted to $1,800,000, and total liabilities were $900,000.
    a. Calculate the asset turnover ratio and profit margin.
    b. Calculate the equity multiplier ratio.
    c. Show how the two ratios in part a can be used to determine the rate of return on assets.
    d. Expand the return-on-assets model expressed in part c to a return-on-owners'-equity model.

2. The Basic Biotech Corporation wants to determine its weighted average cost of capital. Its target capital structure weights are 50 percent long-term debt and 50-percent common equity. The before-tax cost of debt is estimated to be 10 percent and the company is in the 30 percent tax bracket. The current risk-free interest rate is 8 percent on long-term government bonds. The after-tax cost of common equity capital is 14.5 percent.
    Calculate the after-tax weighted average cost of capital.

SUGGESTED READINGS

Helfert, Erich A. *Techniques of Financial Analysis*, 6e. Homewood, IL: Richard D. Irwin, 1987. Chap. 8.

Schall, Lawrence D., and Charles W. Haley. *Introduction to Financial Management*, 5e. New York: McGraw-Hill, 1988. Chaps. 7 and 18.

Van Horne, James C. *Fundamentals of Financial Management*, 7e. Englewood Cliffs, NJ: Prentice-Hall, 1989. Chaps. 21 and 22.

Walker, Ernest W., and J. William Petty II. *Financial Management of the Small Firm*, 2e. Englewood Cliffs, NJ: Prentice-Hall, 1986. Chaps. 10 and 16.

Weston, J. Fred, and Eugene F. Brigham. *Essentials of Managerial Finance*, 9e. Hinsdale, IL: The Dryden Press, 1990. Chaps. 17, 18, and 19.

ANSWERS TO SELF-TEST QUESTIONS   1. b   2. b   3. d   4. a   5. d

SOLUTIONS TO SELF-TEST PROBLEMS

1. a.
   $$\text{Asset turnover} = \frac{\$2,000,000}{\$1,800,000} = 1.111$$

   $$\text{Profit margin} = \frac{\$100,000}{\$2,000,000} = 0.05 \text{ or } 5\%$$

   b.
   $$\text{Equity multiplier} = \frac{\$1,800,000}{\$900,000} = 2$$

   (Note: Total assets of $1,800,000 minus $900,000 in total liabilities gives owners' equity of $900,000.)

   c.
   $$\text{Rate of return on assets} = 1.111 \times 5\% = 5.56\% \left(\text{or: } \frac{\$100,000}{\$1,800,000} = 5.56\%\right)$$

2. After-tax cost of long-term debt: $10\%(1 - .30) = 7\%$

	WEIGHT	AFTER-TAX COST	COMPONENT COST
Long-term debt	0.50	0.070	0.035
Common equity	0.50	0.145	0.073
		Cost of capital =	0.108 = 10.8%

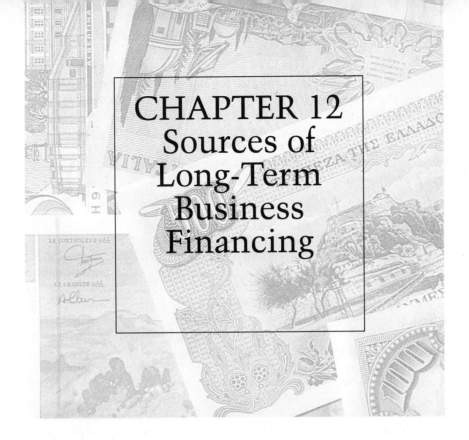

CHAPTER 12
Sources of Long-Term Business Financing

After studying this chapter, you should be able to:

- Discuss the characteristics and importance of term loans.
- Define the role and classifications of investment companies.
- Explain the business activities of trust institutions.
- Discuss the types and importance of life insurance and describe how life insurance company funds are invested.
- Describe the types of property insurance and indicate how property insurance company funds are invested.
- Explain how corporations provide long-term capital for other businesses.
- Describe the types of development companies and explain the role of each in providing long-term business funds.
- Describe how lease arrangements and equipment trust financing are used by businesses.

Commercial banks are an important supplier of business loans that extend beyond one year, as well as the major provider of short-term funds. Institutional investors have played a major role as purchasers of corporate stocks and bonds during the past several decades. The primary suppliers of long-term debt and equity capital are investment companies, trust companies, and insurance companies.

Some business corporations also provide long-term capital for other businesses, as we will see shortly. Other important suppliers of long-term funds include nonprofit development companies, small-business investment companies, and investment development companies. Leasing and equipment trust financing, while not provided by a specific form of financial institution, also represent important sources of long-term debt financing.

TERM LOANS

The term loan represents an interesting and significant development in the lending practices of banks and other financial intermediaries. The **term loan** is a contract under which a borrower agrees to make a series of interest and principal payments on specific dates to a lender. It differs from the usual bank business loan in that it has a maturity exceeding one year. Also, the term loan is usually repaid in monthly or quarterly installments over the life of the loan.

term loan
has a maturity exceeding one year; the borrower makes payments on specific dates

Term lending by commercial banks began during the depression years of the 1930s. Although the term loan was contrary to generally accepted concepts of bank lending activity, there were several reasons for its rapid growth and acceptance by the banks of the nation. First, banks used the term loan arrangement as a convenient means of investing their surplus funds. These surplus funds accumulated in large part from a decline in the demand of businesses for short-term credit. Second, a higher return could be realized on term loans than on the usual business loan. Third, the Securities Act of 1933 made it more difficult for the nation's corporations to secure money through public distribution of securities. The incentive was strong for business corporations to negotiate directly with banks to finance their intermediate-term (between short- and long-term) capital needs. Fourth, the reports of government bank examiners recommended that commercial banks engage in this type of lending activity. Finally, the term loan provided banks with an alternative to investment in the securities of the federal government, states, and municipalities, for the yields on government securities were at all-time lows.

By 1940 the tremendous growth and popularity of term loans had established them as one of the most important lending innovations by the banks of the nation. During World War II, term lending declined because businesses couldn't establish long-range expansion plans and because special government lending programs were established to finance war production. In the postwar period, however, the volume of loans increased at a very rapid rate. The American Bankers Association lent its support to term lending and encouraged its members to explore more fully the potential these loans offered.

Today term bank loans represent an important source of long-term funds for businesses. They provide over $10 billion annually to business corporations, ranking third behind new bond issues and mortgages as a source of long-term debt funds. In recent years, term loans have also been made by insurance companies and pension funds.

Term Loan Agreements

The *term loan agreement* is a detailed written contract between the lender and the borrower that specifies the conditions of the loan. Term loans may be secured by specific property as collateral or they may be unsecured, depending upon the situation. Among other things, the lender frequently requires a business to maintain a certain minimum amount of net working capital. In the event the net working capital of the business should fall below the stated amount, dividends or the salaries of executives may be reduced or cut off until the appropriate level of net working capital is reestablished.

It is also frequently stipulated in the agreement that the business is not to dispose of its fixed assets or incur other indebtedness without the permission of the lender. Another common provision is that insurance must be carried on the lives of key individuals in the business with the lender as beneficiary. Some lenders carry blanket insurance policies on the lives of executives of companies receiving term loans. Another requirement may be that proposed changes in management personnel, changes in production methods or items of production, or increases in executive salaries or bonuses be first approved by the lender.

Despite the restrictions that usually accompany term loans, businesses have generally found the arrangement advantageous. In most cases the conditions only establish fair and reasonable protection against undesirable business activities of management. Also, the simplicity of the term loan arrangement, as well as its cost, often renders it far more desirable than securing funds through the public sale of securities.

Calculating Term Loan Payments

The standard term loan arrangement calls for a constant periodic payment that will fully amortize, or pay off, the loan at maturity. In Chapter 10 we discussed the process for determining the periodic payment for an annuity. Our example used a $20,000, 10 percent, three-year loan requiring annual payments. If this were a term loan, we solve for the annual payment as follows:

$$\text{Annual payment} = \frac{\text{PV annuity}}{\text{PVIFA}} = \frac{\$20,000}{2.487} = \$8,041.82$$

Based on a present value interest factor of an annuity of 2.487 at 10 percent for three years, an annual payment of $8,041.82 would be needed to amortize the loan. For term loans requiring more frequent payments, such as quarterly or monthly, we would need more detailed present value annuity tables or a financial calculator to determine the appropriate payment.

INVESTMENT COMPANIES

investment company
a corporation that
invests the pooled funds
of savers

An **investment company** is a corporation that invests the pooled funds of savers. Investment companies usually purchase the stocks and bonds of other corporations.[1] The funds of many investors are pooled for the primary purpose of obtaining expert management and wide diversity in security investments. Both the number and the size of investment companies have increased rapidly in recent years.

Forerunners of the modern investment company began in the United States during the early 1800s when insurance companies accepted funds from individuals and professionally administered them. Following World War I, the growth in U.S. industry and the tremendous interest in stock market activity gave support to the large-scale development of investment companies. Investment companies in the United States were both victim and cause of the risky practices in the securities market during the 1920s. This was much like the excess speculation at the close of the 19th century in Great Britain. Following the depression of the 1930s, investment companies again attracted public attention and increased in numbers and strength.

Classification of Investment Companies

Investment companies come in two types: closed-end funds and mutual, or open-ended, funds, which are much more popular. Both types have the common objective of achieving intelligent diversification, or variety of investments, for the pooled funds of individuals. However, the methods by which this objective is accomplished, and the way in which shares are purchased and exchanged, are different.

CLOSED-END FUNDS

closed-end fund
investment company
that issues a single offer-
ing of stock, which it
does not redeem

Ordinarily, the stock or ownership shares issued by a **closed-end fund** is sold in a single public offering and additional shares are seldom issued. The investment company itself will not redeem shares. Holders of closed-end fund shares may liquidate their investment just as they

1. Money market mutual funds, a form of investment company that invests in securities, specialize in holding short-term commercial paper, bank CDs, and U.S. Treasury bills. Our focus here is on long-term business financing sources.

Two important developments occurred in the financial markets during the 1980s. First, there was an increased opportunity for corporations to issue low-quality debt. Second, an opportunity to use international markets in the form of corporate Eurobonds developed.

Corporate bonds rated below investment grade, which is a minimum of BBB by Standard & Poor's Corporation and Baa by Moody's Investors Service, had traditionally found little acceptance in the public debt markets. Instead, these corporations had to rely on private placement of their bonds with institutional investors, or they had to turn to banks for term loan financing. However, beginning in the late 1970s, public acceptance of "junk bonds" allowed the issuance of large amounts of low-quality debt in conjunction with mergers, takeovers, and corporate restructurings. Investors were willing, at least in the short run, to ignore the higher probability of issuer default for the expectation of higher yields or returns. Furthermore, several underwriting firms undertook substantial efforts to market new issues of low-quality bonds.

As the 1990s began, a near collapse of the junk bond market occurred due to defaults on interest and principal payments by several large issuers. In addition, several investment bankers were indicted for illegal junk bond practices. Many financial analysts now question the future of low-quality bonds during the 1990s.

The second major long-term financing development involved the increased integration of world financial markets. U.S. and foreign corporations are now able to issue Eurobond debt in large amounts in foreign financial markets. Eurobonds are primarily denominated in U.S. dollars but also are issued in a variety of other currencies. Differences in tax treatments and other regulations allowed U.S. corporations to borrow in foreign markets at lower interest rates relative to the domestic market.

DEVELOPMENTS IN LONG-TERM FINANCIAL MARKETS DURING THE 1980S

would with any corporate security, that is, by selling the securities to other investors. The shares of closed-end funds are traded either on an organized securities exchange or in the over-the-counter market. Bonds and preferred stock, as well as common stock, may be issued by the closed-end fund company.

Closed-end funds place great emphasis on portfolio management, that is, the handling of shares invested in the equity and debt securities of other companies. Dividends and interest received by a closed-end fund from the securities it holds are paid out to its shareholders in the form of dividends. The total asset value of a closed-end fund increases through the growth in market value of its securities and/or through the retention of a small proportion of the earnings obtained by the company. Today the assets of closed-end funds total less than $10 billion.

MUTUAL FUNDS

mutual fund
investment company
that continuously offers
an increasing number
of shares, which are
redeemable by the
company

A **mutual fund** also invests in equity and debt securities, and it uses dividends and interest from these securities to pay dividends to shareholders. In contrast with closed-end funds, mutual funds allow an increasing number of shares to be issued, and they generally offer only a single class of shares to investors. Shareholders may redeem their shares with the mutual fund at any time. The bylaws, or trust agreement, of the mutual fund company provide for the redemption of shares at their net asset value. Hence, the price at which shares are redeemed depends upon the market value of the securities it holds. New shares in the mutual fund are offered to the public continuously. The price of these new shares is determined, as with shares that are redeemed, by the current value of the securities held by the mutual fund.

In handling investments and redemptions, mutual funds fall into two main categories: load and no-load mutual funds. *Load mutual funds* sell their stock through brokers. The price is equal to the net asset value plus a selling charge, called a load. For example, an 8 percent load charge means that the purchase of shares having a net asset value of $1,000 would require an additional fee or load of approximately $80. Usually, as larger amounts of shares are purchased, the load charge as a percentage of the purchase price is reduced. Some mutual funds charge a redemption fee, known as a back-end load. The shares of *no-load mutual funds* are sold at a price equal to their net asset value with no selling charge. No-load funds operate by mail and telephone and have no sales force to compensate. Both load and no-load funds charge management fees to compensate the fund's management and employees.

Because mutual funds redeem their shares, they are not listed on the securities exchanges. It is unnecessary to find other buyers for the shares when they can be promptly and easily redeemed by the fund itself. In order to know the price at which shares should be redeemed or sold, the mutual fund must calculate the total value of its portfolio of securities daily. Daily quotes of the net asset value per share of many mutual funds can be found in the *Wall Street Journal* and many other newspapers.

Mutual funds also place great emphasis on portfolio management, but they differ widely with respect to management objectives. If income is the objective, an extremely conservative portfolio, comprised largely of government debt securities, is maintained. Other mutual funds may try to balance a somewhat above-average yield with reasonable stability of market value. These funds hold high-grade debt and equity securities of well-known companies. Still others have the objective to maximize profits through the purchase and sale of securities. The bulk of these funds' investments are placed in common stocks. Securities and Exchange Commission data indicate that mutual funds hold assets in the form of corporate and government securities well in excess of $400 billion.

Tax Status of Investment Companies

Under the Revenue Act of 1936, corporations, like individuals, are subject to income tax on any dividends they receive. Strictly applied, this tax would make it difficult for investment companies to function in their present form. It would mean triple taxation: taxation first on the income of the corporation invested in, again when the investment company receives its dividends or interest, and finally when these profits are distributed to the holders of shares of the investment company. However, a special supplement to the Revenue Act of 1936, called Supplement Q, provides that investment companies are the agents through which earnings of a corporation flow to the ultimate shareholders. This regulation allows many closed-end investment companies and mutual funds to be exempt from federal income taxation. To qualify for this treatment, the investment company must register with the Securities and Exchange Commission and must distribute at least 90 percent of its taxable income to its shareholders each year. Individuals are then taxed on the proceeds they receive from the closed-end fund or mutual fund.

TRUST INSTITUTIONS

Trust institutions administer and control great amounts of wealth, and they account for a significant portion of securities purchased. A **trust institution** serves in a fiduciary capacity for the administration and disposition of assets and for the performance of specified acts for the beneficiaries of trust arrangements. A **fiduciary** is one who acts in a capacity of trust and undivided loyalty in the management of assets for another. It implies integrity of the person or institution trusted, and it suggests good faith rather than legal obligation as the dominant basis for transactions.

*trust institution
serves in a fiduciary
capacity for the benefi-
ciaries of trust arrange-
ments*

*fiduciary
one to whom assets have
been entrusted for the
benefit of another*

It was not until approximately 100 years ago that the institutional form of trustee became important. In earlier times, trust duties were performed primarily by family, friends, or attorneys. As the country grew, there was a growing complexity of legal and financial matters, making it increasingly difficult to find individuals capable of properly administering trusts. The amount of trust administration by individuals in the United States now is minor compared with that of trust companies and trust departments of banks.

Most of the estimated 3,000 U.S. corporations actively engaged in the trust business are also engaged in banking. This is because the experiences and skills required for banking and trust work are very much the same. Nearly half of all corporations engaged in the trust business are national banks that operate trust departments; state-chartered banks account for most of the remaining institutional trustees. Estimates of trust assets held by commercial banks now exceed $400 billion. About one half of this total is in the form of common stock holdings.

Trusts may be classified according to their functions, which may be broadly grouped into those of a personal nature and those of a corporate nature. Under both classifications, their functions are tremendously important to the financial structure of the economy because they involve the transfer and management of huge sums of money. The personal trust is established for the direct benefit of one or more persons, while the corporate trust exists to handle certain affairs of corporations.

Personal Trust Business

Personal trust business is confined largely to the care of assets included in trust estates and to settling estates of deceased persons. The three principal types of personal trusts are living trusts, testamentary trusts, and insurance trusts.

LIVING TRUSTS

living trust
a trust that is operative during the maker's lifetime

A *living trust* is one that is operative while the maker of the trust is still alive. In recent years there has been a tremendous increase in the number of living trusts. In the first place, living trusts are a convenient means of providing a reasonably assured income for beneficiaries without immediately giving them the property from which the income is derived. Under these circumstances, the beneficiary of the trust, who may be a widowed spouse or a minor child, will receive only the income from the trust principal during the term of the trust. The principal itself is given to the beneficiary only upon the occurrence of a specified event set forth in the trust agreement.

Living trust agreements are often used by persons of advanced age who have reason to doubt their continuing ability to manage their financial affairs. In other cases, trusts may be established for the benefit of minor children or for persons who are incapable of managing their affairs because of physical or mental disability. Or, a business person may establish a trust that will provide a reasonably comfortable income for a specified period of years to protect against undue hardship that might result from a risky business venture.

Under the laws of most states, living trusts can be revocable, irrevocable, or something in between that are called short-term trusts. As the term implies, a *revocable trust* is one in which the maker of the trust has the right to revoke, or cancel, the trust arrangement after its creation. Such an agreement makes it possible to plan the transfer of assets and reduces the time required for passing the property to the beneficiaries when the maker dies. Also, the extra expenses and publicity associated with a will may be avoided by the use of a revocable trust.

revocable trust
a trust that can be revoked by the maker

An *irrevocable trust*, on the other hand, provides for the complete and final transfer of assets to the trustee. In addition to the advantages cited for the revocable trust, the irrevocable trust may involve substantial tax advantages. As a rule, the maker of the trust is freed from taxation on the income from assets transferred to the trust institution. However, the trust must pay taxes on its income. In addition, the property in trust escapes estate taxes upon the death of the trust's maker. The maker of such a trust must pay a gift tax on amounts placed in trust in excess of $10,000 annually for each beneficiary. Nevertheless, this limit allows a significant amount to be placed in trust over a period of years, free of estate or gift taxes.

irrevocable trust
a trust that provides for the complete and final transfer of assets to the trustee

A *short-term trust* represents a compromise between the revocable and irrevocable trust. In brief, it is an irrevocable trust established for a specified number of years. Short-term trusts are often established for tax purposes. If the trust meets all requirements of the tax laws, the maker pays no tax on the income derived from its assets, assuming such income is paid to a person or institution other than the maker of the trust. At the end of the trust term, the assets that have been placed in trust return to maker. Short-term trusts can be used for many purposes, such as the support of parents, contributions to charities, accumulating an estate for one's family, or carrying insurance on another person's life.

short-term trust
an irrevocable trust lasting for a specified number of years

TESTAMENTARY TRUSTS

The testamentary trust, also called a *trusteeship under will*, represents a second major classification of personal trust business. The *testamentary trust* is created within a will and goes into effect on the death of its maker. This type of trust may be used by an individual who prefers that his or her estate be maintained and administered for the benefit of heirs rather than turned over to them directly. The maker of the trust can be reasonably assured that beneficiaries will be properly cared for and at the same time the estate will be protected against irresponsible administration.

testamentary trust
a trust in which an estate is administered for the benefit of heirs

A trust institution may also be designated the *executor* in a will. The duties of the executor are: handling and accounting for all the assets in the estate, liquidating any assets of a perishable nature, paying all debts, including taxes owed by the estate, and distributing the assets of the estate as specified in the will. The trust institution may also act as administrator, guardian, or conservator under authority of a court appointment.

INSURANCE TRUSTS

insurance trust
when the proceeds of an insurance policy are placed with a trust institution upon the death of the maker

The insurance trust represents a third classification of personal trust business. An **insurance trust** results when the maker places in trust one or more insurance policies with an agreement that the proceeds of the insurance will be paid to the trust institution upon the death of the maker. The trust institution is then bound by the terms of the agreement to administer the benefits of the insurance policies for the beneficiaries of the trust. Insurance trusts are generally used when the maker has reason to doubt the ability of the beneficiary to properly handle the large sum of money that would be received under the terms of the life insurance policy.

Investment Policies of Trust Institutions

prudent-man rule
states that trust institutions are responsible for making careful investment decisions

State laws that apply to the administration of trust funds are many and varied and are generally considered to be very restrictive. In addition to the laws, the terms of the trust agreement itself may establish limitations on the trustee's management of the assets placed in trust. Traditionally, trust institutions were required to limit the investment of assets to the securities on a legal list prepared by the state, which included only high-grade bonds and other designated fixed-income investments. Only a few states continue to impose restrictions of this nature on trust institutions. Most states now follow the **prudent-man rule**, which requires that a trust institution be held responsible for the same degree of judgment that a prudent person would exercise in investing personal funds.

Commingled Trust Funds

Of particular importance to the administration of trust assets was a modification of the law to permit national banks to commingle, or pool, the trust funds of their customers. Since a long-established legal principle required that assets of separate trusts should not be mingled, this represented a major change in trust administration activities. New additions to the federal tax laws were also necessary so that income from such invested assets would not be taxed as income to both the trust institution and the individuals named as beneficiaries of the trusts.

Although assets invested under the common trust fund plan are subject to the same regulatory limitations as the investment of individual trust assets, substantial advantages are offered both to the trust institution and to beneficiaries. The common trust fund was established primarily for the benefit of smaller trusts. Originally, under the regulations of the Federal Reserve System the maximum amount of any single trust that could be placed in a common trust fund was $25,000. This was raised successively to $50,000, $100,000, and then maximum limits were removed entirely, although few common trust accounts are for amounts in excess of $100,000.

One primary advantage of the common trust fund is that it is possible for trust institutions to handle smaller trusts with principal amounts of only a few thousand dollars. Small trusts placed with a trust institution under a common trust agreement receive the same quality of supervision as much larger trusts. Costs are reduced and greater diversification is obtained through the common trust arrangement than is possible for the individual handling of small trust assets. Total assets of the commingled trusts are administered under the centralized supervision of the trust department's investment section.

Several trust institutions offer three separate common trust funds. One of the funds ordinarily has all of its assets invested in bonds, the second fund all of its assets in common stocks, and the third fund has its assets in both bonds and common stocks. The maker of a trust, therefore, may choose between a fund that emphasizes stability of principal and one that emphasizes higher income and appreciation, or growth, possibilities. Under this arrangement of multiple common trust funds, the similarity of the operations of trust institutions to investment companies becomes readily apparent. In addition to the common trust fund operations of national banks, all states authorize state-chartered trust corporations to operate common trust funds.

Trust Services for Corporations

Trust services for corporations are an important phase of the trust business. By law all corporations subject to regulation by the Securities and Exchange Commission must use the services of trust corporations. One of the principal forms of trust service provided for corporations is that of *trustee under indenture*, referred to in Chapter 11. The duties of the trust institution as trustee under indenture generally involve holding the mortgage against which bonds are issued by the corporation and the enforcement of and responsibility for all provisions of the trust indenture.

Trust institutions also serve corporations as transfer agents by handling the details relating to the issuance and recording of stock transfers, and they act as dividend distribution agents. Trust institutions may also serve corporations as registrars. Many of the stock exchanges require that corporations having stock listed on their exchanges maintain separate registrars and transfer agents. The registrar's responsibility, among other things, involves supervising the issuance of new stock of the corporation. This ensures that the corporation will not issue more stock than is authorized by the charter. The transfer agent and the registrar, therefore, provide an effective check on each other's operations and assure that the security holder's interests are being responsibly administered.

In the event of corporate reorganization, it is customary for creditors, pending the final reorganization, to deposit bonds and other credit instruments with a corporate trustee. In return, they are given transferable certificates of deposit. The property of a corporation in bankruptcy is generally transferred to a trust institution, which provides, if necessary, for the liquidation and distribution of funds to the creditors of the corporation.

Trust institutions maintain safe-deposit facilities, administer security holdings, keep complete records of all security transactions, make monthly reports to customers, and provide investment counsel. The numerous additional services provided by trust institutions for corporations cannot be covered in this text. Further reference, however, is made to trust activities in connection with pension funds and corporate financing through the use of equipment trust arrangements.

LIFE INSURANCE COMPANIES

This section begins with a brief discussion of the importance of life insurance. Then we cover basic types of life insurance before considering life insurance companies as a source of long-term business funds.[2] The characteristics and operations of life insurance companies are covered in Chapter 18.

One of the most important functions of life insurance is providing an immediate estate for the dependents of the head of a household. This function is particularly important in the event of death before sufficient personal resources have been accumulated to provide for dependents. Where the amount of life insurance is quite small, the objective may be a "clean-up fund" which will pay the costs connected with the death of the insured.

Life insurance may also play an important role in business affairs. For example, in a partnership, often each partner's life is insured and the other partners are specified as the beneficiaries. This arrangement permits the surviving partners to buy the interest of the heirs of a deceased member without creating a serious cash drain on the business. A business person may carry life insurance for settling business debts that may exist at the time of death. Finally, life insurance may be

---

2.   Accident and sickness insurance is also an important form of personal insurance because it provides protection against loss of income and for coverage of hospital and surgical expenses. However, companies specializing in this form of insurance are not major suppliers of long-term business funds.

used to offset the drain on an estate as a result of taxes imposed upon business assets.

Over two-thirds of the people in the United States own some form of life insurance. Life insurance in force now exceeds $8 trillion—a figure that is difficult to comprehend in size. There are over 2,300 life insurance companies currently operating in the United States.[3]

Types of Life Insurance

The applications of life insurance to special requirements and situations has spawned a wide variety of types of policies. The principal types of contracts sold by life insurance companies are term insurance, whole life insurance, universal life insurance, endowment insurance, and annuities.

TERM INSURANCE

The basic feature of **term life insurance** is that the policy is issued for a specified period of time. At the end of the policy period, no obligation exists on the part of the insurance company toward the insured. Term life insurance policies are usually issued for one, five, ten, or twenty years.

Term life insurance is often recommended by financial advisers who feel that insurance should be purchased only when needed for protection. Modifications of the basic form, including renewal privileges without further physical examination and privileges for conversion to more permanent forms of insurance, have added to the appeal of this form of insurance. Because no investment program is combined with term insurance, the annual premiums correspond to the basic cost of insurance protection and are less than for other types of insurance. One of the major disadvantages of term insurance is that the premiums are based on standard mortality, or death rate, tables, and they increase with the age of the insured. Term life insurance provides much smaller capital accumulation for the insurance companies than the other types of life insurance since the annual premiums have no savings or cash value component.

WHOLE LIFE INSURANCE

The **whole life insurance** policy differs from term insurance in that it combines an investment program with the insurance contract. The premiums generally remain the same throughout the life of the policy, which may be equal to the life of the insured or a specified number of

term life insurance
insurance policy issued for a specified period of time

only for the insurance benefit

whole life insurance
insurance that combines an investment program with the insurance contract

3. *Life Insurance Fact Book Update* (Washington, DC: American Council of Life Insurance, 1989), pp. 4 and 49.

years. The portion of the premium that applies to insurance protection is small during the early years of the contract. Much of the premium is credited toward the investment program of the policyholder. This savings accumulation is the *cash value* of the policy. The accumulation of this investment portion of the insurance contract makes it possible for an individual to pay a level or fixed premium throughout life or for a specified number of years despite the higher costs of insurance that accompany advancing age.

UNIVERSAL LIFE INSURANCE

universal life insurance insurance that combines death benefits with a tax-deferred savings or investment account

This form of life insurance has grown in popularity in recent years. **Universal life insurance** combines the death benefits provided by term insurance with a savings or investment account that provides for tax-deferred benefits.

ENDOWMENT INSURANCE

endowment insurance policy issued for a specified period, at the end of which the face value is paid to a surviving insured

Like the term plan of life insurance, endowment insurance is written for a specified number of years. In contrast, however, if the insured person survives to the end of the stated period, the face amount of the **endowment insurance** policy is payable to the insured. Such policies may be written as 20-year or 30-year endowment contracts, or for other time spans. The endowment policy may involve a single premium to be paid immediately when the contract is written, with the endowment to be made at some specified future period. Some endowment policies provide for payments of benefits over a period of years rather than in a single lump sum. Such policies involve a combination of the endowment and annuity contracts.

ANNUITY CONTRACTS

annuity contract provides for the disposition of an estate through regular payments to the insured

Annuity insurance has often been described as "insurance in reverse." The basic purpose of life insurance is to create an estate, while the annuity contract provides for the disposition of an estate through its systematic liquidation. Under an **annuity contract**, the purchaser, or annuitant, agrees to pay a specified sum of money to the insurance company, either in the form of a single lump-sum payment or in a series of regular payments. In return, the annuitant receives a regular income from the company for a specified time, such as a number of years or for life. Typically, annuities are purchased to meet the possibility that the buyers may outlive their earnings and will need a regular income to sustain them in the years beyond retirement.

Annuities have become very popular in recent years because the earnings that result when the annuity premium is invested are allowed to grow tax deferred until the payout begins. *Fixed annuities* are like CDs because they pay a fixed rate of return for a specified period of time. *Variable annuities* are also available; the premiums are invested in mutual funds with the hope that the stock market will provide a superior return.

Investment Policies of Life Insurance Companies

Death rates for the population as a whole are predictable with a high degree of certainty. Thus, life insurance companies can accurately predict what their payouts to policyholders will be in the future. Consequently they accumulate vast reserves. It is through the investment of these reserves that life insurance companies make their principal contribution to the flow of long-term capital in the economy. Life insurance companies customarily make investments that are long-term and not particularly liquid. Investments include U.S. government securities, corporate bonds and stock, commercial mortgages, direct investment in real estate, and loans to policyholders.

Life insurance companies are not regulated to any extent by the federal government. Instead, regulation is left to the states in which companies operate. In recent years there has been a slow but gradual easing of restrictions on investments that life insurance companies may make. Among other things, they are now permitted to invest directly in such income-producing assets as housing projects, real estate for lease-back purposes, and, to a limited extent, common stocks. Although there has been considerable controversy about investment in common stocks, it is now permitted in most states.

Business corporations obtain the majority of their new external long-term funds from mortgage loans and by issuing bonds; life insurance companies are major purchasers of both corporate bonds and commercial mortgages. Corporate bonds comprise over one-third of U.S. life insurance company assets, while mortgage holdings account for about one-fifth, with the majority being nonfarm, nonresidential mortgages. Corporate common stocks currently constitute nearly 10 percent of life insurance company assets.[4]

PROPERTY INSURANCE COMPANIES

There are two purposes of **property insurance**: (1) to protect the insured against loss arising out of physical damages to property, including automobiles, and (2) to protect the insured against loss arising from damages to others for which the insured may be held liable. Property insurance companies currently have assets in excess of $100 billion. We will briefly discuss basic types of property insurance before considering these insurance companies as a source of long-term business funds.

property insurance protects against loss from damage to property or liability for damage to the property of others

4.   *Ibid.*, p. 42.

Types of Property Insurance

For the purposes of describing types of property insurance, it will be convenient to follow the broad classification of fire, marine, and casualty and surety insurance.

FIRE INSURANCE

fire insurance
insurance to protect against losses from fire and other perils to property

The basic form of **fire insurance** protects the insured against losses due to destruction of physical property from fire. In addition, fire insurance companies may write policies that include protection against losses from other perils to property, such as explosion, wind storm, and riot. Fire insurance companies find these risks convenient to underwrite, since it is often difficult to determine whether damage has resulted from these disasters or from the fires that often accompany them.

MARINE INSURANCE

marine insurance
protects against losses during the transport of merchandise from seller to purchaser

Marine insurance is one of the oldest forms of property insurance. These policies were written originally to protect against losses resulting from perils of the sea. **Marine insurance** now provides protection against losses in the transport of merchandise from the seller to the purchaser. This includes land transportation as well as marine transportation. Insurance written on shipments over land by carriers such as railroads and trucks, is referred to as *inland marine insurance*. Insurance for shipments that involve the sea is *ocean marine insurance*.

CASUALTY AND SURETY INSURANCE

casualty and surety insurance
all forms of coverage not included in marine, fire, or life insurance

Casualty and surety insurance is of more recent origin than the other forms of insurance discussed. In brief, **casualty and surety insurance** includes all forms of coverage not included under marine, fire, or life insurance. A well-known example of casualty insurance is automobile liability insurance, which protects vehicle owners from claims resulting from injuries to other persons. Another example of casualty insurance is protection from losses resulting from burglary or robbery. Other forms of casualty insurance used by businesses include insurance against excessive bad-debt loss resulting from sales to customers on open account and protection against the breakage of plate glass.

worker's compensation
insurance to protect businesses from claims due to occupational accidents

Business firms protect themselves against claims resulting from occupational accidents through casualty insurance known as **worker's compensation**. Under worker's compensation laws of the various states, employers are liable for most of the accidents that take place in connection with their business operations. Worker's compensation and employer's liability insurance assumes the payment of wages during the employee's lost work time and provides medical, surgical, and hospitalization coverage as determined by the compensation laws of the state.

surety contract
provides coverage for losses suffered by the insured when terms of a contract are not met by another party

A **surety contract** generally provides that one party, the surety company, becomes answerable to a third party, the insured, if the second party fails to perform as required by contract. For example, a business that contracts for the construction of a new building may secure a surety contract to protect against the contractor's failure to complete the structure by a certain time. The contract may also protect against unsatisfied claims of workers or suppliers of materials as a result of the contractor's failure to meet obligations.

The *fidelity bond*, a special form of surety contract, provides that the surety company reimburse employers for losses resulting from the dishonest acts of employees. Banks, S&Ls, and other businesses in which employees have access to large sums of money always carry fidelity bonds for protection.

fidelity bond
provides coverage to employers for losses caused by dishonest acts of employees

Investment Policies of Property Insurance Companies

Property insurance, like life insurance, is big business. In order to provide an extra guaranty of ability to pay losses, property insurance companies maintain large capital funds. In addition, they have the reserves accumulated from insurance policy premiums that are collected in advance. These sources provide the funds that must be invested and which in turn produce income for the companies.

The investment policies of property and casualty insurance companies are affected by two basic facts. First, they are subject to federal income taxes, unlike life insurance companies. Therefore, they hold a large share of their assets in the form of tax-exempt municipal securities. Second, property losses are more uncertain than the death rate, so these companies cannot accurately predict how much they will have to pay policyholders each year. Property insurance companies purchase far fewer new corporate bond issues, but usually more corporate stock, than life insurance companies. While nearly one-fourth of total company assets are in corporate stock holdings, their bond holdings generally focus more on municipal and government bonds. Property companies have little interest in purchasing business real estate mortgages.

CORPORATE INVESTMENTS

U.S. corporations are not only large users of funds, but they also play a significant part in providing long-term capital for other businesses. This capital is provided in several ways. First of all, a corporation may invest capital in another company for purposes of control. In other cases, a corporation may invest in the securities of another company when that company is an important supplier of materials to the investing company. Finally, large sums accumulated by the employee pension funds of corporations are invested primarily in long-term securities.

Employee Pension Funds

The establishment of pension funds for the benefit of workers has been a part of the U.S. economy for many years. Retirement benefits as provided by the Social Security Act are the basis for pension planning today. Somewhat earlier than this act, the Railroad Retirement Act afforded retirement benefits for railroad employees; still other legislation provided for benefits for retired government employees.

Although the first private pension was adopted by the American Express Company in 1875, a large proportion of private pension plans now in existence have been established since 1945. Their rapid development since that time has been due in part to union pressure and to the desire of employers to reduce labor turnover by providing greater economic security for their employees. Corporations have been further motivated to contribute to pension funds because of high corporate income taxes. Corporate pension contributions are treated as deductible business expenses for corporate income tax purposes. It is estimated that there are over 500,000 private pension plans in existence in the United States today, covering about one half of the civilian labor force. As noted above, there are also government pension plans that cover many federal, state, and local government employees.

Investment Policies of Pension Funds

The majority of large pension funds that are primarily private noninsured funds are administered by trust companies or trust departments of banks. Life insurance companies handle private insured pension accounts, usually in the form of annuity contracts. In some cases, large private pension funds are administered by the companies directly.

The pool of savings channeled through pension plans is an important source of funds in the capital markets. Private noninsured pension funds and state and local retirement funds are major purchasers of new corporate bond and stock issues. In recent years, state and local government pension plans have focused relatively more on the purchase of corporate bonds than corporate stocks. On the other hand, private noninsured pension funds concentrate more on corporate stocks. More than one-half of the over $200 billion in total assets held by private noninsured pension funds are in the form of common stocks, while corporate bonds make up about one-fifth of their assets.

Trust institutions generally avoid investing substantially in the securities of the same corporations whose pension funds they are managing. This is in part a matter of sound financial policy and in part as a result of certain requirements on these investments imposed by the U.S. Treasury Department. Pension funds managed by life insurance companies are invested largely in corporate debt securities, residential and commercial real estate mortgages, and common stocks.

Recent legislation in most states allows life insurance companies to maintain separate investment accounts, each set up for a given pension plan or group of plans. Much more investment latitude is permitted for these separate accounts than in life insurance investments generally.

DEVELOPMENT COMPANIES

There are a variety of organizations whose function is to provide equity capital or long-term loans to new or small businesses that would find it difficult to raise capital through other sources. Some of these organizations are profit oriented, while others are nonprofit and seek to develop the economy of a particular area. Some receive assistance from various levels of government, while others operate entirely on private funds. However, a common thread runs through all of these *investment development companies*. They are designed to help establish businesses that have good prospects of success but lack adequate financial resources. In addition, they permit established companies to expand. Although the total amount of long-term funds provided to business through these development companies is not large compared with the total of business credit, it is a strategic outlay of funds for the purposes described above.

Nonprofit Development Companies

Regional and local development companies are nonprofit organizations usually funded by local citizens and business firms or associations. They may also receive assistance from local governments. Their aim is to improve an area's economy and to promote business growth. *State development companies* are chartered for similar purposes by special state legislation. Although privately funded, both local and state development companies increase their leverage by borrowing, using the proceeds to make long-term loans or purchase equity shares of small businesses. The Small Business Administration has a special loan program to assist local and state development companies.

Profit Oriented Development Companies

The Small Business Administration is also authorized to license and regulate privately-owned **small business investment companies** (SBICs). These development companies are established for profit, and the securities of many SBICs are actively traded in the securities markets.

The lenient tax treatment of the SBICs is an important attraction to their promoters and owners. The dividends an SBIC receives from investments in small businesses are exempt from corporate income

small business investment company (SBIC)
a privately owned, profit-seeking firm that provides funds to businesses

taxes. Both the SBIC and its stockholders may apply against ordinary income any losses sustained from price declines in debentures purchased from small firms, stock obtained through conversion of such debentures, or stock obtained by exercising of stock purchase warrants. Any accrued profits are taxed as capital gains.

An SBIC may finance a small business through the purchase of debentures that are convertible into stock of the firm, by the purchase of capital stock or debt securities, or through a long-term loan. Although privately capitalized, an SBIC may increase its financial leverage by borrowing from the SBA.

A small group of similar development companies exists entirely independent of the SBA or other government involvement. These companies, in most cases, represent the association of a few wealthy persons interested in taking advantage of growth opportunities of selected speculative enterprises. These venture capital companies, commonly referred to as **investment development companies**, are privately established profit-seeking organizations whose primary function is to provide capital not otherwise available to new and growing business ventures. They usually supply equity capital, but loan capital may be provided when its use seems appropriate.

investment development company
a private, profit-seeking company that provides venture capital to new and growing businesses

In addition to financially backing new companies, investment development companies take an active and continuing interest in those companies. However, they do not necessarily require voting control. They offer expert management counsel and guidance as well as continuing financial assistance as the companies pass through the various stages of their development. Investment development companies usually dispose of their interests when the success of the venture is assured and the securities can be sold at a substantial profit.

LEASE ARRANGEMENTS AND EQUIPMENT TRUST FINANCING

Lease arrangements and equipment trust financing do not represent special types of credit flowing from any single form of financial institution. Rather, they represent a type of financing arrangement that may be used by various financial institutions.

Lease Arrangements

It has been estimated that more than 80 percent of all retail establishments rent their places of business under lease arrangements. Many manufacturing corporations also find it to their advantage to rent their plant facilities. One type of lease arrangement entails the construction of special facilities for the use of a particular company. For example, Safeway Stores encourages local real estate groups and others with the necessary capital to construct buildings to their specifications. After construction, the buildings are leased to Safeway for a period of years in accordance with a predetermined agreement. The company benefits from new retail facilities without having to make an outlay of cash or to increase its corporate indebtedness.

Lease arrangements occur not only in real estate transactions. Their use now extends down the line through the equipment and facilities of some firms. For example, insurance companies and other financial institutions now lease fleets of automobiles and trucks to many of the nation's leading corporations. There has been increasing use of containers, which are cargo-carrying units the size of truck trailers that are placed directly from trucks onto ships without needing to be unloaded and loaded. Their use in surface and ship transportation has resulted in a huge demand for containers and for sources of financing for them. Container leasing has now reached a significant volume as their use has extended to such bulk commodities as fertilizers, cotton, hides, and manufactured products.

Lease arrangements are also widely used in the electric utility industry. Many companies now lease their nuclear fuel supply, or nuclear cores, for nuclear power plants. Nuclear power production facilities cost billions of dollars and leasing the fuel supply represents an attractive way to finance a portion of the required investment.

MUNICIPAL LEASING

The municipal leasing process involves a city or town constructing plant facilities by a municipality to the specifications of an industrial firm. Financing is arranged through the sale of municipal bonds known as **industrial revenue bonds** to the general public or to financial institutions. The plant facilities are then leased to the industrial company for a period of years at a rental high enough to cover the interest and retirement of the bonds, plus a small reserve. In this way, the municipality can attract desirable industry. The companies benefit by having the use of new and modern facilities with the only immediate outlay of funds being reasonable rental fees. Because interest to the municipal bond purchaser is free from federal and often from state income tax liability, municipalities can sell bonds at a much lower interest cost than a private corporation. This in turn makes it possible for municipalities to offer attractive rental fees to prospective corporate tenants.

industrial revenue bonds municipal bonds that finance construction of facilities for industrial firms

The popularity and rapid growth of this financial device has led to severe restrictions by the federal government. The tax exemptions in this type of industrial aid enabled many large, prosperous firms to obtain low-cost financing. At the same time, the federal government was losing tax revenues from many well-to-do individuals and corporations who purchased these bonds. Federal legislation now eliminates the tax-exempt status of most new issues of industrial revenue bonds over $10 million.

SALE AND LEASE-BACK ARRANGEMENTS

Another lease arrangement involves the sale of property owned by a company and its lease back to the selling company. One important reason for such transactions is to acquire additional working capital for business operations. Funds obtained from the sale of fixed assets may be used to take advantage of opportunities at times when a firm finds it either impossible or undesirable to increase the debt or equity of the business. The earnings from the application of these funds may far outweigh the rental cost of the facilities that the company has sold. Also, the rent that is paid to the new owner of the property is an expense that is chargeable against earnings for income tax purposes. In addition to the benefits that may accrue to a company's working capital position, the sale of fixed assets often makes possible the retirement of existing debt that may be carried against these assets. Under these circumstances, the capital structure of the firm is simplified, which may result in a stronger credit position.

As a rule, under the sale and lease-back arrangement, the lessee, or user of the property, is required to carry an appropriate amount of property insurance, to pay any property taxes, and maintain the property as if he or she were the owner.

Equipment Trust Financing

equipment trust financing
provides for transferring title to equipment from a seller to a trustee who leases the equipment back to the seller

Equipment trust financing is an important method for railroads to finance the purchase of heavy rolling stock, such as locomotives and tank cars, and for other types of businesses to buy expensive equipment in general. As an alternative to purchasing rolling stock outright, this device provides for the seller to transfer title to the equipment to a trustee. The trustee, generally a trust company or the trust department of a commercial bank, purchases and holds title to the equipment but leases it to the business.

The lessee usually pays from 20 to 25 percent of the equipment's cost as an initial rental payment. This is comparable to the down payment that is customarily made for direct purchase. The balance of the equipment cost is financed by selling equipment test obligations, which the trustee issues against the collateral value of its equipment.

It is generally the responsibility of the lessee to maintain the equipment properly, to pay all taxes and insurance charges, and to keep the trustee informed of the location and condition of the equipment. After the stated number of rental payments has been made, title to the equipment is turned over to the lessee. The periodic lease or rental payment is used by the trustee to pay interest on, and gradually retire, outstanding obligations. When a railroad acquires rolling stock under this arrangement, a metal plate showing the name of the trust institution that holds title to the property is usually attached to each piece of equipment.

Equipment trusts are considered to be low risk and very few losses on them have been recorded in recent decades. This excellent record results in part from the fact that railroad rolling stock has been in extremely short supply in recent decades, and a trustee can easily reclaim the equipment in the event of a railroad's default. Earlier, many railroads had to default on their other fixed payments. But more recently they have been very reluctant to miss the regular rental payments on equipment acquired through trust arrangements; loss of this equipment would seriously hurt the efficiency of operations.

Although this financial arrangement originally came into existence as a way to help the weaker railroads obtain new equipment, it is now the typical process by which all railroads acquire rolling stock. Equipment trust financing is also used by oil companies to purchase tank cars and by air transport companies to acquire airplanes.

KEY TERMS

annuity contract
casualty and surety insurance
closed-end fund
endowment insurance
equipment trust financing
fidelity bond
fiduciary
fire insurance
industrial revenue bonds
insurance trust
investment company
investment development company
irrevocable trust
living trust
marine insurance

mutual fund
property insurance
prudent-man rule
revocable trust
short-term trust
small business investment
   company (SBIC)
surety contract
term life insurance
term loan
testamentary trust
trust institution
universal life insurance
whole life insurance
worker's compensation

DISCUSSION QUESTIONS

1. How do commercial bank term loans differ from loans made under regular lines of credit?
2. What benefits do investment companies offer to investors?
3. Identify basic differences between the closed-end fund and the open-end types of investment companies.

4. Briefly describe the three principal types of personal trusts. Also describe the meaning of a common trust fund.
5. What trust services are performed for corporations?
6. Identify and describe the principal types of life insurance.
7. Describe the importance of life insurance companies as suppliers of long-term business funds.
8. What are the major types of property insurance? How do property and casualty insurance companies provide long-term funds to business corporations?
9. To some extent business corporations are both suppliers as well as users of long-term business financing. Explain.
10. Briefly describe the development of pension funds and indicate their investment strategies.
11. What are regional development companies? How do they differ from investment development companies?
12. What are small business investment companies? Distinguish between the activities of SBICs and those of the Small Business Administration.
13. Describe the special features of municipal leasing as a financial device to attract industry. Also indicate what is meant by a sale and lease-back arrangement.
14. Describe the mechanics of financing long-term equipment requirements through the use of the equipment trust arrangement.

PROBLEMS

1. Assume that you have been asked by the president of your firm to obtain a $90,000 term loan from the Third National Bank. The commercial loan officer agrees to a five-year loan at a 14 percent interest rate and will require annual payments. Determine the amount that your firm will have to pay at the end of each year. How would the annual payments have changed if the loan had been for eight years at a 12 percent interest rate?
2. A term loan from a local commercial bank is available in the amount of $100,000. It will be a 16 percent, four-year loan requiring annual payments.
   a. What would be the size of the annual payment needed to fully amortize the term loan? Make use of Table 4 in the Appendix.
   b. Prepare a loan amortization schedule for this loan. Refer to Table 10.5 in Chapter 10.
   c. What will be the total amount of interest and principal repayments over the life of the term loan?
3. Obtain a current issue of the *Federal Reserve Bulletin*.
   a. Determine the dollar amounts of newly issued corporate bonds

and stocks. Compare these figures with the amounts shown in Table 11.1 in Chapter 11 and comment on any changes.
b. The *Federal Reserve Bulletin* also shows the proportion of life insurance company assets held in the form of corporate stocks and bonds. Comment on whether these holdings as a percent of total assets have changed in recent years.
4. A three-year $425,000 term loan requiring monthly payments is available from the Second Bank of Florida at a 15 percent annual interest rate.
a. Use the Present and Future Value of an Annuity tool to determine the monthly payment.
b. Next use the "loan amortization" tool to prepare a loan amortization schedule for this loan.
c. Show how your answers in parts a. and b. would change if the annual interest rate were 11.75 percent.

SELF-TEST QUESTIONS

1. Which one of the following types of investment companies is also referred to as a mutual fund?
a. closed-end fund
b. open-end fund
c. trust institution
d. management investment holding company

2. Which of the following are considered to be principal types of personal trusts?
a. living trusts
b. living trusts and trusteeships under will
c. living trusts, trusteeships under will, and insurance trusts
d. prudent person trusts

3. The terms "revocable trust" and "irrevocable trust" are associated with which of the following types of trusts?
a. living trusts
b. common trusts
c. trusteeships under will
d. insurance trusts

4. A type of insurance described as "insurance in reverse" is called:
a. term life insurance
b. whole life insurance
c. endowment insurance
d. annuity insurance

5. Which of the following would *not* be considered a type of property insurance?
   a. endowment insurance
   b. fire insurance
   c. marine insurance
   d. casualty and surety insurance

SELF-TEST PROBLEM

1. Assume that you have requested a $50,000 term loan from the First National Bank. The loan officer agrees to a five-year loan at 12 percent interest and will require annual payments. How much will you have to pay at the end of each year? How would the annual payments have changed if the loan had been for six years at a 14 percent interest rate? (Use the PVIFA table, Table 4, in the Appendix.)

SUGGESTED READINGS

Edmister, Robert O. *Financial Institutions,* 2e. New York: McGraw-Hill, 1986. Part 3.

Greene, Mark R., and James S. Trieschmann. *Risk and Insurance,* 7e. Cincinnati: South-Western Publishing Co., 1988.

Investment Companies. New York: Wiesenberger Investment Co., published annually.

Life Insurance Fact Book. Washington, DC: American Council of Life Insurance, published annually.

Moyer, Charles, James R. McGuigan, and William J. Kretlow. *Contemporary Financial Management,* 3e. St. Paul, MN: West Publishing Co., 1987. Chap. 15.

Ross, Stephen A., Randolph W. Westerfield, and Jeffrey F. Jaffee. *Corporate Finance,* 2e. Homewood, IL: Richard D. Irwin, 1990. Chaps. 18 and 19.

Shapiro, Alan C. *Modern Corporate Finance.* New York: Macmillan Publishing Co., 1989. Chaps. 19 and 21.

ANSWERS TO SELF-TEST QUESTIONS   1. b   2. c   3. a   4. d   5. a

SOLUTION TO SELF-TEST PROBLEM

1. PVIFA at 12% for 5 years = 3.605

   Annual payment = $50,000/3.605 = $13,870 (rounded)

   PVIFA at 14% for 6 years = 3.889

   Annual payment = $50,000/3.889 = $12,857 (rounded)

CHAPTER 13
Markets for Long-Term Business Funds

After studying this chapter, you should be able to:

- Describe the processes and institutions used by businesses to distribute new securities to the investing public.
- Outline the recent difficulties and changes in structure of the investment banking industry.
- Describe the institutions and practices involved in the exchange of outstanding securities among investors.
- Discuss the options and futures markets.
- Identify the regulatory mechanisms by which the securities exchanges and the over-the-counter markets are controlled.

This chapter examines the processes by which the borrowers and lenders of long-term capital are brought together in the primary and secondary markets. Specifically, we describe the activities of investment bankers concerning the origination, distribution, and sale of long-term corporate securities. Also discussed are the activities of the over-the-counter market and securities exchanges, showing how they facilitate the transfer of outstanding securities.

THE PRIMARY SECURITIES MARKETS

Recall from Chapter 1 that newly created securities are sold in the *primary market* while existing securities are traded in the *secondary market*. The initial sale of newly issued debt or equity securities is called a **flotation**. The average corporation doesn't usually sell long-term securities directly to investors because it is difficult to always know investor attitudes and the legal requirements involved. Corporations usually use the services of professionals whose primary activity is marketing securities. These professionals who market long-term securities are called **investment bankers** or **underwriters**. Investment bankers are the middlepersons between corporations and the general public in helping corporations accumulate investment funds. Some investment banking firms are organized as partnerships, while others are corporations.

flotation
the initial sale of debt or equity securities

investment bankers or *underwriters*
financial intermediaries who help businesses market their bonds and securities in the primary securities market

Primary Functions of Investment Bankers

Although the specific activities of investment bankers may differ depending upon the size and the financial resources of the company, the primary functions of investment bankers in general are originating, underwriting, and selling newly issued securities.

ORIGINATING

Most of the larger investment banking firms engage in originating securities. Before an investment bank decides to originate an issue of securities for a corporation, it makes a detailed study of the corporation in order to determine the feasibility of security distribution. The investment banker assists the issuing corporation by recommending the types, terms, and offering price of securities that should be sold. He or she also aids the corporation in preparing the registration and informational materials required by the Securities and Exchange Commission (SEC). One important and carefully regulated piece of information is the **prospectus**, which details the issuer's finances and must be provided to each buyer of the security.

prospectus
document describing the terms and conditions of a new security issue

UNDERWRITING

Investment bankers not only offer the means by which securities are made available to the investing public; they also assume the risk arising from the possibility that such securities may not be purchased by investors. This risk is assumed when the investment banker enters into an **underwriting agreement** with the issuing corporation. Through this agreement, the securities are purchased by the underwriters, who then sell them to investors at a higher price than their cost.

Under the laws of some states, if a corporation issues additional shares of common stock, or any security that may be converted to

underwriting agreement
an agreement in which an investment banker assumes the risk of selling a securities offering

common stock, the securities must be offered for sale first to the existing common stockholders. That is, the existing shareholders have *preemptive rights* to purchase newly issued securities. The purpose of this regulation is to permit existing stockholders to maintain their proportional share of ownership. Corporate charters may provide for preemptive rights even in states that do not require it. To make new stock issues attractive to existing stockholders, the company will generally offer the securities at a "subscription" price that is lower than the market price.

It may seem, then, that underwriters need only be used for the initial public offering of securities by a company, and that subsequent issues are simply offered to the existing shareholders. However, circumstances may cause the stock's market price to fall below the subscription price. In this case, shareholders will not be likely to purchase the new shares at the subscription price. As a result, the company will not have a successful flotation, and the sale of securities will not produce the money needed by the company to carry out its commitments.

Because of the uncertainty of a flotation's success, even when offered to existing stockholders, the corporation may again employ investment bankers. The investment bankers sign a **standby underwriting agreement**, whereby they agree to purchase all the newly issued securities not taken by the stockholders. The standby agreement allows the corporation to proceed with its plans and be assured it will receive the funds from the sale of securities. The corporation pays the investment bankers a standby fee to purchase the unsold securities. Although there is a clear distinction between purchase underwriting and standby underwriting activities, the term underwriting is usually used to include both.

standby underwriting agreement
when investment bankers agree to buy all newly issued securities not bought by a corporation's stockholders

Another category of underwriting is called best-effort selling. Under a **best-effort underwriting agreement**, investment bankers make a best effort to sell the securities of the issuing corporation, but they assume no risk for a possible failure of the flotation. The investment bankers are paid a fee for those securities they sell. The best-effort agreement is used for either of two reasons: First, the underwriters may anticipate some difficulty in selling the securities and be unwilling to assume the underwriting risk, for example, in the case of a small firm's initial public offering. Second, the strength and reputation of the company may be so great that the issuing company itself is willing to assume the risk of an unsuccessful flotation.

best-effort underwriting agreement
when investment bankers agree to try to sell a corporation's securities but assume no liability

SELLING

The majority of large investment banking houses maintain retail outlets throughout the nation. Retail selling is selling to individual investors. There are also many independently owned and operated retail brokerage outlets not large or strong enough to engage in major originating and underwriting functions. Like the underwriters, they depend upon the resale of securities at a price above their cost to cover expenses and provide profit from operations. A few of the large investment banking houses do not sell to individuals. Rather, they confine their activities entirely to originating, underwriting, and institutional selling. *Institutional selling* involves large investors such as insurance companies, pension funds, investment companies, and other large investors.

Regulatory authorities permit announcements of security offerings to be placed in newspapers and other publications. These announcements, called *tombstones*, are very restricted in wording and must not seem to be soliciting sales. An announcement, published in August 1990, is shown in Figure 13.1. Note that this tombstone is careful to point out that it is "neither an offer to sell nor a solicitation of an offer to buy...." The word tombstone apparently derives from the small amount of information it provides. The underwriters are shown on the bottom of the announcement. Of those listed, Morgan Stanley & Co., The First Boston Corporation, Goldman, Sachs & Co., and Lehman Brothers are representative of firms that originate, underwrite, and engage in institutional selling. The other firms listed maintain multiple retail offices and also have the capacity to originate issues of securities.

The investment bank that is chosen by a company to handle a flotation is called the lead investment banker. In the issue shown in Figure 13.1, Morgan Stanley & Co. is the lead bank. When necessary, several investment banks may work together in a group called a **syndicate** to handle the flotation. For large issues of securities, thirty or forty investment banking firms may be invited by the syndicate to assume part of the risk of the underwriting and to share in the profits resulting from the sale of the securities. For very large issues, two or three hundred firms may participate in the underwriting and distribution efforts.

syndicate
a group of investment banks joining together underwrite a flotation

Competitive Bidding

Private companies may sell securities on either a competitive bid or a negotiated basis. The typical arrangement, however, for private companies is negotiation between the company and the chosen underwriter. Governmental bodies, on the other hand, usually require competitive bidding by investment bankers before awarding underwriting agreements. This is also the case for railroad securities and some public utilities. Under these circumstances, there may be little initial negotiation between the investment houses and the issuer. In these cases, the issuer decides upon the size of issue and the type of security that it wishes to sell. Then it invites the investment banking houses to offer

FIGURE 13.1   A Security Offering Announcement, or Tombstone

This announcement is neither an offer to sell nor a solicitation of an offer to buy any of these Securities.
The offer is made only by the Prospectus.

4,000,000 Shares

Dillard Department Stores, Inc.

Class A Common Stock

Price $84 a Share

Copies of the Prospectus may be obtained in any State from only such of the
undersigned as may legally offer these Securities in compliance
with the securities laws of such State.

3,200,000 Shares

This portion of the offering is being offered in the United States and Canada by the undersigned.

MORGAN STANLEY & CO.
Incorporated

THE FIRST BOSTON CORPORATION	**GOLDMAN, SACHS & CO.**
MERRILL LYNCH CAPITAL MARKETS	**LEHMAN BROTHERS**
SMITH BARNEY, HARRIS UPHAM & CO. *Incorporated*	**STEPHENS INC.**
SANFORD C. BERNSTEIN & CO., INC.	**WILLIAM BLAIR & COMPANY**

C.J. LAWRENCE, MORGAN GRENFELL INC.   **McDONALD & COMPANY**   **PIPER, JAFFRAY & HOPWOOD**
Securities, Inc.   *Incorporated*

PRESCOTT, BALL & TURBEN, INC.   **WHEAT FIRST BUTCHER & SINGER**
Capital Markets

ADVEST, INC.   **EPPLER, GUERIN & TURNER, INC.**   **FIRST OF MICHIGAN CORPORATION**

FURMAN SELZ MAGER DIETZ & BIRNEY   **INTERSTATE/JOHNSON LANE**
Incorporated   *Corporation*

JANNEY MONTGOMERY SCOTT INC.   **LOVETT UNDERWOOD NEUHAUS & WEBB, INC.**

RAUSCHER PIERCE REFSNES, INC.   **RAYMOND JAMES & ASSOCIATES, INC.**

SEIDLER AMDEC SECURITIES INC.   **STIFEL, NICOLAUS & COMPANY**
Incorporated

August 22, 1990

bids for handling the securities. The investment banking group offering the highest price for the securities, while also providing information showing it will be able to carry through a successful flotation, will usually be awarded the contract. From that point on, the process of security distribution is quite similar to the handling of the securities of an industrial corporation.

A great deal of disagreement has existed about the relative advantages and disadvantages of competitive bidding by investment banking houses. Investment bankers strongly contend that the continuing advice they give the corporations they serve is essential to an economical and efficient distribution of the securities of such companies. Others contend that competitive bidding enables corporations to sell their securities at higher prices than would otherwise be the case. However, during periods of rapidly rising interest rates and general uncertainty in the capital markets, negotiated contracts between investment bankers and the corporate issuer can be more desirable than competitive bids. Much evidence has been presented for both sides, making it probable that securities will continue to be distributed under both arrangements.

Market Stabilization

The period after a new issue is initially sold to the public is called the *aftermarket*. This period may vary from a few hours to several weeks. During this period the members of the syndicate may not sell the securities for less than the offering price. To encourage investors to buy the securities, the underwriters want their market price to remain stable. Because a steady flow of the new securities to the market may depress the price temporarily, it may be necessary to offer to buy back the securities in order to prevent a larger price drop. This is called market stabilization. Although the Securities Exchange Act of 1934 prohibits manipulation of this sort by all others, underwriters are permitted to buy shares if the market price falls below the offering price. When market stabilization may be allowed, it is necessary to state that fact in the prospectus. If part of an issue remains unsold after a period of time, for example 30 days, members can leave the syndicate and sell their securities at whatever price the market will allow. The lead underwriter decides when the syndicate is to be broken, freeing selling members to sell at the prevailing market price.

Other Functions of Investment Banking Firms

Investment banking firms engage in many activities beyond their primary function of distributing long-term security instruments. For example, they have traditionally dominated the commercial paper market. Commercial paper, as described in Chapter 9, is an important source of short-term financing for business. Through buying and selling commercial paper, investment bankers participate in the day-to-day cash flow requirements of many businesses. Four investment banking firms dominate commercial activities. They are Goldman, Sachs & Co., Merrill Lynch & Co., The First Boston Corporation, and Lehman Brothers.

In recent years mergers and acquisitions activities (M & A) have increased in importance for many investment banking firms. Firms with strong M & A departments compete intensely for the highly profitable activity of corporate mergers or acquisitions. It is reported that, for a few investment bankers, profits from M & A activity have exceeded those from all other activities. Investment banking firms act on behalf of corporate clients in bringing together firms suitable for, and receptive to, merger. Very large fees are charged for this service.

Other activities of investment bankers include the management of pension and endowment funds for businesses, colleges, churches, hospitals, and other institutions. In many cases, officers of investment banking firms are on the boards of directors of major corporations. In this capacity they are able to offer financial advice and participate in the financial planning of the firm. Investment bankers also provide financial counseling on a fee basis. Not all investment bankers engage in every one of these activities. The size of the firm largely dictates the various services it provides. Some firms, known as "boutiques," specialize in only a few activities.

Investment Banking Regulation

Federal regulation of investment banking is administered primarily under the provisions of the Securities Act of 1933. The chief purposes of the act are: (1) to provide full, fair, and accurate disclosure of the character of newly issued securities offered for sale, and (2) to prevent fraud in the sale of such securities. The first purpose is achieved by requiring that the issuer file a registration statement with the Securities and Exchange Commission (SEC) and deliver a prospectus to potential investors. The SEC, however, does not pass judgment on the investment merit of any securities. It is illegal for a seller of securities to represent the SEC's approval of a registration statement as a recommendation of investment quality. The philosophy behind the Securities Act of 1933 is that the most effective regulatory device is the requirement that complete and accurate information be disclosed on securities on which investment decisions may be made. Although the SEC does not guarantee the accuracy of any statement made by an issuer of securities in a registration statement or prospectus, legal action may be taken against officers and other representatives of the issuing company for any false or incorrect statements. Full disclosure is, therefore, instrumental in accomplishing the second purpose, that of fraud prevention.

blue-sky laws
state laws to protect investors from fraudulent security offerings

In addition to federal regulation of investment banking, most states have **blue-sky laws** to protect investors from fraudulent security offerings. Blue-sky laws apparently get their name from the efforts of some unscrupulous operators for whom the sky is the limit in their security dealings. Because state laws differ in their specific regulations, individual states have difficulty administering interstate security operations. Thus, the federal government is the primary regulator of investment banking. The most common violation of state blue-sky laws is that of misrepresenting the financial condition and asset position of companies.

COMMERCIAL BANKS AND INVESTMENT BANKING

From our discussion to this point it may be assumed that businesses depend primarily on commercial banks for short-term financing needs and on investment banks for long-term financial requirements. However, there are many exceptions. We have noted that a few investment banks deal in the commercial paper—a short-term security—of businesses. So too, commercial banks make many long-term loans to businesses. However, these long-term loans are directly negotiated and are not comparable to activities of investment banking.

The financial collapse of 1929 and the Great Depression of the 1930s brought a great deal of attention to the poor controls over securities dealings in this country. Several laws regulating securities were passed in the 1930s. We have already noted the Securities Act of 1933, and we will discuss some others later in the chapter.

One major piece of 1930s legislation ended the ability of commercial banks to act as underwriters of newly issued securities. There were many commercial bank failures during the Great Depression, and there was evidence that some of these failures resulted from the underwriting activities of the banks. As a result, legislation regulating the securities activities of commercial banks, was passed. The essential provision of the Glass-Steagall Act of 1933 prohibits commercial banks from acting as investment bankers or underwriters of security offerings.

Until the late 1980s, commercial banks were permitted to underwrite only federal government obligations and general obligation bonds of state and local governments. Financial regulatory controls in the nation have now been strengthened to the point where banks may soon be able to again engage in full underwriting activities. Since 1987, commercial banks have been permitted to underwrite new issues of commercial paper and securities backed by mortgages. In 1989, banks were authorized to underwrite corporate bonds, and there is the prospect of this being extended to corporate stock. The easing of restrictions is not complete because the underwriting activities allowed can be carried out only by subsidiaries of the banks and must not exceed 10 percent of the subsidiary's total business. These subsidiaries are wholly owned by and responsible to parent banks.

Commercial banks are understandably anxious to see the Glass-Steagall Act repealed. They want to open new markets and participate in profitable underwriting activities. They argue that participation in investment banking will help them become larger organizations with stronger capital bases. If domestic commercial banks are to compete internationally, they must have such powers. Large European banks have long combined banking and securities businesses under one roof.

Investment banking firms, on the other hand, oppose unlimited underwriting by commercials banks. Possible conflicts between such underwriting and the banks' basic commercial functions could lead to bank failures.

Resistance to expanded powers for commercial banks by the investment banking community, however, has weakened due to the vast difficulties experienced by that industry. Through the boom years of the 1960s and 1970s in the securities markets, investment banking firms expanded in a pell-mell rush to increase their market share of the underwriting business. Since the crash of 1987 many of these firms have gone out of business or merged with other firms. Their demise was accompanied by a displacement of tens of thousands of employees that had been attracted to the field.

Another move into investment banking was made by commercial banks in 1990. J. P. Morgan & Co., a commercial bank, instituted a computer-based system for the distribution of corporate bonds. This system, named CapitalLink, allows issuers of bonds to bypass Wall Street underwriters and reduce distribution costs. The SEC has approved the device and, as might be expected, there has been strong resistance from investment bankers.

THE SECONDARY SECURITIES MARKETS

The distribution of any product is aided if there is a "secondhand" market for it. For securities, it is particularly important. The secondary market for securities consists of organized security exchanges and the over-the-counter (OTC) market, a network of independent dealers and agents. Less well-organized markets, known as the third and fourth markets, also exist. The secondary markets not only allow an investor to shift investment commitments; they provide liquidity as well. To maintain the health of the market economic system, it is necessary that successful firms be rewarded with a steady flow of investment capital. A firm that fares poorly is penalized through pressure brought on the firm's management by its stockholders as market prices of its securities fall. In addition, when the firm seeks new capital, it will have to provide a higher probable yield to the investor by receiving a lower price for the securities it attempts to sell. The position of a firm's management becomes increasingly vulnerable as business deteriorates. Ultimately management may be replaced by the firm's directors, who are, in turn, elected by the stockholders.

Over-the-Counter Market

The security houses that make up the OTC market distribute newly issued securities to the investing public. They also provide the public with a secondary market for securities, that is, they stand ready to buy as well as sell securities. It is important at this point to distinguish between OTC operations and security exchange operations.

In the OTC markets, securities are purchased and sold by dealers who act as *principals*. They buy from and sell for their own account to the public, other dealers, and commission brokers. In a sense, they operate in the manner of any merchant. They have an inventory, comprised of the securities in which they specialize, which they hope to sell at a price high enough above their purchase price to make a profit.

The security exchanges, discussed later in this chapter, provide facilities where only members may buy and sell securities among themselves. The nonmember investor does not have access to the floor of the exchange and so must secure the services of a person or firm that does have membership and floor-trading privileges. The brokers that represent the public in floor-trading activities on the exchange serve as *agents*, and hence must represent their customers to the best of their ability.

SECURITIES TRADED OVER THE COUNTER

Among the securities handled exclusively through the OTC market are real estate bonds, Federal Land Bank and Federal Home Loan Bank bonds, state bonds, municipal bonds, and equipment trust agreement obligations. In addition, the OTC market handles the securities of all types of businesses. Some securities are handled both on the exchanges and through the OTC market.

MAKING A MARKET

making a market
when an OTC dealer is ready to buy or sell securities at specified prices

bid-and-asked price
the prices for which an OTC dealer is willing to buy or to sell a security

When an OTC dealer stands ready to buy or sell a particular security or group of securities at specified prices, the dealer is said to be **making a market** for the security. The quotation that is made by a dealer making a market for a given security is the **bid-and-asked price**—the bid price is that price the dealer is willing to pay for the securities, and the asked price is the price at which the dealer is willing to sell them. Hence, the margin, or spread, between a bid price and asked price for a security is apparent from its quotations. A security that is traded frequently and has a ready market can be expected to have a narrower spread than a security that is traded infrequently.

An OTC dealer cannot possibly make a market for all the many thousands of securities in existence. Thus a dealer's activities are confined to a limited number of securities. At one time this meant that the broker trying to buy or sell a particular stock for a customer may have had to contact several known dealers in that stock for the best possible price. Now this may be necessary only for the securities of small companies, which are seldom traded. The National Association of Securities Dealers Automatic Quotations, referred to as **NASDAQ** serves the OTC market by making available via computer the quotations of all market makers for the stocks of more than 4,000 companies traded over the counter. A broker can immediately identify the dealer with the best price, confirm the quotation, and complete the purchase or sale through that dealer.

NASDAQ
National Association of Securities Dealers Automatic Quotations

In 1982 a new national market system was instituted. This system now accommodates nearly 3,000 NASDAQ securities. It indicates high, low, and closing trade prices and provides constantly updated volume figures to brokers. OTC stocks whose prices are quoted on NASDAQ accounted for 38 percent of all stocks traded in the domestic securities markets during 1989.

REGULATION OF THE OTC MARKET

The Securities Exchange Act of 1934 established the Securities and Exchange Commission (SEC) and gave it authority over the organized exchanges. All brokers and dealers doing business in the organized markets were made to register with the SEC. The Maloney Act of 1938 amended the Securities Exchange Act of 1934 to extend SEC control to the OTC market. The law created the legal basis for OTC brokers and dealers to form national self-regulating trade associations. This was one instance where business itself requested government regulation. It stemmed from the fact that honest dealers in the investment field had little protection against bad publicity resulting from the unscrupulous practices of a few OTC dealers. Under this provision one association, the National Association of Security Dealers, **NASD**, has been formed. All rules adopted by NASD must be reported to the SEC; the SEC has the authority to take away any powers of the NASD.

NASD
the National Association of Security Dealers

The NASD has established a lengthy set of rules and regulations intended to insure fair practices and responsibility on the part of the association's members. Any broker or dealer engaged in OTC activities is eligible to become a member of the NASD as long as a record of responsible operation can be proved and the broker or dealer is willing to accept the NASD code of ethics. A total of 570 market makers were in the NASD system in 1989.

ORGANIZED SECURITY EXCHANGES

An organized securities exchange is a location with a trading floor where all of the trading of stocks takes place under rules created by the exchange. In late 1990 there were eight organized stock exchanges in the United States. These exchanges began as informal arrangements for trading in securities at convenient locations in the nation's cities. The New York Stock Exchange, for example, had its beginning under the shade of a certain buttonwood tree on Wall Street. At a later date, because of the popularity of this meeting place, traders began to do business as agents of others. Eventually these traders moved indoors, and they now enjoy well-equipped facilities.

The stock exchanges appear to have come into existence primarily to aid trading in local issues. Although there are now only eight exchanges in operation, records indicate the existence of more than one hundred exchanges during the nation's history. Of the eight exchanges, only the New York Stock Exchange and American Stock Exchange, in Chicago, may be considered to be truly national in scope. The New York Stock Exchange accounts for approximately 75 percent of the dollar volume of securities trading on all exchanges. The smaller regional exchanges accommodate trading of the securities of regional and smaller firms.

The organized stock exchanges use the latest in electronic communications. The present methods of transmitting information within cities and between cities is in sharp contrast to the devices used before the introduction of the telegraph in 1844. Quotations were conveyed between New York and Philadelphia through signal flags in the daytime and light signals at night from high point to high point across New Jersey. Although cumbersome compared with modern methods, quotations were often transmitted in this manner in as short a time as ten minutes.

Because of its relative importance and because in most respects its operations are typical of those of the other exchanges, the New York Stock Exchange will provide the basis for the following description of exchange organization and activities.

Structure of the New York Stock Exchange

The New York Stock Exchange is a voluntary association of 1,366 members. Like all the stock exchanges in the nation, its objective is to provide a convenient meeting place where buyers and sellers of securities or their representatives may conduct business. In addition, the New York Stock Exchange provides facilities for the settlement of transactions, establishes rules relative to the trading processes and the activities of its members, provides publicity for the transactions, and establishes standards for the corporations whose securities are traded on the exchange.

The New York Stock Exchange, then, serves primarily to ease the transfer of existing securities from investor to investor. In so doing it contributes significantly to the financial processes of the nation. The existence of a highly efficient secondary market allows the purchaser of new securities to know that the investment can be readily sold should other investments appear more attractive, if funds are needed for other purposes, or to realize profits or losses.

The number of memberships or seats on the New York Stock Exchange was increased from 1,100 to its present level of 1,366 in 1929. It is unlikely that the number will soon be increased again because the physical accommodations for trading activities are limited. As might be expected, membership seats carry a great value. In order to purchase a seat it is necessary to negotiate with other shareholders who may be willing to dispose of their memberships. On April 20, 1987 a seat on the New York Stock Exchange sold for a record high price of $1,000,000, while in 1942 seats sold for as low as $17,000. The cost of security trading seats since 1980 has generally been within the range of $300,000 to $700,000. The extremely high volume of trading in 1987 accounted for the attraction of owning a seat on the NYSE at that time; the low level of trading activity and the uncertainty of the outcome of World War II explains the very low cost of a seat in 1942.

BROKERS

The largest group of members on the New York Stock Exchange are the commission brokers. Most maintain offices throughout the country to solicit business from investors. The key function of **commission brokers** is to act as agents for the execution of customers' orders for securities purchases and sales. In return the broker receives a commission for the service.

commission broker
an agent who executes customers' orders for the purchase and sale of securities

There are other brokers who do not act as agents for customers. Independent brokers hold memberships on the exchange primarily for their own use.

SPECIALISTS

Specialists, or assigned dealers, have the responsibility of making a market in an assigned security. The specialist maintains an inventory of the security in question and stands ready to buy or sell at least 100 shares on order of other brokers or traders. The specialist must make a

specialist
a broker who deals in particular assigned securities, buying and selling for other brokers

large financial investment in the shares held in inventory as well as take the risk position in the stock. The specialist maintains bid-and-asked prices for the security, and the margin between the two prices represents the specialist's gross profit. Specialists provide a vital function to the auction market process. They accomplish this service by offering to buy or sell whenever there is a lack of regularity or order in the market for securities.

Listing Securities

All securities must be listed before they may be traded on the New York Stock Exchange. To qualify for listing its security, a corporation must meet certain requirements concerning earning power, total value of outstanding stock, and number of shareholders. The corporation also agrees to the public distribution at certain times of reports and other information that will make possible an intelligent analysis of the security. The corporation also pays a fee for the privilege of being listed. The acceptance of the security by the exchange for listing on the "big board" does not constitute endorsement of its quality. The common stocks of over 1,700 corporations are listed on the New York Stock Exchange.

The American Stock Exchange and all of the regional exchanges permit unlisted trading privileges as well as listed trading privileges. The distinction between these two lies primarily in the method by which the security is placed on the exchange for trading. For unlisted securities, the exchange itself (instead of the issuing corporation) recommends the securities for trading privileges. Unlisted trading privileges must be approved by the SEC. The securities of approximately 1,000 corporations carry unlisted trading privileges on the nation's stock exchanges.

Security Transactions

Orders for the purchase or sale of securities listed on the New York Stock Exchange may be placed with any of the approximately 6,795 offices maintained by members of the exchange throughout the nation as well as in some foreign countries. In addition, orders may be placed with approximately 2,700 other firms that have correspondent relations with members of the exchange. The investor needs to specify the type of order to be placed as well as the number of shares to be traded. Securities orders to buy and sell can be market, limit, or stop-loss orders.

MARKET ORDER
The firm that receives an order to purchase shares of stock listed on the New York Stock Exchange at the best price possible transmits the order

to its New York office, where the order is transmitted to the floor of the exchange. An order for immediate purchase at the best possible price is a ***market order***.

LIMIT ORDER

In a ***limit order***, the maximum buying price or the minimum selling price is specified by the investor. For example, if a commission broker has a limit buy order at 43 from an investor and other brokers are bidding as high as 43¼, the order could not be filled at that moment. The broker will wait until a price of 43 or less becomes available. Usually any limit order that is not quite close to the current market price is turned over to the specialist, who places it in his or her *limit order book*. The specialist will make the trade for the commission broker when the price comes within the limit. Of course, if the price of the stock progresses upward rather than downward, the order will not be completed. Limit orders may be placed to expire at the end of one day, one week, one month, or on a good-until-canceled basis.

STOP-LOSS ORDER

A ***stop-loss order*** is an order to sell stock at the market price when the price of the stock falls to a specified level. The stockholder may protect gains or limit possible loss due to a fall in the price of the stock by placing a stop-loss order at a price a few points below the current market price. For example, the investor in our example may place a stop-loss order on the stock at a price of 40. If the price does fall to 40, the commission broker sells the shares for as high a price as possible. This order does not guarantee a price of 40 to the seller, since by the time the stock is actually sold, the price may have declined rapidly to well below 40. On the other hand, if the stock price does not reach the specified price, the order will not be executed.

RECORD KEEPING

When the transaction takes place, the information is sent to a central computer system which, in turn, sends the information to display screens across the nation. A section of the securities report and an explanation of the symbols are shown in Figure 13.2. This consolidated report includes all transactions on the New York Stock Exchange as well as those of the Midwest Stock Exchange, Pacific Coast Exchange, Boston Exchange, Cincinnati Exchange, and Philadelphia Exchange.

Abbreviations of the securities appear on the upper line of the screen. Immediately below the last letter of the abbreviation are the number of shares and the price. When the sale is for a round lot of 100 shares (amounts less than 100 shares are called odd lots), only the price is shown.[1] For multiples of 100 shares from 200 through 900, the last

market order
an order to buy stock immediately at the best possible price

limit order
an order to buy or sell a stock that states a maximum price for purchase or a minimum price for sale

stop-loss order
an order to sell when the stock's price falls to a specified level

---

1. For a few stocks listed on the New York Stock Exchange, the round lot is ten shares.

FIGURE 13.2   Section of Securities Transaction Report

DI	HLT	GM	LIL	PE
$50\frac{3}{8}$	$49\frac{1}{2}$	$46\frac{1}{4}$	$2s19\frac{1}{8}$	$1000s16$

Explanation: Dresser Industries Incorporated, 100 shares sold at 50⅜; Hilton Hotels, 100 shares sold at 49½; General Motors, 100 shares sold at 46¼; Long Island Lighting, 200 shares sold at 19⅛; Philadelphia Electric Company, 1,000 shares sold at 16.

digit of the sales figure is followed by an "s." All volume figures are shown for sales of 1,000 shares and over. The letters "ss" are used to separate the volume from the price for stocks traded in units of 10 rather than 100. Errors and corrections are written out.

The details of the purchase transaction are also sent to the central office of the exchange and then to the brokerage office where the order was originally placed. Later the customer will receive a stock certificate indicating ownership of the stock. If the investor chooses, the stock may be bought in street name. A security is bought in **street name** when the brokerage house buys the security in its own name on behalf of the investor. The advantage of this is that the investor may sell the securities by simply phoning the broker without the necessity of signing and delivering the certificates.

street name
when securities are bought in the name of the investor's brokerage firm

Short Sales

A **short sale** is sale of securities that the seller does not own. The stock is borrowed and sold in anticipation of a fall in its price. In the event that a price decline does occur, the short seller covers the resulting short position by buying enough stock to repay the lender.

short sale
a sale of securities that the seller borrows rather than owns

As an example, in anticipation of a decline in the price of a particular stock, an investor sells short 100 shares of the stock. The order is placed through a broker, who in turn arranges to borrow the necessary stock. Having sold the borrowed stock, the brokerage house delivers to the lender of the securities the proceeds of the sale. The lender holds the proceeds as collateral. In our example, if the securities were sold at 50, the proceeds from the 100 shares, $5,000, would be turned over to the lender.

If the short seller covers the short position when the stock has dropped to a price of 40, $4,000 is paid for 100 shares to be returned to the lender. The short seller receives the $5,000 that was posted as collateral and has a $1,000 profit from the transaction, minus brokerage fees. If the price of the security moves upward rather than downward, the short seller must still cover the short position at the end of some stated time period. The short seller will pay more for the stock than the price at which it was sold; the result is a loss rather than a gain.

Because short sales have an important effect on the market for securities, the SEC regulates them closely. Among the restrictions on short sales is one relating to selling only on an "uptick." This means that a short sale can take place only when the price of a security rises or is unchanged, when the previous change was an increase. This restriction is designed to prevent an accumulation of short sales that would cause the price of a security to plunge downward. In addition, regulations of the Federal Reserve System, as well as of the New York Stock Exchange, require the short seller to maintain a margin or deposit of 50 percent of the price of the stock with the broker. Loans of stock are callable on 24 hours' notice.

Buying on Margin

Buying on margin means the investor borrows some of the funds to make securities purchases from the brokerage firm. The securities so purchased become collateral for the loan. The *margin* is the minimum percentage of the purchase price that the investor must pay in cash. In order to buy on margin, the investor must have a margin account with the brokerage firm, which in turn arranges the necessary financing with banks.

buying on margin when an investor borrows from a brokerage firm to cover part of the purchase price of securities

Margin buying is used to magnify expected profits based on the investor's actual cash investment. At one time it was possible for an investor to buy securities by paying only 10 percent of the purchase price and borrowing the remainder. The leverage that is obtained from such an action is obvious. If an investor could buy securities having a market price of $10,000 by contributing only $1,000 in cash and by borrowing $9,000, a 10 percent increase in the market price would increase their value to $11,000, and, when sold, would result in a 100 percent gain to the investor.

The speculator knows of course that losses are also magnified when buying on margin. If the price of the securities used as collateral begins to decline, the investor may receive a *margin call* from the brokerage firm for additional cash. If the market price of the pledged securities continues to decline and the investor fails to provide the new margin amount, the bank or brokerage house will sell the securities. In our example in the previous paragraph, if the market price should drop by 10 percent, the investor's entire cash investment is wiped out.

The combination of falling prices, margin calls, and sales of securities can develop into a downward spiral for securities prices. This kind of spiral played an important role in the stock market crash of 1929, which was considered responsible for the onset of the Great Depression.

At that time there was no regulatory restraint on margin sales and, in fact, margins of only 10 percent were common. As a result, the Board of Governors of the Federal Reserve System limits the extent to which securities may be purchased on margin. Since 1974 the margin requirement has been 50 percent, although at times during World War II, margin requirements reached the 100 percent level. At that time, in order to counter inflationary pressures, margin trading was prohibited entirely.

Program Trading

program trading
a combination of techniques using computer programs to trade groups of securities

Around 1975 stocks began to be traded not only individually, but also in packages or *programs*. **Program trading** is a technique for trading stocks as a group rather than individually. At first program trades were simply trades of any portfolio of stocks held by an equity manager who wanted to change the portfolio's composition for any number of reasons. Today the portfolios that are traded in package form are often made up of the stocks included in a stock index, such as the Standard & Poor's 500.

A wide range of portfolio trading strategies are now described as program trading. These strategies for the purchase or sale of a stock portfolio are based on mathematical models. The stock portfolio and mathematical formulas are stored in computers. The computer is used to constantly apply the mathematical models as stock prices change and give an execution signal when appropriate. At the moment the signal is given, the orders for the stocks are sent directly to the NYSE trading floor for execution by the proper specialist. Overall, the use of computers in trading allows trades to be accomplished more quickly. This has at times been a disadvantage, as when the movement of market prices triggered simultaneous sales orders by a number of large program traders. The result was a serious plunge in market prices. As a result there have been efforts to control some aspects of program trading.

THE THIRD AND FOURTH SECURITY MARKETS

It should not be surprising that an activity as broad as the security market would give rise to special arrangements. Just as the secondary market for cars, office equipment, and other merchandise has various facilities, so too, special facilities for the trading of securities have evolved.

The Third Market

third market
a market for large blocks of shares that operates outside the organized exchanges and the OTC market

The **third market** is a market for large blocks of shares that operates outside the confines of the organized exchanges and the OTC market.

Program trading is a technique or combination of techniques for trading groups of securities. Institutional investors and large individual investors use the computer to monitor movements in the market that trigger portfolio changes determined in advance. The following program trading actions for an imaginary institutional investor will give an idea of some of the many forms that such trading may take.

THE POSSIBILITIES FOR PROGRAM TRADING

- First, in managing its portfolio of investments the company may have established a desired balance between stocks and bonds, based on stock prices and bond yields. As stock prices and bond yields change in relation to each other, the computer will dictate and initiate purchases and sales of groups of securities to maintain the desired relationship.

- Second, the company may have an investment fund designed to copy the performance of a stock index such as that of Standard & Poor's 500 stock index. Since the duplication is accomplished with only a sampling of the stocks in the index, it is necessary to monitor these stocks carefully to reflect the performance of the 500. Computerized programs make this possible with a high degree of accuracy and this is considered a form of program trading.

- Third, the company may choose to switch from one money manager to another. In so doing, a huge movement of securities may be required. Program trading will then involve changing the portfolio with the new manager to accomplish a given investment objective.

- Finally, the company withdraws from or adds large amounts of cash to its portfolio from time to time. The securities that are bought with the added cash, or sold to provide the cash withdrawal, must be chosen in such a way that the portfolio is not unbalanced with respect to the stated investment objective. Program trading makes these decisions.

These are only a few examples of program trading. They are used on the securities exchanges and all other markets. Because of the potential for creating wide price swings in the market, as during the market crash in 1987, these trading techniques have come under intense study and pressure. There have been calls for the elimination of program trading, but its widespread use makes this all but impossible. Certain limited controls on program trading, however, have been implemented. Such controls are brought into effect during unusual swings in stock prices, especially those on the stock indexes.

The participants in the third market are large institutions that often need to move large blocks of shares. In the third market, brokers assist the institutions by bringing buyers and sellers together and, in return, receive a fee. The third market arose in the late 1960s and early 1970s in response to the fixed commission structure of the organized exchanges. The commission structure required commissions for large trades to be the same percentage as the commission for 100 share trades. Large trades resulted in huge commissions. In an effort to avoid the high commissions set by the New York Stock Exchange, larger institutions began to execute their trades in the third market, effectively bypassing the exchange.

The Fourth Market

fourth market
a market in which large institutional investors buy and sell without using brokers

The **fourth market** is even further removed from the world of organized securities trading. Under this arrangement certain large institutional investors arrange purchases and sales of securities among themselves without the benefit of a broker or dealer. A third party maintains an electronic network among these institutions in which offers to buy or sell are made known to the group. The offers are made by code, and institutions wishing to accept a buy or sell offer know the identity of the other party only upon acceptance of the offer. A fee is paid to the third party when the trade is completed. Those who support fourth market trading argue that transfers are often quicker and more economical, but the confidentiality is an important feature to many firms.

The policy of fixed commissions was brought to an end by the SEC in 1975 when it forced the exchange to allow its members to charge whatever commissions they wished. Brokers willing to negotiate on commissions have attracted much of the large institutional trading back to the New York Stock Exchange, but the third and fourth markets are still widely used.

THE OPTIONS AND FUTURES MARKETS

option
contract that allows the holder to buy or sell goods at a specified price and specified time

Closely related to the secondary markets for the exchange of securities are the markets for options. **Options** are financial contracts that allow the owner to buy or sell a particular good at a specified price during a certain period of time. Most of us are familiar with option arrangements of one sort or another. The owner of real estate may be paid a certain amount of money in return for a contract to purchase property within a certain time period at a specified price. If the option holder does not exercise the purchase privilege according to the terms of the contract, the option expires.

A contract for the purchase of securities, a **call contract**, operates much the same way. In like manner, **put contracts** provide for the sale of a certain amount of stock within a specific time period and at a specified price. Until the Chicago Board Options Exchange introduced structured trading of options, however, the option trading activity was at a relatively modest level. Today, options are traded on individual stocks, bonds, currencies, metal, and a wide variety of financial indexes. While the Chicago Board Options Exchange remains the main market, the New York, American, Pacific, and Philadelphia exchanges now deal in option contracts.

call contract
an option to purchase a security at a specified price and time

put contract
an option to sell a security at a specified price and time

Traditionally, most individual investors were limited to put and call option purchases. Through the organized exchanges the individual investor can now sell or create the options. The seller of option contracts is called the *option writer*. Option writers are seeking an opportunity to increase the income from their investment. The buyer of option contracts, on the other hand, is seeking a potentially large profit for a relatively small investment. The option buyer knows precisely how much is at risk. Speculation for profit or hedging to minimize are both part of an investment strategy. The individual investor may be a writer at one time and a buyer of options at another time, depending on the analysis of market prospects.

A **futures** is a contract to buy or sell goods at a certain price, with payment and delivery taking place at a specified time in the future. Basically, a futures contract permits control over large volumes of assets with minimal initial investment. The drawback used to be that it could be difficult to find a trading partner and to get out of the contract arrangement if circumstances changed. The futures market originated in the United States in the mid-1800s as a way to cope with these problems. The futures market involves standardized contracts, which can always be sold to eliminate the obligation. Today, futures contracts are traded not only on agricultural goods and precious metals, but they are also traded on oil, stock indexes, interest rates, and currencies.

futures
a contract to buy or sell a good at a certain price, with payment and delivery in the future

The seller of a futures contract agrees to make a delivery of a particular asset at a specified price and time. A partial payment is received, with the balance to be paid at the time of delivery. The buyer then owns a highly liquid investment item that may be held or traded in the market. If the value of the asset increases during the life of the contract, the futures holder will benefit; if it declines in value a loss will be experienced.

Futures market contracts can be fulfilled by making or taking delivery or by making a reversing trade. A reversing trade is a trade that brings one's position in a futures contract to zero and ends all obligations. Any trader may execute a reversing trade at any time prior to delivery, and that is exactly what most traders do.

The futures contract differs from the option contract in that the holder of an option may simply allow the contract to expire if the value of the asset under contract decreases. In so doing, the amount of the loss is the cost of the option. The futures contract, however, obligates a person to buy or sell a particular asset on the stated date at a particular price. Unlike losses by the holders of option contracts, losses from futures contracts are not limited.

INSIDE INFORMATION AND THE LAW

The temptation for persons who deal in securities and have inside sources of information to exploit this information is great. Furthermore, the financial results of such actions can be of tremendous magnitude. These factors, combined with the ease with which inside information can be used, explain why insider trading is not allowed under provisions of the Securities Exchange Act of 1934. The most obvious opportunity for insider trading is that for personnel of a corporation who, by virtue of their duties, have knowledge of developments that are destined to have an impact on the price of the corporation's stock.

Taking advantage of inside information for trading purposes is not limited to corporate personnel. Investment bankers, aware of corporate difficulties, major officer changes, or merger possibilities, by virtue of their relationship with such corporations, must take great care to avoid taking advantage of such information. From time to time an especially outrageous violation of the law comes to light. This was the case in mid-1986 when an investment banker dealing primarily in mergers masterminded a massive insider-trading scheme. The actions of the investment banker involved not only himself but a host of others to whom he provided such inside information and who shared in the benefits of the scheme.

Because the insider-trading law is not very clear, it is often difficult to tell when it is illegal to turn a tip into a profit. For example, a stock analyst may discover, through routine analysis of a company's financial condition, information destined to have an impact on the price of the company's stock. Such information conveyed to the analyst's clients may be, and has been considered to be, insider trading. The almost frantic efforts of large firms to control insider trading is understandable in light of the damage that can occur to their reputations. It is understandable, too, that the SEC has resorted to very strong efforts to resolve the question that continues to exist with respect to a meaningful and fair definition of "insider information." After all, it is the investing public without access to this information that pays the price for insider information abuses. The efficiency of the securities markets also suffers.

CHANGES IN THE STRUCTURE OF THE STOCK MARKET

The SEC has for twenty years actively promoted major changes in the structure of stock market activities and institutions. Many of the changes proposed have met with resistance from existing interests, who fear the effect such changes will have on their particular role in market activities. This fear has been especially expressed by the New York Stock Exchange. It stems from its possible loss of trading on the exchange. However, many of the SEC's recommendations have been adopted and many more will be instituted in due time.

One important change relates to electronic technology. Since the technology is now at hand to link registered exchanges and OTC markets electronically, the SEC would like to see the stock market take the form of one giant trading floor, all at the command of the broker. The broker would be able to tell which market has the best quote on each stock by punching the quotation machine. Bid and asked prices on covered stocks would be available in all markets. Opponents offer strong arguments against the plan. They claim that not only will many existing market institutions be destroyed, but that in the long run costs for the investor may be higher than under present market arrangements.

Highly efficient securities exchanges now exist in the major money center cities of the world, permitting trading on a global basis. Because of the varying time zones around the world, trading is now possible on a twenty-four-hours-a-day basis.

In mid-1990 the New York Stock Exchange announced that for the first time in its 200-year history trading is permitted at night. The American Stock Exchange, the Chicago Board Options Exchange, and the Cincinnati Stock Exchange have started a computerized, nighttime trading market for stocks and stock options. These plans are part of an effort to regain trading volume that has been lost to foreign markets, particularly London and Tokyo, as the world moves toward global, round-the-clock trading.

KEY TERMS

best-effort underwriting
  agreement
bid-and-asked price
blue-sky laws
buying on margin

call contract
commission brokers
flotation
fourth market
futures

investment bankers or underwriters
limit order
making a market
market order
NASD
NASDAQ
options
program trading
prospectus

put contract
short sale
specialists
standby underwriting agreement
stop-loss order
street name
syndicate
third market
underwriting agreement

DISCUSSION QUESTIONS

1. Why do corporations employ investment bankers in distributing new issues of securities rather than distribute such securities through their own efforts?
2. Outline the steps taken in the typical investment banking process.
3. Discuss how investment bankers assume risk in the process of marketing securities of corporations. How do investment bankers try to minimize these risks?
4. When additional stock of a company is to be offered to existing stockholders at a discount from the market price, why would the services of investment bankers be used?
5. Would competitive price bidding for securities by groups of investment bankers provide a higher price to the issuing company than would result from negotiations with investment bankers who knew in advance they had been chosen to distribute the securities? Explain.
6. Describe the inroads into investment banking being made by commercial banks.
7. The OTC market has been described as a secondary market. As a secondary market, what is the contribution of the OTC market to the economic growth of the nation?
8. Describe some of the types of securities traded in the OTC market.
9. Describe the steps involved in an OTC transaction.
10. Explain how OTC market operations are regulated.
11. Describe the nature of operations of the nation's securities exchanges.
12. List the advantages of owning a membership seat on one or more of the nation's stock exchanges.
13. Describe the steps involved in the completion of a round-lot market order on the New York Stock Exchange.
14. Margin purchases of a security are usually made in expectation of a

price rise. Short sales are made in expectation of a price drop. Explain.

15. Explain the motivation for an investor to purchase an option to sell common stock. What would be the motivation for writing or creating such an option?

16. Describe some of the changes now taking place in the structure of stock market activities and institutions.

PROBLEMS

You are the president and chief executive officer of a family-owned manufacturing firm with assets of $45 million. The company articles of incorporation and state laws place no restrictions on the sale of stock to outsiders.

An unexpected opportunity to expand arises that will require an additional investment of $14 million. A commitment must be made quickly if this opportunity is to be taken. Existing stockholders are not in a position to provide the additional investment. You wish to maintain family control of the firm regardless of which form of financing you might undertake. As a first step, you decide to contact an investment banking firm.

1. What considerations might be important in the selection of an investment banking firm?

2. A member of your board has asked if you have considered competitive bids for the distribution of your securities compared with a negotiated contract with a particular firm. What factors are involved in this decision?

3. Assuming that you have decided upon a negotiated contract, what are the first questions that you would ask of the firm chosen to represent you?

4. As the investment banker, what would be your first actions before offering advice?

5. Assuming the investment banking firm is willing to distribute your securities, describe the alternative plans that might be included in a contract with the banking firm.

6. How does the investment banking firm establish a selling strategy?

7. How might the investment banking firm protect itself against a drop in the price of the security during the selling process?

8. What follow-up services will be provided by the banking firm following a successful distribution of the securities?

9. Three years later as an individual investor you decide to add to your own holding of the security, but only at a price that you consider appropriate. What form of order might you place with your broker?

SELF-TEST QUESTIONS

1. In the investment banking process, a standby underwriting agreement refers to:
   a. the preemptive rights of stockholders
   b. the purchase and resale of a company's securities by an investment banking group
   c. a guarantee of a price to be received by a company when it sells securities to its existing security holders
   d. a best-effort sales contract

2. The investment banking firm that is selected by a company to handle the distribution of its securities is called the:
   a. originating house
   b. selling agent
   c. monitoring firm
   d. winner of a competitive bid

3. In recent years several large investment banking firms have received an increasing proportion of their income from:
   a. competitive bidding
   b. merger and acquisition activities
   c. the underwriting of foreign companies
   d. the sale of mutual fund shares

4. The regulation of new security sales by individual states is referred to as:
   a. the registration process
   b. a "truth-in-securities" requirement
   c. the rating of security quality
   d. "blue-sky" laws

5. Commercial banks were for many years prohibited from full-fledged investment banking by the:
   a. Glass-Steagall Act
   b. Garn-St Germain Depository Institutions Act
   c. Securities Act of 1933
   d. National Association of Securities Dealers

SELF-TEST PROBLEM

You are the fortunate owner of a listed common stock that has increased substantially in recent months. Although you are concerned about the ability of the stock to hold its price, you hesitate to sell because of the possibility of further increases in its market price. Describe the process by which you may be able to achieve some protection against a price decline while at the same time remaining in a position to benefit from further increases in the price of the stock.

SUGGESTED READINGS

Brealey, Richard A., and Stegard C. Myers. *Principles of Corporate Finance*, 3e. New York: McGraw-Hill, 1988. Chap. 15.

Gitman, Lawrence J., and Michael D. Joehnk. *Fundamentals of Investing*, 3e. New York: Harper & Row, 1988. Chap. 2.

Kaufman, George G. *The U.S. Financial System*, 4e. Englewood Cliffs, NJ: Prentice-Hall, 1989. Chap. 20.

Kidwell, David S., and Richard L. Peterson. *Financial Institutions, Markets, and Money*, 4e. Hinsdale, IL: The Dryden Press, 1990. Chap. 14.

Mayo, Herbert B. *Finance: An Introduction*, 3e. Hinsdale, IL: The Dryden Press, 1989. Chap. 6.

Ross, Stephan A., Randolph W. Westerfield, and Jeffrey F. Jaffe. *Corporate Finance*, 2e. Homewood, IL: BPI/Irwin, 1990. Part 5.

Weston, J. Fred. and Eugene E. Brigham, *Essentials of Managerial Finance*, 3e. New York: McGraw-Hill, 1988. Chap. 15.

ANSWERS TO SELF-TEST QUESTIONS   1. c   2. a   3. b   4. d   5. a

SOLUTION TO SELF-TEST PROBLEM

You may attempt to limit your loss from a decline in the market price of your stock by instructing your broker to use a stop-loss order. By setting a "trigger price" for the sale of your stock somewhat below the current market price, your broker has your authority to sell the stock without further contact with you once the stock falls to that price or below. It should be recognized, however, that this does not provide a guaranteed sale price since the stock may be falling so quickly that by the time your broker places your order the price may be far below your stop-loss point. Notwithstanding, your broker will sell the stock at the best price available once the trigger point has been breached. It should be also recognized that if you set the stop-loss price too close to the present market price, a minor decline in the price of the stock may initiate its sale after which the price of the stock may climb to greater heights (probably to your considerable distress).

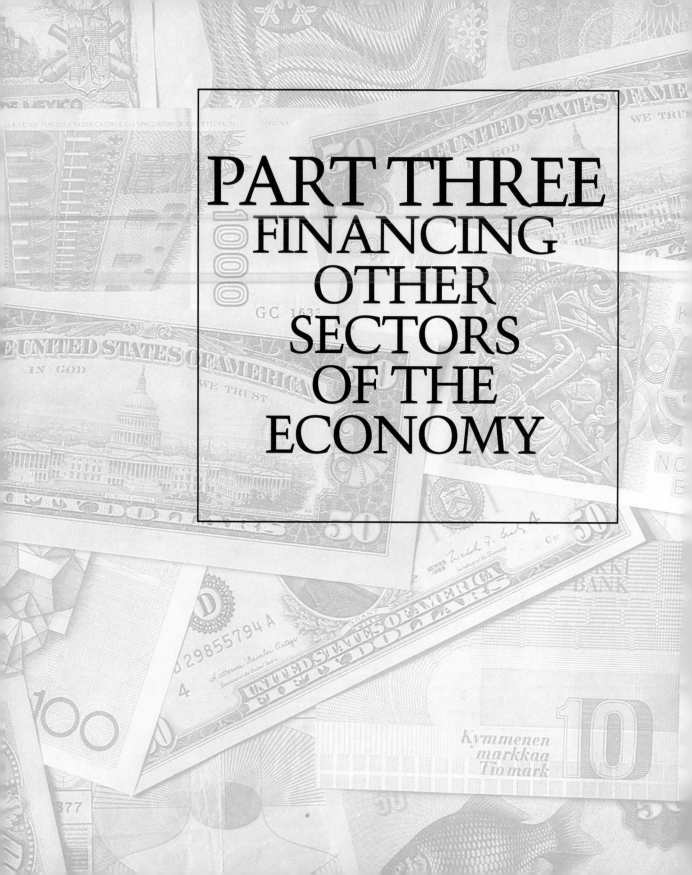

PART THREE
FINANCING OTHER SECTORS OF THE ECONOMY

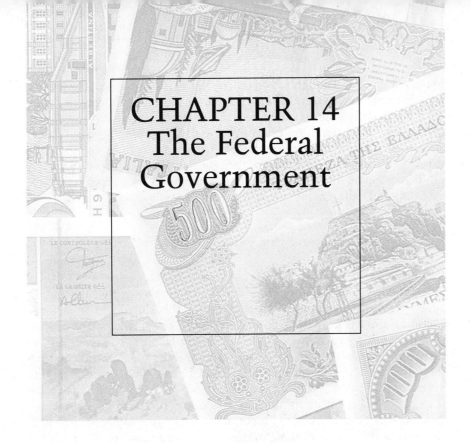

CHAPTER 14
The Federal Government

After studying this chapter, you should be able to:

- Indicate the scope and magnitude of the federal budget and identify the principal sources of revenues and expenditures.
- Explain the nature of federal government borrowing, and describe recent trends in borrowing and the significance of the growing national budgetary deficit.
- Describe the various forms of obligations issued by the federal government, and their tax status, ownership, and distribution.
- Discuss the dealer system and explain its function.

The magnitude of federal government expenditures is such that those of all other institutions and governments seem small in comparison. Therefore, financing these expenditures is equally impressive. The federal government relies primarily on tax revenues to support its various expenditure programs. In addition, revenues for general expenditures are received for specific services benefiting the persons charged. Examples of these revenues include postal receipts, rental receipts from federal housing projects, and food and housing payments collected from some government employees. The federal government also receives substantial insurance trust revenues from contributions to such programs as Old-Age, Survivors, and Disability Insurance. In turn, it makes large disbursements from these revenues. Although these trust fund receipts and expenditures represent a tremendous flow of funds, we are primarily concerned here with the general revenues and expenditures of the federal government. Finally, the federal government relies on borrowing to bridge the gap between revenues and expenditures. Since 1960 the federal government has depended upon borrowed funds to support its program of expenditures in every year except 1969. The national debt has increased accordingly.

EXPENDITURES AND RECEIPTS OF THE FEDERAL GOVERNMENT

For many years national defense expenditures constituted the largest single item in the budget. As a result of the slowdown in defense spending and the growth of general expenditures, however, the proportion of defense expenditures fell to second place in the late 1980s, as shown in Figure 14.1. In order to better see the expenditure picture, refer to Table 14.1, which breaks down federal budget outlays into seventeen categories and also accounts for sources of income. The most important expenditure items are those for the welfare of specific groups, under the heading of "income security." It is interesting to note that one of the smallest items in the budget is general operations of the government itself. This item includes the operations of the judicial system, the executive branch, the Congress, all regulatory agencies, and most departments of government with the exception of the Department of Defense.

FIGURE 14.1   Federal Outlays

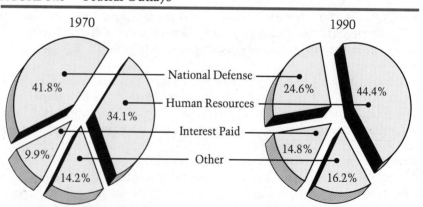

Source: *Budget of the United States Government, Fiscal Year 1991*, U.S. Office of Management and Budget.

TABLE 14.1   Federal Budget Receipts, Outlays, and Total Public Debt (in Millions of Dollars)

	FISCAL YEAR	
	1978	**1989**
BUDGET RECEIPTS BY SOURCE	$399,561	$ 990,789
Individual income taxes	180,988	445,690
Corporation income taxes	59,952	103,292
Social insurance taxes	120,967	359,416
Excise taxes	18,376	34,386
Estate and gift taxes	5,285	8,745
Customs duties	6,573	16,334
Miscellaneous receipts	6,641	22,927
All other	778	1,480
BUDGET OUTLAYS BY FUNCTION	$458,729	$1,142,777
National defense	104,495	303,551
International affairs	7,482	9,596
General science, space, and technology	4,926	12,891
Energy	7,992	3,745
Natural resources and environment	10,983	16,084
Agriculture	11,357	16,948
Commerce and housing credit	6,254	27,810
Transportation	15,521	27,623
Community and regional development	11,841	5,755
Education, employment, and social services	26,710	35,697
Health, medicare, and social security	135,153	365,897
Income security	61,488	136,765
Veterans' benefits and services	18,978	30,066
Administration of justice	3,810	9,396
General government	3,576	8,940
General purpose fiscal assistance	8,442	—
Interest	35,441	169,314
Undistributed offsetting receipts	−15,720	37,212
TOTAL SURPLUS OR DEFICIT (−)	$−59,168	$ −151,988
OUTSTANDING DEBT, END OF PERIOD	$780,425	$2,866,200

Sources: U.S. Office of Management and Budget and Treasury Department.

As noted in the next chapter, local governments depend for revenues primarily on property taxes, while state governments depend largely on sales taxes and special taxes such as those on motor fuel, liquor, and tobacco products. In contrast, the federal government relies primarily on income taxes for its revenues. For the past twenty years personal income taxes have provided approximately 45 percent of general revenue. Corporate taxes currently provide approximately 10.5 percent of revenue, whereas in 1978 they provided 15 percent.

THE BUDGET

Until 1968 the form of budget presented annually to Congress did not include the expenditures and receipts of the various federal government trust funds, such as Old Age, Survivors, and Disability Insurance. As such it failed to reflect the full effect of government activity on the economy. Therefore, many economists preferred to use the so-called "cash budget" to analyze the economy. The cash budget recorded transactions with the public, and included such items as trust fund expenditures and receipts. It was concerned primarily with cash transactions between the public and the federal government. But even the cash budget did not include all cash expenditures and receipts. For example, the various enterprises operated by the federal government were reflected on a net earnings or net deficit basis rather than on the basis of total expenditures and receipts.

In October 1967, the President's Commission on Budget Concepts recommended the use of a new "unified budget" to replace all the older budget concepts. The resulting budget incorporates the best features of several previous budget concepts. All receipts and expenditures are included on a consolidated cash basis. The unified budget covers lending as well as spending, but these two categories are shown separately to facilitate analysis. Lending is included because of the obvious impact it has on the economy. It is separated from spending because it is believed that these two types of outlays differ significantly in their impact on economic activity.

The excess of total expenditures, excluding net lending, over total receipts reflects the deficit in expenditures. The relationship of total outlays to total receipts reflects the total budget surplus or deficit. Political as well as economic considerations enter into structuring the federal budget. The size of the federal deficit is a key political issue. For example, the inclusion of the Old Age, Survivors, and Disability Insurance in the budget as revenue serves to reduce the size of the federal deficit. It is argued by many that these funds should be set aside for their future use as needed. At this time receipts of social insurance taxes far exceed payments but as the population of the nation ages, payments will far exceed revenues. It is estimated that this reversal will exist as early as the year 2020.

Off-Budget Outlays

off-budget outlays funding for some government agencies that is not included in the federal budget

The unified budget concept was designed to be comprehensive in coverage. However, since 1973 the funding for some federal agencies has been excluded from budget totals. These are called ***off-budget outlays***. The existence of off-budget receipts and outlays, which showed a surplus of nearly $90 billion in 1990, prevents the unified budget from completely achieving its objective. Among the off-budget agencies are the U.S. Postal Service, the U.S. Railway Association, the Rural Telephone Bank, and the Federal Financing Bank. The Federal Financing Bank is by far the most important and active of the off-budget agencies, accounting for the bulk of these agencies' outlays.

There is some pressure for the return of these accounts to the basic budget. While some arguments can be made for their continued off-budget status, a stronger case can be made for their inclusion in the basic budget. The existence of off-budget federal agencies adds confusion to the government's financial statements, and it is acknowledged that programs financed outside the unified budget receive less congressional scrutiny than programs contained within the budget. This may explain why the off-budget outlays' recent growth rate is higher than that for unified budget outlays.

It is nearly impossible to obtain a clear understanding of off-budget outlays without recourse to the basic budget document. While periodic publications of the federal government—such as the *Treasury Bulletin*, *Economic Indicators*, the *Survey of Current Business*, and the *Federal Reserve Bulletin*—provide summary data on off-budget outlays, details are not available. This may add to the increasing concern over lack of control by independent budget analysts.

DEBT FINANCING

As we have observed, the federal government obtains funds for expenditures primarily through tax revenues. When these tax and other general revenues fail to meet expenditures, **budgetary deficits** are incurred. Until recent years these deficits have been of modest size compared to total government expenditures. However, their cumulative impact has created a vast increase in the total federal debt. Although **federal statutory debt limits** have been set by Congress, it has been necessary to raise the limits at frequent intervals to accommodate the continuing deficits of the federal government. For example, in October 1989 the President signed a bill raising the temporary public debt limit to $3.1 trillion. Figure 14.2 shows the growth of budgetary deficits over the course of the last 40 years. From 1950 until 1961 relatively small surpluses and deficits prevailed, but from 1961 to the present (except for 1969, as indicated earlier) deficits have been increasing dramatically.

In contrast with some nations, the federal debt of the United States is owned to a large extent by its own citizens and institutions. Indeed, part of our debt is due to our role as a creditor nation from 1918 until 1985. Until World War I the United States depended heavily upon foreign investment, and it was not until 1985 that liabilities to foreign

budgetary deficit
when expenditures are greater than revenue

federal statutory debt limits
limits on the federal debt set by Congress

FIGURE 14.2   Federal Budget Deficits and Surplus Since 1950

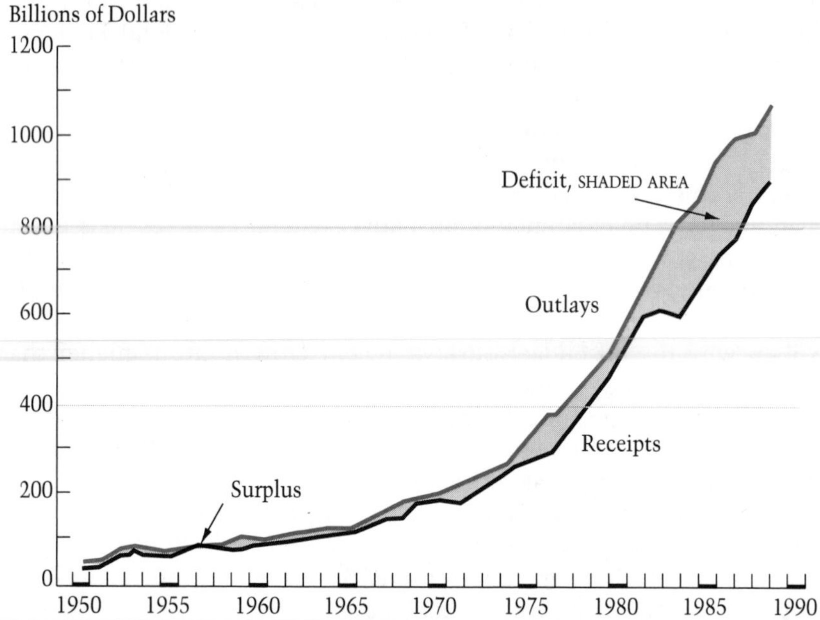

Billions of Dollars

Source: *1989 Historical Chart Book*, Washington, DC: Board of Governors of the Federal Reserve System, p. 50.

creditors again exceeded claims against foreign creditors. Our return to being a debtor nation has been due in large measure to high domestic interest rates, relative political stability in the world arena, and the development of an extremely unfavorable balance of trade. The nation's excess of imports relative to exports since 1964 has been in excess of $100 billion each year. To the extent that foreign claims resulting from a surplus of imports are invested in federal obligations, the federal debt is directly increased. International trade is discussed in detail in Chapter 20.

The burden of the national debt is reflected in part in Table 14.2. Although the federal debt relative to the gross national product increased by 1.7 times from 1970 to 1989, interest relative to total federal outlays has more than doubled. This dramatic increase in the interest burden is due in part to the increasing debt but principally to rising interest rates during this period.

Gramm-Rudman-Hollings
requires yearly reductions of the national deficit with the intention of balancing the budget by 1993

The persistent growth of the federal deficit has met with increasing concern but little meaningful action. In an effort to make progress in reducing federal spending and the deficit, Congress passed the Balanced Budget and Emergency Deficit Control Act of 1985. This act, now commonly referred to as **Gramm-Rudman-Hollings** (GRH), was designed to produce a balanced budget by 1991. By an amendment to the

TABLE 14.2   Interest Paid as a Percentage of Federal Outlays; Federal Debt as a Percentage of Gross National Product

YEAR	INTEREST RELATIVE TO FEDERAL OUTLAYS	FEDERAL DEBT RELATIVE TO GNP
1970	6.8%	36.3%
1971	6.1	35.9
1972	5.8	35.1
1973	6.7	33.6
1974	6.8	32.1
1975	6.3	33.3
1976	6.8	34.7
1977	6.8	35.0
1978	7.5	34.1
1979	8.2	32.7
1980	8.7	33.2
1981	10.3	32.6
1982	10.8	36.0
1983	11.3	40.4
1984	12.9	41.3
1985	13.3	45.6
1986	13.2	50.4
1987	13.4	51.8
1988	14.3	53.3
1989	14.8	54.8
1990	14.7	62.3

Source: *Economic Report of the President*, 1991.

GRH act in 1987, the date was changed to 1993. Targets, however, have not been met because of continuing congressional resolutions providing funds for federal activities. By the end of the second week of the 1990 fiscal year, lacking a legislated budget from Congress with a genuine deficit reduction, President Bush ordered a *sequester* as required by the GRH act. A sequester is a legal impounding of property or money to resolve the disputed matter. This sequester would have required an across-the-board cut in expenditures by all functions of the government except for social security and Medicare. On the very last day, when these cuts were to have been made, budget negotiators reached a compromise. Thus the sequester did not go into effect. The prospect of radical employee cuts in many essential government functions brought immense pressure from the public for a legislated budget. The Omnibus Budget Reconciliation Act of November 1990 represents another effort to reduce future deficits. It is discussed in the final chapter of this text.

Nowhere in the economy is the significance of a smoothly functioning financial system more apparent than in connection with the federal debt. Not only does the financial system accommodate the

THE GRAMM-
RUDMAN-
HOLLINGS
PROCESS: HOW
IT WORKED IN
FISCAL 1990

Under Gramm-Rudman-Hollings, the Federal Office of Management and Budget reviews the budget and estimates the deficit. GRH allows for a $10 billion cushion or "margin of error" except in 1993, when there is no margin of error. If the projected deficit exceeds the target by more than this amount, the administration calculates automatic spending cuts needed in each program to meet the GRH deficit target. If legislation does not achieve this reduction by the end of the second week of the fiscal year, the President orders a sequester.

For fiscal 1990, the GRH deficit target was $100 billion. In October 1989, the administration estimated a deficit of $116.1 billion—$6.1 billion above the target plus "cushion." Hence a sequester designed to reduce outlays by $16.1 billion was brought into operation, and President Bush stated that he would continue with a sequester until a satisfactory budget reconciliation bill was passed.

To meet the target, total outlays had to be reduced by 1.4 percent. GRH splits these reductions evenly between defense and nondefense spending, thus requiring an $8 billion reduction in each. However, 35.4 percent of defense outlays and 73.7 percent of nondefense outlays, largely entitlements and interest payments, are exempt by law from a sequester. To achieve the $8 billion reduction, nonexempt nondefense programs had to be cut by 5.3 percent and nonexempt defense programs by 4.3 percent.

Under the Reconciliation Act, the President issued a revised order that required a sequester of 1.5 percent for defense programs and 1.4 percent for nondefense programs. The revised sequester was designed to achieve outlay reductions equivalent to keeping the original sequester in effect until early February 1990. Hence, the administration established the important precedent, or pattern, of not restoring previously sequestered amounts after the sequester period.

Source: *Economic Report of the President*, 1990.

federal government by financing its frequent budgetary deficits, but it also provides for the smooth transition from old debt issues that mature to the new issues that replace them. The financial markets face a greater challenge in such refunding of government issues than in absorbing net new debt. Just as the nation's industrial development has depended upon an equally efficient development of financial institutions, so too, many of the financial activities of modern government depend upon these same institutions.

It is notable that public borrowing is a relatively modern development. During the Middle Ages, governments were forced to borrow from wealthy merchants and others on an individual basis. Often crown jewels were offered as collateral for such advances. Large public borrowing by governments, as for businesses, became possible only when monetary systems were refined and efficient financial institutions developed that could facilitate the transfer of monetary savings.

In the following pages of this chapter, we are concerned with how the federal government finances its debt and the financial system that makes this possible. The impact of the federal debt on the nation's economy is great indeed. This impact is discussed at length in Part 4. It is important here to note only that federal debt growth has taken place in an expanding economy, and that the burden of the debt is a function of the interest on the debt relative to the ability of the nation to pay.

OBLIGATIONS ISSUED BY THE UNITED STATES

The obligations that constitute the federal debt have become the largest and most important single class of investment instruments. These obligations dominate both short-term and long-term capital markets and play an important role in the investment patterns of most financial institutions. Commercial banks, for example, invest heavily in short-term federal government obligations for liquidity and safety. The short-term obligations provide the investor with a near-cash position and an income as well. Life insurance companies and pension funds invest heavily in long-term federal obligations for safety and income.

Because federal government obligations are the highest quality available to any investor and because of the large market for these obligations, interest rates on all securities are geared to those of federal obligations. Table 14.3 shows the rate structure at the end of 1989 for selected short-term and long-term obligations. In both instances, the rate on the federal obligations becomes the base for the spread of rates. As the interest rates on federal obligations increase or decrease, there is pressure on other obligations for similar movement.

The obligations issued by the federal government may be described as marketable, nonmarketable, and special issues. Special issues include those obligations issued specifically for ownership by government agencies and government trust funds. In addition to these direct issues of the federal government, the obligations of certain federal government-controlled agencies are either general obligations of or guaranteed by the federal government.

One such agency, the Federal Financing Bank, was created by Congress in December 1973. It coordinates under a single agency the

TABLE 14.3
Interest Rates for Selected Obligations on November 30, 1990

SHORT-TERM OBLIGATIONS	RATE
Three-month federal obligations (Treasury bills)	7.04%
Prime bankers' acceptances-3 months	7.99
Prime commercial paper-3 months	8.06

LONG-TERM OBLIGATIONS	RATE
Government bonds-10 years	8.29%
Aaa corporate bonds (highest grade)	9.20
Baa corporate bonds (medium grade)	10.53

Source: *Federal Reserve Bulletin* (February 1991): A24.

marketing of several federal credit programs including the obligations of the Farmers Home Administration, Rural Electrification Administration, and Amtrak. These obligations issued to the public are backed by the full faith and credit of the federal government. The consolidation of the financing requirements of the many agencies provided greater convenience and simplicity for the investors and a resulting lower interest cost.

Marketable Obligations

marketable securities
securities that may be
bought and sold through
the usual channels

Marketable securities, as the term implies, are those that may be purchased and sold through customary market channels. Markets for these obligations are maintained by large commercial banks and securities dealers. In addition, nearly all other securities firms and commercial banks, large or small, will help their customers purchase and sell federal obligations by routing orders to institutions that do maintain markets in them. The investments of institutional investors and large personal investors in federal obligations are centered almost exclusively in the marketable issues. These marketable issues are bills, notes, and bonds, the difference between them being their maturity at time of issue. Although the maturity of an obligation is reduced as it remains in effect, the obligation continues to be called by its original descriptive title. Thus, a 30-year Treasury bond continues to be described in the quotation sheets as a bond throughout its life.

TREASURY BILLS

Treasury bills
Treasury obligations that
bear the shortest original
maturities

Treasury bills bear the shortest maturities of Federal obligations. They are typically issued for 91 days, with some issues carrying maturities of 182 days. Treasury bills with a maturity of one year are also issued at auction every four weeks. Issues of Treasury bills are offered each week by the Treasury to refund the part of the total volume of bills that matures. In effect, the 91-day Treasury bills mature and are "rolled over" in 13 weeks. Each week, approximately 1/13 of the total volume of such bills is refunded.

When the flow of cash revenues into the Treasury is too small to meet expenditure requirements, additional bills are issued. During those periods of the year when revenues exceed expenditures, Treasury bills are allowed to mature without being refunded. Treasury bills, therefore, provide the Treasury with a convenient financial mechanism to adjust for the lack of a regular revenue flow into the Treasury. The volume of bills may also be increased or decreased in response to general surpluses or deficits in the federal budget from year to year.

Treasury bills are issued on a discount basis and mature at par. Each week the Treasury bills to be sold are awarded to the highest bidders. Sealed bids are submitted by dealers and other investors. Upon being opened, these bids are arrayed from highest to lowest. Those bidders asking the least discount (offering the highest price) are placed high in the array. The bids are then accepted in the order of their position in the array until all bills are awarded. Bidders seeking a higher discount (offering a lower price) may fail to receive any bills that particular week. Investors interested in purchasing small volumes of Treasury bills ($10,000 to $500,000) may submit their orders on an "average competitive price" basis. The Treasury deducts these small orders from the total volume of bills to be sold. The remaining bills are allotted on the competitive basis described above. Then these small orders are executed at a discount equal to the average of the successful competitive bids for large orders.

The investor is not limited to purchasing Treasury bills on their original issue. Because Treasury bills are issued weekly a wide range of maturities in the over-the-counter market is available. A look at the Treasury bonds, notes, & bills section of the *Wall Street Journal* shows available maturities of from one week to one year. The bid and ask quotations are shown in terms of annual yield equivalents. The prices of the various issues obtained from a dealer would reflect a discount based on these yields. Because of their short maturities and their absence of risk, Treasury bills provide the lowest yield available on taxable domestic obligations.

Although some business corporations and individuals invest in Treasury bills, by far the most important holders of these obligations are the commercial banks of the nation.

TREASURY NOTES

Treasury notes are issued at specified interest rates usually for maturities of more than one year but not more than ten years. These intermediate-term federal obligations are also held largely by the commercial banks of the nation.

Treasury notes obligations issued for maturities of one to ten years

TREASURY BONDS

*Treasury bonds
obligations of any matu-
rity but usually over five
years*

Treasury bonds may be issued with any maturity but generally have an
original maturity in excess of five years. These bonds bear interest at
stated rates. Many issues of these bonds are callable, or paid off, by the
government several years before their maturity. For example, the 25-
year, 8 percent bonds issued in 1976 are described as having a maturity
of 1996–01. This issue may be called for redemption at par as early as
1996 but in no event later than 2001. As of 1991 the longest maturity of
Treasury bonds was 29 years. As for the other marketable securities of
the government, active markets for their purchase and sale are maintained by dealers.

All marketable obligations of the federal government, with the
exception of Treasury bills, are offered to the public through the federal
reserve banks at prices and yields set in advance. Investors place their
orders for new issues, and these orders are filled from the available
supply of the new issue. If orders are larger than available supply,
investors may be allotted only a part of the amount they requested.

Nonmarketable Obligations

*nonmarketable
government securities
issues that cannot be
transferred between per-
sons or institutions*

As the name implies, **nonmarketable government securities** are those
that cannot be transferred to other persons or institutions and can be
redeemed only by being turned in to the U.S. government. The bulk of
nonmarketable issues are U.S. savings bonds, which are owned by
nearly 55 million Americans, making them the world's most widely
held security. As of year-end 1990 they were outstanding in the
amount of $117 billion. Other nonmarketable securities of the federal
government include those issued to foreign governments, U.S. Government special accounts, and those available only to state and local
governments.

*savings bonds
nonmarketable govern-
ment obligations de-
signed for small investors*

Savings bonds are redeemable at the option of the holder. They are
not marketable because they may be redeemed only by the person to
whom they were issued. Some savings bonds are sold at a discount
while others pay interest semiannually, or twice a year. Savings bonds
sold at a discount earn interest according to a fixed schedule. The
interest is paid and taxed by the federal government only when the
bond is redeemed. For investors nearing retirement and the prospect of
lower tax brackets, this offers a special advantage.

The most popular series of savings bonds has been the Series E.
Since January 1980 a new Series EE savings bond has been sold by the
Treasury in place of the Series E bonds. Series E bonds were sold at a
discount of 25 percent of their redemption value. The smallest denomination of Series E bonds was $25 and they were sold to the public for
$18.75.

The new Series EE differs from the Series E in that the bonds are
sold at a 50 percent discount, thus maturing at twice the purchase

price. Initially the Series EE bonds carried a yield of 6 percent maturing in eleven years. In November 1, 1982, however, an entirely new rate structure on these bonds was introduced. The newer Series EE bonds have a maturity of twelve years at twice their purchase price. Unlike the former system, which set a fixed rate of interest, the new system allows savers to keep pace with market interest rate changes. Every six months, the rate on the bonds is pegged at 85 percent of the average market rate on five-year Treasury securities. At the end of five years, the ten semiannual averages are added, averaged, and compounded to determine a bond's five-year yield. Bonds held longer have additional semiannual market averages added in. Although not knowing in advance what the earnings will be, a saver will be guaranteed a minimum yield of 6 percent a year, compounded semiannually on bonds held five years or longer. This combination of a guaranteed minimum yield of 6 percent coupled with the possibility of increased yields has accounted for much of the popularity of these savings bonds.

Other savings bonds outstanding are the Series G, H, HH, and K. Although these bonds will remain outstanding until maturity or until redeemed, they are no longer being issued.

The appeal of savings bonds to the small investor stems in part from their ease of redemption, lack of risk, and relative ease of replacement in case of loss, theft, or destruction. One of the most significant attractions of savings bonds, however, is the convenience with which they may be purchased. Commercial banks and other institutions sell and redeem savings bonds without charge. Furthermore, automatic payroll deductions offered by many employers now cover approximately 8 million payroll savers and provide a convenient way to buy bonds. The fact that more than one-half of all savings bonds are more than ten years old suggests that many holders are keeping them as part of their retirement programs.

Savings bonds were offered to the public as early as 1935. Their original purpose was to more evenly distribute the public debt. The program of savings bonds as we know it, however, was begun in May 1941 before U.S. entry into World War II. Although the program was started to help finance World War II, it was expanded and adapted to the peacetime financial requirements of the federal government. During the war, savings bonds provided nearly 20 percent of all borrowed funds. They continue to be an important segment of the federal debt.

The Dealer System

The **dealer system** for marketable U.S. government securities occupies a central position in the nation's financial markets. The smooth operation of the money markets depends on a closely linked network of dealers and brokers. The market for U.S. government securities centers

dealer system depends on a small group of dealers in government securities with an effective marketing network throughout the U.S.

on the dealers who report activity daily to the Federal Reserve Bank of New York. In 1990 there were 44 such dealers, eighteen of which were commercial banks and the remaining 26, nonbank dealers. New dealers are added only when they can demonstrate a satisfactory responsibility and volume of activity. The dealers buy and sell securities for their own account, arrange transactions with both their customers and other dealers, and also purchase debt directly from the Treasury for resale to investors. Dealers do not typically charge commissions on their trades. Rather they hope to sell securities at prices above the levels at which they were bought. The dealers' capacity to handle large Treasury financing has expanded enough in recent years to handle the substantial growth in the government securities market. In addition to the dealers' markets, new issues of federal government securities may be purchased directly at the federal reserve banks.

Tax Status of Federal Obligations

Until March 1941, interest on all obligations of the federal government was exempt from all taxes. The interest on all federal obligations is now subject to ordinary income taxes and tax rates. The Public Debt Act of 1941 terminated the issuance of tax-free federal obligations. Since that time, all issues previously sold to the public have matured or have been called for redemption. Income from the obligations of the federal government is exempt from all state and local taxes. Federal obligations, however, are subject to both federal and state inheritance, estate, or gift taxes.

OWNERSHIP OF THE FEDERAL DEBT

The federal debt plays a role in the holdings of most of the financial institutions of the nation, many business corporations, and millions of individuals. Indeed, the very size of the federal debt dictates that it be represented in almost all investment programs. Ownership of the debt by groups as a percentage of the total debt is shown in Table 14.4.

Much of the challenge in managing the federal debt has centered around the individual ownership of obligations, particularly savings bonds. Throughout World War II, the very effective savings-bond sales drives resulted in more than $10 billion in sales each year. Following the war, not only did bond purchase slow down markedly, but vast numbers of bonds were redeemed by individuals anxious to acquire homes and durable goods that had been in short supply during the war. In addition, alternative investments became more attractive as interest rates increased and as the stock market began a growth that would continue for many years. Commercial banks, too, were finding profit-

TABLE 14.4   Ownership of the Federal Debt at Year-end 1989

	PERCENT OF TOTAL DEBT
U.S. Government agencies and trust funds	24.1
Foreign and international investors	13.4
State and local governments	11.2
Federal Reserve banks	7.8
Individuals	7.1
Commercial banks	6.5
Insurance companies	3.7
Money market funds	.5
Other miscellaneous groups of investors*	<u>25.7</u>
	100.0

*Includes savings and loan associations, credit unions, mutual savings banks, corporate pension trust funds, government-sponsored agencies, and nonprofit institutions.

Source: *Treasury Bulletin* (March 1990): 54–55.

able alternative investments for their funds, and they reduced their commitments to federal debt obligations. Although the expenditure requirements of the federal government were reduced substantially in the postwar period, they remained relatively high compared with the prewar period. It became necessary for the Treasury to make strong efforts to stabilize the redemption of savings bonds.

Successive actions begun in 1951 by the Treasury to halt the drain of cash due to savings bond redemptions included the first of the ten-year extension privileges on Series E bonds and the introduction of the Series EE savings bonds at higher interest rates. Notwithstanding the difficulties of the Treasury in maintaining the volume of savings bonds since World War II, it is obvious that had their sale been terminated at the end of the war, the task of selling other obligations in the financial markets would have been increased greatly. In short, the Treasury has needed the investment money of all possible groups of investors.

The subject of national savings was discussed in detail in Chapter 6. The importance of savings to the capital formation processes and to meeting the borrowing requirements of government was emphasized. The failure of the nation to produce enough savings to meet these needs is reflected in Table 14.4. It shows that ownership of the federal debt by foreign and international investors ranks second only to agencies and trust funds of the federal government. Of even greater significance is that this percentage of foreign ownership of the federal debt has been increasing dramatically from year to year. Further, the annual increase in foreign ownership is due primarily to the flow of Japanese capital to this country. Japanese investment in real estate and corporate securities is well publicized. But not so obvious is the dependence of the U. S. Treasury on such foreign capital. This factor explains, in part, the increasing pressure to achieve a balanced federal budget. A balanced budget will not only reduce borrowing requirements but will also instill confidence in the financial soundness of the economy. Continuing large budgetary deficits will not only make the nation increasingly dependent on foreign investment but may also cause those investors to lose confidence and become less willing to support our deficits. Policy makers must, therefore, walk a fine line between the burden and difficulty of achieving fiscal discipline or the possibility of losing foreign investment capital if budgetary discipline is not achieved.

MATURITY DISTRIBUTION OF THE FEDERAL DEBT

maturity distribution
the remaining life for all
outstanding obligations
at a particular time

Earlier in this chapter we described the various types of marketable obligations of the federal government. However, the terms "bills," "notes," and "bonds" describe the general maturity ranges only at the time of issue. In order to determine the **maturity distribution** of all obligations, therefore, it is necessary to observe the remaining life of each issue regardless of its class. The maturity distribution and average length of marketable interest-bearing federal obligations are shown in Table 14.5.

The heavy concentration of debt in the very short maturity range poses a special problem for the Treasury. This is a problem for the securities markets as well because the government is constantly selling additional securities to replace those that mature. The heavy concentration of short-term maturities will not be changed by simply issuing a larger number of long-term obligations. Like all institutions that seek funds in the financial markets, the Treasury has to offer securities that will be readily accepted by the investing public. Furthermore, the

TABLE 14.5   Average Length and Maturity Distribution of Marketable Interest-Bearing Federal Obligations at Year-end 1989

MATURITY CLASS	PERCENT OF TOTAL MARKETABLE DEBT
Within 1 year	33.6
1-5 years	34.5
5-10 years	14.8
10-20 years	4.9
20 years and over	12.2
	100.0

Average maturity of all marketable issues: 6 years and 0 months

Source: *Treasury Bulletin* (March 1990): 33.

magnitude of federal financing is such that radical changes in maturity distributions can upset the financial markets and the economy in general. The management of the federal debt has become an especially challenging financial problem, and much time and energy are spent in meeting the challenge. The influence of the Treasury's debt management policies on the financial system and on the economy will be described in Chapter 21. At this point we are concerned only with generally describing the maturity distribution of the debt.

If the Treasury refunds maturing issues with new short-term obligations, the average maturity of the total debt is reduced. As time passes, longer-term issues are brought into shorter-dated categories. Net cash borrowing resulting from budgetary deficits must take the form of maturities that are at least as long as the average of the marketable debt if the average maturity is not to be reduced. The average length of the marketable debt reached a dangerously low level in 1975, as shown in Figure 14.3. Since that time, progress has been made in raising the length of maturities by selling long-term obligations.

One of the new debt-management techniques used to extend the average maturity of the marketable debt without disturbing the finan-

FIGURE 14.3   Average Length of the Privately Held Marketable Debt

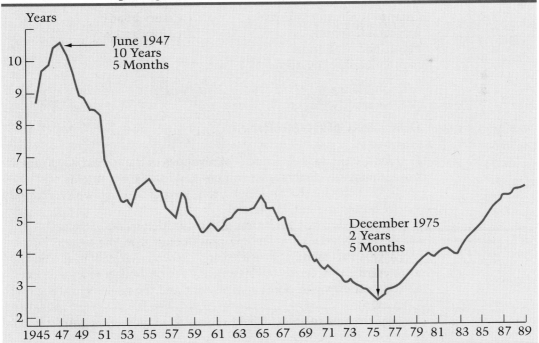

Source: *Treasury Bulletin* (March 1990): 34.

cial markets is advance refunding. This occurs when the Treasury offers the owners of a given issue the opportunity to exchange their holdings well in advance of the holdings' regular maturity for new securities of longer maturity.

In summary, the Treasury is the largest and most active single borrower in the financial markets. The Treasury is continuously in the process of borrowing and refinancing. Its financial actions are tremendous in contrast with all other forms of financing, including that of the largest business corporations. Yet, the financial system of the nation is well adapted to the smooth accommodation of its requirements. Indeed, the very existence of a public debt of this magnitude is predicated upon the existence of a highly refined monetary and credit system.

KEY TERMS

budgetary deficit
dealer system
federal statutory debt limits
Gramm-Rudman-Hollings
marketable securities
maturity distribution
nonmarketable government
   securities

off-budget outlays
savings bonds
Treasury bills
Treasury bonds
Treasury notes

DISCUSSION QUESTIONS

1. Identify the various sources of revenues of the federal government.
2. Although the federal government and local governments rely heavily on taxes for their revenues, the types of taxes on which they rely are quite different. Explain.
3. Comment on the evolution of the "unified federal budget."
4. Why is government lending now included in the federal budget? Why is this lending identified and shown separately in the budget?
5. Describe the nature and significance of off-budget federal outlays.
6. Trace the growth of the federal debt and the reasons for its growth patterns.
7. Explain how the federal debt relates to a study of the monetary and credit system of the United States.

8. Although we concede that the magnitude of the federal debt poses a problem for the federal budget, the securities represented by this debt do serve a useful purpose in the financial system. Explain why this is true.

9. Refer to the *Federal Reserve Bulletin,* the *Wall Street Journal,* or other sources of financial information and construct schedules of interest rates for both short-term and long-term obligations of the federal government and of business enterprises.

10. Using the *Federal Reserve Bulletin* and the *Wall Street Journal,* compare the yields available on high-grade corporate obligations with the yields on obligations of the federal government. How do you explain the differential?

11. Describe the dealer system for marketable U.S. government obligations.

12. Explain the mechanics of issuing Treasury bills, indicating how the price of a new issue is determined.

13. What are the factors that determine the volume of Treasury bills in existence at a particular time?

14. What have been the special contributions of savings bonds to financing the federal government over the years? Has the nature of these contributions changed?

15. Explain the tax status of income from federal obligations.

16. Describe the significant changes in the ownership pattern of the federal debt.

17. Describe the process of advance refunding of the federal debt.

PROBLEMS

1. As one of several advisors to the U.S. Secretary of the Treasury, you have been asked to submit a memo in connection with the average maturity of the obligations of the federal government. The basic premise is that the average maturity is far too short. As a result, issues of debt are coming due with great frequency and needing constant reissue. On the other hand, the economy is presently showing signs of weakness. It is considered unwise to issue long-term obligations and absorb investment funds that might otherwise be invested in employment-producing construction and other private sector support. Based on these conditions, what do you recommend as a course of action to the U.S. Secretary of the Treasury?

2. Table 14.4 of the text reflects the ownership distribution of the federal debt. Why would each of these groups invest in federal government obligations?

SELF-TEST QUESTIONS

1. Expenditures of the federal government rank as follows in terms of dollar amount:
   a. national defense, human resources, interest on the national debt
   b. interest on the national debt, human resources, national defense
   c. human resources, national defense, interest on the national debt
   d. human resources, administrative expenses of government operations, national defense

2. With respect to revenues of the federal government:
   a. corporate income taxes is the major source
   b. individual income taxes are about equal to the revenues produced by corporate taxes
   c. individual income taxes produce more than four times the revenues of corporate taxes
   d. over the last decade the revenue-producing magnitude of individual income taxes has been decreasing relative to that of corporate taxes

3. The federal debt is owned primarily by:
   a. foreign investors
   b. holders of U.S. Savings Bonds
   c. insurance companies
   d. citizens and institutions of the United States

4. Interest on obligations of the federal government:
   a. is not taxable by state or local governments
   b. is not taxable by the federal government
   c. is taxable by both the federal and state governments
   d. except for U.S. Savings Bonds is taxable by the federal government

5. The average maturity of the marketable debt of the United States:
   a. is of little importance, unlike that of private corporations
   b. has been decreasing for the last two decades
   c. remains unchanged unless new obligations are issued
   d. decreases day by day unless new obligations are issued to offset such decreases

SELF-TEST PROBLEM

As an advisor to the United States Treasury you have been asked to comment on a proposal for easing the burden of interest on the national debt. This proposal calls for the elimination of federal taxes on federal obligations. Comment on the proposal.

SUGGESTED READINGS

Brick, John R., H. Kent Baker, and John A. Haslem. *Financial Markets*, 2e. Reston, VA: Reston Publishing Co., 1986. Chaps. 4 and 10.

Buchanan, James M., and Marilyn R. Flowers. *The Public Finances: An Introductory Textbook*, 6e. Homewood, IL: Richard D. Irwin, 1987. Parts 4 and 5.

Facts and Figures on Government Finance, 1990. Tax Foundation, Inc., 1990. Section III.

Kidwell, David S., and Richard L. Peterson. *Financial Institutions, Markets, and Money*, 4e. Hinsdale, IL: The Dryden Press, 1990. Chap. 19.

Rose, Peter S. *Money and Capital Markets*, 3e. Homewood, IL: BPI/Irwin, 1989. Part 4 and Chap. 25.

Treasury Bulletin. Washington, DC: Department of the Treasury, quarterly.

ANSWERS TO SELF-TEST QUESTIONS   1. c   2. c   3. d   4. a   5. d

SOLUTION TO SELF-TEST PROBLEM

If the proposal applies to all U.S. obligations, existing as well as new issues, two things would happen. First, holders of existing obligations would experience a significant increase in the market value of their obligations since the stated interest rate on each series of obligations is fixed. They would, therefore, become much more attractive as investments. Second, the revenue of the government would decrease dramatically when tax revenue from interest is eliminated. To be sure, the interest cost on new issues of obligations would be reduced, but the shrinkage of revenues would be totally unworkable.

If the proposal applies only to new issues of obligations, many problems would arise. First, the savings in interest expense would be offset by the loss of tax revenues on these obligations. Whether the offset would be a complete trade-off would have to be determined by a thorough statistical study. It might by argued that many federal government obligations are purchased by nontaxed institutions and that therefore the revenue picture would not change. But these institutions would surely be less inclined to purchase the tax-free obligations at their lesser interest rates. Since these institutions represent a large segment of demand for such obligations, their shift to investment in higher rate taxable securities would presumably result in upward pressure on interest rates on the tax-free obligations as new issues come to market. A host of other problems would surely develop. Such considerations were undoubtedly studied in 1941 when the decision was made to tax federal obligations.

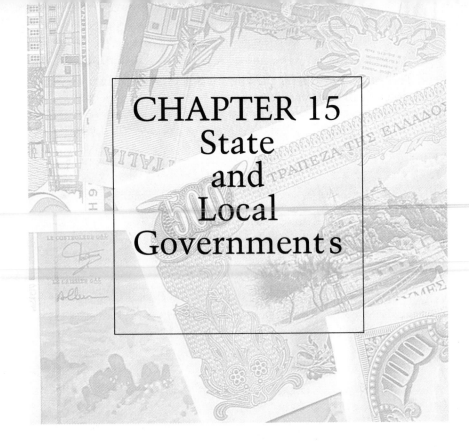

CHAPTER 15
State
and
Local
Governments

After studying this chapter, you should be able to:
- Discuss the nature of financing the operations of state and local governments.
- Identify the sources of revenues for state and local governments.
- Describe the expenditure patterns of these governmental units.
- Explain the special financial problems of state and local governments and how they are handled.
- Discuss the debt financing used to cover spending when current revenues are insufficient to obtain funds for capital spending.
- Describe the various types of and distribution methods for bonds issued by state and local governments.
- Identify the types of investors that buy municipal bonds.
- Describe the cyclical changes that affect state and local government borrowing.

In this chapter we will discuss the financing of state governments and all political subdivisions within the state. These political subdivisions include municipalities (cities, towns, and townships), counties, and special tax districts. ***Special tax districts*** are governmental units that are set up to fill a particular community need, such as school districts, fire districts, and districts for financing sewers or watershed areas.

special tax district
governmental unit that is set up to fill one particular community need

346

MAGNITUDE OF STATE AND LOCAL GOVERNMENT FINANCING

Total outlays of state and local governments have grown at a very rapid rate since World War II. Until the late 1970s outlays at these governmental levels, in fact, increased at a greater rate than federal government spending. The percentage increases are shown in Figure 15.1. As measured in national income accounts, outlays increased from $24 billion in 1951 to more than $700 billion in 1988.

Some of these increased outlays have been due to the higher cost of providing services at constant levels. For the most part, however, the increased spending represents state and local governments' expanded responsibilities and the continuing pressure placed upon existing facilities. Another major factor in post-World War II increases in state and

FIGURE 15.1   Average Ten-Year Percentage Changes in Federal, State, and Local Government Debt, 1949–50 to 1987–88

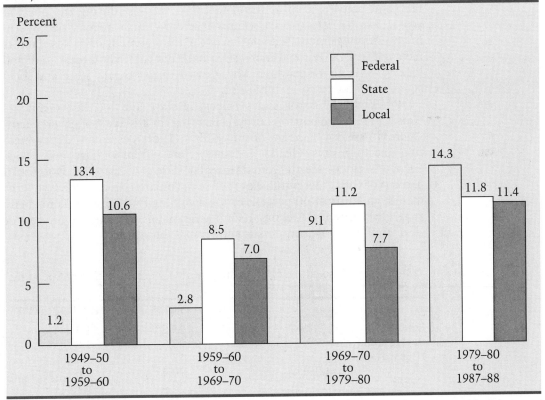

Source: Tax Foundation, Inc. *Facts & Figures on Government Finance*, 1990 Ed., Baltimore, MD: The Johns Hopkins University Press, 1990.

TABLE 15.1   Per Capita Spending by State and Local Governments (for Twelve Months Ending June 30)

	TOTAL SPENDING	EDUCATION	HIGHWAYS	PUBLIC WELFARE	OTHER
1973	$ 863	$332	$ 89	$112	$ 330
1979	1,488	543	129	190	626
1983	1,988	700	157	253	878
1987	2,685	931	214	329	1,210

Source: U.S. Department of Commerce, Bureau of the Census.

local government spending was the huge number of projects undertaken. The financial effects of the 1930s depression and the shortage of building materials during the war left practically all state and local governments with large backlogs of urgent needs.

After most of the projects were completed, general urban expansion and the population movement toward suburban areas continued to necessitate increased government spending. The growing suburbs created demands for various new public facilities such as schools, hospitals, and highways. In addition to these reasons, during the postwar years 1945 to 1975 the age groups that draw most heavily on governmental services increased relative to the total population. These factors have led to a fairly rapid increase in both per capita and total state and local government spending. The growth in per capita state and local spending is reflected in Table 15.1.

Purchases of goods and services by state and local governments constitute a large portion of total spending for all levels of government. Approximately 43 percent of the goods and services are used for education and highways. Health and sanitation, public welfare, and police and fire services are the remaining major areas of spending. Nearly 75 percent of the direct purchases for education are made by local governments, and almost 60 percent of the spending for highways is made by state governments. A comparison of the major items in the budgets of state and local governments is shown in Table 15.2.

TABLE 15.2   Percentage of State and Local Government Direct Spending by Function (Fiscal Year 1987)

	STATES	MUNICIPALITIES
Education	23.5%	42.2%
Public welfare	23.3	4.8
Highways	12.0	5.3
Health and hospitals	10.4	7.6
Other	30.8	40.1
	100.0%	100.0%

Source: U.S. Department of Commerce, Bureau of the Census.

METHODS OF FINANCING

In its simplest form, government financing means securing the funds needed to pay for the goods, services, and benefits governments provide for their citizens. The basic source of financing is derived from taxes, fees, licenses, and in some cases, special charges for providing such things as electrical service, trash collection, and other special services. There are occasions, however, when it is necessary or desirable for governments to borrow funds to meet their needs. One such situation is when a highly uneven flow of receipts is combined with a generally stable expenditure pattern. This often necessitates short-term borrowing by the government in anticipation of the next tax collection period.

Financing capital improvements is the second major reason for government borrowing. The logic behind such action is that these improvements will benefit those who live in the community over a long period of time. Therefore future benefits from these improvements justify spreading their payment over the useful life of the improvement.

The types of spending out of current revenues and the capital spending being financed through borrowed funds largely dictate the sources of funds for state and local governments. In many ways, this is comparable to financing a business enterprise. A government's use of operating revenues is similar to internal financing by a business, while borrowing funds is much like a business's external financing. The credit reputations of both state and local governments are based on the extent of their indebtedness and their ability to meet debt obligations. In short, financing government operations depends upon tax revenues and borrowed funds. Ultimately, tax revenues must provide the basis for all financing. Grants-in-aid to state and local governments must also be supported by tax revenues of the granting units.

Tax Revenues

The major sources of revenue for state and local governments are sales, income, property, and other taxes. With the increase in spending mentioned earlier, it has been a challenge for these governments to increase revenues at the same rate. Many states have enacted an income tax for the first time, while others have either increased the tax rate or started a withholding procedure to achieve greater effectiveness of the existing tax.

Sales taxes, too, have been increased by states, cities, and counties in order to finance the waves of increased spending. Local governments, however, depend largely upon property taxes for current revenues. They have become a generally reliable source of revenues because of more realistic property assessments, higher tax rates, and a larger tax base arising from new construction. Table 15.3 shows the relative importance of various sources of revenue for state and local governments.

TABLE 15.3   Distribution of State and Local Government Taxes and Fees

	FISCAL YEAR		
	1973	1980	1987
STATE GOVERNMENTS			
Sales	38.2%	31.5%	32.3%
Income (personal and corporate)	21.6	36.8	39.2
Motor vehicle licenses	3.5	3.9	6.3
Property	1.4	2.1	1.9
Death and gift	1.5	1.5	1.2
Other taxes and fees	33.8	24.2	19.1
Total	100.0%	100.0%	100.0%
LOCAL GOVERNMENTS			
Property	54.1%	53.3%	45.9%
Sales	6.1	9.0	9.6
Income (primarily personal)	3.0	3.7	3.8
Other taxes and fees	36.8	34.0	40.7
Total	100.0%	100.0%	100.0%

Source: U.S. Department of Commerce, Bureau of the Census.

Grants-in-Aid

grants-in-aid
grants of funds from one governmental unit to another

An important source of revenue for state and local governments has been **grants-in-aid**, or grants from one governmental unit to another. Substantial grants-in-aid have been made by the federal government to states for such purposes as unemployment compensation and highway construction. And state governments give funds to local governments. There may also be direct grants-in-aid to municipalities (cities and towns) by the federal government for such purposes as public housing and urban renewal.

There are two reasons for such grants-in-aid. The first is to enhance state and local services and, second, to increase their equality among the states. The revenue-producing capacity of some states is inadequate to maintain an appropriate level of services as measured by services in other states. Early in the 1980s the expanded federal budgetary emphasis on defense, international affairs, and debt service resulted in a reduction of grants-in-aid. In recent years, however, grants resumed an upward trend. But the purposes for which these grants were and are being made have changed significantly. The share of grants for health and income security jumped from 36 percent to 55 percent of the total during the 1980s. Transportation grants have also shown a relative increase. Thus funds for all remaining functions have decreased. Figure 15.2 shows the changes in mix of federal grants from 1977 to 1988. In 1990 federal grants-in-aid amounted to $126.6 billion and covered about 18 percent of the total direct outlays of state and local governments.

FIGURE 15.2
Federal Grants to State and Local Governments, Fiscal Years 1977 and 1988

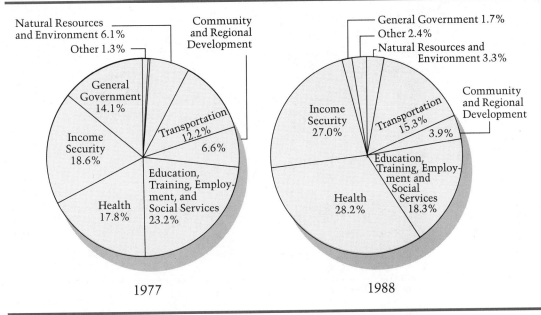

1977

1988

Source: U.S. Office of Management and Budget, *Budget of the United States Government, Fiscal Year 1989.* Prepared by *New England Economic Review.*

Debt Financing

In recent years large sums have been borrowed on a short-term basis to bridge the time gap between current spending and tax collection. For a particular community, such short-term financing is repaid out of tax revenues and total debt is not increased. Because of the general increase in operating budgets of state and local governments, the amount of short-term borrowing has increased each year. Since 1986, however, the amount of both short- and long-term borrowing has increased dramatically. Figure 15.3 shows clearly that state and local governments, like the federal government, are now incurring large deficits.

STATE AND LOCAL GOVERNMENT BONDS

The obligations issued by state and local governments not only play an important role in supporting the functions of these governments, but they also constitute a major outlet for the investment funds of many investors. The obligations of state and local governments are variously

FIGURE 15.3
State and Local Government Operating Surpluses and Deficits

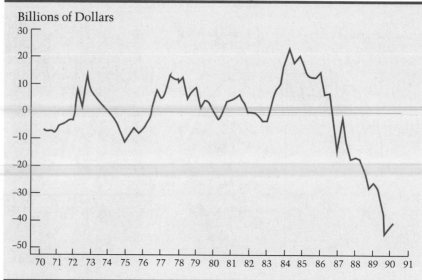

Source: U.S. Department of Commerce.

municipal bonds
*obligations of the state
or any of its subdivisions*

referred to as **municipal bonds,** municipal securities, or simply as
municipals. To refer to a state obligation as a municipal is not technically correct, but it is understood by all parties in the investment
world. Municipal bonds are seldom issued with a maturity that exceeds
the estimated life of the capital improvement. Exceptions to this rule,
such as issuing bonds to finance veterans' aid programs, account for a
very small part of total long-term debt financing. Laws stating specific
maturity limits for various types of capital projects have been passed by
many states.

serial maturity bonds
*bonds with regular
installment dates on
which issues mature*

Most state and local governments issue **_serial maturity bonds_**, that
is, bonds that mature in installments, or at stated times, over the
scheduled life of the issue. For example, an issue of bonds for
$20,000,000 may have maturities ranging from one to twenty years,
with $1,000,000 making up each maturity group. This in effect consti-
tutes 20 separate bond issues, each maturity having its own rate of
interest. Typically, the interest rate is lowest on the shorter maturities.
The serial bond arrangement permits the issuing government to pay off
its indebtedness on a set schedule. It also serves the investor well in
that it allows the selection of maturities to meet special requirements
or preferences. Serial maturity bonds do have the disadvantage to the
issuing government of making the repayment schedule more rigid,
resulting in possible nonpayment during years when revenues are
unusually low or current spending very high.

Although more typical of corporations, state and local governments occasionally use **sinking fund bonds**. This requires the issuer to set aside regularly a certain sum for the purpose of retiring the outstanding bonds. Such sinking fund payments are generally paid to a trustee who may invest them pending ultimate redemption of the issue. More frequently, however, the trustee may partially retire the issue at specified times through purchases in the market or through the call of selected bonds for sinking fund purposes. As with the serial arrangement, sinking funds lend some assurance to investors of the ultimate retirement of the bonds.

sinking fund bonds
bonds that require the issuer to regularly set aside funds to retire the issue

Tax Appeal of Municipal Bonds

The interest income on state and local government bonds is not subject to federal income taxes. In turn, the states and municipalities cannot tax the interest income on obligations of the federal government. There is no specific statement of reciprocal tax immunity in the Constitution, but the U.S. Supreme Court has consistently recognized the doctrine of reciprocal immunity over a long period of years as essential under our dual system of government. This tax status of state and local government bonds is of special significance to investors who are in the higher income tax brackets.

Because of federal tax deductibility of interest on municipals, yields on them are lower than for taxable securities. As indicated by Figure 15.4, "Aaa" grade municipal obligations have an average yield of approximately 2 to 3 percent less than the yield on comparable quality corporate bonds. Organizations such as Moody's Investors Service and Standard & Poor's Corporation rate the quality of municipal securities as well as corporate obligations in general.

Major Types of Municipal Bonds

The extent of the liability of the issuing governmental unit for the payment of principal and interest and the sources of revenue for such payments distinguish the major classes of municipal bonds. The two major classes of municipal bonds are general obligation bonds and limited obligation bonds.

GENERAL OBLIGATION BONDS
A **general obligation bond** is secured by the full faith and credit of the issuing governmental unit, that is, the bond is unconditionally supported by the full taxing power of that government. Although such issues have at times resulted in losses to investors, states, their municipalities, and other political subdivisions are very unwilling to permit such defaults to occur. Very seldom have defaults on municipal bonds resulted from bad faith on the part of the issuing unit. Rather, the primary cause has been economic pressure on a community resulting

general obligation bonds
bonds that are secured by the taxing power of the issuing governmental unit

FIGURE 15.4
Average Yields of Long-term Treasury, Corporate, and Municipal Bonds

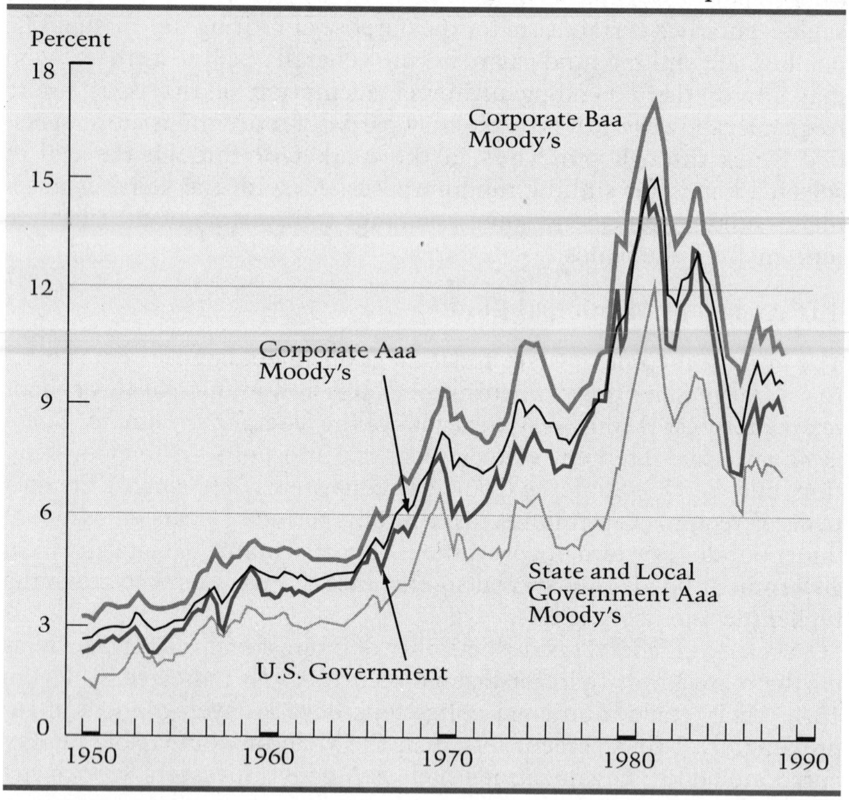

Source: *1989 Historical Chart Book*, Washington, DC: Board of Governors of the Federal Reserve System, p. 97.

in an inability to meet its financial obligations. If governmental units default on their obligations, there is severe damage to their credit ratings—damage not easily or quickly repaired. The governmental unit has a special incentive for maintaining its good credit rating: unlike a business, it cannot reorganize under another name. The credit reputation of most general obligation municipals has been strong historically; such securities play a prominent role in the investment portfolios of some of the most conservative investors. Figure 15.5 is an offering statement for general obligation municipal bonds with serial maturities. It includes information on the bonds' rating, purpose, tax status, underwriters, availability date, and the interest/maturity schedule.

LIMITED OBLIGATION BONDS

revenue bonds
bonds issued by state or
local governments to
finance specific projects

The principal limited obligation bonds are **revenue bonds**, which are issued by a state or local government for the purpose of financing a

FIGURE 15.5   Offering Statement for a Municipal Bond Issue

New Issue   Moody's Rating: Aa
Bank Qualified

In opinion of the Bond Counsel, interest income derived from the Bonds will be exempt from Federal and State of Missouri income taxation under existing laws as now construed.

$5,000,000
(of $17,750,000 authorized)

SCHOOL DISTRICT OF COLUMBIA
BOONE COUNTY, MISSOURI
SCHOOL BONDS

Dated: September 1, 1990   Due: March 1 as shown below

The Bonds will be issued in fully-registered form in the denomination of $5,000 or any whole multiple thereof. Interest on the Bonds will be payable on March 1, 1991, and semi-annually thereafter on September 1 and March 1 in each year. Both the principal of and interest on the Bonds shall be payable in lawful money of the United States of America by check of or draft upon the Mark Twain Bank, in the City of Ladue, St. Louis County, Missouri (the ''Paying Agent''), to the person in whose name such Bond is registered at the close of business on the 15th day next preceding the interest payment date.

The Bonds are issued for the purpose of purchasing schoolhouse sites and other land for school purposes, erecting schoolhouses, building additions to and repairing old buildings, and furnishing schoolhouses in said District and were authorized at an election held in said District on the 4th day of April, 1989, by a vote of 10,580 for their issuance to 3,089 against their issuance.

The Bonds, in the opinion of Messrs. Charles and Trauernicht, St. Louis, Missouri, Bond Counsel, will constitute valid and legally-binding general obligations of the School District of Columbia, Boone County, Missouri, payable, both as to principal and interest, from ad valorem taxes which may be levied, without limit as to rate or amount, upon all taxable, tangible property within the territorial limits of the said District.

MATURITY SCHEDULE

Year	Amount	Rate	Yield	Year	Amount	Rate	Yield
1997	$150,000	7.75%	6.25%	2004	$375,000	6.70%	6.70%
1998	150,000	7.75%	6.30%	2005	400,000	6.80%	6.80%
1999	150,000	7.75%	6.40%	2006	425,000	6.85%	6.85%
2000	275,000	7.75%	6.50%	2007	450,000	6.75%	6.90%
2001	300,000	7.75%	6.55%	2008	350,000	6.75%	6.95%
2002	325,000	6.60%	6.60%	2009	400,000	6.75%	7.00%
2003	350,000	6.65%	6.65%	2010	900,000	6.75%	7.00%

(Plus Accrued Interest)

The Bonds are offered, when, as, and if issued and received by the Underwriters, subject to receipt of an unqualified approving opinion of Messrs. Charles and Trauernicht, Bond Counsel. It is expected that Bonds in definitive form will be available for delivery on or about October 11, 1990.

This Final Official Statement is dated September 20, 1990.

Harris Trust and Savings Bank, Manager

Oppenheimer & Co., Inc.   Smith, Moore & Co.

First St. Louis Securities, Inc.   Mark Twain Bank

TAX EXEMPTION
FOR INTEREST
ON MUNICIPAL
BONDS

"It is admitted that there is no express provision in the Constitution that prohibits the general government from taxing the means and instrumentalities of the states, nor is there any prohibiting the states from taxing the means and instrumentalities of that government. In both cases the exemption rests upon necessary implication, and is upheld by the great law of self preservation; as any government, whose means employed in conducting its operations, if subject to the control of another and distinct government, can exist only at the mercy of that government. Of what avail are these means if another power may tax them at discretion?"

Stated by the Supreme Court in 1871 in Collector v. Day, 11 Wall. 113.

limited obligation bonds
bonds that can be repaid
only from revenues of
the projects they finance

specific project. Examples of such projects are bridges, transportation terminals, sewer facilities, and general public utilities. These bonds are called **limited obligation bonds** because their principal and interest is to be paid only from the revenues produced by the projects. In other words, the source of funds is limited to these revenues, and the issuing governmental unit has no contingent or direct liability for payment. A much publicized kind of revenue bond are those sold to pay for the construction of toll roads. States and municipalities may also issue revenue bonds to construct industrial plants for lease to private industry (a type of financing described in Chapter 12).

The proportion of revenue bonds to total municipal issues has increased greatly since World War II—it is now about equal to that of general obligation bonds. Among the reasons for the increasing volume of revenue bonds may be the expanding scope of public services sponsored by state and local governments and the feeling that the cost of new projects should be borne by their users. The users of these projects pay for the bond costs that support each project.

special assessment bonds
bonds retired by special
assessments that are
used to finance commu-
nity improvements

Special assessment bonds are issued for the purpose of financing improvements that in turn increase adjacent property values. For example, the construction of streets and highways, although for the benefit of all users, is expected to increase the value of nearby properties. These bonds are paid for from assessments on the properties that are assumed to have increased in value. Since the safety of special assessment bonds depends upon the ability and willingness of individuals and corporations to pay their assessments, these securities have found less favor with the investing public. Some special assessment bonds are issued with contingent general liability of the issuing governmental unit, that is, the issue's obligations are met from general revenues if assessments are not adequate for the purpose. This type is more appropriately classified as a general obligation bond.

There are many sources of statistical information relating to municipal bonds. The investment banking firm that sells the bonds when they are originally issued usually maintains financial information on the issue and on the issuer. These firms may be contacted for such information.

FINDING STATISTICAL INFORMATION ON MUNICIPAL BONDS

Several services, principally Dun & Bradstreet, Moody's Investment Service, and Standard & Poor's Corporation, provide detailed information about individual issuers. These publications are available in most libraries, brokerage offices, and some banks. *Moody's Municipal and Government Manual* contains detailed financial statements and information on a very large number of outstanding bond issues, including maturities, the principal tax sources, and the various state laws applying to municipal issues.

In many states there are local organizations that assemble detailed financial information on municipalities within their respective states. In some states these organizations were formed and are maintained by investment banking firms in order to provide current financial information about municipalities.

The rules governing approval for the sale of bonds by state and local governments vary between jurisdictions. For the most part, voter approval is required either for the bond issue or the tax or revenue source necessary to service the indebtedness.

Underwriting State and Local Bond Issues

New issues of municipal obligations are generally sold to investment banking syndicates on the basis of competitive bids. The issuing municipality first obtains counsel to confirm the legality of the issue. The issuing unit then consults specialists to determine appropriate timing, suitable interest rates, and other technical aspects of the issues.

Having decided upon the appropriate terms and timing of the issue, the governmental unit advertises it in local newspapers and financial trade papers and sends special notices (see Figure 15.5) to investment banking houses and large commercial banks with bond departments. These notices clearly set forth the terms of the issue and the date by which competitive bids from underwriting firms must be received. After bids are opened, the award is made to the highest bidder, who then offers the bonds to the public.

The Market for Municipal Bonds

The ownership of municipals is concentrated in banks, property and casualty insurance companies, individuals, and mutual funds. In the early 1970s banks held more than 50 percent of all municipal obligations, reflecting the increased corporate tax rates during that period. Their shares decreased steadily thereafter, and since 1980 banks' share of municipal holdings has dropped dramatically. The share held by insurance companies has also decreased. Ownership of municipal obligations by individuals and mutual funds now exceeds the holdings of either banks or insurance companies. Decreased investment on the part of banks is due to several reasons. The most important has been a reduction in corporate income tax rates and also because special tax rules applicable to banks limit tax deductibility of interest on their investments in municipal obligations. Other things remaining the same, the higher the federal corporate tax rate the more attractive are tax-exempt securities. Another factor in the reduced investment of banks and insurance companies in municipal securities is that they have discovered other more attractive tax shelters such as the leasing of equipment.

CYCLICAL CHANGES IN BORROWING

Although state and local government outlays for construction have until recently been increased at a relatively steady rate, it has not been necessary for them to borrow at the same rate. During periods of expansion and general prosperity, budgetary surpluses have made it unnecessary to borrow as much as at other times. During periods of economic contraction and recession, on the other hand, budgetary surpluses disappear and governments borrow more heavily to sustain planned long-term construction programs.

State and local government borrowing may, therefore, be described as countercyclical—that is, borrowing levels fall during economic expansions and rise during periods of economic contraction. Borrowing more heavily than usual during periods of recession has certain advantages for state and local governments. Because bank reserves and loanable funds increase during such periods, loans are more readily available and interest rates decline. The decline in interest rates encourages borrowing on a long-term fixed rate basis rather than on a short-term basis. Both availability and rates are highly beneficial to governmental units. A reduction in interest rates is especially significant for the issue of revenue bonds. The feasibility of revenue-producing projects is primarily related to those projects' debt-servicing capacity. As the interest burden on the financing is decreased, the feasibility of the project is improved.

The fact that state and local governments have traditionally pursued construction programs at a relatively steady rate and have engaged in borrowing on a countercyclical basis has provided a cushioning effect for the economy. That is, both economic expansions and contractions are less vigorous because of this effect, which lends greater overall stability to the economy. This cushioning effect, however, failed to take place during the 1980 and 1981–82 recessions. Previous tax reductions and reduced federal grants resulted in reduced spending on the part of state and local governments during these two recessions. Figures are not currently available for the 1991 recession. This apparent reversal of the longstanding countercylical influence of state and municipal spending is important from the standpoint of coordinating future fiscal policies at all levels of government.

KEY TERMS

general obligation bond
grants-in-aid
limited obligation bonds
municipal bonds
revenue bonds

serial maturity bonds
sinking fund bonds
special assessment bonds
special tax district

DISCUSSION QUESTIONS

1. Although the spending of the federal government is well publicized, state and local governments also account for significant expenditures. Comment.
2. In recent decades the pressure on state and local governments to increase spending has been great. Describe some of the pressures on their budgets.
3. Name the various sources of financing for state and local governments, and comment on the role that each plays in the overall spending of these governmental units.
4. Federal grants to state and local governments have been a longstanding practice, but the purposes for which such grants are made have changed substantially. Comment.
5. Account for the fact that long-term borrowing has been increasing as a percentage of the funding for capital expenditures of state and local governments.
6. A reduction in personal income tax rates may have a significant effect on the yields of municipal securities relative to those of the federal government and corporations. Explain.

7. The term municipal bond refers to securities issued by what types of political jurisdictions?
8. The typical municipal bond issue involves serial maturities. How do such maturities differ from those of the typical industrial bond issue?
9. Describe the special appeal of municipal bonds to investors in high income tax brackets.
10. Distinguish between general obligation and limited obligation municipal bonds. Would it be safe to say that general obligation bonds are always preferred by investors over limited obligation bonds?
11. Contrast the yields on high-grade municipal bonds with those of federal government bonds.
12. Describe the factors that influence the yields on municipal bonds at any particular time.
11. Describe the cyclical pattern of state and local government borrowing.

PROBLEMS

1. As the mayor of a city having a population of approximately 25,000, you are preparing for a session with the finance committee. Among the financial commitments that will have to be made for the coming year are these: a general increase in salaries for city employees and for teachers in the public schools; the paving of streets in outlying areas of the city; the improvement of parks and playgrounds; a celebration for the 100th anniversary of the city; a proportional share in the construction of a regional airport; and extensive improvements in the city's sewer system. What would you propose to the finance committee as possibilities for the financing of each of these projects?
2. You are a member of the finance committee of a local community that plans to sell bonds in the amount of $24,000,000 for park and educational facilities. You are told that such an issue should be on a serial basis, and so you plan to retire the bonds each year over a 24-year period. Explain the nature of serial bonds and the expected effect of such an arrangement on interest costs.

SELF-TEST QUESTIONS

1. The spending of state governments differs from that of local governments in that:

   a. public welfare spending claims a larger share of budgets

   b. outlays for education represent a slightly higher percentage of total outlays

   c. spending for highways is basically not a state responsibility

   d. health and hospital spending is basically not a state responsibility

2. The most important revenue source for local governments are:

   a. property taxes

   b. sales taxes

   c. Income taxes

   d. Death and gift taxes

3. Grants-in-aid by the federal government to state and local governments is designed primarily to:

   a. reward state and local officials for political support

   b. reduce the burden of education and other facilities that results from the placement of military bases

   c. encourage controls on pollution and other environmental problems

   d. achieve some degree of equalization of services among the states

4. State and local governments are not free to tax the interest income of:

   a. federal obligations

   b. obligations of states and local governments other than their own

   c. obligations of their own jurisdictions

   d. revenue bonds issued to build and support educational facilities

5. The safety of special assessment bonds depends primarily upon:

   a. credit guarantees by commercial banks

   b. the threat of foreclosure on properties so assessed

   c. the willingness of the local government to assume the liability for assessments

   d. the ability and willingness of individuals and corporations to pay assessments

SELF-TEST PROBLEM

A local government finds that its revenues are generally adequate to support its spending on an annual basis. Spending, however, is generally done before revenues are collected. How does the local government handle this problem?

SUGGESTED READINGS

Buchanan, James M., and Marilyn Fr. Flowers. *The Public Finances: An Introductory Textbook,* 6e. Homewood, IL: Richard D. Irwin, 1987. Part 8.

Edmister, Robert O. *Financial Institutions.* New York: McGraw-Hill, 1986. Chap. 8.

Facts and Figures on Government Finance, Tax Foundation, Inc., 1990. Section IV.

Garbade, Kenneth. *Securities Markets.* New York: McGraw-Hill, 1982. Chap. 3.

Mayo, Herbert B. *Investments: An Introduction,* 2e. Hinsdale, IL: The Dryden Press, 1988. Chap. 12.

Rose, Peter S. *Money and Capital Markets,* 3e. Homewood, IL: BPI/Irwin, 1989. Chap. 26.

Tennenwald, Robert. "The Changing Level and Mix of Federal Aid to State and Local Governments," *New England Economic Review.* Federal Reserve Bank of Boston (May/June 1989): 41–55.

ANSWERS TO SELF-TEST QUESTIONS   1. a   2. a   3. d   4. a   5. d

SOLUTION TO SELF-TEST PROBLEM

An important form of financing by state and local governments is short-term borrowing arrangements. This is usually provided by local commercial banks, although banks in larger cities may also participate. Bond financing for such short-term purposes would not be appropriate since borrowed funds would lie idle for various times of the year while interest payments would continue throughout the year.

CHAPTER 16
Consumer Credit in the Economy

After studying this chapter, you should be able to:
- Define consumer credit and discuss problems associated with credit classifications.
- Identify the basic function of consumer credit and describe how this credit provides assistance to consumers.
- Describe how consumer credit developed historically in terms of cash lending and lending for durable goods and real estate purchases.
- Explain the importance of credit to consumers in terms of the household sector's balance sheet.
- Name the major holders and types of consumer installment credit.
- Describe the relationship between consumer credit and overall economic activity.

Consumer credit plays an important role in the financial system of the United States since individuals usually make major purchases like automobiles and homes on credit. This permits the use and enjoyment of these consumer assets while they are being paid for. Consumer credit serves to smooth the process between the production or provision of consumer goods and services and their consumption or use. An exceptionally large amount of consumer credit, however, may be inflationary if it leads to excess demand relative to the available supply of goods and services.

This chapter considers the nature of consumer credit and its role in the financial structure of our economy. Consumer credit is distinguished from other forms of credit, and its functions are considered, showing how it developed and adapted to meet changing needs. The last section of this chapter discusses the volume of consumer credit and its relationship with economic activity.

THE NATURE OF CONSUMER CREDIT

consumer credit
credit used by consumers to purchase goods or services for personal use

Consumer credit may be defined as credit used by consumers to finance or refinance the purchase of goods and services for personal consumption. Its use to finance personal consumption or services distinguishes it from business credit. For example, when an individual uses credit to buy an automobile for personal or family use, the credit extended to her or him is consumer credit; when a cab driver uses credit to buy an automobile for business use, the credit is business credit.

Problems of Classification

Defining consumer credit in terms of the use of goods and services presents several practical problems. Credit extended to farmers who are operating a family farm may be used for personal consumption, for production, or for both. It is often difficult for a farmer to specify just how the money will be divided among different uses. Therefore, banks and the many institutions that loan money exclusively to farmers make no attempt to divide farm loans into consumer or producer credit, treating it instead as a separate category.

A similar credit classification problem arises at times in the nonagricultural sector. A consumer may use credit to buy an automobile that is primarily for personal use but may be used in part for business purposes. Since there is no simple way of allocating such credit to consumption and production, all of it is classified as consumer credit.

Long-term Consumer Credit

Our definition of consumer credit includes credit used to purchase residential real estate as well as that to repair or to improve it. The major difference between financing the purchase of an automobile and a home is in the time period for repayment of the loan. Both are durable goods—goods that are not consumed and last for an extended period of time—but obviously a house lasts much longer than a car and costs much more. Therefore, house payments are made over a longer period of time.

Credit used to purchase homes, or **mortgage debt**, is treated as long-term consumer credit; that used for other purposes is intermediate- or short-term credit. Such distinctions are made in studies of consumer credit. This credit for home repairs and improvement is treated as short-term or intermediate-term consumer credit. Mortgage debt for financing the purchase of a home is the only type of long-term consumer financing and will be discussed separately in Chapter 18.

*mortgage debt
long-term consumer
credit used to buy homes*

FUNCTIONS OF CONSUMER CREDIT

The basic function of consumer credit is to enable consumers to increase the buying power of their income. This is accomplished through (1) the provision of a convenient form of payment, (2) help in periods of financial stress, and (3) the option to pay for durable goods while they are being used.

Convenient Form of Payment

One reason consumers buy on credit is the convenience of using charge accounts or bank credit cards, such as MasterCard and VISA, for multiple purchases throughout the month. The user usually pays off these accounts every month with a single check. Since many people are paid wages or salaries monthly or every two weeks, it is convenient for them to be able to pay for goods and services at the same time. At times credit cards or charge accounts may carry the consumer for longer than a month, especially after the heavy purchasing of the Christmas season. Interest is typically charged at a monthly rate of 1½ percent (or higher) on the unpaid balance. Credit limits are based upon an analysis of the financial position of the credit card or charge account applicant.

Services are frequently offered on a charge basis. This is true of electric, gas, and telephone services that are billed once a month. As a rule, doctors, dentists, lawyers, and other professional people also send out statements once a month, thus providing a convenient method of monthly payment for their patients or clients.

Aid in Financial Emergencies

A second function of consumer credit is that it can help consumers through periods of financial stress. This has been referred to as the safety-valve function of consumer credit. Many families do not have sufficient liquid assets to meet financial emergencies. They may have such assets as a home, a life insurance policy, automobiles, and valuable household equipment, but they do not always have enough cash for unexpected needs. When an emergency strikes—such as a serious illness, an accident, loss of a job, or uninsured loss of property due to an earthquake, a tornado, or theft—the cash reserves of some families may be soon depleted. Consumer credit can perform a valuable function by meeting the family's immediate needs. Unpaid bills probably accumulate, and a consumer loan to consolidate these bills may provide a way out of the difficulty.

Buying Consumer Durables on Installments

The third function of consumer credit is to aid consumers in financing the purchase of durable goods by paying for them in installments. In our economy, the demand for housing, refrigeration, transportation, and so on is satisfied by consumer goods that provide such services for varying periods of time. A house may provide a place to live for 40 or 50 years, while an automobile may provide transportation for only five or ten years.

Consumers can enjoy the benefits from durable goods in several ways. They can rent houses, cars, and some appliances; or they may purchase them, either new or used. These goods may be bought with cash or on the installment plan. To pay cash, the average consumer has to save for a period of time to accumulate the purchase price. For most people, this is not a feasible method for acquiring a home. By the time a sufficient amount could be saved, the family would have likely already raised its children. Therefore, houses are usually being paid for while the owners are living in them.

The situation with certain other durables is similar. Most consumers would need several years to save enough to buy an automobile or other major durable good. In the meantime, the price of doing without these goods could be very high or prohibitive. It does little good to save enough money to buy a car necessary for getting to a new job three years after the job has begun. Nor can we wait to buy a refrigerator a year after the old one has stopped working. Therefore, a system of paying for such durables as they are being used is a real service to consumers.

Under most payment plans, these durable goods are paid for in a period that is shorter than their useful life. For example, a house that is serviceable for 40 or more years is usually paid for in installments over 30 years; a washer and dryer, which last fifteen years or more, may be paid for in two years. Financing such purchases on installments, therefore, is also an aid to the consumer in building up a stock of durable goods; when the article is fully paid for, a substantial period of service still remains.

An important effect of selling new durable goods on installments is the acceleration of the movement of manufactured goods. Consumers buy such goods sooner than if they first had to save the full purchase price. Thus manufacturers are able to achieve volume sales more rapidly than they could in a cash-sale economy.

THE DEVELOPMENT OF CONSUMER CREDIT

Consumer credit is probably as old as the human race itself. Before money was used, primitive peoples developed credit to make barter for goods more flexible. A form of consumer credit based on a barter system is still used by some primitive societies in remote parts of the world today. For nomadic people—those who move from place to place—it is difficult to carry around excess goods, such as food and clothing. If such articles are repaid in kind later on, the borrower and the lender both benefit. The borrower has the goods when needed, and the lender does not have to move them around.

Cash Lending in the United States

Records indicate that the lending of money for use in buying consumer goods occurred almost simultaneously with the development of money as a medium of exchange. In the United States the business of organized cash lending to wage earners began after the Civil War in the cities of the Midwest. The structure of our society was undergoing some pronounced changes during this period. One of the most important was the shift of workers from rural to urban areas. A farmer could get along for a period of time with practically no cash. The urban dweller, however, was dependent upon current income, past savings, credit, or charity. Thus, growing city populations led to a demand for cash loans to meet emergencies.

The need for cash was further increased by the changing character of industry and the position of the laboring class. In 1860 this country was primarily agricultural, but by 1900 it had an established factory system and a permanent body of industrial workers. The average size of the factory increased a great deal, and relationships between employers and employees became more impersonal. Small independent producers began to disappear, and laborers were organized into plants of a thousand workers or more. In some cases, employers continued to finance employees during periods of difficulty. In others, workers could not rely on employers for help in financial emergencies.

Loans were made for short periods of time, the smallest payable in a week, two weeks, or a month; the largest were payable in less than a year. There were various methods to ensure repayment in this early business of cash lending. One group of lenders attached wages as security, that is, they had the borrower sign an agreement to have a part of future wages paid to the lender in the event the loan was not paid on time. Another group loaned on unsecured notes, relying on their ability to get a court order to attach wages to collect on defaulted loans. A third group used chattel mortgages on household furniture as security. These loans generally ranged from $15 to $300, and the interest charges were between 5 percent and 40 percent a month.

This loan business was illegal under the usury laws—laws to prevent excessive rates of interest—that existed in most states. But it was difficult to prove the usurious nature of certain transactions. Interest charges could be disguised as fees for services, notes often had to be signed before the loans were completed, the cash being loaned was turned over without witnesses, receipts were not given, and so on. Also, many borrowers were so glad to be accommodated that they did not press charges of usury.

As these abuses were brought to light, small-loan legislation was passed in state after state. Legal lending of cash to consumers was begun first by consumer finance companies and later by commercial banks.

Early Financing of Durable Goods Purchases

The use of credit for the purchase of durable goods also developed early in our economy. At first it was extended in the form of sales credit with long periods for repayment. A very large part of the trade in colonial Philadelphia involved credit sales. For example, the records of a cabinetmaker for the period from 1775 to 1811 show that 92 percent of all sales were on credit. A linen merchant of the same period expected few customers to pay in less than a year. Benjamin Franklin took over nine months, on average, to pay for the books he bought.

Under such conditions, the volume of bad debts was bound to be high, and some people misused credit and got into financial difficulties. The debts of some southern planters to mercantile houses in London were passed from father to son for several generations. Debts that could not be repaid during a lifetime gave rise to a peculiar marriage custom in colonial days. When a man married a widow whose former husband left unpaid debts, the marriage ceremony took place in the middle of the King's highway. The bride wore only her petticoat so that the groom could avoid taking on her former husband's debts.

The first known examples of installment selling occurred in eastern cities. Stores that sold factory-made furniture on installments were established, but no records remain to show the extent of such trade or the terms of such sales. Early in the nineteenth century, clock manufacturers in New England also began to sell their products on installments. By 1850 a large business was done in the sale of pianos and organs on installments. By that year, Singer Sewing Machine Company had also begun to sell its machines on the installment plan through agents, and its competitors soon copied this practice. By the end of the century, the installment system had spread to most of the country east of the Mississippi and, in some cases, even west. This plan was used for a wide variety of goods and was available to consumers with relatively low incomes.

The real giant of installment sales, the automobile, appeared shortly after 1890, but it did not develop into a widely used consumer good until the end of World War I. In 1900 fewer than 4,200 cars were built in the United States; the total production of cars and trucks first passed 100,000 in 1909. Sales of cars on installments began around 1910, and advertisements offering cars on time payments appeared in New York City in 1914. Thereafter such financing developed at an extraordinary rate, especially after the end of World War I in 1918. As new consumer goods such as refrigerators, vacuum cleaners, washing machines, and air conditioners were developed, they were also sold on installments, which helped increase the volume of such financing.

Growth of Installment Buying

The basic reason for the growth of installment credit was the increase in purchases of durable goods by consumers. In 1860 in the typical home of a better-housed worker in a northern city, a kitchen range was generally the only true durable good in the house. Candles frequently were the only source of light. Furniture was usually homemade or poor quality factory-made, and the house was sparsely furnished. Dishes, silverware, and cooking utensils were of the cheapest grade. The poor got by with even less equipment. Farmers, especially those in the West, often lived in log houses. What little furniture they had was homemade, and a fireplace served both for cooking and for heat.

The stock of durable equipment in American homes increased between 1860 and 1900, but at the turn of the century it was still not large by today's standards. The moderately well-to-do household in 1900 probably had an investment of not over $200 in such devices as a sewing machine, an ice box, a cooking stove, and a few pieces of laundry and cleaning equipment. Today such a home probably has one or more automobiles, a refrigerator and stove, a vacuum cleaner, a washing machine and dryer, a microwave oven, a television set and other audio/video equipment, many small appliances, and perhaps other items. This increase in the ownership of durable goods has created a large total investment in such goods, as we will see later in the chapter.

Reasons for Increased Investment in Durables

Several factors were responsible for the increased spending on consumer durables since World War II. Methods of producing durable goods in large quantities at a low price were developed. A market had to exist for these large quantities of goods to make the economics of large-scale, assembly-line production possible, and the development of installment financing helped to provide such a market.

This market existed because incomes were increasing and money was available for items other than the necessities of food, clothing, and

shelter. Changing patterns of living also provided incentives to purchase certain goods. As more people moved to the cities, they wanted
conveniences equal to those of their neighbors. Increased activities put
a greater value on leisure time, thus leading to a demand for labor-saving devices.

Development of Urban Home Financing

The growth of manufacturing and of urban population after the Civil War
led to an increased demand for housing in the cities. It was not possible
in urban areas, as in the country, to build a log house with the help of
neighbors. The demand for housing was also increased by the many
immigrants entering the U.S., most of whom were between 15 and 45
years of age. Some immigrants moved onto farms, but the majority remained in eastern cities. Few families had the necessary cash to buy or
build a house. Many families rented, yet over the years an increasing
number became homeowners. This was possible not only because incomes increased but also because financial institutions offered plans by
which homes could be paid for while the owners lived in them.

Lending money to individuals to buy homes appears to have begun
in the U.S. almost as soon as people established communities. The
earliest form of real estate financing was through loans from one
individual to another. Such direct loans are still one source of financing
in this field. The first formal organization for home financing was
organized in Frankford, Pennsylvania (now part of Philadelphia) in
1831. It was a cooperative agency for the purpose of lending shareholders' pooled funds for building or purchasing houses. It was not an
American invention but was patterned after similar European institutions with which some of the immigrant members were familiar. As
time went on, more of these organizations were established; they
developed into the present-day savings and loan associations. Over the
years, other institutions including banks and credit unions have
entered the field of home financing.

THE VOLUME OF CONSUMER CREDIT

Consumer credit has become one of the most important segments of
financing. We begin this section by exploring the most significant
portions of short- and intermediate-term consumer credit. Then we
focus on the relationship between consumer credit and economic activity.

Balance Sheet of the Household Sector

The importance of credit to consumers in recent years is depicted in
the balance sheet of Table 16.1. Consumers continue to hold well over

TABLE 16.1   Balance Sheet of the Household Sector in 1985 and 1988 (in Billions of Dollars, End of Period)

	1985	1988
FINANCIAL ASSETS		
Demand deposits and currency	$ 418.9	$ 515.7
Time and savings accounts	2,050.0	2,115.2
Money market fund shares	207.5	301.5
Life insurance and pension fund reserves	1,959.8	2,884.5
Government securities	760.4	1,067.9
Corporate and foreign bonds	74.7	66.1
Corporate stock, market value	1,843.0	2,229.8
Equity in noncorporate business	2,476.7	2,410.5
Other financial assets (net)	309.9	505.5
Subtotal	$10,100.9	$12,096.7
TANGIBLE ASSETS		
Owner-occupied housing	$ 2,377.8	$ 2,999.6
Owner-occupied land	951.1	1,259.8
Consumer durable goods	1,395.2	1,846.2
Other tangible assets	375.7	432.7
Subtotal	$ 5,099.8	$ 6,538.3
Total assets	$15,200.7	$18,635.0
LIABILITIES		
Home mortgages	$ 1,453.3	$ 2,070.3
Consumer installment credit	673.1	746.2
Bank loans, insurance loans, etc.	332.7	372.0
Total liabilities	$ 2,459.1	$ 3,188.5
NET WORTH	$12,741.6	$15,446.5

Source: Federal Reserve Board of Governors.

one-half of their total assets in the form of financial assets. Equity held in business proprietorships and partnerships currently represents the second largest type of financial asset after life insurance and pension funds. Then come major holdings of corporate stock (subject to wide changes in value) followed by time and savings accounts. As would be expected, owner-occupied housing represents the largest type of tangible, or real, asset. Furthermore, these housing assets, exceed even consumer equity in business proprietorships and partnerships.

Table 16.1 also shows that consumer liabilities, dominated by home mortgages, increased by about 30 percent between 1985 and 1988. Since total assets increased by about 23 percent over the same period, consumer liabilities increased more rapidly than consumer net worth. This is reflected in the ratio of liabilities to total assets, which was 17.1 percent in 1988 compared with 16.2 percent in 1985. Even so, consumer net worth remains at a level that is nearly five times the level of liabilities.

CONSUMER
DEBT AND
PERSONAL
INCOME

Economists and others have two concerns when consumer debt relative to personal income, is at high levels. First is the concern that borrowers might have difficulty in meeting their debt obligations as they come due. Second is the direct impact of high debt burdens on spending.

One way of examining consumer repayment difficulties is in terms of changes in rates of mortgage foreclosure (when property is taken away from a borrower by a lender to pay off the debt). Following are mortgage foreclosures as a percentage of total mortgage loans for selected years as reported in the 1989 *Savings Institutions Sourcebook*:

YEAR	FORECLOSURE PERCENTAGES
1965	.40%
1970	.33
1975	.38
1980	.38
1985	.81
1988	.95

Notice that while the recent foreclosure rate has been less than 1 percent of total mortgage loans, by 1988 the rate had more than doubled compared to the rates for the 1960s and 1970s. This finding supports the concern that consumers are having trouble meeting debt obligations.

The second concern is that high debt levels may serve to reduce spending. As more personal income has to be used for servicing debt instead of current consumption, the likely result is downward pressure on economic activity.

Installment Credit

The most important portion of short- and intermediate-term consumer credit is in the form of installment loans. Table 16.2 shows total consumer installment credit outstanding in December 1990 of $749.9 billion. Noninstallment consumer credit, which is credit to be repaid in a lump sum (such as charge accounts, service credit, and single-payment loans), is also an important source of financing.

Commercial banks represent the primary source or holder of consumer installment credit with holdings of about 47 percent of the total. Finance companies are the second most important supplier of installment credit (about 18 percent) to consumers. Next come credit unions with about 12 percent of the total. Savings institutions account for about 7 percent of outstanding consumer installment credit.

Automobile installment credit represents the single most important type of consumer credit, as shown in Table 16.2. This type of credit is extended primarily by commercial banks and finance companies. Credit unions rank third in importance as suppliers of automobile installment credit. Rapid growth in bank revolving credit, particularly credit cards, provides further evidence of the dominance of commercial banks as suppliers of consumer installment credit.

Personal loans, contained within the "other" category in Table 16.2, also represent a significant use of consumer installment credit. Finance companies rank behind commercial banks as suppliers of consumer credit in this category. Consumers also rely on short- to intermediate-term installment loans to finance the purchase of mobile homes and to make home improvements.

Consumer Credit and the Economy

The volume of consumer credit changes in response to changes or expected changes in economic activity. While outstanding intermediate-term credit and home mortgage debt takes a relatively long time to discharge, new consumer borrowing can fluctuate widely from year to year. Figure 16.1, which depicts changes in household borrowing in recent years, shows that during 1969 and 1970 a slowdown in household borrowing occurred, particularly in terms of installment credit and home mortgages. This was a period of tight money characterized by

TABLE 16.2   Consumer Installment Credit by Holder and Type in 1985 and 1990 (in Millions of Dollars)

	1985	1990
TOTAL:	$535,098	$749,852
MAJOR HOLDERS		
Commercial banks	$240,796	$351,198
Finance companies	120,095	135,641
Credit unions	75,127	91,203
Retailers	39,187	42,111
Savings institutions	55,555	49,594
Gasoline companies	4,338	4,747
Pools of securitized assets	n.a.	75,358
MAJOR TYPES OF CREDIT		
Automobile	$206,482	$284,841
Revolving	118,296	230,769
Mobile home	25,461	21,671
Other	184,859	212,571

Source: *Federal Reserve Bulletin* (April 1991): A38.

high interest rates and limited credit supplies. The economy likewise turned down near the end of 1969 and continued in a recession throughout most of 1970.

Another sharp downturn in household borrowing occurred at the beginning of 1973 and preceded the severe economic recession of 1974–1975. Consumer borrowing as a percent of disposable personal income then rose rapidly from its low of close to 3 percent in 1975 to about 12 percent by 1978. Then in 1979 household borrowing fell sharply until it again reached about 3 percent of disposable personal income in early 1980 and again in 1982. These sharp drops in household borrowing also preceded economic downturns, those of 1980 and 1981–82. Notice that after reaching the 1982 low, household borrowing reached a record high of almost 14 percent of disposable personal income by late 1985 before the general decline during the remainder of the 1980s.

The general upward trend in household borrowing as a percentage of disposable personal income during the 1970s and the first half of

FIGURE 16.1   Household Borrowing as a Percent of Disposable Personal Income

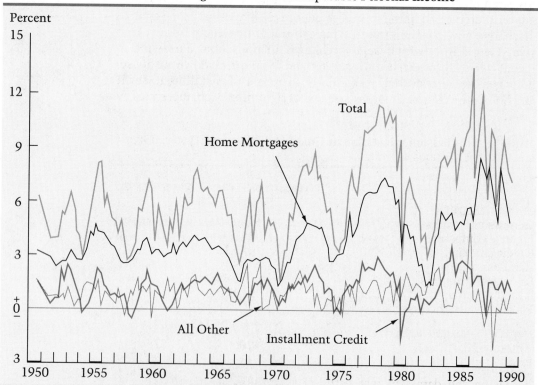

Source: *1989 Historical Chart Book*, Board of Governors of the Federal Reserve System, p. 70.

the 1980s caused some economists to voice concern over the ability of consumers to meet their debt obligations. This concern is supported by a substantial increase in the number of personal bankruptcies in recent years.

KEY TERMS

consumer credit   mortgage debt

DISCUSSION QUESTIONS

1. How does consumer credit differ from other types of credit?
2. Briefly discuss several problems that arise when describing consumer credit.
3. How does long-term consumer credit differ from other types of consumer credit?
4. What economic functions are performed by consumer credit?
5. Describe the early development of consumer lending.
6. Describe the development of cash lending to consumers in the United States.
7. Briefly trace the development of the financing of durable goods.
8. Discuss the factors responsible for the growth of installment buying.
9. What factors have been responsible for the growth of lending on urban real estate in the United States?
10. Briefly describe what has happened in recent years in terms of the household sector's "balance sheet."
11. Identify the major types and holders of consumer installment credit.
12. What has been the relationship between consumer credit and economic activity during recent years?

PROBLEM

Obtain a current issue of the *Federal Reserve Bulletin.*
a. Find the amounts of consumer installment credit by type and holder for the most recently available year.
b. Using the data you just gathered, express each major holder of consumer installment credit as a percentage of the total amount

outstanding. Compare your percentages with those cited in this chapter.

c. Compare the relative importance of the major types of consumer installment credit with the data presented in the chapter.

SELF-TEST QUESTIONS

1. Which one of the following is not considered to be a basic function or reason for using consumer credit?
   a. convenient form of payment
   b. aid in financial emergencies
   c. buying durables on installments
   d. purchasing nondurable goods with installment payments

2. When did lending money for use in buying consumer goods develop?
   a. before the development of money as a medium of exchange
   b. after the development of money as a medium of exchange
   c. almost simultaneously with the development of money as a medium of exchange
   d. after World War I in the United States

3. The increase in consumer spending on durables was the major factor leading to:
   a. an increase in installment credit
   b. a decrease in installment credit
   c. an increase in short-term consumer credit
   d. a decrease in short-term consumer credit

4. When referring to the balance sheet of the household sector, which one of the following financial asset categories would have the largest dollar value?
   a. life insurance and pension fund reserves
   b. government securities
   c. corporate and foreign bonds
   d. demand deposits and currency

5. Which one of the following companies or financial institutions would be the largest holder of consumer installment credit?
   a. savings institutions
   b. credit unions
   c. finance companies
   d. commercial banks

SUGGESTED READINGS

Greene, Mark R., and Robert R. Dince. *Personal Financial Management*, 2e. Cincinnati: South-Western Publishing Co., 1987. Part I.

Griffith, Reynolds. *Personal Finance*. Reston, VA: Reston Publishing Co., 1985. Part II.

Luckett, Charles A. "Personal Bankruptcies." *Federal Reserve Bulletin* (September 1988): 591–603.

Luckett, Charles A., and James D. August. "The Growth of Consumer Debt." *Federal Reserve Bulletin* (June 1985): 389–402.

Rose, Peter S. *Money and Capital Markets*, 3e. Homewood, IL: BPI/Irwin, 1989. Chap. 18.

Savings Institutions Sourcebook, 1989. Chicago: United States League of Savings Institutions.

ANSWERS TO SELF-TEST QUESTIONS   1. d   2. c   3. a   4. a   5. d

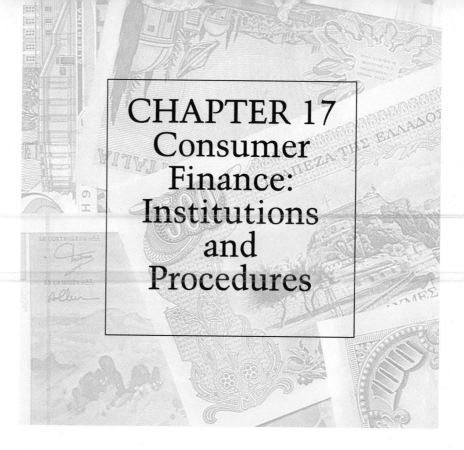

CHAPTER 17
Consumer Finance: Institutions and Procedures

After studying this chapter, you should be able to:
- Identify and describe the financial intermediaries that operate in the consumer installment loan industry.
- Describe the organization and operation of firms in the consumer finance industry.
- Define the term *credit union* and indicate how credit unions developed over time and how they are organized and operated.
- Describe the role and operations of commercial banks in supplying consumer credit.
- Explain the roles of credit exchanges, credit bureaus, and insurance agencies in the consumer credit field.
- Describe recent developments in consumer credit regulation.

The development and present status of each of the types of institutions that finance the consumer for short-term and intermediate-term needs are analyzed in this chapter. We also consider their organization and methods of operation, the results of their operations, and their current characteristics.

First to be considered are the institutions in the consumer installment loan industry, which include consumer finance and sales finance companies. Next to be discussed are credit unions, followed by com-

378

mercial banks in their consumer lending role. Also considered are institutions that facilitate consumer financing, including various credit-checking agencies that report on the credit standing of individuals and specialized insurance companies that insure consumer loans of various types. Recent developments in consumer credit regulation are discussed in the last section of the chapter.

THE CONSUMER INSTALLMENT LOAN INDUSTRY

Many financial intermediaries are involved in making personal loans to consumers and financing consumer purchases of goods and services. Some of the intermediaries, such as banks and credit unions, are depository institutions. They collect the savings of individuals and use the savings as the major source of funds for lending to consumers and others. The consumer installment credit industry also includes finance companies, whose primary role is to make installment credit available to consumers. The institutions in the consumer credit industry were started to meet different needs, but by the 1970s many of the early distinctions had disappeared. The development of each type of institution will be considered first, beginning with consumer finance companies.

Consumer Finance Companies

Consumer finance companies are financial intermediaries that were developed originally to provide aid in time of financial emergency. In the early years of their existence they made loans primarily to low-income borrowers who found it impossible to obtain credit elsewhere. As time went on they expanded their scope of operations until today most of them make loans to a cross section of middle-income as well as low-income families.

consumer finance company
financial intermediary that lends money to middle- and low-income families

As pointed out in the previous chapter, organized cash lending to consumers probably began in midwestern cities after the Civil War. The laws of the states not only made no provisions for institutions to lend money to consumers but also made profitable legal operation impossible because of stringent usury laws. Thus consumer lending was carried on in violation of the law. Usurious lending by loan sharks was extensive because there was a need for loans for emergencies that was not being met in any other way.

Several steps were taken to combat the loan-shark problem before World War I. Late in the 19th century, legislation was passed to encourage the establishment of semi-philanthropic, or charitable, organizations to make small loans to consumers. As a result, in several cities *remedial loan societies* were sponsored by socially-minded citizens who donated their time to these organizations. Although these societies helped many people, they hardly made a dent in the loan-shark problem.

The first comprehensive small-loan legislation was passed in Massachusetts in 1911, and New Jersey followed suit in 1914. In the next year, similar legislation was passed in New York, Ohio, and Pennsylvania. With the experience in these states as a guide, the Russell Sage Foundation published a model Uniform Small Loan Law in 1916.

Several features are basic in small-loan laws if illegal lending is to be eliminated. Maximum charges must be set, but these must be high enough to permit profitable operations. The charge is an overall fee for expenses, services, and interest; it is the only charge permitted. It is computed on the unpaid balance of the loan each month or more often if payments are made more frequently. Provision must be made for licensing lenders on the basis of character, fitness to conduct the business, and financial responsibility. There must also be state supervision of the business and penalties against nonlicensees and licensees who violate any provisions of the law.

Sales Finance Companies

sales finance company
company that finances
installment plan buying
and wholesale purchases

A few years after consumer finance companies came into being, the **sales finance company** was developed to finance the sale of consumer durable goods on installments. A new type of institution was necessary for installment sales financing because commercial banks did not engage in this activity. The sales finance company buys from retail merchants the promissory notes signed by consumers who have bought goods on time payments. Another function of sales finance companies is financing a merchant or dealer's wholesale purchases from the manufacturer. Since cash payment is required by the manufacturer for automobiles and most appliances, the majority of dealers need continuous financing of their inventory. Such financing is business credit, but for convenience it is provided by the same company that finances retail sales.

The sale of durable goods on installments goes back to the early 19th century when furniture was sold by some cabinetmakers on that basis. It grew more rapidly during the last part of that century when sewing machines, pianos, and sets of books were frequently sold on installments.

The biggest growth of sales financing came with the development of the automobile industry. The first corporation to finance auto sales, organized in 1915, was immediately swamped with business. Shortly thereafter, the Commercial Credit Company, which had been founded earlier to finance accounts receivable for manufacturers and wholesalers, developed a plan to finance automobile sales. Its automobile sales

Along with sales and consumer finance companies, the *industrial banking company* was an early member of the consumer installment loan industry. These institutions were sometimes called Morris Plan companies, a name associated with one of the earliest of such institutions.

The first industrial banking company was established in the United States in 1901 when an immigrant from Latvia, David Stein, founded the Merchants and Mechanics Savings and Loan Association in Newport News, Virginia. It was patterned after the consumer banks and loan associations developed in Europe to make loans to workers. It made small general consumer loans and also offered savings accounts.

Other banks of this type were not started until 1910, when Arthur J. Morris set up the Fidelity Savings and Trust Company in Norfolk, Virginia. This institution lent money to people employed in industry—hence the term industrial bank. Morris obtained part of his funds by selling investment certificates that carried a definite rate of interest. Since these certificates could be paid for in installments, they provided a means of saving in small amounts.

In 1911 Morris copyrighted the name "Morris Plan" and began to promote his units actively throughout the country. By 1917 he had established over 70 companies in major cities and some smaller ones. While the Morris Plan banks were being developed, other organizations and individuals were setting up similar units. Several other industrial banking systems were established, but they have all been dissolved.

A number of states currently have industrial-loan laws that provide for the charter or operation of industrial banking companies. However, only eleven states, led by California and Hawaii, have industrial banks with sizable asset holdings. Depending on the state, these companies operate under such names as industrial loan company, Morris Plan bank, or industrial bank. Industrial banking firms continue to emphasize consumer installment loans. In some states they also purchase retail installment contracts, while in others they are active in real estate second mortgage loans and home repair and improvement loans.

As consumer finance companies were able to make larger loans, the distinction between them and industrial banking companies largely disappeared. Industrial banks continue to decline as a separate class of institution, with many becoming regular state banks offering a broad range of services.

THE GROWTH AND DECLINE OF INDUSTRIAL BANKING COMPANIES

financing activities grew rapidly, and today it is still one of the major companies in the sales finance field. General Motors Acceptance Corporation was incorporated in 1919 to do sales financing and also to make wholesale loans to General Motors dealers who were having trouble raising funds to purchase cars from the manufacturer. Many other sales finance companies were established, especially during the 1920s.

Commercial banks did not offer automobile financing until well after the sales finance companies pioneered its development. The commercial banks' basic philosophy held that they should restrict themselves to short-term business loans that were self-liquidating. Automobile and other installment financing for consumers was a new type of business that required new methods and a different outlook from regular banking. Since risks were likely to be great until a substantial volume was built up, bankers had to consider their obligation to depositors, a constraint that did not exist in sales finance companies. It was not until the Great Depression had run its course that commercial banks realized that sales credit could be extended safely.

The ability of sales finance companies to set up branches where they chose also gave them an advantage over banks, which could have no branches in many states and were greatly restricted in others. A last factor was the usury laws that limited banks to rates lower than those necessary to cover costs of this type of lending. These laws were changed and regulations revised when banks began to enter the field.

The Consumer Installment Loan Industry Today

By the middle 1970s many of the distinctions between consumer finance and sales finance companies disappeared. The trend was clearly toward finance companies with a wide range of activities. Consumer finance companies entered the sales finance field primarily by discounting the sales finance paper of companies selling household durables. Sales finance companies also entered the direct cash loan field, and some independent companies began to handle their own sales financing. This happened in part because some manufacturers and retail chains established their own sales finance subsidiaries and also because commercial banks entered the automobile financing field in a significant way.

The companies in the consumer installment credit industry vary in size and ownership from one-office concerns to large national chains operating hundreds of offices. Some companies and chains are independently owned, while others are subsidiaries of industrial and commercial firms, bank holding companies, or insurance companies. Today, most finance companies have a wide range of lending operations and obtain funds from a variety of sources.

Organization and Operations

In the early years of licensed lending, most of the lenders were proprietorships or partnerships, and most lending was done by individual offices. But since 1920, the corporate form and chain operations have become increasingly important. Chains have grown because they enjoy some advantages over independent offices. They have easier access to capital because they can raise funds in the security markets and because they also can obtain short-term bank loans more cheaply. In addition they benefit from mobility of capital, since they can shift funds from office to office as needed. Chains gain a further advantage from spreading their risks over a large geographic area.

ASSET AND LIABILITY STRUCTURES

The Federal Reserve gathers balance sheet data on consumer finance companies, including sales finance and other firms providing consumer installment credit, and commercial finance companies, including factors.[1] These data are presented in aggregate form for recent years in Table 17.1. Finance company assets are primarily composed of accounts

TABLE 17.1   Assets and Liabilities of U.S. Finance Companies (in Billions of Dollars, End of Period)

	1985	1987	SEPT. 1989
ASSETS			
Accounts receivable, gross:			
Consumer	$111.9	$141.1	$140.9
Business	157.5	207.4	275.4
Real estate	28.0	39.5	57.7
Total	$297.4	$388.1	$474.0
Less: Reserves for unearned income	39.2	45.3	55.1
Reserves for losses	4.9	6.8	8.6
Accounts receivable, net	$253.3	$336.0	$410.3
All other	45.3	58.3	102.8
Total assets	$298.6	$394.2	$513.1
LIABILITIES			
Bank loans	$ 18.0	$ 16.4	$ 15.6
Commercial paper	99.2	128.4	148.6
Debt	107.1	165.1	238.6
All other liabilities	41.5	52.8	68.7
Capital, surplus, and undivided profits	32.8	31.5	41.6
Total liabilities and capital	$298.6	$394.2	$513.1

Source: *Federal Reserve Bulletin* (April 1991): A35.

1.   Commercial finance companies and factors were discussed in Chapter 9.

receivable, reflecting the extension of consumer, business and real estate credit. Notice the rapid growth in these loans in recent years.

Finance companies rely very heavily on borrowed funds for their loans to consumers and businesses. This is shown by the fact that finance company equity—capital, surplus, and undivided profits—is less than 10 percent of total assets. This heavy dependence on financial leverage is further compounded by the fact that it is not uncommon for over one-half of the outstanding borrowed funds to be short-term funds. Finance companies' major source of short-term funds is commercial paper, most of which is placed directly, and they also rely on loans from commercial banks. Long-term debt continues to average roughly one-third of total assets.

Because of their heavy dependence on short-term funds, consumer finance companies are severely affected by periods of rapidly rising short-term interest rates. Finance company rates charged to consumers are relatively stable over time while their financing costs fluctuate widely. Rising finance costs cause an industry-wide squeeze on profits (or even losses), as occurred during the 1974–1975 period and at the beginning of the 1980s. To counter the profit sensitivity to changes in short-term borrowing costs, finance companies often offer variable-rate loans to consumers and businesses.

OPERATING CHARACTERISTICS—CASH LOANS

The major purpose of finance company cash loans is to tide consumers over a period of financial emergency. Before a loan is made, the applicant's complete financial position is usually reviewed. It may be possible to plan the applicant's finances in such a way that with a larger loan the most pressing debts can be paid off while reducing monthly payments to a manageable level.

In the early days of consumer finance lending, all loans required chattel mortgages on automobiles, furniture, or store fixtures as collateral or a comaker, the guarantor of repayment. But today a large portion of loans are made unsecured and without a comaker. Originally, consumer finance companies had the borrower repay monthly an equal amount of principal plus a declining amount of interest as the balance was reduced. Most lenders now have loan schedules that provide for equal rather than different payments each month.

Early consumer finance laws stated charges in terms of a maximum percent per month on the unpaid balance and often allowed rates that were higher for the first portion of a loan. For example, a state's small loan law may have called for a maximum rate of 3 percent per month on the first $150 of a loan, 2.5 percent per month on the amount between $150 and $300, and 1 percent per month on the amount between $300 and $2,500. Many states used instead a maximum dollar add-on system. For example, a state law could provide for an annual maximum add-on of $17 per $100 up to $300 and $11 per $100 per year on amounts between $300 and $1,800. However, since passage of the Truth in Lending Act in 1968, rate quotations that give the actual percentage rate on the loan are required. This will be discussed later in the chapter.

Table 17.2 shows average finance rates for various kinds of consumer installment loans during recent years. In general, interest rates on auto, personal, mobile home, and credit card loans declined from 1985 to 1987 and then increased. As auto loan rates fluctuated during the 1985–1990 period, both the average amount and maturity of auto loans were increasing.

OPERATING CHARACTERISTICS—INSTALLMENT PURCHASES

Financing the purchase of consumer durable goods is somewhat different from making cash loans. Since most retailers do not have sufficient capital to carry credit obligations to maturity, they refinance them through sales finance companies or other financial institutions. The time payment contracts between seller and buyer are sold to financial institutions at a discount. The courts hold that this sale of paper is the sale of a thing rather than a loan of money. Thus, this process is not regulated by the usury laws. However, beginning with Indiana in 1935, most states have passed special statutes dealing with installment sales

TABLE 17.2   Terms of Consumer Installment Credit During the 1980s

	1985	1987	1990
INTEREST RATES			
Commercial bank loans:			
48-month new car	12.91%	10.45%	11.78%
24-month personal	15.94	14.22	15.46
120-month mobile home	14.96	13.38	14.02
Credit card	18.69	17.92	18.17
Auto finance companies:			
New car	11.98%	10.73%	12.54%
Used car	17.59	14.60	15.99
OTHER TERMS			
Maturity in months:			
New car	51.5	53.5	54.6
Used car	41.4	45.2	46.1
Loan-to-value ratio:			
New car	91%	93%	87%
Used car	94	98	95
Amount financed:			
New car	$9,915	$11,203	$12,071
Used car	6,089	7,420	8,289

Source: *Federal Reserve Bulletin* (April 1991): A39.

and financing. About half of these statutes govern the sale of all goods on installments; the rest apply only to automobiles. Some of the laws control actual charges that can be made, while others require only a detailed explanation of the items added to the cash price to establish the installment sale price. Practically all of the statutes have provisions for the refund of some charges if the contract is paid in full before final maturity. Some govern repossession practices or delinquency charges.

Most of the state laws require sales finance companies to be licensed. Generally, the licenses are issued upon application and payment of a license fee, but without specific requirements that must be met or investigation of the applicants. In general, the licenses can be canceled for a material misstatement in the application, a willful violation of the law, or fraud.

conditional sales contract
contract for purchasing consumer goods in which the seller retains title to the durable until it is fully paid for

The basic procedures for financing the sale of an automobile, as well as other consumer goods, are the same. The sales contract is drawn up and signed by the purchaser. Usually this is a **conditional sales contract**, which provides that the seller retain title to the car until the agreed-upon purchase price has been paid. In some cases, a separate note is signed for the unpaid balance; in others, the sales contract is all that is required. The purchaser usually makes payments directly to the finance company.

As part of their service, sales finance companies also handle the financing of dealers' or retailers' inventories. The rate for wholesale financing is usually just about equal to costs. It consists of a small flat charge plus interest for the actual time that the money is used. Low charges for wholesale financing are generally used as a way to promote retail financing business. The major difference in appliance wholesale financing as opposed to automobile financing is that manufacturers or distributors may agree to buy back unsold merchandise. Therefore, advances for appliances are usually for only 90 percent of the wholesale price, whereas they are typically 100 percent for cars. Because of a greater risk of default, charges are higher in appliance financing, especially the flat charge, and the interest rate may also be somewhat higher.

CREDIT UNIONS

credit union
a nonprofit cooperative organization that provides credit and accepts savings

Another type of consumer credit supplier is the **credit union**, which is a cooperative nonprofit organization chartered either by the federal government or a state. The credit union operates as a thrift institution for its members and provides credit at moderate rates of interest. It is comprised of individuals who possess common bonds in terms of occupation, place of residence (e.g., same neighborhood), or other form of association such as membership in the same church. Over three fourths of all credit unions are of the occupational type involving manufacturing industries, government, and educational institutions.

Development and Current Status

American credit unions are based on the cooperative financial institutions that developed in Germany and other parts of Europe in the latter half of the nineteenth century. The first credit union in North America was established in 1900 near Quebec by a member of the Canadian Dominion legislature, Alphonse Desjardins. He also helped French Canadians living in Manchester, New Hampshire, organize one of the first credit unions in the United States, which was chartered in 1909. Prior to that time, several cooperative credit associations had been operating in Massachusetts, and in 1909 that state passed the first credit union law. Real progress began in 1921 when the late Edward A. Filene, a Boston merchant, became interested in credit union development and set up the Credit Union National Extension Bureau. Filene put a large sum of money into his organization and, under the outstanding leadership of an excellent promoter, Roy F. Bergengren, adequate credit union laws were subsequently passed in state after state.

In 1934 Congress passed the Federal Credit Union Act. A Credit Union Division was initially created under the Farm Credit Administration to supervise credit unions and to provide various services to them. At present, the Federal Credit Union Act is administered by the National Credit Union Administration (NCUA), which operates as an independent regulatory agency. NCUA is responsible for chartering new federal credit unions and supervising and examining operating practices and financial conditions of existing ones. The National Credit Union Administration also administers the National Credit Union Share Insurance Fund, which was established by law in 1970. Prior to 1970, no national insurance program comparable to the Federal Deposit Insurance Corporation was available to credit unions. Credit union deposit insurance is currently $100,000 per account. All federal credit unions are required to obtain insurance, and state-chartered credit unions may join the National Credit Union Share Insurance Fund.

In addition to federal organizations, a state credit union league, the Credit Union National Association (CUNA), was formed in 1935. This association plays an active role in interlending activities among member credit unions, and it provides certain financial market services.

Credit unions grew rapidly after World War II. During the 1950s, they doubled in number, more than doubled in membership, and increased their assets by over six times. The 1960s also saw rapid growth, with membership nearly doubling and assets increasing over three times. By 1970, membership in credit unions was approaching 22 million people and assets were almost $16 billion. Approximately 21,000 credit unions are operating today; they have over 45 million members and hold over $80 billion in assets.

The total assets of credit unions remain small relative to the asset sizes of other depository institutions and finance companies. However, their rapid growth in recent years suggests that credit unions will play an increasingly important role in the U.S. financial system—particularly in the consumer credit area.

Organization and Operation

As noted above, credit unions may obtain a federal or state charter. All states except Alaska, Delaware, South Dakota, and Wyoming have provisions for chartering credit unions. Close to 60 percent of credit unions have federal charters. Over 80 percent of all credit unions have federal deposit insurance and 97 percent have either federal or state insurance.

ASSET AND LIABILITY STRUCTURES

Table 17.3 contains some selected asset and liability data for both state and federally chartered credit unions during recent years. Loans outstanding to members are the primary assets of both types of credit unions. In terms of total size, in 1990 federally chartered credit unions held about $61 billion more in assets. Data for 1990 also show that approximately 65 percent of total assets for all credit unions were in the form of loans to members. At the same time, credit unions rely almost exclusively on savings by members to finance or support assets. In 1990 member savings accounted for 90 percent of the total liabilities and capital held by federal and state credit unions.

TABLE 17.3   Assets and Liabilities of Credit Unions (in Billions of Dollars, End of Period)

	1985	1987	SEPT. 1990
TOTAL ASSETS	118.0	160.6	197.3
Federal	77.9	104.1	129.1
State	40.1	56.5	68.2
LOANS OUTSTANDING	73.5	90.9	127.3
Federal	47.9	58.4	82.8
State	25.6	32.5	44.5
MEMBER SAVINGS	106.0	148.3	177.5
Federal (shares)	70.9	96.1	115.5
State (shares and deposits)	35.1	52.2	62.1

Source: *Federal Reserve Bulletin* (April 1991): A26.

Loans to members are for personal expenses, purchasing of autos and other durable goods, residential repair and improvement, and so forth. Credit unions also invest a portion of their assets in U.S. government and federal agency securities, make loans to or hold deposits in other credit unions, and hold cash and miscellaneous assets. On the liability side of their balance sheets, checkable deposits have grown rapidly in importance and thrift certificates also make up a large portion of total credit union members' savings. Debt in the form of accounts payable and notes payable remain only a small portion of total liabilities and capital. Thus credit unions, in contrast with finance companies that supply consumer credit, rely very little on borrowed funds and financial leverage.

OPERATING CHARACTERISTICS

Since the credit union is a cooperative, the power to run it rests with the members. All who have subscribed to at least one share, the par value of which is usually $5, are eligible to vote at the general meetings. The general administration of the credit union is in the hands of a board of directors elected at an annual meeting.

An elected credit committee, which must pass on all loan applications, is the heart of the organization. Also elected is a supervisory committee that goes over the books at frequent intervals to be sure that operations are being conducted in line with the association bylaws and the law under which it was chartered. Many credit unions also have an education committee to educate members in thrift and the proper use of credit.

The funds and financial records of the credit union are handled by a treasurer, who is elected at the annual meeting and is the only elected official who receives compensation. The treasurer may also employ clerical assistance to aid in carrying out required duties. Most of the time spent on the credit union affairs is donated by the elected officers and committees, and office space is often donated by the firm or organization sponsoring the credit union. Thus, business expenses can be kept at a relatively low level. These types of financial aid are another difference between credit unions and other depository institutions and finance companies.

Credit unions also differ in that they pay no federal or state income taxes, only real property taxes. Probably their cooperative nonprofit nature and their relatively small average size have kept them free of income taxation. Other financial intermediaries have argued against this advantage, and as credit unions become larger and broaden their operations they may find their income tax-exempt status being threatened.

Federal and most state credit unions have a maximum monthly rate they are legally allowed to charge on the unpaid balance of a loan. This rate must include all charges involved in granting the loan. The maximum rate is often charged for small unsecured loans, while lower rates may apply to loans secured by chattel mortgages (automobiles and other durable goods), pledged shares, and comakers. The maximum amount loaned to one individual cannot exceed 10 percent of the assets of the credit union. Life insurance to cover the remaining balance of the loan in event of death is provided at no additional cost to the borrower by most credit unions through a mutual insurance company, Cuna Mutual Insurance Society.

During 1977 major revisions were made in the Federal Credit Union Act. Federal credit union lending powers were substantially broadened by permitting the extension of secured and unsecured loan maturities to twelve years and by allowing credit unions to make first-mortgage residential real estate loans for periods up to 30 years. A second major legislative development established a share draft program. Under this program, federal credit union members are permitted to write drafts—similar to checks available through other depository institutions—on their share accounts. Credit union share drafts are "cleared" like checks except that canceled drafts are not returned to members. Draft writers periodically receive itemized statements.

Passage of the Depository Institutions Deregulation and Monetary Control Act in 1980 also impacted substantially on the operations of credit unions. As noted in previous chapters, credit unions and other depository institutions can borrow from the Federal Reserve at the discount rate and are being required to hold reserves at a federal reserve bank against their checkable deposits, including share drafts. Likewise, interest-rate and dividend-rate ceilings on savings deposits have been phased out in an orderly manner by the Depository Institutions Deregulation Committee.

COMMERCIAL BANKS

The largest volume of consumer credit in the United States is granted by commercial banks. At the end of 1990, banks had total outstanding loans of $2,094 billion. Commercial loans accounted for 31 percent of this total. Mortgage loans were 40 percent, and loans to individuals 18 percent, which indicates the significance of consumer loans to commercial banks.[2] Banks have achieved the leading position even though they entered the field of consumer financing long after specialized institutions had been developed in it. Banks now make all types of consumer loans and most banks compete strongly for them.

2. *Federal Reserve Bulletin* (April 1991): A16.

Past and Current Consumer Lending

Before consumer financing became widespread, some banks made loans to individuals on a 30-, 60-, or 90-day basis in the same way that they made commercial loans to business. In the mid-1920s a few smaller banks set up personal loan departments, but the growth was slow. In 1928 the movement gained force when the National City Bank of New York, one of the largest banks in the country, set up a personal loan department. In 1929 the Bank of America in San Francisco, which had branches all over California, entered the field.

In the summer of 1934, the federal government initiated a program to expand bank lending to consumers. In an effort to stimulate employment and economic activity in general, the Federal Housing Administration was authorized to guarantee loans to certain lenders who extended credit for home repair and improvement. These loans, which had to be repaid in equal monthly installments, were known as FHA Title 1 loans. During the first couple of years, losses paid to the banks by the FHA were less than 3 percent of the loan volume, and a substantial part of these losses was later recovered by the FHA. The record of FHA loans and their experiences with them convinced many bankers that consumer loans could be made without undue losses and yield a reasonable profit.

The Bankers Association for Consumer Credit, which was formed in 1938, assisted the movement. In 1940 it merged its activities with those of the American Bankers Association, which had recognized the importance of consumer financing. Consumer lending by banks continued to grow, especially during World War II.

At the present time almost all commercial banks make consumer loans. As we saw in Table 16.2, commercial banks held nearly one-half of the consumer installment credit outstanding as of 1990. Approximately 38 percent of the $351.2 billion consumer credit held by commercial banks was automobile installment credit. Bank revolving credit (credit cards) accounted for another 38 percent of the total.

Loan Types and Procedures

Banks generally have a separate department to handle consumer loans. As personal loan departments have gained experience and tried to increase volume, they have shifted from comaker loans to loans on an individual signature. Some personal loans are made with collateral, but banks rely much less on chattel mortgages than do other intermediaries. Collateral may consist of savings accounts, marketable securities, the cash value of life insurance policies, S&L accounts, and the like.

The most important field for many larger banks is automobile financing. Under an arrangement with a dealer, a bank usually finances the dealer's stock of cars. In return, the bank buys the promissory notes signed by consumers who have bought the autos. (The methods used closely follow those developed by the sales finance companies.) The practice of making direct car loans to individuals has grown into a major outlet for funds of many commercial banks. Banks also do a substantial volume of business in financing other durable goods, most of which arise from the purchase of notes from dealers.

In the mid-1960s bank credit card plans began spreading throughout the country. Today, the two largest national plans are VISA and Master-Card. Another form of bank credit is check credit or overdraft plans, which provide for automatic credit within preset limits—the customer simply writes a check larger than the balance on deposit.

OTHER FINANCIAL INTERMEDIARIES

The marketing function plays only a minor role in the intermediate- and short-term consumer credit fields. Some larger companies sell consumer paper to other institutions or individuals. Some sellers of consumer durables carry their own paper for a period and later look for a purchaser for the paper, but there is little organized activity of this kind carried on by brokers or separate institutions. Several other organizations, however, play an important role in the consumer credit field.

Credit Reporting Organizations

credit exchange
an organization set up by consumer finance companies to provide information on loans

In most cities of any size consumer finance companies have set up a **credit exchange** to provide information on the status of existing loans. Some of the earliest of these exchanges operated on a one-loan plan under which an individual or a married couple could have only one loan from a finance company outstanding at any time. This was in keeping with the philosophy that one of a finance company's functions is to help a person plan his or her finances to get out of debt and that this can best be done by dealing with only one company.

The one-loan plan met with opposition from new companies entering a territory. When finance companies entered the field of durable goods financing, there was more opposition to the one-loan plan since these loans were of a different nature from the loans to help an individual in financial difficulty. As a result, some credit exchanges amended their rules to allow several loans to an individual as long as the same collateral was not used as security for more than one loan. More recently, the consumer finance companies in some cities, for example, St. Louis, have developed clearinghouse exchanges in which no restrictions are placed on loans. But each company must furnish the exchange with complete information on all loans and all notes they purchase.

Another important credit-reporting organization is the retail credit bureau. It is organized by local merchants and finance companies to serve as a central exchange for data on individuals and the credit extended them. When more detailed information is required, a special report may be prepared that gives information on such things as the applicant's age, marital status, length of time in one residence, type of housing, estimated income, investments, bank accounts, suits or liens against the applicant, and charge-account buying and paying habits. For information on an individual who lives in another town, data may be obtained from a credit bureau in that town. Several national concerns also prepare reports on the financial status of individuals, primarily for insurance purposes but also for credit evaluation.

Credit bureaus work well when all major credit-granting agencies cooperate. But it is especially difficult to get some used-car dealers to furnish information; their data is very important since a used-car loan may be by far the largest debt of a borrower, especially if the person does not own a home.

Insurance Companies

Insurance of some type, such as fire, theft, or comprehensive, must usually be carried on durables when they are financed. This may be handled by regular insurance companies or by special companies that write insurance only in connection with financing. In automobile financing, collision insurance is required.

To an increasing extent, group life insurance is being used to insure the unpaid balance of consumer loans. Special companies are active in this field and some of the leading life insurance companies have entered it. There is also increasing emphasis on group accident and disability insurance to protect borrowers against these possibilities.

Even though all types of consumer finance insurance coverage are growing, there is disagreement as to the value of some types. Some feel that while group life insurance is desirable, accident, disability, and similar forms of insurance are of limited usefulness.

REGULATION OF THE CONSUMER CREDIT INDUSTRY

Historically, regulation of institutions financing the consumer has been done by state governments. Most state consumer installment loan laws evolved out of the Russell Sage Foundation's efforts in the development of the Uniform Small Loan Law and the National Consumer Finance Association's Model Consumer Finance Act of 1948. The U.S. Congress did give the Federal Reserve temporary powers to regulate two aspects of consumer credit (down payments and repayment periods) during World War II and to regulate real estate credit during the Korean War.

Consumer Credit Protection Act

In 1968 Congress passed the Consumer Credit Protection Act, which requires the clear explanation of consumer credit costs and garnishment procedures—taking wages or property by legal means—and prohibits overly high priced credit transactions. Regulation Z, which was drafted by a Federal Reserve task force, enacts the Truth in Lending section of the act. The purpose of the law and Regulation Z is to make consumers aware of, and able to compare, the costs of alternate forms of credit. Regulation Z applies to consumer finance companies, credit unions, sales finance companies, banks, S&Ls, residential mortgage brokers, credit card issuers, department stores, automobile dealers, hospitals, doctors, dentists, and any other individuals or organizations that extend or arrange credit for consumers.

The law requires a breakdown of the total finance charge and the annual percentage rate of charge. The finance charge includes all loan costs including not only interest or discount but service charges, loan fees, finder fees, insurance premiums, and points (an additional loan charge). Fees for such items as taxes not included in the purchase price, licenses, certificates of title, and the like may be excluded from the finance charge if they are itemized and explained separately. The annual percentage rate of charge is the relationship of total finance charges to the amount financed and must be computed to the nearest one-quarter of 1 percent annually. The creditor must also explain to the customer the method of determining the balance on which the finance charge is calculated, the conditions under which a creditor may acquire a security interest in any property pledged by the customer, and the nature of such an interest.

Calculating Percentage Rates On Loans

The annual percentage rate (APR) must be calculated using the actuarial method. Extensive tables are provided by the Federal Reserve for purposes of computing the APR for installment loans with level monthly payments. One needs only to know the dollar amount of the finance charge, the total amount to be financed, and the number of monthly payments. Table 17.4 is a portion of a Federal Reserve table. The example in the table shows that a $200 loan, with finance charges of $35 and requiring 24 monthly payments would have an APR of 16 percent.

The APR also can be approximated with the following constant ratio formula:

$$R = \frac{2MI}{P(N+1)}$$

where

R = annual effective interest rate expressed in decimal form
M = number of installment payments in a year
I = total dollar amount of interest charged
P = net principal amount of loan available to the borrower
N = total number of installment payments over the life of the loan

In the example above, the effective interest rate would be estimated as

$$R = \frac{2(12)\$35}{\$200(24 + 1)} = \frac{\$840}{\$5000} = 0.168 \text{ or } 16.8 \text{ percent}$$

It should be noted that the formula overstates the true APR calculated by using the Federal Reserve actuarial method. The degree of error increases with higher interest rates and longer loan maturities. However, even with such limitations, the formula does provide the user with a quick estimate of the APR.

Other Legislation

Another important development in 1968, with revisions in 1974, was publication of the Uniform Consumer Credit Code (UCCC) by the National Conference of Commissioners on Uniform State Laws. Nine states have adopted substantial portions of the UCCC, although the law as adopted varies from state to state. Other states have adopted parts of the UCCC in their own state statutes. The UCCC is much like the Federal Consumer Credit Protection Act and covers consumer credit sales, loans, garnishment, and insurance provided in relation to a consumer credit sale of up to $25,000. Its truth-in-lending provisions require full disclosure to the consumer of all aspects of the credit transaction and that charges be computed and disclosed as an annual percentage rate. The UCCC does not prescribe specific rates, but it sets maximums based on unpaid balances—36 percent per year on $300 or less, 21 percent per year for balances of $300 to $1,000 and 15 percent for unpaid balances in excess of $1,000.

Several additions and changes have been made to improve and strengthen the Consumer Credit Protection Act of 1968. Action was taken by Congress in the fall of 1970 to prohibit the distribution of credit cards not requested by a prospective user and to limit the liability of credit card owners for purchases made by others on lost or stolen cards. In 1971 Congress also passed the Fair Credit Reporting Act, designed to protect consumers by keeping credit agencies from distributing incorrect or outdated information.

TABLE 17.4   Partial Federal Reserve Table for Computing the APR for Level Monthly Payment Plans

EXAMPLE
  Finance charge = $35.00; Total amount financed = $200; Number of monthly payments = 24.
SOLUTION
  Step 1—Divide the finance charge by the total amount financed and multiply by $100. This gives the finance charge per $100 of amount financed. That is, $35.00 ÷ $200 = .1750 × $100 = $17.50.
  Step 2—Follow down the left hand column of the table to the line for 24 months. Follow across this line until you find the nearest number to $17.50. In this example $17.51 is closest to $17.50. Reading up the column of figures shows an annual percentage rate of 16%.

NUMBER—ANNUAL PERCENTAGE RATE OF

Payments	14.50%	14.75%	15.00%	15.25%	15.50%	15.75%	16.00%	16.25%
	(Finance Charge per $100 of Amount Financed)							
1	1.21	1.23	1.25	1.27	1.29	1.31	1.33	1.35
2	1.82	1.85	1.88	1.91	1.94	1.97	2.00	2.04
3	2.43	2.47	2.51	2.55	2.59	2.64	2.68	2.72
4	3.04	3.09	3.14	3.20	3.25	3.30	3.36	3.41
5	3.65	3.72	3.78	3.84	3.91	3.97	4.04	4.10
6	4.27	4.35	4.42	4.49	4.57	4.64	4.72	4.79
7	4.89	4.98	5.06	5.15	5.23	5.32	5.40	5.49
8	5.51	5.61	5.71	5.80	5.90	6.00	6.09	6.19
9	6.14	6.25	6.35	6.46	6.57	6.68	6.78	6.89
10	6.77	6.88	7.00	7.12	7.24	7.36	7.48	7.60
11	7.40	7.53	7.66	7.79	7.92	8.05	8.18	8.31
12	8.03	8.17	8.31	8.45	8.59	8.74	8.88	9.02
13	8.66	8.81	8.97	9.12	9.27	9.43	9.58	9.73
14	9.30	9.46	9.63	9.79	9.96	10.12	10.29	10.45
15	9.94	10.11	10.29	10.47	10.64	10.82	11.00	11.17
16	10.58	10.77	10.95	11.14	11.33	11.52	11.71	11.90
17	11.22	11.42	11.62	11.82	12.02	12.22	12.42	12.62
18	11.87	12.08	12.29	12.50	12.72	12.93	13.14	13.35
19	12.52	12.74	12.97	13.19	13.41	13.64	13.86	14.09
20	13.17	13.41	13.64	13.88	14.11	14.35	14.59	14.82
21	13.82	14.07	14.32	14.57	14.82	15.06	15.31	15.56
22	14.48	14.74	15.00	15.26	15.52	15.78	16.04	16.30
23	15.14	15,41	15.68	15.96	16.23	16.50	16.78	17.05
24	15.80	16.08	16.37	16.65	16.94	17.22	17.51	17.80
25	16.46	16.76	17.06	17.35	17.65	17.95	18.25	18.55
26	17.13	17.44	17.75	18.06	18.37	18.68	18.99	19.30
27	17.80	18.12	18.44	18.76	19.09	19.41	19.74	20.06
28	18.47	18.80	19.14	19.47	19.81	20.15	20.48	20.82
29	19.14	19.49	19.83	20.18	20.53	20.88	21.23	21.58
30	19.81	20.17	20.54	20.90	21.26	21.62	21.99	22.35
31	20.49	20.87	21.24	21.61	21.99	22.37	22.74	23.12
32	21.17	21.56	21.95	22.33	22.72	23.11	23.50	23.89
33	21.85	22.25	22.65	23.06	23.46	23.86	24.26	24.67
34	22.54	22.95	23.37	23.78	24.19	24.61	25.03	25.44
35	23.23	23.65	24.08	24.51	24.94	25.36	25.79	26.23
36	23.92	24.35	24.80	25.24	25.68	26.12	26.57	27.01

Source: "Truth in Lending—Consumer Credit Cost Disclosure," Exhibit G, Board of Governors of the Federal Reserve System.

In 1974 the Fair Credit Billing Act was passed to aid consumers in having billing errors corrected. The Equal Credit Opportunity Act was also passed in 1974 and prohibited creditors from discriminating on the basis of marital status or sex. Amendments in 1976 extended the list of factors which cannot be used for rejecting credit applications to include religion, race, color, national origin, age, or source of income (such as public assistance programs). Applicants also cannot be discriminated against if they have exercised "in good faith" any rights granted under the Consumer Credit Protection Act, including the truth in lending section.

Consumer protection legislation has also been passed in the area of long-term consumer financing involving real estate. The Real Estate Settlement Procedures Act was passed by Congress in 1974, amended in 1975, and amended in its current form in mid-1976. Federally regulated lenders must comply with the Act, which is designed to protect purchasers of residential homes and condominiums. Lenders must provide the loan applicant with "good faith" estimates of closing costs (such as loan origination fees, credit reports, and title searches) when a loan application is being made. And, if the borrower requests it, a standard settlements form containing all known settlement costs must be provided by the lender one day before settlement or closing actually takes place.

Other relevant legislation includes the Community Reinvestment Act of 1977, which was passed to encourage depository institutions to help meet the credit needs of the communities in which they operate. In 1979 changes in the National Bankruptcy Act provided for greater protection of assets when personal bankruptcies are filed—since then personal bankruptcies have soared. The Truth in Lending Act was also modified in 1980 to make it easier for creditors to comply with disclosure requirements and to make annual percentage rates more understandable to borrowers.

KEY TERMS

conditional sales contract
consumer finance companies
credit exchange

credit union
sales finance company

DISCUSSION QUESTIONS

1. Which institutions are included in the consumer installment credit industry?

2. Why did consumer finance companies develop in the United States? What were the legislative developments that paralleled the growth of consumer finance companies?
3. Briefly describe the functions of sales finance companies and trace their development.
4. Discuss the development and current status of industrial banking companies in the consumer financing field.
5. What are the major sources of funds used by finance companies to finance their consumer and business loans?
6. Briefly indicate how rates charged by finance companies during recent years differ by type of loan and length of loan.
7. Define what a credit union is and briefly trace the development of credit unions.
8. Discuss the operations of credit unions, including their organizational structure, sources of funds, and recent legislative developments.
9. How important is the role of commercial banks in financing consumers?
10. Identify and briefly describe the facilitating agencies that play a role in the consumer credit field.
11. Describe the main provisions of federal legislation in the consumer credit field since 1968.

PROBLEMS

1. Assume that you have the opportunity to borrow $21,000 for five years. Total finance charges will be $2,000 per year or $10,000 over the five years. Use the constant ratio formula to approximate the actual percentage rate if equal semiannual payments are required. Also show how your answer would change if monthly payments had been required.
2. A one-year, $1,000 loan is offered to you. The finance charge will be $85 and you are required to make level monthly payments. Use Table 17.4 on page 396 to determine the annual percentage rate on this loan. How would your answer change if the lender allowed you to make 24 level monthly payments with a finance charge of $175?
3. Calculate the effective annual rate of interest on the following loan: $850 loaned for a period of 1½ years to be repaid with a total loan financing charge of $105 ($70 per year) in equal monthly installments. Use Table 17.4 to determine the annual percentage rate. Also estimate the rate using the constant ratio formula.

4. Obtain a current issue of the *Federal Reserve Bulletin*.

   a. Find the assets and liabilities for domestic finance companies for the most recent available year. How do your figures compare with the data presented in the chapter?

   b. Find the current terms of consumer installment credit. Compare these against the terms presented in the chapter. Comment on any trends or changes in consumer installment interest rates and other terms.

   c. Find the data on credit union assets and liabilities for the most recently available year. How do your figures compare with the data presented in the chapter?

SELF-TEST QUESTIONS

1. Consumer finance companies were developed to perform which one of the following basic consumer credit functions?

   a. convenient form of payment
   b. aid in financial emergencies
   c. buying durables on installments
   d. purchasing nondurable goods with installment payments

2. A so-called Morris Plan company would be associated with which one of the following types of institutions in the consumer installment loan industry?

   a. consumer finance company
   b. sales finance company
   c. industrial banking company
   d. credit union

3. Which one of the following suppliers of consumer credit is a cooperative nonprofit organization?

   a. consumer finance company
   b. sales finance company
   c. industrial banking company
   d. credit union

4. The largest volume of consumer credit is granted by which one of the following financial institutions?

   a. commercial banks
   b. consumer finance companies
   c. sales finance companies
   d. credit unions

5. Regulation Z is associated with the Truth in Lending section of which one of the following legislative Acts?
   a. Consumer Credit Protection Act
   b. Fair Credit Billing Act
   c. Equal Credit Opportunity Act
   d. National Bankruptcy Act

SELF TEST PROBLEM

You have a business opportunity that will require you to borrow $10,000 for four years. Total finance charges will be $1,000 per year or $4,000 over the four years. Use the constant ratio formula to approximate the actual percentage rate if equal quarterly payments are required. Also show how your answer would change if monthly payments are required.

SUGGESTED READINGS

Edmister, Robert O. *Financial Institutions*, 2e. New York: McGraw-Hill, 1986. Chap. 10.
Goldfaden, Lynn C., and Gerald P. Hurst. "Regulatory Responses to Changes in the Consumer Financial Services Industry." *Federal Reserve Bulletin* (February 1985): 75–81.
Griffith, Reynolds. *Personal Finance*. Reston, VA: Reston Publishing Co., 1985. Chap. 8.
Rose, Peter S. *Money and Capital Markets*, 3e. Homewood, IL: BPI/Irwin, 1989. Chap. 18.
U.S. Department of Commerce. "Consumer Credit—Factors Influencing Its Availability and Cost." Washington, DC: U.S. Government Printing Office, 1976.

ANSWERS TO SELF-TEST QUESTIONS   1. b   2. c   3. d   4. a   5. a

SOLUTION TO SELF-TEST PROBLEM

$$R = \frac{2(4)\$4,000}{\$10,000(16+1)} = \frac{\$32,000}{\$170,000} = 0.1882 \text{ or } 18.82\%$$

$$R = \frac{2(12)\$4,000}{\$10,000(48+1)} = \frac{\$96,000}{\$490,000} = 0.1959 \text{ or } 19.59\%$$

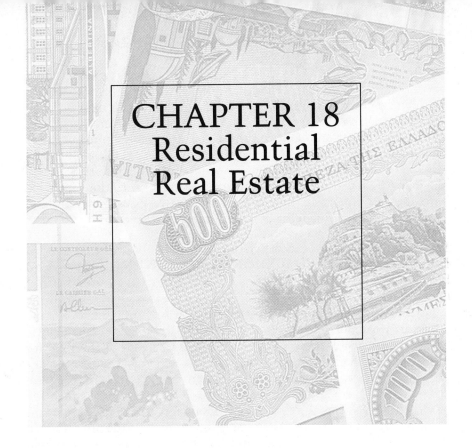

CHAPTER 18
Residential Real Estate

After studying this chapter, you should be able to:
- Describe the recent sources and uses of mortgage funds.
- Explain the procedures used in residential real estate financing.
- Describe the role and operations of S&Ls in supplying real estate credit.
- Describe the role and operations of commercial banks in supplying real estate credit.
- Describe the role and operations of savings banks in supplying real estate credit.
- Describe the role and operations of life insurance companies in supplying real estate credit.
- Identify the merchandising and facilitating agencies involved in the mortgage markets.
- Explain how governmental assistance is involved in real estate financing.
- Discuss the roles played by government agencies in the secondary mortgage market.

Financing the purchase of residential real estate is classified as long-term consumer financing. Home mortgage debt outstanding is almost

twice that of short- and intermediate-term consumer debt, both installment and noninstallment combined, as we saw in Table 16.1.

In this chapter we begin with a discussion of the amount of real
estate funds raised annually and also consider the roles of major financial institutions in supplying mortgage funds. Then we discuss residential real estate financing procedures and follow with an examination of
the major financial institutions and facilitating organizations involved
in real estate financing. In the final section we focus on the role of
government in the financing of residential real estate.

SOURCES AND USES OF MORTGAGE FUNDS

In Chapter 6 we discussed the importance of mortgage borrowing
relative to the total net borrowing by domestic nonfinancial sectors.
Mortgages accounted for about 37 percent of the 1989 net borrowings.
This figure was followed in magnitude by 22 percent of the total for
federal government borrowing through the issue of U.S. government
securities. Funds raised through corporate bond issues in 1989 accounted for 16 percent of the total.

Table 18.1 shows the amounts of mortgage funds raised in recent
years by type of mortgage. Home mortgages represent the primary type
of mortgage funds and now account for about three-quarters of the total
mortgage funds raised annually. Commercial property mortgages rank
second in importance and are followed by multifamily residential
mortgages. The recent difficulties in the farming industry are indicated
by the reduction in farm mortgage funds in recent years. The value is
negative because redemptions exceed new mortgages.

Depository institutions and life insurance companies are the major
suppliers of mortgage funds. Table 18.1 shows these financial institutions held over 54 percent of the total mortgage debt outstanding in the
United States in 1989. Savings institutions (S&Ls and savings banks)
continue to rank first as holders of mortgage debt with 26 percent of the
1989 total. Commercial banks rank second with over 21 percent of the
total mortgage debt. Life insurance companies account for approximately 7 percent of the total.

In addition to financial institutions, mortgage pools or trusts have
been increasing in importance and now account for about 26 percent of
total mortgage debt holdings according to the data in Table 18.1. Mortgages in the pools are guaranteed or insured by agencies such as the
Government National Mortgage Association (GNMA), the Federal
Home Loan Mortgage Corporation, the Federal National Mortgage Association (FNMA), and the Farmers Home Administration (FMHA).

Individuals and others account for about 13 percent of total holdings. "Others" includes mortgage companies, real estate investment

TABLE 18.1   Mortgage Funds Raised and Mortgage Debt Outstanding (in Billions of Dollars)

	1985	1987	1989
MORTGAGE FUNDS RAISED			
Home mortgages	$ 156.8	$ 234.9	$ 218.0
Multifamily residential	29.8	24.4	16.4
Commercial	62.2	71.6	42.7
Farm	– 6.6	– 6.4	– 1.5
Total	$ 242.2	$ 324.5	$ 275.6
MORTGAGE DEBT OUTSTANDING			
1- to 4-family	$1,467.6	$1,958.4	$2,404.3
Multifamily	213.9	272.5	304.1
Commercial	479.8	651.3	744.6
Farm	105.6	88.8	85.3
All holders	$2,266.9	$2,971.0	$3,538.3
Percent of debt by holder:			
Commercial banks	18.9%	19.9%	21.5%
Savings institutions	33.7	28.9	26.2
Life insurance companies	7.5	7.1	6.8
Total financial institutions	60.1%	55.9%	54.5%
Mortgage pools or trusts	18.3	24.1	26.4
Individuals and others	14.2	13.5	13.1
Federal and related agencies	7.4	6.5	6.0
All holders	100.0%	100.0%	100.0%

Source: *Federal Reserve Bulletin* (April 1991): A37 and A40.

trusts (REITs), noninsured pension funds, state and local retirement funds, and credit unions.

Finally, federal and related agencies account for about 6 percent of the outstanding mortgage funds. These agencies include the GNMA, FNMA, FMHA, the Federal Housing Administration (FHA), the Veterans Administration (VA), the Federal Land Banks, and the Federal Home Loan Mortgage Corporation. Governmental assistance programs have been developed over the years to aid in both the primary and secondary real estate markets, as we will see later in the chapter.

PROCEDURES IN RESIDENTIAL REAL ESTATE FINANCING

As in all lending operations, the procedures used in residential real estate financing are determined in large part by the characteristics of the financing used. This financing traditionally has been long-term except for construction loans, and even these are now being replaced by long-term, fixed-rate mortgage loans. Long-term loans are possible because houses last for 40 or 50 or more years. However, because of volatile interest rates and the liquidity problems faced by S&Ls, there has been a trend towards offering variable-rate mortgages and/or maturities shorter than the traditional 30 years.

Special risks are involved in real estate financing: The value of the collateral is affected by changes in the desirability of the geographic area and the neighborhood, as well as by business fluctuations, changing price levels, and the like. Sometimes there are technical difficulties to overcome before the potential borrower can get clear title. The property must be maintained adequately if it is to hold its value. And the present and future income and other obligations of the borrower must be correctly judged to determine the safety of a loan.

The Mortgage

Purchasers of residential real estate usually are able to make only a partial payment on the purchase price. A loan made to finance the difference between the purchase price and the down payment is typically secured by means of a mortgage against the property. Thus, a mortgage is an interest in real property used as security for payment of a debt. The borrower in such a loan transaction is called the **mortgagor**; the lender is the **mortgagee**.[1]

mortgagor
the borrower in a mortgaged loan transaction

mortgagee
the lender in a mortgaged loan transaction

The form of mortgage used in this country is patterned after that of English common law and equity law. In early England, a borrower of money would actually turn over possession of the land to the lender, and the lender would have use of the land until the debt was paid. The word mortgage, which stems from *mort gage*, or "dead-pledge," was therefore appropriate in that the land was, to all intents and purposes, dead so far as the borrower was concerned until such time as the loan was repaid.

Modifications of this mortgage arrangement provided in some cases that the income from the land should apply to payment of the debt, and in other cases that possession of the land by the lender was not to occur unless the borrower defaulted, that is, failed to meet the terms of the contractual agreement. Later the English Court of Equity began to take the view that it was unjust that a mortgagee should always retain the property in full if the borrower defaulted. Since the property was merely transferred to the mortgagee to secure a debt, a mortgagor had a right in equity to redeem it upon full payment of the obligation, even though the maturity date of the loan had passed. This right is known as the **equity of redemption**.

equity of redemption
the right of a mortgagor who has lost property through default to redeem it by paying all money owed

---

1. In some states a *deed of trust* conveys real property used as loan security while in other states a lender has a choice of using either a mortgage or deed of trust. The deed of trust involves three parties: the beneficiary (lender), the trustor (borrower), and the trustee, who forecloses on behalf of the beneficiary in the event of default.

Along with the equity of redemption came the procedure of **foreclosure**. Foreclosure is a legal proceeding that bars or ends a mortgagor's equity of redemption, or right to redeem his mortgaged property. The foreclosure was necessary to prevent an undue burden upon the lender because of the uncertainty of the period of equity of redemption. It provided that on the formal request of the mortgagee the courts would fix a time within which the mortgagor was required to pay the debt. If the mortgagor failed to pay within this time, the decree provided that his equity of redemption was thereby "barred and foreclosed."

foreclosure
a legal action that ends a mortgagor's equity of redemption

SECOND MORTGAGES

At times a mortgagor may want to borrow more money on a piece of property than the mortgagee is willing to lend. Then the borrower may find a lender who will lend the additional sum, usually at a higher rate of interest, provided the mortgagor gives the second lender a claim on equity in the property that is not covered by the existing mortgage. When this is done, the existing mortgage is called the first mortgage, and the new mortgage is the second or junior mortgage. At times three or more mortgages may be placed on one piece of property. Second or subsequent mortgages may also be taken out at various points in time after the initial mortgage has been negotiated.

State laws provide for the recording of mortgages in order to protect the interests of all parties. An unrecorded mortgage is binding between the parties to the agreement, but the law provides that the first mortgage to be recorded is the senior mortgage, so all mortgages should be recorded promptly.

FORECLOSURE PROCEDURE

In the event the mortgagor doesn't make one or more payments, the mortgagee will usually try to work out an arrangement with him for making the payments in default. If the mortgagee feels that his or her interests are at risk, a lawsuit may be filed asking the court to foreclose on the mortgage and to hold a foreclosure sale. The mortgagee may bid at the foreclosure sale if it is believed that other bids are not adequate. Foreclosure costs are paid first out of the proceeds of the sale of the property. If a surplus remains after the foreclosure costs and the mortgage debt are paid, the mortgagor is entitled to it. If part of the debt is unpaid, the court grants the mortgagee a *deficiency judgment* for the amount, which the mortgagee attempts to collect from other assets of the mortgagor. The use of deficiency judgments has been abolished by several states in recent years.

GOVERNMENT GUARANTEES

During the depression of the 1930s, the federal government set up the Federal Housing Administration to stimulate home building by insuring mortgages on residential real estate. A prospective borrower can apply for an FHA loan at an S&L, commercial bank, or other lending institution approved for such loans. The required application papers are sent for approval to the local FHA office which appraises, or judges the value of, the property and checks the applicant's ability to make payments.

The Servicemen's Readjustment Act of 1944, or GI Bill as it is popularly called, authorized the Veterans Administration to guarantee loans on homes purchased by veterans. VA loans were first made available to World War II veterans and more recently to all veterans. Details of FHA-insured and VA-guaranteed loan programs are covered later in this chapter in the discussion of governmental assistance in real estate financing.

AMORTIZED LOANS

amortized loan
loan that is paid off in regular payments of principal and interest

conventional mortgage loan
an amortized loan that is not insured or guaranteed by a government agency

Any loan guaranteed by the Federal Housing Administration or the Veterans Administration must be an *amortized loan*, that is, a loan on which the borrower agrees to make regular payments on principal as well as on interest. Other amortized mortgage loans that are neither FHA-insured nor VA-guaranteed are referred to as *conventional mortgage loans*. Today, many conventional loans are guaranteed or insured by private mortgage insurance companies. The payments are calculated so that the loan is retired within an agreed-upon period of time. Often the lender also requires that the borrower add to each payment an amount equal to one-twelfth of the annual property insurance and property taxes.

Monthly principal plus interest payments get considerably smaller as the time period of the loan is extended. For example, a $1,000 amortized loan at 12 percent interest requires monthly payments of $14.35 if amortized in 10 years and $10.53 if amortized in 25 years. While these payments could be calculated using formulas, it is more convenient to use real estate loan amortization tables or computer software.

adjustable rate mortgage
a loan in which the interest rate varies with market conditions

A variation of the fixed-rate, amortized mortgage loan is the *adjustable rate mortgage* (ARM), also known as a variable rate mortgage. Instead of agreeing to, say, a 12 percent interest rate, the home buyer agrees to pay the "going rate," which is tied to some reference interest rate that changes with changing conditions in the money and capital markets. When market interest rates are rising, the home buyer expects to pay a higher interest rate on his or her mortgage loan, and vice versa.

Land Contracts

land contract
a contract for the sale of property in which the deed does not pass to the buyer until all terms have been met

In some cases when traditional financing is not available, a land contract is used to finance the purchase of real estate. A *land contract* is a

Interest rates on conventional new home mortgages were quite volatile during the first half of the 1980s but stabilized during the latter part of the decade. The Department of Housing and Urban Development (HUD) maintains a list of average annual yields on conventional mortgages that were reported in the *Federal Reserve Bulletin* as follows:

YEAR	INTEREST RATE	YEAR	INTEREST RATE
1980	13.95%	1986	10.07%
1981	16.52	1987	10.17
1982	15.79	1988	10.30
1983	13.43	1989	10.21
1984	13.80	1990	10.08
1985	12.28		

INTEREST RATES ON CONVENTIONAL MORTGAGES DURING THE 1980S

Rates for 1980 averaged slightly under 14 percent before reaching a peak of 16.5 percent for 1981. After that the rates declined dramatically in 1986 to about the 10 percent level and remained there for the rest of the decade.

contract for the sale of property in which the deed to the property does not pass from the seller to the buyer until the terms of the contract have been fulfilled. The contract generally provides for regular monthly payments of interest and part of the principal. If a buyer does not have a sufficient down payment to secure a mortgage, a land contract may represent the only available source of financing. In this way the buyer can build up enough equity to get standard mortgage financing, or to pay the full cost of the property. The advantage to the seller is that the property is sold, but the seller holds the deed to the property until the terms of the land contract have been fully met.

SAVINGS AND LOAN ASSOCIATIONS

After the first savings and loan association was established in the Philadelphia area in 1831, the movement spread to surrounding towns and cities and gradually to most of the eastern part of the country. Many of these early associations were called building and loan associations, and this name is still used by some associations today. After 1855, S&Ls were established in the Mississippi and Ohio valleys and also in Texas, California, and a few other states.

Between 1880 and 1890, S&Ls were chartered at a rapid rate in all sections of the country. Up to this time, all S&Ls were local institutions serving their immediate communities. Late in the century many national associations were chartered, often as promotional ventures for the benefit of the organizers. Many of these organizations were poorly managed and failed during the periods of depressed business activity between 1890 and 1901. As a result, several states passed laws that prevented national savings and loans from doing business in their states. Renewed development and interest in S&Ls came after 1920 and again after World War II. Today there are several thousand S&Ls operating over 10,000 branch offices in the United States.

An S&L may be established under a state charter or, since 1933, under a federal charter in accordance with the Homeowners Loan Act. At the end of 1988, about 52 percent had state charters. The average size of the federal associations was larger than that of the state associations, and they held 59 percent of total S&L assets.[2]

Regulation and Control

Regulation and control of S&Ls was conducted solely by state authorities prior to the early 1930s. Federal involvement began in 1932 with the passage of the Home Loan Bank Act, which created the Federal Home Loan Bank System. The FHLB System was structured along the lines of the Federal Reserve System. It had a governing board and twelve regional banks. Federal S&Ls were required to belong to the FHLB System. State-chartered S&Ls, life insurance companies, and savings banks could also join if they met the qualifications.

The Federal Home Loan Bank Board governed and regulated the FHLB System until recently. In response to the large number of savings and loan failures during the latter part of the 1980s, the Financial Institutions Reform, Recovery, and Enforcement Act (FIRREA) of 1989 was passed. This act retained the twelve regional Federal Home Loan Banks but abolished the FHLB Board and replaced it with the Office of Thrift Supervision (OTS). The OTS placed many failed savings institutions into its conservatorship program, and then they were turned over to the Resolution Trust Corporation (RTC) for the liquidation of remaining assets. All federally chartered and most state-chartered S&Ls are now insured up to $100,000 per account by the Savings Association Insurance Fund which is under the control of the Federal Deposit Insurance Corporation.

Usually five or more citizens may apply for an S&L charter. To obtain a state charter, they must demonstrate their fitness to receive it and the need for the services of the proposed S&L. To qualify for a federal charter, they must show: (1) the good character and responsibility of the applicants, (2) the necessity for such an institution in the community, (3) the reasonable probability of its usefulness and success,

2. *Savings Institutions Sourcebook* (Chicago: United States League of Savings Associations, 1989), 47.

and (4) that it can operate without undue advantage over properly conducted existing local thrift and home-financing institutions.

Organization and Operation

S&Ls are of two types—mutuals which are owned by the depositors and corporations owned by shareholders. Most of the associations with a federal charter are mutuals, and over 75 percent of all S&Ls are mutual companies. Fewer than 900 S&Ls have issued shares of stock and are controlled by shareholders. However, the trend is towards conversion from mutual to stock institutions as a popular method to increase capital.

Both savers and borrowers are members of mutual S&Ls. Since these associations are cooperatives, the savings put into them are shares of ownership, and payments on these shares are dividends, not interest. This distinguishes them from deposits in a commercial bank, which are liabilities of the bank.

In 1968 the Housing and Urban Development Act authorized federal S&Ls to call their savings accounts "deposits." This act also expanded the power of the Federal Home Loan Bank to authorize new forms of savings accounts and savings certificates for federal S&Ls. Regulations have changed periodically to provide for a variety of certificate accounts that pay higher rates of return than passbook accounts and have maturity restrictions and a minimum balance.

The Federal Home Loan Bank Board was given authority under the Interest Rate Adjustment Act passed in 1966 to set maximum interest rates on various types of S&L passbook accounts and savings certificates. However, as we previously discussed, passage of the 1980 Monetary Control Act substantially reduced the regulation of interest and dividend rate ceilings on deposits held at depository institutions. The Depository Institutions Deregulation Committee has since phased out rate ceilings on time and savings deposits. The Act further authorized S&Ls and the other depository institutions to offer negotiable order of withdrawal (NOW) accounts and automatic transfer service (ATS) accounts.

The primary source of funds available to S&Ls is savings deposits. Table 18.2 shows that at the end of 1989 savings deposits accounted for about 76 percent of total liabilities and net worth. Of even greater importance is the change in savings mix in recent years. The past emphasis on passbook savings has been replaced by rate-sensitive deposits such as money market accounts and large certificates of deposit (CDs), which now account for about two-thirds of all savings.

Federal Home Loan Bank advances, along with other borrowed money, ranks second in importance as a source of funds for S&Ls. Net worth represents a relatively small and declining portion of the total source of available funds. This is due in part to the fact that most S&Ls are organized as mutual associations. Therefore, general reserves set aside to protect savers against possible asset losses, plus undivided profits, account for most of the net worth. Other liabilities include accrued taxes payable and advance payments of taxes and insurance by borrowers.

Loans and Investments

Savings and loans specialize in conventional mortgage loans; they seldom make FHA-insured and VA-guaranteed mortgage loans. S&L assets are primarily made up of mortgage loans, as is shown in Table 18.2. Specifically, residential property loans of the one-to-four units type account for over three-fourths of the total dollar amount of mortgage loans held by S&Ls. The remaining loans, multi-unit residential properties and commercial properties, are roughly equal in size.

Many S&Ls make loans to finance the construction of new homes in addition to making mortgage loans on those already built. In recent years, however, shorter-term construction loans have represented only a small portion of their loans. Construction lending, which was done primarily by S&Ls during the 1950s, has been largely taken over by commercial banks and mortgage banking firms.

TABLE 18.2   Assets and Liabilities of Savings and Loan Associations (in Billions of Dollars)

	1985		1989	
	AMOUNT	PERCENT	AMOUNT	PERCENT
ASSETS				
Mortgage loans	$ 645.5	60.3%	$ 734.4	58.7%
Cash and investment securities	143.5	13.4	165.9	13.3
Mortgage-backed securities	115.5	10.8	170.7	13.7
Nonmortgage loans	60.7	5.7	90.9	7.3
Other assets	104.8	9.8	88.2	7.0
Total assets	$1,070.0	100.0%	$1,250.1	100.0%
LIABILITIES AND NET WORTH				
Savings deposits	$ 843.9	78.9%	$ 945.6	75.6%
FHLB and other advances	157.7	14.7	252.2	20.2
Other liabilities	21.7	2.0	27.5	2.2
Net worth	46.7	4.4	24.8	2.0
Total liabilities and net worth	$1,070.0	100.0%	$1,250.1	100.0%

Source: *Savings Institutions Sourcebook* and *Federal Reserve Bulletin.*

Cash and certain investment securities qualify as liquid assets for S&Ls under requirements established by the Federal Home Loan Bank Act of 1950. Liquidity ratios (legally acceptable liquid assets to savings deposits and short-term borrowings) can be set between 4 percent and 10 percent. The successor to the Federal Home Loan Bank Board, the Office of Thrift Supervision, specifies these ratios and determines the composition and maturity of assets that can be used to meet liquidity requirements. Thus, while S&Ls can legally hold many kinds of securities, most of them are short- to intermediate-term U.S. government and federal agency securities, bankers' acceptances, commercial bank time deposits, and relatively short-term state and municipal securities.

Other assets formerly included any other types of loans made by S&Ls. Then the 1980 act permitted federally chartered S&Ls to invest up to one-fifth of their assets in consumer loans, commercial paper, and corporate debt securities. Now nonmortgage loans have their own category and it has been growing over recent years. This is due in part to the increase in loans for purposes other than mortgages. These consumer loans have been largely mobile home loans, home improvement loans, and education and other loans secured by savings accounts.

COMMERCIAL BANKS

National banks were not permitted to loan money on real property as security under the National Banking Act of 1864, but some banks did so anyway. The Federal Reserve Act of 1913 allowed loans on farmland, and an amendment in 1916 provided for one-year loans on urban real estate. Later, much more liberal provisions for real estate loans were enacted, allowing national banks to make FHA and VA loans.

State banks have made loans on real estate mortgages almost from their beginning, helping to finance the westward movement of the population. State banking laws are much more liberal than national banking laws, with over half the states having no restrictions on the length of the loan or on the loan-to-value ratio. Those states that do have restrictions have more liberal provisions, as a rule, than those of the national banking acts.

The regulation, control, organization, and operation of commercial banks have been discussed in detail in previous chapters. However, commercial banks deserve some additional discussion since they represent the second most important supplier of mortgage funds. Table 18.3 shows selected assets and liabilities for commercial banks in recent years. Several observations can be made. Even though commercial banks are an important supplier of mortgage funds, real estate loan holdings accounted for only about 23 percent of total assets in 1989. The vast majority of mortgage loans made by commercial banks are of the conventional type rather than FHA or VA. In contrast with S&Ls, commercial banks have a relatively larger commitment in their mortgage loan portfolios to commercial property loans. Consumer loans and business loans (included in the other loans category) are also very important to banks. In terms of dollar amounts outstanding, commercial loans rank first, followed by real estate loans and then consumer loans.

In Chapter 8 we discussed the importance of hedging in successful financial management. Recall that this principle involves matching the average maturities of assets with the maturities of equity and liabilities. Table 18.3 shows that at the end of 1989 commercial banks held about 70 percent of their liabilities and capital in demand or time and savings deposits. These short- and intermediate-term liabilities are largely offset by cash and bank balances, large holdings of short-term U.S. government securities, and short- and intermediate-term consumer and business loans.

This has not traditionally been the case for S&Ls. Table 18.2 indicates that at the end of 1989, about 76 percent of total liabilities and net worth were held in the form of savings deposits, while long-term mortgage loans accounted for about 59 percent of total assets. Thus, while commercial banks are reasonably capable at practicing the hedging principle, S&L asset maturities still tend to be longer than the average maturities on their liabilities. As a result, various forms of U.S. governmental assistance to S&Ls have been necessary in the past.

TABLE 18.3
Assets and Liabilities of Commercial Banks (in Billions of Dollars)

	1985		1989	
	AMOUNT	PERCENT	AMOUNT	PERCENT
ASSETS				
Cash and bank balances	$ 213.3	8.6%	$ 258.0	7.9%
Securities investments	420.4	16.9	549.0	16.9
Real estate loans	423.7	17.1	758.3	23.3
Other loans	1,224.5	49.3	1,471.6	45.3
Other assets	201.9	8.1	212.7	6.6
Total assets	$2,483.8	100.0%	$3,249.6	100.0%
LIABILITIES AND CAPITAL				
Demand deposits	$ 536.9	21.6%	$ 641.5	19.7%
Time and savings deposits	1,235.6	49.7	1,626.0	50.0
Other liabilities	543.6	21.9	774.1	23.8
Capital accounts	167.7	6.8	208.0	6.5
Total liabilities and capital	$2,483.8	100.0%	$3,249.6	100.0%

Source: *Federal Reserve Bulletin.*

SAVINGS BANKS

Savings banks are an important source of real estate credit in certain areas of the country. Of almost 500 such banks in operation, practically all are in the New England states, New York, and New Jersey. This concentration can be traced back to 1812 when savings banks were organized in Boston and Philadelphia. Savings banks have always stressed thrift savings, safety of principal for their members, and real estate mortgage loans.

Savings banks are traditionally mutual organizations. They are managed by boards of trustees and are operated for the mutual benefit of their depositor-owners.

Regulation

Savings banks are all state chartered and thus are regulated by authorities in the states where they operate. Although there are no federal or national savings bank charters, they may elect to become members of the Federal Home Loan Bank System which would make them eligible to borrow from their region's FHL Bank. They can also elect to be insured like commercial banks under the Bank Insurance Fund (BIF), which is administered by the Federal Deposit Insurance Corporation. Approximately 70 percent of all savings banks have their savings deposits insured by the BIF. Virtually all others are insured under state programs.

State legal restrictions have historically been responsible for the lack of widespread distribution of savings banks throughout the United States. This is partly offset by the fact that several states now permit their savings banks to acquire or participate in mortgages made on properties located in other states.

Loans and Investments

As of 1989 about 78 percent of the total liabilities and reserves of savings banks were in the form of deposits, as shown in Table 18.4. These are largely short-term in nature. General reserves of approximately 8 percent of total liabilities and reserves are held as protection against possible asset losses.

As one might expect, changes in savings flows, particularly those associated with disintermediation (using withdrawn savings for alternative investments), have been of concern to savings banks. Savings banks that belong to the Federal Home Loan Bank System can take advantage of the System's credit facilities. Borrowing opportunities for maintaining liquidity are also provided by New York and Massachusetts to their state-chartered savings banks. Passage of the 1980 Monetary Control Act has helped reduce disintermediation through elimination

TABLE 18.4
Assets and Liabilities of Savings Banks (in Billions of Dollars)

	1985		1989	
	AMOUNT	PERCENT	AMOUNT	PERCENT
ASSETS				
Mortgage loans	$110.4	50.9%	$144.7	56.2%
Other loans	30.9	14.3	34.5	13.4
U.S. government and municipal securities	15.4	7.1	12.1	4.7
Corporate and other securities	40.8	18.8	46.0	17.9
Cash and other assets	19.3	8.9	20.2	7.8
Total assets	$216.8	100.0%	$257.5	100.0%
LIABILITIES AND RESERVES				
Deposits	$186.0	85.8%	$199.8	77.6%
Other liabilities	18.0	8.3	37.8	14.7
General reserve accounts	12.8	5.9	19.9	7.7
Total liabilities and reserves	$216.8	100.0%	$257.5	100.0%

Source: *Federal Reserve Bulletin.*

of savings rate ceilings and liquidity problems through access to the Federal Reserve's discount window, where loans are available at the Fed's discount rate.

Table 18.4 also shows that in 1989 mortgage loans accounted for about 56 percent of total assets. Well over half of savings bank mortgage loans are the one-to-four unit residential property type. They also commit a sizable portion of their funds to multi-unit and commercial property loans. In contrast with commercial banks and S&Ls, approximately one-third of the mortgage loans of savings banks are FHA-insured or VA-guaranteed. Nonmortgage loans by savings banks also have been growing rapidly.

In recent years savings banks have been putting a substantial portion of their funds into corporate and other securities, including those issued by foreign governments and multinational corporations. These are primarily purchases of corporate bonds with an increasing commitment to corporate stocks.

LIFE INSURANCE COMPANIES

The first private life insurance company was established in the colonies in 1759. Life insurance companies may be stock companies that are owned by their stockholders or mutual companies whose policyholders elect their boards of directors since there are no stockholders. Mutual life insurance companies began operating during the early 1840s. Life insurance companies have been lending substantial sums on real estate for over a century. In 1890 over 40 percent of their assets were in mortgages. This figure declined, especially after the crash of 1929, to as low as 15 percent. After increasing to about the 30 percent level, recent levels have been below 20 percent of total assets.

Life insurance companies, while an important supplier of mortgage funds, differ substantially from depository institutions. Unlike S&Ls and savings banks, they were not organized with the primary objective of meeting mortgage needs. Savings flows and resulting periods of inter-mediation and disintermediation are not as important to life insurance companies. Instead, their loans and investment policies are primar-ily determined by the receipt of premium payments from policyholders.

Regulation and Control

All life insurance companies are state chartered and thus regulated by state authorities, usually insurance commissions. The states regulate com-panies to whom they issue charters, as well as out-of-state life insurance companies that do business within their boundaries. Many states fol-low what is considered to be model legislation initially developed in New York. State laws often focus on setting detailed standards concerning the types of acceptable investments and the quality of such investments.

Corporate bond holdings are regulated as to type and quality, while common stocks are tightly restricted in terms of amount and quality. Life insurance companies are permitted to hold FHA and VA mortgage loans. They also hold conventional mortgage loans, on which maxi-mum loan-to-value ratios are generally set. Additional restrictions may also be placed on income-producing real estate investments.

Loans and Investments

Life insurance companies may be either stock companies or mutual organizations. Over 90 percent of the approximately 2,300 companies are stockholder owned. Mutual companies, which number less than 150, are generally much larger than stock companies and continue to hold over half of the life insurance industry's total assets.[3]

Life insurance companies are required by law to hold reserves to back the life, health, and annuity policies they write. The amount of these policy reserves is determined by actuarial calculations to assure that policy obligations can always be met. Policy reserves account for about 80 percent of total liabilities and surplus. Other obligations include policy dividend payments, funds set aside to meet next year's

3. *Life Insurance Fact Book* (Washington, DC: American Council of Life Insurance, 1989), 49–50.

policy dividends, incurred expenses, prepaid insurance premiums, and reserves to cover changes in security values. Surplus funds provide extra safeguards against unexpected developments, such as changes in mortality rates.

Table 18.5 shows that mortgage loans held by life insurance companies rank second only to their holdings of corporate bonds. Approximately 25 percent of the mortgages held by life insurance companies are farm mortgages, 1- to 4-unit home mortgages, or multi-unit mortgages; the remaining 75 percent are nonresidential properties. This latter group includes mortgages on office buildings and factories, shopping centers, and medical centers. In the 1950s, one- to four-unit residential mortgages accounted for over one-half of the total mortgages held by life insurance companies. Since then, these companies have been committing an increasing amount of funds to multifamily residential mortgages and business property mortgages.

Insurance companies make some mortgage loans directly through either the home office or branch offices. Most loans, however, are purchased from brokers, mortgage banking companies, or other institutions. This may be done through branch offices, by appointing a broker or mortgage banking company as a correspondent to bring loans to the attention of the insurance company's loan department or by buying mortgages in blocks from mortgage banking companies that have made the loans with the intention of selling the mortgages to permanent investors.

MORTGAGE MERCHANDISING AND FACILITATING

primary mortgage market
market where new real estate loans are negotiated

The mortgage market consists of three phases or areas of activity. The origination or creation of new mortgages is carried out in the **primary mortgage market**, which we have emphasized up to this point in the

TABLE 18.5   Assets of Life Insurance Companies (in Billions of Dollars)

	1985		1989	
	AMOUNT	**PERCENT**	**AMOUNT**	**PERCENT**
Government securities	$124.6	15.0%	$ 84.4	6.5%
Corporate bonds	296.8	36.0	642.4	49.3
Corporate stocks	77.5	9.4	135.0	10.4
Mortgages	171.8	20.8	246.3	18.9
Real estate owned	28.8	3.5	39.4	3.0
Other assets	126.4	15.3	155.8	11.9
Total	$825.9	100.0%	$1,303.3	100.0%

Source: *Life Insurance Fact Book* and *Federal Reserve Bulletin*.

chapter. Mortgage merchandising and services that facilitate financing represent the essential intermediate activities. In some instances, the originators of new mortgage loans are not necessarily the final investors or holders. Instead, they may act as agents and merchandise mortgages to investors. Several agencies and organizations also facilitate the mortgage financing process.

The third phase or activity area involves the **secondary mortgage market**, where real estate mortgages can be resold, thus providing some liquidity to mortgage holders. This area of the mortgage market will be discussed in the final sections of the chapter.

secondary mortgage market
market where real estate mortgages can be resold

Mortgage Banking Companies

The growth of mortgage banking companies is one of the developments that has created a national market for real estate mortgages. **Mortgage banking companies** not only negotiate the loans but continue to service them by collecting interest and principal payments for the mortgage owners. This requires facilities for receiving payments and for sending out notices of accounts due and past due. Servicing also includes making sure that proper insurance is carried and that all taxes are paid.

mortgage banking company
company that arranges real estate loans and often collects payments for the mortgage owners

Mortgage banking began with the introduction of FHA mortgage insurance in 1934. These companies initially concentrated their activities on FHA loans and later included VA loans, but they now also handle conventional loans. Mortgage banking companies are usually closely held private corporations. They have a relatively small capital investment compared with the volume of business they do, mostly utilizing short-term bank borrowing for the money to hold mortgages until they are placed with lenders.

Mortgage brokers differ from mortgage bankers. Mortgage brokers perform the loan origination function by bringing borrowers and lenders together, but, in contrast with mortgage banking companies, they generally do not service loans after delivery to the lenders.

mortgage broker
a firm or individual who originates real estate loans but does not service them

Real Estate Investment Trusts

A type of organization that grew rapidly during the 1968–1973 period was the **real estate investment trust**, known as REIT. They came into being in 1960 under the Real Estate Investment Trust Act, when Congress extended them the same exemption from double taxation that had been granted earlier to mutual funds if they distribute at least 90 percent of their income to shareholders. REITs engage in a variety of lending activities in the real estate field and some have taken equity positions in real estate projects. Most activity, however, is in financing construction, from land purchase through project completion. Then

real estate investment trust
a shareholder fund that is primarily engaged in financing real estate construction

the mortgages are often sold to more traditional lenders such as insurance companies.

In the past, REITs have relied heavily on commercial paper issues, lines of credit, and term loans from commercial banks for funds to finance their real estate loans. Therefore, REITs have been hit particularly hard during periods of tight money and high interest rates. These trusts have not been important suppliers of mortgage funds in recent years.

Facilitating Agencies

Several agencies are also involved in the process of mortgage financing. Professional *appraisers* make careful appraisals, or judgments of value, of all types of property based on such factors as location, the economic condition of the neighborhood, type of construction, and condition of the property. For FHA and VA loans, this is done by government appraisers.

Another facilitating agency, the *title company*, assures the purchaser of real estate, and the mortgagee who is loaning money on it, that the title to the property is clear. There are so many chances for defects in a title that checking the records has become a specialized activity. For a fee, title companies search the records and issue an opinion on the character of the title being examined.

The title to most land in the United States was originally held by a state or by the federal government. The land has gone through a series of title transfers, which are recorded in public record books in the order in which they occurred. The present title will be clear only if: (1) all titles in the series of sales were defined completely and accurately at the time a transfer was made, (2) all the required documents that might affect the title were properly recorded, and (3) all complicating factors—such as lawsuits over title—were properly handled.

There are very few titles about which there is absolutely no question, but most defects are minor and do not affect the transfer of title. Since it is impossible in most cases to be absolutely sure about a title, some companies now offer *title insurance*. They insure only titles that they believe from their examination are sound. The amount of insurance is stated in the policy and is usually for the full value of the property at the time the insurance is written. The premium is paid only once, when the policy is purchased.

Mortgage insurance was first developed by the federal government for FHA loans. In 1956 the Mortgage Guaranty Insurance Corporation (MGIC) was formed to provide insurance for conventional mortgages. The relatively low premiums charged by private insurers have contributed to a reduction in the volume of FHA-insured mortgages in recent years.

In the summer of 1974 a new facilitating agency was set up in the form of a computerized central information system for offers to buy and sell residential mortgage investments. It is called the *Automated Mortgage Market Information Network*, or AMMINET. It provides a central data bank on secondary mortgage markets useful to both buyers and sellers. It is not an exchange, but provides information to buyers and sellers who conduct their transactions privately, usually by telephone.

GOVERNMENTAL ASSISTANCE IN REAL ESTATE FINANCING

Several agencies of the federal government assist in the financing of residential real estate. Included under the new regulatory structure are the Office of Thrift Supervision and the twelve regional Federal Home Loan Banks. Other agencies include the Federal Housing Administration, the Federal National Mortgage Association, the Government National Mortgage Association, and the Federal Home Loan Mortgage Corporation. The Veterans Administration is also engaged in facilitating real estate financing through its program of loan guarantees under the GI Bill. And the Farmers Home Administration guarantees loans and makes some loans in rural areas.

Office of Thrift Supervision and the FHLB System

As we saw earlier in the chapter, the Home Loan Bank Act of 1932 established the Federal Home Loan Bank System which was comprised of a board and twelve regional Federal Home Loan Banks. The System's primary responsibility was to provide a central credit facility for its savings and loan association members.

However, this old structure was substantially changed with passage of the Financial Institutions Reform, Recovery, and Enforcement Act (FIRREA) of 1989. This act ended the FHLB Board and replaced it with the Office of Thrift Supervision (OTS), a part of the U.S. Treasury under the new regulatory structure. The OTS establishes S&L regulations, charters federal S&Ls, and supervises both federal and state-chartered S&Ls.

The twelve regional Federal Home Loan Banks, while retained under FIRREA, were placed under the management of a newly created agency called the Federal Housing Finance Board. Each of the twelve district banks is administered by a board of twelve directions, four of whom are appointed for terms of four years and eight of whom are elected by the members for terms of two years.

The funds for federal home loan banks are obtained from the proceeds of sales of their capital stock to members, retained earnings, sales of consolidated Federal Home Loan Bank obligations to the public, and deposits of surplus cash by member institutions.

The excess cash of a district federal home loan bank may be deposited with another of the district banks in the System. This is one means by which credit may be transferred from a region of surplus funds to an area where funds are needed.

The district banks make long-term or short-term advances to their member institutions on the security of members banks' home mortgages or the security of government bonds. These advances to members are particularly important during periods of disintermediation.

Under the old regulatory structure, all federally chartered and most state-chartered savings and loan associations were insured by the Federal Savings and Loan Insurance Corporation (FSLIC). FIRREA replaced the FSLIC with the Savings Association Insurance Fund (SAIF), which was placed under the control of the Federal Deposit Insurance Corporation (FDIC). The SAIF insures deposits of S&Ls and will manage the assets and liabilities of insolvent S&Ls after 1992.

FIRREA also provided for the establishment of the Resolution Trust Corporation (RTC), which is responsible for managing the assets and liabilities of S&Ls that became insolvent between 1989 and the end of 1992. Although the Resolution Trust Oversight Board oversees the RTC, it is managed by the Federal Deposit Insurance Corporation (FDIC). The RTC is to use funds raised by the Treasury and the Resolution Funding Corporation, which can issue long-term bonds to resolve S&L problems. The RTC will cease to operate by the end of 1996, when its responsibilities will be shifted to the SAIF.

Federal Housing Administration

The Federal Housing Administration was established under the provisions of the National Housing Act of 1934 for the purposes of stabilizing the mortgage market and making money available to finance both the construction of new homes and repairs and improvements to existing homes and other property. This organization was to accomplish its objectives through insuring certain loans made by private lending institutions.

The Federal Housing Administration currently operates under the jurisdiction of the Department of Housing and Urban Development (HUD). Its principal activity is insuring mortgages on both newly constructed and existing one-to-four-unit homes, authorized under Title II of the National Housing Act. All FHA loans are amortized loans. The payments include part of the principal, interest, a mortgage insurance premium of ½ percent, fire and other hazard insurance premiums, real property taxes, and any special assessments. Maximum interest rates were set by law until 1968, when the Secretary of the Department of Housing and Urban Development was authorized to set ceilings at levels to meet changing market conditions. The maximum maturity on FHA loans is now 30 to 35 years, but the Commissioner of the FHA may reduce it when desirable. The maximum loan-to-value ratio permitted is 97 percent of appraised value on the first $25,000 and 95 percent on the value over $25,000. On a $60,000 home, for example, the loan may be as high as $57,500 or nearly 96 percent of the appraised value. The current maximum FHA loan limit on single-family dwellings is $101,250. This maximum changes from time to time and varies from state to state.

The FHA is also authorized to insure mortgages on cooperative housing projects. The mortgagor must be a nonprofit housing corporation organized for the purpose of building homes for its members, who must occupy the dwellings. Special, more liberal provisions are made if such cooperative housing is for occupancy by elderly persons.

FHA insurance is also available to assist in financing the rehabilitation of existing housing, the replacement of slums with new housing, and the construction of housing for essential civilian employees of some defense installations. Insurance of property improvement loans is authorized under Title I of the National Housing Act. The FHA also insures mortgages on certain types of rental property both during and after construction. Beginning in 1965 the FHA was authorized to aid some housing in these special categories through interest rate subsidies, or contributions, and rent supplements.

Veterans Administration

The amended Servicemen's Readjustment Act of 1944 was passed by Congress to aid returning World War II veterans in the areas of housing, education, and employment training. One objective was to enable veterans to purchase homes without having to make down payments. This was accomplished by the Veterans Administration guaranteeing a percentage of mortgage loans made by private lending institutions to veterans. Congress sets and can change the maturities, interest rates, and maximum loan guarantees on VA mortgage loans.

The large surpluses of loanable funds at the end of World War II resulted in widespread participation in the VA loan guarantee program. As these funds were substantially reduced, however, the interest rate limitation set by Congress on such loans caused many lenders to be less willing to continue lending on this basis. In 1968 the interest rate ceiling was removed and the VA was given power to set the ceiling at levels that were competitive with other mortgage loans.

The Veterans Administration currently offers qualified veterans a guarantee on real estate loans of 40 percent of the loan or $36,000, whichever is the lesser. In 1991 the maximum amount for a VA loan with no down payment was $144,000. This maximum amount is changed from time to time by Congress.

Farmers Home Administration

The Farmers Home Administration is an agency of the Department of Agriculture which provides insured loans and some grants and direct financing for rural housing programs. To qualify, the real estate must be in a town of not more than 10,000 people and the family must show that credit is not available elsewhere. Most loans are made on an insured basis and then sold to private lenders. Guarantees are also available for loans on commercial and industrial property in small towns. Additional discussion is presented in Chapter 19.

SECONDARY MORTGAGE MARKET INSTITUTIONS

Secondary markets for stocks and bonds are well developed. The New York Stock Exchange, for example, began operating during the 1800s. In contrast, there was no organized secondary mortgage market and lack of liquidity was a real problem for mortgage lenders. While some legal provisions for its establishment date back to the 1930s, a well-developed secondary mortgage market did not really begin until the early 1970s. Three major institutions or organizations support and facilitate this market. These are the Federal National Mortgage Association, the Government National Mortgage Association, and the Federal Home Loan Mortgage Corporation.

Federal National Mortgage Association

Federal National Mortgage Association a corporation that buys and sells FHA and VA mortgages and mortgages under special housing programs

The **Federal National Mortgage Association** (FNMA or "Fannie Mae") was organized in 1938 as a part of the Reconstruction Finance Corporation and was later transferred to the Housing and Home Finance Agency. Its original purpose was to provide an additional market for the FHA-insured mortgages of lenders. In the postwar period its authority was broadened to include VA-guaranteed mortgages and mortgages under special housing programs, such as urban renewal projects, housing for the armed forces, cooperative dwellings, and housing for the elderly. The plan was to help to maintain a more stable construction industry by providing a reservoir of funds that would supplement the flow of mortgage money when it was low or drain off an excess flow at other times through the sale of mortgages previously purchased.

The FNMA accumulated a substantial portfolio of mortgages prior to World War II, but during the war this process was reversed because construction of new homes was largely stopped. Following the war, the Association again began to purchase large numbers of mortgages guaranteed by the VA or insured by the FHA. As credit became more difficult to obtain from private institutions after 1955, especially at the maximum rates established on FHA and VA loans, the FNMA greatly increased its activities.

FNMA has several sources of funds for its mortgage-buying activities. The principal source is debenture bonds that are sold to private investors and some notes that are also sold at a discount. A second source is preferred stock and a third is common stock.

The Housing and Urban Development Act of 1968 divided the FNMA into two organizations, one of which kept the original title and the other named the Government National Mortgage Association. The new FNMA is a government-sponsored private corporation that has taken over the secondary market operations in FHA and VA residential mortgages.

Government National Mortgage Association

The **Government National Mortgage Association** (GNMA or "Ginnie Mae") took over the functions of assisting in the financing of special areas and the management and liquidation operations of the portion of the FNMA portfolio acquired before 1954.

Government National Mortgage Association corporation that took over the FNMA secondary market operations, also deals in conventional loans, and operates a mortgage-backed securities program

The 1970 Emergency Home Finance Act also authorized it to operate as a secondary market for conventional loans. FNMA introduced the Free Market System Auction under which it deals in commitments to buy mortgages four or twelve months in the future. The amount of mortgages it will buy is announced; mortgage-holding institutions state the price at which they are willing to sell, thus allowing market forces to set the price.

GNMA has developed a highly successful mortgage-backed securities program involving the sale of pass-through securities backed by FHA and VA mortgage pools. GNMA guarantees the passing through to security holders the interest and principal payments from the mortgages held. This program has been very important to the development of an effective secondary mortgage market. In 1981, FNMA initiated a program of conventional mortgage-backed pass-through securities patterned after the GNMA pass-through securities.

GNMA and FNMA have at times cooperated in a special Tandem Program to absorb some of the risks in investing in mortgages. When interest rates rise, mortgages sell at a discount like all fixed-rate obligations. To cushion some of the risk in a period of rising interest rates, GNMA issues a commitment to purchase a mortgage at a fixed price. It is then sold to FNMA at the market price prevailing at the time of the sale, with GNMA absorbing any discount from the price paid to the seller.

Federal Home Loan Mortgage Corporation

The 1970 Emergency Home Finance Act also created the **Federal Home Loan Mortgage Corporation** (FHLMC or "Freddie Mac"). It was origi-

Federal Home Loan Mortgage Corporation corporation that deals primarily in the secondary market for conventional mortgages

nally an arm of the Federal Home Loan Bank and funded by a stock subscription of $100 billion purchased by the regional Federal Home Loan Banks. It is now under the control of the Resolution Trust Corporation and gets additional funding by issuing bonds backed by GNMA-guaranteed mortgages and by borrowing from the U.S. Treasury. FHLMC provides a secondary mortgage market for S&Ls and others by purchasing conventional, FHA, and VA mortgages and by participating in conventional loans. It also makes commitments for future purchases of mortgages and is a major seller of mortgages.

KEY TERMS

adjustable rate mortgage	land contract
amortized loan	mortgage
conventional mortgage loan	mortgage banking company
equity of redemption	mortgage broker
Federal Home Loan Mortgage Corporation	mortgagee
	mortgagor
Federal National Mortgage Association	primary mortgage market
	real estate investment trust
foreclosure	secondary mortgage market
Government National Mortgage Association	

DISCUSSION QUESTIONS

1. Discuss the relative importance of mortgage funds by type raised annually in the United States.
2. Indicate the importance of various financial institutions as suppliers of mortgage funds.
3. Describe a typical mortgage and explain its use in real estate financing. How does a mortgage differ from a deed of trust and a land contract?
4. Briefly describe the following real estate terms or concepts: (a) foreclosure procedure, (b) government guarantees, and (c) amortized loans.
5. How are S&Ls regulated and controlled?
6. Briefly describe the organization and operation of S&Ls today.
7. What is the role of commercial banks in real estate financing? How well do commercial banks and S&Ls practice the principle of hedging?

8. Discuss the role of savings banks in real estate financing and describe how their asset structures differ from those of savings and loan associations.

9. Describe the activities of life insurance companies as suppliers of mortgage funds by type of mortgage loan and relative to other asset holdings.

10. Identify and briefly describe several merchandising and facilitating agencies that play a role in the real estate field.

11. What is the role of the Federal Home Loan Bank System in assisting the process of financing real estate?

12. Briefly discuss the operations of the Federal Savings and Loan Insurance Corporation.

13. What are the home mortgage loan policies of the Federal Housing Administration and the Veterans Administration?

14. Discuss the functions of the Federal National Mortgage Association, the Government National Mortgage Association, and the Federal Home Loan Mortgage Corporation in terms of their secondary mortgage market activities.

PROBLEMS

1. Assume that you can qualify for an FHA mortgage loan on a home that is appraised at $87,000. What is the dollar amount of the maximum loan that you could obtain on the home? What would be the loan-to-value percentage? How would your answers have changed if the appraised value had been $100,000?

2. The Smiths are seeking a mortgage loan of $40,000 on a new house, while the Joneses would like a house with a $60,000 mortgage. If both can qualify for VA-guaranteed loans, indicate the dollar amount of guarantee in each case. What percentage of each mortgage loan would be guaranteed?

3. Obtain a current issue of the *Federal Reserve Bulletin*.
    a. Find data for the most recently available year on savings and loan association assets and liabilities. Compare these data with the amounts presented in Table 18.2. Comment on any major changes in percentage weights of assets and liabilities.
    b. Find recent asset and liability data for commercial banks. Compare these data against the amounts shown in Table 18.3 and comment on any changes in percentage weights of major components.
    c. Find recent asset and liability data for savings banks. Compare these data against the amounts shown in Table 18.4 and comment on any changes in percentage weights of major components.

d. Find recent asset data for life insurance companies. Compare these data against the amounts shown in Table 18.5 and comment on any changes in percentage weights of major components.

4. The Wright family is considering borrowing $125,000 in addition to their down payment from the Second National Bank to finance the purchase of a new home. The mortgage loan will be for 30 years and will require monthly payments.

    a. Use the Present and Future Value of an Annuity tool to determine the monthly mortgage payment (interest and principal) if the quoted annual interest rate is 11.25 percent.

    b. Next use the Loan Amortization tool to prepare a loan amortization schedule for this loan.

    c. Show how your answers in parts a. and b. would change if the annual interest rate were 10.63 percent.

SELF-TEST QUESTIONS

1. Which one of the following institutions, agencies, or companies represent the largest holder of mortgage debt?
    a. commercial banks
    b. savings institutions
    c. life insurance companies
    d. federal and related agencies

2. Which of the following identifies the parties involved in a real estate mortgage loan?
    a. mortgagor and mortgagee
    b. mortgagor and trustee
    c. mortgagee and trustor
    d. beneficiary, trustor, and trustee

3. Which one of the following asset categories represents the largest dollar value for savings and loan associations?
    a. cash and investment securities
    b. mortgage-backed securities
    c. mortgage loans
    d. nonmortgage loans

4. Which one of the following asset categories represents the largest dollar value for commercial banks?
    a. cash and bank balances
    b. securities investments

   c. real estate loans

   d. other loans (consumer, business, etc.)

5. The origination, or creation, of new mortgages is carried out in which of the following mortgage markets?

   a. primary mortgage market

   b. secondary mortgage market

   c. both the primary and secondary mortgage markets

   d. the third mortgage market

SELF-TEST PROBLEM

Assume that you qualify for an FHA mortgage loan on a home that is appraised at $75,000. What is the dollar amount of the maximum loan that you could obtain on the home? What would be the loan-to-value percentage?

SUGGESTED READINGS

Canner, Glenn, Charles A. Luckett, and Thomas Durkin. "Home Equity Lending." *Federal Reserve Bulletin* (May 1989): 333–344.

Curry, Timothy, and Mark Warshawsky. "Life Insurance Companies in a Changing Environment." *Federal Reserve Bulletin* (July 1986): 449–460.

Goodman, John L., Jr., and Charles A. Luckett. "Adjustable-Rate Financing in Mortgage and Consumer Credit Markets." *Federal Reserve Bulletin* (November 1985): 823–835.

Life Insurance Fact Book. Washington, DC: American Council of Life Insurance, published annually.

Savings Institutions Sourcebook. Chicago: United States League of Savings Associations, published annually.

Unger, Maurice A., and George R. Karvel. *Real Estate: Principles and Practices,* 9e. Cincinnati: South-Western Publishing Co., 1991.

Unger, Maurice A., and Ronald W. Melicher. *Real Estate Finance,* 3e. Cincinnati: South-Western Publishing Co., 1989.

ANSWERS TO SELF-TEST QUESTIONS   1. b   2. a   3. c   4. d   5. a

SOLUTION TO SELF-TEST PROBLEM

$25,000 × 0.97 = $24,250

  50,000 × 0.95 =   47,500

Maximum loan = $71,750

Loan-to-value percentage = $71,750/$75,000 = 95.7%

CHAPTER 19
Agriculture

After studying this chapter, you should be able to:
* Briefly describe the importance of finance to agriculture and the historical difficulties of farm financing.
* Discuss the nature of current agricultural problems and their impact on financing.
* Identify the sources of funds for agriculture.
* Describe the roles of the many governmental facilities established to finance farm purchase and operation.
* Describe the role of secondary mortgage markets in agricultural financing.

The rapid shift of the population of the United States to urban living since the turn of the century has been one of the results of an expanding industrial economy. Agriculture, with a decreasing proportion of the population devoted to it, has had to provide ever-increasing quantities of food and fibers to sustain a rapidly increasing population. Such production has been made possible by the more efficient utilization of land through the use of modern machinery, and by improved methods of storing and preserving farm products and of transporting them to population centers. Just as industrial productivity has increased due to scientific research and technological advances, agricultural production has also increased. Agriculture has, in fact, become increasingly businesslike.

AGRICULTURE AS A BUSINESS

The demands for greater productivity in agriculture have made it necessary for farmers to invest ever-increasing sums of capital in land, buildings, machinery, livestock, fertilizers, and general supplies. Because the typical farm in the United States remains a combination of home and business, operational funds must include the home as well.

As of year-end 1989, total assets invested in agriculture in the United States approximated $973 billion. Table 19.1 reveals the pattern of agricultural assets for selected years. Note that the machinery and motor vehicles category increased from 5.3 percent of total assets in 1945 to 8.3 percent in 1989. As a percentage of non-real estate physical assets, this item increased from 20 percent in 1945 to more than 38 percent in 1989. Such an increase reflects the increasing capital requirements for mechanization.

Methods of Engaging in Agriculture

The person who is intent on farming but has neither a farm nor sufficient capital to acquire one may work for others. Another alternative is to establish a partnership with one or more persons in order to

TABLE 19.1   Comparative Assets of U.S. Agriculture for January 1, 1945 and 1989 (in Billions of Dollars and in Percentages)

ASSETS	1945		1989	
PHYSICAL ASSETS				
Real estate	$ 61.0	59.3%	$703.0	72.3%
Non-real estate:				
Livestock	9.7	9.4	67.0	6.9
Machinery and motor vehicles	5.4	5.3	81.0	8.3
Crops stored on and off farms	6.3	6.1	22.0	2.2
Household furnishings and equipment	5.5	5.3	41.0	4.2
FINANCIAL ASSETS				
Deposits and currency	9.4	9.1	28.0	2.9
United States savings bonds	4.2	4.1	5.5	.6
Investments in cooperatives	1.4	1.4	25.5	2.6
Total assets	$102.9	100.0%	$973.0	100.0%

Source: *Economic Report of the President.* (Washington, DC: U. S. Government Printing Office, 1990), 408.

finance the purchase of farmland and equipment. Or land may be leased for farming, on the basis of either a fixed rental or a fixed proportion of the crops grown on the land. The latter method is generally referred to as sharecropping. Finally, the farmer may borrow. We are concerned here primarily with borrowing for agricultural production and the purchase of farm assets.

The Need for Credit

Although many farmers own their farms and have adequate financial resources, others are repaying debts during many years of their lives. This indebtedness arises from the purchase of land, machinery, livestock, and household needs. Indebtedness should not necessarily be avoided if a farm is to operate efficiently. The farmer who has the capacity and equipment to cultivate 120 acres but has only 80 acres of land may do well to acquire additional land with borrowed capital (if the land and loan costs are both reasonable). By the same token, the farmer with much land but little equipment may be wise to acquire equipment on credit in order that his land may be fully utilized.

The farmer who has financial resources sufficient only to carry the family through the year would be foolish to reduce crops because of a lack of cash to harvest them. The farmer would be expected to borrow prior to the harvest period in anticipation of expected income. Without ample credit, farms could no more function efficiently than could the business institutions of the nation. Farming, in fact, is simply another form of business activity, operating generally as a sole proprietorship. However, recently there has been a striking increase in the number of publicly held farm corporations.

PROBLEMS AND SPECIAL CONSIDERATIONS IN AGRICULTURAL FINANCING

Most farm production is highly seasonal in nature. Therefore, the farmer may receive the bulk of annual farming income within a few weeks during each year. It may be both necessary and profitable to borrow to meet the operational costs of farming, repaying the loan after the crops have been harvested. The traditional source of such financing for the farmer has been the commercial bank.

Banks in farming regions have at times found it difficult to adequately meet farmers' heavy seasonal demands for operating capital. In addition, the term of agricultural loans must be adjusted to the growing period of crops and livestock, a term that is generally longer than for a typical industrial loan. The small size of the average farm loan compared to industrial loans and the difficulty of appraising farm resources have resulted in bank interest charges being somewhat higher than those for industry. Also, the purchase of farmland requires a long amortization period, due to the uncertain year-to-year volume and value of agricultural production. Amortization periods as long as 40 years have been common.

Because of the complexities and difficulties of agricultural finance, there have been recurring complaints that agricultural financing is inadequate. This problem was recognized by the government as early as World War I. Since that time the government has sponsored several special agencies to address the special needs of farmers.

Farm Crisis in the 1980s

While the 1970s was considered a golden age in agriculture, the 1980s was a time of major distress. It not only became extremely difficult for many farm operators to obtain adequate financing, but it was also difficult to simply carry the burden of payments on loans taken out in past years. Newspaper accounts of farm bankruptcies and foreclosures appeared regularly, and the farm problem quickly became a political as well as an economic problem. It affected agricultural banks, grain and tool dealers, and the farm communities in general.

Rapidly rising prices and growing export markets of the 1970s had encouraged farm operators to expand operations both in acreage and in production. Vast indebtedness was undertaken both for the purchase of land at inflated prices and for increasingly expensive farm equipment. Unfortunately farm income to support such indebtedness did not keep pace. As a result, the value of farm land dropped sharply in 1985 along with a drop in commodity prices, while interest rates remained high. Since long-term farm borrowing is based on farm values, the ability to refinance or to take on additional debt was severely limited. The international competition for markets of food and fibers became intense as other nations increased agricultural productivity, adding to the decline in commodity prices. The prices of farm products were also influenced by political actions designed to bring pressure on foreign governments. The freeze on the sale of grain to Russia in the 1980s, for example, not only brought pressure on that country but on U.S. grain producers as well because it resulted in lower prices in domestic markets.

Recovery from Recession

The farm recession that began in 1981 lasted until 1987. The recovery was supported by heavy government spending on farm programs and a number of favorable market developments. Export sales of farm products increased both as a result of government subsidies, or financial aid, and the improved economic growth in key U.S. markets such as Asia

FINANCIAL STRESS AND FARM EXITS IN THE 1980S

During much of the 1980s, financial stress in agriculture was demonstrated by increased exits from farming because of bankruptcy, foreclosure, or other involuntary reasons. Between 1980 and 1988, an estimated 200,000 to 300,000 farm businesses failed, representing 8 to 12 percent of all farms at the beginning of the decade. Exits from farming in the 1980s were slowed by a variety of new federal and state programs and policies, many of which were specially introduced in response to the farm financial crisis. Farm numbers declined by 266,600 during the 1980s, compared with 1.7 million during the 1950s, 1 million during the 1960s, and 510,000 during the 1970s. When adjustments are made in farm numbers because of the 1973 change in farm definition, the average annual decline for 1980–89 was almost the same as for 1970–80.

Source: Stam, Jerome M., and Steven R. Koenig. *Agricultural Income and Finance—Situation and Outlook Report*, U.S. Department of Agriculture (February 1990): 27.

and Latin America. Farm income increased and farm debt was reduced by more than a quarter. Much of the debt reduction was borne by lenders, who wrote off many failed farms. As a result of the increase in farm income and reduction of debt and the historic financial restructuring of the 1980s, agriculture now appears to be on a solid foundation. Both farm assets and liabilities have adjusted to a more competitive worldwide agricultural market. With the recovery of land values and lower interest rates, farm financing has again taken on a more conventional form. In the following pages we shall describe the private and government-sponsored facilities for farm financing.

PRIVATE SOURCES OF FARM CREDIT

The sources of farm credit may be grouped broadly as private and public. Although most discussion of farm financing seems to center on the public agencies that serve that purpose, private sources still provide most of the non-real estate agricultural credit. Among the principal sources of agricultural credit are commercial banks, life insurance companies, individuals, merchants, and dealers.

Commercial Banks

Commercial banks in rural areas have been the primary source of short-term agricultural credit throughout our country's history. In addition, they provide a substantial amount of long-term farm mortgage credit. Unlike larger urban communities with many types of financial institutions, the small town in an agricultural area may have the commercial bank as its only financial institution. It is not surprising then that until 1970 commercial banks played the major role in agricultural financing. But with a changing regulatory environment and growing competition for loanable funds, the smaller rural banks may be less able to serve the agricultural community in the future.

Because their assets need to be highly liquid, the principal contribution of commercial banks to farm finance has been short-term loans for production and operating purposes. Short-term loans are generally based on the current earnings prospects of the farm rather than on land or equipment as mortgage collateral. The restrictions on national banks and many state-chartered commercial banks in connection with real estate lending have made long-term real-estate loans less suitable than short-term loans. As indicated by Table 19.2, in 1989 commercial banks provided only 11.3 percent of all real estate farm loans, but 21.1 percent of non-real estate farm loans.

Life Insurance Companies

For many years life insurance companies have been a significant source of long-term mortgage loans for the farmer. As shown in Table 19.2, they held approximately 6.5 percent of the farm real estate debt at the end of 1989. Yet, because of the huge resources of life insurance companies, farm mortgages represent but a small percentage of their total assets.

Since the objective of life insurance companies for most of their farm mortgage investments is safety and a modest yield, it is not surprising that their volume of long-term farm mortgage lending has lessened during periods of agricultural difficulties. Some financial

TABLE 19.2   Distribution of Farm Debt, Year-End 1989

| LENDERS | TYPE OF DEBT AS PERCENT OF TOTAL | | |
	REAL ESTATE	NON-REAL ESTATE	TOTAL
Commercial banks	11.3%	21.1%	32.4%
Farm Credit System	19.2	6.7	25.9
Farmers Home Administration	6.2	8.7	14.9
Life insurance companies	6.5	—	6.5
Individuals and others	11.6	8.7	20.3
Total	54.8%	45.2%	100.0%

Source: *Agricultural Income and Finance—Situation and Outlook Report*, U.S. Department of Agriculture (February 1990).

authorities believe, however, that insurance companies have been far more lenient toward distressed mortgagors than most other private mortgagees. Because life insurance companies emphasize safety in lending, they restrict farm mortgage loans to the better farming areas and to more profitable farms.

At present, long-term life insurance company loans to the farmer carry maturities of up to forty years, with varying repayment arrangements. In addition to an equal-payments amortization schedule, the payments may decrease in size from year to year, while in cases where it is expected that ability to repay will increase, the principal payments increase. The fact that insurance companies restrict their mortgage loans to the better risks makes it possible for them to charge lower interest rates than most other private farm mortgage lenders. The low interest rates together with the fact that prepayments (early payments) of principal are generally permitted without penalty make these loans very attractive to farmers.

The large insurance companies that have headquarters far from agricultural areas make farm loans through branch offices, local banks, or local loan agents. Branch offices in choice agricultural areas make high-grade, long-term farm loans. These branch offices, which are generally responsible to the home office, are staffed with personnel trained both in the mortgage loan field and in agriculture. Farmers needing loans are contacted by the insurance company's local underwriters, or casualty and property insurance underwriters who generally receive a finder's fee.

Individuals, Merchants, and Other Lenders

This group of lenders accounts for well over 20 percent of all short-and long-term agricultural loans. Loans from individuals generally arise out of a property sale in which the seller takes a mortgage to finance part of the sale price, or when the purchaser borrows from a friend or relative. There are various lending practices among individuals, but as a group they generally don't have the property appraised.

Merchants and dealers typically offer loans to purchase heavy farm equipment, such as tractors and combines. These loans permit systematic repayment over a period of time; lending agencies rely mainly on the collateral value of the equipment for their safety. While interest rates on equipment loans are usually quite high, many farmers are unable to secure financing through other channels and have no alternative. Merchants may also extend credit for such purchases as fertilizers, feed, other farm supplies, and the family's household needs.

"Other lenders" includes companies that make long-term farm mortgage loans with the express purpose of reselling them to institutional investors. Such mortgage companies may continue to service the loans by collecting the payments for a fee. Endowment funds of educational and other institutions sometimes invest in farm mortgages.

THE FARM CREDIT ADMINISTRATION

The Federal Farm Loan Act of 1916 gave rise to many governmental credit institutions established to aid the farmer. In 1933 most of these federal credit institutions were consolidated in the **Farm Credit Administration**, and others have been added since that time. The Farm Credit Administration functioned as an independent agency of the government until 1939, when it was placed under the control of the Department of Agriculture. Under the provisions of the Farm Credit Act of 1953, the Farm Credit Administration again became an independent agency in the executive branch of the government.

Farm Credit Administration
federal agency that supervises the system of farm credit banks, land bank associations, production credit associations, and banks for cooperatives

Farm Credit Banks

Eleven **farm credit banks** serve specific areas of the country. Their functions were carried out by the Farm Credit Administration's land banks and intermediate credit banks until 1987. Each farm credit bank is authorized to make 5- to 40-year loans secured by first mortgages on farm or rural real estate. Loans may not exceed 85 percent of the appraised market value of the real estate security, or 97 percent if the loan is guaranteed by a government agency. Farm credit banks are also authorized to provide short- and intermediate-term loans with maturities of up to ten years. They make loans to farmers, ranchers, rural homeowners, commercial fishermen, and certain farm-related businesses. The banks obtain the bulk of their loan funds by selling securities, called Consolidated Systemwide Bonds and Notes, through the Federal Farm Credit Banks Funding Corporation. Loans are channeled through voluntary borrower associations as described in the following pages.

farm credit banks
eleven federal banks throughout the country that make farm and farm-related loans

Federal Land Bank Associations

Farm credit bank loans are negotiated through **federal land bank associations**. These associations exist to provide the connection between the farmer and the credit bank and aid in the orderly and prompt consideration of loan applications. They are cooperative credit organizations composed of groups of farmers who assume certain responsibilities in order to provide a source of long-term farm mortgage credit for their community. The primary duties of federal land bank associations consist of assisting the farmer in determining loan needs, initiating the loan application, and servicing the loan by collecting payments, placing insurance, and in some cases disposing of property upon default.

federal land bank associations
cooperative credit organizations that arrange and administer long-term farm mortgage loans

Federal land bank associations are chartered and supervised by the Farm Credit Administration in accordance with the provisions of the Federal Farm Loan Act. They are usually organized on a community or county-wide basis. The stockholders of each association elect a board of directors, which in turn appoints a president, a secretary-treasurer, and a loan committee. The secretary-treasurer, who handles most of the administrative work, is not required to be a stockholder.

MEMBERSHIP

Each borrower is required to purchase association stock equal to 5 percent of the amount of the loan. A stockholder-borrower is entitled to one vote no matter the amount borrowed. Each loan a farm credit bank makes through a federal land bank association is guaranteed by the association. These guarantees can be made because the association is required to hold stock of its farm credit bank in an amount equal to 5 percent of total loans made through the association. Any mortgage losses are paid first out of dividends due; if losses exceed dividends, funds may be drawn from the stock held by the borrower-stockholders. This system of requiring a joint responsibility for all loans of an association by all borrowers results in a more careful selection of risks and a local control otherwise difficult to achieve.

FUNCTIONING

An example of a loan application and approval will illustrate the functioning of the farm credit bank system. Assume that a farmer applies for a loan of $50,000 for the purchase of land for agricultural use. The association's loan committee examines the application to establish a preliminary value of the property to be mortgaged and the acceptability of the applicant as a mortgagor. If the loan application is acceptable to the loan committee, it is presented to the board of directors. If acceptable to the board, the application is forwarded to the district's farm credit bank. The farm credit bank then has the property appraised by one of its own appraisers, a requirement established by the Federal Farm Loan Act. Since the maximum nonguaranteed loan-to-value ratio is 85 percent, the property must have an appraised value of at least $58,824.

If the appraiser submits a favorable report and the application is satisfactory in other respects, the loan is granted. When title to the property is cleared and transferred, the $50,000 is delivered to the federal land bank association. The association in turn brings together the parties to the transaction and delivers the money to the seller after the loan settlement arrangements are completed.

The farmer must purchase association stock in the amount of $2,500 (5 percent of $50,000). This amount in turn is paid by the association to the farm credit bank for stock. The farmer is liable, therefore, not only for the $50,000 but also for up to $2,500 for the loans of other members. If losses of the association have been very small, the farmer may redeem his stock when the loan is paid off. If the association has had large losses because of defaults, the borrower may recover only a part or none of the stock investment. Under the Federal Farm Loan Act, the contract interest rate on loans made through federal land bank associations cannot be more than 1 percent above the interest rate on the last series of bonds issued by the bank making the loans, except with the approval of the Governor of the Farm Credit Administration.

Production Credit Associations

The Farm Credit Administration is authorized to charter cooperative lending organizations, known as **production credit associations**, that make short-term agricultural loans to farmers and ranchers. Typically, the loans are used for breeding, raising, and fattening livestock and poultry; dairy production; growing, harvesting, and marketing crops; purchasing and repairing farm machinery; purchasing and repairing rural homes; and refinancing short-term debts. Associations now serve every rural county in the United States and Puerto Rico, as prescribed by the Farm Credit Administration.

production credit associations
cooperative lending organizations that make short-term loans to farmers

CAPITAL STOCK
Each production credit association has two classes of capital stock: nonvoting Class A and voting Class B. Class B stock may be owned only by borrowing farmers. The Class A stock, owned by the Farm Credit Administration, is preferred as to assets in case of liquidation of an association, but all stocks share proportionately in dividends. Borrowers are required to purchase an association's Class B stock in the amount of $5 for each $100 of loan. The stock may be retained and reused for future borrowing. As with members of the land bank associations, each borrower has one vote. Holders of Class B stock are required to sell their stock two years after the loan has been repaid if no new loan has been negotiated. The purpose of this limitation is to restrict control of the production credit association to active borrower members.

MANAGEMENT
Voting stockholders elect their association's board of directors at annual meetings. The board is generally composed of five members, each selected for three years beginning at different times. It is the responsibility of these directors to elect the association officers and appoint its employees.

SOURCES OF FUNDS
The production credit associations secure loan funds by borrowing from their district's farm credit bank. These loans are generally secured by the liens on crops, livestock, and equipment that the production credit

associations hold as a result of loans to their member borrowers. Interest is charged only on the amount of the loans actually outstanding.

Production credit associations also charge a loan service fee to cover the cost of appraising, reviewing, and administering the loans. Short-term credit secured from the production credit associations is often sufficient to cover a member's entire credit needs for a season or a year. Farmers draw down their loans as they need the money and repay them when they sell the products financed. By so doing, the number of days each dollar is borrowed is reduced and the interest paid is reduced accordingly.

Banks for Cooperatives

banks for cooperatives
banks that provide credit to agricultural cooperatives

For many years the federal government has encouraged the establishment of farmers' marketing and purchasing cooperatives. This has taken the form of immunity from the antitrust laws—laws passed to prevent business monopolies—offering tax advantages, and providing financial assistance. The provision of financial assistance is accomplished through a system of **banks for cooperatives**.

Under the provisions of the Farm Credit Act of 1933, the governor of the Farm Credit Administration chartered twelve district banks and one central bank in Washington, DC, to provide a permanent system of credit for farmers' cooperatives. The Agricultural Credit Act of 1987 initiated a proposal for the merger of these banks into a National Bank for Cooperatives. Ten of the district banks along with the Central Bank for Cooperatives voted for this merger. They formed the National Bank for Cooperatives, located in Denver, Colorado. Stockholders of the Springfield, Massachusetts and the St. Paul, Minnesota Banks for Cooperatives voted to remain independent.

FUNCTIONS
The banks make loans to cooperatives engaged in marketing agricultural products, purchasing farm supplies, and furnishing farm business services. To be eligible to borrow from a bank for cooperatives, a cooperative must be operated for the mutual benefit of its members. Farmers must act together in doing one or more of the following: (1) processing, preparing for market, handling, or marketing farm products; (2) purchasing, testing, grading, processing, distributing, or furnishing farm supplies; or (3) furnishing farm business services.

TYPES OF LOANS
Three types of loans are made to cooperatives: (1) short-term loans secured by appropriate commodities in storage; (2) operating capital loans to supplement the borrowing cooperatives' working capital; (3) loans to finance the cost of construction, to purchase or lease land, and

to purchase buildings, equipment, or other physical facilities. Although maturities of 20 years are permitted, in most cases they are for much shorter periods.

SECONDARY FARM MORTGAGE INSTITUTIONS

By definition, secondary mortgage institutions are those that do not deal directly with the public. Their activities support those institutions that do deal with the public. In the farm mortgage field there are two such institutions, the Federal Agricultural Mortgage Corporation and the Farm Credit System Assistance Board. These two secondary mortgage institutions exist to provide funds for other institutions of the Federal Credit System.

The first of these, the Federal Agricultural Mortgage Corporation, informally known as **Farmer Mac**, was created under the Agricultural Credit Act of 1987. It accomplishes its objective by guaranteeing the payment of interest and principal for pools, or groups, of qualified loans. Simply stated, farm mortgage lenders may sell their mortgage holdings to "pooling agencies." They in turn receive principal and interest guarantees on the mortgages. The poolers then sell securities backed by the collateral of the pooled mortgages to investors. In this way mortgage originators dealing with agricultural borrowers have access to a supplementary flow of funds to support their farm mortgage lending. Figure 19.1 shows the flow of money through Farmer Mac.

*Farmer Mac
the Federal Agricultural Mortgage Corporation which supports the secondary market for farm mortgages*

The second support institution, the Farm Credit System Assistance Board, was also created by the 1987 act. Its purpose is to provide financial assistance to troubled Farm Credit System institutions so they can continue providing credit at reasonable and competitive rates. This institution obtains its funds by selling 15-year bonds guaranteed by the U.S. Treasury.

OTHER FEDERAL AGRICULTURAL CREDIT FACILITIES

In recent years there has been a trend toward centralizing under the Farm Credit Administration the many sources of agricultural credit. However, several financial organizations operate directly under the control of the Secretary of Agriculture. Two of these are the Commodity Credit Corporation and the Farmers Home Administration.

Commodity Credit Corporation

The **Commodity Credit Corporation** was organized in 1933 to provide a more orderly and stable market for farm products. It makes loans and

*Commodity Credit Corporation
federal agency that supports prices of commodities and markets for them*

FIGURE 19.1   How Money Flows Through Farmer Mac

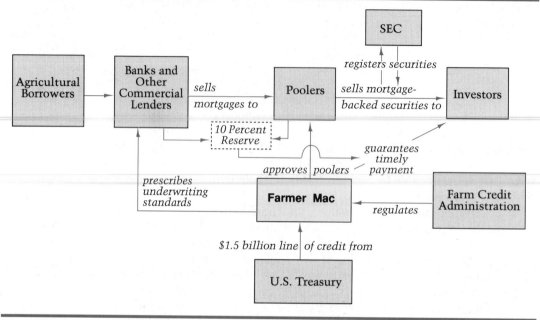

Source: U.S. Department of Agriculture.

loan guarantees to support the price of basic commodities such as wheat, tobacco, corn, and cotton. These commodities serve as collateral for the Corporation's loans. The maximum loan value on farm products is based on a percentage of "parity" prices—prices adjusted to allow farmers to maintain the purchasing power of a previous period—established at the beginning of each year. To qualify for a loan, the farmer must have complied with the governmental restriction on his acre allotment for the planting of that crop. A stated percentage of the parity value of the crop, which may be higher than the current market value, can be borrowed from the Commodity Credit Corporation. If the loan is not repaid, the government takes title to the farm products used as collateral for the loan. This amounts to a conditional purchase plan by the government to effect a price floor on farm products equal to the amount loaned on the basis of the collateral.

The Commodity Credit Corporation also supports farm prices through the direct purchase and storage of crops. It has participated in general supply programs in cooperation with other federal agencies, foreign governments, and international relief organizations. The $100 million capital of the Commodity Credit Corporation is provided entirely by the U.S. government. It is authorized to borrow an additional $30 billion from the government.

Farmers Home Administration

The *Farmers Home Administration* (FMHA) was created in 1946 by the merger of the Farm Security Administration and the Emergency Crop and Feed Loan Division of the Farm Credit Administration. It is authorized to make loans and to insure loans for farmers who are otherwise unable to obtain credit at suitable interest rates and maturities. The FHA makes loans for terms up to 40 years for purchasing, improving, or repairing farms and farm buildings. Preference is given to veterans to enable them to purchase farms.

Farmers Home Administration agency that makes and insures farm loans

The Farmers Home Administration is responsible for: (1) administering rural resettlement projects; (2) financing purchases of farm property by tenant farmers; (3) financing emergency loans to low-income farmers; and (4) financing loans to aid farmers' community and cooperative enterprises that are rehabilitation or resettlement projects. Loans of up to $200,000 are made for purchases of livestock, seed, fertilizer, farm equipment, supplies, and other farm needs, as well as for financing indebtedness and family subsistence. The loans have maturities of from 1 to 15 years. Farmers Home Administration loans plus other debts against the security property may not exceed $200,000. Borrowers may make advance payments in good years so they will be protected against falling behind in difficult years. Funds for the loans of the Farmers Home Administration are obtained from certain revolving loan funds and the sale of obligations to the Federal Financing Bank.

KEY TERMS

banks for cooperatives
Commodity Credit Corporation
Farm Credit Administration
Farmer Mac

farm credit banks
Farmers Home Administration
federal land bank associations
production credit associations

DISCUSSION QUESTIONS

1. Explain the increasing capital requirements of agricultural activities.
2. Farm financing is often described as being especially difficult. Explain the problems associated with it.
3. Discuss the importance of commercial bank lending for agricultural purposes. Do commercial banks provide credit for all agricultural purposes?

4. To what extent and for what purposes do life insurance companies provide funds for agriculture?
5. How do the life insurance companies of the nation maintain contact with farmers for purposes of extending mortgage loans?
6. Name some of the private sources of agricultural credit other than commercial banks and life insurance companies.
7. Describe the evolution and present structure of the principal governmental facilities for farm credit.
8. Trace the principal steps involved in a farm credit bank loan, from the original application by the farmer to the receipt of the loan.
9. Discuss the method by which the farm credit banks shift part of the risk of mortgage lending to other groups.
10. Discuss the sources of loan funds for the farm credit banks. To what extent are the obligations of these organizations liabilities of the federal government?
11. Describe the role of the production credit associations in agricultural financing.
12. For what purposes were the banks for cooperatives established?
13. Describe the purposes and operations of the Commodity Credit Corporation.
14. Outline the types of loans available to farmers through the Farmers Home Administration.
15. Describe the special problems of agriculture at the present time and how these problems impact on agricultural financing.

PROBLEMS

1. Having graduated recently from a well-known agricultural college, you are intent on a farming career. Your savings will permit you to purchase only about 40 acres of a 600-acre parcel now on the market in a good location. You are aware that "economies of scale" are such that 40 acres devoted to grain production (your special area of interest) are not adequate. You believe that at least 400 acres will be needed to justify the purchase of farm implements and other equipment. Furthermore, it will be necessary to finance seed and fertilizer as well as to meet other current operating expenses. Outline the types and sources of financing for these various needs.
2. You have returned from military service and are attempting to take up farming. The old homestead is in need of extensive repair, as are the various barns and sheds. You have exhausted your savings on the repairs and still need substantial funds for equipment, additional land next to your property, and working capital for general operating purposes. The local commercial bank is understandably reluctant to extend you credit since it now has a large volume of

overdue farm loans on its books. You seem to have no personal sources of credit available. Your situation is so difficult that you fail to qualify for credit through the voluntary associations of the farm credit bank of your district. What is your next step in attempting to establish a source of credit?

SELF-TEST QUESTIONS

1. Farm loans by insurance companies are characterized by:
   a. an emphasis on good quality loans and modest yields
   b. unusual terms and conditions
   c. generous terms and conditions
   d. short-term maturities

2. Farm credit bank loans are:
   a. limited to short-term loan maturities
   b. limited to long-term loan maturities
   c. extended directly to farmers and ranchers
   d. channeled through voluntary borrower associations

3. Borrowers from federal land bank associations:
   a. must purchase association stock
   b. must accept variable interest rate terms
   c. typically use loans for operating purposes
   d. must obtain third-party guarantees

4. Secondary farm mortgage institutions:
   a. deal only in second mortgages
   b. are served primarily by the Farmers Home Administration
   c. exist to provide support for lenders dealing with the public
   d. are among the oldest of the federal farm credit institutions

5. The Farmers Home Administration:
   a. makes only home loans to qualifying farmers
   b. is the basic source of funds for farm purchases
   c. may make or insure loans to farmers who are otherwise unable to obtain credit on reasonable terms
   d. came into existence during the depression of the 1930s

SELF-TEST PROBLEM

As a farmer or rancher in need of financing to acquire additional acreage, you have decided to explore the possibility of obtaining a loan

through the facilities of the farm credit bank of your district. To whom
do you make application and what are some of the terms and conditions to which you would be subject?

SUGGESTED READINGS

A Brief History of Farmers Home Administration, U.S. Department of Agriculture,
    (February 1986).
Agricultural Finance Review, published annually by the Agricultural Research Service,
    U.S. Department of Agriculture.
Annual Reports of the Farm Credit Administration.
Drabenstott, Mark, and Marvin Duncan. "Farm Credit Problems: The Policy Choices,"
    Economic Review, Federal Reserve Bank of Kansas City (March 1985): 3–16.
Drabenstott, Mark, and Alan D. Barkema. "U.S. Agriculture charts a new course for the
    1990s," *Economic Review*, Federal Reserve Bank of Kansas City (January/February
    1990): 33–49.
Smith, Allerton G. *The Farm Credit System.* New York: The First Boston Corporation,
    July 1988.

ANSWERS TO SELF-TEST QUESTIONS   1. a   2. d   3. a   4. c   5. c

SOLUTION TO SELF-TEST PROBLEM

Since you need financing to support land purchase, a long-term mortgage will be required. A local federal land bank association, which serves as the intermediary for farm
credit bank mortgage loans, should be contacted. Among other things, you will be told
that if you qualify for the loan the amount will be no greater than 85 percent of the
appraised value of the mortgaged property. Further, you will be required to purchase stock
in the federal land bank association in an amount equal to 5 percent of your loan. Current
interest rates will be quoted, possible maturities discussed, and other terms of the
proposed loan will be described.

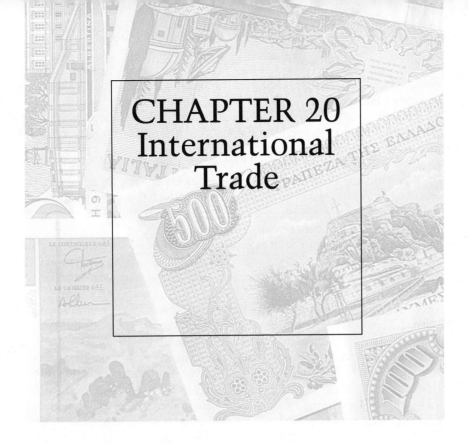

CHAPTER 20
International
Trade

After studying this chapter, you should be able to:
- Explain the importance of finance to the effective conduct of international commerce and investment.
- Describe how international payments are made.
- Describe the nature of foreign exchange markets.
- Discuss the effect of exchange rates on international trade and explain arbitrage and exchange quotations.
- Explain the role of financial managers of businesses in reducing foreign exchange risks.
- Describe how the banking systems of the world facilitate the financing of sales by exporters and purchases by importers.
- Show how the Export-Import Bank aids in financing international trade.

The productive capacity of the U.S. economy is the result of many factors, including vast natural resources, suitable weather conditions, and a population that has had the motivation and the ability to profit by these natural advantages. Of equal importance to the productive growth of the nation is a form of government that has encouraged individual effort. The government has made a major contribution in this respect by facilitating trade throughout the nation. Thus each geographical area can specialize in the activities for which its natural resources best equip it.

It is difficult to imagine the situation that would exist if each of the fifty states tried to be self-sufficient. Under these circumstances, the northern states would not enjoy citrus fruits. Floridians would not eat beef from Kansas, and houses in Oklahoma could not be built with lumber from the Northwest. Nor could we expect the tobacco-growing states to have modern farm machinery, since the market for large machines in a single state would not warrant production on a scale necessary for economical manufacture.

While these principles of specialization are obvious enough within the United States, it may be less easy to appreciate their application beyond the nation's borders. Yet what is true about specialization of effort within a nation holds true with equal force among nations. The very size of the United States might lead a person who is unfamiliar with the country's vast foreign trade to believe that the nation is nearly self-sufficient. It is true that many items that were formerly imported are now produced in our country, making us less dependent upon foreign sources. But there is an effective limit to the self-sufficiency that any nation can attain. For example, it would probably be impossible to produce enough coffee within the nation to satisfy the current domestic demand. In addition to the many items for which other nations possess a natural productive advantage, certain resources are simply not available within U.S. borders. Such things include tin, magnesium, and extracts from certain tropical plants used in the preparation of medicines. Although there may be legitimate reasons for stopping certain trade flows temporarily, or even permanently, it is undoubtedly true that specialization of effort on the part of the nations of the world benefits all of them.

The benefits of specialization depend on whether the persons or companies participating are assured of a market. Any market is effective only if adequate financial facilities exist to settle claims of indebtedness between the parties. The United States has developed a complex and smoothly operating system of finance to provide for the exchange of goods and services among persons and institutions. So, too, there is a system of international finance for settling international claims. It is this process of international claims settlement that this chapter explores.

INTERNATIONAL TRANSACTIONS

The U.S. dollar is important in international trade and can be easily converted into other currencies. Therefore, foreign exporters are usually quite willing to accept dollars in payment. In contrast to the

International finance appears to have developed as early as economic transactions took place. As far as can be determined, it began about 5000 years ago in Babylonian civilization in Mesopotamia, now known as Iraq. Historical information is obtained from writings on clay tablets and artifacts that have escaped weather and human destruction. The level of sophistication even at that time is surprising.

THE BEGINNINGS OF INTERNATIONAL FINANCE

Babylonian cities rose to importance as centers of trading between the Mediterranean and the East. Clay tablets contain references to financial accounts, drafts, contracts, letters of credit, credit money, and commodity money. The first institution engaged in international banking activity was probably the temple of Samas in the Babylonian city of Sippar. The temple had business as well as religious interests. It appears that whenever international trade developed, financial institutions came into existence and international bankers followed. Centers of international finance shifted to Athens around 500 B.C. and to Rome around 100 B.C. International economic activity and finance declined during the Dark Ages but revived during the commercial revolution that started around A.D. 1000.

Instruments and documents similar to those in use today were designed to control movement of cargo, insurance against losses, government requirements, and the transfer of funds. Financial centers shifted to the northern European cities during the 1500s, and in later years to London and New York.

Source: Fraser, Robert D. *International Banking And Finance*, 6th ed. Washington, DC: R & H Publishers, 1984. Chapter 2.

United States, importers in many countries must arrange payments in the currency of the exporter's country. The strength of the U.S. dollar makes it popular for the settlement of transactions among other countries as well as between the United States and foreign countries.

Payments by Individuals

In the United States, those who offer goods and services expect payment in dollars. Likewise, a U.S. citizen who orders leather goods from Mexico, glassware from Italy, or a year's subscription to the *London Times* may at times need to arrange payment in the appropriate foreign currency. When it is necessary or desirable to make a payment in the currency of another country, actual possession of that currency is unnecessary. In the situation of a U.S. resident subscribing to the *London Times*, the following example illustrates how this works.

If the person subscribing to the *Times* needs a claim for 250 pounds, she or he might find a British tourist willing to write a check against a bank in England for that amount. In return, the American would give the tourist the appropriate number of dollars, which the visitor could spend while touring this country. The subscriber would then send the check together with the order to England, where the check would be deposited for collection at the newspaper's bank.

To carry out this transaction with a tourist would be an awkward process, however. It is much more likely that the subscriber would go to a bank and, using dollars, buy a claim against British pounds sterling equivalent to the subscription cost of the paper. This claim is in the form of a bill of exchange, an order by telegraph, or similar instrument. Banks and foreign exchange brokers provide this service for a small fee. Although not all banks have foreign exchange departments, practically all have correspondent relations with banks that do offer the service. Hence, one can buy a foreign money claim at a local bank.

Banks that deal directly in foreign exchange may do so by maintaining monetary deposits in foreign banks, against which they may write drafts for sale to their home customers. In other cases, banks may operate branches in foreign countries, as authorized by the Federal Reserve. At year-end 1990 there were more than 700 foreign offices of U.S. banks. Likewise, foreign banking corporations have a network of contacts outside their countries. In addition to maintaining correspondent relations with U.S. banks, foreign banks are permitted to operate agencies and to set up subsidiaries in this country. These foreign banking corporations are not subject to any special U.S. restrictions.

Foreign Exchange Markets

foreign exchange markets electronic network that connects the major financial centers of the world

We ordinarily think of a market as a specific place or institution, but this is not always so. **Foreign exchange markets** are in reality electronic communication systems connecting the major financial centers of the world. When an individual or business firm engaged in a foreign transaction deals with a local bank, it is, in effect, dealing with the exchange markets of the world. Transactions throughout the world may be completed in only a few minutes by virtue of the effective communications network serving the various financial institutions, including central banks of every nation.

Exchange Rates

The conversion ratio or exchange rate, as it is generally referred to, is the rate at which a unit of foreign currency is quoted in terms of domestic currency. For example, if the British pound is quoted at $1.70 in the foreign exchange rate section of a newspaper, it means that purchases of claims on pounds sterling were made for $1.70 for one British pound.

Since the newspaper records the exchange ratio of large unit transfers within the foreign exchange market, an individual buying foreign currency claims would not get exactly the same ratio. The prices for an individual always favor the seller, who makes a margin of profit.

The balance in the foreign account of a U.S. bank is subject to constant drain as the bank sells claims to individuals who import goods or obtain services from other countries. These banks may reestablish a given deposit level in their correspondent banks either through selling dollar claims in the foreign countries concerned or by buying claims from another dealer in the foreign exchange. There are times when the volume of trading is strongly unbalanced, and this affects the exchange ratio. For example, the demand for claims against British pounds may be substantially greater than the corresponding demand by British businesses and individuals for U.S. dollars. Since the exchange ratio reflects the forces of supply and demand, such a situation would likely cause the dollar-to-pound ratio to rise above the dollar amount at which it had been trading. At some point, the dollars offered in exchange for pounds would become high enough to induce owners of pounds to invest in U.S. dollars.

Like the prices of all commodities, exchange rates vary, although the degree of change is generally not large over a short period of time. Changes of a few cents may be noticed in weekly comparisons of the exchange ratios of foreign currencies with dollars. Varying exchange rates may financially benefit or hurt the importer or exporter in much the same manner as changes in commodity price levels. Although changes from day to day are usually small, devaluations, political crises, wars, and other major events may give rise to wide swings in exchange rates over short periods of time. Foreign exchange rates between the United States and 31 other countries of the world as of February, 1991 are shown in Table 20.1.

ARBITRAGE

Arbitrage is the simultaneous, or nearly simultaneous, purchasing of commodities, securities, or bills of exchange in one market and selling them in another where the price is higher. In international exchange, variations in quotations between countries at any time are quickly brought into alignment through the arbitrage activities of international financiers. For example, if the exchange rate in New York was reported at £1 = $1.71 and in London the rate was quoted at £1 = $1.70, alert international arbitragers would simultaneously sell claims to British pounds in New York at the rate of $1.71 and have London correspondents sell claims on U.S. dollars in London at the rate of $1.70 for each pound sterling. Such arbitrage would be profitable only when dealing in large sums. If an arbitrager, under these circumstances, sold a claim on £100 million in New York, $171 million would be received. The corre-

arbitrage
buying commodities, securities, or bills of exchange in one market and immediately selling them in another to make a profit from price differences in the two markets

sponding sale of claims on American dollars in London would be at the rate of £100 million for $170 million. Hence, a profit of $1 million would be realized on the transaction. A quotation differential of as little as one sixteenth of one cent may be sufficient to encourage arbitrage activities.

The ultimate effect of large-scale arbitrage activities on exchange rates is the elimination of the variation between the two markets. The sale of large amounts of claims to American dollars in London would drive the price for pounds sterling up, and in New York the sale of claims to pounds sterling would force the exchange rate down.

QUOTATION VARIANCE AMONG INSTRUMENTS

If you ask at the local bank about the exchange rate for a foreign currency, you will generally be given a banker's sight draft rate. A *banker's sight draft*, or banker's check as it is commonly called, differs from the common bank check only in that it is drawn by one bank on another bank. When the draft is presented for payment at the foreign bank, the balance of the drawing bank is reduced. Several days or weeks may elapse between the time the check is issued by the bank and the time it is presented for payment at the foreign bank or foreign correspondent bank. During this interval, the foreign balance of the issuing bank is not affected by the transaction.

TABLE 20.1   Foreign Exchange Rates, February 1991

COUNTRY	U.S. DOLLAR EQUIVALENT	COUNTRY	U.S. DOLLAR EQUIVALENT
Australia (Dollar)	.7835	Malaysia (Ringgit)	.0270
Austria (Schilling)	.1042	Netherlands (Guilder)	.0167
Belgium (Franc)	.3048	New Zealand (Dollar)	.6012
Brazil (Cruzado)	.4590	Norway (Krone)	.0579
Canada (Dollar)	.0116	Portugal (Escudo)	1.3045
China (Yuan)	.0524	Singapore (Dollar)	.0172
Denmark (Krone)	.0570	South Africa (Rand)	.0254
Finland (Markka)	.0359	South Korea (Won)	7.2397
France (Franc)	.0504	Spain (Peseta)	.9261
Germany (Deutsche Mark)	.0148	Sri Lanka (Rupee)	.4060
Greece (Drachma)	1.5882	Sweden (Krona)	.0555
Hong Kong (Dollar)	.0779	Switzerland (Franc)	.0127
India (Rupee)	.1886	Taiwan (Dollar)	.2711
Ireland (Punt)	1.7981	Thailand (Baht)	.2514
Italy (Lira)	11.1119	United Kingdom (Pound)	1.9641
Japan (Yen)	1.3054		

Source: *Federal Reserve Bulletin* (April 1991): A69.

If requested, the quotation may be based on a cable rate. The bank may cable a certain amount of money to its foreign correspondent or branch to credit to the account of a specified individual or business. The cost of a cable order is more than a banker's check because it reduces the balance of the bank's foreign deposit almost immediately. A reduction in deposits reduces the earnings that would otherwise result from the investment of the deposits—another example of the time value of money.

The *banker's time draft* provides a rate that is lower than either the banker's sight draft or cable rate. This instrument, sometimes called long exchange or a long bill, is payable at a specified future date, usually thirty days or some multiple thereof. The quotations on these time drafts are, of course, lower because they reduce the balance of the foreign branch or correspondent only after a specified period of time.

BUSINESS MANAGEMENT OF FOREIGN EXCHANGE

The firm that has foreign sales must concern itself with the stability of the governments and changing values of currency in the countries in which it does business, with commodity price changes, and other uncertainties related to monetary systems.

Large firms usually have special departments that handle international transactions. These firms may engage in foreign exchange speculation as opportunities arise, but risk reduction is their primary goal. Among the possible actions of skilled foreign exchange specialists are hedging, adjusting accounts receivable and payable procedures, cash management, and borrowing and lending activities. Existing or anticipated variations in the value of the foreign currencies guide all of these actions. For example, a seller with a claim for payment within 90 days may anticipate a possible decline in the currency value of his customer's country. The seller can hedge by entering into a "futures contract" for the delivery of that currency at the existing exchange rate on the day of the contract. By so doing, a loss in the collection process is offset by a gain in the delivery process 90 days hence. The fee for the futures contract becomes a cost of the transaction.

Large multinational companies enjoy special opportunities for risk reduction and speculation since they can move cash balances from one country to another as monetary conditions warrant. For example, if a decline in the value of a particular currency is expected, cash in the branch in that country may be moved back to the U.S. Or, a firm may borrow funds in a foreign market and move them immediately to the U.S. (or to another country) with the expectation of repaying the loan at a reduced exchange rate. This is speculation rather than a risk reduction activity. An expected decline in a currency may lead to an attempt to accelerate collection of accounts receivable, with funds transferred quickly to another country. Payments on accounts payable may be delayed in the expectation of a decline in exchange rates. If, on the other hand, a foreign currency is expected to increase in relative value, the preceding actions would be reversed. In the following sections we describe the various instruments of foreign exchange and their uses.

FINANCING INTERNATIONAL TRADE

One of the substantial financial burdens of any industrial firm is the process of manufacture itself. When a U.S. manufacturer exports goods to distant places such as India or Australia, funds are tied up not only for the period of manufacture but also for a lengthy period of transportation. In order to reduce costs, manufacturers may require the foreign importer to pay for the goods as soon as they are on the way to their destination. In this way, a substantial financial burden is transferred to the importer.

Financing by the Exporter

If the exporter has confidence in foreign customers and is in a financial position to sell to them on open-book account, then sales arrangements should operate very much as in domestic trade, subject, of course, to the complex nature of any international transaction.

SIGHT AND TIME DRAFTS

draft (bill of exchange)
an unconditional order for the payment of money from one person to another

As an alternative to shipping merchandise on open-account financing, the exporter may use a collection draft. A **draft**, or **bill of exchange**, is an unconditional written order, signed by the party drawing it, requiring the party to whom it is addressed to pay a certain sum of money to order or to bearer. A draft may require immediate payment by the importer upon its presentation—on demand—or it may require only acceptance on the part of the importer, providing for payment at a specified future time. Instruments requiring immediate payment are classified as **sight drafts**; those requiring payment later are **time drafts**. Drafts may require remittance, or payment, in the currency of the country of the exporter or of the importer, depending upon the transaction's terms. An example of a sight draft form is shown in Figure 20.1

sight draft
draft requiring immediate payment

time draft
draft that is payable at a specified future date

documentary draft
draft that is accompanied by an order bill of lading and other documents

Drafts may be either documentary or clean. A **documentary draft** is accompanied by an order bill of lading and other papers such as insurance receipts, certificates of sanitation, and consular invoices. The **order bill of lading** represents the written acceptance of goods for shipment by a transportation company and the terms under which the goods are to be transported to their destination. In addition, the order

order bill of lading
document given by a transportation company that lists goods to be transported and terms of the shipping agreement

FIGURE 20.1 Sight Draft or Bill of Exchange

$2,500.00 New Orleans, Louisiana, August 15, 19 --

At sight - PAY TO THE

ORDER OF Mervin J. Mansfield

Two thousand five hundred no/100 - - - - - - - - - - - - - - - - DOLLARS

VALUE RECEIVED AND CHARGE TO ACCOUNT OF

TO Brazilian Import Company
No. 11678 Rio de Janeiro, Brazil

NEW ORLEANS EXPORT COMPANY
Theresa M. Jones

bill of lading carries title to the merchandise being shipped, and only its holder may claim the merchandise from the transportation company. (See Figure 20.2.) The documentary sight draft is generally referred to as a D/P draft (documentary payments draft), while the documentary time draft is referred to as a D/A draft (documentary acceptance draft).

A ***clean draft*** is one that is not accompanied by any special documents and is generally used when the exporter has confidence in the importer's ability to meet the draft when presented. Once the merchandise is shipped to the importer, it is delivered by the transportation company regardless of any action taken by the importer concerning the draft.

clean draft
a draft that is not accompanied by any special documents

BANK ASSISTANCE IN THE COLLECTION OF DRAFTS

An importer will generally try to avoid paying for a purchase before the goods are actually shipped because several days or perhaps weeks may elapse before the goods arrive. But the exporter is often unwilling to send the draft and documents directly to the importer. Therefore, the exporter usually works through a commercial bank.

A New York exporter dealing with an importer in Portugal with whom there has been little past experience may ship goods on the basis of a documentary draft that has been deposited for collection with the local bank. That bank, following the specific instructions regarding the manner of collection, then forwards the draft and the accompanying documents to its correspondent bank in Lisbon. The correspondent bank holds the documents until payment is made in the case of a sight draft, or until acceptance is obtained if a time draft is used. When collection is made on a sight draft, it is remitted to the exporter.

FINANCING THROUGH THE EXPORTER'S BANK

It is important to recognize that throughout the preceding transaction the banking system only provided a service to the exporter and in no

FIGURE 20.2   Order Bill of Lading

UNITED STATES LINES CO.		
(SPACES IMMEDIATELY BELOW FOR SHIPPERS MEMORANDA – NOT PART OF BILL OF LADING)		

FORWARDING AGENT – REFERENCES
John Doe Shipping Co., #E6776 F.M.B. #9786

EXPORT DEC. No.
X67-90687

DELIVERING CARRIER TO STEAMER:
Penn Central Company

CAR NUMBER – REFERENCE
876528

BILL OF LADING
(SHORT FORM)

(NOT NEGOTIABLE UNLESS CONSIGNED "TO ORDER")

SHIP   American Banker   FLAG
PORT OF DISCHARGE FROM SHIP Liverpool   AM.
(Where goods are to be delivered
to consignee or On-carrier)
If goods to be transhipped beyond Port of Discharge, show destination   Here ►► To

PIER
61 N.R.
THROUGH BILL OF LADING

PORT OF LOADING
NEW YORK

SHIPPER   Midwest Printing Company

CONSIGNED TO: ORDER OF   M.T. Wilson & Co.

ADDRESS ARRIVAL NOTICE TO   Same at 15 Dock St., Liverpool, E.C. 3

PARTICULARS FURNISHED BY SHIPPER OF GOODS

MARKS AND NUMBERS	NO. OF PKGS.	DESCRIPTION OF PACKAGES AND GOODS	MEASUREMENT	GROSS WEIGHT IN POUNDS
M. T. W. & Co. Liverpool	56	Books		10,145
		SPECIMEN		

FREIGHT PAYABLE IN   NEW YORK

(10,145) @ ____ PER 2240 LBS.... $ ____
_____ @ ____ PER 100 LBS.... $ ____
_____ FT. @ ____ PER 40 CU. FT... $ ____
545 FT. @ $1.05 PER CU. FT. ...... $ 572 | 25
_____ $ ____
_____ $ ____
_____ $ ____
_____ $ ____
TOTAL .... $ ____

(TERMS OF THIS BILL OF LADING CONTINUED FROM REVERSE SIDE HEREOF)
IN WITNESS WHEREOF,
THE MASTER OR AGENT OF SAID VESSEL HAS SIGNED 3
BILLS OF LADING, ALL OF THE SAME TENOR AND DATE, ONE OF WHICH
BEING ACCOMPLISHED, THE OTHERS TO STAND VOID.

UNITED STATES LINES COMPANY
BY_____ J.H.
FOR THE MASTER
B/L No.   ISSUED AT NEW YORK, N. Y.
M-105

January   12   19--
MO.   DAY   YEAR

way financed the transaction itself. The exporter's bank, however, may offer financing assistance by allowing the exporter to borrow against the security of a documentary draft. Such loans have the financial strength of both the exporter and the importer to support them, since documents for taking possession of the merchandise are released only after the importer has accepted the draft.

The amount that the exporter can borrow is less than the face amount of the draft and depends mainly on the credit standing of both the exporter and the importer. When the exporter is financially strong enough to offer suitable protection to the bank, a substantial percentage of the draft may be advanced even though the importer may not be known to the exporter's bank. In other cases, the advance may be based on the importer's financial strength.

The character of the goods shipped also has an important bearing on the amount loaned, since the goods offer collateral security for the advance. Goods that are not breakable or perishable are better as collateral. And goods for which there is a ready market are preferable to those with a very limited market.

Financing by the Importer

Like the exporter, the importer may also arrange payment for goods without access to bank credit. When an order is placed, payment in full may be made or a partial payment offered. The partial payment gives some protection to both the exporter and the importer. It protects the exporter against rejection of the goods for no reason. And it gives the importer some bargaining power in the event the merchandise is damaged in shipment or does not meet specifications. When the importer is required to make full payment with an order but wants some protection in the transaction, payment is sent to a bank in the exporter's country. The bank is instructed not to release payment until certain documents are presented to the bank to prove shipment of the goods according to the terms of the transaction. The bank, of course, charges a fee for this service.

FINANCING THROUGH THE IMPORTER'S BANK

In foreign trade, because of language barriers and the difficulty in obtaining credit information about companies in foreign countries, the use of the *banker's acceptance* is common. The banker's acceptance is a draft drawn on and accepted by a bank rather than the importing firm. An example of a banker's acceptance is shown in Figure 20.3. The importer must, of course, make arrangements with the bank in advance. The exporter, too, must know before shipment is made whether or not the bank in question has agreed to accept the draft. This arrangement is facilitated by the use of a **commercial letter of credit**. It is a bank's written statement to an individual or firm guaranteeing acceptance and payment of a draft up to a specified sum if the draft is presented according to the terms of the letter. (See Figure 20.4).

commercial letter of credit
statement by a bank guaranteeing acceptance and payment of a draft up to a stated amount

IMPORTER BANK FINANCING—AN EXAMPLE

The issue of a commercial letter of credit and its use in international finance is shown in this example. The owner of a small exclusive shop

FIGURE 20.3 Banker's Acceptance

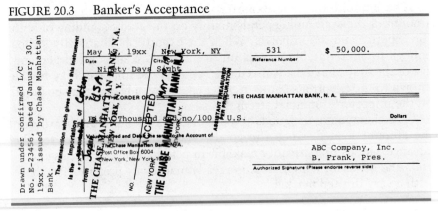

Courtesy The Chase Manhattan Bank, N.A.

in Chicago wishes to import expensive perfumes from Paris. Although the shop is well known locally, its financial reputation is not known widely enough to permit it to purchase from foreign exporters on the basis of an open-book account or drafts drawn on the firm. Under these circumstances the firm would substitute the bank's credit for its own through the use of a letter of credit. Upon application by the firm, the bank issues the letter if it is entirely satisfied that its customer is in a satisfactory financial condition.

The letter of credit is addressed to the French exporter of perfumes. The exporter, upon receipt of the commercial letter of credit, would not be concerned about making the shipment. Although the exporter may not have heard of the Chicago firm, the bank issuing the commercial letter of credit may be known to the exporter or to his bank. (International bank directories provide bank credit information.) The French exporter then ships the perfumes and at the same time draws a draft in the appropriate amount on the bank that issued the letter of credit. The draft and the other papers required by the commercial letter of credit are presented to the exporter's bank. The bank sends the draft and the accompanying documents to its New York correspondent, who forwards them to the importer's bank in Chicago. The importer's bank makes a thorough inspection of the various papers that accompany the draft to make sure that all provisions of the letter of credit have been met. If the bank is satisfied that the terms have been met, the draft is accepted and the appropriate bank officials sign it. The accepted draft, now a banker's acceptance, may be held until maturity by the accepting bank or returned to the exporter on request. If the acceptance is returned to the exporter, it may be held until maturity and sent to the accepting bank for settlement, or it may be sold to other investors. An active market for bankers' acceptances exists in the world's money centers.

FIGURE 20.4   Irrevocable Commercial Letter of Credit

| Irrevocable Commercial Letter Of Credit | The Chase Manhattan Bank, N.A. P.O. Box 6004, Church Street Station New York, New York 10249 | ⬛ CHASE | Cable Address: Chamanbank | Letter Of Credit Division |

May 2, 19-- $50,000.

Drafts drawn hereunder must be marked:
"Drawn under the Chase Manhattan Bank, N.A., New York,
L/C Ref. E-23456   and indicate the date hereof."

ABC Company, Inc.

B. Frank, President

SPECIMEN

Gentlemen:
We hereby authorize you to draw on The Chase Manhattan Bank, N.A., New York City

by order of J. R. Doe & Company, New York, N.Y.

and for account of   J. R. Doe & Company

up to an aggregate amount of Fifty Thousand Dollars U.S. Currency

available by your drafts at 90 days sight, for full invoice value, in duplicate
accompanied by   Commercial Invoice in triplicate . . .
                 Consular Invoice in duplicate . . . .
                 Full set of onboard Bills of Lading to order of The
Chase Manhattan Bank, New York, marked Notify J. R. Doe & Company, New York,
N. Y., and bearing a separate onboard endorsement signed by the Master and
also marked freight collect at port of destination . . . . .

Relating to shipment of Cotton.

. . . Any charges for negotiation of the draft(s) are for your account.
. . . Marine and war risk insurance covered by buyers.

Drafts must be drawn and negotiated not later than October 2, 19--

The amounts thereof must be endorsed on this Letter Of Credit.
We hereby agree with the drawers, endorsers, and bonafide holders of all drafts drawn under and in compliance
with the terms of this credit, that such drafts will be duly honored upon presentation to the drawee.
This letter of credit is subject to the Uniform Customs and Practice for Documentary Credits (1974 Revision) International Chamber Of Commerce Publication No. 290.

Yours very truly,

D.E. Price

D. E. Price
Vice President

Authorized Signature

Courtesy The Chase Manhattan Bank, N.A.

After having accepted the draft, the Chicago bank notifies its customer that it has the shipping documents and that arrangements should be made to take them over. As the shop sells the perfume, it builds up its bank account with daily deposits until they are sufficient to retire the acceptance. The bank can then meet its obligation on the acceptance without having advanced its other funds at any time.

In releasing shipping documents to a customer, some banks prefer to establish an agency arrangement between the firm and the bank whereby the bank retains title to the merchandise. The instrument that provides for this is called a **trust receipt.** Should the business fail, the bank would not be in the position of an ordinary creditor trying to establish its claim on the business assets. Rather, it could repossess, or take back, the goods and place them with another agent for sale since title had never been transferred to the customer. As the merchandise is sold under a trust receipt arrangement, generally the business must deposit the proceeds with the bank until the total amount of the acceptance is reached.

trust receipt
an instrument through which a bank retains title to goods until they are paid for

In summary, the banker's acceptance and the commercial letter of credit involve four principal parties: the importer, the importer's bank, the exporter, and the exporter's bank. Each benefits to a substantial degree through this arrangement. The importer benefits by securing adequate credit. The importer's bank benefits because it receives a fee for issuing the commercial letter of credit and for the other services provided in connection with it. The exporter benefits by being assured that payment will be made for the shipment of merchandise. Thus, a sale is made that might otherwise have been rejected because of lack of guaranteed payment. Finally, the exporter's bank benefits if it discounts the acceptance, since it receives a high-grade credit instrument with a definite, short-term maturity. Acceptances held by commercial banks provide a low but certain yield, and they can liquidate them quickly if funds are needed for other purposes.

The Volume and Cost of Bankers' Acceptances

The Board of Governors of the Federal Reserve System authorizes member banks to accept drafts that arise in the course of certain types of international transactions. These include the import and export of goods, the shipment of goods between foreign countries, and the storage of highly marketable staple goods in any foreign country. The maturity of member bank acceptances arising out of such transactions may not exceed six months. This authority to engage in bankers' acceptance financing is intended to encourage banks to participate in financing international trade and to strengthen the U.S. dollar abroad.

Bankers' acceptances are used to finance international transactions on a wide variety of items, including coffee, wool, rubber, cocoa, metals and ores, crude oil, jute, and automobiles. Due to the growth of international trade in general and the increasing competition in foreign markets, bankers' acceptances have become increasingly important. Exporters have had to offer more liberal terms on their sales to compete effectively; the banker's acceptance permits them to do so without undue risk.

The cost of financing an international transaction with the banker's acceptance involves not only the interest cost involved in the exporter's discounting the acceptance but also the commission charge of the importer's accepting bank. From 1961 through 1985 interest costs on bankers' acceptances moved from slightly less than 3 percent to more than 15 percent and back down to below 7 percent in early 1991. Foreign central banks and commercial banks regard bankers' acceptances as attractive short-term funds commitments. In recent years, more than half of all dollar acceptances have been held by foreign banks, with most of the remainder held by domestic banks. Nonfinancial corporations have played only a small role as investors in acceptances. There are relatively few firms that deal in bankers' acceptances. These dealers arrange nearly simultaneous exchanges of purchases and sales.

OTHER AIDS TO INTERNATIONAL TRADE

The Export-Import Bank

The **Export-Import Bank** was authorized in 1934 and became an independent agency of the government in 1945. The bank's purpose is to aid in financing and facilitating exports and imports between the United States and other countries. It is the only U.S. agency engaged solely in financing foreign trade.

Export-Import Bank bank established to aid in financing and facilitating trade between the U.S. and other countries

The Export-Import Bank is a government-owned corporation with capital of $1 billion in nonvoting stock paid in by the U.S. Treasury. It may borrow from the Treasury on a revolving basis and sell short-term discount promissory notes. It pays interest on these loans and dividends on the capital stock. In performing its function, the bank makes long-term loans to private enterprises and governments abroad to finance the purchase of U.S. equipment, goods, and services. The Export-Import Bank also aids substantially in the economic development of foreign countries by giving emergency credits to assist them in maintaining their level of U.S. imports during temporary balance-of-payments difficulties. In addition, the bank finances or guarantees the payment of medium-term commercial export credit extended by exporters and, in partnership with private insurance companies, offers short- and medium-term credit insurance. It lends and guarantees only where repayment is reasonably assured and avoids competition with sources of private capital.

Traveler's Letter of Credit

A firm's buyer who is traveling abroad may not know in advance from which individuals or firms purchases will be made—for example, an art buyer touring several countries. The buyer could carry U.S. currency, but this involves possible physical loss of the money and a sometimes substantial discount for its conversion into the local currency. A traveler's letter of credit is a convenient and safer method for travelers who need large amounts of foreign currency.

traveler's letter of credit *issued by a bank to banks in other countries authorizing them to cash checks or purchase drafts presented by the bearer*

The ***traveler's letter of credit*** is issued by a bank in one country and addressed to a list of foreign banks. These banks are usually correspondents of the issuing bank and have agreed to purchase sight drafts presented to them by persons with appropriate letters of credit. When a bank issues a letter of credit, it sends a copy of the signature of the person to whom the letter is issued to each of its foreign correspondent banks. When someone presents a draft for payment in foreign currency to one of these correspondent banks, his or her signature is compared with that the bank already has. The bank may also ask the individual for supplementary identification.

As with a commercial letter of credit, a maximum total drafts amount is stated in a traveler's letter of credit. In order that an individual with such a letter does not exceed authorized withdrawals, each bank to which the letter is presented enters on it the amount of the draft it has honored.

Travelers' Checks

Travelers' checks, which are offered by banks, express companies, and other agencies in the United States, are generally issued in denominations of $10, $20, $50, and $100. These checks, generally purchased by an individual before leaving for a foreign country, promise to pay on demand the even amounts indicated on the face of the checks. Each check must be signed by the purchaser twice, once when it is bought and again in the presence of a representative of the business, hotel, or financial institution where it is presented for payment. This allows the person cashing a traveler's check to determine whether the signature is authentic.

The use of travelers' checks is widespread and offers several advantages to the traveler, including protection in the event of loss and almost certain acceptance when they are presented for payment. Travelers' checks are usually sold for their face amount plus a charge of one percent. They can now be purchased in the U.S. in major foreign currency denominations—for example, British pounds. This eliminates a traveler's exposure to changing exchange rates and the extra amount that is often charged (in the form of a less favorable exchange rate than the official rate) when U.S. dollar checks are cashed in a foreign country.

KEY TERMS

arbitrage   foreign exchange markets
clean draft   order bill of lading
commercial letter of credit   sight draft
documentary draft   time draft
draft (bill of exchange)   traveler's letter of credit
Export-Import Bank   trust receipt

DISCUSSION QUESTIONS

1. A smoothly functioning system of international finance makes possible specialization of productive effort by the nations of the world. Why is such specialization of effort desirable?
2. How do commercial banks provide for the financial settlement of international transactions? Describe the arrangements of commercial banks for maintaining deposits in foreign countries.
3. Explain the role of supply and demand as it relates to the establishment of exchange rates between countries.
4. Describe the activities and economic role of the arbitrager in international finance.
5. Foreign exchange quotations may be given in terms of sight drafts, cable orders, and time drafts. What is the relative cost of these different types of drafts? Why should such cost differences exist?
6. Describe the nature of foreign exchange markets.
7. Why should managers of multinational companies be concerned with foreign relationships?
8. Describe the various ways by which an exporter may finance an international shipment of goods. How may commercial banks assist the exporter in the collection of drafts?
9. How do importers protect themselves against improper delivery of goods when they are required to make payment when placing an order?
10. Describe the process by which an importing firm may substitute the credit of its bank for its own credit in financing international transactions.
11. How may a bank protect itself after having issued a commercial letter of credit on behalf of a customer?
12. Describe the costs involved in connection with financing exports through bankers' acceptances.
13. Describe the ultimate sources of funds for export financing with bankers' acceptances. How are acceptances acquired for investment by these sources?

14. Explain the role played by the Export-Import Bank in international trade. Do you consider this bank to be in competition with private lending institutions?

15. Commercial letters of credit, travelers' letters of credit, and travelers' checks all have an important role in international finance. Distinguish among these three types of instruments.

PROBLEMS

1. As an exporter of relatively expensive electronic equipment you have a substantial investment in the merchandise that you ship. Your foreign importers are typically small- or medium-size firms without a long history of operations. Although your terms of sales require payment upon receipt of the merchandise, you are concerned about the possible problem of nonpayment and the need to reclaim merchandise that you have shipped. How might the banking system assist and protect you in this situation?

2. As an importer of merchandise you depend upon the sale of the merchandise for funds to make payment. Although customary terms of sale are 90 days for this type of merchandise, you are not well known to foreign suppliers because of your recent entry into business. Furthermore, your suppliers require almost immediate payment to meet their own expenses of operations. How might the banking systems of the exporter and importer accommodate your situation?

SELF-TEST QUESTIONS

1. Foreign exchange markets may be described as:
   a. specific locations in major industrial cities
   b. major financial centers connected by good communications
   c. money markets outside of the U.S.
   d. facilities of central banks for foreign exchange

2. Quotations of foreign exchange rates in the many cities of the world are identical or nearly so because of:
   a. central bank control
   b. price fixing
   c. clearinghouse activities
   d. arbitrage activities

3. The least costly form of claim in foreign exchange is a:
   a. banker's sight draft
   b. cable order
   c. time draft
   d. bill of exchange

4. A documentary draft is accompanied, among other things, by a(n):
   a. order bill of lading
   b. manifest
   c. trust receipt
   d. letter of credit

5. A banker's acceptance differs from a trade draft in that:
   a. it is drawn on a bank rather than on an importer
   b. it is always accompanied by a bank letter of credit
   c. its acceptance depends entirely on the goodwill of the importer
   d. (There is no difference.)

SELF-TEST PROBLEM

You are the owner of a business that has offices and production facilities in several foreign countries. Your product is sold in all of these countries, and you maintain bank accounts in the cities in which you have offices. At present you have short-term notes outstanding at most of the banks with which you maintain deposits. This borrowing is to support seasonal production activity. One of the countries in which you have offices is now strongly rumored to be on the point of a devaluation, or lowering, of their currency relative to that of the rest of the world. What actions might this rumor cause you to take?

SUGGESTED READINGS

Brealey, Richard A., and Stewart C. Myers. *Principles of Corporate Finance*, 3e. New York: McGraw-Hill, 1988. Chap. 34.

Brick, John R., H. Kent Baker, and John A. Haslem. *Financial Markets*, 2e. Reston, VA: Reston Publishing Co., 1986. Chap. 23.

Edmister, Robert O. *Financial Institutions*. New York: McGraw-Hill, 1986. Chap. 15.

Eiteman, David K., and Arthur I. Stonehill. *Multinational Business Finance*, 5e. Reading, MA: Addison-Wesley, 1990. Chaps. 4 and 7.

Hempel, George H., Alan B. Coleman, and Donald G. Simonson. *Bank Management*, 2e. New York: John Wiley & Sons, 1986. Chap. 13.

Kaufman, George G. *The U.S. Financial System*, 4e. Englewood Cliffs, NJ: Prentice-Hall, 1989. Part 5.

Kidwell, David S., and Richard L. Peterson. *Financial Institutions, Markets, and Money*, 3e. Hinsdale, IL: The Dryden Press, 1987. Part 7.

Mayo, Herbert B. *Finance: An Introduction*, 3e. Hinsdale, IL: The Dryden Press, 1989. Chap. 5.

Quarterly Review, Federal Reserve Bank of New York. Each issue, published quarterly, presents an article on Treasury and Federal Reserve foreign exchange operations.

Rose, Peter S. *Money and Capital Markets*, 3e. Homewood, IL: BPI/Irwin, 1989. Part 8.

Ross, Stephan A., Randolph W. Westerfield, and Jeffrey F. Jaffe. *Corporate Finance*, 2e. Homewood, IL: Irwin, 1990. Chap. 29.

ANSWERS TO SELF-TEST QUESTIONS   1. b   2. d   3. c   4. a   5. a

SOLUTION TO SELF-TEST PROBLEM

You could try to hedge against your financial claims in that country losing value by moving some of the funds in your bank account to another country. In anticipation of moving the funds, you could try to accelerate the collection of your receivables. You might also slow down your payments on liabilities with the expectation of moving funds back into the country after devaluation, receiving more local funds in so doing. Other devices, such as dealing in futures contracts, may also be available to you.

PART FOUR
MONETARY, FISCAL, AND DEBT MANAGEMENT POLICIES

CHAPTER 21
Policy Instruments of the Federal Reserve and Treasury

After studying this chapter, you should be able to:

- Discuss the objectives of national economic policy and the conflicting nature of these objectives.
- Describe the relationship between the policymaking groups, the types of policies and decisions these groups make, and the primary objectives of each.
- Identify the specific instruments of monetary control exercised by the Federal Reserve System and evaluate their relative effectiveness.
- Identify the policy instruments of the U.S. Treasury, and provide brief explanations of how the Treasury manages cash balances and budgetary surpluses and deficits.
- Describe U.S. Treasury tax policy and debt management responsibilities.

Part 1 of this text described the financial system of the United States. It included a discussion of the monetary system, the banking structure, and the operation of the central banking system. The nature and sources of the nation's money supply, along with the savings and investment process, were explained in detail. In Part 4 we will examine the way in which the policies of the federal government and the Federal Reserve System (Fed) influence the operation of the financial system and the economy. In this chapter we will discuss the nature of the decisions these two bodies must make. The remainder of Part 4 describes the ways that these decisions influence the economy, including their effect on interest rates and prices. The final chapter illustrates these concepts by reviewing the development of economic policy and events over the last several decades.

NATIONAL POLICY OBJECTIVES

The broad range of economic policy objectives for the nation can be described in different ways and with different degrees of emphasis. The government's major involvement in the economy influences its course and affects the lives of everyone. While people with differing views debate the proper role of government, there is broad agreement that the decisions of policymakers have a significant effect in certain areas. There is also a strong tradition in our system that the objectives should be pursued with minimum interference with the economic freedom of individuals. Economic policy actions are directed toward the four general goals of economic growth, high and stable employment levels, price stability, and international financial equilibrium.

Economic Growth

The standard of living of the nation's citizens has increased dramatically over our history as a result of the growth of the economy and its productivity. But growth means more than merely increasing total output. It requires that output increase faster than the population so that the average output per person expands. Growth is a function of two components: an increasing stock of productive resources—the labor force and stock of capital—and improved technology and skills.

High and Stable Levels of Employment

Unemployment represents a loss of potential output and imposes costs on the entire economy. The economic and psychological costs are especially hard on those who are unemployed. While there is some disagreement over what we should consider full employment, it is a stated objective of the government to promote stability of employment and production at levels close to our potential. It seeks to avoid large changes in economic activity, minimizing the hardships that accompany loss of jobs and output.

Price Stability

In recent years the importance of stable prices has become well accepted but difficult to achieve. Consistently stable prices help create an environment in which the other economic goals are more easily reached. Inflation discourages investment by increasing the uncertainty about future returns. Therefore high inflation rates are no longer considered acceptable as a price to pay for high levels of employment.

International Financial Equilibrium

The increasing importance of international trade and international capital markets has resulted in a new emphasis on worldwide financial affairs. The U.S. economy is so large that the actions taken with respect to our own affairs influence the economies of other nations as well. Economic policymakers therefore must always maintain a world view rather than a narrow nationalistic approach.

ECONOMIC POLICIES AND GOVERNMENT INFLUENCE ON THE ECONOMY

The federal government plays a dual role in the economy. In its traditional role it provides services that cannot be provided as efficiently by the private sector. In this role it acts like a firm, employing resources and producing a product. The magnitude of this role and its influence on economic activity have led to its more modern role: guiding or regulating the economy. The decisions of a number of policy-making entities must be coordinated in order to achieve the desired economic objectives.

A government raises funds to pay for its activities in three ways: levies taxes, borrows, or prints money for its own use. Since this last option has tempted some governments, with disastrous results, Congress delegated the power to create money to the Fed. Our federal government collects taxes to pay for most of its spending, and it borrows, competing for funds in the financial system, to finance its deficits.

To illustrate the complex nature of the government's influence on the economy, consider the many effects of the federal deficit. To finance it, the government competes with other borrowers in the financial system. This absorbs savings, and it may raise interest rates. Private investment may be reduced if it becomes more difficult for firms to borrow the funds needed. On the other hand, a deficit stimulates economic activity. The government is either spending more or collecting less in taxes, or both, leaving more income for consumers to spend. The larger the deficit, the more total spending, or aggregate demand, there will be. In some circumstances this stimulation of the economy generates enough extra income and savings to finance both the deficit and additional investment by firms.

Furthermore, the Fed may buy government securities, financing some of the deficit and providing additional reserves to the banking system, thus increasing the money supply. This process is known as **monetizing the deficit**. The Fed has at past times monetized some of the deficit, especially during World Wars I and II. It does not now do so since that would be counter to current monetary policy. It would also have a significant impact on the financial markets. The competition for funds would make it more difficult for some borrowers to meet their financing needs. The characteristics and maturities of debt sold by the Treasury would determine which sectors are most affected.

monetizing the deficit when the Fed increases the money supply by purchasing government securities

The Policymakers

The decisions of policymakers enter this process at a number of points. The President and the Council of Economic Advisors formulate a program of *fiscal policy*: the relationship of the Treasury's tax plans to its expenditure plans to influence the economy of the nation. Congress must pass legislation authorizing the Treasury's plans or a variation of it. The Treasury has responsibility for actually collecting taxes and disbursing funds. The Treasury is also responsible for the huge task of debt management, which includes financing current deficits and refinancing the outstanding debt of the government. The Fed contributes to the attainment of the nation's economic goals by formulating **monetary policy**. It uses its powers to regulate the growth of the money supply and thus influence interest rates and the availability of loans. Figure 21.1 shows the relationship between policymakers and policy objectives.

fiscal policy government influence on economic activity through taxation and expenditure plans

monetary policy formulated by the Fed to regulate the growth of the money supply

The principal responsibilities of these policymakers have not always been the same. When the Fed was established in 1913, most of the power to regulate money and credit was placed in its hands. However, as the public debt grew during World War I, the Great Depression of the 1930s, and World War II, the Treasury became vitally interested in

FIGURE 21.1   Policymakers and Policy Objectives

Policymakers	Types of Policies or Decisions	Policy Objectives
Federal Reserve System		Economic Growth
The President	Monetary Policy	High Employment
The Congress	Fiscal Policy	Price Stability
U.S. Treasury	Debt Management	International Equilibrium

credit conditions. Policies that affect interest rates and the size of the money supply affect the Treasury directly, since it is the largest borrower in the nation. Therefore, the U.S. Treasury took over, and continues to have, primary responsibility for management of the federal debt. In managing the large public debt and various trust funds placed under its jurisdiction, the Treasury has the power to influence the money market materially. The Fed came back into its own in the 1950s and is now the chief architect of monetary policy.

When it is felt that the Fed is not being responsive to the needs of the economy, the President will usually exercise pressure. The President also formulates budgetary and fiscal policy, but Congress must enact legislation to implement these policies. Congress regularly exercises its authority to modify presidential proposals before enacting legislation. In short, there is much overlap of influence among those who make policy decisions. All three types of policies, however, are directed toward achieving the four objectives of economic growth, high employment, price stability, and international financial equilibrium.

It should not be surprising that the policy instruments of the various policymakers at times put them at cross-purposes. A longstanding debate continues over the balance between full employment and price stability. A particular policy that leads toward one may make the other more difficult to achieve, yet each objective has its special supporters. As in all governmental policy, economic objectives are necessarily subject to compromise and tradeoffs.

Dynamic, Defensive, and Accommodative Functions

Public discussions of Fed and Treasury operations are almost always directed toward *dynamic actions* that stimulate or repress the level of prices or economic activity. However, we should recognize that this area is but a minor part of the continuous operation of these systems. Far more significant in terms of time and effort are the defensive and accommodative functions of the Fed and the Treasury. *Defensive activities* are those that contribute to the smooth everyday functioning of the economy. Unexpected developments and shocks are continuously imposing themselves upon the economy; unless these events are countered by appropriate monetary actions, disturbances may develop. Large unexpected shifts of capital out of or into the country and very large financing efforts by big corporations may significantly alter the reserve positions of the banks. Similarly, buyouts and acquisitions of one corporation by another, supported by bank financing, also affect reserve positions. In our competitive market system unexpected developments contribute to the vitality of our economy. Monetary policy, however, has a special responsibility to smoothly absorb these events and avoid many of their traumatic short-term effects.

The *accommodative function* of the nation's monetary system is the one with which we are the most familiar. One of the original purposes of the Fed was to provide flexibility in meeting the requirements of money and credit for an expanding economy. Meeting the credit needs of individuals and institutions, clearing checks, and supporting depositories and other institutions (described in detail in Chapters 3 and 4) represent accommodative activities.

FEDERAL RESERVE POLICIES

The basic policy instruments of the Fed are setting reserve requirements for depository institutions (banks, for short), lending to banks, and open market operations. By setting reserve requirements, the Fed establishes the maximum amount of deposits the banking system can support with a given level of reserves. The amount of reserves can be affected directly through open market operations, thereby causing a contraction or expansion of deposits by the banking system. Discount rate policy also affects the availability of reserves to banks and influences the way they adjust to changes in their reserve positions. Thus the Fed has a set of tools that together enable it to influence the size of the money supply in working to attain its broader economic objectives.

Reserve Requirements

Banks are required to hold reserves equal to a specified percentage of their deposits. The assets which may be counted as reserves are vault cash and deposits with the Reserve Banks. If a depository institution has reserves in excess of the required amount, it may lend them out. This is how they earn a profit, and it is also the way in which the money supply is expanded.

In Chapter 5 the mechanics of money supply expansion and contraction were explained in detail. We observed that in our system of fractional reserves, control of the volume of checkable deposits depends primarily on reserve management. Recall that the total deposits that can be supported by a given level of reserves is the reciprocal of the reserve requirement. Thus, a required reserve ratio of 10 percent can give rise to a tenfold increase in deposits for each dollar of additional reserves placed in the system. A 15 percent ratio can give rise to an increase in deposits of 6.67 times.

The reserve ratio is essential to the Fed's control. The closer to the required minimum the banking system maintains its reserves, the tighter the control the Fed has over the money creation process through its other instruments. If the banking system has close to the minimum of reserves (that is, if excess reserves are near zero), then a reduction of reserves forces the system to tighten credit in order to reduce deposits. If substantial excess reserves exist, the pressure of reduced reserves is not felt so strongly. When reserves are added to the banking system, depositories may expand their lending but are not forced to do so. However, since depositories earn no interest on reserves, profit maximizing motivates them to lend out excess reserves to the fullest extent consistent with their liquidity requirements. When interest rates are high this motivation is especially strong.

The ability to change reserve requirements is a powerful tool that the Fed uses infrequently. For a number of reasons, the Fed prefers to use open market operations to change reserves rather than change reserve requirements. If reserve requirements are changed, the maximum amount of deposits that can be supported by a given level of reserves changes. Total deposits and the money supply can be contracted by holding the amount of reserves constant but raising the reserve requirement. Lowering reserve requirements provides the basis for expansion of money and credit.

It has been argued that changing reserve requirements is too powerful a tool and that its use as a policy instrument would destabilize the banking system. The institutional arrangements through which the banking system adjusts to changing levels of reserves might not respond as efficiently to changing reserve requirements. Another advantage of open market operations is that they can be conducted quietly, while changing reserve requirements requires a public announcement. The Fed feels that some of its actions would be opposed if public attention were directed toward them.

Changing reserve requirements has been used as a policy instrument on occasion. In the late 1930s the nation's banks were in an overly liquid position because of excessive reserves. Banks had large amounts of loanable funds that businesses did not wish to, or could not qualify to, borrow because of the continuing depression. The reserves were so huge that the Fed could no longer resolve the situation through its other policy instruments. Therefore it increased reserve requirements substantially in order to absorb excess reserves in the banking system.

Reserve requirements were lowered during World War II in order to assure adequate credit to finance the war effort. But they were raised again in the postwar period to absorb excess reserves. In the 1950s and early 1960s reserve requirements were lowered on several occasions during recessions. In each case, the lowering made available excess reserves to encourage bank lending, ease credit, and stimulate the economy. By using this policy tool, the Fed was publicly announcing its intention to ease credit, in hopes of instilling confidence in the economy.

In the late 1960s and 1970s, reserve requirements were selectively altered to restrain credit because the banking system was experimenting with new ways to get around Fed controls. Banks were using more negotiable certificates of deposit, Eurodollar borrowings, and other sources of reserve funds. This prompted the Fed to impose restraint on the banks by manipulating the reserve requirements on specific liabilities.

The evolution of the banking system eventually led Congress to pass the Depository Institutions Deregulation and Monetary Control Act of 1980, which makes significant changes in reserve requirements throughout the financial system. Up to this time the Fed had control over the reserve requirements of its members only. Nonmember banks were subject to reserve requirements established by their own states, and there was considerable variation among states. As checks written on member banks were deposited in nonmember banks, and vice versa, funds moved among banks whose deposits were subject to different reserve requirements. This reduced the Fed's control over the money supply.

The 1980 act applies uniform reserve requirements to all banks with certain types of accounts. For banks that were members of the Fed, these requirements are, in general, lower now than they were prior to the act. A schedule of these revised reserve requirements is shown in Table 21.1.

The Discount Rate

One of the most important Fed policy instruments in the minds of the framers of the 1980 act is the use of the discount rate for making the amount of currency and loans available correspond to the needs of business. The discount power was given to the Reserve authorities as a basic part of the monetary and credit system because it was felt that it would be effective in regulating the volume of money and loans in the economy.

Stated in somewhat oversimplified terms, discount policy was intended to work in the following fashion. If the Fed wanted to cool an

TABLE 21.1   Reserve Requirements of Depository Institutions after Implementation of the Monetary Control Act (Effective 12/18/90)

TRANSACTION ACCOUNTS* DEPOSITS	PERCENT OF DEPOSITS
$0 million–$41.1 million	3%
More than $41.1 million	12%

*Transaction accounts include all deposits on which the account holder is permitted to make withdrawals by negotiable or transferable instruments, payment orders of withdrawal (in excess of three per month) for purposes of making payments to third persons or others.

inflationary boom, it would raise the discount rate. An increase in the discount rate would lead to a general increase in interest rates for loans, decreasing the demand for short-term borrowing for additions to inventory and accounts receivable. This in turn would lead to postponing the building of new production facilities and, therefore, to a decreased demand for capital goods. As a consequence, the rate of increase in income would slow down. In time, income would decrease and with it the demand for consumer goods. Holders of inventories financed by borrowed funds would liquidate their stocks in an already weak market. The resulting drop in prices would tend to stimulate the demand for, and reduce the supply of, goods. Thus economic balance would be restored. A reduction in the discount rate was expected to have the opposite effect.

Discount policy is no longer a major instrument of monetary policy and, in fact, is now regarded more as an adjustment or fine tuning mechanism. As an adjustment mechanism, the discount arrangement does provide some protection to depository institutions in that other aggressive control actions may be temporarily moderated by the ability of banks to borrow. For example, the Fed may take a strong restrictive position through open market operations. Individual banks may counter the pressure by borrowing from their Reserve Banks. The Reserve Banks are willing to tolerate what appears to be an avoidance of their efforts while banks are adjusting to the pressure being exerted. Failure to reduce their level of borrowing can always be countered by additional Fed open market actions. Discount borrowing fluctuates rapidly, but typically is in a range of 1 to 5 percent of total reserves. For several years borrowed reserves have exceeded excess reserves for the banking system as a whole. In other words, nonborrowed reserves have not been large enough to meet requirements. Figure 21.2 shows borrowed reserves and excess reserves in recent years.

Open Market Operations

The most used instrument of monetary policy is open market operations. Open market operations involve the purchase of securities by the Reserve Banks to put additional reserves at the disposal of the banking system or the sale of securities to reduce reserves. The original Federal Reserve Act did not provide for open market operations. In order to maintain stability in the money supply, this policy instrument developed out of the experience of the early post-World War I period.

From the beginning of their operations, Reserve Banks bought government securities with funds at their disposal to earn money for meeting expenses and to make a profit in order to pay dividends on the stock held by member banks. All twelve banks usually bought and sold the securities in the New York market. At times their combined sales

FIGURE 21.2   Excess Reserves and Borrowings

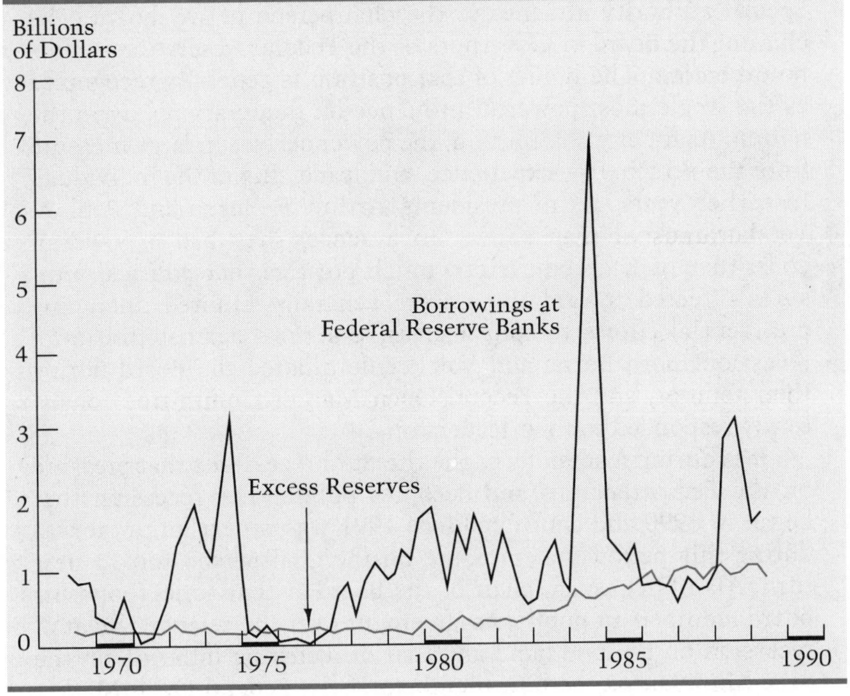

were so large that they upset that market. Furthermore, the funds used to buy the bonds ended up in New York member banks and enabled them to reduce their borrowing at the Reserve Bank of New York. This made it difficult for the Reserve Bank of New York to maintain effective credit control in its area. As a result, an open market committee was set up to coordinate buying and selling of government bonds. In 1933 the Federal Open Market Committee was established by law. In 1935 its present composition was established: the Federal Reserve Board of Governors plus five of the presidents of the twelve Reserve Banks, who serve on a rotating basis.

Although not provided for in the original organization of the Fed, open market operations have become the most important and effective means of monetary and credit control. These operations can take funds out of the market and thus raise short-term interest rates and help restrain inflationary pressures. Or they can provide for easy money conditions and lowered short-term interest rates. Of course, such monetary ease will not necessarily start business on the recovery road after a recession. When used with discount policy, open market operations are an effective way of restricting credit or making it more easily available.

Special authority attaches to the chairperson of any board. The chair of the Board of Governors of the Federal Reserve System is no exception. The holder of that position is generally recognized as the single most powerful influence on monetary policy in the nation. As for any chairperson, the power derives in large measure from the personality, experience, and leadership of the individual. In earlier years, Board presidents Arthur F. Burns and Paul A. Volcker ran one-man shows. In a sense, they had a powerful constituency. Each enjoyed so much prestige that political pressures directed toward them were generally blunted, including presidential efforts to spur aggressive actions against threats of recession. Both Burns and Volcker dominated the Board during their tenures, and the Federal Open Market Committee consistently responded to their leadership.

It is during recessions or the threat of recessions that pressure on the Fed intensifies and becomes public. The recession that began in 1990 and continued into 1991 was no exception; it was during this period that pressure on the chairperson took a new turn. Alan Greenspan, chair of the Board at that time, found his board members in public disagreement over the relative threat of recession on the one hand and that of recurring inflation on the other. In addition, certain members of the Federal Open Market Committee challenged some of his decisions. All members of the Board as well as the presidents of five of the reserve banks are members of the FOMC. Some of these reserve bank presidents participated in the resistance.

These challenges to Chairman Greenspan resulted not from a lack of competent leadership but rather from a leadership style in which he encouraged open debate. Although some contrary opinions resulted from this debate, Chairman Greenspan's decisions have largely prevailed. It is highly likely that this technique of open debate will set the tone for future decision making at the Fed.

INCREASING OR DECREASING RESERVES

Open market operations differ from discount operations in that they increase or decrease reserves at the initiative of the Fed, not of individual banking institutions. The process in simplified form works as follows. If the Open Market Committee wants to buy government securities, it contacts dealers to ask for offers and then accepts the best offers that meet its needs. (The Fed restricts its purchases to U.S. government securities, primarily because of their liquidity and safety.)

The dealers receive wire transfers of credit for the securities from the Reserve Banks. These credits are deposited with member banks. The member banks, in turn, receive credit for these deposits with their Reserve Banks, thus adding new reserves that form the basis for additional credit expansion.

If the Fed wants to reduce reserves, it sells government securities to the dealers. The dealers pay for them by a wire transfer from a depository to a Reserve Bank. The Reserve Bank then deducts the amount from the reserves of the depository.

Open market operations don't always lead to an immediate change in the volume of deposits. This is especially true when bonds are sold to restrict deposit growth. As bonds are sold by the Reserve Banks, some banks lose reserves and are forced to borrow from their Reserve Bank. Since they are under pressure from the Fed to repay the loan, they use funds from maturing loans to repay the Reserve Bank. Thus, credit can be gradually restricted as a result of the adjustments banks must make to open market operations.

DEFENSIVE SECURITIES TRANSACTIONS

The Fed also uses open market purchases and sales to carry out its accommodative and defensive functions. In fact, a majority of the Fed's open market operations are for defensive purposes. Over an extended period, purchases of securities exceed sales, and these net purchases provide for growth in banking system reserves and growth in the money supply to accommodate a growing economy. On any given day, however, purchases or sales may take place as the Fed reacts defensively to fluctuations in reserves originating from sources beyond its control. For example, when the Treasury makes large purchases and pays with checks drawn on its account at the Fed, bank reserves are increased substantially. To prevent this sudden increase from disrupting the money supply and credit conditions, the Fed sells securities to absorb some of the increase in reserves.

POLICY INSTRUMENTS OF THE U.S. TREASURY

The Treasury has vast power to affect the supply of money and credit. The very magnitude of Treasury operations, however, dictates that it must play as defensive or neutral a role as possible. The power to regulate the money supply has been placed primarily in the hands of the Fed; close cooperation between the Treasury and the Fed must exist if Treasury operations are not to disrupt the money supply. Consider the impact on monetary affairs of a massive withdrawal of taxes from the banking system without offsetting actions. The decrease in bank deposits would result in a temporary breakdown of the system's ability to serve the credit needs of the public. Yet, taxes are periodically claimed by the federal government without significant impact on lending institutions. In like manner, borrowing by the government or the refunding of maturing obligations could be traumatic in their effect on money and credit, but such is not the case. In short, the Fed efficiently manages these dynamic aspects of money and credit while the Treasury largely limits its actions to taxing, borrowing, paying bills, and refunding maturing obligations. The Treasury carries out these functions with as little interference with the conduct of monetary affairs as possible. This is no small challenge.

Managing the Treasury's Cash Balances

Treasury operations involve spending nearly one trillion dollars a year. It is necessary to maintain a large cash balance, since Treasury receipts and payments do not occur on a regular basis throughout the year. This makes it critical for the Treasury to handle its cash balances in such a way that it will not create undesirable periods of credit ease or tightness. In order to affect bank reserves as little as possible, the Treasury has developed detailed procedures for handling its cash balances.

TREASURY TAX AND LOAN ACCOUNTS

The Treasury's primary checkable deposit accounts for day-to-day operations are kept at Reserve Banks. Most cash flows into the Treasury through Treasury Tax and Loan Accounts of banks, S&Ls, and credit unions (referred to as banks, for short). Employers deposit withheld income taxes, social security, and railroad retirement taxes in these Treasury Tax and Loan Accounts. They have the option of depositing these government receipts either with Reserve Banks or one of the other banks. Most employers make their payments to the latter.

The Treasury may also make payments of income and eligible profits taxes in Tax and Loan Accounts. Many excise taxes may also be paid either to a Reserve Bank or to a qualified bank with a Tax and Loan Account. The proceeds from a large portion of the sales of new government securities also flow into Tax and Loan Accounts. Proceeds from the sale of nonmarketable securities are always eligible for deposit in the accounts; most marketable issues are also eligible. Sales of Treasury bills, however, have rarely been eligible for credit to Tax and Loan Accounts. If the Treasury feels its balances at the Reserve Banks are too large, it can transfer funds to its accounts at the banks.

TREASURY RECEIPTS AND OUTLAYS

The Treasury tries to handle its cash receipts, outlays, and balances so as to avoid large changes in bank reserves. To do this, the Treasury tries to keep balances in its accounts at the Reserve Banks relatively stable.

Almost all Treasury disbursements are made by checks drawn against its deposits at the Reserve Banks. Most Treasury receipts are deposited in Tax and Loan Accounts at the various banks, but some are deposited directly in the Treasury accounts at the Reserve Banks. The Treasury adjusts the withdrawal of funds from its accounts at the banks in such a way as to keep its balances at the Reserve Banks as stable as possible. This means that the funds shifted from banks and the funds deposited directly in Reserve Banks must closely correspond to the volume of Treasury checks that are likely to be presented to the Reserve Banks.

If the Treasury accounts at the Reserve Banks are kept at about the same level, bank reserves are not changed. This is possible only if accurate forecasts are made of the daily receipts and spending from the Treasury account so that funds from the Tax and Loan Accounts may be shifted in the right amounts at the right time. If the forecasts were not worked out with a reasonable degree of success, Treasury operations would cause bank reserves to change a great deal over short periods of time. Despite these precautions, the Treasury's account frequently does fluctuate by as much as several billion dollars from day to day. The Fed closely monitors the Treasury account and takes any changes into consideration in conducting daily open market operations in order to minimize the effect on bank reserves.

Powers Relating to the Federal Budget and to Surpluses or Deficits

The government may also influence monetary and credit conditions indirectly through taxation and expenditure programs, especially by having a significant cash deficit or surplus. Decisions in the budget-making area rest with Congress and are usually based on the needs of the government and political considerations, without giving much weight to monetary and credit effects. Because of the magnitude of the federal budget, government income and spending may be one of the most important factors in determining credit conditions.

GENERAL ECONOMIC EFFECTS OF FISCAL POLICY

Economic activity depends to a large extent on aggregate demand, or total spending in the economy. An increase in aggregate demand will generally cause an increase in production and employment but may also cause prices to rise. If the economy is already close to full employment, increases in aggregate demand will be likely to increase prices more than output. Similarly, decreases in aggregate demand will result in lower employment and reduced prices.

Fiscal policy has a significant effect on aggregate demand and economic activity. Not only is government spending itself a large component of aggregate demand, but any change in government spending has a multiplied effect on aggregate demand. An increase in government spending increases employment and incomes, and thus also increases consumer spending. Not only does spending increase in a downturn, but tax receipts of all types, including those for Social Security, decrease when fewer people are at work because these taxes are based on payrolls. Changes in taxes also have a direct impact on disposable income and affect aggregate demand through consumer spending.

Various programs of the federal government act in such a way as to help stabilize disposable income and, in turn, economic activity in general. Some act on a continuing basis as **automatic stabilizers**. Other government fiscal actions are discretionary and depend on specific congressional actions.

automatic stabilizers
continuing federal pro-
grams that stabilize eco-
nomic activity

One of the automatic stabilizers is the unemployment insurance program, funded in large part by the states. Under this program, payments are made to workers who lose their jobs, thus providing part of their former incomes. Another stabilizer is welfare payments under federal and state aid programs. Both unemployment and welfare benefits are examples of **transfer payments**, or income payments for which no current productive service is rendered.

transfer payment
government payment for
which no current ser-
vices are given in return

Another important automatic stabilizer is the "pay-as-you-go" progressive income tax. Pay-as-you-go refers to the requirement that tax liabilities of individuals and institutions be paid on a continuing basis throughout the year. The progressive nature of our income tax means that as income increases to various levels, the tax rate increases. In other words, as incomes increase, taxes increase at a faster rate. The reverse is also true: at certain stages of decreased income, the tax liability decreases more quickly. The result is generally immediate since, for most wages subject to withholding taxes, tax revenues change almost as soon as incomes change.

These programs are a regular part of our economy. In times of severe economic fluctuations, Congress can help to stabilize disposable income. Income tax rates have been raised to lower disposable income and to restrain inflationary pressures; they have been lowered during recessions to increase disposable income and spending. Government spending can also be increased during recessions to increase disposable income. Likewise, it could be cut during prosperity to reduce disposable income, but for political reasons attempts to do this have not been successful.

When a recession is so severe that built-in stabilizers or formulas are not adequate to promote recovery, there is seldom complete agreement on the course of action to take. A decision to change the level of government spending and/or the tax rates must be made. Increased spending or a comparable tax cut would cost the same number of dollars initially, but the economic effects would not be the same. When income taxes are cut, disposable income is increased almost immediately under our system of tax withholding. This provides additional income for all sectors of the economy and an increase in demand for many types of goods.

Congress may decide to increase government spending. But the effects of increased government spending occur more slowly than those of a tax cut since it takes time to get programs started and put into full operation. The increased income arises first in those sectors of the economy where the money is spent. Thus, the initial effect is on specific areas of the economy rather than the economy as a whole.

The secondary effects of spending resulting from a tax cut or from increased government spending depend on how and what proportion the recipients spend. To the extent that they spend it on current consumption, aggregate demand is further increased in the short run. The goods on which recipients spend the income determine the sectors of the economy that receive a boost. If they invest the added income and later use it to purchase capital goods, spending is also increased. But in this case there is a time lag and different sectors of the economy are affected. If the money is saved—thus added to idle funds available for investment—there is no secondary effect on spending.

The effects must also be considered if economic activity is to be restrained by a decrease in government spending or by a tax increase. A decrease in spending by the government will cut consumer spending by at least that amount; the secondary effects may cut it further. A tax increase may not cut spending by a like amount since some taxpayers may maintain their level of spending by reducing current saving or by using accrued savings. A tax increase could, however, cut total spending more if it should happen to discourage specific types of spending, such as on home building or on credit purchases of consumer durable goods. This could lead to a spending cut that is substantially greater than the amount of money taken by the higher taxes.

EFFECTS OF TAX POLICY

The **tax policy** and tax program of the federal government have a direct effect on monetary and credit conditions which may work in several ways. The level of taxes in relation to national income may affect the volume of saving and thus the funds available for investment without credit expansion. The tax structure also determines whether saving is done largely by upper-income groups, middle-income groups, or by all groups. This in turn can affect the amount of funds available for different types of investment. Persons in middle-income groups may be more conservative than those with more wealth. Therefore they tend to favor bonds or mortgages over equity investments. Persons in high tax brackets on the other hand tend to invest in securities of state and local governments, the income from which is not subject to income taxes. Or they may invest for capital gains since taxes on the gains may be deferred until the asset is sold.

tax policy
setting the level and structure of taxes to affect the economy

Changes in corporate tax rates may also affect the amount of funds available for short-term investment in government bonds and the balances kept in bank accounts. The larger the tax payments, the less a corporation has available for current spending. Also, if tax rates are raised with little advance warning, as sometimes happens, a corporation may be forced to use funds it had been holding for future use. Businesses that are short of funds may be forced to borrow to meet their taxes. In either case, a smaller amount of credit is available for other uses.

EFFECTS OF DEFICIT FINANCING

deficit financing
how a government finances its needs when spending is greater than revenues

crowding out
lack of funds for private borrowing caused by the sale of government obligations to cover large federal deficits

The government spending program affects not only the overall economy but also monetary and credit conditions. When the spending rate is faster than the collection of taxes and other funds, **deficit financing** will affect the monetary and banking system. The effect will depend on how the deficit is financed. Budgetary deficits result in government competition for private investment funds. When credit demands are great, there may be a threat of **crowding out** private borrowers from the capital markets. When credit demands are slack, the sale of Treasury obligations puts idle bank reserves to use. When deficit financing is so large that the private sector cannot or will not absorb the Treasury obligations offered, the Fed may purchase a significant portion of the issues.

DEBT MANAGEMENT

debt management
various Treasury decisions connected with refunding debt issues

Debt management includes determining the types of refunding to carry out, the types of securities to sell, the interest rate patterns to use, and decision making on callable issues. Since World War II, federal debt management has become an important Treasury function affecting economic conditions in general and money markets in particular. The economy and the money markets are affected in several ways by the large government debt. First, interest must be paid on government securities. This has become one of the major items in the federal budget, estimated at nearly $175 billion for fiscal year 1991. Interest payments do not transfer resources from the private to the public sector, but they do represent a transfer of funds from taxpayers in general to security holders. When the debt is widely held, there is little or no redistribution of income among groups. However, the taxes levied to pay the interest may have a negative effect on the taxpayer incentive and so affect economic activity. This could lead to less risk taking and thus slow down economic growth.

One of the basic objectives of debt management is to handle it in such a way as to help establish an economic climate that encourages orderly growth and stability. In order to avoid inflation in boom periods, large numbers of individuals have been encouraged to save and to buy bonds. During recessions, the Treasury can borrow in ways that are least likely to compete with private demands for funds. For instance, the Treasury can sell short-term securities to attract idle short-term funds, especially idle bank reserves. Thus, there will be no restriction of credit for business and individuals. Credit will be available in larger amounts to the extent that bank purchases of bonds lead to credit expansion.

Some suggest that the Treasury should go further and affect the supply of long-term funds so as to promote stability. If long-term government bonds are issued at attractive rates, funds can be taken out of the long-term market. This action could reduce the supply of available funds for home construction, capital development, and the like and, therefore, help restrain a boom. The Treasury can also do more short-term financing when it wants to increase the amount of funds available for capital improvements. Since there is no agreement that the Treasury should use debt management in this way, no serious attempt to apply these policies over a period of time has been made.

Another objective of debt management policy is to hold down Treasury interest costs. The influence of Treasury policies may also tend to reduce all interest rates. Lower interest rates tend to stimulate home building, the construction of business plant and equipment, commercial building, and so forth. This objective and the first one may, however, conflict when higher interest rates may be helpful to restrain inflationary pressures.

A lesser Treasury objective is to maintain satisfactory conditions in the government securities market through maintaining investor confidence. It also tries to discourage wide price swings and maintain orderly buying and selling.

Among the more technical objectives are issuing securities to fit the needs of various investor groups and obtaining an evenly spaced scheduling of debt maturities to ease debt retirement if funds are available, or refunding when that is necessary. Our heavy dependence on foreign investors to purchase new issues in recent years has added a special dimension to the problem of U.S. debt management. Terms of new issues must now be geared to the special needs of foreign investors, especially the Japanese.

TREASURY PROBLEMS—AN OUTLOOK

Even assuming some budgetary cutbacks and reasonable growth of the economy, there is a high probability of large budgetary deficits through 1994. These huge deficits will be almost equal to the entire amount of savings by individuals, leaving state and local saving, corporate saving, and foreign saving to finance whatever private capital formation occurs. During a period of economic growth significant reductions in the absolute size of the deficit are typically an important source of net saving to finance inventory growth and capital formation. It is for this reason that there is so much concern over the budgetary deficit outlook. The difficulty of ending entitlement programs, danger of drastic cuts in national defense spending, and political unattractiveness of tax increases all converge to virtually assure large continuing deficits. Furthermore, a continuing antiinflationary position by the Fed may serve to slow growth in the economy. Strong economic growth is perhaps our best hope for reducing deficits. Growth will increase tax revenues, but even that possibility is not without its problems. A strong economic recovery could reverse the nation's recent progress in reducing inflationary pressures.

KEY TERMS

automatic stabilizers
crowding out
debt management
deficit financing
fiscal policy

monetary policy
monetizing the deficit
tax policy
transfer payments

DISCUSSION QUESTIONS

1. List and describe briefly the economic policy objectives of the nation.
2. In what ways does the federal government attempt to promote and attain these objectives?
3. How does the government raise the funds to pay for its activities?
4. Describe the relationship between policymakers, types of policies, and policy objectives.
5. It is said that economic policymakers sometimes work at cross-purposes in achieving desirable objectives. Comment.
6. Distinguish among the dynamic, defensive, and accommodative functions of the Fed and the U.S. Treasury.
7. Evaluate the use of discount policy by the Fed.
8. To what extent is borrowing from the Fed on the part of banks a privilege or a right?

9. How may changes in reserve requirements be used to carry out Fed policy?
10. Discuss the process by which open market operations affect monetary conditions, and evaluate their effectiveness.
11. Although the U.S. Treasury has vast power to affect the supply of money and credit, the dynamic aspects of monetary control are delegated to the Fed. Comment.
12. How do commercial banks accommodate Treasury cash operations as depositories?
13. Describe the effects of tax policy on monetary and credit conditions.
14. Federal government deficit financing may have a very great influence on monetary and credit conditions. Explain.
15. Discuss the various objectives of debt management.
16. Do you see any relationship between the nation's trade deficit and management of the national debt?

PROBLEMS

1. The Federal Reserve Board of Governors has decided to "ease" monetary conditions to counter early signs of an economic downturn. Because price inflation had been a burden in recent years, the Board is anxious to avoid any action that the public might interpret as a return to inflationary conditions. How might the Board use its various powers to accomplish the objective of monetary ease without drawing unfavorable publicity to its actions?
2. An economic recession has developed and the Federal Reserve Board has taken several actions to retard further declines in economic activity. The U.S. Treasury now wishes to take steps to assist the Fed in this effort. Describe the actions the Treasury might take.

SELF-TEST QUESTIONS

1. Government financing of large budgetary deficits:
   a. absorbs savings and decreases interest rates
   b. may temporarily stimulate economic activity
   c. is known as monetizing the deficit
   d. reduces total consumer spending and demand

2. The Fed has responsibility for:
   a. formulating a program of fiscal policy
   b. debt management
   c. formulating monetary policy
   d. collecting taxes and disbursing funds

3. The Fed spends most of its time and effort on:
    a. activities characterized as defensive
    b. activities described as dynamic
    c. clearing checks for the public
    d. supervision and examination of member banks

4. Bank assets that may be counted as required reserves are:
    a. cash in bank vaults
    b. deposits with a Reserve Bank
    c. Treasury bills
    d. cash in vaults and deposits with the Fed

5. Depository institutions borrow from Reserve Banks for many reasons but most often to:
    a. meet seasonal loan demands
    b. meet emergency needs
    c. adjust reserve positions
    d. obtain funds at a lower cost than the returns on loans made with the funds

SELF-TEST PROBLEM

Important policy objectives of the federal government include economic growth, high employment, price stability, and international financial equilibrium. These objectives are functions of monetary policy, fiscal policy, and debt management. These policies and objectives are addressed by the Federal Reserve System, the President, the Congress, and the U.S. Treasury. How is the responsibility for each allocated among these areas of government?

SUGGESTED READINGS

The Federal Reserve System—Purposes & Functions, Washington, DC: Board of Governors of the Federal Reserve System, 1984.

Friedman, Milton. *A Program for Monetary Stability.* New York: Fordham University Press, 1960.

Gilbert, R. Alton. "Operating Procedures for Conducting Monetary Policy," *Review*, The Federal Reserve Bank of St. Louis (February 1985): 13–21.

Kaufman, George G. *The U.S. Financial System*, 4e. Englewood Cliffs, NJ: Prentice-Hall, 1989. Part 6.

Kidwell, David S., and Richard L. Peterson. *Financial Institutions, Markets, and Money*, 4e. Hinsdale, IL: The Dryden Press, 1990. Chap. 23.

Meulendyke, Ann-Marie. *U.S. Monetary Policy and Financial Markets.* New York: Federal Reserve Bank of New York, 1990.

Rose, Peter S. *Money and Capital Markets*, 3e. Homewood IL: BPI/Irwin, Inc., 1989. Chaps. 22–24.

Rose, Peter S. and Donald R. Fraser. *Financial Institutions*, 3e., Homewood, IL: Richard D. Irwin, 1988. Chap. 5.

ANSWERS TO SELF-TEST QUESTIONS   1. b   2. c   3. a   4. d   5. c

SOLUTION TO SELF-TEST PROBLEM

The President of the United States along with his advisors formulates fiscal policy. Congress enacts legislation to implement fiscal policy (after exercising its authority to modify the policy). The Fed has primary responsibility for monetary policy, while the Treasury handles debt management.

CHAPTER 22
Interest Rate Levels and Structure

After studying this chapter, you should be able to:
- Describe the characteristics and the yield and price relationships of interest rates.
- Explain the loanable funds theory of interest rates.
- Explain the liquidity preference theory of interest rates.
- Explain *term structure of interest rates.*
- Describe the money market, various money market instruments, and their rates.
- Discuss the effect of inflation and risk premiums on the level of long-term interest rates.

The basic price that equates the demand for and supply of loanable funds in the financial markets is the interest rate. An understanding of interest rates, what causes them to change, and how they relate to changes in the economy is of fundamental importance in the world of finance. We begin with a discussion of some of the factors influencing interest rates and their patterns over time. Then our attention turns to theories used to explain the level of interest rates. Next we discuss the term structure of interest rates, showing the relationship between maturity and yields. We then consider interest rates in the money market and how these rates influence one another. The last section of the chapter focuses on how inflation, the economy, and other factors affect differences between interest rates in capital markets.

INTEREST RATE CHARACTERISTICS AND PATTERNS

The quoted interest rate for any type of loan is a result of several costs, including the administrative cost of making the loan, and the cost of paying for the risk involved. If inflation is likely, part of the cost is to offset the resulting decline in purchasing power of the borrowed dollars during the term of the loan. The remaining cost is what the borrower pays for the use of the money itself during the period of the loan. It compensates the lender for loss of liquidity. Instead of having money to invest or spend at will, the lender now has a claim for repayment in the future.

Risk, Marketability, and Maturity Factors

Quoted interest rates for different types of loans also vary according to how the funds are to be used. The costs of making loans to business, to government, and to consumers to buy real estate, finance the purchase of durable goods, or tide them over during emergencies vary significantly. These variations account for differences in quoted interest rates. The same is true of how lenders assess the risk involved in different loans. Differences in the quality or credit rating of borrowers will lead to differences in the interest rates that they are charged.

Interest rates also differ according to the degree of marketability of the instruments. For example, U.S. government bonds are more marketable—that is, there are more people willing to buy them—than bonds of a major corporation such as IBM; both of these are more marketable than the bonds of a less well known corporation. The more marketable the bond, the lower the interest rate that it will have to pay.

Interest rates also vary according to the maturities of loans. At times short-term rates are below long-term rates, and at other times the reverse is true. This occurs partly because there are differences in the supply of and demand for funds of various types. In other words, the market is divided into submarkets for funds of varying maturities. But funds are shifted between markets even though some lag is involved. Differences in rates also depend on expectations of lower or higher interest rates in the future.

Various factors affect interest rates in different sectors of the market. However, the part of the quoted interest rate that is paid for the use of the money itself is determined by supply and demand in the market for loanable funds.

Historical Changes in U.S. Interest Rate Levels

Interest rates for loanable funds have varied throughout our history as the result of shifting supply and demand. Since just after the Civil War, there have been four periods of rising or relatively high long-term interest rates and three periods of low or falling interest rates on long-term loans and investments. The rapid economic expansion after the Civil War caused the first period of rising interest rates from 1864 to 1873. The second period, from 1905 to 1920, was based on both large-scale prewar expansion and the inflation associated with World War I. The third period, from 1927 to 1933, was due to the economic boom from 1927 to 1929 and the unsettled conditions in the securities markets during the early part of the depression, from 1929 to 1933. The rapid economic expansion following World War II led to the last period, from 1946 to the present.

The first period of falling interest rates was from 1873 to 1905. As the public debt was paid off and funds became widely available, the supply of funds grew more rapidly than the demand for them. Prices and interest rates fell, even though the economy was moving forward. The same general factors were at work in the second period, 1920 to 1927. The third period of low interest rates, from 1933 to 1946, resulted from the government's actions in fighting the Great Depression and continued during World War II, when interest rates were "pegged," or set.

Beginning in 1966 interest rates entered a period of unusual increases, leading to the highest rates in our history. This increase in rates began as a result of the Vietnam War. It continued in the 1970s because of a policy of on-again, off-again price controls and increased demands for capital arising from ecological concerns and the energy crisis. Furthermore, several periods of poor crops coupled with sharp price increases for crude oil caused worldwide inflation. Interest rates peaked at the beginning of the 1980s, with short-term rates above 20 percent and long-term rates in the high teens. To sum up, double-digit inflation, a somewhat tight monetary policy, and heavy borrowing demand by business contributed to these record levels.

Short-term interest rates generally move up and down with the business cycle. They therefore show many more periods of expansion and contraction. Both long-term and short-term interest rates tend to rise in prosperity periods during which the economy is expanding rapidly. The only major exception was during World War II, when interest rates were pegged. During this period the money supply increased rapidly, laying the base for postwar inflation.

Yield and Price Relationships

Most debt instruments and securities have a stated interest rate. Exceptions include U.S. Treasury bills and commercial paper issued by corporations, along with other loans made on a discount basis. U.S. Treasury and corporate bonds have coupon interest rates stated on the certificates. Most bonds are issued in $1,000 denominations, and par values are also usually stated in $1,000 denominations. Coupon rates then are expressed as a percentage of the bond's par value. For example, a $1,000 par value bond with a 10 percent coupon rate pay $100 in interest per year. Typically, interest is paid in $50 amounts twice a year. The issuing organization also agrees to redeem, or pay off, the bond at its par value at the maturity date.

Because the coupon rates, maturity dates, and par redemption values of most debt instruments are fixed, prices vary inversely with changes in financial market interest rates. For example if, because of economic changes, interest rates rise for other bonds similar to the one described above, the bond's price will fall. The "new" price will reflect the yield now being demanded in the marketplace.

The present value process for determining the value or price of a bond was described in Chapter 10. Remember that when the market interest rate is the same as the coupon rate for a particular quality of bond, the bond will be priced at its $1,000 par value. For example, assume a bond has a 10-year life, the market interest rate is 10 percent, and the bond pays $100 annually. Using present value tables from Chapter 10 (Tables 10.4 and 10.3) or the Appendix, for the $100 annuity and the one-time receipt of $1,000 at maturity, we calculate the bond value as $1,000.[1]

Now let's assume that the bond falls in price to $887 because of rising interest rates. The bond now has a "current yield" to a new purchaser of 11.3 percent ($100/$887). However, this current yield estimate fails to consider that the bond will be redeemed for $1,000 at maturity even though it costs the new purchaser only $887. To take this cost-versus-maturity price difference into consideration, we need to calculate the **yield to maturity** on the bond. Finding the yield to maturity is just like finding the internal rate of return, as discussed in Chapter 10. We need to find the discount rate that will make the present value of the cash inflows (interest and maturity payments) equal to the investment or cost. As before, we use a trial and error process to find the rate that makes the net present value zero.

yield to maturity
rate of return based on interest and principal payments of a bond held to maturity

For our bond example we begin by choosing a discount rate greater than 10 percent because the current price is less than $1,000. Let's try 12 percent for ten years. Using the appropriate factors from present value Tables 3 and 4 in the Appendix gives us the following:

---

1. For semiannual, or twice-yearly, interest payments of $50 ($100/2), we would use the present value interest factor for a 5% (10%/2), 20 periods (10 years × 2) annuity of 12.462 from Table 4 in the Appendix. Likewise, the $1,000 amount at maturity would be multiplied by the 5%, end of 20 periods factor of .377 taken from Table 3 in the Appendix. Notice that the price would still be $1,000 for this example.

$$\$100 \times 5.650 = \$565$$
$$\$1,000 \times 0.322 = \underline{322}$$
$$\$887$$

In this case the internal rate of return or yield to maturity is right at 12 percent, because the present value of cash inflows of $887 is equal to the current price or cost of $887. In many instances we would not be so "lucky" as to find the yield to maturity so easily. For example, if the current bond price were $800, the yield would be greater than 12 percent. We would try higher discount rates until the present value of cash inflows approached $800. We may need to estimate an amount in between two percentage points.

This simple formula also approximates the average annual yield to maturity (YM):

$$YM = \frac{I + \dfrac{PV - CP}{N}}{\dfrac{CP + PV}{2}}$$

where

I = annual dollar amount of interest
PV = par value of bond
CP = current price of bond
N = the number of years remaining to maturity

We would estimate the yield to maturity on our $887 bond example as follows:

$$YM = \frac{\$100 + [(\$1,000 - \$887)/10]}{(\$887 + \$1,000)/2} = \frac{\$100 + \$11.30}{\$1,887/2} = \frac{\$111.30}{\$943.50} = 11.8\%$$

Thus, while this formula does not consider the time value of money, the 11.8 percent estimate in this case is reasonably close to the true 12 percent yield to maturity.

Bonds and other debt instruments and securities trade in the marketplace at prices that reflect yields to maturity investors require. As interest rates rise, the prices of existing bonds will fall, and vice versa. Understanding this relationship is crucial to understanding how debt instruments and securities trade in secondary markets.

DETERMINING INTEREST RATE LEVELS

loanable funds theory
states that interest rates
are a function of the sup-
ply of and demand for
loanable funds

Two theories are often used to explain the level of interest rates. The **loanable funds theory** holds that interest rates are a function of the supply of and demand for loanable funds. This is a "flow" theory, in that it focuses on the relative supply and demand of loanable funds during a specified period of time. The **liquidity preference theory** contends that interest rates depend on the supply of and demand for money. This is a "stock" theory in that it focuses on the amount or stock of money at a point in time.

liquidity preference theory
states that interest rates are determined by the supply of and demand for money

These theories are not considered to be incompatible; that is, one is not right and the other wrong. The choice is often made on the basis of objective or convenience. Let us consider these theories in greater detail.

Loanable Funds Theory

The loanable funds theory focuses on the "market" for loanable funds. The interest rate is the price borrowers pay to lenders for the use of these funds. As is true in any market, how the supply of and the demand for loanable funds interact determines both this price and the quantity of funds that flows through the market during any period. If the supply of funds increases, holding demand constant, interest rates will tend to fall. Likewise, an increase in the demand for loans will tend to drive up interest rates.

SOURCES OF LOANABLE FUNDS

There are two basic sources of loanable funds: (1) current savings and (2) the expansion of deposits by depository institutions. The supply of savings comes from all sectors of the economy, and most of it flows through our financial institutions. Individuals may save part of their incomes, either as voluntary savings or through contractual savings programs such as purchasing whole life or endowment insurance policies or repaying installment or mortgage loans. Governmental units and nonprofit institutions sometimes have funds in excess of current expenditures. Corporations may have savings available because they are not paying out all their earnings as dividends. Depreciation allowances that are not being used currently to buy new capital equipment to replace older equipment may also be available for lending.

Pension funds, both governmental and private, provide another source of savings. These funds, which are building up large reserves to meet future commitments, are available for investment.

Some savings are invested as ownership equity in businesses either directly in single proprietorships or partnerships or by buying stock in corporations. This is, however, only a small part of total savings; the bulk of the total savings each year is available as loanable funds. Funds may be loaned directly: for example, when someone lends money to a friend to enable the friend to expand business operations. However, most savings are loaned through financial institutions, one of whose basic functions is the accumulation of savings.

The other basic source of loanable funds is that created by the banking system. Banks and other depository institutions not only channel savings to borrowers, but they also create deposits, which are the most widely used form of money in our economy. This process was discussed in detail in Chapter 5. Net additions to the money supply are a source of loanable funds; during periods when the money supply contracts, the flow of loanable funds drops below the level of current savings.

Loanable funds can be grouped in several ways. They may be divided into short-term funds and long-term funds. We can also group funds by (1) use, such as business credit, consumer credit, agricultural credit, and government credit, and by (2) the institutions supplying each type, as this book has done.

FACTORS AFFECTING THE SUPPLY OF LOANABLE FUNDS

Many factors affect the supply of loanable funds. Both sources of funds have some tendency to increase as interest rates rise. However, this effect is often small compared to other factors that limit or otherwise affect the volume of savings or the ability of the banking system to expand deposits.

Volume of Savings

The major factor that determines the volume of savings, corporate as well as individual, is the level of national income. When income is high, savings are high; when it is low, savings are low. The pattern of income taxes—both the level of the tax and the tax rates in various income brackets—also influences savings volume. Furthermore, the tax treatment of savings itself influences the amount of income saved. For example, the tax deferral (postponement of taxes) of savings placed in individual retirement accounts (IRAs) increases the volume of savings.

The age of the population has an important effect on the volume of savings. As we learned in Chapter 6, little saving is done by young adults, especially those with school-age children. Therefore, an economy with a large share of young couples with children will have less total savings than one with more late middle-aged people.

The volume of savings is also dependent on the factors that affect indirect savings. The more effectively the life insurance industry promotes the sale of whole life and endowment insurance policies, the larger the volume of savings. The greater the demand for private pension funds, which are built up during working years to make payments on retirement, the larger the volume of savings. The effect of interest rates on such savings is often just the opposite of the normal effect of price on supply. As interest rates decrease, more money must be paid for insurance for the same amount of coverage, because a smaller amount of interest will be earned from the reinvestment of premiums and earnings. Inversely, as interest rates rise, less money need be put into reserves to get the same objectives. The same is true of the amount of money that must be put into annuities and pension funds.

When savings result from the use of consumer credit, the effect of interest rates is delayed. For example, assume a car is bought with a three-year auto loan. Savings, in the form of repaying the loan, must go on for three years regardless of changes in interest rates. There may even be an opposite effect in the case of a mortgage because, if interest rates drop substantially, the loan can be refinanced. At the lower interest rate the same dollar payments provide a larger amount for repayment of principal, that is, for saving.

Expansion of Deposits by Depository Institutions

The amount of short-term credit available depends largely on the lending policies of commercial banks and other depository institutions, and on the policies of the Federal Reserve System. Lenders are influenced by such factors as present business conditions and future prospects. But the Federal Reserve has great control over the ability of the banking system to create new deposits, as discussed in Chapter 5.

How much long-term credit of different types is available depends on the policies of the different suppliers of credit. Since depository institutions do not play a major role in this field, the money supply is not expanded directly to meet long-term credit demands. Indirectly, however, their policies and those of the Federal Reserve are very important because, if the banking system expands the money supply to meet short-term needs, a larger proportion of the supply of loanable funds can be used for long-term credit.

Liquidity Attitudes

How lenders see the future has a significant effect on the supply of loanable funds, both long-term and short-term. Lenders may feel that the economic outlook is so uncertain that they are reluctant to lend their money. This liquidity preference can be so strong that large amounts of funds lie idle, as they did during the depression of the 1930s. Lenders may also prefer liquidity because they expect interest rates to go up in the near future, or opportunities for direct investment to be more favorable. Thus, liquidity attitudes may result in keeping some funds idle that would normally be available for lending.

EFFECT OF INTEREST RATES ON THE DEMAND FOR LOANABLE FUNDS

The demand for loanable funds comes from all sectors of the economy. Business borrows to finance current operations and to buy plant and equipment. Farmers borrow to meet short-term and long-term needs. Institutions such as hospitals and schools borrow primarily to finance new buildings and equipment. Individuals finance the purchase of homes with long-term loans and purchase durable goods or cover emergencies with intermediate and short-term loans. Governmental units borrow to finance public buildings, bridge the gap between expenditures and tax receipts, and meet budget deficits.

The factors affecting the demand for loanable funds are different for each type of borrower. We have considered such factors in detail when analyzing the various types of credit. Therefore, this discussion will only cover how interest rates affect the major types of borrowing.

One of the biggest borrowers is the federal government, and Congress is generally little influenced in its spending program by interest rate considerations. Minor changes in interest rates do not affect short-term business borrowing. However, historical evidence shows that large increases in short-term interest rates do lead to a decrease in the demand for bank loans and other forms of short-term business borrowing.

Changes in long-term interest rates also affect long-term business borrowing. Most corporations put off long-term borrowing when rates have gone up, if they expect rates to go down in the near future.

Likewise, minor changes in interest rates have little effect upon consumer borrowing. For short-term installment loans the monthly repayments of principal are so large compared to the interest cost that the total effect on the repayment schedule is small. However, larger interest rate changes have strongly influenced consumer borrowing in the past. This happened in recent years when home mortgage rates reached historically high levels and new housing starts declined sharply.

ROLES OF THE BANKING SYSTEM AND THE GOVERNMENT

While the effect of interest rates on loanable funds varies, both the supply of and the demand for loanable funds are affected by the actions of the banking system and the government. When depository institutions expand credit by increasing the total volume of short-term loans, the supply of loanable funds increases. When credit contracts, the supply of loanable funds decreases. The actions of the Federal Reserve in setting discount rates, buying securities in the open market, and changing reserve requirements also affect the supply of loanable funds. In fact, all actions that affect the level of banking system reserves and creation of checkable deposits, as described in Chapter 5, affect the supply of loanable funds in the market.

Government borrowing has a major effect on demand for funds. Government borrowing has now become a major influence and will remain so in the foreseeable future. Government surpluses or deficits make funds available in the market or take them out of the market in substantial amounts. Treasury debt management policies that affect the supply-and-demand relationships for short-term, intermediate, and long-term funds were discussed in Chapter 21.

The financial markets are thus under the influence of the Treasury and the Federal Reserve strongly influences the supply of funds. The Treasury, through tax policies and other government programs, also has some role on this side of the market. However, the Treasury's major influence is on the demand for funds, as it borrows heavily to finance federal deficits.

INTERNATIONAL FACTORS INFLUENCING INTEREST RATES

Interest rates in the United States are now no longer only influenced by domestic factors. The large trade surplus of Japan, with its accumulation of funds to invest, has had an important influence on the rates the federal government pays in issuing new securities. This international influence adds to the critical need to balance the national budget and avoid the frequency of financing. The unification of West and East Germany is expected to lead to a large flow of investment funds to East Germany to help its economy. Until now, such investment funds have been directed partly to the United States. As production has shifted to many other countries, investment has also shifted. In short, the Treasury and the Federal Reserve must now carefully consider the influence of international movements of funds on domestic interest rates.

Liquidity Preference Theory

Some economists prefer to analyze interest rates from the viewpoint of money supply and demand rather than loanable funds. The two approaches are related, since an increase in the demand for money tends to increase the holding of money balances and thus reduce the flow of loanable funds.

The factors that determine the supply of money were considered in detail in Chapter 5 and therefore need not be reviewed here. Instead, we will focus on a brief review of the demand for money, also considered to some extent in Part 1. There are three basic motives for holding money: (1) the transactions motive, (2) the speculative motive, and (3) the precautionary motive. The transactions motive has already been considered in some detail and refers to the need for money to meet the gap between the time when payments must be made and the receipt of income. The amount of money held for the transactions motive varies with the level of national income. It responds more to changes in such income than to changes in interest rates. The speculative motive is the desire to hold money in the belief or hope that better investment opportunities will arise in the near future. The precautionary motive refers to holding cash for emergency needs. Most businesses, institutions, and individuals hold some money to meet emergencies. However, the amount held varies with confidence in the future of the economy and of the monetary unit. In a severe depression, there is large-scale hoarding, or holding, of cash. On the other hand when inflation is very high, money is spent as soon as possible to avoid loss of value. If carried to the extreme, this lack of confidence in money leads to uncontrolled inflation.

The demand for money is also influenced by the existence of "near" money (marketable securities) and the markets that buy and sell such highly liquid investments. If short-term investments can be made and converted back into cash quickly and with little or no risk, there is less demand to hold money than when such investment possibilities do not exist.

The interest rate can be analyzed from either point of view: the liquidity preference theory or the loanable funds theory. Many economists prefer to use the liquidity preference theory since it fits more easily into their analyses of change in national income. Analysts in the financial markets usually make short-run forecasts from the point of view of loanable funds. This approach requires an analysis of the money supply and the amount of money held in idle balance since these both affect the supply of loanable funds.

Long-run Relationship Between Changes in Money Supply and Interest Rates

The short-run effect of an increase in money is a decrease in interest rates. If there is an unexpected increase in the money supply, investors may want to make some changes in their portfolios. The holders who have more cash than they expected will try to convert some of it into corporate and government securities. This bids up the price of these securities and lowers the interest rate. Since someone must hold the cash, interest rates tend to drop until there is a new balance between the desire to hold money and the interest rates.

This process also follows the actions of the Federal Reserve in increasing the money supply by buying more U.S. government securities. These increased purchases will add to reserves in the banking system, increasing the supply of loanable funds and tending to reduce interest rates.

But this short-run effect is not the only effect of an increase in money supply. Lower interest rates and more money lead to increased economic activity and higher national income, followed by an increase in the demand for goods and services. At first, inventories are reduced; production then increases to replenish stocks of goods. The increase in the level of production leads to an increased demand for credit to finance it. If the increased demand for credit that results from an expansion of the money supply is greater than the supply of credit that is created, the net result, after some lag, will be a rise in interest rates.

If the money supply and total demand increase faster than output, prices will rise. This increase in prices leads to further demands for credit since more funds are needed to finance the production of a given volume of goods. Wages will also rise, with little delay in labor groups whose union contracts call for cost-of-living adjustments but with greater delay in other groups. Wage hikes raise costs and thus increase the demand for credit.

The expectation of inflation also affects interest rates. Borrowers are willing to pay higher rates since they expect to repay the loan with cheaper dollars, and lenders expect higher rates in order to get the same real return as before. In addition, in an inflationary period rising prices increase the cost of holding cash. Therefore, smaller cash balances are held in relation to income; more funds are available for spending and investing, thus reinforcing the increase in economic activity already in progress.

In summary, rapid increases in size of the money supply cause interest rates to be lower in the short run than they otherwise would be. However, a sustained increase in the rate of growth of the money supply works in the opposite direction, if the growth rate is greater than the supply of money desired to be held as cash balances. The result is a rise in the demand for goods, services, and credit—and in prices. The rise in prices is most severe when the economy is operating at nearly full employment. As a result, market interest rates rise in response to increased credit demands. In the long run, increased money growth does not necessarily lead to lower interest rates.

TERM STRUCTURE OF INTEREST RATES

Term structure of interest rates refers to the impact of loan maturities on interest rates. This relationship is generally described by three basic theories: (1) expectations theory, (2) market segmentation theory, and (3) liquidity premium theory. No single theory completely explains term structure of interest rates. Rather, all three are important in explaining term structure changes over time.

Yield Curves

Before examining each of these theories, we need to describe how the term structure of interest rates is expressed. This is often shown through the graphic presentation of *yield curves*. A properly constructed yield curve must first reflect securities of similar risk. (Default risk is another factor that affects interest rate differentials and will be discussed later). Second, the yield curve must represent a particular point in time, and the interest rates should reflect yields to

yield curve
graphic presentation of the term structure of interest rates at a given point in time

maturity. That is, the yields should not only include stated interest rates but should also consider that instruments and securities could be selling above or below their par values. Third, the yield curve must show yields on a number of securities with differing lengths of time to maturity.

Yield curves show at a glance how yields to maturity compare at different points in time. A higher line means higher yields. An upward sloping line means long-term rates are higher than short-term rates, while the reverse is true for downward sloping lines. U.S. government securities provide the best basis for constructing yield curves because Treasury securities are considered to be risk-free in terms of **default risk**—the likelihood that a bond issuer will not meet its payment obligations—and because there is a large number of these securities with differing maturities outstanding at any point in time. Figure 22.1 shows yield curves, or the term structure of interest rates, that existed at five different points in time as we entered the 1980s. Although

default risk
the probability that a bond issuer will not meet its payment obligations

FIGURE 22.1
Selected Historical Yield Curves for U.S. Government Securities

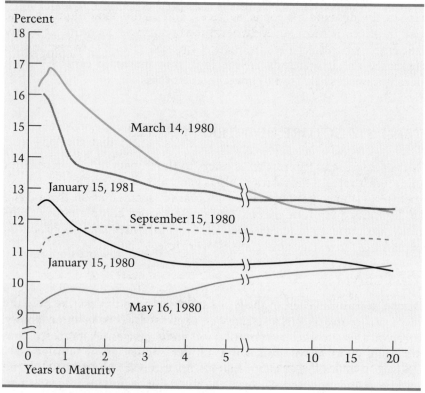

Source: Federal Reserve Bank of St. Louis.

interest rates were at a historic high in mid-January 1980, they increased rapidly across all maturities by mid-March 1980. A rapid decline followed, particularly in short-term rates, by mid-May 1980. Interest rates then rose during the rest of 1980 and into 1981.

After reaching new highs during the second half of 1981, interest rates showed a downward trend through 1986 (not shown), followed by a more recent increase. Short-term interest rates fell more rapidly than did long-term interest rates. Consequently, the term structure of interest rates generally has been upward sloping (short-term rates were lower than long-term rates) in recent years.

Relationship Between Yield Curves and the Economy

Historical evidence suggests that interest rates generally rise during periods of economic expansion and fall during economic contraction. Therefore the term structure of interest rates—or yield curves—shifts upwards or downwards with changes in economic activity; interest rate levels are the lowest at the bottom of a recession and the highest at the top of an expansion period. Furthermore, when the economy is moving out of a recession, the yield curve slopes upward. The curve begins to flatten out during the latter stages of an expansion and typically starts sloping downward when economic activity peaks. As the economy turns downward, interest rates begin falling and the yield curve again goes through a flattening-out phase, to become upward sloping when economic activity again reaches a low point.

Term Structure of Interest Rates Theories

There are three theories commonly used to explain term structure of interest rates. The **expectations theory** contends that the long-term interest rates at any point in time reflect the average of the current short-term interest rates plus short-term rates expected in the future. Thus, over the long run then, a series of consecutive short-term securities should have the same yield as a long-term security of similar default risk. This implies that if short-term rates are lower than long-term rates in a given period, and vice versa, the gaps will close in the future. Historical evidence, however, shows that upward-sloping yield curves are more common than downward-sloping yield curves. Thus the expectations theory does not completely explain the term structure of interest rates.

The **liquidity premium theory** is sometimes used along with the expectations theory. It holds that, because of uncertainty in the future, the yield curve should be mostly upward sloping. Investors should be willing to trade off some yield—in the form of higher long-term interest rates—for the greater liquidity that comes with short-term securities. Likewise, borrowers should prefer to borrow long-term and thus reduce

expectations theory
states that long-term interest rates reflect average current short-term rates and expected future rates

liquidity premium theory
states that investors should be willing to lose some yield to gain the liquidity of short-term securities

RECENT YIELD CURVE RELATIONSHIPS FOR U.S. SECURITIES

In recent years the shape of the structure of yields on U.S. government securities has been upward sloping. Furthermore, yields over the whole range of maturities have declined substantially since the early 1980s. Following are yields on U.S. government securities by maturity taken from selected issues of the *Federal Reserve Bulletin*:

DATE	1-YEAR TREASURY BILLS	5-YEAR TREASURY SECURITIES	LONG-TERM TREASURY SECURITIES
Dec. 1983	10.11%	11.54%	12.02%
Dec. 1986	5.87	6.67	7.67
Dec. 1987	7.17	8.45	9.12
Dec. 1988	8.99	9.09	9.13
Dec. 1989	7.72	8.12	8.39
Dec. 1990	7.05	7.73	8.24

Notice that all rates had shifted downward by over four percentage points between December 1983 and December 1986. This reflects lower inflation rates, a relatively slow real growth in economic activity, and a relatively easy monetary policy. A low-level, upward-sloping yield curve is generally seen as leading to future economic expansion.

If we plotted the above data, each depicted yield curve would be upward sloping since the yields on one-year Treasury bills are lower than the yields on five-year Treasury securities in each time period. This upward-sloping relationship also holds when yields on five-year Treasury securities are compared with long-term Treasury securities yields.

At the end of an economic expansion the whole yield curve usually shifts upward in position and then becomes downward sloping in shape. This would be consistent with the shape of the term structure of interest rates during earlier business cycle peaks.

their own liquidity risks associated with maturing securities. These supply and demand pressures suggest that short-term rates should be lower than long-term rates and that the yield curve should slope upward.

market segmentation theory
states that securities of different maturities are not perfect substitutes for each other

The **market segmentation theory** holds that securities of different maturities are not perfect substitutes for each other. For example, commercial banks concentrate their activities on short-term securities because of their demand and other deposit liabilities. On the other hand, the nature of insurance company and pension fund liabilities allows these firms to concentrate holdings in long-term securities. Thus, supply-and-demand factors in each market segment affect the shape of the yield curve.

The shapes of the yield curves shown in Figure 22.1, and what is historically known about yield curves, suggest that all three theories are needed to explain the term structure of interest rates. In any case, time to maturity is an important factor in explaining how interest rates vary among securities of similar quality.

RELATIONSHIPS AMONG INTEREST RATES IN THE MONEY MARKET

The money market mainly trades in deposits and debt instruments of one year or less. There are both primary and secondary money markets. Short-term bank loans are made in the primary money market but are seldom traded in the secondary money market. Short-term debt instruments that do trade in the secondary money market include U.S. Treasury bills, negotiable certificates of deposit, bankers' acceptances, and commercial paper. These money market instruments, first mentioned in Chapter 1, are summarized in this section.

We must understand several other interest rates in addition to those established in the money market in order to see how the overall money market operates. One such rate is the **prime rate** charged by commercial banks to their best business customers. This short-term bank loan rate sets a "floor" interest rate for other loans to less qualified business borrowers. Interest rates commercial banks charge security dealers and brokers are also closely tied to other money market rates. The discount rate controlled by the Federal Reserve is also important to the money market. In the past, maximum rates on time and savings deposits set by regulatory agencies directly affected the processes of intermediation and disintermediation. However, with the phasing out of dividend and interest-rate ceilings on depository institution deposits, the impact of regulatory control will diminish and money market operations will depend even more heavily on free market supply and demand factors.

prime rate
interest rate charged by banks to their best business customers

New York Money Market Activities

While there are informal markets for short-term debt instruments all over the United States, major money market activities are carried out in New York City through telephone and electronic transfers. The national money market in New York is not a definite organization as is the New York Stock Exchange, but is a loose network of various participants that demand and supply funds in this market. The New York money market is located mainly on or near Wall Street.

Wall Street itself is surprisingly short, running only seven blocks in lower Manhattan from Broadway's old Trinity Church to the East River. Most of the purely financial institutions of the New York money market are located in the area a few hundred yards on either side of Wall Street. The buildings house the Federal Reserve Bank of New York, the great stock and commodity exchanges, the head offices of the nation's largest banks, government security dealers, investment bankers, corporate and municipal bond houses, foreign exchange dealers, and many subsidiary financial specialists. This small area is probably the most intensively used half square mile in the world. So much steel, stone, brick, concrete, and mortar are packed on each square foot that engineers once feared the island would sink from the weight. So many people work here that they could not all crowd into the streets at one time.

As is to be expected in a market of final money adjustments, most credit is extended for short periods of time, some of it on a day-to-day basis. The procedure is usually handled by telephone or electronic transfer. Borrowers and lenders do not have a regular demand for and supply of funds but are in and out of the market as necessary to adjust their finances.

Money Market Instruments and Rates

U.S. Treasury bills are the single most important debt instruments bought and sold in the money market. Also important in dollar amount and trading activity are commercial paper, negotiable certificates of deposit (CDs), bankers' acceptances, and Eurodollar time deposits. Federal funds are excess reserves held by banks (or other depository institutions) that are lent on a short-term basis to reserves-short depository institutions. These funds also have a major impact on the money market.

Interest rates on Treasury bills and these other money market instruments change freely with changing supply-and-demand forces, with Treasury bill rates setting the floor, or minimum, for the other instruments. In contrast, the Federal Reserve's discount rate and the bank prime rate do not change freely but rather are administered or set. The discount rate historically has been kept below the Treasury bill rate while the prime rate has been set above the Treasury bill rate. That the prime rate is higher is consistent with higher default risk on bank loans than on Treasury bills.

U.S. TREASURY BILLS
As we have previously discussed, Treasury bills are sold at a discount through competitive bidding in a weekly auction. These bills are

offered in all parts of the country, but sell mostly in New York City. Treasury bills are also actively traded in secondary money markets, again mostly in New York.

Figure 22.2 shows the levels and volatility—or tendency to change rapidly—of three-month Treasury bill yields in recent years. Notice that they were over 8 percent in early 1985, dropped to near the 5 percent level in late 1986, and rose to about 9 percent in early 1989 before dropping again. U.S. Treasury bills are considered to be essentially risk-free in that there is virtually no risk of default. Consequently, interest rates are, as we would expect, higher for other money market instruments of similar maturity at the same point in time.

FEDERAL FUNDS

As a result of normal operations some commercial banks and other depository institutions find they have reserves that are temporarily

FIGURE 22.2   Selected Money Market Rates

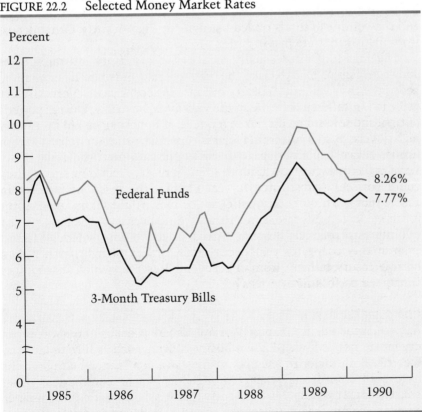

Source: Federal Reserve Bank of St. Louis.

greater than their required reserves. These temporary excess reserves, or federal funds as they are called when loaned, are lent on a day-to-day basis to other depository institutions that are temporarily short of reserves.

The lending for a one-day period is generally done by an electronic funds transfer and can be illustrated with an example involving two commercial banks. The deal may be made by one or more telephone calls from the bank wanting to borrow funds, or it may be arranged through a federal funds broker. Funds are electronically transferred from the lending bank's reserve account to the borrowing bank's reserve account at the Federal Reserve Bank. Repayment of the loan plus interest occurs the next day. Many of these transactions are between New York City banks, but banks in other cities also enter the New York money market, usually as lenders but also as borrowers.

The most common trading unit for federal funds is $1 million, but this is often exceeded. Trades may at times be made for $250,000 or multiples thereof; they are almost never made for less. The number of banks trading federal funds has increased substantially in recent years and the volume of funds traded has gone up significantly. Other depository institutions are just beginning to participate.

Federal funds rates usually parallel U.S. Treasury bill rates, as is shown in Figure 22.2. Notice that the federal funds rate has remained above the three-month Treasury bill rate in recent years. Normally the "spread" or difference between the two rates is narrow. During periods of tight money and credit, however, federal funds can be bid up to very high levels. Banks and other depository institutions choose, within limits, between borrowing at the discount rate from the Federal Reserve and borrowing federal funds to meet reserve requirements. If they could be freely substituted for each other, the discount rate set in accordance with monetary policy objectives would set an upper limit for the federal funds rate, since banks would borrow at the lower of the two rates. In practice, however, banks prefer to borrow federal funds, even at the high rates that occur when money is tight, rather than borrow too frequently from the Federal Reserve, which discourages continued use of this alternative.

COMMERCIAL PAPER

As we discussed in Chapter 9, commercial paper is the short-term, unsecured notes of well-known business firms such as IBM or General Electric. Both major finance companies and nonfinancial corporations have sold commercial paper through dealers or commercial paper houses for many years. More recently many issuers, particularly finance companies, have begun to issue or sell their own commercial paper.

Interest rates on commercial paper tend to closely follow Treasury bill rates over time. Of course, because of somewhat greater default risk, commercial paper rates for similar maturities are higher than Treasury bill rates at any point in time. Since commercial paper rates are typically below bank prime rates, they are a valuable short-term financing source for high quality business firms.

NEGOTIABLE CERTIFICATES OF DEPOSIT

One of the major new developments in the money market in the 1960s was the greatly increased use of negotiable certificates of deposit, or CDs. A certificate of deposit is in essence a receipt issued by a bank in exchange for a deposit of funds. The bank agrees to pay the amount deposited plus interest to the bearer of the receipt on the date specified on the certificate. Many banks had issued such certificates as early as the turn of the century, but before 1960 they were rarely issued in negotiable form. Negotiable CDs can be traded in the secondary market before maturity.

Within a short time after CDs were issued in substantial amounts, a government securities dealer decided to trade in outstanding negotiable certificates of deposit. This beginning of a secondary market was followed by trading by other security dealers so that by 1969 virtually all of the nonbank dealers and many of the bank dealers in U.S. government securities bought, sold, and maintained an inventory in CDs.

The volume of negotiable CDs (usually issued in denominations of $100,000 or more) has increased dramatically in recent years. Interest rates on these CDs usually parallel rates on other money market instruments, such as commercial paper and bankers' acceptances, and are above the less risky Treasury bill rates.

BANKERS' ACCEPTANCES

The origination and use of bankers' acceptances were discussed in Chapter 20. As we know, this form of business paper primarily finances exports and imports and, since it is the unconditional obligation of the accepting bank, generally has a high quality rating. Yields on bankers' acceptances closely follow yields on commercial paper.

In the mid-1970s, the volume of bankers' acceptances increased greatly because they were used in domestic transactions. Most of this activity involved goods in storage or transit within the United States.

EURODOLLARS

Eurodollars are deposits placed in foreign banks that remain denominated in U.S. dollars. A demand deposit in a U.S. bank becomes a Eurodollar when the holder of such a deposit transfers it to a foreign bank or an overseas branch of an American bank. After the transfer, the foreign bank holds a claim against the U.S. bank, while the original deposit holder (usually a business firm) now holds a Eurodollar deposit. It is called a Eurodollar deposit because it is still denominated in U.S.

dollars rather than being denominated in the currency of the country in which the foreign bank operates.

In recent years, and especially since 1966, large commercial banks have raised money by borrowing from the Eurodollar market through their overseas branches. Overseas branches of U.S. banks and banks outside the United States get funds in the Eurodollar market by accepting dollars in interest-bearing time deposit accounts. These dollar deposits are lent anywhere in the world, usually on a short-term basis. Banks generally transfer funds by telephone or electronically, lending large sums without collateral between banks. Banks that handle Eurodollars are located in Europe, with London as the center, and in other financial centers throughout the world, including such places as Singapore and the Bahamas.

Eurodollar deposit liabilities have arisen because the dollar is widely used as an international currency and because foreigners are holding more dollars due to ongoing U.S. balance-of-payment problems. Eurodollars are supplied by national and international corporations, banks, insurance companies, wealthy individuals, and some foreign governments and agencies. Eurodollar loan recipients are also a diverse group, but commercial banks, multinational corporations, and national corporations are heavy users.

There are several major reasons why U.S. banks have entered the Eurodollar market by means of their overseas branches: to finance business activity abroad, to switch Eurodollars into other currencies, and to lend to other Eurodollar banks. The most important reason, and the one that has received the most publicity in the United States, is for banking offices in the United States to borrow Eurodollars from their overseas branches. In this way they get funds at lower costs and during periods of tight money.

Relationship of Monetary Policy to the Money Market

As the final money market, the New York money market is affected directly or indirectly by all factors that affect the supply of and the demand for loanable funds. A demand for additional funds in St. Louis, for example, is first met locally. If it continues, however, funds are obtained from balances held by New York correspondent banks and by the sale of short-term government securities, usually in the New York market. Similarly, excess funds of banks and businesses tend to flow to New York. The most important factor in day-to-day conditions in that market is the reserve position of New York City banks. When excess reserves exist, they become available; when reserves are low, credit is tight in this market.

Conditions in the New York and other markets are also equalized—or balanced out—quite rapidly. If reserves are short in New York but available elsewhere, funds will flow to the money market. Likewise, if funds are available in New York, they will be loaned out and find their way into the channels of trade throughout the country. Therefore, any policy that affects the money market affects the supply of loanable funds throughout the country.

Changes in Federal Reserve policy have a pronounced effect upon this market. In fact, the direct impact upon the economy of changes in Federal Reserve policies is often through this New York money market. Changes in reserve requirements directly affect the market for federal funds. Changing the discount rate affects the rate on federal funds; this most sensitive of all rates affects the whole market. Open market operations have their first impact almost entirely in the New York money market, because government securities are bought and sold here. Treasury financing by means of short-term securities also takes place largely in this market. Thus, Treasury policies regarding money and debt management have an important influence. In fact, all types of changes in monetary policy influence the money market materially. Since it is a sensitive market, even minor changes affect it substantially. Monetary policy has a more direct and immediate effect on the availability of funds than it would have if this final market for balancing supply and demand did not exist or was not organized so well.

INFLATION AND INTEREST RATE DIFFERENTIALS IN THE CAPITAL MARKETS

It is important to distinguish between the money and capital markets when discussing long-run inflation expectations and interest rate differences between securities. Supply and demand in the money market are influenced greatly by Federal Reserve actions and objectives. In contrast, interest rates change more slowly in the long-term capital markets and traditionally have been only indirectly affected by monetary policy.

Long-term Treasury securities, like Treasury bonds, are considered risk-free in a default risk context. At any point in time this risk-free rate is composed of a real return component and a long-run inflation expectations component. Economists usually contend that the real return required to cause investors to convert cash into investments is about 3 percent. Therefore, the remaining portion of the risk-free rate usually reflects long-run inflation expectations.

Figure 22.3 shows the interest rates on long-term Treasury securities during recent years. Notice that these rates peaked at about 12 percent in early 1985. This suggests that investors then expected long-run inflation to be about 9 percent (12% − 3%) and, in fact, inflation was relatively high at that time. Long-term Treasury rates dropped to below the 8 percent level by 1986, as it became clearer to investors that inflation could be controlled.

Figure 22.3 also shows the interest rate differentials, which reflect differences in quality or risk of default, between risk-free long-term Treasury securities and Aaa (highest quality) corporate bonds. Default risk is the probability that the issuer of a security will fail to make payments. The difference between the risk-free rate and the interest rate on a risky corporate bond is called a **risk premium**. Notice that the risk premium is typically far less than one percentage point for Aaa corporate bonds. These interest rate differentials generally narrow during periods of economic expansion and widen during economic downturns, when defaults and bankruptcies increase.

Corporate securities of lower quality than Aaa have higher yields and larger risk premiums when compared with long-term government securities. Default risk depends on such factors as the firm's profit-

risk premium
difference between the Treasury security interest rate and the rates on more risky securities

FIGURE 22.3   Selected Capital Market Rates

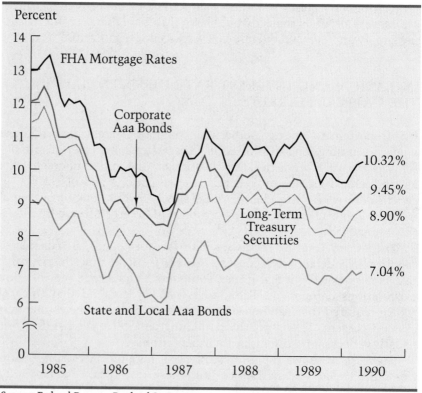

Source: Federal Reserve Bank of St. Louis.

Bond risk premium relationships change with changes in investor optimism—positive feelings—or pessimism—negative feelings—about expected economic activity. When investors are pessimistic about the economy and expect a recession, risk premiums tend to widen. Because bond issuers are more likely to default during periods of economic downturn, investors require greater expected compensation, in the form of higher interest, before they will invest in riskier securities. The opposite is true when investors are optimistic about the economy: When the economy is expanding, fewer firms default on their bond obligations and therefore investors are willing to accept lower expected added returns for investing in risky securities.

BOND RISK PREMIUMS AND THE ECONOMY

The following yields on long-term U.S. government securities and Aaa-rated and Baa-rated long-term corporate bonds were reported in selected issues of the *Federal Reserve Bulletin*:

DATE (YEAR-END)	LONG-TERM TREASURY SECURITIES	Aaa CORP-ORATE BONDS	RISK PREMIUM	Baa CORP-ORATE BONDS	RISK PREMIUM
1983	12.02%	12.57%	.55%	13.75%	1.73%
1986	7.67	8.49	.82	9.97	2.30
1987	9.12	10.11	.99	11.29	2.17
1988	9.13	9.57	.44	10.65	1.52
1989	8.39	8.86	.47	9.82	1.43
1990	8.24	9.05	.81	10.43	2.19

The decline in the long-term Treasury rates indicates a decline in investor long-run inflation expectations since the end of 1983. If we use an average real interest rate of 3 percent, then the long-run inflation expectations at the end of 1983 was about 9 percent versus below 5.3 percent at the end of 1990.

After the 1981–82 economic recession, the economy expanded slowly in real terms until the end of 1990. The low and stable risk premiums in 1988 and 1989 began increasing in 1990. By the end of 1990, the risk premium for the highest quality (Aaa) corporate bonds was around 0.8 percentage points. Likewise, the risk premium on the lowest investment grade (Baa) corporate bonds increased to about 2.2 percentage points by year-end 1990. When investors become pessimistic about the outlook for the U.S. economy, these risk premiums increase, as they have when the economy turned down in the past.

ability, its debt-to-equity ratios, and its ability to cover interest expenses.

FHA mortgage rates are consistently higher than the rates on long-term Treasury securities and Aaa corporate bonds. This higher rate reflects higher default risk as well as other differences between the bond and real estate mortgage capital markets.

Interest rate differentials may also be influenced by other factors such as marketability, taxability, and whether or not the issuing organizations can call or refund the debt issue before maturity. Taxability, for example, accounts for the much lower interest rates on state and local Aaa bonds shown in Figure 22.3. Interest on these securities is excluded from federal income taxes. Marketability impacts most heavily on smaller firms that find it difficult to issue debt securities because of their size and the size of their issues. Small issues usually have little marketability in secondary markets and thus must carry higher interest rates.

KEY TERMS

default risk	market segmentation theory
expectations theory	prime rate
liquidity preference theory	risk premium
liquidity premium theory	yield curves
loanable funds theory	yield to maturity

DISCUSSION QUESTIONS

1. Briefly discuss why interest rates for different types of loans are likely to vary.
2. Identify major periods of rising interest rates in U.S. history and describe some of the underlying reasons for these interest rate movements.
3. Describe the relationship between yields and prices for debt securities.
4. Identify the two basic theories used to explain the level of interest rates. Discuss how these theories differ from each other.
5. What are the main sources of loanable funds? Indicate and briefly discuss the factors that affect the supply of loanable funds.
6. Indicate the sources of demand for loanable funds and discuss the factors that affect the demand for loanable funds.
7. Discuss the three basic motives for holding money. What other factors affect the demand for money?

8. The short-run effect of a change in money supply on interest rates may differ from its long-run effect. Explain this statement.
9. What is meant by term structure of interest rates and how is it expressed? Identify and describe the three basic theories used to explain the term structure of interest rates.
10. Define and describe the money market.
11. Identify and briefly describe the major debt instruments that trade in the money market.
12. Explain how Federal Reserve policies affect the money market.
13. Describe how inflation has affected capital market interest rates in recent years. Indicate and describe other factors that influence interest rate differentials between debt securities trading in the capital markets.

PROBLEMS

1. A $1,000 par value, 11 percent bond issued by the Energy Conservation Corporation is currently selling for $800. The bond has a remaining life of 8 years. What is the coupon rate and the current yield on this bond? Also estimate the approximate average annual yield to maturity using the approximation formula.
2. Assume that interest is paid annually on an 11 percent, $1,000 par value, 10-year bond issued by the Rotary Tool Corporation. If the market rate of interest is 14 percent on bonds of similar quality, what will be the bond's current price or value? How would the price change if interest payments of $55 occurred twice a year?
3. Two $1,000 par value corporate bonds with 10-year lives are available for investment purposes. The Alpha Corporation bond pays annual interest of $90 while the Beta Corporation pays $140 in interest annually on its bond.
    a. Determine the yield to maturity or internal rate of return on Alpha's bond if its current price is $939.
    b. If Beta's bond has a current price of $1,200, what would be the yield to maturity on the bond?
4. Use a current copy of the *Federal Reserve Bulletin* to find interest rates on U.S. government securities and on corporate bonds with different bond ratings.
    a. Prepare a yield curve or term structure of interest rates.
    b. Identify long-run inflation expectations and the size of interest rate differentials between long-term U.S. Treasury securities and corporate bonds.
5. A $1,000 face value bond issued by the Ricoa Company currently pays total annual interest of $128.50 per year and has a 17-year life. Use the Bond Yield to Maturity and Bond Valuation tools.

a. What is the yield to maturity of this bond if the current market price is $776.50?

b. How would your answer in part a change if the Ricoa Company makes interest payments semiannually (i.e., $64.25 every six months)?

c. What would be the yield to maturity three years from now if interest payments are made semiannually and the bond then has a market price of $1,119.00?

SELF-TEST QUESTIONS

1. The process of calculating the yield to maturity on a bond is comparable to finding the:
   a. payback period
   b. present value of cash inflows
   c. net present value
   d. internal rate of return

2. The loanable funds theory used to explain the level of interest rates holds that interest rates are a function of the:
   a. supply of loanable funds and the demand for money
   b. supply of loanable funds and the demand for loanable funds
   c. supply of money and the demand for loanable funds
   d. supply of money and the demand for money

3. Which one of the following is not considered to be a basic motive for holding money?
   a. interest rate motive
   b. transactions motive
   c. speculative motive
   d. precautionary motive

4. The yield curve or term structure of interest rates is downward sloping when:
   a. short-term Treasury interest rates are lower than long-term Treasury interest rates
   b. short-term and long-term Treasury interest rates are the same
   c. long-term Treasury interest rates are lower than short-term Treasury interest rates
   d. long-term Treasury interest rates are higher than short-term Treasury interest rates

5. Which one of the following money market instruments would consistently have the lowest interest rate levels?

a. U. S. Treasury bills
b. federal funds
c. commercial paper
d. bankers' acceptances

SELF-TEST PROBLEM

A $1,000 par value, 9 percent bond issued by a corporation is currently selling for $900. The bond has a remaining life of 5 years. What is the coupon rate and the current yield on this bond? Also estimate the approximate average annual yield to maturity using the approximation formula.

SUGGESTED READINGS

Cook, Timothy Q., and Bruce J. Summers (eds.). *Instruments of the Money Market*, 5e. Federal Reserve Bank of Richmond, 1981.

Henning, Charles N., William Pigott, and Robert H. Scott. *Financial Markets and the Economy*, 5e. Englewood Cliffs, NJ: Prentice-Hall, 1988. Chaps. 12, 13, and 14.

Jensen, Frederick H., and Patrick M. Parkinson. "Recent Developments in the Bankers Acceptance Market." *Federal Reserve Bulletin* (January 1986): 1–12.

Madura, Jeff. *Financial Markets and Institutions*. St. Paul, MN: West Publishing Co., 1989. Chaps. 2, 3, and 4.

Rose, Peter S. *Money and Capital Markets*, 3e. Homewood, IL: BPI/Irwin, 1989. Part 3.

Van Horne, James C. *Financial Market Rates and Flows*, 3e. Englewood Cliffs, NJ: Prentice-Hall, 1990.

ANSWERS TO SELF-TEST QUESTIONS   1. d   2. b   3. a   4. c   5. a

SOLUTION TO SELF-TEST PROBLEM

Coupon rate: $90/$1,000 = 9%

Current yield: $90/$900 = 10%

$$YM = \frac{\$90 + (\$1,000 - \$900)/5}{(\$900 + \$1,000)/2} = \frac{\$110}{\$950} = 11.58\%$$

CHAPTER 23
Price Level Changes and Developments

After studying this chapter, you should be able to:
- Recount the broad historical price level changes of various economies and discuss their causes.
- Describe the influence of monetary and fiscal factors on price level changes.
- Explain how price level movements affect markets, interest rate levels, and economic activity.
- Describe the various theories of the relationship between monetary and fiscal policies and changes in the price level.
- Describe the various types of inflation and their causes.
- Explain the basis for the nation's long-run inflationary bias.

Monetary and fiscal policies try to guide the economy of the United States toward economic growth, high employment, and stable prices. Since the Employment Act of 1946 adopted these goals, the world's economies have come to depend on each other more and more. This new interdependence requires a fourth goal: international financial balance.

This chapter is concerned with the relationship of monetary and fiscal policies to price changes and the effects of such changes on the economy. The next chapter explores the impact of monetary and fiscal policies on business fluctuations, or cycles, and on international financial balance.

Anything that changes the value of the money unit or the supply of money and credit affects the whole economy. The change affects first the supply of loanable funds and interest rates and, later, both the demand for and the supply of goods in general. The price changes caused by changes in the monetary system are the topic for this chapter. As a background for understanding such changes, we will briefly examine some unusual ways in which price levels have changed in the past, especially in the United States.

HISTORICAL PRICE MOVEMENTS

Changes in the money supply or in the amount of metal in the money unit have influenced prices since the earliest records of civilization. The money standard in ancient Babylon was in terms of silver and barley. The earliest available price records show that one shekel of silver was equal to 240 measures of grain. At the time of Hammurabi, about 1750 B.C., a shekel in silver was worth between 150 and 180 measures of grain, while in the following century it declined to 90 measures. After Persia conquered Babylonia 539 B.C., the value of the silver shekel was recorded as between 15 and 40 measures of grain.

The greatest inflationary period in ancient history was probably caused by Alexander the Great, when he captured the large gold hoards of Persia and brought them to Greece. Inflation was high for some years; but twenty years after the death of Alexander, a period of deflation began that lasted over fifty years.

The first recorded cases of deliberate currency debasement, (lowering the value), occurred in the Greek city states. The government would debase currency by calling in all coins and issuing new ones containing less of the precious metals. This must have been a convenient form of inflation, for there are many such cases in the records of Greek city states.

Ancient Rome

Similar inflation occurred in Roman history. Caesar Augustus brought so much precious metal from Egypt that prices rose and interest rates fell. During the Punic wars devaluation led to inflation, as the heavy bronze coin was reduced in stages from one pound to one ounce. From the time of Nero, debasements were frequent. The weight of gold coins was gradually reduced, and silver coins had baser metals added to them so that they were finally only 2 percent silver. Few attempts were made to arrest or reverse this process of debasement of coins as the populace adjusted to the process. When Aurelian tried to improve the coinage by adding to its precious metal content, he was resisted so strongly that armed rebellion broke out.

The Middle Ages and Early Modern Times

During the Middle Ages princes and kings debased the coinage to get more revenue. The rulers of France used this ploy more than others, and records show that profit from debasement was sometimes greater than the total of all other revenues.

An important example of inflation followed the discovery of America. Gold and silver poured into Spain from Mexico and Peru. Since the riches were used to buy goods from other countries, they were distributed over the continent and to England. Prices rose in Spain and in most of Europe, but not in proportion to the increase in gold and silver stocks. This was because trade increased following the discovery of America and because many people hoarded the precious metals.

Paper money was not used generally until the end of the seventeenth century. The first outstanding example of inflation due to the issuing of an excessive amount of paper money was in France. In 1719 the government gave Scottish banker John Law a charter for a bank that could issue paper money. The note circulation of his bank amounted to almost 2,700 million livres,[1] against which he had coin of only 21 million livres and bullion of 27 million livres. Prices went up rapidly, but they fell just as fast when Law's bank failed. Afterwards, the money supply was again restricted.

The next outstanding period of inflation was during the American Revolution, which is discussed in the section on American monetary history. Shortly after this American inflation, the government of the French Revolution issued paper currency in huge quantities. This currency, called *assignats*, declined to one-half of one percent of its face value.

Inflation in Modern Times

The next outstanding period of inflation before World War I was in the United States during the Civil War, 1861–1865. Inflation during World War I was widespread, but it was held in check somewhat by government action. Between the two world wars, spectacular inflation took place in Germany in 1923, when prices soared to astronomical heights.

Governments acted to control inflation during World War II, and they were somewhat successful. Runaway inflation did take place, however, especially in China and Hungary.

---

1.   The livre was the monetary unit in use at that time in France.

MAJOR MOVEMENTS OF PRICES IN THE UNITED STATES

Monetary factors have often affected price levels in the United States, especially during major wars.

Revolutionary War

The war that brought this nation into being was financed mainly by inflation. The Second Continental Congress had no real authority to levy taxes and thus found it difficult to raise money. As a result the congress decided to issue notes for $2 million. They issued more and more notes until the total rose to over $240 million, and the individual states issued $200 million more. Since the notes were crudely engraved, counterfeiting was common, adding to the total of circulating currency. Continental currency depreciated in value so rapidly that the expression "not worth a continental" became a part of the American language.

War of 1812

During the War of 1812, the government tried to avoid repeating the inflationary measures of the Revolutionary War. But since the war was not popular in New England, it was impossible to finance it by taxation and borrowing. Paper currency was issued in a somewhat disguised form: bonds of small denomination bearing no interest and having no maturity date. The wholesale price index, based on 100 as the 1910–1914 average prices, rose from 131 in 1812 to 182 in 1814. Prices declined to about the prewar level by 1816 and continued downward as depression hit the economy.

Civil War

The Mexican War (1846–1848) did not involve the total economy to any extent and led to no inflationary price movements. The Civil War, however, was financed partly by issuing paper money. In the early stages, Congress could not raise enough money by taxes and borrowing to finance all expenditures, and therefore it resorted to inflation by issuing United States Notes with no backing, called "greenbacks." In all, $450 million was authorized. Even though this was but a fraction of the cost of the war, prices went up substantially. Wholesale prices on a base of 100 increased from 93 in 1860 to 185 in 1865. Attempts to retire the greenbacks at the end of the war led to deflation and depression in 1866. As a result, the law withdrawing greenbacks was repealed.

World War I

Although the government did not print money to finance World War I, it did practice other inflationary policies. About one-third of the cost of the war was raised by taxes and two-thirds by borrowing. The banking system provided much of this credit, which added to the money supply. People were even persuaded to use Liberty bonds as collateral for bank loans to buy other bonds. The wholesale price index rose from 99 in 1914 to 226 in 1920. Then, as credit expansion was finally restricted in 1921, it dropped to 141 in 1922.

World War II and the Postwar Period

The government used fewer inflationary policies to finance World War II. Nevertheless, the banking system still took up large sums of bonds. By the end of the war, the debt of the federal government had increased by $207 billion. Bank holdings of government bonds had increased by almost $60 billion. Prices went up by only about one-third during the war because they were held in check after the first year by price and wage controls. They then rose rapidly when the controls were lifted after the war. In 1948 wholesale prices had risen to 236 from a level of 110 in 1939.

Wholesale prices increased during the Korean War and again during the 1955–57 expansion in economic activity, as the economy recovered from the 1954 recession. Consumer goods prices continued to move upward during practically the entire postwar period, increasing gradually even in those years in which wholesale prices hardly changed.

Recent Decades

Wholesale consumer goods prices again increased substantially when the Vietnam War escalated after mid-1965. Prices continued upward after American participation in the Vietnam War was reduced in the early 1970s. After American participation in the war ended in 1974, prices rose at the most rapid levels since World War I for the reasons discussed in Chapter 22. Inflation was worldwide in the middle 1970s; its effects were much worse in many other industrial countries than in the United States.

As the 1970s ended, economists realized the full impact of a philosophy based on a high inflation rate. Many economists thought high inflation could keep unemployment down permanently, even though history shows that it does not. The government's efforts to control interest rates by increasing the money supply reinforced people's doubts that such policies would reduce inflation and high interest rates. By October 1979, the Federal Reserve System abandoned this failed approach to interest rate control and adopted a policy of monetary growth control. The result was twofold. First, there was a far greater volatility in interest rates as the Federal Reserve concentrated on monetary factors. Second, during the first three quarters of 1980 some monetary restraint was exercised. This monetary restraint had a depressing effect on production and employment. The Federal Reserve System quickly backed off from this position of restraint, and by the end of 1980 a far greater level of monetary stimulus had driven interest rates to new peaks.

By this time the prime rate had risen to 21.5 percent and three-month Treasury bills had doubled in yield from their midyear lows. These high interest rates had a profound negative effect on such interest-sensitive industries as housing and automobiles. The Reagan Administration reversed the rapid growth of money supply throughout 1981 and until late in 1982. Unemployment climbed as the effects of monetary restraint were imposed on the economy, but the back of inflation was broken. Figure 23.1 shows the steep decline in the Consumer Price Index at this time. By the end of 1982, economic recovery was in place—along with an easing of monetary restraint. Although inflation stayed moderate through mid-1986, the recovery showed signs of weakening. In July 1986 the Fed began to take positive steps to ease monetary restraint to counter weakness in the economy. Specific measures of M1, M2 and M3 were clouded, however, as their definitions changed. M1 showed a dramatic increase in mid-1986, even before the Fed actions, while M2 and M3 were well within their target ranges. All measures of money supply moderated from 1986 to mid-1989, when

FIGURE 23.1   Consumer Price Index, 1960–1990

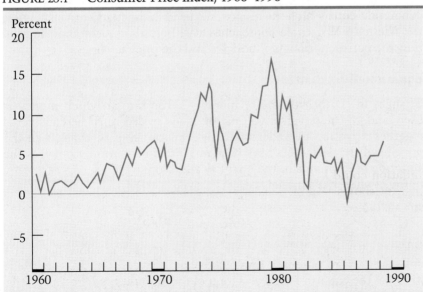

Source: *1989 Historical Chart Book*, Board of Governors of the Federal Reserve System.

rates of both M1 and M2 started increasing significantly. Concern for a weakening of the economy led to the decision to increase the money supply again.

MONETARY AND FISCAL FACTORS THAT AFFECT THE PRICE LEVEL

The record of history shows that inflation usually occurs because the supply of money is increased faster than the supply of goods. In the earliest cases this happened when rulers acquired large stocks gold and silver as part of the spoils of war. Later on, governments increased the money supply by lessening the precious metal content of existing coins and using the extra metal to issue more coins. Beginning in the 18th century paper money was issued in quantity, which led to higher prices. In the last half of the nineteenth century, and especially in the twentieth century, banks created inflation by expanding credit. On the other hand, credit contraction caused deflation.

Such changes in the volume of money probably had the most important effect on the price level. They were by no means the only influence, however; prices did not always go up in proportion to the increases in money supply. For instance, when the money supply in Europe increased as gold and silver flowed from the New World, trade also increased. Then more money was needed to meet the demands of such commerce. Also, many people hoarded precious metals, slowing down the rate at which the money was used in the market to buy goods.

The following three approaches will help us understand the relationship between monetary policies and the price level.

Equation of Exchange

equation of exchange shows how changes in the volume of money, rate at which money is used, and volume of goods and services being exchanged interact to affect the price level

Changes in (1) the volume of money, (2) the rate at which money is used, and (3) the physical volume of goods traded must be considered together if we are to understand their relationship to changes in the price level. These factors have been put into an equation, known as the **equation of exchange** or the quantity equation, which serves as a ready frame of reference for analysis:

$$MV = \Sigma pq$$

In this equation M is the total supply of money, and V is the velocity of money. Velocity is the average number of times per year a dollar is used to purchase final goods and services. On the goods side (right) of the equation there is a total of the amounts spent on all goods, which is equal to the average price of each article sold—for example, bushels of wheat—multiplied by the physical quantity traded. For convenience, the right side of the equation may be written as PT with P, the price level, a weighted average of all average prices, or ps, and T the sum of all the physical quantities traded. The equation then becomes

$$MV = PT$$

This equation can help us understand factors involved in changes in the price level. It shows two equal quantities from different points of view. The total money value of goods and services traded can be seen first from the point of view of the total price of all the goods (PT) and then from the point of view of the sum of the money transactions (MV) to buy such goods. These two amounts must of course be equal, but we can gain valuable information from looking at the factors at work on each of them.

It is important to recognize that when one factor such as M changes, other factors will probably also change so that the effect on prices may not be proportionate, or a price change may not occur at all. For example, the supply of money may double; but the rate of use, or V, may be cut in half. In such a case the other side of the equation would not be affected at all. Or, V could decrease somewhat and prices go up somewhat to again balance the equation.

So far the effect of a change in M or V has been assumed to be on P. It is possible, however, for T to be affected. If in a period of unused resources M is increased and V does not decrease, or at least not proportionately, T can go up, to balance the PT side of the equation. So the situation is usually far more complex than a simple change in M or V leading to a proportionate change in P.

Cash Balances Approach

Another way of analyzing the effect of money changes on prices is the **cash balances approach**, which focuses on the public's demand for cash balances. Several equations are used to explain the relationship of money to prices and trade. One of the most useful is the following:

$$M = kTP$$

cash balances approach *method of analyzing the effect on price levels of money held as cash balances*

In this equation M is the money supply, T is the physical volume of trade to be transacted with money during a year, and P is the price level of the things included in T. The new factor, k, is the amount of money held in the form of cash balances, that is, cash plus bank deposits. It is expressed as the fraction representing the ratio of cash balances to the amount of transactions in a given period of time, such as a year, a quarter, or a month.

The value of k is thus related to the velocity of money. If the amount of cash balances held is equal to one-fifth of a year's transactions, V is 5 and k is 1/5. In other words, k and V are reciprocals of one another, that is, $k = (1/V)$. The cash balances equation can therefore be written

$$M = (1/V)(TP) \text{ or } MV = TP$$

Thus, the cash balances equation and the quantity equation are just different ways of looking at the same thing. However, both equations are useful ways of showing the factors that affect prices. The equation of exchange focuses on the rate at which money is spent and the reasons for spending it at that rate. The cash balances equation puts special emphasis on the reasons for holding money as cash balances, as well as on the reasons for spending it, by showing the money supply on one side and the demand for money (to be held as cash balances or used in trade) on the other side. Thus, we can understand what is happening to prices from the point of view of supply-and-demand.

The cash balances approach can be useful in analysis. For example, increases in the government deficit and the money supply (M) are likely to affect cash balances. If there is less than full employment at that time, the volume of trade (T) will go up. But what if business people do not feel that future business prospects are good and, therefore, do not spend as much on inventory, maintenance, and capital expenditures? In that case, cash balances (k) will increase abnormally. As a result, the increased government expenditures at such a time will not have the same effect on the volume of business as they would have had if the outlook for the future were more positive. This was the situation during the 1930s when government deficits led to abnormal increases in cash balances.

However, if government deficits and increases in the money supply take place when business volume (T) and prices (P) are expected to increase, as is true during a war, cash balances, or k, will not increase. They may even drop as business people rush to buy raw materials and equipment before prices go up. On the other hand, if prices are held in check by price controls as they were during World War II and for a time after the Vietnam War, cash balances, or k, will increase greatly. When price controls are lifted, these additional cash balances are used to buy goods and services, and prices rise. Thus, inflation has not been avoided but only delayed until more goods are available.

To sum up, these equations show how four elements of the economy are always in balance. If values increase on one side of the equation, they must increase by the same amount on the other side. And if a value on one side goes up or down, the other values on that side must adjust to keep the balance. Keeping these equations in mind can make the effects of changes in the economy a little more understandable.

The Quantity Theory

One of the oldest, and also one of the currently most popular, theories about the relationship of money to prices is the **quantity theory**. It holds that changes in the quantity of money are the main cause of changes in the price level. All versions of this theory rely partly on some form of the equation of exchange to develop their relationships. In its crudest form, the quantity theory holds that changes in the money supply lead to equal, proportionate changes in the same direction in the price level. This may be true for an idealized free-enterprise economy where output (T) is always at full-employment level and V does not change. But such an economy does not exist today and probably never did. Irving Fisher of Yale University was one of the early advocates in America of a more refined quantity theory. He recognized that V and T might change at times, offsetting the effect of changes in the money supply on the price level. But he held that such changes took place mainly during the upswing and downswing of the business cycle and, therefore, were cyclical in nature. That is, Fisher felt that V and T would have about the same level at a given stage in any cycle.

quantity theory states that the quantity of money is the primary determinant of changes in price level

The behavior of the economy during the depression, which began in 1929, and the writings of J. M. Keynes of Cambridge University convinced most economists that the quantity theory could not adequately explain general price changes during periods of less than full employment. However, it has come back into favor in recent decades, mainly because of the work of economist Milton Friedman and others, who refer to themselves as **monetarists**. Friedman holds that the money supply is the major influence of the *value* of output, that is, PT, rather than P alone. This means that the velocity of money or its reciprocal, the demand for cash balances, is fairly stable, or at least reasonably predictable.

monetarists economists who believe that price level is determined by money supply

This version of the quantity theory is based on the idea that an outside influence that changes the prices and quantities of some assets causes the prices and quantities of other assets to adjust so that these amounts stay in balance. If there is a given level of income, interest rates, prices, and profits received from holding real assets, then spending units—businesses, governmental units, or individuals—will want to hold given amounts of real assets, money, and other financial assets. They will want to buy a given amount of goods and services. Any amount of money they receive in excess of the amount they desire to hold is used to acquire real and financial assets and to buy goods and services. Changes in the rate of spending are part of the adjustment, tending to close the gap between desired and actual money balances.

Assets are generally produced in changing quantities in response to changes in demand, but in the short run, changes in the money stock are largely independent of changes in the demand for money. When the

Federal Reserve increases the money stock by supplying banks with additional reserves, they have more reserves than they want and, therefore, invest them or increase their lending. Spending units sell securities or borrow as long as the interest rate banks charge is less than the yield from hiring labor and from buying and using other assets. These spending units in turn use their demand deposits to buy additional services and goods and to invest in real and financial assets. And so other spending units receive more additions to money balances than they want. This process leads to an increase in spending or investing to eliminate the excess. But spending or investing does not destroy the money balances; it merely passes them on to someone else. The process continues until new levels of income, prices, interest rates, and services received from holding real assets are reached and spending units want to hold the expanded stock of money.

The demand to hold money need not be the same as it was before the money stock was expanded, because the demand to hold money changes in relationship to income and wealth and changes in the price level. People usually want to hold more money when personal income or real wealth is greater than when it is smaller. Price level increases may increase the wealth of an individual or a corporation, and thus the desire is to hold more money. When prices have not increased, but are likely to increase in the future, the demand for money will tend to decline since the cost of holding it becomes higher. Interest rates also affect the amount of money an individual or corporation wants to hold, since at higher interest rates it costs more to hold money. These and other factors will affect the level of money that the community wants to hold.

FACTORS INFLUENCING THE MONEY SUPPLY, VELOCITY, AND THE VOLUME OF TRADE

In Chapter 5 we analyzed in detail the factors affecting the supply of money, but we will review them briefly here. The total currency supply (M) is influenced primarily by people's demand for cash. The largest part of the money supply today is demand and checkable deposits. The amount of deposits is determined by the demand for checkable accounts and for individual and government loans, and by the policies of the banks and central bank authorities that govern its availability. The basic reasons for holding a certain level of money in checking accounts usually relate to the timing of receipts and disbursements and to expectations about the future.

The velocity of money (V) is the relationship between two factors: the volume of monetary transactions and the amount of cash balances (cash and bank deposits) that individuals, business units, institutions, and the government feel they must keep on hand to meet demands for funds and emergencies. These factors in turn depend on the organization of the financial system of the community and expectations about the future.

The organization of the financial system is an important factor in determining the needs for money and bank credit. If individuals, businesses, and government can borrow money easily, quickly, and at a reasonable cost, they will keep smaller money balances. A system of savings institutions that provides safety, liquidity, and some income on savings also increases velocity because people will put money in such institutions rather than hoard it. Also, the more such institutions invest their funds, the more the velocity increases.

Another major factor affecting velocity is how consumers feel about the future of the economy. Consumers spend more freely when they feel that income will remain stable or increase than they do when they expect income to decrease. They also spend their money more rapidly when they feel prices are likely to increase. Business people keep smaller sums of money on deposit to meet emergencies when they feel the outlook is good than when it is doubtful. This is especially true when they expect the prices of the goods they have to buy to increase. They also put off buying capital equipment and inventory when they expect business to decline. This reduces the velocity of money. Likewise, velocity increases or decreases according to whether expectations regarding interest rates and the future level of security prices make new financing more or less desirable.

The physical volume of trade (T) is likewise subject to many influences, some of which lead to changes in prices. The basic volume of trade depends on such factors as (1) the size of the population and the labor force and its technical abilities, (2) the quantity and the quality of the natural resources and man-made capital, and (3) the techniques of production, distribution, and administration. The extent to which resources are fully used is equally important. This, in turn, depends on the ability of producers to sell their output, or the total demand for goods and services in the economy.

The price level is thus the result of the interaction of all of the factors that affect M, V, and T. Changes in the money supply can lead to changes in the price level, but many other factors are involved.

ANALYSIS OF CHANGES IN THE PRICE LEVEL

On the basis of all of these factors that affect the price level, it is possible to further analyze various types of changes in the price level.

Price Changes Initiated by a Change in Costs

The price level can sometimes increase without the original impulse coming from either the money supply or its velocity. If costs rise faster than productivity increases, as when wages go up, businesses with some control over prices will try to raise them to cover the higher costs. Such increases are likely to be effective when the demand for goods is strong compared to the supply. The need for more funds to meet production and distribution at higher prices usually causes the money supply and velocity to increase. This type of inflation is called *cost-push inflation*. So this rise in prices comes from the cost side, not from increases in the money supply. Prices may not go up, however, if the monetary authorities restrict credit expansion. In that case only the most efficient businesses will have enough demand to operate profitably. As a result, some resources will be unemployed.

cost-push inflation occurs when prices are raised to cover rising production costs, such as wages

Cost-push inflation is different from inflation caused by an increase in the money supply, which is called *demand-pull inflation*. Demand-pull inflation may be defined as an excessive demand for goods and services during periods of economic expansion as a result of large increases in the money supply. In actual practice, both aspects of inflation are likely to be operative at the same time, since cost-push can occur only in industries in which labor negotiations are carried out on an industry-wide basis and in which management has the ability to increase prices.

demand-pull inflation occurs during economic expansions when demand for goods and services is greater than supply

Demand-pull inflation may also be caused by changes in demand in particular industries. The demand for petroleum, for example, may be greater than demand in general, so that prices rise in this industry before they rise generally. The first raise is likely to be in the basic materials themselves, leading to increased profits in the industries that produce them. Labor will press for wage increases to get its share of the total value of output, and thus labor costs also rise. Price rises in basic industries lead to price increases in the industries that use their products. Wage increases in one major industry are also likely to lead to demands for similar increases in other industries and among the non-organized workers in such industries. Thus, a process is set into motion which can lead to general changes in prices, provided the monetary authorities do not restrict credit so as to prevent it.

Price Changes Initiated by a Change in the Money Supply

The way in which factors that affect prices relate to one another is quite complex. In this discussion we consider the adjustments that take place when the primary change is in the money supply or its velocity. In the following chapter we will consider the more complex relationships arising out of changes in both the money supply and goods side of the equation during business cycles.

An increase in the supply or velocity of money can cause several types of inflation. Inflation may result when the supply of purchasing power increases. In modern times such inflation is often initiated by government deficits financed by creating deposits, and at other times by private demands for funds.[2] If this happens when people and resources are not fully employed, the volume of trade goes up; prices are only slightly affected at first. As unused resources are brought into use, however, prices will go up. When resources such as metals become scarce, their prices rise. As any resource begins to be used up, the expectation of future price rises will itself force prices up, because attempts to buy before such price rises will increase demand above current needs. Since some costs, such as interest costs and wages set by contract, will lag, profits will rise, increasing the demand for capital goods. We will consider such changes more fully in the discussion of monetary factors in business cycles in Chapter 24.

Once resources are fully employed, the full effect of the increased money supply will be felt on prices. Prices may rise out of proportion for a time as expectations of higher prices lead to faster spending and so raise V. The expansion will continue until trade and prices are in balance at the new levels of the money supply. Velocity will probably drop somewhat from those levels during the period of rising prices, since the desire to buy goods before the price goes up has disappeared.

Even if the supply of money is increased when people and resources are fully employed, prices may not go up proportionately. Higher prices increase profits for a time and so lead to a demand for more capital and labor. Thus, previously unemployed spouses, retired workers, and similar groups begin to enter the labor force. Businesses may use capital more fully by having two or three shifts use the same machines.

Speculative and Administrative Inflation

When an increased money supply causes inflation, it can lead to additional price pressure called **speculative inflation**. Since prices have risen for some time, people believe that they will keep on rising. Inflation becomes self-generating for a time because, instead of higher prices resulting in lower demand, people may buy more to get goods before they go still higher, as happened in the late 1970s. This effect may be confined to certain areas, as it was to land prices in the 1920s

speculative inflation caused by the expectation that prices will continue to rise, resulting in increased buying to avoid even higher future prices

2. Demand-pull inflation traditionally exists during periods of economic expansion when the demand for goods and services exceeds the available supply of such goods and services. A second version of inflation also associated with increases in the money supply occurs because of "monetization" of the U.S. government debt. The reader should recall from Chapter 21 that the Treasury finances government deficits by selling U.S. government securities to the public, commercial banks, or the Federal Reserve. When the Federal Reserve purchases U.S. government securities, reserves must be "created" to pay for the purchases. This, in turn, may lead to higher inflation because of an increase in money supply and bank reserves.

Florida land boom or to security prices in the 1928–1929 stock market boom. Such a price rise leads to an increase in V as speculators try to turn over their funds as rapidly as possible and many others try to buy ahead of needs before there are further price rises.

For three decades, until the early 1980s, price pressures and inflation were continuous despite occasional policies of strict credit restraint. During this long period, in fact, prices continued upward in recession periods, though at a slower rate than in prosperity periods. The need to restrain price rises hampered the Fed's ability to promote growth and fight recessions. Prices and other economic developments during this period led many to feel that the economy had developed a long-run **inflationary bias**. Even though prices actually declined slightly in early 1986, many economists expect the long-run inflation to continue.

inflationary bias
assumption that a long history of price increases, even during recessions, will continue

Economists base their expectations that long-run inflationary bias will continue on the following factors: (1) Prices and wages tend to rise during periods of boom in a competitive economy. This tendency is reinforced by wage contracts that provide escalator clauses to keep wages in line with prices and by wage increases that are sometimes greater than increases in productivity. (2) During recessions, prices tend to remain stable rather than decrease. This is because major unions have long-run contracts calling for annual wage increases no matter what economic conditions are at the time. The tendency of large corporations to rely on nonprice competition (advertising, and style and color changes) and to reduce output rather than cut prices also keeps prices stable. Furthermore, if prices do decline drastically in a field, the government is likely to step in with programs to help take excess supplies off the market. There is little doubt that prices would decline in a severe and prolonged depression. Government takes action to counter resulting unemployment, however, before the economy reaches such a level. Thus we no longer experience the downward price pressure of a depression.

administrative inflation
the tendency of prices, aided by union-corporation contracts, to rise during economic expansion and to resist declines during recessions

The inflation resulting from these factors is called **administrative inflation**. This is to distinguish it from the type of inflation that happens when demand exceeds the available supply of goods, either because demand is increasing faster than supply in the early stages of a recovery period, or because demand from monetary expansion by the banking system or the government exceeds available supply.

Traditional monetary policy is not wholly effective against administrative inflation. If money supplies are restricted enough, prices can be kept in line; but this will lead to long-term unemployment and slow growth. It is also difficult for new firms and small growing firms to get credit since lending policies are likely to be conservative. The government must develop new tools to deal with administrative inflation effectively.

The Relationship Between Growth in Money Supply and Inflation

We have seen that the factors that affect prices interact in a complex way. In addition, there are several different types of inflation at work in the U.S. economy. Even with these complexities, however, we can gain some valuable insights by examining the relationship between money supply growth and inflation over a period of time.[3]

Figure 23.2 shows a close parallel between inflation rates and money growth until the early 1970s. This suggests that underlying the

FIGURE 23.2   Rates of Change of Money and Prices

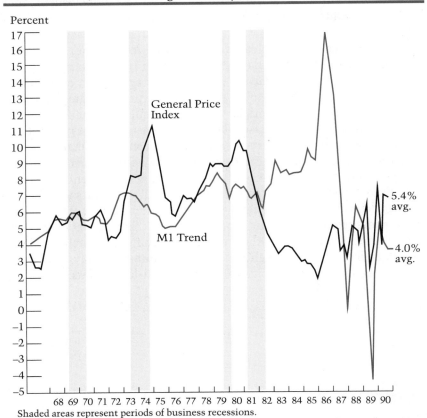

Shaded areas represent periods of business recessions.

Source: Federal Reserve Bank of St. Louis.

3.   Inflation rates can be estimated in a number of ways. For example, a consumer price index (CPI) or a producer price index could be used. Many economists, however, prefer using the GNP price deflator because it is comprehensive; gross national product measures the total output of goods and services in the United States for a specified time period. The GNP deflator reflects the ratio of GNP, measured in terms of current prices, to GNP using last year's prices or some base-period prices.

complex relationship between prices and other factors, the inflation rate seems to follow the growth rate in money supply or stock.

Substantial differences between money growth and inflation did occur over the 1971–75 time period. Several reasons, however, seem to account for this. First, wage and price controls were instituted in 1971 and mandatory and voluntary versions were maintained until early 1974. These controls held inflation rates artificially below money growth rates during 1971 and part of 1972. Inflation then "caught up" with the growth in money supply. In addition, an OPEC embargo on oil shipments to the United States caused a rapid rise in energy costs, leading to the sharp inflation of 1973.

From 1976 until 1980, the relationship between money supply and prices returned to its historical closeness, but from 1980 to early 1990 a wide departure developed. While the money stock as measured by M1 increased a great deal, increases in the price level fell dramatically. Since early 1990 a closer relationship between the general price level and the money supply as measured by M1 has again been established. Economists offer several explanations for the previous breakdown in the relationship between prices and money supply. One is that the velocity of money has decreased. Because decreasing interest rates have made it less costly to hold money, individuals and businesses want to hold more. Another explanation is that money stock definitions have changed, and the yields that banking institutions can offer on deposits have been deregulated. The introduction of NOW accounts and time or savings deposits bearing unregulated rates of interest disrupted conventional measures of the money supply after 1981. Some economists have shifted their attention to other money supply figures, such as M2 or M3, to explain the relationship between the money supply and prices. A recovery of money velocity to more normal levels since 1986 supports this approach.

KEY TERMS

administrative inflation
cash balances approach
cost-push inflation
demand-pull inflation
equation of exchange
inflationary bias

monetarists
quantity theory
speculative inflation

DISCUSSION QUESTIONS

1. Describe the process by which inflation took place before modern times.
2. Discuss the early periods of inflation based on the issue of paper money.
3. Discuss the basis for inflation during World Wars I and II.
4. Discuss the causes of the major periods of inflation in American history.
5. State the equation of exchange and identify each factor in it. Why are the two sides of the equation equal?
6. State the cash balances equation and identify each factor in it. Also indicate how this approach can be useful in analyzing the factors affecting the price level.
7. Discuss various versions of the quantity theory of money. Explain, step by step, how the Friedman version of the quantity theory is supposed to work.
8. Outline and discuss major factors that affect the money supply, the velocity of money, and the physical volume of trade.
9. Explain the process by which price changes may be initiated by a general change in costs.
10. Explain the process by which a change in the money supply leads to a change in the price level.
11. Discuss the speculative type of inflation.
12. What factors are used to support the case for a long-run inflationary bias?
13. Discuss the relationship between money supply growth and inflation rates.

PROBLEMS

1. Assume a condition in which the economy is strong, with relatively high employment. For one reason or another the money supply is increasing at a high rate and there is little evidence of money creation slowing down. Assuming the money supply continues to increase, describe the evolving effect on price levels.
2. At long last, the inflationary spiral appears to have been broken. Notwithstanding, the money supply continues to increase rapidly, contradicting the general assumption of a direct link between price levels and the supply of money. As a member of the Board of Governors of the Federal Reserve System you are pleased with price level developments but concerned about the growth of the money supply. In casting your vote for monetary action would you favor a

strong reduction of the growth of the money supply? Explain your reasoning.

SELF-TEST QUESTIONS

1. Price inflation has been characteristic of:
    a. modern industrial society
    b. our post gold-standard period
    c. the history of prices since earliest recorded history
    d. only industrialized societies

2. One of the most spectacular examples of price inflation is:
    a. that of Germany in the early 1920s
    b. the period following the Civil War in this country
    c. the post-World War I period
    d. the post-World War II period

3. The record reveals that inflation usually occurred:
    a. during periods of large gold discoveries
    b. first on the west coast, then moving to the east coast
    c. as a result of international trade deficits
    d. because the supply of money was increased faster than the supply of goods

4. The cash balances approach to price movements:
    a. focuses on the cash demands of the public
    b. emphasizes the velocity of money
    c. places equal emphasis on the supply of money, its velocity and the volume of goods traded
    d. is known as the equation of exchange

5. The quantity theory of money is:
    a. of recent origin
    b. held by a few key authorities
    c. dependent on stable or predictable velocity and trade levels in its most basic form
    d. the basis for most Federal Reserve actions

SELF-TEST PROBLEM

As an economist for a major bank you are asked to explain the present substantial increase in the price level, notwithstanding the fact that neither the money supply nor the velocity of money have increased. Explain.

SUGGESTED READINGS

Black, Robert P. "In Support of Price Stability," *Economic Review*, Federal Reserve Bank of Richmond (January/February 1990): 3–6.

"The Costs of Inflation and Recession," *Economic Report of the President*, (February 1990): 79 and 80. (The annual President's reports typically provide a commentary on price level movements.)

Haslag, Joseph H. "Money Aggregates and the Rate of Inflation," *Economic Review*, Federal Reserve Bank of Dallas (March 1990): 1–12.

Kaufman, George G. *The U.S. Financial System*, 4e. Englewood Cliffs, NJ: Prentice-Hall, 1989. Chaps. 2 and 34.

Kidwell, David S., and Richard L. Peterson. *Financial Institutions, Markets, and Money*, 4e. Hinsdale, IL: The Dryden Press, 1990. Chap. 24.

Rose, Peter S. *Money and Capital Markets*, 3e. Homewood, IL: BPI/Irwin, Inc., 1989. Chap. 9.

ANSWERS TO SELF-TEST QUESTIONS   1. c   2. a   3. d   4. a   5. c

SOLUTION TO SELF-TEST PROBLEM

This situation may be described as cost-push inflation. During periods of great demand for goods relative to the supply, the demand for wage increases may be met. Such increased costs will then be passed on in the form of higher prices. Though this results in an increase in the money supply and velocity, the basic influence is one of cost-push. It is also possible that prices have increased because of changes in demand in particular industries. Wage increases may be generated in those industries and spread to other industries with the result of overall cost increases.

CHAPTER 24
Business Fluctuations and International Payment Problems

After studying this chapter, you should be able to:
- Define business cycles and explain the processes that lead to expansions and recessions in economic activity.
- Describe the effects of monetary and fiscal policies on business cycles.
- Discuss the relationship of prices and wages to unemployment rates.
- Explain what is meant by international financial equilibrium and its importance to the domestic U.S. economy
- Briefly describe the U.S. balance of payments and the evolution of the international financial system.

In the two previous chapters, we analyzed how changes in monetary and fiscal policies affect interest rates and the money market and the price level. Because price changes and fluctuations in interest rates are key factors in the continually recurring cycles in business activity, we will analyze more thoroughly the role of monetary and fiscal policies in the cyclical process in the first part of this chapter. The latter part of the chapter explores our nation's international financial relationships. The final chapter in this text traces recent monetary and fiscal policy actions to achieve the four economic goals of: (1) sustained economic growth, (2) high levels of employment, (3) stable prices, and (4) international financial balance.

BUSINESS FLUCTUATIONS AND CYCLES

Ever since business activity began taking place almost exclusively through monetary or credit transactions, economic activity has alternated between prosperity and recession or depression. These recurring fluctuations in economic activity are called **business cycles**, even though they are not of equal length or intensity. They have ranged from such mild recessions as those in 1927 and 1960, which many people hardly noticed, to the Great Depression of the early 1930s, when about one-third of the labor force was out of work. Business cycles can vary from a little over a year to more than nine years.

business cycles recurring fluctuations in economic activity between periods of recession and expansion

Most people, including economists, like sustained economic growth, particularly when prices do not go up with the growth. This "real" economic growth traditionally leads to higher living standards. In this section we will emphasize the impact of monetary and fiscal policies on economic activity in the United States.

The Circular Flow of Economic Activity

Economic activity is a circular flow in which the act of producing goods and services generates income. This income allows those who receive it to buy goods and services; the spending leads to production to satisfy wants; production generates more income; and so on in a continuous circular process. One person's spending is another person's income.

At any given time, a nation has facilities to produce goods and services of all kinds for consumers, businesses, and governments. Some goods and services are traded for other goods and services from foreign countries. This structure for producing goods and services developed over a long period of time, and only a part of it is changing at any one time. Various parts of the structure are related to each other. The steel mills we have, for example, provide different types and quantities of steel to meet the demands of consumers, producers, and the government. Some parts of the production structure are changing constantly as the demand for steel changes. The pattern of production of goods and services refers to the amounts and types of goods being produced in any period of time.

In the act of producing goods and services, income is paid to the factors of production in the form of wages, interest, rent, and profits. Money is paid to the government as taxes and other fees. Some money is also transferred to others as gifts and grants. Businesses keep the remaining funds as depreciation allowances to replace equipment and as retained profits to increase the equity of the owners. This pattern of distributing income is called the flow of money payments, and it has developed over time. Tax structures, for example, evolved gradually; business and consumer decisions adjust to them. Wage rates are set by bargaining, which is affected by the relative strengths of business and labor bargaining units in general and within each industry.

The funds from the flow of money payments continue in the circular flow when they are spent on goods and services. Those who receive the money include consumers, nonprofit institutions, businesses, and the government. They, in turn, decide how they will spend this money on goods and services, and how much of it they will save. They may also use credit and, in this way, spend more money for a while than they receive. At other times, they may pay off debts faster than new credit is extended. The goods and services that consumers, businesses, governments, and institutions buy and the prices they can pay determine what is produced in the next round.

Depreciation allowances and retained earnings kept in businesses and the savings of individuals and institutions also enter the spending stream to complete the circular flow of money payments. Depreciation allowances and retained earnings that the business spends on plant and equipment or inventory enter into the spending stream. If the business does not have an immediate need for these funds, it may offer them for investment in the money market; the borrower will then spend them. Savings may enter the spending stream by being invested directly in real estate, equipment, or other assets. Or they may be put into financial institutions and entered into the spending stream by a borrower. The amount and type of all spending by those who receive the flow of money payments constitute the pattern of spending in any period of time.

Individuals, governments, and businesses use the monetary and banking system to transfer money in the circular flow of activity. Banks can create a problem in the equilibrium, or balance, since money sometimes accumulates in the banking system rather than being spent or invested. At other times individuals, businesses, or governments may have funds to spend that did not arise out of the circular flow of economic activity, but that came from deposit creation by the banking system.

The Role of Monetary and Fiscal Policy in Cyclical Fluctuations

As we have seen in Chapter 22, monetary changes are important in the cyclical process because of how they affect interest rates. Their influence is more widespread than this, however. In fact, modern business cycles can exist only in an economy whose banking system can expand

and contract the money supply. In analyzing the factors at work in the cyclical process, we will consider expansion first.

FACTORS LEADING TO AN EXPANSION

Many factors can initiate an expansion in economic activity. Any change in the pattern of production, of money flow, or of consumption (buying of goods and services) can be the factor that initiates the expansion. Such factors might include unusually good crops or new inventions.

The effects of increased spending during wartime need no further explanation. Increases in government spending, except during periods of full employment of resources, also cause increases in economic activity, though of a smaller magnitude. The same is true of changes in the methods of financing the spending. A shift from funding government spending through taxation to funding by borrowing affects the economy by increasing the incomes of those whose taxes have been cut. The way the government responds to the public debt likewise has a strong economic effect. Higher taxes to reduce the public debt have a deflationary effect, cutting income available for consumer spending. Lower income means less consumer demand followed by less production.

A change in transfer payments affects the flow of money payments and, in turn, the patterns of spending and production. This happens, for example, when social security taxes are raised and more is paid to those receiving benefits under the social security programs. The government can also cause changes in economic activity by actions in the housing area. Making more money available for financing, or making financing easier to get, changes the flow of money payments, spending, and production.

Government can also influence business conditions by changing laws, such as tariff and banking laws that regulate business. Introducing a high protective tariff after the rates have been low causes a demand for materials with which to produce what was formerly imported. The higher prices for the domestically produced goods likewise causes a change in consumer spending patterns.

Changes in monetary policies can also cause fluctuations in the economy. If loans become easier to get at lower rates, investment spending will increase. If the Federal Reserve does something to restrict lending, business investment will be slowed down. Monetary policy also affects the housing market, especially by severe lending restriction, and it has some effect on the durable consumer goods market.

Some of the initiating factors first affect business; others first affect consumers and their spending. As businesses adjust to changes in consumer buying, they also change the pattern of production and, in turn, the income distribution and the flow of money payments. This again affects the pattern of consumption.

THE CUMULATIVE PROCESS DURING EXPANSION

After one of the initiating factors has begun an expansion, other inten-sifying, or increasing, factors may strengthen the upward movement. One of the most important is the **multiplier**, that is, the process by which an increase in spending leads to a multiplied effect on national income. For example, as investment spending goes up, national income increases, leading to an increase in consumption spending. This in turn raises national income, which leads to more spending on consumption, and so on. If investment spending does not increase further as a result of the derived effect of consumer spending, the total effect on income will depend on the *marginal propensity to consume*, that is, the rela-tionship of consumption spending to changes in income. Suppose the increase in investment spending is $5 billion and the marginal propen-sity to consume is 0.8. That is, 80 percent of the increased income derived from the investment is spent on consumption. This means that in the next round $4 billion is spent on consumption and $1 billion is saved, and this increases national income by $4 billion. Of this amount $3.2 billion is then spent in the next round, and so on. If all other factors remained constant, this process would go on until the total change in income would be $25 billion, of which $5 billion is the increase in investment spending and $20 billion is the derived increase in consumption spending.

multiplier
process by which an increase in spending leads to a multiplied effect on national income

Another factor that intensifies expansion is the resulting demand for additional production facilities. The demand for production facili-ties increases by a larger percentage than that for consumer goods because of the **accelerator principle**. Since production facilities last for a relatively long time, only some of them need to be replaced each year. For example, if production facilities last for ten years, an average of 10 percent will be replaced each year. When all of the production facilities are being used fully, a 10 percent increase in consumer demand can cause the demand for production facilities to double—10 percent of the production facilities for normal replacement and another 10 percent to meet the added consumer demand.

accelerator principle
the demand for producer goods increases more than the demand for con-sumer goods

In the final analysis, all intensifying factors are related to (1) money creation, (2) the reduction of cash balances, (3) an increase in the velocity of money, or (4) the level of interest rates. When businesses build up inventories because they expect price rises, or expand produc-tion as profits increase, they either use idle funds or increase short-term borrowing. This borrowing has been an important source of added spending in past cycles.

Money expansion also aids speculation in commodity and security markets. The same is usually true of government deficit financing during an expansion. Long-term business financing mainly uses cur-rent savings; but in the early stages of an expansion, funds held in short-term investments are drawn into the capital markets. Money from bank loans may also find its way into permanent investment in plant and equipment.

FACTORS LEADING TO A RECESSION

A recession may be brought about by something from outside the circular flow of economic activity. The government may decrease spending or bank loans may become harder to get and more expensive. However, expansion itself causes changes that tend to slow business down or even cause a recession. Costs tend to rise faster than selling prices after a period of time, and the lower profits reduce the motive for expansion. Less productive workers are drawn into the labor force and inefficiency increases. Profits, in turn, are reduced.

Furthermore, forecast errors made during an expansion do not show up while activity is expanding rapidly. After a while, however, it may become apparent that not all of the goods that some business people thought would be demanded in their field can be sold at a reasonable profit. This factor also slows down expansion.

During a period of expansion interest rates go up because the demand for funds rises faster than the supply. This makes it less profitable to finance expansion with bonds. It also makes capital investment less desirable. While interest rates are rising, the marginal efficiency of capital—the expected rate of return which can be earned by adding units of capital equipment—falls, first in a few fields and then in others. This happens because expectations of future profits go down as supply outpaces demand and costs get closer to selling prices. The result is a decrease in new plant and equipment spending.

THE CUMULATIVE PROCESS DURING RECESSION

Decreasing profits and future expectations of smaller profits, money contraction, and an increasingly negative outlook intensify a recession, just as their opposites do to an expansion. The fall in prices causes businesses to buy less than they need to meet current demands, since they want to cut inventory losses. They reduce inventories to the level of the current volume of business so as to cut losses from future price declines. Hoarding takes funds out of the current economic stream, whereas money creation adds funds during an expansion. In the Keynesian terminology, liquidity preference is increased, and this intensifies the recession.

Furthermore, funds that would normally be used to buy consumer goods are used to pay off debts because of the fear of the future, and people save more and spend less. As profits and gross errors of forecast become apparent in some fields, many businesses must be liquidated. This leads to a forced sale of assets to pay off debts.

FACTORS LEADING TO ANOTHER EXPANSION

In many past cycles, initiating factors arising outside the circular flow of economic activity have started business on a new upward movement. These include such things as new inventions leading to more business spending, new consumer goods leading to more consumer and business spending, more foreign purchases in the United States, and more government spending. Even with no outside forces, the economy will gradually generate the momentum for an expansion.

After liquidation has gone so far that only reasonably strong businesses remain and some of these are again operating at reasonable profits, confidence gradually returns. This leads to more spending for repairs and replacement of some equipment. After a while, this replacement demand will grow because many producer goods do not last more than a few years and have to be replaced if production is to continue. At the same time, the drive to further reduce costs is likely to lead to the introduction of cost-cutting devices, thus adding to the demand for new capital. Lower interest rates and greater profits will also lead to more investment spending.

Monetary and Fiscal Policies and the Level of Economic Activity

The discussion of the cyclical process indicates clearly that monetary actions and fiscal policy play an important role in the cycle. Either can act as an initiating factor leading to an expansion or a recession. They are also related to the intensifying factors.

There are basically two different approaches to the relationship between monetary policy and economic activity. One approach holds that the major effect works through interest rates, the other that it works through changes in the money stock.

KEYNESIAN ECONOMICS

The standard Keynesian national income analysis puts major emphasis on interest rates. Government spending is thought to be largely independent. Consumer spending depends on income and the consumption function, that is, how consumption spending compares to income. Investment spending depends on the expected profitability of the investment, that is, the relationship of investment outlays to income resulting therefrom. This relationship, in turn, depends on many factors, including the price levels of products to be sold, interest costs, wages rates, and other costs of production.

Different rates of interest induce different rates of investment and, in turn, different equilibrium levels of income. Therefore, the level of interest rates is one of the key variables in the economic process, and a change in interest rates leads to a change in economic activity. When Federal Reserve policy, for example, leads to lower interest rates, the level of investment spending goes up. Forces are set in motion through the multiplier and accelerator which increase the national income until a new equilibrium is reached at the lower interest rates. Fiscal policy is extremely important in the Keynesian framework since government and investment spending are what mainly set the level of national income. No economist believes that relationships in the real world are as simple as the simplified national income model, but the rate of interest and government spending are still of highest importance, even after many other factors come into play.

QUANTITY THEORY

The other approach is the modern quantity theory or monetarist approach, which holds that the most significant factor affecting the economy is the effect of Federal Reserve policies on the money stock. We considered some aspects of this theory in the previous chapter in the discussion of how changes in money supply affect prices. In Chapter 5 we discussed the relationship between changes in money supply and economic activity. Recall that recessions are usually preceded by declines in the growth rates in money stock, while increasing growth rates usually occur with expansion. However, a too rapid rate of increase in money stock may lead to higher inflation rates.

The monetarist approach holds that increases in the money stock result directly and indirectly in increased spending on a whole range of capital and consumer goods. Most important is the relationship between income and the amount of money people and businesses choose to hold. When money supplies change, spending adjusts to bring money balances to desired levels. The adjustments affect the relative prices of goods. Since individuals and institutions hold the total money supply, changes in income occur until actual money holdings are in line with desired holdings.

According to modern quantity theory, monetary policy is far more important than fiscal policy. The size of the federal budget, or even of a deficit, is not very important. Changes in the interest rate and in real and nominal wealth may affect total spending, but the relationship is not clear. When a deficit is financed by the monetary system, the economy expands. But it expands because the money supply expands, not because of the federal deficit itself.

It is impossible at this stage to choose between these conflicting viewpoints, since the evidence is not all in. It's likely that both interest rates and the size of the money stock have an important effect on economic activity. And the effect may well vary at different times and under differing conditions. Interest rates may be more important than the money stock when the economy is operating at less than full employment of resources. Changes in the money stock may be more important in boom periods when resources are being used to the fullest.

The Relationship of Prices, Wages, and Employment

Phillips curve
graphical representation of a theory that inflation is necessary for high employment

Another unresolved problem is how unemployment relates to wages and prices. The trade-off view holds that it is impossible to have high employment without inflation, and that policymakers must choose between some degree of unemployment and some degree of inflation. By this theory, if we plot the relationship of unemployment and inflation on a graph, the curve slopes downward from left to right and is usually shaped like a rounded "L." This curve is often called the **Phillips curve**, after the British economist who first stressed the relationship between levels of unemployment and wages. The long-run equilibrium view holds that the relationships are stable. It states that when the economy reaches a high employment range, excessive wage increases and inflation are caused by expansionary fiscal policies, not by further reductions in unemployment.

THE TRADE-OFF VIEW
Figure 24.1 shows the annual relationship between inflation and unemployment in the United States from 1963 to 1990. It can be seen that a rounded "L" Phillips curve fits nicely for the 1963–1969 time period, supporting the notion of a somewhat simplified trade-off relationship. However, since 1970 the relationship seems to have dramatically changed. Some economists suggest that the Phillips curve has shifted upward and to the right in the short run because of higher inflation expectations. The relationship of price inflation to unemployment since 1982, however, casts further doubt on the accuracy of the Phillips curve, since both inflation and unemployment rates show a decline.

THE LONG-RUN EQUILIBRIUM VIEW
The long-run equilibrium view holds that if proper policies are followed, inflation need not result. This view suggests that there is a "natural" rate of unemployment based on supply-and-demand factors and that this rate is independent of inflation. In other words, the long-run Phillips curve would be a vertical line at the "natural" rate of unemployment.

For example, suppose the economy is at the stage of a cycle in which there is significant unemployment. Monetary or fiscal action starts an expansion. Spending begins with the expectation that prices will stay as they are, and for a time output and employment rise more rapidly than wages or prices. But as demand increases and prices rise, real wages go down and workers demand—and get—higher wages during times of high employment. If inflationary monetary and fiscal policies are pursued, wages will continue to rise and inflation will result. But as wages rise, employers are less willing to hire workers or raise wages as rapidly as early in the expansion; they also try to use more labor-saving equipment.

If some degree of deflationary action is pursued after the expansion has lost momentum, unemployment will increase, but only temporarily. As soon as a new price trend not only becomes a reality but is expected to continue in the future, nominal and real wages will be the same and unemployment will again fall. According to this view, inflation is not necessary or desirable to achieve high employment. Economists do not yet know which view, if either, is the correct one or if monetary and fiscal policies can be utilized to achieve long-run equilib-

FIGURE 24.1   Inflation and Unemployment Relationships, 1963–1990

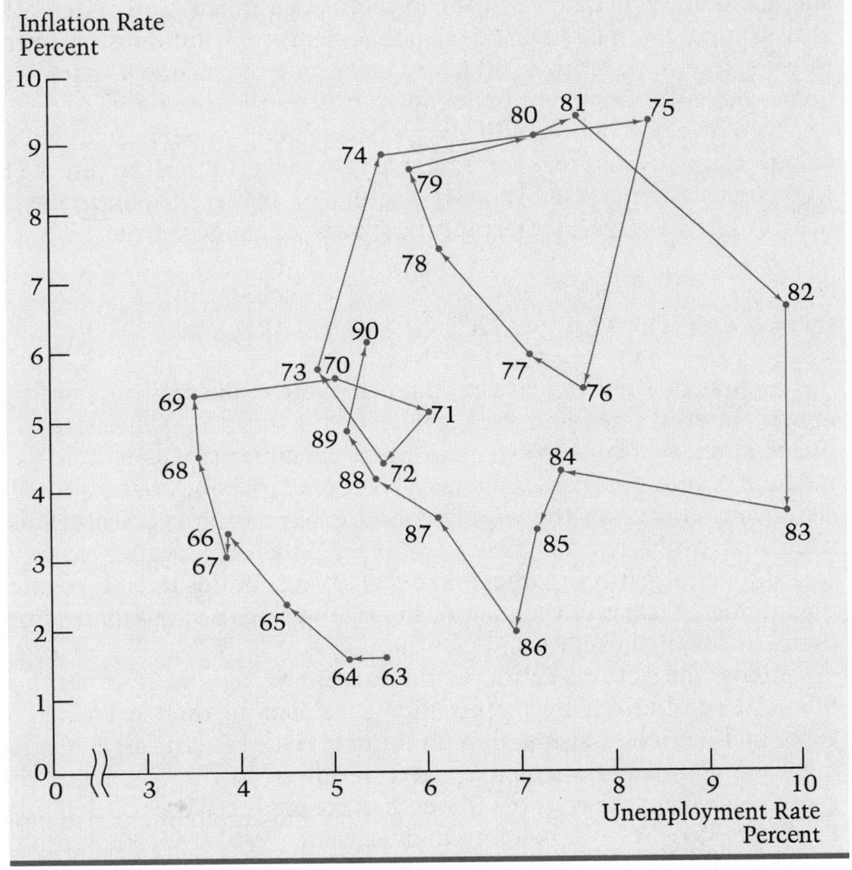

Source: *Economic Indicators*, various years.

rium. Therefore, policymakers should be cautious about assuming any set relationship between employment and wages and the resulting price levels.

No More Business Cycles?

Until the beginning of the recession in July 1990, many observers had begun to believe that severe recessions or depressions may be a thing of the past. It seems likely instead that most future recessions will take the form of a slowdown in growth rather than an outright decline in GNP. Even reduced growth rates, though, can be troublesome.

One reason that recessions have been short and moderate since World War II is that output has shifted from manufacturing to services. The demand for most services is less sensitive to changes in income than the demand for goods. Also, government spending as a percentage of GNP has increased dramatically. This has had a cushioning effect, because the public sector does not shrink during recessions. Retailers and manufacturers can now control their stock much more efficiently with computers, reducing the chance of dangerous buildups of inventory. We like to think that monetary management has now reached the point where it can prevent major downturns in the economy.

Even so, the economy will always be affected by unexpected shocks of one form or another. For example, skyrocketing oil prices, trade wars, and vast increases in debt defaults by industrial and financial institutions all serve to interrupt the growth of the economy.

INTERNATIONAL FINANCIAL EQUILIBRIUM

Just as monetary policy plays an important role in the nation's stability, growth, interest rates, and price levels, so, too, it can keep international financial relationships in balance. Since the dollar is widely held as a medium of international exchange, U.S. monetary policy has especially significant effects on the world economy. No nation is a world unto itself, nor can a nation pursue whatever policies it desires without regard to other nations. Policymakers of all economies must recognize the interdependence of their actions in attempting to maintain international financial equilibrium.

Briefly, the nations of the world attempt to achieve international financial equilibrium by maintaining a balance in their exchange of goods and services. In general, international trade benefits all countries involved. Consumers benefit by getting lower cost goods, since the goods come from the country where they are produced most efficiently. Producers benefit by expanding their markets. Well over one-tenth of the U.S. national income comes from selling goods to foreigners, and a like amount of our needs are met through imports. However, individuals and firms make the decisions to import and export, and problems arise if they are out of balance over a period of time.

The Nature of the Problem

Exports are sales to foreigners; they are a source of income to domestic producers. Imports divert spending to foreign producers and therefore represent a loss of potential income to domestic producers. When the two are in balance there is no net effect on total income in the economy. However, an increase in exports over imports tends to expand the economy just as an increase in investment or government spending does. An excess of imports tends to contract the economy.

As in the domestic economy, goods and services are not exchanged directly in international trade; payment flows through monetary or financial transactions. We discussed methods of making payments and financing international trade in Chapter 20. Other short- and long-term lending and investment are conducted across national boundaries on a large scale. In addition, government grants for both military and civilian purposes and private gifts and grants are sources of international financial flows. These flows can have an important impact on domestic economies and may affect monetary policy.

Since producers, consumers, and investors in different countries use different currencies, the international financial system requires a mechanism for establishing the relative values, or exchange rates, among currencies, and for handling their actual exchange. Under the system of **flexible exchange rates** that began in 1973, rates are determined in the actual process of exchange, by supply and demand in the foreign exchange market. This system reduces the impact of international financial transactions on domestic money supplies. Still, changes in exchange rates do affect imports and exports and can thus affect domestic production, incomes, and prices. International financial markets strongly influence domestic interest rates, and vice versa, so that domestic monetary policy still involves international considerations.

flexible exchange rates a system in which international exchange rates are determined by supply and demand

In short, domestic economies are linked to each other in a worldwide economic and financial system. The United States has played a leading role in the development and growth of that system. Before we take a closer look at that role, we should examine the accounting system used to keep track of international financial transactions.

Balance-of-Payments Accounts

The U.S. **balance of payments** involves all of its international transactions, including foreign investment, private and government grants, U.S. military spending overseas, and many other items besides the buying and selling of goods and services. The single most important

balance of payments a summary of all economic transactions between one country and the rest of the world

balance of trade
the net value of a
country's exports of
goods and services com-
pared to its imports

merchandise trade
balance
the net difference
between a country's
import and export of
goods

element of the balance of payments is the ***balance of trade***, which is the net balance of exports and imports of goods and services. A more narrow view considers only the import and export of goods and is termed the ***merchandise trade balance***, depicted in Figure 24.2. The merchandise trade balance was consistently favorable between the 1950s and the beginning of the 1970s. In recent years, however, imports of goods has exceeded exports. This imbalance has been particularly severe since 1977. A major reason is our dependence on oil imports. In addition, the United States has had greater economic growth compared to growth abroad, which also caused us to import more than we exported.

We can better understand the U.S. balance of payments by examining Table 24.1. To find the goods and services balance, the merchandise trade balance is adjusted for military transactions, foreign investment income, and other service transactions that include tourism, transportation, and banking activities. Next, we find the current account balance by adjusting the goods and services balance for unilateral, or

FIGURE 24.2   U.S. International Transactions

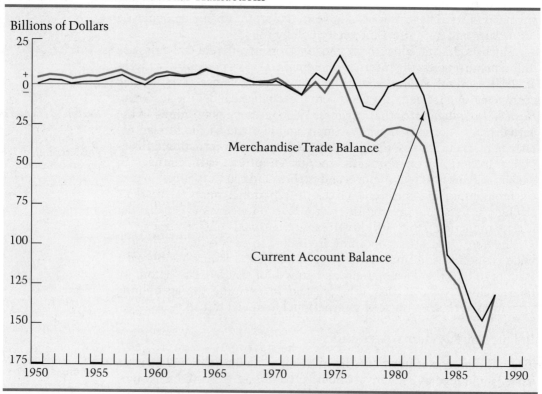

Source: *1989 Historical Chart Book*, Board of Governors of the Federal Reserve System, p. 100.

TABLE 24.1
United States Balance of Payments in 1989 (Millions of Dollars)

	INCOME (+)	PAYMENTS (−)	NET
CURRENT ACCOUNT			
Merchandise exports	$360,465		
Merchandise imports		$475,329	
Merchandise trade balance			−$114,864
Military transactions, net		6,319	
Investment income, net		913	
Other service transactions, net	26,783		
Balance on goods and services			− 95,313
Remittances, pensions, and other transfers		3,758	
Government grants		10,963	
Balance on current account			−110,034
CAPITAL ACCOUNT			
Changes in U.S. government ownership of foreign assets (−)		24,108	
Changes in U.S. private ownership of foreign assets (−)		102,953	
Changes in foreign government ownership of U.S. assets (+)	8,823		
Changes in foreign private ownership of U.S. assets (+)	205,829		
Balance on current and capital account			− 22,443
Statistical discrepancy	22,443		
Total	$624,343	$624,343	

Source: *Federal Reserve Bulletin* (April 1991): A54.

one-way, transfers. These transfers include remittances, pensions, private gifts and grants, and U.S. government grants (excluding military). Thus, the **current account balance** shows the flow of income into and out of the United States during a specified time period. The **capital account balance** includes all foreign private and government investment in the U.S. netted against U.S. investments in foreign countries.

Deficits or surpluses in the current account must be offset by changes in the capital account. That is, changes in the current account and the capital account must be equal except for statistical discrepancies caused by measurement errors and the inability to keep track of all international transactions. Thus, in Table 24.1, the item "Balance on current and capital account" would be zero except for the statistical discrepancy of $22,443 million.

current account balance *the flow of income into and out of the United States during a specified time period*

capital account balance *foreign government and private investment in the U.S. netted against similar U.S. investment in foreign countries*

The first item in the capital account section, changes in U.S. government ownership of assets in foreign countries, covers gold, Special Drawing Rights, the reserve position in the International Monetary Fund, and convertible foreign currencies held by the U.S. Treasury and Federal Reserve. The second item, changes in U.S. private ownership of foreign assets, reflects private investments abroad. Both items represent changes that result in outflows of capital.

The third and fourth items reflect foreign ownership changes, both government and private, in investments in the United States. Among those changes are increases in bank deposits, purchases of government and corporate securities, loans, and direct investment in land and buildings. Both of these items give rise to inflows of capital.

From an international monetary management point of view, U.S. government ownership of foreign assets is of special interest. Under the current system of flexible exchange rates, a country's central bank does not have to redeem its currency. However, it may try to control its exchange rate by entering the foreign exchange market to buy or sell that currency, thus adding to demand or supply. Intervention by central banks in the flexible exchange rate system is called a managed or **dirty float**.

dirty float
intervention by central banks to control exchange rates in the foreign exchange market's flexible exchange system

Under a pure flexible system in which central banks do not enter the foreign exchange market at all, there would be no change in the official government ownership of foreign assets. Note, however, that the rest of the accounts would still balance. Any surplus or deficit in current accounts would be balanced by the capital accounts. For example, a trade deficit might be balanced partly by an increase in foreign assets in the United States, including deposits in U.S. banks.

The International Financial System

For many years after World War II the United States enjoyed a favorable merchandise trade balance. During this period, however, the United States also engaged in massive international aid to countries whose productive facilities were destroyed by the war. The United States also gave great amounts of assistance to developing nations of the world. One of the results of these efforts was the accumulation of foreign claims to U.S. dollars and the loss of a large amount of gold reserves.

Even with loss of gold reserves, the United States had far greater reserves than any other nation. Also, the accumulation of claims against U.S. dollars was long considered desirable. Indeed, one of the most serious difficulties facing international trade in the early post World War II period was the "dollar gap" or shortage as the world increasingly relied on the dollar as an international currency. Gold had been the world's international reserve currency and the basic medium of exchange in international commerce. But as the volume of world trade increased over the years, the supply of gold failed to keep pace. Without some form of supplementary international money, the result would have been international deflation.

The U.S. balance of payments problem and the world's need for a growing monetary base to support increasing international liquidity came into sharp focus in the early 1970s. The year-by-year growth in short-term financial claims on the dollar resulting from our continuing unfavorable merchandise trade balance served foreign central banks well. It provided them with a growing base of reserve assets. Since these claims to U.S. dollars could be converted into gold at a fixed rate, the claims were considered to be as good as gold. But just as the world's monetary gold supply was not increasing fast enough to accommodate expanding international trade, eventually the U.S. stock of monetary gold was no longer adequate to support the vast increase in claims against it.

SPECIAL DRAWING RIGHTS

In January 1968, recognizing that the dollar could no longer serve as a steadily increasing international money, the principal nations of the world agreed to a supplementary world money, **Special Drawing Rights (SDRs)**. The SDRs, sometimes called "paper gold," can be created freely by the International Monetary Fund. The SDRs are assets that the member banks accept from one another up to specified limits. Like gold, they are claims on the world's resources and go to participants in proportion to their International Monetary Fund quotas.

Special Drawing Rights (SDRs)
international reserve assets created by the International Monetary Fund that can be drawn upon by member nations

THE END OF THE GOLD STANDARD

In 1971, as a result of strong inflation, the U.S. trade balance fell into deficit. Furthermore, higher interest rates in Europe than in the United States created a rush of capital outflows to Europe. As a result, the dollar declined so much that on August 15, 1971, President Nixon stopped the dollar from being converted into gold to protect our declining gold stock.

FLEXIBLE INTERNATIONAL EXCHANGE RATES

Suspension of dollar convertibility in the summer of 1971 was a significant milepost in the worsening U.S. international monetary situation. Equally important was the decision to allow the dollar to "float" in relation to its exchange rate with other currencies. Under the previous rules of the International Monetary Fund a nation could only alter the established (or pegged) exchange ratio with other currencies with the Fund's approval. The arguments for and against flexible exchange rates had been debated in academic circles for a dozen years. Under flexible exchange rates, some contended, supply and demand would establish appropriate exchange rates between nations, and cost and price structures as well as changing monetary policy would be reflected in the supply-and-demand relationships.

A primary objection to flexible exchange rates is the chance of wide swings in response to changes in supply and demand, with a resulting uncertainty in international trade. After only four months of flexible exchange rates, a group of ten representatives of central banks in leading industrial nations met at the Smithsonian Institution in Washington in December 1971 to express their concern for monetary stability. Out of this so-called Smithsonian Agreement came a new alignment of fixed exchange rates. Major currencies were officially revalued against the dollar, and the dollar was devalued in terms of gold. However, the Smithsonian Agreement was completely out of use by March 1, 1973 as a result of change of policy. Rather than attempt to establish another realignment of fixed exchange rates, the leading industrial nations decided to again let their currencies float.

RECENT FOREIGN EXCHANGE DEVELOPMENTS

The dollar remains the main currency for international commercial and financial transactions. Because of this, both the United States and the rest of the world benefit from a strong and stable U.S. dollar. Its strength and stability depend directly on the ability of the United States to pursue noninflationary economic policies. In the late 1960s and the 1970s the United States failed to meet this objective. Continuing high inflation led to a dollar crisis in 1978, which, in turn, threatened the stability of international financial markets.

As inflation was brought under control in 1982, the dollar rose against other major currencies to its highest level since the reestablishment of flexible exchange rates in 1973. The renewed strength of the dollar helped the U.S. economy by reducing import prices and thus working against inflation. On the other hand, the increasing strength of the dollar caused exported U.S. goods to be less cost competitive. The dollar reached its maximum value in international exchange in 1985. The value of the dollar in relation to the major currencies of the world, such as the yen, mark, and pound, then declined steadily until 1987. Since 1987 the value of the dollar in international exchange has continued to fluctuate, but within a fairly narrow range.

A stronger dollar leads to concern about the deficit in our trade balance but at the same time offers hope of lower inflation. A stronger dollar results in more imports of foreign merchandise since it requires fewer dollars for purchase. Just as a U.S. tourist abroad finds it cheaper to travel when the dollar is strong, importers find prices reduced when their dollars increase in relative strength. When the dollar weakens, inflation may follow, countered by a reduced balance of trade deficit.

KEY TERMS

accelerator principle
balance of payments
balance of trade
business cycles
capital account balance
current account balance

dirty float
flexible exchange rates
merchandise trade balance
multiplier
Phillips curve
Special Drawing Rights

DISCUSSION QUESTIONS

1. Describe the circular nature of economic transactions.
2. Describe the circular flow of money in the total economy.
3. Identify and analyze various factors that may initiate an expansion in economic activity.
4. Discuss possible intensifying factors that may reinforce expansion in economic activity.
5. Discuss the factors that may lead to an economic recession.
6. Briefly describe the cumulative process during contraction and the factors that will lead to another expansion.
7. Identify and describe the two approaches used to explain the relationship of monetary and fiscal policies to economic activity.
8. Discuss the two views concerning the relationship of unemployment rates to wages and prices.
9. Briefly indicate the problems facing the United States in its attempt to maintain international financial equilibrium.
10. The U.S. international balance of payments position is measured in terms of the current account balance. Describe the current account balance and indicate its major components. Also indicate developments in the current account balance during recent years.
11. Discuss the meaning of the capital account balance and identify its major components.
12. A great deal of concern has been expressed about the lack of international monetary stability in recent years. In connection with this concern, describe some of the developments in terms of gold and flexible exchange rates in relation to the U.S. dollar.
13. Discuss some of the recent foreign exchange developments as they affect the United States and its recent balance of trade deficits.

PROBLEMS

1. Assume that the economy of the nation has been relatively stable for eighteen months; that is, the gross national product, employ-

ment levels, and industrial production have varied only modestly. Employment, however, is less than full. Production is substantially below capacity. A new consumer product based on a recent invention has developed so quickly and with such an impact on the economy that the gross national product has shown an unexpected increase with further strong increases in prospect. Assuming that this technological advance does generate a general economic expansion, trace the various forces that may support the expansion process, the limiting factors that may eventually bring the expansion to a halt, and the reinforcing factors that may precipitate a general contraction in the economy.

2. For the entire year the nation's balance of trade with other nations has been in a substantial deficit position, yet, as always, the overall balance of payments will be in balance. Describe the various factors that accomplish this overall balance, in spite of the deficit in the balance of trade.

SELF-TEST QUESTIONS

1. Alternating expansions and contractions of the economy:
   a. are of varying durations and magnitudes
   b. consistently show durations of contractions to be greater than those of expansions
   c. consistently show the magnitudes of contractions to be greater than those of expansions
   d. are generally predictable with respect to duration

2. Modern business cycles can only exist:
   a. in an economy with a modern banking system
   b. in nations with strong central governments
   c. when government intrudes on business activity
   d. when tax rates fluctuate widely over the years

3. A reinforcing factor during the process of economic expansion is:
   a. an increase in corporate tax levels
   b. the multiplier effect
   c. an increase in interest rates
   d. cost-push inflationary factors

4. Factors contributing to the cumulative process during an economic contraction include:
   a. the expansion of the money supply
   b. decreasing supplies of consumer goods

    c. businesses' attempt to decrease their debt levels

    d. consumers' attempt to increase their debt levels

5. The Phillips curve:

    a. refers to the topping out of an expansion of the economy

    b. tries to establish a relationship between interest rates and employment

    c. refers to an unusually favorable leverage buy-out

    d. suggests an inverse relationship between inflation and unemployment

SELF-TEST PROBLEM

Explain the concept of "balance" as it relates to a nation's balance of payments.

SUGGESTED READINGS

Burnham, James B. *International Challenges for American Banking*, Center for the Study of American Business, Washington University, St. Louis, MO: 1989.

Eiteman, David K., and Arthur I. Stonehill. *Multinational Business Finance*, 5e. Reading, MA: Addison-Wesley Publishing Co., 1990. Chaps. 3 and 10.

Fraser, Donald R., and Peter S. Rose. *Financial Institutions and Markets in a Changing World*, 3e. Homewood, IL: Richard D. Irwin, 1987. Part V.

Garner, C. Alan, and Richard E. Wurtz. "Is the Business Cycle Disappearing?" *Economic Review*, Federal Reserve Bank of Kansas City (May/June 1990): 25–39.

International Financial Statistics Yearbook. Washington, DC: International Monetary Fund, published annually.

Meyer, Stephen A. "The U.S. as a Debtor Country: Causes, Prospects, and Policy Implications." *Business Review*, Federal Reserve Bank of Philadelphia (November/December 1989): 19–31.

"Treasury and Federal Reserve Foreign Exchange Operations." Published in each issue of *Quarterly Review*, The Federal Reserve Bank of New York.

Weston, J. Fred, and Thomas E. Copeland. *Managerial Finance*, 8e. Hinsdale, IL: The Dryden Press, 1989. Chap. 32.

ANSWERS TO SELF-TEST QUESTIONS   1. a   2. a   3. b   4. c   5. d

ANSWER TO SELF-TEST PROBLEM

In one sense there is never a precise count that establishes a balance since it is impossible to record all transactions that enter into the schedule. Hence, an item referred to as "statistical discrepancy" solves that problem nicely. Aside from the practical matter of counting, however, the schedule must always be in balance in a theoretical sense. It's true that we can have deficits in our current account. In other words, our export of goods and services may fall short of our imports, but this must be made up in one or both of the other parts of the schedule. It can be made up by a reduction in our gold reserves or other reserve assets, or we can increase the amount that we owe abroad. Like a three-piece jig-saw puzzle with fixed boundaries, the change in the shape of one piece must result in the change in shape of one or both of the other two pieces.

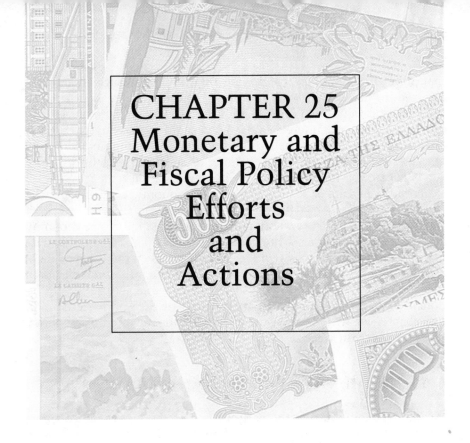

CHAPTER 25
Monetary and Fiscal Policy Efforts and Actions

After studying this chapter you should be able to:
- Understand how the policies of the Federal Reserve System have changed over the years.
- Identify the monetary problems resulting from the Vietnam War.
- Describe why monetary and fiscal conditions in 1990 make solutions extremely difficult.

Monetary theorists try to learn from the successes and failures of monetary and fiscal actions taken throughout our history. Because of the importance of the Federal Reserve Act in 1913, they devote special attention to economic affairs following that major change in the structure of banking practices and policies. And since wars place great strain on the resources of a nation, theorists continue to study the monetary policies in effect during World Wars I and II.

Postwar periods also interest us as we try to gain insight for more appropriate future actions. During and shortly after World War II, for example, the U.S. Treasury and the Fed could not agree on a course of action. The Fed wanted to restrict the growth of the money supply to discourage inflation. The Treasury, however, wanted to keep interest rates low, requiring the Fed to buy all government securities offered that were not purchased by private buyers. This disagreement was resolved in March 1951 with an accord between the Treasury and the Fed. The Fed would no longer be obligated to buy government securities to maintain set interest rates. The accord required only that the Fed continue to buy and sell some securities to maintain an orderly market. The accord was the beginning of an era in which monetary policy became an independent force in managing the economy.

For fifteen years or so after the accord, economic conditions in the United States were relatively calm. This allowed increasing use of fiscal and monetary policy. Both policies tried to stabilize the economy by influencing the demand for goods and services. The Fed described its role as **leaning against the wind**, easing credit when the economy was contracting and applying monetary restraint when inflation built up. In mid-1965, however, the economy entered a new and very serious inflationary period as a result of military spending on the war in Vietnam. In this chapter we will focus on the effects of monetary and fiscal policy since the Vietnam War.

leaning against the wind a term used by the Fed to mean easing credit during economic contraction and applying monetary restraint during inflation

EARLY IN THE VIETNAM WAR TO THE END OF 1969

Military spending during the early phases of the war added to rising spending for plant, equipment, and inventories. This led to much greater demands for funds, and to labor shortages and price increases. The Fed took steps to restrict bank credit expansion, and interest rates moved up. Since little was done by Congress to impose fiscal restraint, the burden of restraining inflation fell on monetary policy. As monetary policy tightened more and more during the first half of 1966, interest rates reached their highest levels in forty years. Many people who normally put their money in savings and loan associations and mutual savings banks bought money market securities instead, which paid a higher rate. As a result, the mortgage market was seriously short of funds. Construction dropped sharply, with resulting unemployment in that field. This effect was called the "credit crunch."

Though prices continued to rise, the overheated economy began to cool off in the fall of 1966. Economic activity began to moderate and the GNP remained about level through the first quarter of 1967. It rose little during the second quarter, and industrial production dropped somewhat. Monetary policy began to ease up in November 1966, and government fiscal policy also played a counter-cyclical role in 1967 by increasing outlays for goods and services.

Though private spending went up, increased federal government spending was the main cause of higher inflation in 1968. The federal deficit in fiscal 1968 was in excess of $25 billion. President Lyndon Johnson asked for a surtax to be added to personal and corporate income taxes in the summer of 1967, but Congress took no action until June 1968.

Inflation continued in 1969 at an even greater rate. Wholesale prices rose sharply in the first quarter, and the consumer price index rose to its highest level in years. This renewed inflation could not be blamed on federal government spending, since the budget for fiscal 1969 showed a small surplus. But business spending on new plant and equipment was up sharply. Private spending, in general, continued to increase rapidly. By midyear the Fed was following a policy of severe restraint on the money and credit markets, in some respects more severe than in 1966. Interest rates rose to even higher levels than in 1966 and in some cases were the highest since Civil War days. Capital spending dropped somewhat from plans announced earlier in the year, but still stayed at very high levels. Once again, credit for mortgage financing decreased, and housing starts declined.

The economy suffered a recession from late 1969 through almost all of 1970. This recession was mainly caused by the restrictive credit policy the Fed followed in late 1968 and 1969 as it tried to slow down inflation. It appears in retrospect that monetary policy was too strict in 1966 and too easy in early 1968. It should have been much tighter during most of 1968, when it was relaxed to cushion the effects of fiscal policy. As a result, monetary policy had to be very restrictive in 1969, and this helped bring on a recession.

MONETARY AND FISCAL ACTIVITIES DURING THE 1970s

The situation at the end of the 1960s was an omen for the coming years. The consumer demand approach to monetary and fiscal policies as a measure of the strength of the economy had worked well for the last two decades when applied to either inflation or recession. But when both problems existed at the same time, attacking either one with the old tools would only make the other worse. Economic policy since 1970 was marked by a variety of attempts to deal with this and other problems policymakers faced.

The First Half of the 1970s

The recession of 1969–1970 was unusually mild and recovery began near the end of 1970. The Fed had decided to ease credit to slow the 1970 decrease in economic activity and to stimulate recovery. Inflation was so strong, however, that prices kept rising even during the recession. The economy began a slow recovery in late 1970, helped by a rapidly increasing money supply in the first half of the year. Prices moved up sharply, the consumer price index increasing by more than 5 percent during the year. To combat inflation, President Nixon ordered a 90-day price freeze in mid-August and set up wage and price controls when the freeze ended. The goal was to cut price increases to an average of 2.5 percent per year while wages rose on average by 5.5 percent. This goal was based on the assumption that average productivity in the economy would increase at 3 percent annually. To help restrain prices, the growth of the money supply was cut substantially after midyear.

The economy continued to have balance-of-payments problems, which had persisted for several years. In order to correct what appeared to be an imbalance in the relationship of the dollar to major foreign currencies, the dollar was devalued by 12 percent in December of 1971.

Economic recovery accelerated in 1972, and by the end of the year real growth was increasing rapidly. Consumer prices went up by only about 3.5 percent. It was the best year for price restraint since 1967, mainly because of wage and price controls. Fed monetary policy was expansive in the early part of the year, but late in 1972 money growth was slowed because of renewed inflation.

Inflation became greater in 1973, a year in which consumer prices increased some 9 percent. Early in the year, American involvement in the Vietnam War ended, and it looked as if 1973 might be a good year for the economy. The dollar was devalued by 10 percent in February and was allowed to float against other currencies in March; the balance-of-payments problem seemed to be nearing solution as America again developed a surplus trade balance with the rest of the world. Mandatory price controls, administered by the Cost of Living Council, were replaced in January with mainly voluntary controls. The Council had been created under authority of the Economic Stabilization Act of 1971. The growth of Fed credit was slowed and the federal government had a surplus by the second quarter.

However, economic activity increased rapidly and in many fields demand was greater than supply. Unemployment, which was at about 6 percent at the beginning of 1972, dropped below 5 percent in 1973. Price controls also led to problems in many sectors of the economy, thus adding to shortages in some areas. Prices moved up so rapidly that a new 60-day price freeze by the Cost of Living Council was put into effect in June 1973. At the end of this period prices were again frozen but were allowed to increase for the amount of higher production costs. Provisions were made for price decontrol on an industry-by-industry basis.

The price situation got worse as 1973 progressed, for several reasons. Poor crops in many parts of the world caused food prices to go up. Grain prices rose, as large amounts of wheat were sold to Russia and China. In October another Arab-Israeli War broke out. Though the war was short, it had a marked effect on our economy. The Arabs, in order to put pressure on the United States and other countries to support their cause, put an embargo, or restriction, on oil shipments and raised oil prices. The embargo was lifted in March 1974, but prices went to several times their prewar levels. As the demand for credit remained high, its supply was restricted by the Fed, and investors feared continued inflation as interest rates reached new highs.

High interest rates and tighter credit would probably have slowed the economy somewhat in 1974. But the oil crisis compounded the problem, since it affected all industries based on petroleum products. Because of the gasoline shortage, people also bought fewer cars, especially full-sized "gas hogs." High interest rates led to a major decrease in residential construction and slowed some industrial plans for expansion.

Price controls were removed in April, not because inflation was under control, but because many believed that controls were a failure. Prices moved up after decontrol; they rose even more when the Midwest farm belt was hit by a severe drought. By summer, prices were increasing at a faster rate than at almost any time since during World War I. The prime interest rate on short-term business loans reached 10.8 percent, a historic high, and the consumer price index increased 11 percent during the year. The economy suffered a decline in real growth and was in deep recession during 1974.

From the End of 1974 to 1979

Unemployment, which was under 5 percent in 1973 and 5.6 percent in 1974, went above 8 percent in 1975 before it started to drop as the economy began recovering. U.S. Treasury fiscal policy moved to stimulate the economy in 1975 by reducing corporate income taxes and increasing the investment tax credit from 7 percent to 10 percent. In addition, there were certain personal income tax cuts and a rebate on some of the 1974 taxes. The result of these tax cuts and increased government spending was a substantial budget deficit in 1975.

Monetary policy also eased somewhat during 1975. The Fed, which had allowed the money stock to increase only at a 3.4 percent rate between the second quarter of 1974 and the first quarter of 1975, began increasing the money stock at a rate of over 5 percent.

Fiscal policy continued to stimulate the economy in 1976. Congress passed the Tax Reform Act of 1976, providing tax credits for individuals and extending the corporate income tax changes enacted in 1975. In 1977, the Tax Reduction and Simplification Act extended for one year the temporary provisions passed in the 1976 act. This legislation was followed by the Revenue Act of 1978, which reduced capital gains tax rates for individuals, boosted investment tax credits, and reduced corporate income tax rates. These income tax policies, along with U.S. government spending programs, produced fiscal year budget deficits of $66 billion in 1976, $45 billion in 1977, and $49 billion in 1978.

The Fed also stimulated the U.S. economy by increasing the money stock at an 8 percent rate between the third quarter of 1976 and the third quarter of 1978. These monetary and fiscal policies caused inflation to accelerate, economic activity to grow, and unemployment to fall below 6 percent during 1978. However, as we discussed in Chapter 24, the high rate of U.S. economic expansion caused imports to outpace exports and produce very large current-account deficits in the U.S. balance of payments in 1977 and 1978. These deficits, coupled with growing U.S. inflation compared to the rates in many other major countries, also caused the exchange rate value of the U.S. dollar to drop steeply in 1978, 1979, and 1980.

By the latter part of 1978, the Fed had moved to a much tighter monetary policy and the Fed and U.S. Treasury were attempting to support the U.S. dollar in foreign exchange markets. The Carter administration also was proposing to slow the economy by reducing government spending, resulting in smaller budget deficits. As the United States entered 1979, growth in economic activity continued while inflation and interest rates returned to high levels.

MONETARY AND FISCAL ACTIVITIES DURING THE 1980s

As indicated in Chapter 23, in October 1979 the Fed abandoned its longstanding efforts to control interest rates by monetary accommodation. It began to focus on controlling monetary growth instead of interest rates. The strength of this approach not only reduced interest rates but also caused a brief recession. The real gross national product (GNP) declined sharply in the second quarter of 1980, but then advanced rapidly after a quick reversal of restrictive monetary control. Both interest rates and prices again increased to record levels. Figure 25.1 reflects a decline in GNP in early 1980 as measured in both current and 1982 dollars. Remember that the difference between the growth rates of these two GNP measures reflects inflation as measured by the GNP price deflator.

In 1981 the new administration changed the direction of economic policy. It attempted to increase the total supply of goods and services by promoting economic growth and efficiency. Monetary restraint was to hold inflation in check, and tax reductions would stimulate investment and production. These expected effects of tax cuts were not immediately felt, but the Fed substantially reduced the growth of the money supply relative to its record high growth rate in late 1980. This monetary restraint reduced inflation and short-term interest rates but also caused a decline in economic activity in late 1981. As reflected in Figure 25.1, real output fell sharply in the last quarter of 1981. The administration believed that this recession would be over by the second

FIGURE 25.1   Gross National Product

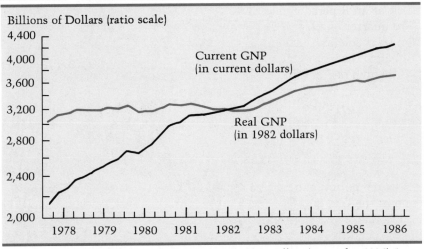

Source: *Economic Indicators*, U.S. Government Printing Office, (November 1986): 1.

quarter of 1982.[1] Such was not the case. The recovery did not begin until much later in the year, by which time unemployment had surged to nearly 11 percent, as Figure 25.2 shows. The effects of the recession, the reduced tax rates, and the failure of the government to reduce its spending combined to produce enormous federal budget deficits.

The substantial drop in growth of the money supply was the main cause of the decline in economic activity. But this decline was compounded by a marked reduction in the velocity of money, the largest reduction since the Fed began publishing data on currently defined M1, M2, and M3 monetary aggregates in 1959. The causes of this decline in velocity are still not completely known, but it appears that major changes in demands of individuals and businesses for goods and services played an important role. The new nationwide interest-bearing NOW accounts and the increasing popularity of money market funds offer a partial explanation. The attractive yields on these investments apparently induced people to save money that otherwise would have been spent. The Fed had not expected the decline in velocity and was not inclined to increase the money supply to offset it. It feared creating too much liquidity and a return to high interest rates and prices.

Although the economy showed strong growth throughout 1983, prices and interest rates increased only moderately. By spring of 1984 the growth rate began to slacken and by mid-1986 there was some

1. *Economic Report of the President.* Washington, DC: Government Printing Office, 1982. p. 25.

FIGURE 25.2   U.S. Unemployment Rate

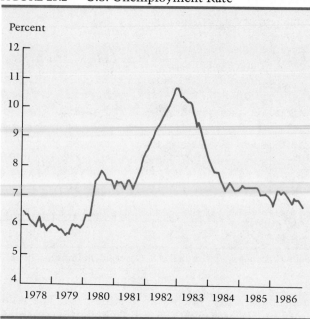

Source: U.S. Department of Labor.

concern about the prospect of a recession. Policymaking was complicated by very large federal deficits.

The Tax Reform Act of 1986 (TRA) was enacted by Congress in a
further effort to reduce the federal deficit. It was considered to be the
most important reform of the federal income tax since its inception in
1913. The hope was that it would restore incentives to work, save, and
invest, thereby substantially boosting economic growth and individual
well-being. Among the principal features of the TRA is a significant
lowering of tax rates on personal income, a broadening of the personal
tax base, strong limitations on tax-sheltered activities, and substantial
increases in the standard deduction. Notwithstanding the high hopes
for this reform, federal deficits continued to increase.

President Reagan signed a bill on September 29, 1987 which, among
other things, pushed the original Gramm-Rudman-Hollings deadline
for a balanced budget back two years, from 1991 to 1993. The GRH law
was discussed in detail in Chapter 14.

Concern over the prospect of a recession continued into mid-1987,
as the cyclical expansion passed the four-year mark. The large federal
deficit, an expansive domestic monetary policy, and restrictive monetary
policies by our industrial allies had caused the dollar to decline in foreign
exchange markets. This stimulated some areas of domestic produc-

tion as foreign customers paid effectively less for U.S. goods. But, because foreign imports became more expensive, it also raised consumer prices in the United States. Furthermore, the declining value of the dollar threatened the flow of foreign investment into the United States—investment that we had depended on to finance the federal deficits.

The Fed chose to strengthen the dollar by reducing the growth rate of the money supply, which in turn increased interest rates. This action was taken to prevent inflation and to preserve the attraction of foreign investment to the United States. The danger of this course of action was the chance that higher interest rates would start a recession by reducing the demand for such things as automobiles, housing, and plant and equipment for business. A recession would certainly make the federal deficit more difficult to control, since tax revenues would decline and government spending increase. To counter this threat, the administration appealed to other nations, especially West Germany and Japan, to stimulate their economies in order to provide more markets for U.S. products abroad and reduce the danger of a U.S. recession.

CRISIS FOR THE 1990s

By 1990 the emphasis for damage control had shifted to fiscal policies instead of monetary actions. Everyone agreed that something had to be done about the large continuing federal deficits. The national budget became the subject of debate. Should we increase taxes or cut spending? The Fed continued to emphasize inflation control, while the administration openly expressed concern with the Fed's actions. The negative political consequences of the recession resulted in confrontations between the Fed and the administration.

The day-to-day operations of the Fed shifted to intermediate indicators rather than long-term targets. Because of a loss of confidence in the relationship between money supply and economic activity, the Fed began to follow developments of the economy and prices directly. It now studies monetary aggregates along with a variety of economic statistics.

The budget problems of 1990 stemmed from long-delayed actions to establish a balanced economy. The problems were compounded because corrective actions hurt even when taken during times of economic well-being. In late 1990 the economy was entering a recession—hardly the time to apply strong measures. Further, the series of budget deficits resulted in a national debt that claims a major portion of tax revenues just to meet interest payments.

As discussed in previous chapters, the value of the dollar in international exchange was at a low point. The nation's trade balance was unfavorable and foreign claims to U.S. assets continued to climb. And the U.S. Treasury's ability to sell new issues of debt and to refinance maturing debt depended largely on the willingness of foreign investors, mainly the Japanese, to purchase the new issues.

Courses of action taken in late 1990 to attack these problems were entered into with much fanfare. In the opinion of some economists, however, some of these actions attack certain problems in a constructive way but tend to aggravate other problems. The principal effort to resolve the nation's problems was enactment of the Omnibus Budget Reconciliation Act in November 1990. This new budget law was expected to reduce future deficits substantially from what they would have been without the act. These deficit reductions were to be effected over a five-year period.

Most of the deficit reduction called for in the 1990 law was to come from slowing the growth of expenditures. Discretionary spending—the spending Congress sets each year—was expected to account for roughly 40 percent of the total reduction. Much of this total was to have come from reductions in defense outlays. (The expenses of the Gulf War in early 1991 was the first problem with reductions in military expenditures. Aside from the war's costs, it led to reconsiderations of the wisdom of too deep a cut in defense outlays.) Statutory obligations such as medicare and agriculture programs were expected to account for about 20 percent of the five-year reduction.

The new budget law was to raise almost $150 billion in additional tax revenue over the fiscal 1991–1995 period. In general, the marginal tax rate on the extreme upper income levels was increased from 28 to 31 percent. In addition, the affluent were required to pay higher taxes as a consequence of a new phaseout of personal exemptions, a limitation on itemized deductions, and new excise taxes levied on selected luxury items, such as expensive furs, jewelry, and cars. About one-quarter of the total new revenue was to come from increased excise taxes on gasoline, alcohol, and tobacco. The Omnibus Budget Reconciliation Act, like the Tax Reform Act of 1986, does not override the budget targets established by Gramm-Rudman-Hollings. The 1986 and 1990 laws represent attempts to meet the GRH requirements.

By May of 1991, monetary policy was directed toward easing interest rates and banks responded by decreasing the prime rate. This action was taken, notwithstanding some disagreement on the Federal Reserve Board regarding the seriousness of the recession relative to the threat of recurring inflation. The easing of interest rates by the Fed along with a hoped-for improvement in the credibility and stability of fiscal policy was expected to provide support for an early end to the recession.

As time plays out over the 1991–1995 period, we will know how effective these actions have been. An early recovery from the recession will be a key factor in the outcome because increasing incomes and profits result in increased tax revenues. Among those with dissenting opinions were some who argued strongly that since recovery from the recession was such an important factor in the success of the plan, taxes should have been lowered rather than raised. This argument was the basis for President Bush's request for a lower capital gains tax rate. But, as stated earlier, the resolution of certain problems runs counter to the solution of others. Tax increases were expected to reduce the budgetary deficit, unquestionably a desirable outcome. The presumption is that levying increased taxes on the wealthy will not impede recovery from the recession. But if tax increases add to the severity of the recession, then lower tax revenues will increase the deficit.

The situation described here fully qualifies as a crisis. It also qualifies as a challenge. There continues to be underlying strengths in the economy, but it is often difficult to look beyond the nation's immediate problems. Excessive pessimism, an easily understood attitude during periods of economic difficulty, can be harmful, just as excessive optimism during economic boom periods can be harmful. It is our responsibility to try to reason through the economic circumstances of our condition in a constructive way. We hope that an understanding of the nation's monetary and fiscal system and the functioning of its financial institutions as presented in this text will provide a firm basis for analyzing economic circumstances.

KEY TERM

leaning against the wind

DISCUSSION QUESTIONS

1. Describe the significance of the accord that was reached between the U.S. Treasury and the Fed in 1951.
2. When officials of the Fed state that they are "leaning against the wind," what are they describing?
3. A condition described as a "credit crunch" developed following the Vietnam War. What is meant by the phrase and how did it develop?
4. Review monetary and fiscal policy during the period from mid-1965 to the 1969–1970 recession. Evaluate policy decisions during this period.
5. Briefly describe the economic developments during the 1971–1973 expansionary period. Also, indicate the factors that contributed to the severity of the economic downturn during 1974 and early 1975.

6. Tax legislation in the years 1975, 1976, 1977, and 1978 provided both a stimulus for the economy and an increase in the budgetary deficit. Describe the nature of this tax legislation.
7. The recession of early 1980 is reported to have been one of the shortest on record. How do you account for this?
8. Describe the nature and primary cause of the recession that started in 1981.
9. Although price inflation had been brought to a very low level in 1983, real interest rates remained very high. Explain.
10. In 1987 there was some concern about the possibility of a recession. Describe the special circumstances that created conflicting views as to what actions the Fed should take.
11. By the early 1990s concern for continuing budget deficits caused a shift from monetary actions to fiscal actions. Explain.
12. Describe some of the conflicting pressures that made budgetary considerations extremely difficult in 1990.

PROBLEMS

1. Recent commentators have suggested that in spite of the generally low level of U.S. unemployment, low productivity continues to be a drag on economic growth. They suggest that the U.S. economy staggers along with an obsolete capital assets base and that if productivity is to increase, better "tools" must be placed in the hands of workers. Comment on this position. If you agree, suggest steps that might help resolve the problem.
2. Using your knowledge of the successes and failures of economic policy in financing past wars (and with the hope that no more armed conflict experiences will ever have to be recorded), how could our present understanding have contributed to a less inflationary long-term monetary and fiscal experience?

SELF-TEST QUESTIONS

1. Close cooperation and coordination of efforts between the Fed and the U.S. Treasury:
   a. has existed since the creation of the Fed in 1913
   b. has never been achieved
   c. has prevailed only during periods of armed conflict
   d. was achieved in 1951 after much disagreement during World War II

2. Efforts to moderate the "credit crunch" that followed the Vietnam War:

    a. were made jointly by the Fed and the U.S. Treasury
    b. were primarily a U.S. Treasury operation
    c. were primarily a Fed operation
    d. were not made by either the Fed or the U.S. Treasury

3. To counter the inflationary pressures that developed in 1971 as a result of the rapidly increasing money supply:

    a. wage and price controls were instituted
    b. price controls were instituted
    c. the Fed imposed credit controls on consumer durable goods
    d. the U.S. Treasury restricted new debt issues to those with short maturities

4. When the Fed abandoned its longstanding efforts in 1979 to control interest rates by monetary accommodation:

    a. emphasis was placed on monetary growth control
    b. interest rates moved to higher levels
    c. prosperity was achieved, as reflected by rising GNP figures
    d. the U.S. Treasury cooperated by issuing only securities with long maturities

5. The Gramm-Rudman-Hollings amendment:

    a. required yearly reductions of budget deficits to zero by 1993
    b. established legal limits to the national debt
    c. has now been completely repealed
    d. removes from the Congress responsibility for balancing the national budget

SELF-TEST PROBLEM

During the Vietnam War, as during all previous wars, the U.S. Treasury supported costs by issuing debt securities and increasing budgetary deficits. Reflecting on past war financing efforts and looking to the future, a think tank has submitted a proposal that would place the personal and financial burden of future conflicts directly on the civilian population. In effect, they propose a current sacrifice and "pay as you go" policy. Do you agree with such a proposal?

SUGGESTED READINGS

Kaufman, George G. *The U.S. Financial System*, 4e. Englewood Cliffs, NJ: Prentice-Hall, 1989. Chap. 32.

Leigh-Pemberton, Robin. "Europe 1992: Some Monetary Policy Issues," *Economic Review*, Federal Reserve Bank of Kansas City (September/October, 1989): 3–8.

Tobin, James. "Social Security, Public Debt, and Economic Growth." Frank M. Engle Lecture in Economic Security, The American College, Bryn Mawr, PA, April 19, 1990.

Yellen, Janet L. "Symposium on Budget Deficit," *The Journal of Economic Perspectives* (Spring 1989): 17–23.

ANSWERS TO SELF-TEST QUESTIONS   1. d   2. c   3. a   4. a   5. a

SOLUTION TO SELF-TEST PROBLEM

A good case can be made for such a financing policy if the war is expected to be brief and relatively minor. Past experience, however, shows that we cannot plan either the length or seriousness of a war. Wars are much easier to start than to end, and history shows that they often drag on longer than expected. So the answer must account for the strong possibility that any armed conflict will be expensive and lengthy.

In any conflict the population bears the cost one way or another. The energy of the work force must be concentrated on major war efforts. Attention to the domestic infrastructure—roads, bridges, buildings, parks, schools, and other facilities—must be delayed. For a short time a work force will respond well to the challenge. As time progresses, however, the dedication of most people begins to flag. Moving to a new location, working overtime, or leaving the home to work in a factory all require considerable personal sacrifice. People will respond with more energy if monetary reward is present (this is no reflection on their patriotism). Therefore, debt financing by the government to pay the work force for its special efforts must remain an important element in the financing of any long conflict. It is also true that even short but intensive conflicts require financing through long-term borrowing.

APPENDIX

Table 1
Future Value of $1 (FVIF)

Table 2
Future Value of a $1 Ordinary Annuity (FVIFA)

Table 3
Present Value of $1 (PVIF)

Table 4
Present Value of a $1 Ordinary Annuity (PVIFA)

TABLE 1 Future Value of $1 (FVIF)

YEAR	1%	2%	3%	4%	5%	6%	7%	8%	9%
1	1.010	1.020	1.030	1.040	1.050	1.060	1.070	1.080	1.090
2	1.020	1.040	1.061	1.082	1.102	1.124	1.145	1.166	1.188
3	1.030	1.061	1.093	1.125	1.158	1.191	1.225	1.260	1.295
4	1.041	1.082	1.126	1.170	1.216	1.262	1.311	1.360	1.412
5	1.051	1.104	1.159	1.217	1.276	1.338	1.403	1.469	1.539
6	1.062	1.126	1.194	1.265	1.340	1.419	1.501	1.587	1.677
7	1.072	1.149	1.230	1.316	1.407	1.504	1.606	1.714	1.828
8	1.083	1.172	1.267	1.369	1.477	1.594	1.718	1.851	1.993
9	1.094	1.195	1.305	1.423	1.551	1.689	1.838	1.999	2.172
10	1.105	1.219	1.344	1.480	1.629	1.791	1.967	2.159	2.367
11	1.116	1.243	1.384	1.539	1.710	1.898	2.105	2.332	2.580
12	1.127	1.268	1.426	1.601	1.796	2.012	2.252	2.518	2.813
13	1.138	1.294	1.469	1.665	1.886	2.133	2.410	2.720	3.066
14	1.149	1.319	1.513	1.732	1.980	2.261	2.579	2.937	3.342
15	1.161	1.346	1.558	1.801	2.079	2.397	2.759	3.172	3.642
16	1.173	1.373	1.605	1.873	2.183	2.540	2.952	3.426	3.970
17	1.184	1.400	1.653	1.948	2.292	2.693	3.159	3.700	4.328
18	1.196	1.428	1.702	2.026	2.407	2.854	3.380	3.996	4.717
19	1.208	1.457	1.754	2.107	2.527	3.026	3.617	4.316	5.142
20	1.220	1.486	1.806	2.191	2.653	3.207	3.870	4.661	5.604
25	1.282	1.641	2.094	2.666	3.386	4.292	5.427	6.848	8.623
30	1.348	1.811	2.427	3.243	4.322	5.743	7.612	10.063	13.268

Note: The basic equation for finding the future value interest factor (FVIF) is:

$$FVIF_{i,n} = (1 + i)^n$$

where i is the interest rate and n is the number of periods in years.

TABLE 1   (*continued*)

10%	12%	14%	15%	16%	18%	20%	25%	30%
1.100	1.120	1.140	1.150	1.160	1.180	1.200	1.250	1.300
1.210	1.254	1.300	1.322	1.346	1.392	1.440	1.563	1.690
1.331	1.405	1.482	1.521	1.561	1.643	1.728	1.953	2.197
1.464	1.574	1.689	1.749	1.811	1.939	2.074	2.441	2.856
1.611	1.762	1.925	2.011	2.100	2.288	2.488	3.052	3.713
1.772	1.974	2.195	2.313	2.436	2.700	2.986	3.815	4.827
1.949	2.211	2.502	2.660	2.826	3.185	3.583	4.768	6.276
2.144	2.476	2.853	3.059	3.278	3.759	4.300	5.960	8.157
2.358	2.773	3.252	3.518	3.803	4.435	5.160	7.451	10.604
2.594	3.106	3.707	4.046	4.411	5.234	6.192	9.313	13.786
2.853	3.479	4.226	4.652	5.117	6.176	7.430	11.642	17.922
3.138	3.896	4.818	5.350	5.936	7.288	8.916	14.552	23.298
3.452	4.363	5.492	6.153	6.886	8.599	10.699	18.190	30.288
3.797	4.887	6.261	7.076	7.988	10.147	12.839	22.737	39.374
4.177	5.474	7.138	8.137	9.266	11.974	15.407	28.422	51.186
4.595	6.130	8.137	9.358	10.748	14.129	18.488	35.527	66.542
5.054	6.866	9.276	10.761	12.468	16.672	22.186	44.409	86.504
5.560	7.690	10.575	12.375	14.463	19.673	26.623	55.511	112.46
6.116	8.613	12.056	14.232	16.777	23.214	31.948	69.389	146.19
6.728	9.646	13.743	16.367	19.461	27.393	38.338	86.736	190.05
10.835	17.000	26.462	32.919	40.874	62.669	95.396	264.70	705.64
17.449	29.960	50.950	66.212	85.850	143.371	237.376	807.79	2620.00

TABLE 2   Future Value of a $1 Ordinary Annuity (FVIFA)

YEAR	1%	2%	3%	4%	5%	6%	7%	8%
1	1.000	1.000	1.000	1.000	1.000	1.000	1.000	1.000
2	2.010	2.020	2.030	2.040	2.050	2.060	2.070	2.080
3	3.030	3.060	3.091	3.122	3.152	3.184	3.215	3.246
4	4.060	4.122	4.184	4.246	4.310	4.375	4.440	4.506
5	5.101	5.204	5.309	5.416	5.526	5.637	5.751	5.867
6	6.152	6.308	6.468	6.633	6.802	6.975	7.153	7.336
7	7.214	7.434	7.662	7.898	8.142	8.394	8.654	8.923
8	8.286	8.583	8.892	9.214	9.549	9.897	10.260	10.637
9	9.369	9.755	10.159	10.583	11.027	11.491	11.978	12.488
10	10.462	10.950	11.464	12.006	12.578	13.181	13.816	14.487
11	11.567	12.169	12.808	13.486	14.207	14.972	15.784	16.645
12	12.683	13.412	14.192	15.026	15.917	16.870	17.888	18.977
13	13.809	14.680	15.618	16.627	17.713	18.882	20.141	21.495
14	14.947	15.974	17.086	18.292	19.599	21.015	22.550	24.215
15	16.097	17.293	18.599	20.024	21.579	23.276	25.129	27.152
16	17.258	18.639	20.157	21.825	23.657	25.673	27.888	30.324
17	18.430	20.012	21.762	23.698	25.840	28.213	30.840	33.750
18	19.615	21.412	23.414	25.645	28.132	30.906	33.999	37.450
19	20.811	22.841	25.117	27.671	30.539	33.760	37.379	41.466
20	22.019	24.297	26.870	29.778	33.066	36.786	40.995	45.762
25	28.243	32.030	36.459	41.646	47.727	54.865	63.249	73.106
30	34.785	40.568	47.575	56.805	66.439	79.058	94.461	113.283

Note: the basic equation for finding the future value interest factor of an ordinary annuity (FVIFA) is:

$$FVIFA_{i,n} = \sum_{t=1}^{n} (1 + i)^{t-1} = -\frac{(1 + i)^n - 1}{i}$$

where i is the interest rate and n is the number of periods in years.

Future Value of a $1 Annuity Due (FVIFAD)

The future value interest factor of an annuity due (FVIFAD) may be found by using the following formula to convert FVIFA values found in Table 2:

$$FVIFAD_{i,n} = FVIFA_{i,n+1} - 1$$

where i is the interest rate and n is the number of periods in years.

TABLE 2   (continued)

9%	10%	12%	14%	16%	18%	20%	25%	30%
1.000	1.000	1.000	1.000	1.000	1.000	1.000	1.000	1.000
2.090	2.100	2.120	2.140	2.160	2.180	2.200	2.250	2.300
3.278	3.310	3.374	3.440	3.506	3.572	3.640	3.813	3.990
4.573	4.641	4.779	4.921	5.066	5.215	5.368	5.766	6.187
5.985	6.105	6.353	6.610	6.877	7.154	7.442	8.207	9.043
7.523	7.716	8.115	8.536	8.977	9.442	9.930	11.259	12.756
9.200	9.487	10.089	10.730	11.414	12.142	12.916	15.073	17.583
11.028	11.436	12.300	13.233	14.240	15.327	16.499	19.842	23.858
13.021	13.579	14.776	16.085	17.518	19.086	20.799	25.802	32.015
15.193	15.937	17.549	19.337	21.321	23.521	25.959	33.253	42.619
17.560	18.531	20.655	23.044	25.733	28.755	32.150	42.566	56.405
20.141	21.384	24.133	27.271	30.850	34.931	39.580	54.208	74.327
22.953	24.523	28.029	32.089	36.786	42.219	48.497	68.760	97.625
26.019	27.975	32.393	37.581	43.672	50.818	59.196	86.949	127.91
29.361	31.772	37.280	43.842	51.660	60.965	72.035	109.69	167.29
33.003	35.950	42.753	50.980	60.925	72.939	87.442	138.11	218.47
36.974	40.545	48.884	59.118	71.673	87.068	105.931	173.64	285.01
41.301	45.599	55.750	68.394	84.141	103.740	128.117	218.05	371.52
46.018	51.159	63.440	78.969	98.603	123.414	154.740	273.56	483.97
51.160	57.275	72.052	91.025	115.380	146.628	186.688	342.95	630.17
84.701	98.347	133.334	181.871	249.214	342.603	471.981	1054.80	2348.80
136.308	164.494	241.333	356.787	530.312	790.948	1181.882	3227.20	8730.00

Example: You are planning to deposit $100 at the beginning of each year for five years in a savings account that pays 7 percent. The value of this account at the end of the fifth year is $100 $\times$ FVIFAD$_{i,n}$ where i is 7 percent and n is 5.

$$FVIFAD_{7\%,5} = FVIFA_{7\%(5+1)} - 1$$

Table 2 gives the value of the FVIFA at 7 percent for six years as FVIFA$_{7\%,6}$ = 7.153, so

$$FVIFAD_{7\%,5} = 7.153 - 1 = 6.153$$

Your account after five years will be worth

$$\$100 \times 6.153 = \$615.30$$

TABLE 3   Present Value of $1 (PVIF)

YEAR	1%	2%	3%	4%	5%	6%	7%	8%	9%	10%
1	.990	.980	.971	.962	.952	.943	.935	.926	.917	.909
2	.980	.961	.943	.925	.907	.890	.873	.857	.842	.826
3	.971	.942	.915	.889	.864	.840	.816	.794	.772	.751
4	.961	.924	.888	.855	.823	.792	.763	.735	.708	.683
5	.951	.906	.863	.822	.784	.747	.713	.681	.650	.621
6	.942	.888	.837	.790	.746	.705	.666	.630	.596	.564
7	.933	.871	.813	.760	.711	.665	.623	.583	.547	.513
8	.923	.853	.789	.731	.677	.627	.582	.540	.502	.467
9	.914	.837	.766	.703	.645	.592	.544	.500	.460	.424
10	.905	.820	.744	.676	.614	.558	.508	.463	.422	.386
11	.896	.804	.722	.650	.585	.527	.475	.429	.388	.350
12	.887	.788	.701	.625	.557	.497	.444	.397	.356	.319
13	.879	.773	.681	.601	.530	.469	.415	.368	.326	.290
14	.870	.758	.661	.577	.505	.442	.388	.340	.299	.263
15	.861	.743	.642	.555	.481	.417	.362	.315	.275	.239
16	.853	.728	.623	.534	.458	.394	.339	.292	.252	.218
17	.844	.714	.605	.513	.436	.371	.317	.270	.231	.198
18	.836	.700	.587	.494	.416	.350	.296	.250	.212	.180
19	.828	.686	.570	.475	.396	.331	.276	.232	.194	.164
20	.820	.673	.554	.456	.377	.312	.258	.215	.178	.149
25	.780	.610	.478	.375	.295	.233	.184	.146	.116	.092
30	.742	.552	.412	.308	.231	.174	.131	.099	.075	.057

Note: The basic equation for finding the present value interest factor (PVIF) is:

$$PVIF_{i,n} = \frac{1}{(1 + i)^n}$$

where i is the interest or discount rate and n is the number of periods in years.

TABLE 3   (*continued*)

12%	14%	15%	16%	18%	20%	25%	30%
.893	.877	.870	.862	.847	.833	.800	.769
.797	.769	.756	.743	.718	.694	.640	.592
.712	.675	.658	.641	.609	.579	.512	.455
.636	.592	.572	.552	.516	.482	.410	.350
.567	.519	.497	.476	.437	.402	.328	.269
.507	.456	.432	.410	.370	.335	.262	.207
.452	.400	.376	.354	.314	.279	.210	.159
.404	.351	.327	.305	.266	.233	.168	.123
.361	.308	.284	.263	.225	.194	.134	.094
.322	.270	.247	.227	.191	.162	.107	.073
.287	.237	.215	.195	.162	.135	.086	.056
.257	.208	.187	.168	.137	.112	.069	.043
.229	.182	.163	.145	.116	.093	.055	.033
.205	.160	.141	.125	.099	.078	.044	.025
.183	.140	.123	.108	.084	.065	.035	.020
.163	.123	.107	.093	.071	.054	.028	.015
.146	.108	.093	.080	.060	.045	.023	.012
.130	.095	.081	.069	.051	.038	.018	.009
.116	.083	.070	.060	.043	.031	.014	.007
.104	.073	.061	.051	.037	.026	.012	.005
.059	.038	.030	.024	.016	.010	.004	.001
.033	.020	.015	.012	.007	.004	.001	.000

TABLE 4   Present Value of $1 Ordinary Annuity (PVIFA)

YEAR	1%	2%	3%	4%	5%	6%	7%	8%	9%	10%	12%
1	0.990	0.980	0.971	0.962	0.952	0.943	0.935	0.926	0.917	0.909	0.893
2	1.970	1.942	1.913	1.886	1.859	1.833	1.808	1.783	1.759	1.736	1.690
3	2.941	2.884	2.829	2.775	2.723	2.673	2.624	2.577	2.531	2.487	2.402
4	3.902	3.808	3.717	3.630	3.546	3.465	3.387	3.312	3.240	3.170	3.037
5	4.853	4.713	4.580	4.452	4.329	4.212	4.100	3.993	3.890	3.791	3.605
6	5.795	5.601	5.417	5.242	5.076	4.917	4.767	4.623	4.486	4.355	4.111
7	6.728	6.472	6.230	6.002	5.786	5.582	5.389	5.206	5.033	4.868	4.564
8	7.652	7.325	7.020	6.733	6.463	6.210	5.971	5.747	5.535	5.335	4.968
9	8.566	8.162	7.786	7.435	7.108	6.802	6.515	6.247	5.995	5.759	5.328
10	9.471	8.983	8.530	8.111	7.722	7.360	7.024	6.710	6.418	6.145	5.650
11	10.368	9.787	9.253	8.760	8.306	7.887	7.499	7.139	6.805	6.495	5.938
12	11.255	10.575	9.954	9.385	8.863	8.384	7.943	7.536	7.161	6.814	6.194
13	12.134	11.348	10.635	9.986	9.394	8.853	8.358	7.904	7.487	7.103	6.424
14	13.004	12.106	11.296	10.563	9.899	9.295	8.745	8.244	7.786	7.367	6.628
15	13.865	12.849	11.938	11.118	10.380	9.712	9.108	8.559	8.061	7.606	6.811
16	14.718	13.578	12.561	11.652	10.838	10.106	9.447	8.851	8.313	7.824	6.974
17	15.562	14.292	13.166	12.166	11.274	10.477	9.763	9.122	8.544	8.022	7.120
18	16.398	14.992	13.754	12.659	11.690	10.828	10.059	9.372	8.756	8.201	7.250
19	17.226	15.678	14.324	13.134	12.085	11.158	10.336	9.604	8.950	8.365	7.366
20	18.046	16.351	14.877	13.590	12.462	11.470	10.594	9.818	9.129	8.514	7.469
25	22.023	19.523	17.413	15.622	14.094	12.783	11.654	10.675	9.823	9.077	7.843
30	25.808	22.397	19.600	17.292	15.372	13.765	12.409	11.258	10.274	9.427	8.055

Note: The basic equation for finding the present value interest factor of an ordinary annuity (PVIFA) is:

$$PVIFA_{i,n} = \sum_{t=1}^{n} \frac{1}{(1+i)^t} = \frac{1 - \dfrac{1}{(1+i)^n}}{i}$$

where i is the interest or discount rate and n is the number of periods in years.

Present Value of a $1 Annuity Due (PVIFAD)

The present value interest factor of an annuity due (PVIFAD) may be found by using the following formula to convert PVIFA values found in Table 4:

$$PVIFAD_{i,n} = PVIFA_{i,n-1} + 1$$

where i is the interest or discount rate and n is the number of periods in years.

TABLE 4   *(continued)*

YEAR	14%	16%	18%	20%	25%	30%
1	0.877	0.862	0.847	0.833	.800	.769
2	1.647	1.605	1.566	1.528	1.440	1.361
3	2.322	2.246	2.174	2.106	1.952	1.816
4	2.914	2.798	2.690	2.589	2.362	2.166
5	3.433	3.274	3.127	2.991	2.689	2.436
6	3.889	3.685	3.498	3.326	2.951	2.643
7	4.288	4.039	3.812	3.605	3.161	2.802
8	4.639	4.344	4.078	3.837	3.329	2.925
9	4.946	4.607	4.303	4.031	3.463	3.019
10	5.216	4.833	4.494	4.193	3.571	3.092
11	5.453	5.029	4.656	4.327	3.656	3.147
12	5.660	5.197	4.793	4.439	3.725	3.190
13	5.842	5.342	4.910	4.533	3.780	3.223
14	6.002	5.468	5.008	4.611	3.824	3.249
15	6.142	5.575	5.092	4.675	3.859	3.268
16	6.265	5.668	5.162	4.730	3.887	3.283
17	5.373	5.749	4.222	4.775	3.910	3.295
18	6.467	5.818	5.273	4.812	3.928	3.304
19	6.550	5.877	5.316	4.843	3.942	3.311
20	6.623	5.929	5.353	4.870	3.954	3.316
25	6.873	6.097	5.467	4.948	3.985	3.329
30	7.003	6.177	5.517	4.979	3.995	3.332

Example: The present value of a ten-year lease with annual payments of $1000. with the first payment due immediately and the remaining nine payments due at the beginning of each year, discounted at a 9 percent rate, is $1000 × PVIFADi,n where i is 9 percent and n is 10.

$$\text{PVIFAD}_{9\%.10} = \text{PVIFA}_{9\%.(10-1)} + 1$$

Table 4 gives the value of the PVIFA at 9 percent and nine years as PVIFA9%.9 − 5.995, so

$$\text{PVIFAD}_{9\%.10} = 5.995 + 1 = 6.995$$

The present value of the ten-year lease discounted at 9 percent is $1000 × 6.995 = $6995.

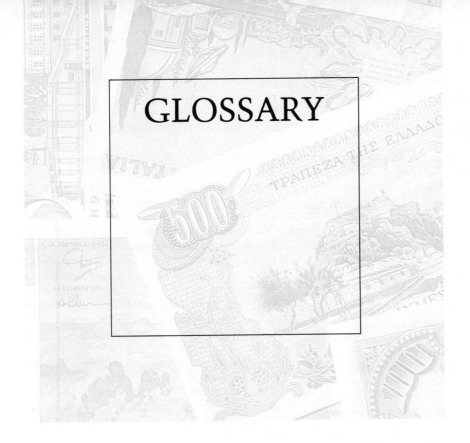

GLOSSARY

A

Accelerator principle. A concept expressing the relationship between investment in real capital assets such as plant and equipment and demand for output from such assets. If demand for consumer goods is growing, new producer assets must be added to meet this new demand plus worn-out (depreciated) equipment must be replaced. This, in turn, leads to accelerated economic activity.

Acceptance. A type of receivable instrument that arises out of the sale of merchandise to a business customer and which may be sold to a bank. Also see bankers' acceptances.

Accounts payable. Accounts arising primarily from the purchase of goods by a business on credit terms.

Accounts receivable. Accounts arising from the sale of products, merchandise, or services on credit and which reflect a promise of the customer to pay.

Accrued liabilities. Amounts owed but not yet paid for, including such items as wages and salaries, taxes, and interest on notes.

Acid-test ratio. A liquidity ratio that is calculated by dividing the residual of current assets minus inventories by the firm's current liabilities.

Adjustable rate mortgage. Also called variable rate mortgage. A mortgage where instead of agreeing to a certain fixed interest rate, the home buyer agrees to pay the "going rate" which is tied to a reference interest rate that changes with changing conditions in the financial markets. When market interest rates are rising, the home buyer would expect to pay a higher interest rate on the mortgage loan, and vice versa.

Administrative inflation. The tendency of prices to rise during periods of economic expansion but remain stable during periods of contraction; explained in part by the existence of fixed-wage contracts with escalator clauses and the preference of businesses to avoid price competition whenever possible.

Amortized loan. A loan in which the borrower agrees to make regular payments on principal as well as on interest.

Annuity. A constant or level cash flow amount in each time period. With an ordinary annuity the cash flow is at the end of each time period; in an annuity due the cash flow occurs at the beginning of each time period.

Annuity contract. Described as "insurance in reverse," it provides for the disposition of an estate through its systematic liquidation. The purchaser agrees to pay a stipulated sum of money to the insurance company in return for a regular income from the company for a specified time, such as a number of years or for life.

Arbitrage. The simultaneous, or nearly simultaneous, purchase of commodities, securities, or bills of exchange in one market and selling them in another market where the price is higher. In international exchange, variations in quotations between countries at any time are quickly brought into alignment through the arbitrage activities of international financiers.

Assets. All money, property, and rights to money owned by a person or a business. Assets include 1) fixed, which are items such as buildings that cannot be easily converted to cash, and 2) current, which are cash and items such as accounts receivable and goods for sale that can be reasonably expected to be turned into cash in the near future.

Asset utilization ratios. Financial ratios that show how well a firm uses its assets to support or generate sales.

Automatic stabilizers. Programs and progressive income tax schedules that automatically serve to counter inflationary or deflationary conditions. Among them are the unemployment insurance program, federal and state welfare payments, and the progressive income tax, which results in vast increases in tax revenues during boom times and results in a reduction in taxes during periods of economic recession.

Average collection period. The average amount of time that accounts receivable are outstanding. It is found by dividing the accounts receivable balance by the average daily credit sales (which are net sales divided by 360).

B

Balance of payments. A summary of all international transactions including foreign investment, private and government grants, expenditures of the U.S. military forces overseas, and many other items in addition to the purchases and sales of goods and services.

Balance of trade. The net balance of exports and imports of goods and services; the single most important element in the balance of payments.

Balance sheet. The summary or report that shows the assets and the sources of financing of a business at a particular point in time. It reveals two broad categories of information: (1) the properties owned by a business (assets) and (2) the creditors' claims (liabilities) and the owners' equity in the business.

Bankers' acceptances. Instruments used to finance exports and imports arising from foreign trade and representing the unconditional obligation of the accepting or guaranteeing bank. These financial claims to wealth may be traded in secondary money markets.

Bank holding company. A company which directly or indirectly owns, controls, or holds the power to vote 25 percent or more of the voting shares of each of two or more banks.

Banking system. A general term referring to a composite of the four depositories; that is, commercial banks, savings and loan associations, mutual savings banks, and credit unions.

Banks for cooperatives. A system of twelve district banks and one central bank established in 1933 to provide credit to agricultural cooperatives. In 1987 the central bank and ten of the district banks merged into the National Bank for Cooperatives, which is in Denver, Colorado.

Barter. The process of directly trading or exchanging goods and services without the use of money in such transactions.

Best-effort underwriting agreement. An arrangement whereby the investment bankers make a best-effort to sell the securities of the issuing corporation, but they assume no risk for a possible failure of the securities issue.

Bid-and-asked price. The quotation which is made by a dealer making a market for a given security. The "bid" is that price the dealer is willing to pay for the securities and the "asked price" is the figure at which the dealer is willing to sell the security.

Bimetallic standard. A monetary standard based upon two metals such as silver and gold.

Blue-sky laws. State laws to protect investors from fraudulent security offerings.

Branch banks. Banking offices that are controlled by a single parent bank. One board of directors and one group of stockholders control the home office and the branches.

Budgetary deficit. The excess of federal government expenditures over income reflected in the federal budget.

Business cycles. The fluctuations in economic activity between prosperity and recession or depression. These recurring fluctuations have come to be known as business cycles even though they are not of equal intensity or equal length.

Buying on margin. The use of borrowed funds to support part of the purchase price of a security. The security so purchased serves as the collateral for the borrowed funds.

C

Callable preferred stock. Preferred stock that can be retired, or paid off, at any time by the issuing corporation.

Call contract. An option to buy a security at a specified price during a specified period of time.

Capacity. One of the five C's of credit analysis. Capacity reflects the financial ability of a borrower to pay bills as they come due.

Capital. The accumulated wealth of a business or individual. In credit analysis it refers to the adequacy of equity relative to liabilities and is therefore a measure of credit worthiness.

Capital account balance. The balance, including changes, in foreign government and private investment in the United States. Netted against this are similar U.S. government and private investments in foreign countries.

Capital asset pricing model. (CAPM) A model that measures risk differences by comparing a stock price to an overall market average to find the stock's expected return.

Capital formation. The creation of physical productive facilities such as buildings, tools, equipment, and roads.

Capital markets. Markets where longer-term (in excess of one year maturities) debt securities (notes and bonds) and instruments (mortgages) as well as corporate stocks are traded.

Cash balances approach. In determining the causes of changes in prices this approach places primary emphasis on the reasons that individuals and businesses hold money as well as their reasons for spending it. The approach therefore lends itself to supply-and-demand analysis.

Cash transactions statement. A financial statement showing only the receipt and disbursement of cash. It is used by firms to manage their cash activities and to plan for short-term borrowing needs.

Casualty and surety insurance. Includes all forms of coverage not included as marine, fire, or life insurance. Examples would be automobile liability insurance and insurance protection against burglary or robbery.

Certificates of deposit. Depository printed receipts having stated maturities, which either bear interest or are issued at discounts.

Character. One of the five C's of credit analysis. Character is an assumption about the willingness of the applicant to pay his or her bills.

Clean draft. A time or sight draft that is not accompanied by other documents that specify conditions under which the draft is payable.

Closed-end fund. A type of investment company that obtains funds from the public by issuing its own common shares, typically all at one time. The asset value of the closed-end fund changes primarily through changes in the market value of the securities that it holds. A closed-end fund may also offer bonds and preferred stock.

Closed-end mortgage bonds. Sold in a single issue that prevents further sale of bonds secured by the same mortgage.

Collateral. Assets pledged as security for the payment of a loan. One of the five C's of credit analysis.

Commercial finance company. An organization without a bank charter that makes loans to business firms by: advancing funds to business firms by discounting accounts receivable; making loans secured by chattel mortgages on machinery or liens on inventory; and financing deferred-payment sales of commercial and industrial equipment.

Commercial letter of credit. A written statement on the part of the bank to an individual or firm guaranteeing acceptance and payment of a draft up to a specified sum if presented to the bank in accordance with the terms of the commercial letter of credit.

Commercial paper. Short-term unsecured promissory notes of well-known business concerns with strong credit ratings.

Commercial paper house. An organization that purchases the promissory notes of reputable dealers or business organizations for the purpose of resale to other lenders (i.e., individuals and organizations desiring to invest in or hold commercial paper).

Commission brokers. The members of the securities exchanges that serve the public in effecting purchases and sales of securities on the exchanges. They act as agents for the execution of customers' orders and receive commissions for this service.

Commodity Credit Corporation. Federal agency that stabilizes farm products prices and the market for them through commodity loans and loan guarantees, regulating how land is used, and buying and storing crops.

Common stock. Shares representing an ownership claim in the assets of a business corporation and a claim to the profits of the business that remain after the holders of all other classes of debt and equity instruments have received their stipulated returns. The common stockholders vote to select the board of directors of a corporation.

Compensating balance. The average deposit that may be required of a borrowing business by a lending bank.

Compounding. Interest earned each period plus the principal is reinvested at the stated interest rate so that interest will be earned on interest as well as on the principal.

Conditional sales contract. An agreement providing that a seller retain title to assets until the full purchase price has been paid.

Conditions. Refers to the prevailing economic climate or business cycle state. It is one of the five

C's of credit analysis and is important in assessing whether credit obligations can be met.

Consumer credit. Credit used by consumers to finance or refinance the purchase of goods and services for personal consumption. Its use to finance personal consumption distinguishes it from business credit used for production purposes.

Consumer finance companies. Organizations that provide credit to consumers. Originally developed to provide aid in time of financial emergency, they now loan money to middle- and low-income families.

Contractual savings. Savings that are accumulated on a regular schedule by prior agreement for such purposes as insurance premiums, pension fund, or loan repayments. Typically they are automatically withheld from wages or withdrawn from bank accounts.

Controller. The person responsible for a firm's accounting and tax-record activities.

Conventional mortgage loan. An amortized mortgage loan that is neither FHA-insured nor VA-guaranteed. Today these loans are usually insured by private mortgage insurance companies.

Convertible preferred stock. Preferred stock that can be converted by its holders into common stock.

Corporate equity capital. The financial capital supplied by the owners of a corporation, whose ownership claims are represented by stock certificates.

Corporation. A business that exists in perpetuity as a separate legal entity owned by shareholders who buy its stock and who are not liable for claims against the corporation.

Cost of capital. The combined rate of return necessary for a firm to cover its cost of debt and equity funds.

Cost-push inflation. If costs are increased faster than productivity increases, as in the case of rising wages, businesses that have some say about prices will attempt to raise them in order to cover the increased costs. The result is cost-push or wage-push inflation.

Credit bureau. An organization set up by local merchants and finance companies to serve as a central exchange for data on the credit history of businesses or individuals.

Credit exchange. An agency set up in most cities by consumer finance companies to provide information on loans.

Credit money. Money which has a greater value than the value of the material out of which it is made.

Credit union. A cooperative nonprofit organization that provides its members with consumer credit at moderate interest rates and also accepts savings. It is comprised of individuals who share common bonds, such as occupation, residential ties, or other forms of association like church affiliation.

Crowding out. A condition that occurs when the sale of government obligations to cover large federal deficits threatens the flow of funds to the private sector for investment purposes.

Cumulative preferred stock. Shares requiring that before common stock dividends may be paid, preferred dividends must be paid not only for the dividend period in question but also for all previous periods in which no preferred dividends were paid.

Current account balance. Shows the flow of income into and out of the United States during a specified time period. It is calculated by adding one-way remittances, pensions and other transfers, and government grants to the current negative balance of goods and services.

Current assets. Cash and other assets (such as accounts receivable and inventory) of a business that may be reasonably expected to be converted into cash, sold, or used in the near future through the normal operations of the business.

Current liabilities. Business obligations that must be satisfied within a period of one year. They are the liabilities that are usually met out of current funds and operations of the business.

Current ratio. A measure of the short-term financial position of a firm. It is found by dividing total current assets by total current liabilities.

D

Dealer system. A small group of large securities dealers through which the Fed affects its purchase and sale of U.S. obligations.

Debenture bonds. Bonds which are dependent upon the general credit and strength of the corporation for their security. They represent no specific pledge of property, but rather their holders are classed as general creditors of the corporation.

Debt capital. Business funds obtained from creditors rather than from owners. Such capital may be obtained through direct negotiation with a lender or the sale of notes or bonds to many lenders.

Debt management. A Treasury function affecting economic conditions and money markets through the refunding of debt issues. Decisions about advance refunding, types of securities to sell, interest rate patterns to use, and call provisions are involved in connection with debt management.

Debt ratio. Calculated as total liabilities divided by total assets, which is a way of measuring a firm's financial leverage.

Deed of trust. Used as security on a real property loan. It differs from a mortgage in that three parties are involved: the beneficiary (lender), a trustor (borrower), and a trustee, who is responsible for the lender's interests.

Default risk. The likelihood or probability that a bond issuer will fail to meet its interest or principal payment obligations.

Deficit financing. The manner in which the government chooses to finance the excess of expenditures over revenues in any fiscal period.

Deficit reserves. Deficit reserves are created when the amount of required reserves for a depository institution is greater than its total reserves. The deficit is the difference between the two amounts.

Demand deposits. The checking accounts of individuals, businesses, and other organizations held at commercial banks.

Demand-pull inflation. This type of inflation occurs when the demand for goods and services exceeds the available supply of them.

Depository institutions. Units of the banking system consisting of commercial banks, savings and loan associations, mutual savings banks, or credit unions.

Depreciation. The reduction in some of the economic value of plant and equipment as it is used. Depreciation is charged off against the original cost of that plant and equipment.

Derivative deposits. Deposits that occur when reserves created from primary deposits are made available through bank loans to borrowers who leave them on deposit in order to write checks against the funds.

Direct securities. Contracts between savers and borrowers themselves such as corporate stocks and bonds.

Dirty float. The attempt by central banks to influence or control exchange rates in the foreign exchange market's floating exchange rate system.

Discounting. The opposite of compounding whereby the focus is on finding the present value of cash flows that are to be received in future time periods by discounting or reducing them by a stated interest rate.

Disintermediation. The process whereby savings are withdrawn from thrift institutions and commercial banks and are channeled into alternative investments.

Dissave. To liquidate accumulated savings for consumption uses.

Documentary draft. The documentary draft, in contrast with a clean draft, is accompanied by an order bill of lading and other papers such as insurance receipts and consular invoices.

Draft (bill of exchange). An unconditional order in writing, signed by the party drawing it, requiring the party to whom it is addressed to pay on demand or at a fixed or determinable future time a certain sum of money to order or to bearer.

E

Electronic funds transfer systems. EFTS provide for the receiving and disbursing of funds electronically instead of through the use of checks.

Eligible paper. Short-term promissory notes of commercial, industrial, and agricultural customers of banks, eligible for discounting with the Federal Reserve banks. Such paper may also be used as collateral against advances from Federal Reserve banks, although in practice U.S. government and agency securities are generally used.

Endowment insurance. Insurance written for a spec-ified number of years. If the insured person survives to the end of the stipulated period, the face amount of the policy is payable to the insured.

Equation of exchange. The equation $MV = PT$, or $MV = \Sigma pQ$, which shows how the volume of money, the rate at which money is used, and the volume of goods and services being exchanged all interact to affect price changes.

Equipment trust financing. A device providing for the transfer of title to equipment by the seller to a trustee. The trustee, generally a trust company or a trust department of a commercial bank, holds title to the equipment but leases it to the business.

Equity multiplier ratio. Shows the extent to which a firm's assets are financed by borrowed funds by dividing total assets by owners' equity.

Equity of redemption. A mortgagor's right in equity to redeem property lost through default on the mortgage loan against the property. Payment in full must take place within a time period specified by a decree of foreclosure.

Eurobonds. Bonds that are denominated in currencies other than those of the countries where they are sold.

Eurocurrencies. Money from one country that is deposited in banks of other countries—for example, when German marks are deposited in a Swiss bank. About three quarters of Eurocurrency deposits are made in U.S. dollars (Eurodollars).

Eurodollars. Deposits placed in foreign banks that remain denominated in U.S. dollars. A demand deposit in a U.S. bank becomes a Eurodollar when the holder of such a deposit transfers it to a foreign bank or an overseas branch of an American bank. After the transfer the foreign bank holds a claim against the U.S. bank, while the original deposit holder (possibly a business firm) now holds a Eurodollar deposit.

Excess reserves. The difference between the total reserves of the banking system and those required to be held at Federal Reserve banks. These constitute the excess reserves available for credit expansion.

Exchange rate. The rate at which a given unit of foreign currency is quoted in terms of domestic currency and vice versa.

Expectations theory. Theory contending that the long-term interest rates at any point in time reflect the average of the prevailing short-term interest rates plus short-term rates expected in the future. Thus, over the long-run, short-term and long-term interest rates should be equal for securities that have comparable default risks.

Export-Import Bank. A bank authorized in 1934 which became an independent agency of the government in 1945. Its purpose is to aid in financing and to facilitate exports and imports between the United States and other countries. It is the only agency engaged solely in the financing of the foreign trade of the United States. The Ex-Im Bank makes intermediate- and long-term loans and loan guarantees abroad, offers credit insurance, and assists developing foreign countries with credits for maintaining their level of U.S. imports.

F

Factor. An organization that engages in accounts receivable financing for business enterprises by purchasing the accounts outright and by assuming all credit risks.

Farm Credit Administration. Federal agency established in 1933 to consolidate the facilities created under the Farm Loan Act. It supervises the system of farm credit banks, land bank associations, production credit associations, and banks for cooperatives.

Farm credit banks. Nationwide system of eleven banks under the Farm Credit Administration that makes long- and short-term farm loans. Loans may be made to farmers, ranchers, rural homeowners, commercial fishermen, and certain farm-related businesses.

Farmer Mac. The Federal Agricultural Mortgage Corporation. It was established in 1987 to support a secondary market for farm real estate mortgages by guaranteeing the payment of interest and principal for groups of qualified loans. The loans are then used as collateral to back securities sold to investors, providing a supplementary flow of funds to support farm mortgage lending.

Farmers Home Administration (FMHA). Created in 1946 to make loans to farmers otherwise unable to obtain credit at appropriate rates of interest and suitable maturities. Loans are made for purposes of purchasing, improving, or repairing farm land and buildings.

Federal Deposit Insurance Corporation (FDIC). An agency which insures deposits in and supervises member commercial banks.

Federal funds. Temporary excess reserves that are loaned on a day-to-day basis to banks that are temporarily short on reserves. This process involves the transfer of reserve balances on the books of the federal reserve bank from the reserve account of the lending bank to the reserve account of the borrowing bank.

Federal Home Loan Mortgage Corporation (FHLMC). An agency providing a secondary market for conventional mortgages written by savings and loan associations that are members of the Federal Home Loan Bank System.

Federal Housing Administration (FHA). An agency providing mortgage loan insurance on homes that meet FHA requirements and standards.

Federal land bank associations. Cooperative credit organizations serving communities or counties, made up of groups of farmers and supervised by the Farm Credit Administration. They assist farmers in determining loan needs, processing loan applications, and servicing the loans. Member-borrowers are required to purchase association stock in the amount of 5% of their loans.

Federal National Mortgage Association (FNMA). Also called "Fannie Mae," FNMA was organized in 1938 under the Reconstruction Finance Corporation to provide an additional market for FHA-insured mortgages and, after World War II, VA-guaranteed mortgages and mortgages under special housing programs. By buying and selling these mortgages the FNMA helped stabilize the housing construction industry. In 1968 the FNMA was divided into two organizations. The first, which retained the original title, is a government-sponsored private corporation responsible for secondary market operations in FHA and VA residential mortgages. The other part became the Government National Mortgage Association.

Federal Reserve float. The temporary increase in bank reserves that results when checks are credited to the reserve accounts of banks that deposited them before they were debited to the accounts of banks on which they are drawn.

Federal Reserve System (Fed). The central banking system in the United States. It performs important functions for the banking system and it establishes and administers monetary policy.

Federal Savings and Loan Insurance Corporation (FSLIC). An agency which until 1989 insured deposits in member savings and loan associations. It was replaced by the Savings Association Insurance Fund.

Federal statutory debt limits. Debt limits of the federal government established by Congress. Such limits are frequently raised on a "temporary" basis to meet the needs of the U.S. Treasury and at rare intervals on a permanent basis.

Fiat money. Money based on the general credit of an issuing government and proclaimed to be money by law or fiat.

Fidelity bond. A special form of surety contract which provides that the surety company reimburse employers for losses incurred from the dishonest acts of employees.

Fiduciary. One who has been empowered with the control of assets for another and acts in a capacity of trust and undivided loyalty for that person or organization.

Field warehouse. A temporary warehouse set up by a lender on the premises of the borrowing business firm to store inventory used as collateral against the loan.

Finance. The study of financial institutions and markets and their operation within the financial system (macro level); financial planning, asset management, and fund raising (micro level).

Finance company. A company that makes loans directly to consumers and businesses.

Financial assets. Claims against (obligations or liabilities of) individuals, businesses, financial institutions, and governments who issued them. Examples would be debt obligations issued by businesses and savings accounts held at commercial banks by individuals.

Financial intermediaries. Institutions such as banks and credit unions, whose financial activities aid the flow of funds from savers to borrowers.

Financial investment. When claims to wealth in the form of financial assets, such as securities, are purchased or when debt obligations are repaid.

Financial leverage ratios. Financial ratios that indicate the extent to which assets are financed by borrowed funds and other liabilities.

Fire insurance. Insurance offering protection to the insured against the destruction of physical property as a result of fire. It may also provide for protection against related perils, such as explosions, or "acts of God," such as hurricanes.

Fiscal agent. The role of the Fed that involves collecting taxes, issuing checks, maintaining records, distributing U.S. obligations, and other such activities for the U.S. Treasury.

Fiscal policy. Government influence on economic activity through the Treasury's expenditure and taxation programs. The policy is formulated by the President and the Council of Economic Advisors and must be approved by Congress.

Fixed assets. Physical facilities used in the production, storage, display, and distribution of the products of a firm. These assets normally provide many years of service to the firm. The principal fixed assets are equipment, land, and buildings.

Fixed costs. Expenses such as general and administrative expenses that must be incurred regardless of the volume of sales generated by a firm.

Flexible exchange rates. A system established in 1973 in which international exchange rates are determined by supply and demand in the foreign exchange market. This system reduces the impact of international financial transactions on the domestic money supply.

Float. The amount payable on checks already written but not yet deducted from the accounts on which they are drawn. Federal Reserve float is the temporary increase in bank reserves that results when checks are credited to the reserve accounts of banks that deposited them before they are debited to the accounts of banks on which they are drawn.

Flotation. The initial sale of newly issued debt or equity securities. These sales are usually made through investment bankers.

Foreclosure. Provides that a mortgagor's equity of redemption right is "barred and foreclosed" after a court-specified time period. This occurs when payments to the lender are not made as agreed by the borrower.

Foreign exchange markets. Electronic communication systems that connect the major financial centers of the world. The network can be accessed through most financial institutions, thus enabling businesses to complete transactions throughout the world within minutes.

Fourth market. A market in which large institutional investors arrange purchases and sales of securities without using brokers or dealers. Transactions are quick and economical; an electronic network is maintained to make offers known and to allow transactions to take place anonymously.

Fractional reserve system. A system whereby banks are required to hold reserves equal to some portion or fraction of their deposits rather than on a dollar-for-dollar basis.

Full-bodied money. Circulating coins that have their full monetary value of metal in them, under a gold, silver, or bimetallic standard. Their value as a commodity thus is as great as their value as money.

Futures. A contract to buy or sell a good, such as soybeans, oil, or currencies, at a certain price, with payment and delivery at a specified time in the future. Ownership is traded and profits are made from the paper value of the goods, not from actual possession.

G

General obligation bond. A bond secured by the full faith and credit of the issuing governmental unit, that is, the bond is unconditionally supported by the full taxing power of the issuing government. General obligation bonds constitute by far the largest class of municipal obligations.

Government National Mortgage Association (GNMA). A government-owned corporation organized in 1968 under the Housing and Urban Development Act to help finance special housing areas such as urban renewal and to manage and liquidate the pre-1954 mortgages acquired by FNMA. GNMA also operates a secondary market auction for conventional mortgage loans and sells mortgage-backed securities. These securities, the popular "Ginnie Maes,"

are backed by FHA and VA mortgage pools that "pass through" interest and principal payments to investors.

Gramm-Rudman-Hollings. The popular name for the Balanced Budget and Emergency Deficit Control Act of 1985. Its goal was to reduce the federal debt and produce a balanced budget by 1991—later amended to 1993. This is to be accomplished by making annual reductions in federal spending.

Grants-in-aid. Grants of funds from one governmental unit to another, usually transfers of funds from the federal government to state and community levels.

Greenbacks. Paper money officially known as United States notes authorized by Congress to help finance the Civil War.

H

Hedging. In financing assets, the practice in which the average maturities of the assets are matched with the maturity dates of the firm's liabilities.

Housing and Urban Development, Department of (HUD). This department, created in 1965, has a wide range of responsibilities including the regulation of the Federal Housing Administration and the Government National Mortgage Association.

I

Income statement. A statement reflecting the change in a firm's financial position over a specified accounting time period. It shows the net profit or income (or loss) available to the owners of the business.

Indirect financing. Financing created by an intermediary who is a party to separate instruments with lenders and borrowers. For example, business loans and time deposits are indirect instruments created by banks.

Industrial revenue bonds. Bonds issued by municipalities to provide lower-cost financing for construction of plant facilities for businesses as an incentive for the firms to locate in their areas.

Industry comparative analysis. A method that compares financial ratios for a firm against industry ratios.

Inflation. A condition which occurs when a rise or increase in the prices of goods and services is not off set by increases in the quality of those goods and services.

Inflationary bias. A view that the long history of price increases will, because of governmental policy and other reasons, continue upward.

Insurance trust. One or more insurance policies placed in trust with the agreement that the proceeds of the insurance be paid to the trust institution upon death of the maker of the trust. The trust institution will then administer the funds for the beneficiaries of the trust.

Interest rate. The basic price that equates the demand for and the supply of loanable funds in the financial markets. The quoted interest rate for any type of loan is a combination of several factors. Part of it is a fee for the administrative costs of making a loan, and another part of it is payment for the risk involved. The remainder is a payment for the use of money itself.

Interest rate risk. A financial risk relating to short-term financing costs that affect business operations. If interest rates rise significantly in a short period of time, the added cost may affect profit margins unless prices can be raised to offset the added cost.

Interest risk premium. The difference between the interest rate on a comparable maturity U.S. government security (which is viewed as being risk-free) and the interest rate on a security with some risk involved.

Intermediation. The process by which savings are accumulated in financial institutions and, in turn, lent or invested by them.

Internal business risk. Possible financial risk to a business from theft, fire, natural disasters, or, in the case of small companies, the death or incapacitation of a key employee.

Internal rate of return method. The rate of return when the net present value is zero. This occurs when the present value of the cash inflows equals a project's investment or initial outlay.

International Monetary Fund (IMF). An international organization that promotes stability in the world's currencies by maintaining a monetary pool from which member countries can borrow foreign currencies to correct temporary payment imbalances with other countries.

Inventories. The materials and products that a manufacturing enterprise has on hand. Generally, a manufacturing firm categorizes its inventories in terms of raw materials, goods in the process of manufacture, and finished goods.

Inventory turnover. A financial ratio measured as the cost of goods sold divided by the value of inventories.

Investment bankers. Also called underwriters, they are financial intermediaries who help businesses market and distribute their bonds and stocks in the primary securities market. Also called underwriters.

Investment company. An institution that engages principally in the purchase of stocks and bonds of other corporations. This permits the pooling of funds of many investors on a share basis for the primary purpose of obtaining expert management and wide diversification in security investments.

Investment development company. A venture capital company that is a privately established profit-seeking organization whose primary function is to provide capital to new and growing businesses.

Irrevocable trust. A trust that provides for the complete and final transfer of assets to the trustee.

J

Junior lien. When a parcel of real estate has more than one mortgage lien against it, the bonds outstanding against mortgages filed after the first mortgage are junior liens.

L

Land contract. A contract for the sale of property in which the deed to the property does not pass to the purchaser until the terms of the contract have been fulfilled.

Leaning against the wind. A phrase used by the Federal Reserve in describing its strategy of gently easing credit during periods of economic contraction and applying monetary restraint when inflationary pressures begin to appear.

Legal tender. Money backed by the general credit of the government and acceptable to pay taxes and to fulfill contracts calling for payment in lawful money.

Liabilities. All debts a business owes, including creditors' claims (accounts payable), taxes, bank loans, and the like.

Life insurance. Insurance whose main function is providing an immediate estate for the dependents of the head of the household in the event of death before sufficient personal resources have been accumulated to provide for the dependents.

Limit order. An order placed with a broker providing a maximum price that is to be paid for a particular security or a minimum price at which a security may be sold.

Limited obligation bonds. Most of these are revenue bonds, issued to provide funds for specific projects with the understanding that both principal and interest are to be paid only from revenues of the project so financed.

Limited partnership. A statutory modification of the common-law partnership in which one or more general partners combine with one or more limited partners. Limited partners have limited liabilities in terms of the partnership organization.

Line of credit. The loan limit that a bank establishes for each of its business customers.

Liquidity. The ease with which an asset can be exchanged for money or other assets.

Liquidity preference theory. A theory which holds that interest rates are determined by the supply of and demand for money. This is viewed as a "stock" theory in that it focuses on the amount or stock of money at a certain point in time.

Liquidity premium theory. A theory which holds that investors should be willing to trade off some yield for the greater liquidity of short-term securities. Likewise, borrowers would prefer to lend long-term and thus reduce their own liquidity risks associated with maturing securities. These supply-and-demand pressures suggest that short-term rates should be lower than long-term rates and that their yield curve should be upward sloping.

Liquidity ratios. Financial ratios that indicate the ability of a firm to meet its short-term debt obligations as they come due.

Living trust. A trust that operates during the lifetime of its maker. The trust principal is held for a beneficiary, such as a spouse or minor child, until a specified event occurs. The beneficiary receives income generated by the principal in the meantime.

Loanable funds theory. A theory which holds that interest rates are a function of the supply of and demand for loanable funds. This is a "flow" theory in that it focuses on the relative supply and demand of loanable funds over a specified time period.

Long-term liabilities. Business debts with maturities greater than one year.

M

Macroeconomic business risk. The extent to which changes in the economy and the firm's industry impact on the business operations of the firm.

Macro level finance. The financial system in the U.S. and global economies.

Making a market. When an over-the-counter dealer stands ready to buy and/or sell a particular security or group of securities. As such, the dealer is acting as a principal in the transaction in much the same manner as any merchant.

Marine insurance. Provides protection for losses arising from the transportation of merchandise from the seller to the purchaser; includes transportation over land or water.

Marketable securities. Investments that are highly liquid (short maturity and an active secondary market) and of such high quality that there is little chance that the borrower will default.

Market order. An order placed with a commission broker requesting the purchase or sale of a particular security at the best possible price that can be negotiated at the time the order is received.

Market segmentation theory. A theory which holds that securities of different maturities are less than perfect substitutes for each other. Institutional pressures dominate this theory. For example, commercial banks concentrate their activities in short-term securities because of demand and other deposit liabilities. On the other hand, the nature of insurance company and pension fund liabilities allows these firms to concentrate their purchases and holdings in long-term securities. Thus supply-and-demand factors in each segmented market will affect the shape of the yield curve.

Maturity distribution. The length of life remaining at a particular time for all outstanding obligations.

Medium of exchange. The basic function of money in any economy. Money also serves as a store of purchasing power and as a standard of value.

Merchandise trade balance. The net difference between the import and export of goods between one nation and the rest of the trading world.

Micro level finance. The financial system of an individual business or financial institution.

Monetarists. The group of monetary theorists that places primary emphasis on the supply of money as the determinant of price levels.

Monetary base. Reserve deposits held in Federal Reserve banks, vault cash or currency held by banks and other depository institutions, and currency held by the nonbank public. The monetary base (MB) times the money multiplier (m) produces the M1 definition of the money supply and can be expressed in formula form as $MB \cdot m = M1$.

Monetary policy. The policy formulated by the Fed to regulate the growth of the money supply and influence interest rates and the availability of credit.

Monetizing the deficit. The process of increasing the money supply by the Fed's purchasing government debt obligations. The result is equivalent to the government's printing money to pay for its expenditures.

Money. Anything that is generally accepted as a means of paying for goods and services and of discharging debts.

Money markets. Markets where debt instruments of one year or less are traded.

Money multiplier. An adjustment factor influenced by the Federal Reserve, the nonbank public, and the U.S. Treasury which when multiplied times the monetary base results in the M1 money supply definition.

Morris Plan company. Type of early industrial banking company established by Arthur J. Morris in 1910 that grew to a group of banks throughout the U.S. They made small consumer loans and offered savings accounts to people employed in industry.

Mortgage. An interest in real property used as security for payment of a debt. Two parties, a mortgagee and a mortgagor, are involved. The

mortgagor conveys the property deed to a mortgagee, who supplies the loan.

Mortgage banking company. A company that originates or negotiates real estate mortgage loans and often service the mortgages by collecting interest and principal payments and then forwarding them to the owners of the mortgage. These firms are usually closely held private corporations. They have relatively small capital investment compared with the volume of business they do.

Mortgage bonds. Long-term corporate securities that are secured by the pledge of specific real property.

Mortgage broker. A firm or individual who originates real estate loans by bringing borrowers and lenders together but does not usually service these loans.

Mortgage debt. Long-term consumer credit used to purchase homes. Consumer credit used for other purposes is classified as either intermediate- or short-term credit.

Mortgagee. The lender in a mortgaged loan transaction.

Mortgagor. The borrower in a mortgaged loan transaction.

Multiplier. The process by which an increase in investment, government, or consumption expenditures leads to a multiplied effect on national income. For example, as investment expenditures or government expenditures are increased, the level of national income increases, and this leads to an increase in consumption expenditures, which again in turn raises national income, which leads to more expenditures on consumption, and so on.

Municipal bonds. In investment circles, commonly interpreted to mean the obligations of a state itself or of any of its political subdivisions. The description is not technically correct, but it is understood by all parties in the investment world.

Mutual fund. An investment company that usually offers a single class of shares to investors, which can be redeemed at any time. Mutual funds allow an increasing number of shares to be issued, and their price is determined by the current value of the securities held by the fund.

N

NASD. National Association of Securities Dealers, a self-regulating association of firms in the securities industry.

NASDAQ. National Association of Securities Dealers Automatic Quotations, which provides over-the-counter security price quotations.

Negative financial leverage. Situation which occurs when the interest cost of borrowing is more than the return being earned on the investment in assets. If the earnings before interest falls below the amount needed to meet interest obligations on the borrowed funds, the firm might be forced into bankruptcy.

Negotiable certificates of deposit. In essence, receipts issued by a bank in exchange for deposits of funds. The bank agrees to pay the amount deposited plus interest to the bearer of the receipt on the date specified on the certificate. Because the certificate is negotiable ($100,000 or more in amount), it can be traded in the secondary market before maturity.

Net present value method. A way of evaluating a project that considers the time-value of money. It is calculated by finding the present value of all cash inflows and subtracting the initial investment or outlay for the fixed assets which generate the inflows.

Net working capital. An amount determined by subtracting the total of current liabilities shown on the balance sheet from the total of current assets.

Nonbanking financial conglomerates. Diversified financial facilities owned by large commercial or industrial corporations that offer financial services that are in competition with the facilities of the banking system.

Noncumulative preferred stock. A type of preferred stock that does not contain a provision for the accumulation of unpaid dividends.

Nonmarketable government securities. Instruments that cannot be transferred to other persons or institutions and can be redeemed only by being turned in to the U.S. Treasury. Savings bonds comprise the bulk of nonmarketable issues.

Note payable. A liability (debt) in the form of a written promise to pay a specified amount of money to the order of a credit or on or before a certain date.

Note receivable. An asset in the form of money owed the holder of the note by a certain date.

O

Off-budget outlays. Expenditures for several government agencies that are not included in the published budget of the U.S. government.

Open-end fund. Commonly referred to as a mutual fund, an investment company that issues an unlimited number of common shares. The public buys shares in the fund directly from the investment company and redeems shares with that company. This contrasts with a closed-end fund investment company which has a fixed number of shares that are bought and sold in securities markets.

Open-end mortgage bonds. Bonds sold in an issue that provides for continuing sale of bonds against the same mortgage. Frequently there is a stipulation that additional real property which is acquired automatically becomes a part of the property secured under the mortgage.

Open market operations. The buying and selling of large quantities of securities in the open market by the Federal Reserve, for the purpose of increasing or decreasing the supply of money in circulation.

Optimal capital structure. Reflects an industry's ideal mix between long-term debt and equity funds that minimizes the cost of capital and maximizes the value of firms within that industry.

Options. Contracts that give their holders the right to buy (call option) or sell (put option) a security at a specified price before a specified date.

Order bill of lading. This instrument carries title to the merchandise being shipped and only its holder may claim the merchandise at the transportation terminal. The order bill of lading represents the written acceptance and terms of goods for shipment by a transportation company.

Owner's equity. Also called equity capital, it is the personal investment of the owners or owner in a business in the form of cash or other assets such as real estate, machinery, and office equipment. Owners' equity also accrues when profits are allowed to remain with the business.

P

Paid-in capital account. Part of the owners' equity of a corporation, it reflects the surplus from selling shares of common stock above the stated or par value. Also called a surplus account.

Partnership. A form of business organization that exists when two or more persons own a business for the purpose of making a profit.

Par value. A fixed or stated value assigned to shares of common stock in the certificate of incorporation.

Payback period method. A technique for evaluating a potential project that determines the time it will take in years to recover the initial investment in fixed assets.

Phillips curve. A rounded L-shared curve that plots the relationship between employment and wages and prices. It is based on British economist Phillips's theory that it is impossible to have high employment without inflation and that policymakers must choose between some degree of unemployment and some degree of inflation.

Positive financial leverage. Situation which occurs when the interest cost of borrowing is less than the return being earned on the investment in assets. Trading on equity thus is favorable to the firm's stockholders.

Precautionary motive. The demand for marketable securities or cash to handle disruptive developments that otherwise could cause severe short-term liquidity problems.

Preferred stock. A form of stock in a corporation that has a prior claim relative to common stock on a firm's assets but generally carries a limited dividend.

Price-earnings ratio. The relationship (P/E) between a corporation's stock price and its earnings per share. The P/E ratio indicates how a firm is valued in the stock market and is found by dividing the stock price by earnings per share.

Primary deposits. Deposits that add new reserves to the bank where deposited and generally arise when cash and checks drawn against other banks are placed on deposit in a bank.

Primary mortgage market. The market where the origination, or creation, of new mortgages is carried out.

Primary securities market. The market involved in the creation and issuance of new securities, mortgages, and other claims to wealth.

Prime rate. The interest rate charged by commercial banks to their best business customers. This short-term bank loan rate sets a "floor" interest rate for other loans to less qualified business borrowers.

Production credit associations. Cooperative lending organizations under the Farm Credit Administration that make short-term loans to farmers for breeding and raising livestock; dairy production; growing, harvesting, and marketing crops; buying and repairing buildings and machinery; and refinancing short-term debts.

Profitability ratios. Financial ratios that indicate the degree to which firms have been able to generate profits relative to sales, assets, or stockholders' equity.

Program trading. Techniques for trading groups of securities for the purpose of maintaining a desired portfolio balance, profit taking, or avoiding losses. The strategies are often carried out through the use of sophisticated computer programs.

Property insurance. Insurance whose purpose is either to protect the insured against loss arising out of physical damages to the insured's property or loss arising from damages to others for which the insured may be held liable.

Proprietorship. A form of business organization in which the business is owned by one person who is entirely responsible for all its management and for assets and liabilities.

Prospectus. The document that describes the terms and conditions of a new security issue. The Securities Exchange Act of 1934 requires the distribution of prospectuses to buyers of securities coming under regulation of the Securities and Exchange Commission.

Prudent-man rule. Rule which requires that a trust institution be held responsible for the same degree of judgment that a prudent person would exercise in investing personal funds.

Purchasing power risk. A risk which results from changes in the price level. For example, a rise or increase in prices in the form of inflation in the U.S. results in a decline in the purchasing power of the dollar.

Put contract. An option to sell a security at a specific price during a specified period of time.

Q

Quantity theory. One of the oldest theories that attempts to explain the relationship of money quantity to prices. It holds that changes in the quantity of money are the main cause of changes in the price level. This theory relies on the use of the equation of exchange.

R

Real assets. Assets which include direct ownership of land, buildings, machinery, inventory, precious metals, or other items that can be converted into cash.

Real Estate Investment Trust (REIT). A shareholder fund authorized to invest in real estate, primarily construction. REITs are managed and controlled by trustees and are exempt from federal corporate income taxes.

Real investment. When savings are used to create or acquire wealth in the form of real assets.

Regulation Z. The Truth in Lending section of the Consumer Credit Protection Act. It regulates the disclosure of consumer credit costs and also garnishment procedures and prohibits exorbitant credit transactions. Its purpose is to make consumers aware of the cost of credit and to enable them to compare the costs of alternate forms of credit.

Representative full-bodied money. Paper money fully backed by gold or silver.

Repurchase agreements. When securities are bought or sold with an agreement that the transaction will be reversed within a stated period of time. Repurchase agreements are used by the Fed to temporarily increase or decrease the amount of reserves available to banks.

Required reserves. The percentage of total deposits that banks must hold as reserves at their Federal Reserve banks or as cash in their vaults. The percentage is determined by the Fed, which varies the rate as a way of controlling the money supply. A raise in reserve requirements leaves less money for banks to lend, while lowering the reserve requirement encourages lending.

Reserve ratio. The percentage of deposits that a bank must hold as reserves.

Retained earnings. Reflects the retention or accumulation of earnings or profits of a business and is part of the owners' equity.

Revenue bonds. Obligations issued by state or local governments to finance specific projects. The revenues from these specific projects are to provide the funds to service the obligations with liability of the governmental unit being limited to those specific sources of funds.

Revocable trust. A trust in which the maker of the trust has the right to revoke the trust arrangement after its creation.

Revolving credit agreement. A standby agreement for a guaranteed line of credit that a business firm may obtain from a commercial bank.

Risk-adjusted discount rate. Determined by adding a risk premium to the firm's cost of capital for purposes of discounting riskier-than-average projects.

Risk premium. The difference between the risk-free interest rate on a Treasury security and the interest rate on a risky corporate debt security.

S

Sales finance company. An organization developed to finance the sale of durable goods on installments, and also to finance wholesale purchases by merchants or dealers from manufacturers.

Savings. The accumulation of cash and other financial assets such as savings accounts and corporate securities.

Savings and loan associations (S&Ls). Thrift institutions that were established primarily to accept savings deposits and provide home mortgage financing. They have been an important contributor to the growth of housing in the United States.

Savings bonds. A form of nonmarketable U.S. government obligation especially designed to serve as an investment medium for small investors.

Savings deficit. Occurs when an economic unit's investment exceeds its income. This often is the case for business firms as a group or economic unit.

Savings surplus. Occurs when an economic unit, such as individuals taken as a group, has current savings that exceed the group's direct investment in real assets.

Secondary mortgage market. Market where real estate mortgages can be resold, thus providing some liquidity to mortgage holders.

Secondary securities market. Market involving the transfer of existing securities from old investors to new investors. A secondary market also exists for real estate mortgages.

Secured loan. Loan for which specific property is pledged as collateral.

Senior liens. When a parcel of real estate has more than one mortgage lien against it, the first mortgage filed has priority and the bonds outstanding against this first mortgage are senior liens.

Serial maturity bonds. Bonds with stated installment dates, usually annual, on which issues mature. The dates may range, for example, from one to twenty years, with each maturity bearing its own rate of interest. Usually, the shorter the maturity, the lower the interest rate. This arrangement allows investors to choose the maturity best suited to their needs.

Short sale. The sale of securities that the seller does not own but which are borrowed in anticipation of a price decline in the security. The securities must be bought back at a future time.

Short-term trust. A trust that is irrevocable for a specified number of years. It offers a compromise between the revocable and irrevocable trust.

Sight draft. Draft requiring immediate payment.

Sinking fund bonds. Bond contracts that require the setting aside on a regular basis of funds to retire all or a part of an issue during the life of the issue.

Small business investment company (SBIC). A privately owned, profit-seeking firm licensed and regulated by the Small Business Administration that provides long-term funds to other businesses.

Sources and uses of funds statement. A financial statement that shows how a firm obtained funds during an accounting period and how those funds were used. Information for it is derived from both the income statement and the balance sheet.

Special assessment bonds. Generally issued by local governments to finance community improvements. Since such improvements are expected to improve the value of properties adjacent to the improvements, special tax assessments may be levied to provide the funds to service the obligations.

Special Drawing Rights (SDRs). A form of reserve asset or "paper gold" as they are called. They are account entries in the books of the International Monetary Fund, which are separate from all other accounts and are divided among the members in accordance with their quotas in the fund. SDRs can be drawn upon to meet balance-of-payments deficits with other countries.

Specialists. Members of the exchanges who buy and sell for their own accounts, generally limiting their attention to only a few stocks. They also serve as floor brokers for other brokers who place transactions with them.

Special tax districts. Governmental units established to levy taxes for special community needs such as schools, fire districts, and flood control.

Speculative inflation. Inflation that results from the strong expectation that an upward trend in prices will continue. This results in a "buy now" attitude for a time, with increased demand causing attendant price pressures.

Speculative motive. Demand for marketable securities or cash to be able to take advantage of unusual cash discounts or other price bargains.

Standard of value. A function of money whereby prices are expressed in terms of the monetary unit and contracts for deferred payments are expressed in the same way.

Standby underwriting agreement. An agreement in which underwriters buy all newly issued securities not purchased by a corporation's stockholders. Underwriters are paid a fee for this service.

Statement of cash flows. Also called a sources and uses of funds statement. It uses information from the income statement and the balance sheet to show the sources and uses of funds for a particular accounting period.

Stock certificate. Provides evidence of an ownership claim in a corporation.

Stock or bond power. Authorizes a lender to sell or otherwise dispose of assignable stocks and bonds, provided as collateral for a loan by the borrower, should it become necessary to do so to protect the loan.

Stop-loss order. A form of "limit order" for securities in which a price is set slightly below the prevailing market price; when that point is reached, a sale is triggered. By establishing such a limit order the owner of the security attempts to limit a loss.

Store of purchasing power. A function of money which allows money to be held as a liquid asset and provides flexibility in the decision to spend or to invest.

Street name. Securities owned by investors that are issued and retained in the name of the brokerage firm serving the customer. This arrangement facilitates the sale of securities with only a telephone call and eliminates the requirement of careful safekeeping of the securities.

Surety contract. Generally provides that one party, the surety company, becomes answerable to a third party, the insured, as a result of failure on the part of a second party to perform as required by contract.

Syndicate. A group of investment banks that work together to buy large issues of securities. Syndicates may consist of several banks or may include as many as several hundred firms to underwrite very large sales.

T

Tax policy. The raising or lowering of taxes to affect economic conditions and changing the structure of taxes to alter the burden of taxes on various income groups.

Term life insurance. Insurance whose basic feature is that the policy is issued for a specified period of time after which time no obligation exists on the part of the insurance company toward the insured.

Term loan. A contract under which a borrower agrees to make a series of interest and principal payments on specific dates to the lender. Term loans have a maturity that exceeds one year and are usually repaid in monthly or quarterly payments.

Testamentary trust. A trust that provides that an estate be maintained and administered for the benefit of heirs rather than be turned over to the heirs directly. It is designed to provide for heirs while at the same time protecting the estate against irresponsible management.

Third market. A market for large blocks of securities that operates outside the organized exchanges and the OTC market. This market is usually used by large institutions to avoid the high commissions of the organized exchanges.

Thrift institution. A term used in referring to savings and loan associations, mutual savings banks, and credit unions.

Time draft. Draft requiring payment at a specified later date, usually thirty days or some multiple thereof.

Token coins. Coins whose nominal value for exchange purposes is greater than the value of the metal they contain.

Total reserves. Deposits held in Federal Reserve banks plus vault cash or currency held by depository institutions.

Trade credit. The open accounts receivable, together with notes receivable, taken by manufacturers, wholesalers, jobbers, and other business units as sellers of goods and services to other businesses.

Trading on the equity. The process of using borrowed funds in an attempt to increase the percentage return on the investment of existing stockholders in a business.

Transactions motive. Demand for cash needed to carry on day-to-day operations.

Transfer payments. Payments for which no current productive service is rendered. Examples of government transfer payments include pensions, direct relief, and veterans' allowances and benefits.

Traveler's letter of credit. An instrument issued by a bank in one country and addressed to a list of banks abroad. These foreign banks to which the letter is addressed are usually correspondents of the issuing bank and have agreed to purchase upon sight the drafts presented to them by persons displaying such letters of credit. A maximum for total amount of withdrawals is stated in the letter.

Treasurer. The person responsible for managing a firm's cash, acquiring assets, and raising financial capital.

Treasury bills. Treasury obligations with the shortest maturities, typically issued for 91 days, but with some issues carrying maturities of 182 days or one year. They are sold at a discount from their value at maturity.

Treasury bonds. Treasury obligations that may be issued with any maturity but generally have an original maturity in excess of five years. These bonds bear interest at stipulated rates. Many issues of these bonds are callable by the government several years before their maturity.

Treasury notes. Treasury obligations that are usually issued for maturities of more than one year but not more than ten years and are issued at specified interest rates.

Trend (or time series) analysis. A method that compares a firm's financial ratios over several years.

Trust indenture. A document that spells out in detail the contractual terms associated with a bond issue.

Trust institution. Serves in a fiduciary capacity for the administration or disposition of assets and for the performance of specified acts for the beneficiaries of trust arrangements.

Trust receipt. An instrument used by banks in releasing shipping documents to a customer in which the bank retains title to the merchandise until the debt is repaid. In the event of failure of the business, the bank repossesses the merchandise and sells as much of it as necessary to cover the total amount of the debt.

U

Underwriting agreement. An agreement in which investment bankers purchase the newly issued securities of a corporation, with the intention of selling them for a profit.

Universal life insurance. A form of life insurance that provides death benefits during a specified period of time and that is a savings or investment account providing tax-deferred income.

Unsecured loan. A loan that represents a general claim against the assets of the borrower.

V

Variable costs. The types of business expenses that vary directly with sales, such as cost of goods sold.

Velocity of money. A measure of the rate of circulation of the money supply, expressed as the average number of times each dollar is spent on purchases of goods and services and calculated by dividing gross national product (GNP) in current dollars by the money supply.

Voluntary savings. Financial assets set aside for use in the future.

W

Wage and price controls. Governmental efforts to control rapid increases in wages and prices by setting legal limits for such increases. These were used most recently in the United States in 1971.

Weighted average cost of capital. The after-tax cost of a firm's long-term debt and equity capital weighted on the basis of the optimal capital structure mix.

Whole life insurance. Insurance which combines an investment program with the insurance contract. The premiums are generally for a fixed sum each payment period throughout the life of the insured.

Worker's compensation. A form of casualty insurance purchased by business firms to protect themselves against claims resulting from occupational accidents. State laws typically hold employers liable for most of the accidents that take place in connection with their business operations.

Working capital. A firm's total current assets including cash, marketable securities, accounts receivable, and inventories.

World Bank. Founded as an agency of the United Nations in 1945 to help rebuild Europe after World War II. Officially called the International Bank for Reconstruction and Development, the World Bank provides loans and technical advice to help develop the economies of member nations.

Y

Yield curves. Graphic representation of the term structure of interest rates at a given point in time. Interest rates for securities of comparable quality for various maturities are compared as of that point in time.

Yield to maturity. The rate of return based on interest and principal payments that will be received on a bond held to its maturity.

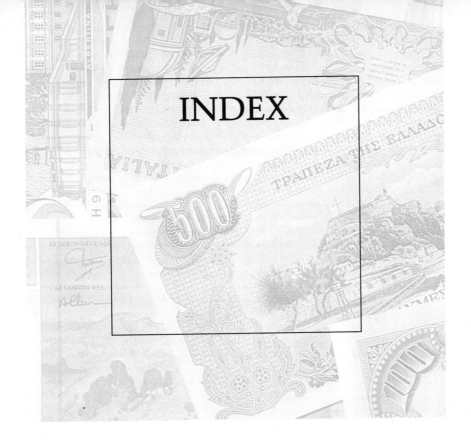

INDEX

This index uses several conventions to help you find information. If the page number appears in boldface (for example, **120**), the citation refers to a definition in the margin of the text page. If the page number appears in italic (*120*), the citation refers to an illustration. The letter *n* after a page number (120n) refers to a footnote on the cited page.